Strange Parallels

Southeast Asia in Global Context, c. 800–1830
Volume 1: Integration on the Mainland

This is the first volume in an ambitious two-volume study of a thousand years of Southeast Asian political, cultural, and economic history. The study has two goals: to overcome the fragmentation of early Southeast Asian historiography and for the first time to connect Southeast Asian to world history in serious and sustained fashion. A blend of detailed archival work and secondary research, of local inquiry and large-scale theorization, Volume 1 argues that each of mainland Southeast Asia's three great lowland corridors experienced a pattern of accelerating integration punctuated by recurrent collapse. These trajectories were broadly synchronized not only between corridors, but, most curiously, between the mainland and other sectors of Eurasia. This volume describes the nature of consolidation – which was simultaneously territorial, religious, and ethnic – and dissects the fluid interplay of endogenous and external pressures encouraging that trend. Volume 2 will explore parallels with Russia, France, and Japan c. 800–1830 and will explain why in yet other areas of Eurasia fragmentation, not integration, became the norm. Here is a fundamentally original analysis of both Southeast Asia and the premodern world.

Victor Lieberman is Professor of Southeast Asian History at the University of Michigan. His publications include *Burmese Administrative Cycles: Anarchy and Conquest, c. 1580–1760*, which won the Harry J. Benda Prize from the Association for Asian Studies, and an edited collection, *Beyond Binary Histories: Re-imagining Eurasia to c. 1830*. Papers in that collection originally appeared as a special edition of *Modern Asian Studies* devoted to an examination of Lieberman's scholarship.

Strange Parallels

Southeast Asia in Global Context, c. 800–1830
Volume 1
Integration on the Mainland

VICTOR LIEBERMAN
University of Michigan

CAMBRIDGE
UNIVERSITY PRESS

PUBLISHED BY THE PRESS SYNDICATE OF THE UNIVERSITY OF CAMBRIDGE
The Pitt Building, Trumpington Street, Cambridge, United Kingdom

CAMBRIDGE UNIVERSITY PRESS
The Edinburgh Building, Cambridge CB2 2RU, UK
40 West 20th Street, New York, NY 10011-4211, USA
477 Williamstown Road, Port Melbourne, VIC 3207, Australia
Ruiz de Alarcón 13, 28014 Madrid, Spain
Dock House, The Waterfront, Cape Town 8001, South Africa

http://www.cambridge.org

First published 2003

Printed in the United States of America

Typeface Palatino 10/13 pt.　　*System* LATEX 2$_\varepsilon$　[TB]

A catalog record for this book is available from the British Library.

Library of Congress Cataloging in Publication Data

Lieberman, Victor B., 1945–
Strange parallels : Southeast Asia in global context, c. 800–1830 / Victor Lieberman.
　　p.　cm. – (Studies in comparative world history)
Includes bibliographical references and index.
ISBN 0-521-80086-2 – ISBN 0-521-80496-5 (pb.)
1. Asia, Southeastern – Historiography. 2. Asia, Southeastern – History.
I. Title. II. Series.
DS524.4.L54 2003
959–dc21　　　2002071481

ISBN 0 521 80086 2 hardback
ISBN 0 521 80496 5 paperback

To Sharon, and to the memory of my mother and father

Contents

List of Figures

List of Figures

Principal Political Eras on the Mainland

Pyu Era, c. 200–840
Pagan, c. 950–1300
Ava Period, 1365–1555
Independent Ra-manya Polity, c. 1300–1539
First Toungoo Dynasty, c. 1486–1599
Restored Toungoo Dynasty, 1597–1752
Kon-baung Dynasty, 1752–1885

Funan, c. 200–600
Dvaravati Period, c. 550–900
Pre-Angkorian Cambodia, c. 600–800
Angkor, 802/889–c. 1440
Early Ayudhya Period, 1351–1569
Late Ayudhya Period, 1569–1767
Taksin, 1767–1782
Chakri Dynasty, 1782–present

Chinese Imperial Period, 43–938
Ly Dynasty, 1009–1225
Tran Dynasty, 1225–1400

Ming Occupation, 1407–1427
Le Dynasty, 1428–1788
Mac Period at Thang Long, 1527–1592
Trinh Period, 1592–1786
Southern Nguyen Period, c. 1600–1802
Tayson Era, 1771–1802
Nguyen Dynasty, 1802–1945

Abbreviations Used in the Notes

A	*Original Inscriptions Collected by King Bodawpaya in Upper Burma and Now Placed Near the Patodawgyi Pagoda, Amarapura* (Rangoon, 1913).
AA-L	Let-we-naw-yahta, "Alaung-min-taya-gyi ayei-daw-bon," in U Hla Tin, ed., *Alaung-hpaya ayei-daw-bon hnasaung-dwe* (Rangoon, 1961), 1–152.
AAS	Association for Asian Studies
AA·T	Twin-thin-taik-wun, "Alaung-min-taya-gyi ayei-daw-bon," in U Hla Tin, ed., *Alaung-hpaya ayei-daw-bon hnasaung-dwe* (Rangoon, 1961), 153–233.
AHR	*American Historical Review*
B I, *B* II	*Inscriptions Copied from the Stones Collected by King Bodawpaya and Placed Near the Arakan Pagoda, Mandalay,* 2 vols. (Rangoon, 1897).
BEFEO	*Bulletin de l'Ecole Francaise d'Extreme-Orient*
BL OR 3464	British Library, London. MS Orient. 3464. Burmese translation of Mon history of Pegu by Monk of Athwa. Composed late 1760s (?), transcribed 1847.
BSOAS	*Bulletin of the School of Oriental and African Studies, University of London*
BTLV	*Bijdragen tot de Taal-, Land- en Volkenkunde*
CC	*Climatic Change*
CEHI	*The Cambridge Economic History of India. Vol. 1: c. 1200–c. 1750,* Tapan Raychaudhuri and Irfan Habib, eds. (Cambridge, 1982).

CHSEA	*The Cambridge History of Southeast Asia. Vol. 1: From Earliest Times to c. 1800*, Nicholas Tarling, ed. (Cambridge, 1992).
CSSH	*Comparative Studies in Society and History*
Dal	*Reprint from Dalrymple's Oriental Repertory, 1791–97 of Portions Relating to Burma* (Rangoon, 1926).
EHR	*Economic History Review*
GRL	*Geophysical Research Letters*
GUBSS	*Gazetteer of Upper Burma and the Shan States*, J. George Scott and J. P. Hardiman, comps. Part I, 2 vols., Part II, 3 vols. (Rangoon, 1900–1901).
HNY	*Hman-nan-daw-u-dwin pyu-zi-yin-ya-thaw maha-ya-zawin-daw-gyi*, vol. 3 (Mandalay, 1908).
I 1089, etc.	Inscriptions numbered according to Chas. Duroiselle, comp. and ed., *A List of Inscriptions Found in Burma. Part I* (Rangoon, 1921).
JAH	*Journal of Asian History*
JAOS	*Journal of the American Oriental Society*
JAS	*Journal of Asian Studies*
JBRS	*Journal of the Burma Research Society*
JEH	*Journal of Economic History*
JEMH	*Journal of Early Modern History*
JESHO	*Journal of the Economic and Social History of the Orient*
JIH	*Journal of Interdisciplinary History*
JRAS	*Journal of the Royal Asiatic Society of Great Britain and Ireland*
JSEAH	*Journal of Southeast Asian History*
JSEAS	*Journal of Southeast Asian Studies*
JSS	*Journal of the Siam Society*
JWH	*Journal of World History*
KBZ	*Kon-baung-zet maha-ya-zawin-daw-gyi*, U Tin (Mandalay), comp., 3 vols. (rpt., London, 1967–68).
LBHK	Thi-ri-u-zana, *Law-ka-byu-ha kyan (In-yon sa-dan)*, U Hpo Lat, ed. (Rangoon, 1968).
LFSG	India Office Records, London. *Records of Fort St. George. Letters to Fort St. George, 1681/82–1744/45.* 29 vols. (Madras, 1916–33).
List	*List of Microfilms Deposited in the Centre for East Asian Cultural Studies, Part 8, Burma* (Tokyo, 1976).
MAS	*Modern Asian Studies*

MMOS	U Tin (Pagan Wun-dauk), *Myan-ma-min ok-chok-pon sa-dan*, 5 vols. (Rangoon, 1931–33).
NL 1950, etc.	National Library, Rangoon, MS 1950, etc.
PP	*Past and Present*
PPA	*Inscriptions of Pagan, Pinya and Ava* (Rangoon, 1892).
REO	*Revue de l'Extreme-Orient*
ROB	*The Royal Orders of Burma, A.D. 1598–1885*, Than Tun, ed., 10 vols. (Kyoto, 1983–1990).
RUL 45235	Rangoon University Library MS 45235, "Nyaung-yan mintaya let-htet-daw-ga-thi Anauk-hpet-lun Tha-lun-min-taya-taing min-thon-zet amein-daw . . ." no transcription date.
SEAR	*South East Asian Research*
SHDMA	Maung Thu-ta, *Sa-hso-daw-mya at-htok-pat-ti* (rpt., Rangoon, 1971).
SMK	Burma, Department of Archaeology, *Shei-haung myan-ma kyauk-sa-mya*, t. 474–1150, 6 vols. (Rangoon, 1972–1991).
TL	Maha-dama-thin-gyan, *Tha-thana-lin-ga-ya sa-dan* (Rangoon, 1897).
UB	*Inscriptions Collected in Upper Burma*, 2 vols. (Rangoon, 1900, 1903).
UK	U Kala, *Maha-ya-zawin-gyi*. Vols. 1, 2, Saya Pwa, ed. (Rangoon, 1926, 1932); Vol. 3, Hsaya U Kin So (Rangoon, 1961).
ZOK	*Zam-bu-di-pa ok-hsaung kyan*, J. S. Furnivall and Pe Maung Tin, eds. (Rangoon, 1960).

To facilitate identification, the first time each nonabbreviated source appears in the notes of a new chapter, that source receives a full citation with author, title, place, and date of publication.

Preface

My strongest academic memory from graduate school – a feeling, I am certain, not unique to me – was a sense that precolonial Southeast Asian historiography was desperately chaotic and difficult to penetrate. Texts available in the 1970s and 1980s offered an endless array of names, battles, and dates with few, if any, long-term patterns discernible for individual realms, much less the region as a whole or major subregions.

I also remember thinking – a more idiosyncratic reverie, no doubt – how very curious it was that the 16th-century unification of Burma coincided with the dramatic annexations of Ivan IV in Russia, and that in both Russia and Burma these conquests yielded to periods of utter chaos at the turn of the 17th century. Preoccupied with Burmese research, I relegated such coincidences to the "useless trivia" section of my mind. But years later, when completion of some Burma projects allowed me to revisit the issue of correlations, it gradually dawned on me that far from being a 16th-century peculiarity, parallel chronologies extended throughout much of Burmese and Russian history. What is more, I began to realize, substantially similar chronologies were shared by other far-flung sectors of Eurasia with no obvious connection to either Burma or Russia.

The present two-volume study *Strange Parallels: Southeast Asia in Global Context, c. 800–1830* addresses these abiding, ultimately interrelated, concerns: What were the principal long-term trends in precolonial Southeast Asian political, cultural, and economic history? How did that history relate to the rest of the world? *Volume One: Integration of the Mainland,* focuses on sustained political and cultural integration in each of the three chief sectors of continental Southeast Asia. Of course, this is hardly the only possible narrative – one could as easily consider trends in gender relations, literature, or Chinese trade, with rather different implications for compartmentalizing Southeast Asia – but it is a critical story that touches on diverse spheres and facilitates novel comparisons between mainland Southeast Asia and other parts of Eurasia. *Volume Two: Mainland Mirrors: Russia, France, Japan, and the Islands* attempts precisely such comparisons. It argues that in terms of linear-cum-cyclic trajectories, chronology, and dynamics, the mainland resembled much of Europe and Japan, but diverged significantly from South Asia and island Southeast Asia.

My own expertise in non-European primary sources is in Burmese. As soon as I decided on this comparative project, I therefore had to decide: should I attempt to write about regions outside Burma, or should I collaborate with other specialists? A concern for expertise instinctively inclined me to the latter approach, which in fact inspired an earlier collection of essays I edited, *Beyond Binary Histories: Re-imagining Eurasia to c. 1830,* in which nine specialists commented on the applicability to their areas, ranging from France to Java, of more general theories of Eurasian development.[1] Yet, despite their authority and despite a preliminary effort to get each contributor to address a common set of themes, in the end these essays, I think, remained rather disparate. One simply cannot expect several scholars, with unique training and temperament, to focus on precisely the same questions, especially if those are questions of Eurasian coordination alien to traditional disciplinary concerns. If a theory of Southeast Asian, much less Eurasian, history is to have any claim to coherence or originality, it cannot be done by committee.

At the same time, any historian attempting this task must accept that her/his work is provisional, designed to stimulate new perspectives but certain to attract specialist criticism. Such a scholar also must do everything to overcome the limits of her/his background by reading widely, thinking deeply – and seeking expert advice wherever possible. Accordingly, in writing this first volume I have accumulated a large number of debts that I am eager to acknowledge.

If Chapter 2, on the western mainland, embodies the fruits of some 25 years of research in Burmese-language primary sources, even here I have benefited from the generosity of other scholars. I spent a year

---

[1] Victor Lieberman, ed., *Beyond Binary Histories: Re-imagining Eurasia to c. 1830* (Ann Arbor, 1999).

interrogating 530 14th- to 16-century inscriptions with Burma's leading historian and epigrapher, U Than Tun, whose erudition is exceeded only by his patience. On many occasions his kind wife Ma Khin Yi assisted us. Michael Aung-Thwin readily made available his recent, exciting research on the Mon kingdom of Lower Burma and answered sundry other questions. U Saw Tun helped me with Pagan cultural history, while U Toe Hla introduced me to the world of Kon-baung commercial contracts (*thet-kayits*) and provided three volumes of unpublished *thet-kayit* manuscripts. Besides drawing my attention to little-known primary sources, Michael Charney offered insights into Arakanese cultural and Burmese military history. Sun Laichen did the same with Ming-Burmese overland trade and Chinese military technology, and Wil O. Dijk provided a cornucopia of information on Burmese-Dutch economic relations in the 17th century. Jörg Schendel widened my understanding of 19th-century Kon-baung trade. Bob Hudson provided data on pre-Pagan archeology, and Patrick Pranke answered questions on Kon-baung Buddhism. Several of these scholars also provided specific citations and working papers, which I gratefully acknowledge in the notes. The late H. L. Shorto furnished translations of two Mon histories of the 16th–18th centuries, the *Uppanna Sudhammavati Rajavamsa-katha* and the *Nidana Ramadhipati katha*, while Ken Breazeale made available translations from the early 19th-century Mon annals, *Phongsawadan Mon Phama*. My Michigan colleague Valerie Kivelson, although an historian of Russia, offered critical readings of Chapters 1 and 2, and over the years has helped me think through a variety of problems in early modern historiography.

In Chapter 3, the sections on Angkor and Cambodia benefited from comments and/or unpublished research provided by Ashley Thompson, Charles Higham, Dan Penny, and most especially David Chandler, Roland Fletcher, and Christophe Pottier. On Thai history Yoneo Ishii, David Wyatt, Richard O'Connor, and Dhiravat na Pombejra answered specialized inquiries and in some cases supplied unpublished materials. In addition, Thongchai Winichakul, Yoneo Ishii, Dhiravat na Pombejra, David Chandler, Junko Koizumi, and Constance Wilson provided painstaking written comments on various drafts of Chapter 3, ensuring a level of expertise I would not have been able to attain on my own.

For Chapter 4, covering Vietnam and the eastern mainland, I am indebted to John Whitmore, my friend and colleague for 35 years, who has guided me in things Vietnamese and has helped shape my ideas on

Southeast Asia in general. Alexander Woodside also provided penetrating written commentary on this chapter, answered questions, and drew my attention to research in Vietnamese and Japanese that I eventually had translated. When I visited Cornell, Keith Taylor, in a display of collegiality and generosity I shall not forget, went over the penultimate draft of Chapter 4 with me page by page and line by line. Likewise, Li Tana, Nola Cooke, and Brian Zottoli supplied highly detailed written comments on this chapter and shared with me their latest scholarship. George Dutton and Charles Wheeler were no less supportive, providing copies of their dissertations and research papers.

My foray into the initially unfamiliar world of paleoclimatology depended on assistance from James C. G. Walker, Philip Meyers, Michael E. Mann, David Godley, Dan Penny, Thomas Crowley, and Pao K. Wang. Kathleen Morrison supplied material on climate and famine in medieval India, while Jack Goldstone's unpublished papers alerted me to his new research on global economic history. I hasten to add that neither these scholars nor any of the Southeast Asian historians who aided me are responsible for shortcomings in the text.

For translations of primary and secondary sources in Japanese I am grateful to Atsuko Naono, Mariko Foulk, and Matthew Stavros. For translations of early Chinese documents I depended on Sun Laichen's expertise. D. N. Dang-vu and John Whitmore translated Vietnamese materials. Fe Susan Go, Michigan's Southeast Asia librarian, has been unfailingly helpful in tracking down obscure sources over the years, while the staff of the 7-FAST service at the library cheerfully supplied me with more than 1,500 special orders.

I am grateful as well for the following grants and fellowships: a National Endowment for the Humanities Summer Stipend, a Social Science Research Council/American Council of Learned Societies Research Grant, a National Endowment for the Humanities Fellowship for University Teachers, a NEH Summer Stipend, an Arthur H. Cole Grant-in-Aid from the Economic History Association; and from the University of Michigan, the Richard Hudson Research Professorship, a Horace H. Rackham Faculty Fellowship, plus translation, travel, and research grants from the Office of the Vice-President for Research, the Center for Japanese Studies, the Center for Southeast Asian Studies, and the History Department. In addition, the History Department and the Office of the Vice-President for Research furnished a subvention for maps and charts, which were skillfully and cheerfully executed by Asligul Gocmen.

The readers of my manuscript, Merle Ricklefs, Ian Brown, and a third anonymous referee, provided much welcome encouragement. Frank Smith, Publishing Director for Social Sciences at Cambridge University Press, agreed to convert what was originally a one-book project into two volumes. For this decision as well as for his editorial support and that of Michael Adas, I am deeply grateful.

Finally, for her intellectual comradeship, tolerance of receding deadlines, and sustained optimism, I thank Sharon, my wife and best friend.

V. L.
January 2002

CHAPTER 1

Introduction

The Ends of the Earth

In 1792 the French monarchy collapsed. Between 1799 and 1815, a new Parisian regime improved the efficiency and penetration of the central apparatus, while dramatically extending French military power. Short-lived though France's conquests were, her continental wars precipitated imitative reforms of administrative and military structures across Europe and a permanent reduction in the number of independent states.

Between 1752 and 1786 the Burmese, Siamese, and Vietnamese kingdoms all disintegrated. In each realm, a new, more dynamic leadership then succeeded in quelling the chaos, increasing the resources and local authority of the state, and enlarging its territorial writ. The ensuing wars between reinvigorated empires in the late 18th and early 19th centuries accelerated competitive reform while diminishing the number of independent polities across mainland Southeast Asia.[1]

How shall we explain these parallels between Europe and Southeast Asia? Surely, one is tempted to say, no explanation is needed: the cultural contexts were so different, the interstate and domestic systems so unique, the trajectories so disparate as to render parallels ultimately meaningless. This is historical flotsam, curious but basically random coincidences, like similarities between Meso-American and Egyptian pyramids or between Jewish and Buddhist cosmogonic explanations for the origin of suffering.

---

[1] The mainland is here defined as present-day Myanmar, Thailand, Cambodia, Laos, and Vietnam; while archipelagic Southeast Asia refers to Malaysia, Singapore, Brunei, Indonesia, and the Philippines.

1

But closer scrutiny suggests rather more was involved. In fact, in mainland Southeast Asia as well as in France, the late 18th and early 19th centuries ended the third and inaugurated the last of four roughly synchronized cycles of political consolidation that together spanned the better part of a millennium. The first synchronized consolidation, which saw extremely rapid demographic and commercial growth across much of Europe and Southeast Asia, began in the 10th or 11th centuries and concluded with a generalized political and social crisis extending from the late 13th to the late 14th or early 15th centuries. Political integration resumed in the mid- or late 1400s, but between c. 1540 and 1610 new states in Burma, Siam, Vietnam, France, as well as Russia again succumbed, this time to a combination of novel cultural and political tensions, overly rapid territorial extension, and/or renewed ecological strains. Reforms in the early to mid-1600s inaugurated a third phase of consolidation – ending with the late 18th century collapse, the dramatic revivals, and the raging continental wars with which I opened the discussion. Why should distant regions, with no obvious religious or material links, have experienced more or less coordinated cycles? If we discount coincidence, what hitherto invisible ties could have spanned the continents?

Moreover, why did interregna in both mainland Southeast Asia and much of Europe tend to become progressively shorter and less disruptive? In most cases the 13th/15th-century collapse was both longer and more profoundly dislocating – territorially, economically, demographically, institutionally – than subsequent crises (see Figures 1.1 and 1.2).[2] Or to reverse the terms of inquiry so as to pose a yet more fundamental problem: Why during the course of the second millennium did local societies in mainland Southeast Asia as well as Europe become more politically and culturally integrated? Whereas Europe as a whole in 1450 had some 500 political units, by the late 19th century the number was closer to 30. Between 1340 and 1820 some 23 independent Southeast Asian kingdoms collapsed into three. Each 19th-century survivor was more effectively centralized than any local predecessor. At the same time across much of western Europe, northeastern Europe, and mainland Southeast Asia alike – in a pattern that was both symptom and

---

[2] Vietnam is the chief exception insofar as 16th-century fragmentation continued, in essence, to 1802. However, both the northern and southern Vietnamese regimes stabilized in the early 1600s, both owed nominal allegiance to the Le dynasty, and both collapsed in the late 1700s, to be reunited by 1802. See Ch. 4 for discussion.

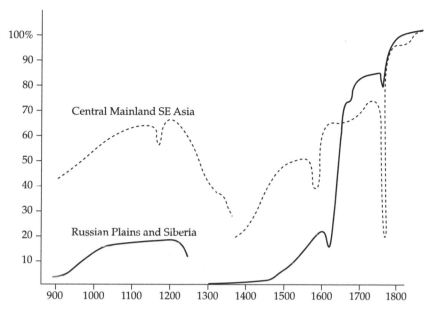

Figure 1.1. Territorial consolidation in central mainland Southeast Asia and in the Russian Plains and Siberia. This chart shows the amount of territory controlled by the dominant power in each region between c. 900 and 1825 C.E. The number of square miles held by the chief regional power in 1825 defines the 100-percent level on the vertical axis, with earlier formations presented as a proportion of that 1825 figure. Thus, for example, since the Russian empire in 1825 controlled roughly 7,000,000 square miles and its Russian predecessor (the Kievan federation) in 1200 controlled in the order of 1,400,000 square miles, in 1200 the graph for the "Russian Plains and Siberia" registers at 20 percent. The 13th-century gap corresponds to the interregnum between the collapse of Kiev and the rise of Moscow, while the late 14th-century gap in the line for "Central Mainland SE Asia" identifies the period separating the decline of Angkor and the early success of Ayudhya. Especially in earlier eras, fluid overlapping frontier loyalties make precise territorial calculations problematic. As a relatively short-lived empire whose center of gravity lay outside the Russian heartland, the Mongol polity is excluded.

Sources: Jan Pluvier, *Historical Atlas of South-East Asia* (Leiden, 1995); David Chandler, *A History of Cambodia* (Boulder, CO: 1992); David Wyatt, *A History of Thailand* (New Haven, 1984); idem, "Relics, Oaths and Politics in Thirteenth-Century Siam," *JSEAS* 32 (2001): 3–66; Jerome Blum, *Lord and Peasant in Russia* (Princeton, 1961); John Cannon, *The Penguin Historical Atlas of Russia* (London, 1995); Janet Martin, *Medieval Russia 980–1584* (Cambridge, 1995).

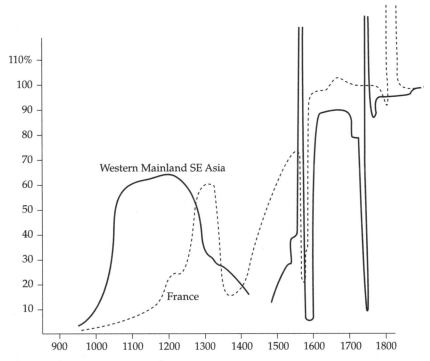

Figure 1.2. Territorial consolidation in Western mainland Southeast Asia and in France. This figure employs the same format as Figure 1.1, with lands held by the chief regional power in 1825 defining the 100-percent level on the vertical axis and with pre-1825 formations presented as a proportion of that 1825 figure. The 15th-century gap in the line for "Western Mainland SE Asia" corresponds to the period between the decline of Ava and the rise of Toungoo. Pre-1700 French territory refers not to the boundaries of the titular kingdom, but of the French royal domain. The same caveat about fluid frontier loyalties applies here as in Figure 1.1.

Sources: G. E. Harvey, *History of Burma* (rpt., London, 1967); Victor Lieberman, *Burmese Administrative Cycles* (Princeton, 1984); Elizabeth Hallam, *Capetian France 987–1328* (London, 1980); Xavier de Planhol, *An Historical Geography of France* (Cambridge, 1994); Louis Bergeron et al., *Histoire de la France. L'espace francais* (Paris, 1989); Roland Mousnier, *The Institutions of France under the Absolute Monarchy 1598–1789, Volume II. The Organs of State and Society* (Chicago, 1984); personal communications, Robin Briggs and Paul Hanson, Oct. 2001.

cause of political integration – the dialect, religion, social conventions, and ethnicity of elites in each capital entered into more sustained dialogue with provincial and popular traditions. Everywhere literacy grew more widespread, vernacular literatures more profuse; cultural as well

4

as commercial circuits denser, more inclusive, and more specialized. In varying degrees in Burma, Siam, Vietnam, France, and Russia alike, centrally-defined cultural norms became a marker of political inclusion.

Why, then, these parallel consolidations between lands at the extremities of Eurasia – in effect, the ends of the earth? Why not uninterrupted construction in one region, permanent collapse in another, and random, directionless oscillations in yet another? Why too should Japan have exhibited some of these same synchronized patterns, including growing cultural unity and an unprecedentedly successful political re-integration from the 17th to 19th centuries? How widespread across Eurasia were such parallels? French consolidation finds obvious echoes elsewhere in Western Europe, but surely as the devolutionary histories of much of archipelagic Southeast Asia and of Mughal India (not to mention the Holy Roman Empire) show, linear outcomes were hardly inevitable. The fact that French, Russian, Japanese, and mainland Southeast Asian states varied considerably in population and size, operated in distinctive physical environments, embraced idiosyncratic religious traditions, and consistently exhibited very different levels of administrative and cultural coherence only deepens the puzzle of their gross convergence. What features linked mainland Southeast Asia to much of Europe and Japan but distinguished the mainland from nearby South Asia and island Southeast Asia? In Europe "early modern" is conventionally used to identify the period c. 1400–c. 1750. Can this same term – with its hint of inexorable progress to full modernity – be shifted from Western Europe to describe areas that proved incapable of generating by themselves some of the core features of true modernity, including industrialization? Conversely, can Asian parallels reshape hitherto encapsulated explanations of European dynamics? Finally, in using analytic models derived from one region, be it Europe or Asia, to examine another, can we avoid contaminating our inquiries at the source?

Potentially, Southeast Asia promises rich insights into such questions, precisely because this region lay at an enormous physical and cultural distance from Europe, and because parallels between mainland Southeast Asia and parts of Europe appear, at first glance, exceptionally striking. The systematic neglect of Southeast Asia in world histories only adds to its allure.

To realize this potential, however, Southeast Asian historiography must be recast. At present there is no way to connect Southeast Asia to other Eurasian regions, because we lack either an overview of regional development during the second millennium or a plausible model of regional dynamics. To be sure, we have country histories, but these are usually encapsulated. We also have one attempt at a regional synthesis for the era 1450–1680, but I shall argue shortly that this does not answer our most pressing needs. This project therefore has two goals which I approach sequentially but which in fact are interdependent. First and most basic, I seek to reconceptualize the history of mainland Southeast Asia during a thousand years, c. 800–1830 C.E. Second, during this same period I compare trajectories and dynamics in mainland Southeast Asia with those in Russia, France, and Japan, in China and South Asia to a lesser extent, and in the archipelago so as to rethink both Southeast Asian marginalization and European exceptionalism. Accordingly, *Strange Parallels: Southeast Asia in Global Context, c. 800–1830* is divided into two volumes, *Integration on the Mainland*, followed by *Mainland Mirrors: Russia, France, Japan, and the Islands*.

This chapter, which serves as an introduction to the entire study, begins with a review of Southeast Asian historiography in an effort to show why new paradigms are needed. The chapter concludes by suggesting how those paradigms connect to the wider world.

PART A: RETHINKING SOUTHEAST ASIA

"Externalist" Historiography

Our understanding of precolonial Southeast Asia has passed through three phases whose successive emphases display a contrapuntal logic.

The earliest historiographic tradition – which was certainly Eurocentric, but for which I believe "externalist" offers a broader, more accurate label – did not articulate its underlying assumptions, both because it lacked an earlier historiography against which to define itself, and because it embraced the positivist assumption that diligence and goodwill alone would eliminate bias and produce history whose truth was self-evident. Nor, in an era when colonial divisions loomed large, was there much concern for the coherence of what academics now treat as a distinctive region. In essence, this historiography reflected the intuitive understandings – joined often to formidable linguistic expertise – of French, British, Dutch, and Indian scholars, many unaware of one another's work, who attempted to write histories of Southeast Asia's several parts. Yet in retrospect we can see that, along with scholars of other parts of Asia, these historians shared certain basic tenets, chief among which was a tendency to explain the astounding East-West power inequalities of their own day with essentialist definitions of culture. Early achievements in India and China were recognized, of course, but these only rendered more stark Asia's subsequent immobility, whose root cause was the despotism, obscurantism, and servile equality of Asian society. With innovation prey to tyranny, history had become cyclic rather than linear. The real goal of European intervention therefore was not to make money, but to liberate Asia from its own past by introducing notions of liberty and progress.[3]

These interpretive approaches were applied to Southeast Asia with a peculiar twist. Here the trope "indigenous incapacity/external benefaction" gained added force from the belief that Southeast Asia, unlike India, China, or the Mideast, had never engendered its own civilization. So dramatic was evidence of Indian architectural and religious influence in Burma, Siam, Cambodia, and Java, and of Chinese influence in Vietnam, that the first Western observers could hardly avoid seeing these civilizations as fundamentally derivative – especially if the observers had been trained in Indology or Sinology. The terms "Farther India" and "Indo-China" were sufficiently emblematic. A preoccupation with external actors, whether Indian, Chinese, or European – hence my term "externalist" – therefore characterized most historiography written in the first half of the 20th century, and to these actors all significant innovation was attributed. Thus, for example, "Indianization" – the process whereby early Indian religious, architectural, and scriptural traditions were transferred to Southeast Asia during the first millennium C.E. – was portrayed by Hendrik Kern, N. J. Krom, G. Coedes, and other leading scholars as primarily the fruit of Indian, rather than Southeast Asian, initiatives. Either Indian traders had provided an indispensable spur, or Indian warriors had established colonies.[4]

Historians of the era after Indianization necessarily examined local dynasties, but with the arrival of European ships at the great regional emporium of Melaka in 1511, once again "the view . . . turned a hundred

[3] Cf. Thomas Trautmann, *Aryans and British India* (Berkeley, 1997), 129.
[4] C. C. Berg, "Javanese Historiography – A Synopsis of Its Evolution," idem, "The Work of Professor Krom," and J. G. de Casparis, "Historical Writing on Indonesia (Early Period)" in D. G. E. Hall, ed., *Historians of South-East Asia* (London, 1961), 13–23, 121–71, esp. 127 n. 38; G. Coedes, *Les Etats hindouises d'Indochine et d'Indonesie* (Paris, 1948), translated as *The Indianized States of Southeast Asia*, Walter Vella, ed. (Honolulu, 1968); J. D. Legge, "The Writing of Southeast Asian History," in *CHSEA*, esp. 3–15. On Southeast Asian historiography, see too Hall, *Historians*; Anthony Reid and David Marr, eds., *Perceptions of the Past in Southeast Asia* (Singapore, 1979); Nicholas Tarling, *Southeast Asia: A Modern History* (Oxford, 2001), 503–27.

eighty degrees and from then on the Indies are observed from the deck of the ship, the ramparts of the fortress, the high gallery of the trading-house."[5] The history of archipelagic Southeast Asia became a history of Portuguese, Dutch, Englishmen, and Spaniards in Asian waters – their wars and trade, their refashioning of local societies – with indigenous peoples reduced to European foils.[6]

On the mainland the indisputably marginal role of Europeans before 1824 rendered indigenous actors more prominent than in the islands. Yet here too histories by Europeans remained "kings and battles" narratives rather than analyses of indigenous social change, in part because colonial scholars felt obliged to establish basic chronologies, but more fundamentally because they too embraced what I term "the law of Southeast Asian inertia": unless acted upon by external forces, native societies remained at rest. "Their ideas remained in the nineteenth century what they had been in the ninth," wrote G. E. Harvey, the doyen of English historians of Burma. "To build pagodas, to collect daughters from tributary chiefs, to sally forth on slave raids, to make wars for white elephants – these conceptions had had their day, and a monarchy which failed to get beyond them was doomed."[7] So a French historian observed of Vietnam: "[After separating from China in 939] the Annamites, throughout the centuries, made no progress on Chinese civilization. Their arts and sciences always remained inferior to those of China. . . . Peoples, like individuals, progress only when provided with the necessary stimulus: they require contact with people of a more refined culture."[8]

My point is not to disparage colonial-era archeologists and historians, who heroically laid the foundations for all subsequent scholarship.

---

[5] J. C. van Leur, *Indonesian Trade and Society* (The Hague, 1955), 261.

[6] See for example R. O. Winstedt, *History of Malaya* (Singapore, 1935, rpt., 1962); F. W. Stapel, ed., *Geschiedenis van Nederlandsch-Indie* (1938–1940), analyzed in de Casparis, "Historical Writing," 145; and the first edition (London, 1955) of D. G. E. Hall's *A History of South-East Asia*, which divided pre-20th century material into "The Pre-European Period" (to 1511), "South-East Asia during the Earlier Phase of European Expansion," and "The Period of European Territorial Expansion."

[7] G. E. Harvey, *A History of Burma* (London, 1925, rpt. 1967), 249. For similar perspectives, see D. G. E. Hall, *Early English Intercourse with Burma, 1587–1743* (1928; rpt., London, 1968), 11–12; W. A. R. Wood, *A History of Siam* (London, 1926); Etienne Aymonier, *Le Cambodge*, 3 vols. (Paris, 1900–1904), I, pt. 2.

[8] A. Schreiner, *Les institutions annamites en Basse-Cochinchine avant la conquete francaise*, 3 vols. (Saigon, 1900–1902), I, 53–54. Cf. C. B. Maybon, *Histoire moderne du Pays d'Annam* (Paris, 1920), P. Pasquier, *L'Annam d'autrefois* (Paris, 1907); and discussion in Nola Cooke, "Colonial Political Myth and the Problem of the Other: French and Vietnamese in the Protectorate of Annam" (Australian National Univ. Ph.D. diss., 1991).

Their research became increasingly sophisticated, and much of it, no doubt, will survive gerontophagy better than the present study. Rather, I seek to identify the assumptions and perspectives animating much of their writing and persisting in many quarters well into the 1970s. First, without external stimuli, Southeast Asian societies existed in space but not in time. Second, with the partial exception of Coedes' *Les Etats hindouises d'Indochine et d'Indonesie* (1948), these writings had no vision of Southeast Asia as a coherent region. Coedes defined pre-1300 Southeast Asia in terms of Indian influence, and for that reason omitted the Philippines and northern Vietnam.[9] But usually the criteria of regional identity, potential or actual, were not discussed. Thus, notwithstanding its title, D. G. E. Hall's authoritative *A History of South-East Asia* (first edition, 1955) remained smaller than the sum of its parts: after a chapter based on Coedes, it became a collection of country histories, without interest in synthesis or regional themes.[10] Third, insofar as colonial-era historiography treated indigenous society, it focused on the courts to the exclusion of villagers and lower social groups. Finally, an ontological difference separated Southeast Asian and European mentalities and ensured that the histories of Europe and precolonial Asia were fundamentally dichotomous.

"Autonomous" Historiography

Despite the externalist orientation of much prewar scholarship, it was from the ranks of colonial historians that an anti-externalist – what I call an "autonomous" – approach began to emerge in the 1930s and 1940s. Some Europeans reacted against the tendency of Indian scholars to overemphasize Indian elements in Indonesian culture. Others, attuned to Southeast Asian political aspirations, grew weary of White Man's Burden ideology. Yet others sought merely to correct what they saw as the simplistic claims of their predecessors.[11] The resultant historiography tended to be both more nuanced and more sympathetic to indigenous agency.

---

[9] Coedes, *Les Etats hindouises*; cf. idem, *Indianized States*, v, xv. A more inclusive geographic vision of "Monsoon Asia" stretching from southern China across Indo-China to southern India inspired Paul Mus, "Cultes indiens et indigenes au Champa," *BEFEO* 33 (1933): 367–410.

[10] This edition also omitted the Philippines. On the evolution of the concept of Southeast Asia, Donald K. Emmerson, "Southeast Asia: What's in a Name?", *JSEAS* 15 (1984): 1–21.

[11] De Casparis, "Historical Writing," 136–40; van Leur, *Trade and Society*, vi–vii.

In analyzing the transfer of Indian culture, for example, the pioneering French scholar Paul Mus and such Dutch researchers as W. F. Stutterheim and J. C. van Leur drew attention away from Indian origins to argue that much Southeast Asian art and architecture revealed quintessentially indigenous conceptions of sanctity. Indianization, they suggested, should be seen as a process by which local rulers themselves took the initiative to summon brahmin priests and artificers for the express purpose of enhancing royal dignity.[12] But van Leur, supported in various contexts by B. Schrieke, systematically extended this emphasis on the autonomy of Indonesian history. Van Leur argued that during the period of Islamization c. 1300–1600, and also more surprisingly during the early Dutch era c. 1600–1830, the basic rhythms of Indonesian economic life continued to reflect internal rather than external forces. Likewise, the deep structures of Javanese culture and psychology resisted Indian, Muslim, and European contacts. In van Leur's memorable dictum, "The sheen of the world religions and foreign cultural forms is a thin and flaking glaze; underneath it the whole of the old indigenous forms has continued to exist . . ."[13] "[A]s long as the magic poison of modern capitalism had not yet enchanted Europe . . . to produce steam, mechanics, and grooved cannon," two equal civilizations coexisted, with the Asian quantitatively superior.[14]

The translation into English in the 1950s of van Leur's and Schrieke's writings helped to popularize this perspective, but its growing influence reflected, above all, shifts in the political and academic climate during the third quarter of the century. The collapse of European imperial ideologies favored a more celebratory, empowering view of the region's past. The view of Southeast Asians as continuously "in charge" of their own destiny appealed to Westerners who sympathized with Southeast Asian nationalism. In American universities the Cold War expansion of area-studies programs, with their emphasis on local languages and cultures as suitable subjects in their own right, also encouraged autonomous at the expense of Sinological or Indological approaches. During the 1960s and 1970s, and lingering into the 1980s, bitter academic hostility to American intervention in Vietnam and to the Domino Theory on which that intervention rested, had much the same effect. Since the

---

[12] Mus, "Cultes indiens," 367–410; van Leur, *Trade and Society*, esp. 89–110; historiograhic discussion at de Casparis, "Historical Writing," 138–40; B. Schrieke, *Indonesian Sociological Studies*, 2 vols. (The Hague, 1955, 1957).

[13] *Trade and Society*, 95.

[14] *Trade and Society*, 284–85. See also Schrieke, *Studies*, I, 7–36, and II, 3–4, 97–101, 230–67.

Domino Theory assumed that Southeast Asians lacked genuine agency, that whichever external power applied the greatest pressure in Vietnam was bound to win, antiwar scholars emphasized the indigenous roots of Vietnamese Communism in particular and of local evolution in general.

"Autonomous" historiography was fairly christened in 1961 and 1962 with two influential essays by John Smail and Harry J. Benda entitled, respectively, "On the Possibility of an Autonomous History of Modern Southeast Asia" and "The Structure of Southeast Asian History: Some Preliminary Observations."[15] Smail extended van Leur's methodological approach into the early 20th century, long after one would have thought Western influence was radically transformative, by arguing that under the surface of colonial rule European categories remained at best marginally relevant to the world view of most local peoples. Likewise insisting that Southeast Asian history be written "from within," Benda proposed a periodization based on cultural and political relations peculiar to Southeast Asia.

Inspired by this new *weltanschauung*, from the late 1960s through the late 1980s an expanded corps of scholars, most trained in American universities, began to explore with unprecedented enthusiasm and archival energy the internal life of precolonial societies. They commonly sought not to exclude foreign influences, but to show how local peoples had been able to absorb, translate, and recontextualize external forces, in short, to maintain control of their environments. Not only did their political vision differ from that of most prewar scholars, but the prewar concentration on the classical period was now balanced by a growing interest in the 16th to early 19th centuries – as if to demonstrate the vitality of indigenous culture even after the arrival of Europeans in Southeast Asian waters.[16]

To cite briefly some representative research: For the central mainland, David Wyatt reconstructed the political histories of Tai-speaking states from the 13th to the mid-19th centuries, an evolution in which Europeans and foreign Asians played a decidedly modest role.[17] Michael Aung-Thwin revolutionized classical Burmese historiography by analyzing the monkhood's tendency to accumulate tax-free religious lands.[18] The

---

[15] Smail, in *JSEAH* 2 (1961): 72–102; and Benda, in *JSEAH* 3 (1962): 106–38.
[16] Insofar as both reacted against an externalist orthodoxy, this perspective corresponds to a trend in Chinese historiography that Paul Cohen, *Discovering History in China* (New York, 1984), ch. 4 labeled "a China-centered history of China."
[17] Wyatt, *Thailand: A Short History* (New Haven, 1982), chs. 1–6.
[18] *Pagan: The Origins of Modern Burma* (Honolulu, 1985).

present author sought to analyze Burmese administrative cycles after 1500 by focusing on intra-elite competition for manpower. Already apparent in Tai historiography, this emphasis on manpower was itself symptomatic of an internal orientation.[19]

For Vietnam, Keith Taylor, John Whitmore, O. W. Wolters, Insun Yu, and most especially Alexander Woodside in his classic *Vietnam and the Chinese Model* began to dissect the complex relation between Chinese and Vietnamese practices. Contrary to early French assumptions that Vietnam had emerged from Chinese occupation in 939 as a "smaller dragon," these historians demonstrated that Vietnam engaged Chinese culture in an open-ended process of resistance, accommodation, and localization. Outcomes remained regionally variable and uncertain, and many patterns, especially at the popular level, differed from Chinese traditions.[20]

In studies of the island world that paralleled revisionist interpretations of Vietnamese-Chinese relations, a number of talented scholars analyzed the relation between indigenous leaders and Chinese, Dutch, English, and Spanish actors.[21] While discounting van Leur's more extreme claims, this new archipelagic historiography accorded indigenes an irreducible independence and treated Europeans as but one element in a complex political and economic mix. Autonomy had a psychocultural as well as a material dimension. Clifford Geertz emphasized the chasm between Western notions of political power as resource

---

[19] Lieberman, *Burmese Administrative Cycles: Anarchy and Conquest, c. 1580–1760* (Princeton, 1984). Cf. Akin Rabibhadana, *The Organization of Thai Society in the Early Bangkok Period, 1782–1873* (Ithaca, 1970).

[20] Taylor, *The Birth of Vietnam* (Berkeley, 1983); Whitmore, "The Development of Le Government in Fifteenth-Century Vietnam" (Cornell Univ. Ph.D. diss., 1968); idem, *Vietnam, Ho Quy Ly, and the Ming (1371–1421)* (New Haven, 1985); Wolters, "Assertions of Cultural Well-being in Fourteenth Century Vietnam, parts I and II," *JSEAS* 10 (1979) and 11 (1980); idem, "Le Van Huu's Treatment of Ly Than Ton's Reign (1127–1137)," in C. D. Cowan and O. W. Wolters, eds., *Southeast Asian History and Historiography: Essays Presented to D. G. E. Hall* (Ithaca, 1976), 203–26; Yu, "Law and Family in Seventeenth and Eighteenth-Century Vietnam" (Univ. of Michigan Ph.D. diss., 1978), republished as *Law and Society in Seventeenth and Eighteeth Century Vietnam* (Seoul, 1990); Woodside, *Vietnam and the Chinese Model* (Cambridge, MA: 1971). For recent work in the same vein, see Li Tana, *Nguyen Cochinchina* (Ithaca, 1998).

[21] Seminal writings included Wolters, *Early Indonesian Commerce* (Ithaca, 1967); idem, *The Fall of Srivijaya in Malay History* (London, 1970); M. C. Ricklefs, *Jogjakarta under Sultan Mangkubumi 1749–1792* (London, 1974); Barbara Watson Andaya, *Perak: The Abode of Grace* (Kuala Lumpur, 1979); Leonard Andaya, *The Kingdom of Johor* (Kuala Lumpur, 1975); idem, *The Heritage of Arung Palakka* (The Hague, 1981); Vicente Rafael, *Contracting Colonialism* (Ithaca, 1988).

command, and the Indic conception of the polity as a theater state crafted to dramatize status pride and hierarchy.[22] Even in the Philippines, where at first glance widespread Christianization would suggest that the Spanish project of acculturation was wholly successful, Vicente Rafael argued that local people appropriated and fundamentally revalorized Spanish concepts so as to mark themselves off from the novel forces confronting them.[23]

In what was arguably the most extended theoretical summary of the autonomous viewpoint, Wolters' *History, Culture, and Region in Southeast Asian Perspectives* (1982, 1999) argued that the constant fracturing and restatement of Indian (and Sinic) materials in local idioms drained them of their original significance and inhibited any common Indic heritage or regional identity. He concluded that the study of dissimilar cultural statements through the patient analysis of local vocabulary was the proper goal of early Southeast Asian historiography.[24]

Taken as a whole, this body of work defiantly rejected the central claim of colonial-era historiography, namely, that Southeast Asians lacked agency. Yet, this attention to difference can obscure the fact that externalist and autonomous histories also shared fundamental, if unspoken assumptions. An emphasis on the self-sufficiency and effortless ability of indigenous peoples to absorb outside influences lapsed easily into a renewed emphasis on social and cultural inertia. Colonial historians assumed Southeast Asians were incapable of linear change, some autonomists implied Southeast Asians were not much interested in change, yet the resultant images were similar. What is the difference between, on the one hand, the aforementioned claim by Harvey, a dyed-in-the-wool imperialist, that Burmese ideas remained in the 19th century what they had been in the 9th, and on the other hand, the claim by Schrieke, a pioneer autonomist, that Indonesian society "cherished no other ideal than to remain as it was, shunning all change.... As a consequence, the Java of around 1700 A.D. was in reality the same

---

[22] Geertz, *Negara: The Theatre State in Nineteenth-Century Bali* (Princeton, 1980).

[23] Rafael, *Contracting Colonialism*. A similar interpretive framework inspired Reynaldo Ileto, *Pasyon and Revolution* (Quezon City, 1979).

[24] Wolters, *History, Culture, and Region in Southeast Asian Perspectives* (Singapore, 1982), chs. 3–5. In the revised edition (Ithaca and Singapore, 1999), Wolters acknowledged, "Perhaps in 1982 I was too anxious to preserve both geographical and historical distance between the sub-regions" (107). But he reaffirmed his basic opposition to those historians "who detect change and especially change in the form of centralizing tendencies" (152).

as the Java of around 700 A.D."?[25] To be sure, this emphasis was not uniform – it was least apparent in Vietnamese historiography, which by virtue of its concern with pulsating Chinese influences was inherently developmental – but it was undoubtedly widespread.

This orientation continued to work against incorporating Southeast Asia into world history. If, as we have seen, Orientalist historians posited a dichotomy between Western dynamism and Eastern inertia, at least their emphasis on the voyages of discovery provided a tie between far-flung sectors of Eurasia. Now, with European activities devalued, connective history – inquiry into contacts between physically distant societies – languished. Comparative history – the investigation of structural similarities between societies regardless of physical linkages – fared no better, precisely because the emphasis on local self-sufficiency militated against a search for features common to Southeast Asia and Europe, or indeed any other region. In the hands of Geertz and other devotees of autonomous cultural worlds, Balinese and Javanese actors, obsessed with ritual potency but indifferent to problems of hard economic power, were fundamentally unlike Western historical figures.[26]

Moreover, notwithstanding Benda's self-consciously regional perspective and the fact that "Southeast Asia" was becoming more widely accepted in the academy, the attention to local statements and particularized experience ensured that the concept "Southeast Asia" itself still had minimal substantive content, at least for the precolonial era. New survey texts remained disjointed assemblages of country histories.[27] Admittedly, anthropologists and some autonomous historians of an anthropological bent identified elements of what they claimed was a persistent Southeast Asian cultural and material substratum, including bilateral kinship, high levels of female autonomy, a concept

---

[25] Schrieke, *Sociological Studies*, II, 99–100. Also ibid., II, 4, 230. Cf. Wolters, *History, Culture* (1982), 22, 27.

[26] Geertz, *Negara*. On claims for the basic incomparability of post-1500 European and Southeast Asian history, see also Benedict R. O. 'G. Anderson, "The Idea of Power in Javanese History," in C. Holt, ed., *Culture and Politics in Indonesia* (Ithaca, 1972), 1–69; Jeyamalar Kathirithamby-Wells, "Restraints on the Development of Merchant Capitalism in Southeast Asia before c. 1800," in Anthony Reid, ed., *Southeast Asia in the Early Modern Era* (Ithaca, 1993), 123–50. The distinction between comparative and connective history I derive from Karen Wigen, "Bringing the World Back In: Meditations on the Space-Time of Early Japanese Modernity," paper prepared for an SSRC-sponsored workshop, December 1995.

[27] E.g., John F. Cady, *Southeast Asia: Its Historical Development* (New York, 1964); Nicholas Tarling, *A Concise History of Southeast Asia* (New York, 1966); and the 2nd, 3rd, and 4th editions (1964, 1968, 1981) of D. G. E. Halls's magnum opus.

of animating "soul stuff," pervasive patron-client ties, leadership by "men of prowess," spirit propitiation, houses resting on poles, and a rice-fish diet.[28] But such traits were not distributed uniformly, northern and central Vietnam providing innumerable thorny exceptions. Beyond this, some elements in this list did not distinguish Southeast Asia from southern China, South Asia, or Melanesia. With the post-1400 progress of textual religions – Theravada Buddhism, Neo-Confucianism, Islam, and Christianity – cultural commonalities, limited to begin with, became ever less encompassing. But above all, the listing of traits emblematic of some enduring regional essence was static and thus unsympathetic to the historian's overriding responsibility to describe changes in structure and perception.

Finally, because cultural inquiry tended to remain divorced from political history, the post-1965 explosion of precolonial research did not seriously challenge the elitist focus enshrined before World War II. Most histories (my own included) still featured courtiers, with commoners barely visible.

The "Age of Commerce" Thesis

Unlike the first two historiographic approaches, the third was the creation of a single scholar, Anthony Reid, whose interpretation of Southeast Asia during the precolonial era, especially the 15th to 17th centuries, to this day remains best known and most widely accepted. Also unlike earlier paradigms, whose exemplars generally wrote of individual countries, Reid sought to develop a master regional narrative, paying particular attention to the relation between Southeast Asia as a whole and the wider maritime world. In part, Reid may have been inspired by East Asia's spectacular economic performance in the 1980s and early 1990s, when revisionist critiques of Eurocentric global economic history began to appear. Starting with articles on urbanization and demography and continuing with his magisterial two-volume *Southeast Asia in the Age of Commerce 1450–1680* (1988, 1993) and his recapitulatory *Charting the Shape of Early Modern Southeast Asia* (1999), Reid attempted, intentionally or not, to redress many of the weaknesses of earlier historiography. These were not only the first book-length studies to offer a coherent

[28] See, e.g., Wolters, *History, Culture*, esp. ch. 1; Charles A. Fisher, *South-East Asia* (London, 1964), chs. 1, 3; Charles Keyes, *The Golden Peninsula* (New York, 1977); and the special edition of *JSEAS* 15, 2 (1984) entitled "Symposium on Societal Organization in Mainland Southeast Asia Prior to the Eighteenth Century."

vision of precolonial Southeast Asia, they were also the first to link indigenous political change, at least temporarily, to global economic shifts, to describe changes in urban, commercial, and religious organization, and to deal extensively with commoners and non-elite merchants. Although far richer and more sophisticated than any externalist work, if we posit a Southeast Asian historiography whose polar dynamics are external maritime influences and indigenous cultural forces, Reid shifted the balance away from the latter and back toward the former – in a move that reversed the "autonomous" shift that began in the 1960s.[29]

In essence, the Age of Commerce thesis argued that from the early 15th century an expansion of Indian Ocean and Chinese demand encouraged throughout Southeast Asia a novel prosperity, together with a cultural cosmopolitanism and a trend toward centralized polities, all of which was reversed by the global economic downturn of the mid-17th century. After describing and attempting to quantify the growth in foreign trade with Southeast Asia between c. 1400 and 1650, Reid systematically analyzed the social and economic repercussions. So marked was urban growth that by 1650 some 5 percent of the region's people lived in large cities, a percentage Reid claimed was greater than in contemporary northern Europe.[30] A significant portion of the population came to depend on international trade for their livelihood and for much of their clothing, while in contrast to later periods, between c. 1450 and 1630 Southeast traders and shippers became major players on international routes.

The political impact of maritime expansion was particularly impressive, as increasing royal revenues joined with foreign-style firearms and naval craft to promote political systems throughout the region that were more absolutist, centralized, and bureaucratic. Moreover, in the archipelago, new cities and market connections created a grid for the dissemination of Islam and Christianity, indeed, for a religious revolution. In lieu of fluid, localized, heavily animist traditions – the "Southeast Asian religion" – the new faiths imposed more precise religious

---

[29] See Reid, ed., *Slavery, Bondage and Dependency in Southeast Asia* (New York, 1983); idem, ed., *Southeast Asia in the Early Modern Era* (Ithaca, 1993); idem, ed., *The Last Stand of Asian Autonomies* (New York, 1997); idem, ch. 8, "Economic and Social Change, c. 1400–1800," in *CHSEA*; idem, *Southeast Asia in the Age of Commerce 1450–1680. Volume One: The Lands Below the Winds. Volume Two: Expansion and Crisis* (New Haven, 1988, 1993); idem, *Charting the Shape of Early Modern Southeast Asia* (Chiang Mai, 1999). For Reid's numerous articles, see bibliographies in these volumes.

[30] *Age of Commerce*, II, 75.

boundaries, universal texts, and a predictable moral universe. To appreciate the originality and seminal power of Reid's research, consider that such concepts as precolonial urbanization, maritime technology, changing import levels, commercial export agriculture, new moral codes, and animist-textual tensions were not even broached in the fourth (1981) edition of Hall's *History of South-East Asia*, which in the early 1990s was still the standard reference.

Finally, Reid borrowed the concept of a 17th century crisis from European historiography to explain what he claimed was a reversal of these trends. What maritime trade bestowed, it could as easily revoke. He identified a series of constraints on Southeast Asian prosperity arising in the early 17th century and peaking in the 1680s: deteriorating climate, falling profit margins, Chinese and European navigational advances with which Southeast Asians had difficulty competing, and – most critical for the archipelago – unprecedented assaults by the Dutch East India Company. In combination, these forces compelled Southeast Asians to retreat from cash-cropping to subsistence agriculture and to disengage from the international economy. Indigenous cities declined, to be replaced in some places by European enclaves culturally divorced from their hinterlands. Deprived of easy access to external authorities, cosmopolitan cultures now yielded to less textually oriented religious expressions and a growing distrust of external ideas.[31]

More dramatic yet was the political transformation, as once-powerful kingdoms fragmented. Although Reid acknowledged that Aceh and the chief mainland kingdoms retained greater freedom of maneuver than places like Banten or Makassar, in virtually every case institutions of central control built during "the time of absolutism" failed to survive the loss of commercial income, as shown by severe political crises in the late 17th and 18th centuries. Even Java, Burma, Siam, and Vietnam failed to "escape impoverishment and eventual collapse under the strain of a bureaucracy more complex than they could maintain without the revenues from trade."[32]

In short, these trends toward economic and cultural impoverishment and political deracination contrasted sharply with the previous era and constituted a fundamental shift in the character of Southeast Asian development that would persist until modern times. In a chapter titled

---

[31] *Age of Commerce*, II, 267–330, esp. 328–29; "Economic and Social Change, c. 1400–1800," 488–501; *Charting the Shape*, 12–14, 217–34.
[32] "Economic and Social Change, c. 1400–1800," 500; *Age of Commerce*, II, 303–11.

"The Origins of Southeast Asian Poverty," Reid concluded, "The important point is that there was a change of direction in the seventeenth century that was not reversed until the twentieth.... The positive interaction between international trade, scriptural religion, and expanding Southeast Asian monarchies was at an end – and with it the age of commerce."[33]

This broad schema, which it must be emphasized was presented as valid for all of Southeast Asia, works best for the archipelago, where Reid's earlier research was focused. With its weak agricultural base and thin populations (outside Java and Bali), its strategic position athwart the world's chief east-west shipping lanes, its monopoly on spices, and its vast coastlines, this zone in fact was exceptionally dependent on maritime revenues and thus unusually vulnerable to European naval strength. To be sure, even for the archipelago problems of interpretation remain. The central and northern Philippines, for example, fit the model poorly, and in key respects actually stand closer to western and central mainland Southeast Asia than to other archipelagic areas. Nor in the Muslim zone can I accept as universally valid the argument that post-1650 Islam grew more parochial. One also wonders whether the emphasis on long-term decline distinguishes sufficiently between major cities and smaller ports, whose marginality afforded them a wider autonomy, and whether it gives enough attention to the post-1750 commercial and political revival in Java and elsewhere. Still, if we contrast the position of indigenous rulers and shippers in much of the Malay-Indonesian world in 1800 with that in 1550, Reid's basic thesis of a 17th-century political and economic decline remains cogent.

When we turn to mainland Southeast Asia, however, more far-reaching questions arise. In his determination to use Malay-Indonesian kingdoms as a template for the entire region, in effect, to overcome Southeast Asia's fragmentation by positing a single trajectory, Reid, I believe, tended to overcompensate in somewhat the same way that van Leur and the early autonomists overcompensated for the excesses of their externalist predecessors. As applied to the mainland, the Age of Commerce thesis, its many virtues notwithstanding, entails four problems.

First, it ignores a number of cultural and political transformations on the mainland without sustained parallel in the Muslim archipelago.

---

[33] *Age of Commerce*, II, 311, 325. See *infra* n. 35 for Reid's subsequent research on post-17th century trade and its implications.

Such was the case, for example, with the tendency, adumbrated at the outset of this chapter, toward ethnic/cultural homogenization – that is to say, the incorporation before 1680 of Mons and Chams into the Burman and Vietnamese majorities, and the integration of diverse peoples in the Chaophraya basin to form a Siamese identity. In each polity not merely religious orthodoxy, but broader patterns of speech, ritual, social organization, and ethnicity tended to diffuse from center to periphery and from elite to lower strata. We learn something about the trend on the mainland toward political "absolutism," but virtually nothing about territorial consolidation, which was arguably the most dramatic political change to 1680. By the same token, although as functional ideologies Neo-Confucianism, Islam, and Christianity were in some ways quite comparable, Reid gave scant attention to the Neo-Confucian revolution of the 15th century, presumably because its origins were independent of oceanic commerce.

Second and by extension from the previous point, the impulses to integration across the mainland between c. 1450 and 1680 were generally more heterogeneous than Reid acknowledged and the relations between them, more fluid and indeterminate. In his emphasis on maritime trade, Reid in effect revived the "law of Southeast Asian inertia": when maritime impulses suffused the region, it prospered, and when they ceased, Southeast Asia languished. Although barely mentioned, overland trade with China was a significant fraction of maritime trade. But more basic, amidst the tumult of the ports, we hear little or nothing about preeminently domestic sources of dynamism – about the elaboration of domestic (as opposed to maritime) commercial networks, rural demographic rhythms, rural educational networks, frontier reclamation, new crops and irrigation systems, agricultural taxation, changes in land tenure. Nor is this emphasis accidental, as the vast bulk of Reid's primary sources were written by European visitors, whose understanding of rural life was, at best, limited. Writing Southeast Asian history from non-Southeast Asian sources may be necessary for much of the archipelago, but probably not for Java,[34] and certainly not for mainland states like Burma and Vietnam, with rich indigenous-language records. Without minimizing the role of foreign guns and trade revenues, I shall argue that integration in the chief mainland states was never purely, and in many contexts not even primarily, a function of maritime commerce.

[34] On the limits of European sources for 18th-century Java, where they are exceptionally abundant, see M. C. Ricklefs, *The Seen and Unseen Worlds in Java* (Honolulu, 1998), 345.

Third, the Age of Commerce chronology invites criticism. In particular, the notion of a mid- to late 17th-century watershed, however attractive it may be for Malay-Indonesian areas, is inapplicable to continental Southeast Asia. By and large, the chief mainland states were too removed from the chief sea routes, too immune to naval pressures, and too well integrated to exhibit the same sensitivity to European pressure as their archipelagic counterparts. In some parts of the mainland, maritime trade did stagnate or decline in the late 17th century. Admittedly too, the mid- to late 1600s saw political disorders in Siam and Burma. However, not only was the loss of maritime revenues less severe than in the archipelago, but these losses were reversed during an expansion that began in the 1710s or 1720s and continued well into the 19th century. Moreover, compared to state breakdowns in the late 1500s and again in the mid- to late 1700s, the disorders on the mainland during the 1600s were insignificant. (Nor were they precipitated by maritime decline). Ironically, if any period in the tumultuous history of the mainland may be termed placid and institutionally conservative, it was precisely the period c. 1650–1720. But even the interregna of the 16th and 18th centuries anticipated a more successful imperial integration in Burma and Siam, and in the latter epoch, Vietnam. In terms of territorial extent, administrative penetration, and economic resources, the Burmese Kon-baung dynasty (founded 1752), the Siamese Chakri dynasty (founded 1782), and the Vietnamese Nguyen dynasty (in national control, 1802) represented the apogee of precolonial vigor. Moreover, within each zone rural education, vernacular literature, ethnic and cultural standardization, and market networks all were far more encompassing and specialized in the early 1800s than in the mid-1600s, which Reid saw as the acme of Southeast Asian cultural and commercial achievement.[35]

---

[35] More recently, seeking to modify the image of unalloyed post-1680 retreat, Reid has called attention to a resurgence of trade during what he calls the "Chinese century" c. 1740–1840. See his "Introduction" and "A New Phase of Commercial Expansion in Southeast Asia, 1760–1840," in Reid, *Last Stand*, esp. 11–14, 57, 70; idem, "Flows and Seepages in the Long-term Chinese Interaction with Southeast Asia," in idem, ed., *Sojourners and Settlers* (St. Leonards, Australia, 1996), 15–49; and David Bulbeck, Reid, Lay Cheng Tan, and Yiqu Wu, comps., *Southeast Asian Exports Since the 14th Century* (Singapore, 1998). But this approach does not help his case for three reasons: a) it continues to exaggerate for all three mainland sectors the decline or stagnation in trade that occurred between c. 1680 and 1740 (see *infra* Chs. 2, 3, 4 for documentation of continued commercial vitality); b) even with an exaggerated 1680–1740 hiatus, the revisionist emphasis on post-1740 vitality undermines the basic Age of Commerce

At the other end of the time line, treating the 15th century as the dawn of a new age, although more plausible than a late 17th-century rupture, also entails risks, because it minimizes continuities between pre-1350 polities and their post-1400 successors. Not only did Theravada communities experience no shift in religious sensibility comparable to the introduction of Islam, Christianity, or Neo-Confucianism, but in the Indic mainland – unlike the islands – the 14th-century transition was but the most disruptive of three increasingly feeble interregna.

Finally, the Age of Commerce thesis beclouds the relation between Southeast Asia and other sectors of early modern Eurasia. Volume Two of *Southeast Asia in the Age of Commerce 1450–1680* attempts *en passant* to connect Southeast Asian to European history by comparing briefly rapid commercial growth in both areas prior to 1680, and by suggesting that European absolutism bore some resemblance to state-strengthening projects in Southeast Asia. But after c. 1680 – once maritime revenues were lost – the emphasis is on thwarted opportunities and Southeast Asian regression.[36] Ultimately, therefore, the Age of Commerce thesis reverts to a model of East-West incomparability.

A Fourth Approach

This book proposes to re-interpret mainland Southeast Asian history from c. 800 to 1830 by examining halting, but sustained, trends to political, cultural, and commercial integration. The approach differs from externalist historiography because it rejects local stasis and denies exclusive agency to foreign actors. It diverges from autonomous historiography because it seeks to connect diverse changes in local structure to global patterns. But it differs also from the Age of Commerce thesis insofar as it: a) explores a variety of hitherto ignored transformations; b) treats maritime influence as one of several dynamics; c) views the period 1450–1680 in the context of accelerating political and cultural consolidations from the 9th to 19th centuries; d) rejects East-West dichotomies to consider sustained, if lethargic, parallels; e) distinguishes

thesis that the late 17th century was a watershed in mainland development; and c) the discussion of economic and political evolution continues virtually to ignore non-maritime factors.

[36] Reid, *Age of Commerce*, II, 267 ff., 329; and idem, "Economic and Social Change, c. 1400–1800," 504: "it was already clear by 1700 that Southeast Asian states were not following the path of European ones. Cosmopolitan urban agglomerations, private concentrations of capital, craft specialization . . . were all less, not more, central to these states than they had been a century earlier."

between mainland trajectories and those in the archipelago as well as between variant patterns on the mainland.

Why focus on long-term multifaceted coalescence? Why make it a prism through which to view an entire region? The benefits, we shall find, are several. A concern with integration can reveal novel connections between ostensibly disparate phenomena – administrative, military, literary, religious, demographic, and economic. There is a tendency to treat these fields in isolation, but I submit that all were transformed by a wider, more rapid market-based circulation of goods and ideas, and this book explores complex feedback loops without which topical inquiries are inadequate. Beyond this, wider market networks and patronage systems modified the ethnic self-images, political visions, concepts of sanctity, and economic roles, in short the life prospects, of virtually all classes and regional groups, not merely capital elites. In retrospect, a concern with precolonial integration helps to explain different nationalist trajectories in much of continental and archipelagic Southeast Asia during the 20th century. Most critical, Southeast Asian consolidation offers uniquely rewarding insights into Eurasia itself as a unified, interactive zone.

But if the payoff is substantial, I am the first to acknowledge that this approach, with its attention to mainland/archipelagic contrasts, is by no means the only possible schema. If the Indonesian-Malay world as a whole did not experience political integration comparable to that on the mainland, in many island and mainland areas demography, frontier reclamation, monetization, and Chinese settlement appear to have followed broadly comparable rhythms. I seek to explain why similar economic contexts produced different political and cultural outcomes, but one could as well focus on economic change in its own right. Likewise, as Barbara Watson Andaya's recent collection of essays on women in early modern Southeast Asia seems to suggest, one may find changes in gender relations – also perhaps in literary representation, popular entertainment, and social categories – that crosscut a simple mainland/archipelago distinction.[37] In short, I approach Southeast

---

[37] Barbara Watson Andaya, ed., *Other Pasts: Women, Gender and History in Early Modern Southeast Asia* (Honolulu, 2000), 23–24, 69–86, 195–268 and *passim*. Insofar as high levels of state intrusion correlated with stricter divisions between male and female roles, one might expect to find such divisions more pronounced in mainland than in island SE Asia (cf. ibid., 232, 240). Yet in fact, Islam, Neo-Confucianism, and Christianity in SE Asia seem to have been rather more consistently insistent on gender discrimination than Theravada Buddhism, so once again we see no clear mainland/archipelagic division.

Asian history from a particular and, I believe, revealing perspective without pretending to an exclusive prerogative.

Territorial Changes on the Mainland to c. 1830: An Overview

The next three chapters examine in detail, respectively, the western, central, and eastern sectors of the mainland. At this point I propose to survey briefly the mainland as a whole in order to provide basic definitions, to identify regional patterns against which individual country histories may be judged, and above all, to develop a theoretical model of long-term integration and periodic collapse.[38]

I begin with territorial consolidation. During most of the period c. 900 to 1350, four major polities ruled large sectors of the mainland. Pagan, centered in Upper Burma, controlled the Irrawaddy basin and a modest upland and peninsular perimeter. Angkor dominated the middle and lower Mekong basin, much of the Chaophraya basin, and more intermittently, parts of what is now northern and peninsular Thailand. Separated from China in 939, the Vietnamese state of Dai Viet ruled the Red River basin and a southern coastal extension. Champa, arguably the weakest polity, controlled the southeast coast (Figure 1.3).[39] In recognition of the fact that these states, in varying degrees, provided a religious, political, and administrative charter for subsequent empires, I term the period prior to c. 1350 the "charter era."

Despite disparate origins – a Chinese provincial legacy in Dai Viet, indigenous adaptations of Indian statecraft elsewhere – these polities, and especially the three about which we have most information, namely, Pagan, Angkor, and Dai Viet, shared a number of developmental and chronological features. In each case, more effective domestic pacification, agricultural colonization, and improved rainfall contributed to what seems to have been substantial population growth, with a corresponding increase in the scale of religious edifices and water control projects. Starting in some cases in the 11th century and with growing vigor in the 12th and 13th centuries, the three chief states also sought to extend their zones of influence. Yet even at their height, they controlled effectively only coasts and lowlands, chiefly the great river valleys that ran in a generally north-south direction. Extensive, often thinly

---

[38] Annotation for this section is accordingly limited. For full documentation, see Chs. 2–4 *infra*.

[39] Yet smaller, more or less independent states, including Arakan, Haripunjaya, and Suphanburi, existed in what is now southwestern Burma, Laos, and western Thailand.

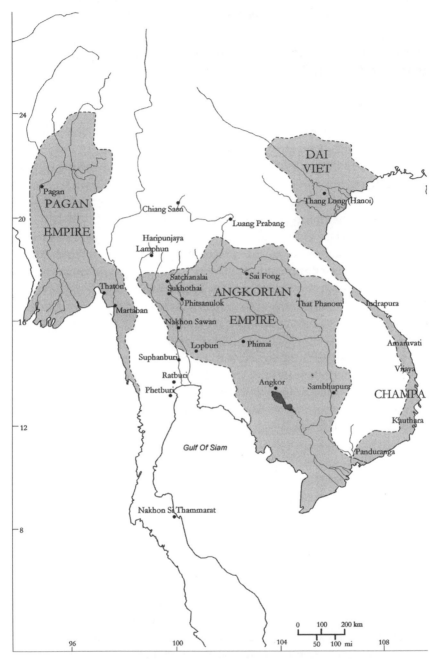

Figure 1.3. Mainland Southeast Asia, c. 1220. The depiction of Angkorian terri-torial authority generally follows David Wyatt, "Relics, Oaths and Politics in Thirteenth-Century Siam," *JSEAS* 32 (2001): 24.

populated regions in the upland interior, the peninsula, and the western Chaophraya basin retained an irreducible independence. Finally, during the late 1200s and 1300s Upper Burma, Angkor, and Dai Viet all suffered internal disorders and external attacks that eventually culminated in the sack of each capital and the collapse of central administration.[40]

These disorders derived from locally specific combinations of: a) ecological constraints, including shortages of quality land, which in turn reflected the combined effects of regional desiccation and a shift to more marginal lands after 200–300 years of sustained population growth; b) increased maritime trade that strengthened coastal principalities at the expense of the imperial heartlands in Upper Burma, Angkor, and Dong Kinh; c) Mongol incursions and more especially, large-scale Tai migrations; d) institutional features that conferred an excessive autonomy on local power-holders. So severe was the ensuing fragmentation that by 1340, as noted, at least 23 mainland kingdoms were independent in the sense that they paid no regular tribute to other Southeast Asian rulers (see Figure 1.4).[41] Most would survive into the 16th century.

---

[40] As Paul J. Bennett, *Conference Under the Tamarind Tree: Three Essays in Burmese History* (New Haven, 1971), 3–53, demonstrated, Upper Burma experienced less decisive political and institutional changes with the "fall" of Pagan in 1287 than with the change of capital in 1312, and more especially with the Shan incursions in the early 1360s that preceded the founding of Ava. Michael Aung-Thwin, "The Myth of the 'Three Shan Brothers' and the Ava Period in Burmese History," *JAS* 55 (1996): 881–901, and idem, *Myth and History in the Historiography of Early Burma* (Athens, OH, 1998), ch. 3, while denying that the Mongols sacked Pagan in 1287, concurs that the so-called Pagan era ended only in 1365. Angkor's "fall" to the Siamese, sometimes dated to 1431, and the shift in the Khmer center of gravity to the southeast climaxed a series of reverses that began in the early 13th century and became particularly serious after Ayudhya's founding in 1351. Dai Viet's travails at the hands of Champa also were concentrated 1360–1390. See discussion in Chs. 3, 4 *infra*. Tentatively I exclude Champa from this discussion, because its internal dynamics are less well understood, and because as beneficiary of Dai Viet's difficulties, Champa did not experience a 14th-century political crisis. However, Momoki Shiro, "Was Champa a Pure Maritime Polity?" (Paper for 1998 Core University Seminar, Kyoto and Thammasat Universities) argues that by the 1300s unsustainable population growth and agricultural overexploitation also were causing severe problems in Champa.

[41] In 1340 we can identify Arakan, Sagaing, Pinya, Martaban, Prome, Toungoo, Mogaung (Mohnyin), Mong Mit, Kenghung, Kengtung, Lan Na, Lopburi, Suphanburi (the latter two would coalesce in Ayudhya in 1351), Phayao, Nan, Sukhothai, Nakhon Si Thammarat (intermittently subject to Sukhothai and Suphanburi), Angkor, Luang Prabang, Vientiane, That Phanom, Champa, and Dai Viet (plus Manipur and Assam beyond the sphere of charter states). Cf. late 13th century map at Wyatt, *Thailand*, 40; Jan Pluvier, *Historical Atlas of South-East Asia* (Leiden, 1995), 12–13. Multiple, conditional allegiances render any count somewhat arbitrary.

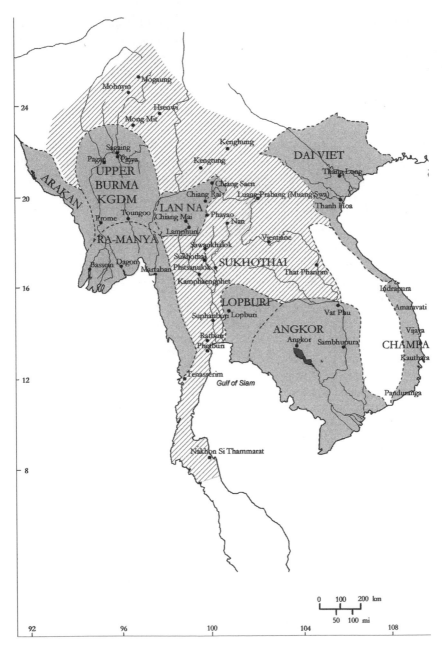

Figure 1.4. Mainland Southeast Asia, c. 1340. The hatched area represents a zone of fluid, generally small-scale Tai polities. At this date Sukhothai was in decline and neither Lan Sang nor Ayudhya had been founded.

In general, those disruptions – religious and ethnic as well as territorial – that attended the 14th-century crisis were more wrenching in the central than in the western mainland, which in turn experienced more prolonged traumas than the east. In the central region, Angkor's extraordinary size and the natural tension between the Mekong and Chaophraya basins ensured that Angkor's domain would remain divided until the late 1700s. Although 14th- and 15th-century polities in the central mainland preserved Angkorian motifs, the novel power of Tai-speaking immigrants and of Theravada Buddhism and the persistence of Mon traditions in the Chaophraya basin encouraged Angkor's heirs to develop an ethnic and cultural profile substantially different from that of Angkor itself. Among these central mainland successors, Ayudhya (Siam) would prove most successful. To the west, the Irrawaddy basin also endured Tai settlement and fragmentation. But the continued prestige of Burman culture, long-standing Theravada sympathies, and the benefits of a single river axis help to explain why the area once controlled by Pagan was reunified in 1555, considerably earlier than the old Angkorian zone, and why cultural change was more limited. In Dai Viet, in contrast to the rest of the mainland, Tais never attempted to settle. For this reason, and also because in 1350 Dai Viet was far smaller and more culturally homogeneous, territorial losses were more modest, and the sense of rupture less profound than in either the Angkorian or Pagan realm.

In a broader sense, however, 14th-century breakdowns across the mainland were analogous insofar as they ushered in regimes in each sector that both recycled and substantially strengthened charter legacies.

Modest, uneven population densities and north-south valleys molded post-1450 polities much as they had the charter states. In the 1680s the king of Golconda in India replied to a Siamese visitor who boasted about the size of his home kingdom. "It is true, I admit," said the Indian prince, "that [it is] of greater extent than mine, but you must agree that the king of Golconda rules over men, while the king of Siam only rules over forests and mosquitoes."[42] This was not wide of the mark. For the mainland as a whole, population densities in 1800 were only 10–20 percent those of India, China, or Japan.[43] With some 80 percent of the mainland consisting of hills either uncultivable or

---

[42] Nicolas Gervaise, *The Natural and Political History of the Kingdom of Siam*, John Villiers, tr. (Bangok, 1989), 27.

[43] I refer to China proper, excluding Chinese Turkestan, Tibet, Manchuria, and Inner Mongolia. Colin McEvedy and Richard Jones, *Atlas of World Population History* (London, 1978), 166–97; Reid, *Age of Commerce*, II, 14.

suited only for swidden, habitation remained heavily concentrated in five lowland wet-rice corridors with access to the coast: a) the Irrawaddy basin, b) the Chaophraya basin, c) the Cambodian plain and the lower-central Mekong, d) the Vietnamese Red River basin and adjacent deltas, e) the present southern Vietnamese littoral (see Figures 2.1, 3.1, and 4.1). Like their charter predecessors, each post-1450 empire naturally centered on one of these lowland corridors that, with the partial exception of the two Vietnamese areas and of the Chaophraya and Cambodian plains, were separated from one another by jungles and uplands. Sustained unity therefore was impossible between the Irrawaddy and Chaophraya basins – repeated Burmese invasions ended in disaster – or between the central mainland and the Vietnamese coast. Even along the latter coast, north Vietnamese–south Vietnamese tensions in some ways reproduced earlier conflicts between Dai Viet and Champa. In short, as in the charter era, a quadripartite or at least a tripartite division of the mainland was, almost literally, written in stone.

Yet a comparison of the late precolonial territorial structure with pre-1300 patterns also reveals long-term changes. In the central sector the lower Chaophraya basin, Siam's heartland, eclipsed the Cambodian plain, which had been dominant under Angkor. With Champa's demise and Vietnam's reunification, the four principal states of the charter era were reduced to three. For the first time, virtually the entire mainland, including upland valleys, was effectively divided among lowland-based empires, so the Burmese, Siamese, and Vietnamese realms of 1820/1830 were considerably larger than their charter predecessors (compare Figures 1.3 and 1.6). Finally, territorial extension required and reflected more effective internal administrative controls.

Broadly speaking, post-charter territorial consolidation fell into three phases, c. 1350–1570, c. 1600–1752, and c. 1760–1830/40, each inaugurated by generalized political collapse and desperate improvisation. During the first phase, c. 1350–1570, in each of the main corridors post-charter successor states carved out modest niches and began a series of drawn-out contests, generally in a north-south direction, for local hegemony. Thus in the western corridor new Shan polities and the freshly founded kingdoms of Ava, Toungoo, and Pegu battled one another. In the center Ayudhya (Siam) fought kingdoms in what is now northern Thailand, Laos, and Cambodia. In the east Dai Viet faced Champa. Until 1440 or 1470, such conflicts remained rather desultory, but thereafter consolidation accelerated so that by 1540 only six or seven major kingdoms remained (Figure 1.5).

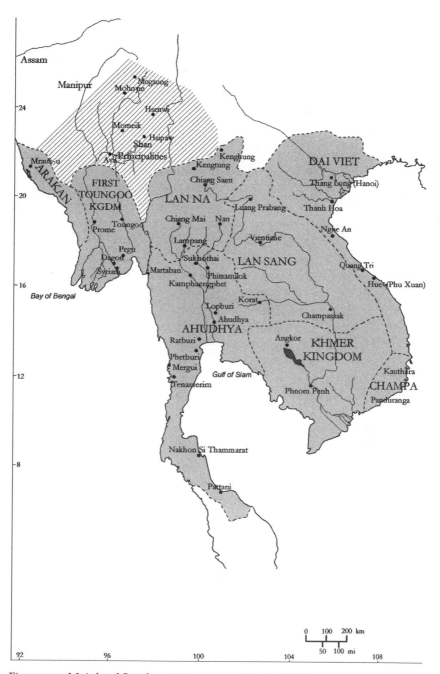

Figure 1.5. Mainland Southeast Asia, c. 1540. The hatched area represents a zone of fluid, small-scale Tai polities.

Of these the most astoundingly successful was Toungoo Burma, which by 1574 had succeeded not only in reuniting all of the Irrawaddy basin for the first time in two and a half centuries, but in conquering much of present-day Thailand and Laos. These breathtaking conquests accelerated the decline of polities in northern Thailand, Laos, and Cambodia to the ultimate benefit of Burma and Siam. Yet in the short term, the vast scale of warfare joined with renewed economic pressures to exhaust not only Siam, Burma's chief victim, but Burma herself, whose armies could not police their overextended domain. Between 1568 and 1599 both kingdoms collapsed, precipitating another, albeit relatively brief, period of acute disorder in the western and central mainland.

Territorial overextension and overly rapid growth, that is to say, an excess of good fortune, likewise weakened Dai Viet, helping to pit southern against northern Vietnamese leaders as early as 1539. But in contrast to the short-lived fragmentation of the western and central mainland, this north–south split would recur and endure to the eve of the 19th century, in part because the Vietnamese lowlands, unlike the Irrawaddy and Chaophraya basins, lacked a unifying riverine artery.

During the second post-charter phase, c. 1600–1752, the differentiation between strong and weak states advanced to the benefit of Burma, Siam, and northern and southern Vietnam (both of which owed nominal loyalty to the same sovereign). Burma tightened its hold over outlying Tai dependencies, while Siam increased demands on its Lao, Malay, and Cambodian tributaries. The southern Vietnamese state also encroached on Cambodia, inaugurating a Vietnamese–Siamese competition reminiscent of the older Burmese–Siamese rivalry farther west. Yet amidst this consolidation, Cambodia, Lao, and Malay principalities retained greater freedom of maneuver than they would enjoy in the 19th century, while on the mainland's western fringe Arakan, Manipur, and Assam remained completely independent.

Between 1752 and 1786 all four principal states again collapsed through local combinations of destabilizing commercial and demographic growth, injudicious efforts at provincial centralization, and exhausting warfare. Coming after those of the 14th and 16th centuries, this last, most closely synchronized region-wide crisis also served as prelude to more ambitious consolidations. By 1824 a resurgent Burma had conquered for the first time or had dramatically tightened its hold over far-flung Arakan, Assam, Manipur, and the Shan uplands. Siam by 1847 had exerted an unprecedented authority over northern Thailand, the chief Lao kingdoms, the northern Malay states, western and central Cambodia, while Vietnam had absorbed the last Cham remnants and the Mekong delta (Figure 1.6). If the French had not arrived in the 1860s, an effective Siamese-Vietnamese frontier might have stabilized along the Mekong. Each empire faced anticentralizing revolts, often by ethnic minorities, but apart from an anti-Vietnamese Khmer rising in 1840–41 that succeeded with help from Siam, these challenges proved counter-productive. With the eclipse of independent principalities and with the reunification of Vietnamese-speaking lands, where in 1340 some 23 king-doms had staked their claims, as early as 1802 only three viable polities were left standing.

This narrative of relentless consolidation should not conceal alternate territorial possibilities. In the western mainland, until 1600 it seemed possible that the center of gravity would remain at the coast rather than in the agricultural interior, which might have occasioned further north–south conflict. In the central mainland, agricultural and maritime superiority afforded Ayudhya a growing advantage over interior Tai rivals, but it is less clear why Ayudhya was able to dominate Cambodia, which enjoyed many of the same geographic assets and which as late as the 1590s remained a credible competitor. In the Vietnamese lowlands, without a series of military and political contingencies in the late 1700s, cultural ties among northern and southern Vietnamese-speakers may have been insufficient to ensure unification.

Administrative Centralization to c. 1830: An Overview

At the same time as privileged cores extended their territorial writ, they commonly sought to strengthen their systems of patronage, extraction, and coercion. External expansion and internal reform were mutually re-inforcing, because larger domains required more efficient control, while the concentration of resources that flowed from better coordination aided colonization and conquest. Yet whereas territorial consolidation had both a linear and cyclic dimension, administrative change between c. 1000 and 1830 tended to be more consistently linear.

I discern four principal administrative patterns, the first three of which were sequential. In practice we will find intermediate patterns, variations within each pattern, and chronological overlap, but the fol-lowing are useful heuristic conventions (Figure 1.7).

Pattern A, "charter administration," characterized Pagan and Angkor throughout their existence. Signature features were also found in Ava

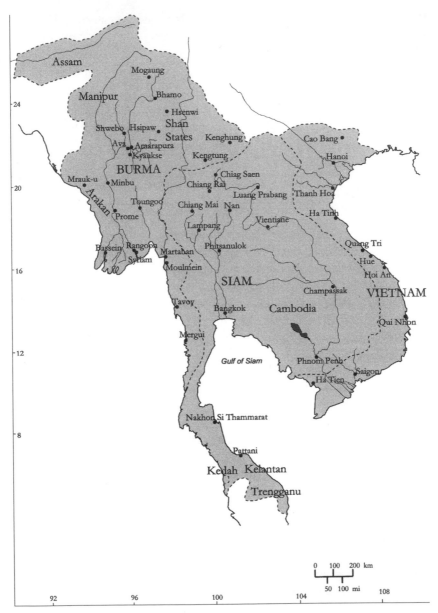

Figure 1.6. Mainland Southeast Asia in 1824.

to c. 1500, in Dai Viet to varying degrees under the Ly (1009–1225) and Tran (1225–1400) dynasties, and apparently in Champa. Each realm was a "solar polity" – this term is more descriptively accurate than S. J. Tambiah's "galactic polity" – in which provincial "planets" revolved around a sun whose "gravitational pull" diminished with distance.[44] Insofar as each planet had its own satellite moons, its gravitational system replicated in decreasing scale the structure of the solar system as a whole. The farthest planets were ruled by hereditary tributaries; less distant realms, by powerful local families or relatives of the High King. All such leaders were tied to the overlord by webs of family, marriage, and patronage whose instability ensured constant fluctuations in the center's territorial influence. Reliable royal control in the sense of resource exaction was therefore confined to the capital zone, which normally included the empire's most populous districts but which might not exceed a 60-mile radius. In Pagan, Angkor, and to a lesser extent perhaps early Champa and Dai Viet, temples and monasteries served simultaneously as agencies of agricultural reclamation, ritual validation, and intra-elite alliance. Because these wealthy, self-regulating religious institutions helped to stabilize labor and to concentrate resources, they tended to compress and, in some ways, to obviate royal administration. Nonetheless, the ruler remained indispensable as ritual intermediary between kingdom and cosmos, as military leader, and as coordinator of temple as well as secular patronage. Thus, while accepting that these were weak forms of the genus, we can still recognize charter-era entities as "states" according to Charles Tilly's minimalist definition: "coercion-wielding organizations that are distinct from households and kinship groups and exercise clear priority in some respects over all other organizations within substantial territories."[45]

After the charter polities collapsed, a modified structure that I term "decentralized Indic administration," Pattern B, emerged in the western and central mainland. It seems to have arisen earlier in the central mainland and in Lower Burma than in Upper Burma, but by the start of the 16th century (outside Dai Viet) Pattern B was nearly universal.

[44] Cf. S. J. Tambiah, *World Conqueror and World Renouncer* (Cambridge, 1976), ch. 7. Unlike our solar system, most galaxies lack a distinct central body and their components defy enumeration. Likewise, I prefer "solar polity" to *mandala.*
[45] Charles Tilly, *Coercion, Capital, and European States, AD 990–1990* (Cambridge, 1990), 1. Cf. Tony Day's emphasis on family networks, rather than formal political institutions, in early modern SE Asian polities, "Ties That (Un)Bind: Families and States in Premodern Southeast Asia," *JAS* 55 (1996): 384–409.

Like all non-Sinic Southeast Asian states, this too was a form of "solar polity," but it diverged from Pattern A either because it took root in areas that lacked an elaborate system of temple complexes and religious lands in the charter era, or because commercial and military pressures in the 15th and 16th centuries had severely eroded that system. Village organizations and lay patrons, chiefly military leaders, assumed many regulatory functions formerly entrusted to religious bodies, and substantial religious wealth fell into lay hands.

Our data on "decentralized Indic" states are richer than for Pattern A. Direct royal control over taxes, corvees, and judicial appeals continued to be restricted to the nuclear zone, with a radius anywhere from 30 to 80 miles. Beyond this core, major lowland towns were still entrusted to senior princes or local dynasts, who ruled with their own quasi-royal insignia, in some cases with the right of hereditary succession, and with independent powers of justice, taxation, and appointment. Compared to Pattern A, the capital tended to acknowledge more readily the pretensions to ritual sovereignty of these lowland viceroys, some of whose territories in fact had become independent kingdoms during the post-charter free-for-all. In viceroy-ruled provinces, therefore, capital officials still lacked direct contact with headmen or direct access to village resources. As in Pattern A, the ambiguity of their status – at one and the same time provincial heads might be self-styled Buddhist rulers (*dhamma-rajas*) and clients of the High King – joined with their independent control of manpower to encourage viceroys to assault the capital during periods of central weakness. Farther afield, in less accessible lowland areas and in the rugged uplands, tributaries, who were generally of a different ethnicity than the king, enjoyed yet greater autonomy and unqualified hereditary succession.

The weaker Indic states, including most Shan, Lao, and Malay principalities, maintained a version of Pattern B throughout their history. But Burma and Siam, possessing greater resources and reacting to the appalling crisis of the late 1500s, undertook a series of energetic reforms that cohered in the early and mid-1600s. With less success, Lan Sang (in Laos) and Cambodia attempted similar reforms, in part perhaps in imitation of their more powerful neighbors. In the principal kingdoms, therefore, the early and mid-17th century, far from ushering in political decline, inaugurated an administrative pattern that proved as durable as it was effective. This I term "centralized Indic administration," Pattern C. From the late 1700s, in response to the third and last great administrative collapse, Burma and Siam sponsored additional reforms,

Name	Approx. Dates	Locales	Key Features
A) Charter Administration	900–1450	Chiefly Pagan, Angkor, early Ava; in some degree, Champa and early Dai Viet	Loose solar polity; semi-independent tributaries; autonomous religious institutions with extensive economic and social functions
B) Decentralized Indic Administration	1450–1840	All of western and central mainland to c. 1600; Khmer, Malay, and weaker Tai states to 1840	Loose solar polity; semi-independent tributaries; autonomous viceroys; reduced economic and social role for temples; still modest central administrative and manpower control
C) Centralized Indic Administration	1600–1840	Chiefly Siam and Burma; in very attenuated form, Cambodia, Lan Sang	More efficient service and tax exactions in nuclear zone; extension of nuclear zone procedures to provinces; wider use of commercial taxes; tighter tributary controls; more elaborate central administration; generally only one level of appointed local officials
D) Chinese-style Administration	1460–1840	Dong Kinh for most of this era; after 1831, all of Vietnam	Nominally bureaucratic supervisory and tax procedures; civil service exams; uniform provincial administration, three levels of appointed local officials

Figure 1.7. Administrative patterns on the mainland.

35

partly of a commercial nature, which advanced the centralizing thrust of 17th-century changes. Especially in Siam, where patronage of Chinese trade transformed the political economy, one could argue that post-1770 structures constituted a fourth pattern. But I hesitate to do so, because Burma did not share these changes to the same degree, because they were more short-lived than Patterns A to C, and because the principal territorial features of Pattern C continued into the second quarter of the 19th century.

Put simply, the differences between Patterns C and B were five-fold. First, in the nuclear zone new systems of censuses, tattoos, popular regimentation, and commercial taxation sought to ensure a more regular flow of taxes and labor service. Second, controls once restricted to the nuclear zone extended into the provinces. August viceroys and their deputies yielded to more humble, centrally appointed officials, while senior princes generally were confined to the capital. Censuses, land inquests, tax farms, and commercial monopolies expanded into outlying areas, and provincial elites competed more directly with nuclear-zone families for appointments and financial privileges. Third, although they were still regarded as enjoying an autonomous sovereignty within a system of nested sovereignties, in practice the nearer tributaries were obliged to provide more revenue and manpower and to accept greater interference in their internal affairs. Fourth, the king tended to become more ceremonially remote and to employ more explicitly Buddhist ideologies. Finally, as administration became more complex, central agencies tended to grow larger, more literate, and more routinized. Needless to say, these successes were relative, for by colonial rather than 16th century standards, the new Indic regimes remained superficial, ramshackle affairs, with hopelessly ill-defined jurisdictions, both departmental and territorial.

Linear administrative trends were less sustained in Vietnam. The late 15th century Neo-Confucian revolution introduced, at least on paper, a full-blooded Chinese-style structure, Pattern D, including civil service examinations, bureaucratic prescriptions, and three levels of appointed lowland officials as opposed to usually one level in Indic states. The Neo-Confucian revolution also reduced the wealth and autonomy of Buddhist institutions in a fashion curiously reminiscent of Patterns B and C. Despite the continued prestige of Neo-Confucian ideals, from the 16th to 18th centuries patrimonial practices and new forms of village leadership joined military pressures to limit their implementation in northern Vietnam. Meanwhile within the breakaway southern regime, a family-led, quasi-military administration, comparable in some ways to Pattern C, rendered Neo-Confucian practices yet less realistic. But there too, Neo-Confucianism gradually acquired a normative appeal, so that after 1802 and in particular from the 1830s, the southern-based Nguyen regime openly embraced Sinic techniques in an effort to integrate its unprecedentedly elongated, fissiparous domain.

Cultural Integration: An Overview

Discussion of territorial and administrative consolidation leads to a third general index of integration within each of the chief mainland societies: a growing uniformity of religious practices, languages, and ethnicity.

I follow Clifford Geertz in viewing culture as an ordered system of rules, instructions, and symbols designed to govern thought and behavior. With Geertz, Ernesto Laclau, Chantal Mouffe, and Johannes Fabian, I regard this system not as a "coherently structured whole," but as an "unsutured" complex of negotiated symbols whose interpretation normally fluctuates with locale, class, corporate group, and individual. At the same time, within any stable population, by definition, such rules permit a measure of common identifications and implicit understandings.[46] The main point is that in each of the chief empires, especially in the lowlands, social labels and signs, instructions and recipes became more standardized along two axes: a) laterally, the political and demographic advantages of each core encouraged the flow of religious, linguistic, and ethnic practices from that region into the provinces, although to be sure, crossfertilization also occurred; b) vertically, select elite practices spread to lower social strata, although here too some popular features ascended.[47] Lateral integration usually involved the partial absorption of one literate complex by another: Khmer notables,

[46] Clifford Geertz, *The Interpretation of Cultures* (New York, 1973), esp. 10–18, 44–5, 144–45; Ernesto Laclau and Chantal Mouffe, *Hegemony and Socialist Strategy* (London, 1985), chs. 3, 4; Johannes Fabian, *Language and Colonial Power* (Cambridge, 1986), chs. 1, 5, 6. On the definition of culture, see also Tessa Morris-Suzuki, "The Invention and Reinvention of 'Japanese Culture,' " *JAS* 53 (1995): 759–80; Jean Comaroff and John Comaroff, *Of Revelation and Revolution* (Chicago, 1991), 20–22; and George Steinmetz, ed., *State/Culture: State Formation After the Cultural Turn* (Ithaca, 1999), 4–8. By extension, I define ethnic group as a collectivity within a larger society that claims a common name and history and that elevates one or more symbolic elements as the epitome of that common identity and as a boundary against outsiders. Cf. Mark J. Hudson, *The Ruins of Identity* (Honolulu, 1999), 6–11; R.A. Schermerhorn, *Comparative Ethnic Relations* (New York, 1970), 12; and Anthony D. Smith, *The Ethnic Origins of Nations* (Oxford, 1986), chs. 2, 3.
[47] Cf. Smith, *Ethnic Origins*, 76–89, contrasting lateral and vertical ethnies.

for example, adopted elements of Siamese court culture. Although vertical (demotic) integration also could involve literate displacements, more frequently it exposed illiterate folk traditions to written norms.

During the charter era elites in each capital supported a set of religious, linguistic, and architectural practices whose normative appeal in the 12th and 13th centuries increased among provincial elites and perhaps to some extent, among lower strata. Yet by comparison with later periods, standardization to 1350 remained limited. In royal cults animist, Theravada Buddhist, Mahayana Buddhist, Saivite, Vaishnava (and in Dai Viet, Confucian) elements mixed promiscuously. As yet there was no sharp divide between Indic and Sinic court traditions. This same fluidity and tolerance characterized elite attitudes toward the substantially animist practices of their own peasantries. Although from an early date imported religions influenced village cultures, before 1300, indeed before 1600 in many areas, village literacy remained rare, and the network of village monasteries and schools characteristic of late precolonial societies was not much in evidence. Knowledge of Pali, Sanskrit, or Chinese texts – together with foreign-derived concepts of political space, literature, architecture, and aesthetics – remained preeminently the preserve of monks or literati attached to the courts and elite temples.[48] Given this high degree of village self-sufficiency, it is not surprising that even in the lowlands ethnicity and language also were more diverse than they later would become. With Tai irruptions and the confusion that accompanied the collapse of the charter polities, ethnicity and religious practice, especially in the west and center, become yet more complex.

However, from the 15th century, and with unprecedented vigor in the 18th and 19th centuries, the progress of both lateral and vertical standardization is easily demonstrated. In terms of language and ethnic self-identification, the Irrawaddy basin in 1400 was a medley in which Burmans may not have been a majority, but by 1830 basin culture and ethnicity had become overwhelmingly Burman. Whereas in the 15th century adjacent Shan-Tai uplands borrowed sparingly from the Irrawaddy valley, by 1830 Burma's Tai tributaries extensively mimicked Burman alphabets, calendars, dress, architecture, and religious practices. Likewise, in the 15th century the lower Chaophraya basin contained a mix of Khmers, Mons, and Tais, with many commoners apparently speaking a Mon language different from that of the Tai elite, but thereafter, and especially in the 18th and 19th centuries, a melded

[48] Cf. Sheldon Pollock, "The Cosmopolitan Vernacular," *JAS* 57 (1998): 6–37.

Siamese ethnicity and dialect dominated the basin and adjacent areas, while non-Siamese tributaries adopted ritual and artistic motifs from Ayudhya and Bangkok. In the eastern lowlands between the Hai Van Pass and Ca Mau, areas originally dominated by Chams and Khmers, it is doubtful whether even 5 percent of lowlanders spoke Vietnamese dialects in 1450, but 400 years later over 70 percent did so. With Vietnamese dialects arrived Vietnamese religious, social, and ethnic practices which, however localized and syncretic they may have become, still had more in common with northern Vietnamese practices than did Cham or Khmer cultures.

As metropolitan cultures expanded, literacy also became more common at all social levels. Insofar as literacy in the first instance meant the ability to read religious/ethical texts, this expansion was inextricably linked to movements of cultic "orthodoxy" as measured against canonical conventions. In Indic villages, courts joined local enthusiasts to construct a network of Theravada Buddhist monasteries and thus to push textual religion deeper into the countryside. In Vietnam, particularly in the north and especially among upper strata, the Neo-Confucian revolution of the 15th century hastened the acceptance of Chinese models of scholarship, law, and family relations. A hitherto barely visible fault line between Theravada and Sinic Southeast Asia now became pronounced. (Even in southern Vietnam, where the relation between Mahayana Buddhism and Confucianism was weighted heavily towards the former, Buddhism itself was largely of Sinic derivation.) Differences in soteriology, ritual language, and social ambition notwithstanding, Theravada Buddhism and Confucianism shared not only an emphasis on texts and orthodox praxis, but an interest in gender differentiation that subjected elite women more completely to male legal control while rejecting female claims to supernatural access.[49]

To be sure, within each area one can easily exaggerate the ensuing standardization of culture, primarily because its social and geographic reach remained limited, but also because where they did operate, those same processes as bred integration nurtured at least four countervailing or crosscutting currents. First, communication and trade links promoted cultural ties not only within, but outside each empire, such as those between Vietnamese and foreign Christians, between Tai courts

[49] But, as noted, this was pursued more systematically in Neo-Confucian Vietnam than in most of Theravada SE Asia. See John Whitmore, "Gender, State, and History: The Literati Voice in Vietnam," in Andaya, *Other Pasts*, 215–30.

throughout the upland interior, or between Theravada communities on the mainland and in Sri Lanka. Second, at the same time as they eroded local self-sufficiency, wider literacy and denser market networks fostered a novel specialization, hence fracture, in artistic and literary production and in patterns of consumption. Third, as capital elites increased their demands for taxes and conformity, subalterns within the heartland were tempted to resist or subvert official norms. Finally, resistance was yet more likely among minorities on the periphery, where the initial distance between official and local cultures was greater than in the core and where incorporation into an imperial social hierarchy often entailed a more serious loss of status.

What, then, were the political and psychological implications of cultural integration? Even where external conformity did develop, to assume that shared rituals, dialects, or other forms of behavior implied subjective identity is absurd.[50] As just indicated, wider literacy might spark greater specialization and wider debate. Old grievances might find new rationales. At most, the growth of networks encompassing larger numbers created a potential identity.

This potential could be critical, however, in several contexts. Most obviously among religious and political elites, closer interaction opened more unified fields for discussion and contestation. By definition, standardization provided a similar set of references. Precisely because the same texts and symbols meant different things to different people, negotiation and exchange to determine normative interpretations became more frequent.

Moreover, insofar as specific languages, rituals, and ethnicities were associated with stable political centers, assimilation could transform these markers into a shorthand for political allegiance. During periods of conflict, contiguous communities were tempted to seize, at times arbitrarily, on cultural symbols in order to reinforce, even to erect, boundaries that could strengthen their common claim to resources in competition with populations judged to be alien and threatening. Exaggerating in-group/out-group differences could enhance the efficiency of group mobilization, while fostering a sense of control over a chaotic environment.[51] Such responses were particularly likely when: a) the costs of

---

[50] Most obviously, geographic balkanization ensured that among Tai-speakers a common linguistic and Theravada heritage never produced an overarching political identity.

[51] Alterity as the basis of political association has inspired a rich literature. See, e.g., A. P. Cohen, *The Symbolic Construction of Community* (London, 1985); Fredrik Barth, ed., *Ethnic*

uncoordinated localism became acutely debilitating; b) a foe could be distinguished by easily recognized external symbols; c) local communities could link their cause to an enduring political entity, be it territorial or dynastic. Without a formal theory of nationality or a system of sustained mobilization, supra-local identities tended to recede once the alien threat disappeared. In any case, such identities usually affected upper strata more than peasants, whose normal frame of reference was local. In Pransenjit Duara's words, ethnic boundaries remained "soft."[52] Yet over time a repeated sense of external danger could combine with thicker communications circuits and more effective patronage to harden boundaries by yoking the welfare of diverse local groups to that of the political center. In varying degrees in Burma, Siam, Vietnam, and smaller states, such emerging linkages were proclaimed in written histories, folk tales, pilgrimage traditions, puppet shows, and national cults devoted to protective deities. For their part, especially in contested border districts, Burman and Vietnamese leaders frequently promoted majority ethnicity and language, in part to improve administrative efficiency, but more basically to strengthen psychological identification with the throne. Thus a discourse of cultural distinction helped to structure political thought and action.

These visions differed from modern nationalism in critical respects. Sovereignty flowed not from the people upward, but from the ruler, sanctioned by the cosmos, downward. In lieu of nationalism's leveling emphasis on uniform citizenship and horizontal equality, the precolonial ethos was implacably hierarchic, anti-entropic, obsessed with innumerable particularities of status and privilege determined by one's distance from the sovereign, hence from the principles of sanctity and morality he embodied. Because universal religious doctrines provided the principal theoretical foundation for authority, ideally and proleptically each ruler's dominion was universal rather than culture-specific. Absent a "natural" cultural space, imperial boundaries remained nebulous, with

Groups and Boundaries (Boston, 1969), esp. 86–100; Partha Chatterjee, *The Nation and Its Fragments* (Princeton, 1983), 138; Mary Douglas, *Purity and Danger* (London, 1966), 1–28; Prasenjit Duara, "Deconstructing the Chinese Nation," *The Australian Journal of Chinese Affairs* 30 (1993): 5–6; Orest Ranum, "Counter-Identities of Western European Nations in the Early Modern Period," in Peter Boerner, ed., *Concepts of National Identity* (Baden-Baden, 1986), 63–78; C. A. Bayly, "The Prehistory of Communalism?" *MAS* 19 (1985): 177–203; Mark Elliott, *The Manchu Way* (Stanford, 2001).

[52] See Duara, "Deconstructing," 20–25; idem, "Historicizing National Identity, or Who Imagines What and When," in Geoff Eley and Ronald G. Suny, *Becoming National* (Oxford, 1996), 151–78.

some tributaries paying homage to more than one overlord.[53] For these reasons, and also because subordinates entered the polity not as a collectivity but through individual ties to the sovereign, at least in Indic realms there was no formal demand that rulers be of the same ethnicity as their subjects. Above all, with politics the more or less exclusive prerogative of elites and with self-replicating microcultures enjoying a long-sanctioned autonomy, official attempts to modify popular culture necessarily remained limited. In recently annexed areas, such efforts normally sought not to extinguish minority cultures (usually an impractical undertaking), but to assert the ritual primacy of the religious or ethnic complex with which the court was most closely associated. Although increasingly influential, the notion of standard imperial culture thus remained in tension both with more cosmopolitan religious-cum-dynastic loyalties above, and with more local identities below. Such considerations enjoin the use of "national," even "proto-national" (with its teleological implications) in favor of some more awkward but neutral term like "politicized ethnicity."

Nonetheless, in their efforts to erect a yawning, unbridgeable gulf between all premodern political identities and post-1750 (or 1789) European-style nationalism, scholars like Benedict Anderson, Ernest Gellner, and Ronald Suny typically overstate their case.[54] While innocent of the French insistence on popular sovereignty, evolving political identities, especially in Burma and Vietnam, shared undeniable similarities with their increasingly coherent European counterparts both before and after 1789. Bear in mind that most European nations also began as heterogeneous dynastic conglomerates whose provinces served as cultural periphery to the metropole, and whose cultural integration

---

53 See Thongchai Winichakul, *Siam Mapped* (Honolulu, 1994), 20–36, 74–88.

54 Benedict Anderson, *The Spectre of Comparisons* (London, 1998), 318: "It is easy to forget that minorities came into existence in tandem with majorities – and, in Southeast Asia, very recently. . . . They were born of the political and cultural revolution brought about by the maturing of the colonial state and by the rise against it of popular nationalism." Cf. idem, *Imagined Communities* (rev. ed., London, 1991), chs. 7, 10, and *passim*. Although ignoring Southeast Asia, the following also stress the utter novelty of post-1789 nationalism: Ernest Gellner, *Nations and Nationalism* (Ithaca, 1983) ["Nationalism . . . owes everything to a decisive and unutterably profound break in human history," p. 125]; Eley and Suny, *Becoming National*, [". . . the novelty of national culture . . . is probably the most important point to emerge from the recent literature," p. 8]; E. J. Hobsbawm, *Nations and Nationalism Since 1870* (Cambridge, 1990). Cf. Smith, *Ethnic Origins*, emphasizing continuities; and Frank Proschan, "Peoples of the Gourd," *JAS* 60 (2001): 999–1032, which argues, *pace* Anderson, for deeply rooted precolonial, preliterate notions of ethnicity in highland Southeast Asia.

was a contested, imperfect affair starting in some cases as early as the 13th century and lasting well into the 20th century.[55]

In mainland Southeast Asian as in West European states, the most obvious long-term trend was for selected cultural/ethnic features to serve as a recognized badge of allegiance among politically active elements, including popular strata during periods of crisis, and for the culture of the dominant ethnic group to acquire normative prestige throughout the realm. Telltale markers fluctuated, depending on the out-group to be excluded. In the 15th and 16th centuries Burmans distinguished themselves from Shans by language and Theravada allegiance, but during subsequent wars against Mons, who were fellow Theravadins, hairstyle and body tattoos became the chief indices of loyalty to the Burman court. Vietnamese conflicts with Chams prior to c. 1470 lacked consistent symbolism, but after the Neo-Confucian revolution official efforts to "civilize" Chams and Khmers focused on the latter's dress, speech, social habits.[56] In both polities, contrary to modern nationalist ideologies but in keeping with pre-1750 European practice, a sense of political community not only proved compatible with, but in fact depended on the maintenance of a deeply hierarchical social ethic. Moreover, *pace* Anderson's emphasis on print capitalism as a prerequisite for national communication,[57] popular cultural mobilization relied overwhelmingly on oral channels of communication supplemented by manuscripts. In their invocation of local myths and symbols, anti-centralizing ethnic rebels – Khmers, Chams, Mons, Malays – held up a mirror to precisely the same marriage of culture and power as their imperial overlords proclaimed.

As in early modern Europe, and again contrary to some recent theorizing, universal religions also proved compatible with projects of ethnic differentiation.[58] The fusion of religion and ethnicity became most

[55] On the evolution of European national cultures, see n. 58 *infra*; Colette Beaune, *The Birth of an Ideology* (Berkeley, 1989); Rainer Babel and Jean-Marie Moeglin, eds., *Identite regionale et conscience nationale en France et en Allemagne du moyen age a l'epoque moderne* (Sigmaringen, Germany, 1997); David Bell, *The Cult of the Nation in France* (Cambridge, MA, 2001); and full documentation in my Vol. 2, Ch. 2.

[56] This volume, Chs. 2–4 for documentation.

[57] Anderson, *Imagined Communities*, esp. ch. 3.

[58] Anderson, *Imagined Communities*, 9–19 postulates an opposition between religious and ethnic/national allegiances. But see Wolfgang Reinhard, "Introduction," in Reinhard, ed., *Power Elites and State Building* (Oxford, 1996), discussing "national" religions in early modern England, Spain, Sweden, Bavaria, and Prussia; and Linda Colley, *Britons* (New Haven, 1992), arguing that Protestant superiority provided an indispensable British national bond well into the 19th century.

obvious in those areas where rival communities supported different religious/cultic traditions, as on the Vietnamese–Cham frontier after c. 1460, on the Burman–Shan frontier prior to 1560, or along the Vietnamese–Khmer interface after c. 1700. In such contexts defense of the faith became synonymous with ethnic self-assertion. But even in zones of ostensibly uniform religious or cultic allegiance, a similar logic could apply: The religion of Gotama Buddha shone only in Burma, whose rulers regretfully were obliged to invade Tai states in order to clean up impure Theravada practices. "Decadent China and orthodox Vietnam" became a favorite conceit of the self-consciously Neo-Confucian Nguyen court.[59]

Finally, in mainland Southeast Asia as in Europe, the growing proportion of inhabitants willing to identify ethnically and culturally with each capital in the centuries prior to c. 1830 anticipated later trends. In Burma and Vietnam, central ethnicities cohered among political elites during the charter era. In the new Tai realms of Ayudhya, Laos, and northern Thailand, an analogous process occurred in the 14th and 15th centuries. Modified identities then diffused vertically and laterally, accelerating sharply in the chief lowland empires after c. 1770. In the 20th century under European intellectual tutelage, concepts of national territory and national culture were secularized, while becoming far more systematic and exclusive.[60] Nonetheless, the 20th-century redefinition of Siamese, Burmese, and Vietnamese loyalties built on pre-1850 foundations in a fashion that depended less on intelligentsia interventions and was incomparably less artificial than the 20th-century construction of Malay or Indonesian nationalism.

A Model of Long-Term Integration: External and Domestic Economic Stimuli

In sum, after a period of post-charter fragmentation whose length varied by region, starting between 1350 and 1480 and accelerating into the 19th century, each of the principal states expanded its territory, centralized its administration, and saw elements of the population adopt more uniform cultural and ethnic identities. Note that the pattern, most readily apparent in the western and central mainland whereby successive

---

[59] Lieberman, *Cycles*, ch. 5; Woodside, *Vietnam*, 121.
[60] Winichakul, *Siam Mapped*; Anderson, *Spectre*, 318–30; David Henley, "Ethnogeographic Integration and Exclusion in Anticolonial Nationalism: Indonesia and Indochina," *CSSH* 37 (1995): 264–85.

interregna grew progressively shorter and less institutionally disruptive, corresponded remarkably well to that of imperial China during the Six Dynasties, Five Dynasties/Ten Kingdoms, Song-Yuan, Yuan-Ming, and Ming-Qing transitions. But so far I have said little, if anything, about the underlying dynamics of Southeast Asian integration. Why was each sector of the mainland more cohesive in 1830 than in 1400? The remainder of "Part A: Rethinking Southeast Asia" develops a general model of integration which Chapters 2–4 will test and particularize.

My basic argument is this: External, including maritime, factors enhanced the economic and military advantages of privileged lowland districts. In reciprocal fashion, multicausal increases in population, domestic output, and local commodification aided foreign trade, while widening further the material gap between incipient heartlands and dependent districts. So too, by stimulating movements of religious and social reform and by strengthening transportation and communication circuits between emergent cores and outlying dependencies, economic change enhanced each core's cultural authority. As warfare between cohering polities grew in scale and expense, and as the subjugation of more alien populations aggravated problems of imperial control, those principalities that would survive were obliged systematically to strengthen their patronage and military systems, to expand their tax bases, and to promote official cultures over provincial and popular traditions. Insofar as sustained warfare increased popular dependence on the throne, it heightened the appeal of ethnic and religious patterns championed by the capital. Pacification and military reforms also had a variety of unplanned economic and social effects generally sympathetic to integration. The Irrawaddy basin in the west and the Chaophraya basin in the center channeled these processes along unifying axes absent in the more geographically fragmented Vietnamese littoral. At first glance, the north–south division of Vietnamese-speaking lands after c. 1600 ran contrary to trends elsewhere on the mainland. Yet in truth, both Vietnamese polities, and especially the rapidly expanding southern state, responded to much the same economic, cultural, and military pressures as other mainland contenders, so whether the south ultimately remained separate or reunited with the north leaves unaltered my basic analysis.

External and domestic factors remained influential throughout the period under study, but their relative weights and interconnections varied widely by time and place. I therefore argue less for a single lockstep pattern than for a loose constellation of influences whose local contours must be determined empirically and without prejudice. We have seen that an oscillating attention to external vs. internal factors, and to local vs. regional perspectives, governed the movement from external-ist to autonomous to Age of Commerce historiography. I continue this contrapuntal rhythm insofar as I, like autonomists but unlike Reid, disaggregate Southeast Asia and refuse to grant automatic priority to maritime factors. Yet mine is hardly a reversion to autonomist views, because the dynamics I emphasize were material as well as cultural, because I emphasize linear change, and because I do not hesitate to acknowledge the critical impact of global currents.

Indeed, let us begin a discussion of integrative dynamics by consid-ering the only factor to have received serious attention in the literature, namely, maritime trade. For the charter era and especially its opening phase c. 900–1100, there is little indication at Pagan, Angkor, or Dai Viet that this was the chief spur to development, but in the 14th and 15th cen-turies evidence of maritime activity, which Reid has sought to quantify, becomes more impressive. Such trade after 1400, and more especially 1470, benefited from growing market demand in key sectors of Eurasia, including Europe, India, south China, and Japan, whose more or less coordinated vitality during the late 15th and 16th centuries is as strik-ing as it is curious. Post-1530 improvements in silver extraction in Japan and the New World provided much of the bullion necessary to lubricate this growth, both directly within Southeast Asia, and indirectly, through silver's contribution to commercialization in China.[61]

Particularly in the west and center, the trade momentum of the 1500s and early 1600s seems to have ebbed during the last third of the 17th century, but in the early 1700s exports picked up at the chief Irrawaddy, Chaophraya, and Mekong delta ports. Most coastal districts then saw an accelerated upswing from the 1720s that lasted, with only tempo-rary vicissitudes, well into the 19th century. During the 17th to early 19th centuries the movement from luxury to bulk exports (rice, timber, metals, and raw cotton) gained ground, balanced by a greater volume of imported bullion and Chinese and then European consumer goods. Such vitality drew strength from a growing appetite for foreign goods

---

[61] For overviews, Reid, *Age of Commerce*, II, ch. 1; Victor Lieberman, "Local Integration and Eurasian Analogies: Structuring Southeast Asian History, c. 1350–c. 1830," *MAS* 27 (1993): 489 ff.; Dennis O. Flynn and Arturo Giraldez, "Born with a 'Silver Spoon': The Origin of World Trade in 1571," *JWH* 6 (1995): 201–21; Andre Gunder Frank, *Re-Orient: Global Economy in the Asian Age* (Berkeley, 1998); William Atwell, "Time, Money, and the Weather: Ming China and the 'Great Depression' of the Mid-Fifteenth Century," *JAS* 61 (2002): 83–113.

in Southeast Asia itself, from the global trade in New World silver, from the opening of British ports at Singapore and Penang, and most especially from the ramified activities of Chinese merchants. The latter provisioned not only China, whose population between 1650 and 1850 rose from c. 130,000,000 to 420,000,000,[62] but new Chinese communities throughout coastal Southeast Asia.

Moreover, from the 1400s, and then with unprecedented vigor in the 1700s and 1800s, Chinese settlement in Yunnan and Guangxi joined with Southeast Asian vitality to promote the overland exchange of Chinese silks and specie for local gems, raw cotton, and textiles. To help meet regional bullion demands, in the 18th century tens of thousands of Chinese also opened mines in Upper Burma and northern Dong Kinh.[63]

By the 18th century if not earlier, we see a tendency for mainland Southeast Asia to exchange raw materials for Chinese manufactures and handicrafts. One is reminded of Immanuel Wallerstein's core/periphery schema. But in basic respects, Wallersteinian categories are here inapplicable. The Southeast Asia/raw materials, China/manufactures dichotomy had numerous exceptions on both sides, and no hierarchically structured manufacturing processes governed the region as a whole. Although coerced labor certainly existed in Southeast Asia, it neither originated with nor depended on Chinese trade. Unlike peripheral or semi-peripheral states in Wallerstein's European-Atlantic world system, Southeast Asian governments faced no serious externally-imposed restrictions. Above all, instead of a methodical periphery-to-core transfer of wealth, we find a system of multifocal Smithian exchange that strengthened the economies and political systems of both mainland Southeast Asia and China.[64]

We shall return to the political implications of economic change, but for now let it suffice to say that foreign trade magnified the income differential between authorities in control of ports and frontier bazaars, on

---

[62] William Lavely and R. Bin Wong, "Revising the Malthusian Narrative," *JAS* 57 (1998): 719. For sources on SE Asian trade, see *infra* Chs. 2–4.

[63] For discussion of overland trade and tentative size comparisons with maritime trade, see Victor Lieberman, "Secular Trends in Burmese Economic History, c. 1350–1830," *MAS* 25 (1992): 15; Sun Laichen, "Ming-Southeast Asian Overland Interactions, 1368–1644" (Univ. of Michigan Ph.D. diss., 2000), chs. 5–6.

[64] Cf. Immanuel Wallerstein, *The Modern World-System I* (Orlando, FL, 1974), esp. 100–103; Victor Lieberman, "Wallerstein's System and the International Context of Early Modern Southeast Asian History," *JAH* 24 (1990): 70–90; and Robert Marks, *Tigers, Rice, Silk and Silt* (Cambridge, 1998), 171. A similar multifocalism informs R. J. Barendse, "Trade and State in the Arabian Seas: A Survey from the Fifteenth to Eighteenth Centuries," *JWH* 11 (2000): 173–226.

the one hand, and interior elites who relied on agricultural taxes and local services, on the other. Although agriculture was by no means static, it is doubtful that it grew as rapidly as foreign trade, especially after 1700. Moreover, because dispersed in-kind resources were more difficult to tax, foreign commerce tended to yield larger per-unit revenues. In a wider sense, by creating wholesale/retail networks that stimulated rural production and by providing novel opportunities for economies of scale and for specialization, long-distance commerce swelled each state's domestic tax base. In the west, 16th-century maritime trade provided the chief spur to the First Toungoo dynasty's explosive conquests. In the center, Ayudhya derived up to a third of its revenues from such trade; while after Burma's conquest of Siam in 1767, Siam based its recovery and its rise to regional preeminence largely on the China connection. In the east, maritime profits helped to underwrite the southern Vietnamese breakaway regime after 1600 and, along with Chinese settlement around the Gulf of Siam, contributed to the Nguyen reconquest of the 1780s and 1790s.

Ports provided unique access to another innovation of fatal consequence: European-style handguns and cannon, which rapidly eclipsed Chinese and Muslim firearms hitherto available. From their introduction by the Portuguese in the late 1510s through the large-scale importation from Penang and Singapore in the 19th century, these increasingly potent weapons (combined in some cases with a European-inspired tactical emphasis on inflicting heavy casualties) offered a major advantage in urban sieges, stockade fighting, field encounters, and naval warfare alike. Firearms thus provided two further spurs to consolidation. First, access again favored coastal principalities. Interior states in Laos, the Shan hills, and northern Thailand could never procure guns of the same quality or quantity as their lowland rivals, nor could local manufacture compensate. Second, even among coastal principalities, the high cost of the new weaponry conferred a cumulative advantage on the wealthiest and most enterprising, as demonstrated by the astonishing records of the First Toungoo empire and the southern Vietnamese state.

Alongside maritime inputs, changes in the composition and size of domestic output strongly influenced political integration. To some degree, a complex synergy rendered artificial the distinction between internal and external stimuli: denser, wealthier mainland populations were better able to supply exports and absorb imports, while foreign demand and bullion were critical to rural commodification. By aiding domestic pacification, guns and trade revenues helped agriculture indirectly.

Nonetheless, before we can hope to disentangle maritime and domestic factors, we must consider that in these overwhelmingly peasant societies some key determinants of political and cultural change were intrinsic to the rural economy. Axiomatic though it may sound, this proposition has rarely been tested. Ports and courts float as disembodied entities above their own countrysides.

Preeminent among domestic economic influences was agricultural extension and intensification, which drew strength from a variety of environmental, political, and social pressures. Chapter 2 uses paleoclimatic studies to argue that fluctuations in solar radiation, volcanism, and oceanic currents affected long-term precipitation and temperature over extensive Eurasian zones. There is some evidence that during all or part of their duration, the same periods – roughly 950–1300, and less dramatically, 1470–1590 and 1710/1720–1805 – that saw warming trends favorable to agriculture in northern Europe produced higher rainfall, aiding harvests and population growth, in much of mainland Southeast Asia as well as parts of southern India and southeast China. Conversely, climate during the 14th century and again in the mid to late 17th century proved generally less favorable.[65] This approach raises the possibility that: a) agricultural and maritime cycles both depended to some extent on a third variable, namely, climate, which helped to coordinate population, hence market, expansion in Southeast Asia and Southeast Asia's chief trading partners; and b) Southeast Asian agricultural cycles must be considered alongside maritime cycles in explaining the rhythms of political-cum-cultural consolidation. The latter perspective is particularly relevant to the charter era, when the florescence of Pagan, Angkor, and Dai Viet correlated roughly with that of medieval Europe, Kiev, and Song China, but when foreign trade seems to have had only a marginal impact on the economies of Southeast Asian cores.

Lest one exaggerate the impact of climate, however, consider: over the long term, population, commercial integration, and economic specialization grew in cumulative ratchet-like fashion, whereas climate had merely a cyclic tendency. By 1830 in most Eurasian rimlands population was significantly larger than in 1130 and political and cultural consolidation was far more effective, but climate in the 12th century was generally more beneficent than in the 19th. Reinforcing the economic advantages of climate when it was beneficent and limiting damage – even stimulating creative adaptations – in periods of deterioration, was a sustained

[65] See Ch. 2 for sources.

accumulation of technical expertise, both agricultural and commercial, to which we shall turn shortly.

Did epidemiological change also affect population trends, and by implication, agricultural performance? In the late first and early second millennia, it is conceivable that more frequent migratory and mercantile contacts with other Eurasian regions allowed Southeast Asians to develop endemic resistance to diseases like measles and smallpox that had once proved almost uniformly lethal. Because endemic illnesses typically affect children more than child-bearing economically productive adults, here as in other outlying sectors of Eurasia, the transition may have intensified demographic growth. This would have aided the mainland as a whole, but especially the lowland cores, where both foreign contacts and population densities needed to sustain endemic disease were greatest.[66]

Less speculative is the argument that lowland agriculture benefited from sustained migration. Richard O'Connor has argued that whereas Mons and Khmers tended to be house-gardening rice farmers who relied on runoff and waterway floods to cultivate what he terms the "flood-farming niche," the Burmans, Tais, and Vietnamese who displaced them were skilled irrigators who diverted moving water through their fields and thus succeeded in occupying more profitable niches at elevations above and below the flood-farming niche. Above were hitherto untapped foothills, while below were floodplains where newcomers could breach levees to drain and irrigate back swamps. Entry of these innovative peoples, together with a tendency among earlier inhabitants to assimilate to the newcomers' social/ritual systems, would help to explain both the north-south ethnic succession in each sector and the simultaneous expansion of lowland populations.[67] Even if the link between ethnicity and agricultural regimes was looser than O'Connor suggests, there is no question that riverine and coastal populations were constantly augmented by migrants from the hills as well as by deportees from conquered principalities and by maritime, chiefly Chinese, immigrants. The lowlands thus served as migratory cul-de-sacs.

Moreover, with centralizing polities better able to defend and pacify their heartlands after the 15th or 16th century, chronic disorders typical

---

[66] See sources in Chs. 2–4 building on William H. McNeill, *Plagues and Peoples* (Garden City, 1976).
[67] Richard O'Connor, "Agricultural Change and Ethnic Succession in Southeast Asian States," *JAS* 54 (1995): 968–96.

of the post-charter era diminished. Studies of Java and the Philippines suggest that warfare, with its disruption of procreation, family and economic routine, was normally one of the most serious depressants of population growth.[68] In conditions of relatively accessible land and early marriage, fertility rates may have begun to gain ground over endemic adult diseases, monastic celibacy, and high infant mortality.

At the same time as acreage expanded, that is to say, as agriculture became more extensive, new crops and improved cultivation regimes permitted more efficient land use. At least four interrelated processes seem to have been at work. First, O'Connor's schema allows for sustained ethnically-linked improvements in land use in such long-settled, but thinly inhabited areas as the middle and lower Irrawaddy basin, central and southern Vietnam. Second, even without immigration, population growth in older centers encouraged agricultural intensification, including more irrigation works, an expansion of double and triple cropping, and the provision of larger labor inputs for planting, weeding, and harvesting. By reducing the role of large estates and providing smallholders with greater incentives, changes in landholding in some areas fostered both population growth and intensification. After several generations in heavily-settled zones like Upper Burma and Dong Kinh, these "density-dependent projects" may have promoted an involutionary pattern in which returns per unit of labor began to decline while output per land unit continued to rise. But when such regimes were new, it is likely that their economies of scale boosted output per work day as well as per land unit.[69] Third, either independently or in combination with rising labor inputs, new crops from Bengal and the New World, including cotton, tobacco, sugar, peanuts, and *indica* rice, helped to raise

---

[68] M. C. Ricklefs, "Some Statistical Evidence on Javanese Social, Economic and Demographic History in the Later Seventeenth and Eighteenth Centuries," *MAS* 20 (1986); 1–32; Norman G. Owen, "The Paradox of Nineteenth-Century Population Growth in Southeast Asia: Evidence from Java and the Philippines," *JSEAS* 18 (1987): 45–57; Reid, *Age of Commerce*, I, 12–18.

[69] Likely examples of the latter pattern included new rice regimes in early-charter Pagan and Angkor, and irrigation-dependent *kauk-gyi* cultivation in 14th–16th century Middle Burma. But in truth data on land and labor productivity are too weak to support more than educated guesses. See discussion *infra*, Chs. 2, 3, plus theoretical analysis of density-dependent efficiencies at Ester Boserup, *The Conditions of Agricultural Growth* (New York, 1965); idem, *Population and Technological Change: A Study of Long-Term Trends* (Chicago, 1981), esp. pts. 1–3. On involution, probably characteristic of Upper Burma in the 18th–19th centuries and Dong Kinh for part of the late 14th, 16th, and 18th centuries, see *infra* Chs. 2, 4, plus Philip C. C. Huang, *The Peasant Family and Rural Development in the Yangzi Delta, 1350–1988* (Stanford, 1990).

the productivity of existing fields as well as hitherto marginal lands. Local experimentation, which yielded hundreds of rice varieties geared to specific ecological niches, offered similar benefits. Finally, by increasing the size of the market and by reducing unit transport costs, expanding overseas and domestic demand encouraged agricultural specialization, especially in urban hinterlands.

According to best estimates – based on respectable records for Dai Viet, but quite fragmentary evidence for Indic areas – the combination between 1400 and 1820 of lateral extension and modified technique permitted (and reflected) a more than three-fold population increase in Vietnam and perhaps a two-fold increase in Burma and Siam.[70] The eras 1450–1560 and 1720–1820 apparently saw the most rapid growth, with the largest increases on the fringes of the Burman dry zone and the Lower Burma frontier, in the lower Chaophraya basin, Dong Kinh, and on the constantly moving Vietnamese frontier.

Population growth in turn helped to invigorate domestic as well as foreign commerce. We cannot prove, as has been claimed for high medieval Europe, Song China, and Tokugawa Japan, that per capita income rose during particular periods in mainland Southeast Asia.[71] But even if we assume, for argument's sake, that in each mainland region during the period under review population growth absorbed most of the surplus and that per capita income therefore tended to stagnate, higher population densities meant larger aggregate demand and lower distribution costs not only for rice and specialized foodstuffs, but for mass consumption items like cotton and silk textiles, pottery, ironware and brassware, and diverse handicrafts. These were produced in specialist centers and disseminated through periodic local markets and a network of permanent markets corresponding broadly to G. William Skinner's

---

[70] Each comparison uses 1820 borders. The Vietnamese population grew from c. 2,000,000 to c. 7,000,000; the Burmese from perhaps 2,000,000 to c. 4,500,000, and the Siamese from a similar starting point to perhaps 4,000,000. Lieberman, "Secular Trends," 11–12; Simon de La Loubere, *The Kingdom of Siam* (rpt., Singapore, 1986), 11; Reid, *Age of Commerce*, I, 14; G. William Skinner, *Chinese Society in Thailand* (Ithaca, 1957), 79; Li, *Cochinchina*, 159–60.

[71] See *supra* n. 69, plus discussion of per capita GDP trends c. 900–1850 elsewhere in Eurasia in Jan Luiten van Zanden, "The Great Convergence from a West-European Perspective," *Itinerario* 24 (2000): 9–28; E. L. Jones, *Growth Recurring* (Oxford, 1988); Jack Goldstone, "Efflorescences and Economic Growth in World History" (ms forthcoming in *JWH*); Edwin Horlings, "Pre-industrial Economic Growth and the Transition to an Industrial Economy," in Maarten Prak, ed., *Early Modern Capitalism* (London, 2001), esp. 97–99; Jan de Vries, "Economic Growth Before and After the Industrial Revolution: A Modest Proposal," in ibid., 177–94.

Chinese macro-region typology.[72] In itself, the expansion of cities, mines, and specialized occupations strengthened commodification insofar as non-cereal producers relied on markets for food and materials more heavily than did the average peasant. The settlement of frontier zones with unique agricultural and mineral products also multiplied the possibilities for specialization and long distance exchange. Meanwhile, foreign traders introduced bullion and specie and opened commercial circuits along which domestic goods could move more easily. By providing accepted measures of value, foreign and domestic specie further reduced transaction costs. The search for comparative advantage was therefore at one and the same time local, regional, and international. Together, these factors encouraged in many contexts a degree of Smithian economic growth, in which the division of labor and economies of scale inherent in market integration joined with incremental technical improvements to create modest advances in productivity within a stable production-possibility frontier.[73]

Evidence of wider specialization and commodity production is readily available, even in interior areas that one might have thought would remain substantially untouched. Specie and bullion circulated more widely. Subsistence agriculture coexisted with growing commodity production in handicrafts, mining, forest extraction, specialty crops, and rice, for domestic as well as overseas markets. Reduced household self-sufficiency and demographic pressure in turn enhanced the number of local and intermediate markets and the complexity of central (capital) markets. In favored lowland districts, more commercially oriented systems of land tenure, credit, and contract took root. The social order grew more mobile, competitive, and commercially oriented; consumer goods began to erode sumptuary laws, and especially in Siam, trade acquired literary and social prestige. Visible as early as the 15th

---

[72] See G. William Skinner, "Marketing and Social Structure in Rural China," Pts. 1–2, *JAS* 24 (1964–65): 3–43, 195–228; Susan Naquin and Evelyn S. Rawski, *Chinese Society in the Eighteenth Century* (New Haven, 1987), ch. 5; and analyses of market structures in Chs. 2–4 *infra*. Cf. discussion of demographically-aided commercialization at Boserup, *Population and Technological Change*, pt. 2; and Horlings, "Pre-industrial Economic Growth," 97, citing K. G. Persson.

[73] Pre-industrial growth as described by Adam Smith was thus distinct from what Simon Kuznets termed "modern economic growth," in which sustained investment and technological advances produced continuous increases in productivity per workday within a constantly changing production-possibility frontier. On Smithian growth, modern economic growth, extensive growth, and involutionary growth, see *supra* nn. 69, 71; Kuznets, *Modern Economic Growth* (New Haven, 1996), 490–509; Joel Mokyr, *The Lever of Riches* (New York, 1990), 3–16.

and 16th centuries, such trends became particularly pronounced in the 1700s and early 1800s.

Political and Cultural Repercussions

How did economic expansion influence political and cultural life? In the short term, by creating land and monetary shortages and by aggravating center-periphery and intra-elite conflicts, economic growth repeatedly destabilized mainland polities. In one realm after another, breakdowns during the 14th, 16th, and 18th centuries followed periods of rapid demographic and/or commercial growth not easily accommodated by existing political arrangements.

Over the long term, however, as central authorities learned to harness larger manpower and commercial reserves, domestic growth reinforced the centralizing impact of firearms and foreign trade. Hence, in part, the cumulative success of political integration between 900 and 1830 and the reduced severity and duration of successive interregna in the western and central mainland. I have argued that increases in population and output were concentrated in politically dominant lowland cores – the Irrawaddy and Chaophraya basins, Dong Kinh, the southern Vietnamese lowlands. Even if the economies of such regions and of more peripheral areas grew at the same rate, the former's initial superiority would have ensured a constantly increasing absolute advantage. For example, if the economies of lowland district A, with output of 100 units in 1500, and of outlying area B, with output of 30 in 1500, both grew during two centuries by 50 percent, the former's absolute advantage by 1700 would have increased from 70 to 105, with the relevant units being soldiers, rice, and cash taxes. Frequently, however, better pacification, easier access to foreign trade, and centripetal resource transfers (via deportations, tribute, and trade) induced more rapid growth in imperial heartlands than in their peripheries. Although overextension could be a problem, such disproportionalities again tended to fuel imperial expansion in circular fashion: conquests strengthened capital districts, which were able to conquer fresh territories.

Two problems, one definitional, the other empirical, arise. First, when I claim that imperial heartlands grew more rapidly than peripheries, does the latter category include Lower Burma and southern Vietnam (Dang Trong), both of which eventually displayed greater demographic and commercial vigor than their original metropoles, namely, Upper Burma and Dong Kinh? Or does "periphery" refer only to upland

54

dependencies and noncompetitive lowland areas like Cambodia? In the western mainland I am inclined to regard the entire Irrawaddy basin, at least by 1800, as a single unit insofar as: a) basin-wide markets and political controls ensured that Upper Burma profited directly from southern prosperity, b) Lower Burma assimilated rapidly to northern culture and administration, so that the lowlands as a whole assumed a character quite distinct from that of the surrounding uplands. In Vietnam, by contrast, ties between Dong Kinh and Dang Trong were not economic, merely cultural and political, and these tended to weaken from 1600 to 1786. Even before reunification in 1802, Dang Trong, which dominated southeastern Cambodia and much of the Annamite chain, benefited from many of the same centripetal impulses as the Irrawaddy and Chaophraya basins. After 1802 Dang Trong dominated the entire eastern coast. In this view, then, the eastern mainland, unlike the other two sectors of the mainland, lacked a stable center, with the original core and periphery eventually reversing roles.

A second problem, critical to the larger Eurasian project, concerns the relation between maritime and domestic economic stimuli. In a word, which set of stimuli more decisively influenced political and cultural evolution? Although after 1450 or 1500 maritime factors became more influential than previously, in many contexts internal factors remained dominant. Upper Burma's demographic superiority explains not only why Burmans dominated Mons, but also why, except for the 16th century, the capital remained in the interior. In the east, if Dang Trong's defense against the north benefited from maritime revenues and firearms, her survival also depended on agricultural and demographic expansion. This was yet more true of Dai Viet's earlier victory over the Chams. Of all mainland capitals, Ayudhya and Bangkok depended most consistently on maritime trade. Yet it is often forgotten that the lower Chaophraya basin also enjoyed a critical agricultural advantage: the floodplain/delta was both more extensive and less dependent on hydraulic engineering than intermontane Tai basins to the north.

At the same time as economic expansion boosted aggregate resources, monetization enhanced each capital's ability to extract and distribute those resources. With markets affording cultivators easier access to cash, the creation of tax-farms and the commutation of notoriously unwieldy in-kind taxes and labor services became more feasible. Like maritime revenues, domestic cash revenues were used to finance military campaigns, to replace corvées with wage labor, to centralize patronage, and to develop new forms of religious donations.

In a wider social and psychological sense, this same mobility of goods and labor helped to erode encapsulated systems, while generating a growing receptivity to supra-local political coordination and cultural norms. The issue of capital-local linkages may be considered from the standpoint of political patronage models and of cultural transfer (including diffusionist) models. In both cases, a rich early modern European historiography, if treated with due caution, offers a useful starting point.

The first approach, associated with such scholars as William Beik, Sharon Kettering, Valerie Kivelson, Gerald Aylmer, Antoni Maczak, and Ruth Mackay,[74] emphasizes the growing inclination of local elites to use the developing apparatus of the state – indeed to help construct that apparatus – so as to buttress their own social position. Admittedly, in Southeast Asia commercial anemia and poorly articulated legal traditions inhibited these processes by European standards. Nonetheless, especially in the lowlands, market expansion, the growing political importance of central tax revenues and market access, the increased threat of foreign incursion, a desire for foreign spoils, and the danger of uncontrolled peasant mobility all made it more difficult for local leaders to maintain their preeminence or to direct affairs without help from a central coordinating apparatus. They therefore negotiated novel arrangements that simultaneously enhanced the flow of resources to the capital, provided them with new sources of patronage, and secured their place in an expanded social hierarchy. Especially from the 15th century in Dai Viet, and from the early 17th century in Burma and Siam, provincial elites joined central officials to reform taxation, mobilize larger armies, guarantee labor services, and regularize access to office, whether through civil service examinations (as in Dai Viet) or central adjudication of hereditary claims.[75] Although, especially on the periphery, coercion remained critical to state building, I believe that

---

74 William Beik, *Absolutism and Society in Seventeenth-Century France* (Cambridge, 1985); Sharon Kettering, *Patrons, Brokers, and Clients in Seventeenth-Century France* (Oxford, 1986); Valerie A. Kivelson, *Autocracy in the Provinces: The Muscovite Gentry and Political Culture in the Seventeenth Century* (Stanford, 1996); Gerald Aylmer, "Center and Locality: The Nature of Power Elites," in Reinhard, *Power Elites*, 59–77; Antoni Maczak, "The Nobility-State Relationship," ibid., 189–206; Ruth Mackay, *The Limits of Royal Authority* (Cambridge, 1999). See too Jonathan Dewald, *Pont-St-Pierre 1398–1789* (Berkeley, 1987), and James Collins, *The State in Early Modern France* (Cambridge, 1995).

75 See, e.g., Lieberman, *Cycles*; Rabibhadana, *Organization*; Nola Cooke, "Nineteenth-Century Vietnamese Confucianization in Historical Perspective," *JSEAS* 25 (1994): 270–312. Nor was this process restricted to elites insofar as tax-payers and servicemen often negotiated their obligations to local patrons.

the process was more local in origin, more consensual – and the state, by implication, more vulnerable to a rupture of elite consensus – than generally has been recognized.

The diffusionist interpretation of cultural change, as in the work of Robert Muchembled and Xavier de Planhol, emphasizes the multifaceted breakdown of local cultural systems under the combined impact of urban-rural trade, wider literacy, official repression, and a process of social differentiation by which successful peasants and notables sought to advertise their superior status by adopting prestigious motifs. Through contagious imitation, gradually local dialects, customs, and religious practices lost ground.[76] Muchembled's schema, in particular, has been criticized for positing binary elite/popular categories when in fact gradations were innumerable, and for minimizing the resilience and plasticity of popular cultures.[77] In lieu of unidirectional flows, it is more useful to theorize a dialogue, weighted in favor of the center, between official norms and popular practices. What Philip S. Gorski has recently termed "third-wave theories" of state formation argue that substantially local and autonomous processes altered popular definitions of legitimate behavior, which then modified the self-images of central actors.[78] Such localized perspectives are even more necessary in Southeast Asia, where urban-rural links and central institutions tended to be weaker than in Western Europe.

That said, the general argument that a thickening web of economic, social, and cultural links "involved an enlargement of social space and a quickening of exchanges within that space" certainly applies to the mainland.[79] Given their superior political, economic, and demographic weight, such exchanges tended to favor urban districts and imperial centers. From an ever wider hinterland, urban trade and pilgrimage networks drew peddlers, peasants, itinerant monks, actors, entertainers,

[76] Robert Muchembled, *Popular Culture and Elite Culture in France 1400–1750* (Baton Rouge, 1985); Xavier de Planhol, *An Historical Geography of France* (Cambridge, 1994).

[77] See Robin Briggs, *Communities of Belief* (Oxford, 1989), 53–57, 384–402. Also Jacques Revel in Steven L. Kaplan, ed., *Understanding Popular Culture* (Berlin, 1984); Edward Muir, *Ritual in Early Modern Europe* (Cambridge, 1997); Nancy Shields Kollman, *By Honor Bound* (Ithaca, 1999), esp. 186–202.

[78] The first wave was Marxist; the second emphasized the influence of war and geopolitics. Philip S. Gorski, "Beyond Marx and Hintze? Third-Wave Theories of Early Modern State Formation," *CSSH* 43 (2001): 851–61. See also Wayne Te Brake, *Shaping History* (Berkeley, 1998); Roger Chartier, *The Cultural Origins of the French Revolution* (Durham, NC, 1991).

[79] Quote is from Dewald, *Pont-St-Pierre*, 284.

and scholars, all agents of cultural exchange and synthesis. In the opposite direction, waves of Burman and Vietnamese colonists swamped outlying peoples. Frontier minorities withdrew, rebelled, and/or accepted majority motifs, but all three responses led to substantial assimilation.

Granted that a more rapid circulation of people and cultural motifs privileged lowland religious norms, why did those norms tend to become more textual and self-consciously orthodox? People leaving their natal villages, where they had been protected by local spirits, needed portable, universal systems of sacrality, which were necessarily textual. New trade routes opened the interior to proselytizing, orthodox, Sinhalese-oriented monks. Improved pacification and more concentrated wealth supported more monasteries, schools, and manuscripts, with a corresponding rise in religious literacy. Even illiterates exposed to sermons and oral accounts acquired a hunger for textual authority. Insofar as economic growth supported larger administrations, which in turn honored and exempted from taxation men who could read approved texts, orthodoxy had an obvious social appeal.

Frequently the extension of literacy transferred the initiative for cultic reform from royal courts to the countryside. Yet Theravada Buddhism and Neo-Confucianism strongly favored political centralization, not least because as a practical matter, both philosophies required supra-local systems of training and instruction. Vietnamese civil service examinations, which were administered by the state, which relied on an approved textual corpus, and which obliged students to leave their villages to write about issues of imperial governance, offer the most obvious example. Theravada monks also studied standard texts and depended on the throne to resolve disputes and to honor provincial talent. More subtly, orthodox teachings probably increased popular sympathy for royal claims of local regulation. By idealizing the throne as bulwark against anarchy, Neo-Confucian and Theravada traditions legitimated royal supervision of local personnel, lay and religious, while devaluing spirits and purely local sources of sanctity.

But if literacy was acquired primarily through monasteries and Confucian tuition, neither in motivation nor expression was it exclusively religious. Legal contracts, loans, and commercial calculation encouraged numeracy and written skills at surprisingly humble social levels. Demands for accurate censuses and tax records and a growing volume of litigation had a similar impact. In response to these impulses, whereas 14th-century rural society had been overwhelmingly illiterate, by the 19th century Burmese male literacy, for which we have the best data, exceeded 50 percent, quite impressive for a pre-industrial society. Perhaps the most dramatic indication of expanding literacy – and a major stimulus to reading in its own right – was the bloom, beginning as early as the 14th century but evident in almost all lowland areas by the 17th or 18th centuries, of vernacular-language literatures appealing to a readership that was both more plebeian and more empire-specific. Besides religious materials, these works included lay chronicles, law codes, books of punctilio, and new forms of fiction and poetry, with the latter exploring novel social dilemmas and a wider array of stylistic forms. While in the Theravada world such works used Burmese and various forms of Tai, especially capital dialects, in lieu of Pali or Sanskrit, in Vietnam demotic writing systems increasingly supplemented Chinese characters. At the same time Pali and Chinese-character writing drew strength from continuing contacts with Sri Lanka and China and from deepening orthodox sensibilities. Thus in the sphere of culture as in the spheres of economy and royal administration, by their very nature larger, more encompassing systems supported greater internal specialization.

Warfare as a Spur

Alongside economic growth and changes in religious and cultural sensibility, military competition provided a major spur to political and cultural integration.

Historians of 15th- and 16th-century Japan credit the era of large-scale warfare known as Sengoku with helping to transform an atomized manorial system into consolidated *daimyo* domains. The need to supply ever larger armies, some equipped with European-style firearms, contributed to basic changes in administration and social structure, which in turn prepared the way for Tokugawa consolidation.[80] In South Asia as well, scholars of the Mughal empire and of post-Mughal successor states have drawn attention to fiscal-administrative changes that flowed from new weapons technology and associated military demands.[81] In Charles Tilly's formulation of early modern European experience, the advantage of states like France over city-states and over more agrarian

[80] John W. Hall, ed., *The Cambridge History of Japan, Vol. IV: Early Modern Japan* (Cambridge, 1991), chs. 1–2; John W. Hall, Nagahara Keiji, and Kozo Yamamura, eds., *Japan Before Tokugawa* (Princeton, 1981).

[81] Marshall G. S. Hodgson, *The Venture of Islam. Vol. 3: The Gunpowder Empires and Modern Times* (Chicago, 1973); Burton Stein, "State Formation and Economy Reconsidered," *MAS* 19 (1985): 387–413; idem, *A History of India* (Oxford, 1998).

eastern polities derived from an ability to combine large domestic armies with commercial wealth. As fresh rounds of warfare whittled down the number of contenders, financial need drove the survivors to penetrate local society ever more deeply, so that standing armies, national cultures, and direct rule came to nourish one another.[82]

In mainland Southeast Asia military technology and strategy were more conservative than in Sengoku Japan or early modern Europe, and perhaps early modern South Asia. With broad, inhospitable marches separating some of the chief potential antagonists, fewer opportunities arose for extended conflict. Whereas in Europe printing, mercenaries, and a common cultural subtext sped the latest techniques from the English Channel to the Urals, and whereas in Japan a relatively unified culture also encouraged a rapid sharing of military advances, in mainland Southeast Asia poor east–west communications and the Indic-Sinic divide prevented a comparable fluidity. Moreover, compared to Japan, Europe, or South Asia, populations were smaller and commercial economies more sluggish, which was critical insofar as: a) Southeast Asia lacked the financial and credit mechanisms to maintain large standing armies and b) the absence of large-scale indigenous gun manufacture reduced the pressure for changes in weapons production, training, and finance.

But if technical innovation was relatively anemic, here too a competitive multistate system provided a frequent catalyst for administrative reform. Following the collapse of the charter states, warfare in the 13th to 15th centuries contributed to changes in service organization, provincial controls, throne-monkhood relations, and the selection of administrative personnel, as illustrated by the onset of Pattern B and Pattern D administration. Then, from the early or mid-1500s much as in Europe, Japan, and South Asia, European-style handguns and cannon accelerated the pyramiding of power inherent in economic growth and contributed to a reduction in the number of independent polities. Each Southeast Asian survivor faced two types of intensifying pressure. First, the incorporation of more geographically and culturally distant communities increased the risk of anticentralizing rebellions. Second, the growing size of infantry forces and the rising cost of firearms and

---

[82] Tilly, *Coercion, Capital*. The literature on military contributions to European state formation is extensive, including Theda Skocpol, *States and Social Revolutions* (Cambridge, 1979); Brian Downing, *The Military Revolution and Political Change* (Princeton, 1992); Thomas Ertman, *Birth of the Leviathan* (Cambridge, 1997); Jeremy Black, *War and the World* (New Haven, 1998).

fortifications rendered warfare more expensive and administratively taxing. The impact after 1550 became most obvious in Indic states, where repeated structural changes responded to the demands of external warfare and/or domestic rebellion. Administrative centralization thus had a convulsive quality, with periods of military challenge and/or collapse followed by intensified projects of reform in a pattern that might be termed creative destruction. The social impact of interstate warfare was also acute. In the absence of salaried professionals, most military tasks in Indic states continued to depend on hereditary services from a substantial part of the general population. The resultant emphasis on stratified control joined with the weakness of family property to encourage royally-defined social ranks more complex than anything attempted in France, for example.

In Vietnam the correlation between military challenge and administrative reform was more complex, in part because Confucianism had a social blueprint demanding implementation regardless of military circumstances, and in part because Vietnam's unique military vs. literati rivalry made literati-led Confucian reform less likely in wartime or its immediate aftermath. Civil wars in the 16th and 17th centuries promoted essentially military regimes in both north and south. Yet the Confucian model also appealed to leaders concerned with interstate competition: by standardizing procedures and pushing administration to the district level, Sinic-style bureaucracy promised to curb regionalism and to bolster Vietnamese regimes in military contests with Champa, Cambodia, and Siam.

As for psychological effects, I have suggested that in many communities intensifying warfare, particularly the chaos of the mid- and late 1700s, strengthened popular identification with the throne and with official culture by generating mythic reminders of communal danger and salvation, by rendering border communities more dependent on the throne for security, by nurturing ethnic stereotypes, and by integrating conscripts from different locales.

State Influences on Economics and Culture: Intended and Unintended Effects

In sum, political integration in mainland Southeast Asia drew strength from an interlocking set of economic, social, and intellectual changes in the local environment. Surely, however, the lines of causation ran in the opposite direction as well: as it acquired greater stability and administrative expertise, each polity modified, consciously and unconsciously, the economic and sociocultural environment in which it operated.

What intellectual resources undergirded state evolution? Administrative expertise derived from at least three sources. First, the inheritance from charter principalities. Insofar as post-1400 ruptures in Vietnam and Upper Burma were relatively modest, those realms had more direct access to charter legacies than did Siam, but even there precedents from Angkor (as well as Suphanburi) were influential. Second, external models. Buddhism's tribulations in India and in Sri Lanka and its relative indifference to practical affairs meant that no Indic state had so detailed or sophisticated an administrative model as Dai Viet found in Ming and Qing China. On the other hand, competition between Indic states did create a channel for the transmission of best military and political practices. This was true, for example, during the intensifying warfare of the late 15th and 16th centuries; and again in the 17th and 18th centuries when Toungoo Burma and Late Ayudhya Siam copied one another's provincial reforms. In a broader sense, I have suggested that the Chinese-inspired Neo-Confucian revolution of the 15th century and Sinhalese-derived movements of Theravada reform nourished popular sympathy for royal claims of enhanced authority. A third source of expertise was local trial-and-error, which was spurred by the growing size of each administration and which became especially intense in the aftermath of military disasters. Thus, administrative expertise – like knowledge of new crops, commercial practices, or firearms – was a resource that could accumulate, that was rarely lost completely, and that further explains the progressive, ratchet-like nature of integration and the shorter duration of successive interregna.

State influences became particularly clear in the economic sphere, where each throne attempted periodically to develop its tax base in order to bolster its patronage and military prospects. To suggest that on balance such interventions were helpful is neither to deny innumerable instances of counterproductive rent-seeking and commercial restriction nor to pretend that such inducements approached the best case institutional and legal conditions that historians like Douglass C. North have postulated for parts of early modern Western Europe.[83] Nonetheless, in order to obtain strategic metals, firearms, and larger revenues,

[83] Douglass C. North and Robert Paul Thomas, *The Rise of the Western World* (Cambridge, 1973); North, *Institutions, Institutional Change, and Economic Performance* (Cambridge, 1990); Horlings, "Pre-industrial Economic Growth," 94–95.

it is clear that Southeast Asian rulers enthusiastically welcomed foreign merchants, sponsored overseas trading expeditions, and in Siam built strategic canals that had commercial spin-offs. To promote urban trade, they encouraged bullion imports and mining, standardized weights and measures, and in some cases reduced royal tolls. In Siam and possibly Burma, new laws tended to favor the private ownership, sale, and mortgage of land at the expense of less commercially oriented communal systems. During the post-charter era and again from the 17th to the 19th centuries, royal courts encouraged diking and irrigation, sponsored new crops, and in Burma and Vietnam, vigorously promoted frontier settlement. ("There is no way to the west, and it is too hard to go north, therefore we should do our best to advance to the south," wrote an 18th-century Vietnamese official advocating southern colonization.[84])

Alongside such self-conscious efforts, the chief empires and some of their smaller rivals encouraged production through activities whose economic impact was incidental to their original purpose and in many cases, probably unnoticed. Political unification tended to lower transaction costs by reducing the number of competing tribute gatherers and by facilitating exchange between zones with unique resource profiles. Demands for cash rather than in-kind levies channeled peasant production toward the market. Into the great capital cities of Ava, Ayudhya, Bangkok, Thang Long, and Hue, governments poured money for patronage and construction, while concentrating officials and support personnel. The resultant growth in urban market demand fostered all manner of specialization and long-distance exchange. Finally, by reducing mortality and raising nuptiality, I have suggested that pacification in each lowland core provided a powerful impetus to population growth.

The same mixture of motives, the same distinction between intended and unintended effects, applies to government influence on culture, including religious practice, literature, language, and ethnicity. Some early modernists emphasize the instrumentalism of cultural policy insofar as homogeneity eased communications and tax collections.[85] But purely functionalist explanations ignore the internal logic of religious commitments.

Whatever its motivation, the impact of cultural coordination is obvious enough. To promote religious orthodoxy, Theravada rulers resolved

[84] Li, *Cochinchina*,14.
[85] Charles Tilly, "Reflections on the History of European State-Making," and Stein Rokkan, "Dimensions of State Formation and Nation-Building," in Tilly, ed., *The Formation of National States in Western Europe* (Princeton, 1975).

monastic disputes, disseminated texts, dispatched missionaries, enforced Buddhist law codes, created official spirit pantheons, and performed an annual cycle of religious donations. In all three mainland realms, Buddhist personnel and wealth became subject to more effective lay control in a pattern with clear analogues to church-state transitions in 16th-century Europe and Japan. To these programs of religious standardization must be added persistent efforts to unify lay hierarchies, to determine aesthetic standards, and to modify lay social practices. Through literary and artistic patronage, Ava, Ayudhya, Bangkok, and Hue made themselves arbiters of taste and cultural magnets for provincial imitators. By indoctrinating villagers in Confucian norms, by promoting specifically Confucian legal notions of inheritance and family organization, and by regulating key status symbols through the examinations, Vietnamese leaders sought with particular vigor to influence settled society. In frontier areas as well, I have noted that late 18th- and early 19th-century Burmese and Vietnamese rulers self-consciously promoted majority ethnicity.

The indirect cultural effects of government action were no less significant. By appealing to a combination of snobbery and practical ambition, political patronage offered a powerful, if implicit, spur to what might be termed self-Burmanization, self-Vietnamization, and self-Siamization. The growing circulation between provincial and capital agencies of documents and legal decisions had a similar standardizing effect. In Burma and Siam the annual rotation of tens of thousands of provincial servicemen at the capital offered another powerful vehicle, largely unintended, of cultural exchange.

To summarize the entire theoretical argument: Each of the chief north–south corridors of mainland Southeast Asia fragmented in the 14th, late 16th, and late 18th centuries, yet these interregna proved compatible with – indeed, through their spur to compensatory experiments, generally aided – cultural and political integration. Riverine arteries peculiar to the western and central mainland ensured that integration was more secure in those sectors than in the east, but there too, both in the lowlands as a whole and in rival Vietnamese-speaking polities, we find comparable tendencies. Consolidation drew strength from several variables, including rising foreign trade, imported guns, population growth and agricultural extension, wider literacy, new religious currents, and the demands of intensifying interstate competition. Most factors had their own etiology, but all modified one another in

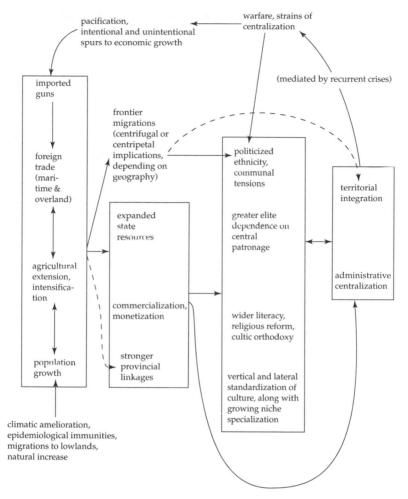

Figure 1.8. Some elements in the integration of mainland realms to 1830 and their potential interactions. Dotted lines indicate the ambiguous, potentially centrifugal implications of frontier settlement in the eastern lowlands during the 17th and 18th centuries.

ways that were both open-ended and potentially cumulative. To take a single thread, agricultural and commercial vitality magnified state resources and encouraged cultural diffusion, both of which processes aided territorial integration, which intensified interstate competition, which reinforced administrative interventions, which frequently promoted economic growth. Figure 1.8 abstracts some of these potential linkages.

This abstract, synchronic presentation should not obscure how widely individual elements differed by time and place. Vietnam's reliance on Chinese models after c. 1450, for example, provided a uniquely sophisticated administrative blueprint, but engendered elite-mass cultural tensions without close Theravada parallel. Whereas post-1600 frontier settlement tended to strengthen the Burmese and Siamese realms, along the eastern littoral the effects were more ambiguous. On the other hand, in both the western and eastern lowlands the relative mildness of post-charter disruptions joined with endemic tensions on the advancing frontier to foster a closer link between ethnicity and political loyalty than in Siam. Likewise, in the Irrawaddy basin and Dong Kinh, maritime stimuli were less consistently influential than in the Chaophraya basin. Thus, depending on criteria, one can organize the chief mainland realms (as well as their less successful competitors) into quite different configurations.

PART B: IMPLICATIONS FOR EURASIA

East–West Incomparability

As I emphasized at the outset, this narrative of cyclic-cum-linear integration has implications beyond Southeast Asia. But to appreciate their significance, it is necessary to gauge the historiographic juncture at which we stand.

A dichotomous distinction between the "West" and the "Rest" (to redeploy Samuel P. Huntington's aphorism[86]) has long been central to intellectualized European understandings of the world. As early as Machiavelli, but more systematically in the works of Montesquieu, Hegel, Marx, Weber, and the externalist historians with whom we began this chapter, European thinkers defined Asia in negative terms by its lack of European traits: an absence of stable private property, juridical restraint, a spirit of rational inquiry, and ultimately, of any true historical dynamic.[87] The resultant necessity for European tutelage provided a charter for late imperialism. But more basically, Eurocentric histories said less about politics than about the overwhelming intellectual – nay,

---

[86] Samuel P. Huntington, *The Clash of Civilizations and the Remaking of World Order* (New York, 1996), ch. 8.

[87] See, e.g., Max Weber, *Economy and Society*, 2 vols., Guenther Roth and Claus Wittich, eds. (Berkeley, 1968), I, 611–30; Perry Anderson, *Lineages of the Absolutist State* (London, 1974), 397–402, 462–549; Edward Said, *Orientalism* (New York, 1978).

emotional – urge to explain the intoxicating power imbalance between Euro-America and Asia from the mid-18th through the mid-20th century. To essentialize these asymmetries, to portray European patterns as a norm whose historic absence in other areas was invariable, yet somehow still puzzling, proved all too irresistible. Hence the compression of societies that were enormously varied but comparably vulnerable into a single artificial category – Asia. Hence too the contrast between European dynamism and Asian stagnation even among scholars with impeccable anti-imperialist credentials, including Marxist advocates of the Asiatic Mode of Production theory, Japanese critics of the Tokugawa era,[88] as well as those "autonomous" historians of Southeast Asia whose sympathy for local independence was compatible with claims of indigenous stasis.

Ironically, because they bore little fruit, efforts by Asianists to find analogues to specifically European features also served to reinforce a sense of profound difference. Popular candidates included feudalism, industrial capitalism, and concepts of civil society and the public sphere. Although Japan exhibited many European-style feudal traits, elsewhere the search for feudalism required such elasticity as to deprive the category of analytic value.[89] With the doubtful exception of Japan, all concede that Asia in 1800 was not moving toward a European-style industrial revolution.[90] Nor have European notions of the public sphere yielded plausible parallels. Although late Ming/Qing China, for example, saw activity by extra-bureaucratic organizations concerned with public welfare, the notion that individuals with defined rights vis-a-vis the state were entitled to enter critical debate on national policy had no real resonance.[91]

---

[88] Timothy Brook, ed., *The Asiatic Mode of Production in China* (Armonk, NY, 1989); Anderson, *Lineages*, Note B, 462–549; John W. Hall and Marius Jensen, eds., *Studies in the Institutional History of Early Modern Japan* (Princeton, 1968), 55–64.

[89] See, e.g., Rushton Coulborn, ed., *Feudalism in History* (Princeton, 1956); Edmund Leach et al., *Feudalism: Comparative Studies* (Sydney, 1985).

[90] Gary Leupp, *Servants, Shophands, and Laborers in the Cities of Tokugawa Japan* (Princeton, 1991); Evelyn Rawski, "Research Themes in Minq-Qing Socioeconomic History – The State of the Field," *JAS* 50 (1991): 84–111; Sanjay Subrahmanyam, "Rural Industry and Commercial Agriculture in Late 17th Century South-Eastern India," *PP* 126 (1990): 76–114.

[91] "Symposium: 'Public Sphere'/'Civil Society' in China?" *Modern China* 19 (1993): 107–215; R. Bin Wong, "Great Expectations," *Chukogu shigakkai* 3 (1993): 7–50; C. A. Bayly, "Rethinking the Origins of the Indian Public Sphere," Univ. of Michigan lecture, Sept. 15, 1995.

In recent years, European exceptionalism has been promoted most enthusiastically not by Asian specialists, but by comparative sociologists, economists, and historians, most trained in European studies, including E. L. Jones, author of the aptly-named *The European Miracle*; Patricia Crone, Michael Mann, Douglass North, Thomas Sowell, Immanuel Wallerstein, Jack Goldstone, and perhaps best known, David S. Landes.[92] Naturally, emphases vary. Jones called attention to the continent's peculiar geography – the "dispersed portfolio" of resources, the high proportion of coastlines – which encouraged competition between commercially sympathetic states. Crone, in an essay titled "The Oddity of Europe," focused on the uniqueness of that region's kinship patterns and the legal empowerment subjects gained under feudalism. Mann analyzed the conjuncture of: a) normative continent-wide Christian pacification; b) a multiplicity of competing states; and c) diversified, intensive economic networks. North stressed the unique success of Western Europe, especially Britain, in creating institutional protection for competitive markets in land, labor, and intellectual property. With a similar insistence on the primacy of culture, Landes, a self-declared neo-Weberian, emphasized the Protestant work ethic; while Goldstone argued for the critical role of empirical science and representative government in nurturing a specifically British "engine science."[93] Different emphases aside, most agreed that the fragmented political structure of early modern Western Europe (or its most advanced sectors) engendered a cultural and legal tradition that placed a unique value on

[92] E. L. Jones, *The European Miracle*, (2nd ed., Cambridge, 1987); Patricia Crone, *Pre-Industrial Societies* (Oxford, 1989), ch. 8; Michael Mann, *The Sources of Social Power*, vol. 1 (Cambridge, 1986), esp. chs. 13–15; idem, "European Development," in Jean Baechler, John A. Hall, and Michael Mann, eds., *Europe and the Rise of Capitalism* (Oxford, 1991), 6–19; North and Thomas, *Rise of the Western World*; Thomas Sowell, *Conquests and Cultures: An International History* (New York, 1998); Wallerstein, *World System*; Goldstone, "Efflorescences and Economic Growth"; idem, "Europe's Peculiar Path: Would the World Be Modern if William III's Invasion of England in 1688 Had Failed?", forthcoming in Ned Lebow et al., eds., *Counterfactual History* (New York, n.d.); David Landes, *The Wealth and Poverty of Nations* (New York, 1998); idem, "Culture Makes Almost All the Difference," in Lawrence E. Harrison and Samuel P. Huntington, eds., *Culture Matters* (New York, 2000), 2–13. While most of these authors focus on Europe, Crone is an Islamicist.

[93] Previous note. See too P. K. O'Brien, "The Reconstruction, Rehabilitation and Reconfiguration of the British Industrial Revolution as a Conjuncture in Global History," *Itinerario* 24 (2000): 117–34, and C.A. Bayly, "South Asia and the 'Great Divergence,'" *Itinerario* 24 (2000): 89–103, arguing that British/West European exceptionalism resided in sustained state commitments to warfare and industry and in the "density of social communication" associated with civil society.

property rights, urban autonomy, and contractual government. This in turn provided the granite foundation for those twin glories of Western civilization, representative government and capitalism.

The flipside of the argument is that in the absence of such traditions, Asian societies – often exemplified by Mughal India, the Ottomans, and Ming/Qing China – could accumulate extensive resources, but could not generate increases in per capita output needed to rescue them from Malthusian/ecological traps. By 1600 – some claim much earlier – most of Asia therefore began to fall behind Europe in key economic indices. In passages whose politics could have been taken from Montesquieu but whose economic assumptions were neo-Smithian, Jones dismissed Asian governments as "revenue pumps" and "plunder machines."[94] If more inclined to explain divergence in terms of self-reinforcing structural advantages, Wallerstein concurred that Europe's economic superiority over China derived in large part from a more favorable institutional heritage: whereas feudalism provided small European states with "leverage for change," in China "crucial decisions were centralized in an imperial framework that had to concern itself first and foremost with short-run maintenance of the political equilibrium..."[95] In comparing Chinese and European economic policy, Landes concluded: "In Asian despotisms... what did ordinary people exist for, except to enhance the pleasure of their rulers?... In these circumstances, the very notion of economic development was a Western invention."[96] The respectful, even deferential, response to Landes's recent work suggests that at the start of the 21st century among professional historians his approach remains popular, and among the educated public, probably dominant.

A Fortress Besieged

Venerable though it be, the fortress of European exceptionalism has come under attack both from within and without.

From within, for reasons that have everything to do with antiformalist trends in European historiography but nothing to do with global or comparative concerns per se, European sappers have begun to undermine a number of famous landmarks. Quite unintentionally, therefore, they have aided anti-Eurocentric assaults. Susan Reynolds's thesis that

---

[94] Jones, *European Miracle*, 228–31; also 153–71.
[95] Wallerstein, *World System*, I, 63.
[96] Landes, *Wealth and Poverty*, 32; also 516.

the system of feudal legal contracts was invented by 16th- and 17th-century lawyers suggests that feudalism was less seminal to European legal tradition than most writers have assumed.[97] Whereas earlier historians sought to contrast the bureaucratic character of West European administrations with the factionalism and inefficiency of Asian patrimonialism, recent scholarship on 17th–18th century France has shown that in fact clientage remained basic at all administrative levels.[98] European class-based analyses translated poorly to Asia. But with the decline of European Marxist historiography in favor of emphases on society-wide cultural and commercial currents,[99] the possibilities for European-Asian comparisons in this respect have widened as well.

Even the division of European history into medieval, Renaissance, and early modern eras, with its emphasis on innovation and dynamism, has been questioned by historians arguing for basic continuities in what Dietrich Gerhard termed "Old Europe," c. 1000–1800. Jean Chapelot and Robert Fossier claimed that the European city and village remained structurally stable from the 11th century until industrialization. According to Georges Duby, by 1220 "the various elements that constituted the political system in France until the end of the ancien regime were all in place."[100] Nor has that telltale harbinger of European modernity, the Industrial Revolution, escaped: once said to be the logical culmination of accelerating economic expansion throughout Western Europe, primary industrialization is now seen by some as a discontinuous, fragile, and contingent outcome specific only to Britain.[101] Without accepting

---

[97] Susan Reynolds, *Fiefs and Vassals* (Oxford, 1994).

[98] Kettering, *Patrons, Brokers, and Clients*; Beik, *Absolutism and Society*; Roger Mettam, *Power and Faction in Louis XIV's France* (Oxford, 1988); Nicholas Henshall, *The Myth of Absolutism* (London, 1992). See similar arguments for Spain in Mackay, *Limits*; and for Russia in Kivelson, *Autocracy*, and Kollman, *Honor Bound*, 17 ff.

[99] See, e.g., Jack Goldstone, *Revolution and Rebellion in the Early Modern World* (Berkeley, 1991), chs. 2, 3; William Doyle, *Origins of the French Revolution* (3rd ed., Oxford, 1999), pt. 1.

[100] Georges Duby, *France in the Middle Ages 987–1460* (Oxford, 1991), 298. See too Dietrich Gerhard, *Old Europe: A Study of Continuity, 1000–1800* (New York, 1981); Jean Chapelot and Robert Fossier, *The Village and House in the Middle Ages* (Berkeley, 1985); C. Warren Hollister, "The Phases of European History and the Nonexistence of the Middle Ages," *Pacific Historical Review* 61 (1992): 1–22; R. I. Moore, "The Birth of Europe as a Eurasian Phenomenon," *MAS* 31 (1997): 583–601.

[101] See, e.g., Kenneth Pomeranz, *The Great Divergence* (Princeton, 2000); Goldstone, "Efflorescences and Economic Growth"; Jan Luiten van Zanden, "Early Modern Economic Growth," in Prak, *Early Modern Capitalism*, 69–87; Horlings, "Pre-industrial Economic Growth." For more gradualist approaches and for overviews of the rather see-saw

all these views, some sharply contested, one can acknowledge that these perspectives threaten the stark opposition between Western dynamism and Eastern stasis.

Meanwhile from outside the citadel – but often unaware of the turmoil in Europeanist ranks – a handful of Asianists and Asian-oriented comparativists have launched open attacks on Eurocentrism. In much the same way as Europe's post-1750 military and commercial ascendancy provided the psychological background for theories of European cultural superiority, so in reverse order, East Asia's economic power in the 1980s and 1990s led some comparativists to naturalize Asian dynamism by rooting it deeply in Asian history and culture.

Given Japan's 1980s role as harbinger of the "Asian miracle," it was to be expected that the earliest such efforts would focus on that country. Comparativists in turn depended on an antecedent revolution in Japanese historiography, which once rejected the Tokugawa as an era of backwardness but which now lauds that very era for engendering the social solidarity and capital accumulation on which later industrial success would rest.[102] E. L. Jones in his second foray into global history, John Powelson, and (with less enthusiasm) David Landes all argued that in Tokugawa Japan as in early modern Western Europe, the emergence of free markets rested on the institutionalized diffusion of political power. Japan and Europe thus contrasted with nonpluralist regimes everywhere else, where political authorities' excessive rent-seeking thwarted innovation. Yet as a model for global history this offered little conceptual advance beyond Eurocentrism: by making Japanese into honorary whites, it preserved intact the age-old chasm.[103]

A more ambitious approach has been pioneered by Marshall G. S. Hodgson, J. M. Blaut, Janet Abu-Lughod, and most recently, Andre Gunder Frank, R. Bin Wong, and Kenneth Pomeranz. These authors have sought to reduce the gap in economic achievement between the West and Asia as a whole, not merely Japan, by minimizing its extent and postponing its onset. When a break did occur, they have explained

---

historiography of the industrial revolution, see N. F. R. Crafts and C. K. Harley, "Output Growth and the British Industrial Revolution," *EHR* 45 (1992): 703–30; O'Brien, "Reconstruction, Rehabilitation."

[102] See Thomas C. Smith, *Native Sources of Japanese Industrialization, 1750–1920* (Berkeley, 1988); Chie Nakane and Shinzaburo Oishi, eds., *Tokugawa Japan* (Tokyo, 1991). In a wider sense, analysts of contemporary East Asia began to praise Confucian legacies, heretofore denigrated as a retarding force.

[103] Jones, *Growth Recurring*; John Powelson, *Centuries of Economic Endeavor* (Ann Arbor, 1994); Landes, *Wealth and Poverty*, ch. 22.

it in terms of the West's geographic good fortune and/or the benefits it drew from extra-European contacts. In this shift from culture
to contingency, they therefore denied the central teleological claim of
European exceptionalists, namely, that the West's unique success was
rooted in its institutional and legal heritage. Hodgson, a scholar of
Islam, claimed that "technicalization" occurred first in the West because
Europe adapted key Eastern inventions, and because western Europe
was uniquely blessed by a combination of well-watered soil, protection against Mongol incursions, and access to New World resources.[104]
Abu-Lughod and Blaut also emphasized the comparability of urbanization and commercial organization in a wide band of Eurasian societies and the critical role of New World capital in Europe's post-1500
takeoff.[105] According to Frank, Asians in general and Chinese in particular actually were more efficient than Europeans, who, lacking anything
of their own to sell, gained entree to Asian markets only through their
monopoly of New World silver. Not until the late 18th century did
Asia enter a downward phase at the same time as Britain – for reasons
Frank could not explain with any clarity – succeeded in substituting its
own for Asian manufactures. The late 1700s, not the early 1500s, therefore marked the beginning of Western ascendancy, but Frank warned
that the center of the world economy is now returning to the Middle
Kingdom.[106]

Without prognosticating, the China specialists Wong and Pomeranz
concurred with Frank's delayed chronology. Until the late 1700s patterns of Smithian growth, consumption, and longevity were entirely
comparable in advanced sectors of Western Europe and China. But
thereafter, Pomeranz argued, Europe's involvement in a vast Atlantic
system, much of which depended on coerced nonmarket labor, relieved
the growing strain on Europe's supply of land and energy and made
possible greater core-periphery differentiation than in China. Ironically,
because more efficient Chinese markets inhibited core-periphery specialization on the Atlantic model, and also because China was endowed
with poorer overall resources than the Atlantic system, the periphery of
the Yangzi basin could provide neither the critical consumer demand nor
the cheap raw materials and food (the "ghost acres") that Britain found
in the New World. Nor did Chinese proto-industry have access to coal

[104] Marshall G. S. Hodgson, *Rethinking World History* (Cambridge, 1993), esp. pt. 1.
[105] Janet Abu-Lughod, *Before European Hegemony* (Oxford, 1989); J. M. Blaut, *The Colonizer's Model of the World* (New York, 1993).
[106] Frank, *Re-Orient*.

on anything like the scale of Britain. In short, colonies and coal were the twin foundations of British industrialization. But outside Britain, most of Western Europe faced the same Malthusian pressures, the same poor prospects as the Yangzi basin, from which British technology alone rescued them. Again, therefore, contingency and structural constraints, not cultural biases were the key variables.[107]

The View from Southeast Asia

This two-volume study also critiques the trope of European exceptionalism, but I adopt a different geographic and chronological perspective, a fresh set of thematic concerns, and a new explanatory dynamic.

Southeast Asia is routinely omitted from world histories, but I offer structured comparisons between that region (both mainland and islands) and France, Russia, Japan, and more briefly, China and South Asia. Whereas most revisionists consider a limited time span, I argue that nine or ten centuries provide the most appropriate framework to recognize a Eurasian-wide pattern of secular integration punctuated by coordinated periods of collapse. As the foregoing summary suggests, the bulk of comparative inquiry has sought to explain the origins of Europe's unique industrialization. By contrast, I concentrate on changes in political organization and communal identities, examining economic change as an agent in this larger transformation.

Furthermore, I propose to turn Southeast Asia's obscurity into a virtue by developing a more generous, less adversarial calculus of Eurasian difference. As is common among revisionists who feel obliged to compensate for the inertia of entrenched opinion, anti-Eurocentric critiques frequently overstated their case by denying that before 1500, 1800, or whatever date is convenient, West European societies enjoyed any distinction whatever. Blaut implied that Columbus was lucky to have

---

[107] R. Bin Wong, *China Transformed* (Ithaca, 1997); Pomeranz, *Great Divergence*; and contributions by those authors to "*AHR* Forum: Asia and Europe in the World Economy,"*AHR* 107 (2002): 419–80. For early modern European/Asian economic comparisons, see too John Lee, "Trade and Economy in Preindustrial East Asia, c. 1500–c. 1800," *JAS* 58 (1999): 2–25; Frank Perlin, *Unbroken Landscape* (Aldershot, UK, 1994); Prasannan Parthasarathi, "Rethinking Wages and Competitiveness in the 18th Century: Britain and South India," *PP* 158 (1998): 79–109; Jack Goody, *The East in the West* (Cambridge, 1996); Daniel Power and Naomi Standen, eds., *Frontiers In Question: Eurasian Borderlands, 700–1700* (New York, 1999); Jerry Bentley, "Hemispheric Integration, 500–1500 C.E.," *JWH* 9 (1998): 237–54; Jack Goldstone's marvelous *Revolution and Rebellion*; Gale Stokes, "The Fates of Human Societies," *AHR* (2001): 508–25.

beaten African and South Asian mariners into the Atlantic.[108] According to Frank, as late as 1750 Europe "remained a marginal player in the world economy," while even in weapons, Europe in 1700 enjoyed no significant superiority. Overwhelming evidence can be marshaled against these and similar claims, but in his enthusiasm to debunk the European Miracle, Frank made everything east of the Urals superior to everything to the west.[109] Notwithstanding the general sophistication of his scholarship, Wong, eager to establish the precocious "modernity" of Chinese political culture, claimed that unlike China, no pre-19th century "European state could imagine an attempt to shape social opinion and cultural practices."[110] (What of the Reformation and Counter-Reformation?) So too, in their emphasis on New World wealth as a contingent explanation of Western economic superiority, most comparativists – Pomeranz is a notable exception – ignored the consensus that the great bulk of industrial capital derived from within, rather than outside, that continent.[111]

Southeast Asianists have their weaknesses, to be sure, but these do not include fantasies of world preeminence. The region's limited population, tortured internal geography, and relative isolation ensured that

---

[108] Blaut, *Colonizer's Model*, 180–83.

[109] Frank, *Re-Orient*, 75, 100–101, 126–30, 179–85, 193, 195–97, 270–71. One may well ask how a region that conducted an extensive internal commerce and that in 1750 dominated the trade of West Africa, the entire New World, and much of maritime Southeast Asia and coastal India could have been marginal to the world economy. Frank equates trade surplus with productive efficiency, when in fact bullion was a commodity that followed price differentials. By Frank's logic, late 18th century Russia, which ran a consistent surplus, was more efficient than Western Europe, when in fact Russia's agricultural yields and industrial methods were noncompetitive.

[110] Wong, *China Transformed*, 282. Also suspect are Wong's claims that pre-1800 European states could not enumerate their populations or expand agrarian taxation (282), and that agricultural production remained "largely beyond the political economy of centralizing [European] states" (143).

[111] Pomeranz, *Great Divergence* emphasizes the American contribution not of capital, but of energy and land. On the role of New World capital, see P. K. O'Brien, "Intercontinental Trade and the Development of the Third World Since the Industrial Revolution," *JWH* 8 (1997): 75–134; Thomas A. Brady, Jr., "The Rise of Merchant Empires, 1400–1700," in James D. Tracy, ed., *The Political Economy of Merchant Empires: State Power and World Trade 1350–1750* (Cambridge, 1991), 119–20. According to Philip C. C. Huang, "Development or Involution in Eighteenth-Century Britain and China?", *JAS* 61 (2002): 501–38, and Robert Brenner and Christopher Isett, "England's Divergence from China's Yangzi Delta," ibid., 609–62, even Pomeranz, in his determination to stress English-Chinese equivalences, glossed over the availability of Chinese coal and minimized differences between English and Chinese labor productivity, consumption, handicrafts, and social-property relations. But see Pomeranz' spirited reply to Huang in that issue. For other evaluations of Pomeranz, see P. H. H. Vries, "Are Coal and Colonies Really Crucial?" *JWH* 12 (2001): 407–46; and *Itinerario* (2000): 9–134.

levels of commercialization would remain modest. By comparison not only with Western Europe, but China, Japan, and India, mainland Southeast Asia lacked the market densities, hence commercial incentives, needed to support extensive specialization in manufacture or technology. In turn, limited markets and military technologies joined dispersed settlement patterns to impose a ceiling on political unity lower than in many European realms or even Japan.

Yet it is this very marginality that renders hitherto ignored comparabilities between Southeast Asia, Europe, Japan, and other regions so intriguing. Preoccupied with differences in industrial potential, comparativists have failed to note, much less explain, widespread Eurasian coordination, in particular, the tendency in many areas, not merely the most advanced, for broadly synchronized increases in production and market activity to support more cohesive political and cultural systems. Why during a thousand years did areas widely separated in space and culture, in economic scale and demography, with minimal commercial ties, join in synchronized gyrations toward greater local cohesion? Why in these far-flung realms did successive interregna not only become shorter, but more tightly coordinated? How could discrepant power capacities have supported apparently similar political processes? In which contexts did domestic population growth, external trade, or intensifying warfare make the most critical contribution to integration? Was the relation between commercialization and integration necessarily linear? After major interregna, how did new polities in Europe, Southeast Asia, and Japan construct the image of previous regimes? In each realm how were social hierarchy and polyethnicity reconciled with changing notions of political community? The neutrality and capaciousness of such inquiries allow us to replace dichotomies with continua that can accommodate any number of idiosyncratic formations, including those that go under the name European exceptionalism.

Rather than insist on a single transcendent criterion of comparison – such as the ability to support a precocious industrialization – I argue that various aspects of integration were distinct and that these often crosscut a simple European/Asian divide (in much the same way as they crosscut the Indic/Sinic divide within the mainland). For example, if France in 1700 was preeminent in administrative and military capacity, in cultural integration it was arguably not very different than the comparably sized realms of Japan and Vietnam. In their relation to older Eurasian core civilizations and the severity of post-charter disruptions, Vietnam and France also had more in common than did Vietnam and Burma. But in terms of provincial conflicts, solar political organization, and the role of foreign merchants, Vietnam in 1810 resembled Burma more than either resembled France. If commerce contributed to more horizontally uniform dialects and customs in France and Japan than in the Burmese empire, Japan lacked the war-induced sense of politicized ethnicity that transformed French and Burmese self-images. In short, as categories of analysis, Europe and Asia may be less useful than Eurasia conceived as an interactive zone of idiosyncratic formations whose affiliations varied with the indices employed.

Nor does my distinction between sustained integration in mainland Southeast Asia and other Eurasian areas, on the one hand, and less linear trajectories in South Asia and island Southeast Asia, on the other hand, create a Eurasian fault line, a bifurcation, comparable to that posited by classical Eurocentrism. For one thing, as I have already suggested, political integration was but one aspect of a more general intensification of communications and exchange that affected South Asia and island Southeast Asia no less than other regions. I seek merely to show how in different geographic contexts, broadly comparable economic trends yielded discrete political outcomes. Moreover, even if we restrict our inquiry to politics, centralizing tendencies in 18th-century South and island Southeast Asia continued to coexist with devolutionary pressures, so again we are dealing not with dichotomies, but with continua of difference. This is yet more obvious if we consider the Mughal empire and Javanese Mataram in their 17th-century heyday.

Finally, I offer a novel take on the dynamics of Eurasian interaction. Insofar as they tried to connect widely separated pre-modern areas, Abu-Lughod, Wallerstein, Dennis O. Flynn, Arturo Giraldez, Frank, and Barry Gills have focused almost exclusively on bullion and commodity flows.[112] But as in mainland Southeast Asia, so in Eurasia at large, for much of the period to 1500 such trade was too marginal, and political convergences too pronounced, to see the latter as fundamentally dependent on the long-distance exchange of goods and bullion. One must first distinguish between: a) the expressly economic, b) indirectly

---

[112] Abu-Lughod, *Before Hegemony*; Wallerstein, *World-System*; Dennis O. Flynn and Arturo Giraldez, "Arbitrage, China, and World Trade in the Early Modern Period," *JESHO* 38 (1995): 429–48; idem, "Born with a Silver Spoon." See also the attempt by Andre Gunder Frank and Barry Gills, *The World System: Five Hundred Years or Five Thousand?* (London, 1993) to explain Eurasian history from 3000 B.C.E. in terms of a unified commercial system.

economic, and c) essentially noneconomic coordinating influences of trade. The first category included commodity and bullion flows per se. The second included technology transmission, new disease pathways, and new crop transfers such as Alfred Crosby, Jr. described.[113] The third included new cultural, religious, and administrative concepts and new weapons. In combination, the latter two categories were at least as important as the first in promoting global synchronization.[114] But one also must distinguish between these three aspects of trade, broadly conceived, and factors that had an etiology partly or entirely independent of trade. I refer, for example, to movements of Central Asian nomads, to parallel but independent institutional responses to intensifying warfare and state breakdown, to pathogen mutations, fluctuations in global climate, demographic spurs to agricultural and commercial intensification, and local agricultural experiments. If trade influenced these factors – except for climate – in gross and subtle ways, the influence was profoundly reciprocal. As a crude generalization, I argue that Eurasian commercial rhythms, especially to 1450 or 1500, depended on demographic trends more heavily than vice versa, and that coordinated demographic trends in turn depended in part on global climate and disease patterns.

What then, in brief outline, is the Eurasian thesis of this study? Volume One *en passant,* and Volume Two explicitly and in detail, make the following broad claims:

1) Lying on the periphery of older civilizations, during the second half of the first and/or the early second millennia C. E., northwestern Europe, northeastern Europe, Japan, and mainland Southeast Asia all domesticated world religions, developed unprecedentedly grand architectural complexes and/or public works, and underwent what Barbara Price terms "secondary state formation."[115] I regard these areas as representative of a Eurasian subcategory that, for reasons to be explained shortly, I term the "protected rimlands." Principalities founded in this period were "charter states" insofar as their religious, dynastic, and/or territorial traditions were regarded by local successor states as normative

---

[113] Alfred W. Crosby, Jr., *The Columbian Exchange* (Westport, CT: 1972).

[114] Cf. William McNeill, "World History and the Rise and Fall of the West," *JWH* 9 (1998): 215–36; Jerry Bentley, "Cross-Cultural Interaction and Periodization in World History," *AHR* 101 (1996): 749–70; Sanjay Subrahmanyam, "Notes Towards a Reconfiguration of Early Modern Eurasia," *MAS* 31 (1997): 735–62.

[115] Barbara Price, "Secondary State Formation: An Explanatory Model," in Ronald Cohen and Elman R. Service, eds., *Origins of the State* (Philadelphia, 1978), 161–86.

and legitimating. Compared to later polities, these were administratively decentralized and tolerated a high degree of cultural diversity, both vertical and horizontal. The florescence of charter states drew strength from locally specific combinations of some or all the following factors: a) climatic conditions c. 900–1300 favorable to agriculture which thus encouraged both local expansion and trade with simultaneously prospering, longer-settled Eurasian cores; b) a stronger, trade-mediated flow of religious and administrative concepts from Eurasian cores to the rimlands; c) the putative conversion of hitherto epidemic diseases to mere endemicity; d) the economic benefits of improved pacification.

2) Following the disintegration of these charter principalities in the 13th and 14th centuries, territorial consolidation resumed at some point between 1450 and 1590 and continued to gain in scope and efficiency well into the 19th century. This in turn meant that, outside Japan and Vietnam, successive interregna tended to grow shorter and less disruptive. Thus, not only the territorial trajectories of different realms, but post-crisis programs of administrative reform – as in early 17th-century Burma, Siam, Russia, France, and Japan – frequently coincided.

3) In each area both political collapse and consolidation were heavily influenced by demographic and commercial expansion. In some contexts, whether by fueling provincial insurgencies or by creating critical shortages of bullion, land, or administrative posts, vigorous growth could intensify popular distress and intra-elite rivalries. This was true in parts of Europe and Southeast Asia in the 13th and 14th centuries at the end of the charter era, and again during the crises of the 16th and 18th centuries. But over the long term the enhanced solidity of each state reflected the combined effects of: a) an expansion in aggregate and most particularly monetized resources, which in turn benefited from synergistic combinations of growing population, domestic, and international trade, b) more inclusive cultural identities; c) cumulative improvements in administrative and military technique, spurred by interstate competition.

4) In each realm starting in the charter era, but with accelerating force from the 16th through 19th centuries, cultural motifs tended to become more vertically uniform in each capital region and (especially among elites) more horizontally uniform in the provinces. Although connected through various feedback loops to political integration, insofar as it depended on local capillary action, cultural standardization

often was more continuous, less episodic. Everywhere this movement benefited from a wider, more rapid circulation of goods, people, and texts, which tended to privilege central norms certified by imperial authorities. Typically too, cultural integration was associated with new religious/educational structures, wider literacy, more vigorous cross-class communication – as well as a marked proliferation of cultural subspecialties. Outside Japan, intensifying warfare infused popular self-images with a sense of ethnic exclusion. We thus revisit a persistent irony: as international linkages grew stronger, the cultural mobilization of ever greater numbers of people whose only tongue was the vernacular created more exclusive, bounded cultural categories. Popular acculturation normally entailed greater peasant acceptance of religious orthodoxy and a corresponding retreat in openly animist practices. But, insofar as the masses could not master Pali, Sanskrit, Latin, or Chinese, the rise of vernacular literatures necessarily reduced the role within the overall culture of these once unrivalled sacred universal languages. Likewise, in all six realms (Burma, Siam, Vietnam, Russia, France, and Japan), the growth of state power compressed the wealth and political autonomy of religious institutions. In France alone, however, secularization produced an explicit transfer of sanctity from church and monarchy to the "nation."

5) The combination of accelerated political integration, firearms-based warfare, broader literacy, religious textuality, vernacular literatures, wider money use, and more complex international linkages (both cultural and material) marks the years between c. 1450 and 1800/1850 as a more or less coherent period in each of the six realms under review. Covering the second and third grand administrative cycles,[116] this era started with recovery from post-charter crises and ended with such watersheds as the French Revolution and European irruptions in mainland Southeast Asia and Japan. What shall we call this period? The European-derived term "early modern," with its suggestion of modernity in embryo, can be problematic because a key feature of genuine modernity, namely the industrial use of fossil fuels, was not the logical outcome of universal processes, but a feature unique to northwest Europe, if not Britain. Nonetheless, insofar as the elaboration of global and local

---

[116] In parts of Europe and mainland SE Asia, recall, the first extended from c. 900 to 1300, the second from c. 1450 to 1570/1600, the third from c. 1600 to 1750/1800. In Japan, the late 15th/16th centuries represented a transition between two long administrative cycles, but Japan, along with Russia, experienced no late 18th century political collapse.

networks during this period anticipated, however weakly, processes in the 19th century, the term early modern has some appeal.[117]

6) Despite wide variations in most indices of integration, with the chief exception of Vietnam, these six realms enjoyed relatively good internal communications and/or an economic/demographic imbalance between the imperial core and outlying areas that was markedly favorable to the capital. From 1450 to 1840 all six also enjoyed substantial protection from external invasion, whether overland from Central Asia or by sea from Europe.

7) In varying degrees China, much of Southwest Asia, the Indian subcontinent, and island Southeast Asia exhibited the same early modern features – identified in point 5 above – as did the other areas under consideration. Nonetheless, insofar as they lacked effective barriers to nomadic or seaborne invaders, these areas differed from the six protected rimlands. In each of the former zones the dominant early modern stratum consisted of a conquest elite – Turkic peoples, Afghans, Persians, Manchus, Dutch, or Iberians – who differed substantially in religion, culture, and ethnicity from the chief populations over whom they ruled. Elite/mass cultural unity was impeded. Furthermore, in South Asia and island Southeast Asia, notwithstanding 17th-century glories, problems of transport and communications rendered centralization less secure than in the six protected rimlands. Indeed, as noted, in Mughal India and much of island Southeast Asia, geography and foreign intervention joined 18th-century economic growth to encourage not sustained unity, but fragmentation. This in turn had long-term cultural correlates. Chapters 2 to 4 of this volume examine integration in, respectively, the western, central, and eastern sectors of mainland Southeast Asia. *Volume Two: Mainland Mirrors* uses the same thematic and chronological format to consider developments in realms, namely Russia and France, which between them captured much of the variety of European experience, as well as in Japan. The second volume concludes by considering how and why these trajectories differed from patterns in South Asia, island Southeast Asia, and other more exposed sectors of Eurasia.

---

[117] On "early modern" as an historiographic category, see Lieberman, ed., *Beyond Binary Histories; Re-imagining Eurasia to c. 1830* (Ann Arbor, MI: 1999), 1–18; "From the Editors," *JEMH* 1 (1997): 1; the special issue on "Early Modernities" in *Daedalus* (Summer, 1998): v–18; Jack Goldstone, "The Problem of the 'Early Modern' World," *JESHO* 41 (1998): 249–84; idem, "Efflorescences and Economic Growth," arguing for "late premodern" rather than "early modern."

Criticisms

Before launching country studies, let me anticipate objections that the approach laid out in this introduction is likely to trigger.

Perhaps the most easily allayed concern goes like this: Precolonial Southeast Asian historiography is still too undeveloped, too immature to support grand syntheses. We have only a handful of monographs, mostly on political and cultural topics, and little detail on domestic economy or rural society. Before working to death these puny, under-nourished fellows by assigning them tasks they cannot possibly fulfill, it would be better to build up their numbers and strength – that is, to accumulate more empirical studies – which alone can provide credibility and texture to larger constructs.

The problem with this approach is its assumption that hypotheses arise automatically from the study of "facts", when in truth the filtering of kaleidoscopic inputs requires a preliminary schema, and the relation between theory and documentation is always dialogic.[118] By alerting archival researchers to patterns that they otherwise might have over-looked entirely and by stimulating new empirical work to test its central contentions, Reid's Age of Commerce thesis, to which I am indebted, has had an impact on Southeast Asian studies that is entirely salutary. In my own schema I am frankly uncertain, for example, which factors best explain the synchronized florescence of charter Southeast Asia with Kiev, medieval Europe, and Song China, but surely it is necessary to move beyond coincidence to consider influences informed by a wider historiography.

A second objection also is concerned with excessive theorization, al-beit of a more specific variety. One could argue that this story of sus-tained political integration has simply grafted onto Southeast Asia (and Japan) the meta-narrative of the European nation-state. The effort to in-terpret Southeast Asia with categories and concepts – Kettering's notion of patronage brokers, Tilly's military dynamic – some of which derive from European historiography contaminates my inquiry at the source. I claim to examine Europe through a Southeast Asian prism, but in truth, one could argue, we are seeing Europe through a Southeast Asian prism through a European prism. In short, this is a neo-modernization project, driven perhaps by a desire to compensate for Southeast Asia's marginal-ity and encumbered with all the weaknesses of modernization theory,

---

[118] Cf. Robert F. Berkhofer, Jr., *Beyond the Great Story: History as Text and Discourse* (Cambridge, MA: 1995).

including a unilinear teleology and an insensitivity to non-European norms.[119]

But if we accept the original goal of comparing European and non-European evolution, obviously we must employ uniform criteria. If some of my categories derive from European experience, these categories are now part of a universal discourse on which Japanese, Chinese, and South Asian historiography are no less dependent. As preliminary topics for inquiry, integration, centralization, cultural diffusion, and so forth carry very little specific baggage, far less certainly than feudalism or civil society. At the same time, fundamental elements in my interpretation of French and Russian experience – including the concepts of charter polities, administrative cycles, progressively less disruptive interregna – derive not from European historiography at all, but from my reading of Chinese and Burmese history. In my view, the pattern of cyclic-cum-linear integration in Pagan, Toungoo, and Kon-baung Burma can tell us more about Capetian, Valois, and Bourbon France than French historiography can tell us about Burma.

If my revisionist goals lead me to examine hitherto ignored parallels between far-flung realms, I am also at pains to describe and explain major differences between these realms in charter legacies, social structure, administrative reach, religious idiom, ethnicity, economic organization, and so forth. I do so within Southeast Asia and Asia, within Europe, and between these regions. The fascination of Eurasian parallels derives precisely from their multiple contexts, limited extent, and idiosyncratic prospects. There is no hint, for example, that Vietnam was but a couple generations behind France en route to political democracy and industrial capitalism. In short, this is not a modernization project at all, but a Darwinian project. I try to show that certain early modern political/cultural animals, so to speak, which until now no one suspected were related, in fact constituted species within a larger genus. I demonstrate that "man" (read "Europe"), who saw himself in the image of God with dominion over all beasts of the field and fish of the seas, is merely a peculiar type of primate. As an historian of mainland Southeast Asia, I first examine those Eurasian countries to which, by my integrative criteria, Burma, Siam, and Vietnam had strongest evolutionary affinities. But, as noted, my interest in diversity also leads me to compare sustained

---

[119] Cf. Anthony Giddens, *The Consequences of Modernity* (Stanford, 1990), esp. 47–53; and the discussion of modernization theory in Downing, *Military Revolution*, 5–6; Lynn Hunt, *Politics, Culture and Class in the French Revolution* (Berkeley, 1984), 205–12.

centralization with more limited or aborted trajectories (other genera, to continue the biological metaphor) and to isolate variables responsible for those outcomes.

Finally, one may imagine that because my concern with centralization privileges capital elites, the experiences of subalterns and peripheral peoples are automatically excluded. "The dirty little secret," James Scott has written referring chiefly to the uplands, "is that for most of 'Burmese' history there was no state in any robust sense of the term. There were, instead, small-scale local chiefs, confederations of villages, warlords, bandits, multiple sovereigns contending. . . . Might it be possible to imagine a history written systematically from this perspective – a kind of anarchist history . . . ?"[120]

Here I plead guilty – but only in part. Following Scott, Keith Taylor, David Wyatt, Eugen Weber, or Peter Sahlins,[121] one could indeed craft narratives of self-sufficient local communities on which the influence of distant capitals easily can be exaggerated. But my concern with integration has at least two large virtues. It lets us deploy existing Southeast Asian historiography to compare hitherto incomparable units within that region and Eurasia at large. And it is concerned with the evolution of cultural and economic as well as political structures that modified in genuinely critical ways the choices and self-images of enormous numbers of people, and not merely central elites. Ultimately, if imperial histories are impossible without a consideration of local contexts, the reverse is also true. After proclaiming his "dirty little secret," Scott himself, without contradiction, acknowledged that even in the hills, even on the peripheries of empire, ethnicity, religion, and settlement were shaped substantially and continuously by their relation to "state-making projects in the valleys."[122] If we consider the more densely populated Burmese lowlands, the value of supralocal perspectives becomes yet more obvious. Likewise in Vietnam, where Taylor has argued eloquently for parochial identities as strong as anywhere in the lowlands, provincial

---

[120] James Scott, "Hill and Valley in Southeast Asia, or . . . why Civilizations Can't Climb Hills," Paper prepared for "Beyond Borders" Workshop sponsored by the Centre d'etudes et de recherches internationals and the SSRC, Paris, June, 2000, p. 3.

[121] Previous note, plus Keith Taylor, "Surface Orientations in Vietnam: Beyond Histories of Nation and Region," *JAS* 57 (1998): 949–78; David Wyatt, "Southeast Asia 'Inside Out,' 1300–1800: A Perspective from the Interior," *MAS* 31 (1997): 689–709; Eugen Weber, *Peasants Into Frenchmen* (Stanford, 1976); Peter Sahlins, *Boundaries: The Making of France and Spain in the Pyrenees* (Berkeley, 1989). See also Deborah E. Tooker, "Putting the Mandala in Its Place," *JAS* 55 (1996): 323–58.

[122] Scott, "Hill and Valley," 9–15, considering Philippine as well as mainland examples.

history requires attention to kingdom-wide loyalties (whether to Dai Viet or the southern realm), to royal fiscal and military pressures, and to those distinctive socio-agricultural patterns that routinely gave Vietnamese-speakers greater expansive potential than their Cham and Khmer neighbors. Moreover, as this chapter has shown, I posit a synergy between royal interventions, on the one hand, and quintessentially local processes of demographic, agricultural, and religious change, on the other. In some measure, political centralization was merely a reflection of these local processes.

CHAPTER 2

One Basin, Two Poles

The Western Mainland and The Formation of Burma

Our detailed examination of mainland history begins with the western sector of the mainland in part because it is convenient to proceed west to east and in part because here I am best able to address regional conundrums with indigenous-language primary sources. Moreover, insofar as any sector can be representative of so varied a region, the western mainland has a good claim. In duration and degree, for example, post-charter disruptions were intermediate between those of the central and eastern mainland. The same may be said of intrasectoral tensions: Upper Burma reemerged as the dominant zone within the western mainland in the 1630s. This was long after Ayudhya had established its preeminence in the central mainland, but almost 170 years before Hue gained a secure authority along the yet more fragmented eastern littoral.

As elsewhere, political change had a cyclic character: periodic breakdowns encouraged administrative reform, but reformed administrations collapsed before destabilizing economic growth, external attacks, and domestic factionalism. Whenever the capital region was in trouble, restive provinces were quick to magnify its difficulties. Thus Lower Burma exploited Upper Burma's problems in the 1280s and 1740s, and when the south faltered in the late 1500s, Upper Burma returned the favor. With the interior home to Burmans[1] and the south to Mons, endemic north–south tensions had an irreducible, if fluid, ethnic component.

---

[1] "Burman" conventionally refers to the principal ethnic group, while "Burmese" refers either to the language and culture of that ethnic group or to the collectivity of peoples, Burman and non-Burman, living in the area of the contemporary Union of Myanmar.

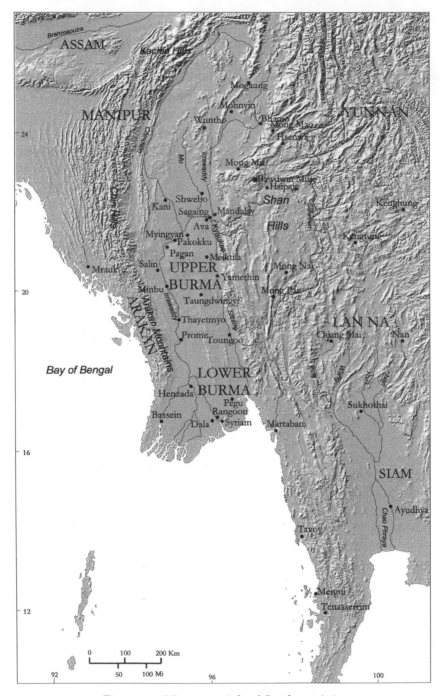

Figure 2.1. Western mainland Southeast Asia.

Over the long term, however, these oscillations accommodated to a larger integrative trend: cumulative organizational expertise joined with firearms and more secure commercial and cultural links to stabilize central authority and to render three interregna progressively shorter and less disruptive. After the charter polity of Pagan collapsed, between c. 1290 and 1530 the basin fragmented, marauders poured in from the eastern hills, and monastic and royal institutions were extensively recast. The second imperial collapse, that of the late 16th century, also led to substantial administrative and geopolitical shifts, but the interregnum itself was short-lived. By comparison, that of the mid-18th century was both brief and institutionally placid. Arising in the aftermath of the latter crisis and flourishing until it ran up against the British in 1824, the Kon-baung dynasty (1752–1885) was the most administratively penetrating and commercially sophisticated in the history of the western mainland.

Compared to these political gyrations, cultural change, substantially dependent as it was on local capillary processes, tended to be more gradual and more consistently linear. In the Pagan era ethnicity and religious practice varied widely by class and locale, village literacy seems to have been rare, and popular religious sensibilities were but nominally Buddhist. Burmans during this period were heavily concentrated in the interior dry zone. But slowly from the 14th century, and then with accelerating vigor in the 17th to early 19th centuries, Burman ethnicity and language came to dominate the entire lowlands at the expense of Mons and other groups, while elite-centered textually-based Theravada norms spread to more humble sectors of the Burman population and to highland valleys inhabited by non-Burman peoples. Particularly in the lowlands, changes in monastic landholding and village monastic organization facilitated unusually high male literacy rates. Notwithstanding the growing complexity of literary and cultural production in Upper Burma itself, by 1830 a vast region that had once been extremely fragmented thus had an indisputable cultural as well as political center.

While the impact on Burmese history of maritime revenues before 1600 has long been recognized, I argue that maritime influences, including imported firearms, continued to strengthen royal authority well into the 19th century, and that overland trade with China may not have been appreciably less significant than maritime contacts. The genius of post-1613 dynasties in Upper Burma resided precisely in their ability to tap coastal revenues while maintaining secure control over the China trade as well as the great agricultural and manpower reserves of the interior. It is usually assumed that Burmese agriculture, like Burmese popular religion, existed "outside history," but in fact post–1350 agriculture had both an extensive and intensive component. Together, the expansion of cotton cultivation, new irrigation works, new rice strains, and frontier colonization raised aggregate output, while encouraging rural commodification and synergistic links to foreign trade. In turn economic growth promoted north–south cultural links and political unification under northern auspices.

Our task then is to chart the evolution of political and cultural forms and their intersection with economic stimuli, both domestic and external.

THE CHARTER POLITY OF PAGAN: SOURCES OF VITALITY

The western mainland is here defined basically as the area now enclosed by the Union of Myanmar (Burma). The perimeter consisted of a vast sparsely-settled upland ring extending from the Arakan Mountains in the west to the Shan hills in the east. Along the Bay of Bengal, the Arakan and Tenasserim regions both have narrow coastal plains, but their mountain-enforced isolation and modest populations rendered these coastal strips peripheral to regional politics. The core of the western mainland therefore was neither the uplands nor the coastal isolates, but the great structural depression drained by the Chindwin, Sittang, and most especially the Irrawaddy, where a combination of excellent riverine communications, maritime access, and extensive cultivable lands supported relatively dense populations and elaborate political systems.

At the same time the rain shadow effect of the Arakan Mountains, which sheltered the interior from the full force of the southwestern monsoon, divided the central basin itself into the dry zone of Upper Burma, extending from roughly 19–23 degrees north latitude, and the wet maritime zone of Lower Burma, including the Irrawaddy delta. Between these two poles, as noted, political authority tended to oscillate. Notwithstanding more abundant rainfall, in Lower Burma the combination of heavy alluvial soils, frequently destructive flooding, and severe malaria depressed population compared to the interior. In an era of limited military specialization, when the number of conscripted cultivators offered the best single indication of military success, the north was the natural center of political gravity. In the central mainland and Java as well, we shall find that easily cultivated dry areas enjoyed an early demographic advantage over wetter maritime districts.[2]

Burmans, the historically dominant ethnic group, were hardly the first to build towns and to develop literate cultures in the central basin. As early as the 1st or 2nd century C.E. the Pyus, who were culturally distinct from the later-arriving Burmans but who apparently also spoke a Tibeto-Burman language, had built water-management systems along secondary streams in central and northern parts of the Irrawaddy basin and had founded one of Southeast Asia's earliest urban centers. Starting perhaps in the 2nd century and with ever greater profusion and refinement from the 4th century, we find architectural and artistic evidence of Pyu contact with Indian culture, directly via eastern India and Sri Lanka and indirectly perhaps via Buddhist centers in the Chaophraya basin. The Pyu ritual system included elements of Sarvastivadin Buddhism, Hinduism, and indigenous urn burial. Archeological surveys of six walled Pyu cities suggest a consistent ecological and urban pattern, perhaps too an increase during the 7th to early 9th centuries in the scale of political organization, but there is no indication that any of these cities, some of which must have been political rivals, exercised authority over more than a limited sector of the basin. The chief Pyu sites included the early city of Beikthano near modern Taungdwingyi, Sri Ksetra near Prome, and the Mu valley town of Halin.[3] By the late first millennium if not earlier, some speakers of

---

[2] See Srisakra Vallibhotama, "The Dry Areas in the Archaeology of Southeast Asia," in Fukui Hayao, ed., *The Dry Areas in Southeast Asia: Harsh or Benign Environment?* (Kyoto, 1999), 17–25; Fukui Hayao, "Historical Cities and Agriculture in Tropical Asia: A Hydrological Examination," *Journal of Sophia Asian Studies* 18 (2000): 27–37. On Burmese precipitation, topography, and early demography, see Charles Fisher, *South-East Asia* (London, 1964), ch. 14; and my *Burmese Administrative Cycles: Anarchy and Conquest, c. 1580–1760* (Princeton, 1984), 16–23.

[3] Note that Pyu sites extended to Lower Burma. On the history of the Pyu (P'iao), also known as the Tircul, see Paul Wheatley, *Nagara and Commandery* (Chicago, 1983), ch. 4; Than Tun, *Hkit-haung myan-ma ya-zawin* (Rangoon, 1969), 39–63; *Achei-pya myan-ma naing-ngan-yei thamaing*, vol. 1 (Rangoon, 1970), 144–85; Aung Thaw, *Report on the Excavations at Beikthano* (Rangoon, 1968), esp. 4–6, 61–62; Janice Stargardt, *The Ancient Pyu of Burma, Vol. 1* (Cambridge, 1990); G. H. Luce, *Phases of Pre-Pagan Burma*, 2 vols. (Oxford, 1985), I, chs. 5–6; Robert L. Brown, "Pyu Art: Looking East and West," *Orientations* 32 (2001): 35–41; Bob Hudson, Nyein Lwin, and Win Maung, "The Origins of Bagan," *Asian Perspectives* 40 (2001): 48–74; Michael Aung-Thwin, "Lower Burma and Bago in the History of Burma," in Jos Gommans and Jacques Leider, eds., *The Maritime Frontier of Burma* (Amsterdam, 2002), 34–37.

Mon, a language akin to Khmer but distinct from Tibeto-Burman, also inhabited parts of the dry zone, Lower Burma, and the trans-Sittang littoral, although the size and extent of their settlement are debated. Insofar as they were in contact with the Pyus and with their Mon-speaking confreres in the Chaophraya basin, these western Mon-speakers would have been familiar with Hindu and Buddhist rituals and Indian-derived scripts.[4]

According to G. H. Luce's reconstruction, large numbers of Burman warriors and their families first entered this quasi-Indianized universe in the 830s and 840s after attacks by the Nanzhao kingdom of Yunnan had weakened the Pyus. Descending into the Upper Burma plains from the northeastern hills, Burmans established themselves in and around key irrigated districts, as well as at the old Pyu site of Pagan near the confluence of the Chindwin and Irrawaddy rivers.[5] The newcomers intensified irrigation-based cultivation, while borrowing extensively from their predecessors' predominantly Buddhist culture. As Pagan's early iconography, architecture, and scripts suggest, there may have been little difference between early Burman and Pyu cultural forms. Nor is there evidence of a sharp ethnic distinction between Burmans and the linguistically linked Pyus. Moreover, as had been true in the Pyu era, for much of the 10th century the political situation remained fragmented and fluid. Dependent for much of its rice on the Kyaukse district some

---

[4] For traditional scholarship emphasizing the antiquity of Mon culture and settlement, Wheatley, *Nagara*, ch. 5; Than Tun, *Hkit-haung*, 81–97; *Myanma-ingaleik abi-dan* (Rangoon, 1993), vi–vii; Luce, *Phases*, I, chs. 1–2; idem, "Old Kyaukse and the Coming of the Burmans," JBRS 42 (1959): 75–112; Myint Aung, "The Excavations of Ayethama and Winka (Suvannabhumi)," *Studies in Myanma History, Vol. 1* (Yangon, 1999), 19–64; Tilman Frasch, "Coastal Peripheries During the Pagan Period," in Gommans and Leider, *Maritime Frontier*, 66–67. Recently, however, Aung-Thwin, "Lower Burma and Bago," 25–57; "The Legend that was Lower Burma" (ms), and personal communications, Aug.–Oct. 2001, has questioned the early existence of a large Mon population, much less a Mon kingdom, in Lower Burma, which he suggests was a substantially empty frontier. According to his reconstruction, Mons began entering the Irrawaddy basin in large numbers from the east only with the decline of Dvaravati starting in the 10th century. Emphasizing the exiguity of early Mon inscriptions, Aung-Thwin also argues that the Mon script of Burma derived from Old Burmese, rather than vice-versa, as Frasch and others (see n. 69 *infra*) contend.

[5] Luce, "Old Kyaukse"; idem, *Old Burma-Early Pagan*, 3 vols. (Locust Valley, NY: 1969), I, ch. 1; idem, *Phases*, I, ch. 9; idem, "Geography of Burma under the Pagan Dynasty," *JBRS* 42 (1959): 32–51, esp. 50–51; Michael Aung-Thwin, *Pagan: The Origins of Modern Burma* (Honolulu, 1985), 17–22; idem, "Lower Burma and Bago," 37. The foundation walls at Pagan are now dated to the 10th century, although this does not rule out earlier Burman penetration. Peter Grave and Mike Barbetti, "Dating the City Wall, Fortification and the Palace Site at Pagan," *Asian Perspectives* 40 (2001): 75–87.

80 miles to the east, Pagan seems to have been but one among several competing city-states.[6]

From the late 900s, however, Pagan grew in authority and grandeur. In a process which certainly involved a combination of force and negotiated alliance among local chiefs but the details of which are poorly elucidated in epigraphic and external sources, Pagan first established its authority throughout the northern interior. Known later as Arimaddana-pura, "The City That Tramples on Enemies," Pagan benefited from its location midway between the rice-growing districts of Kyaukse and Minbu, from its access to north-south river routes, and perhaps too from its proximity to a sacred animist site atop nearby Mt. Popa. According to traditional reconstructions, the celebrated warrior king Anaw-rahta, having solidified control over the north, went downriver in 1057 to conquer the Mon kingdom of Thaton in Lower Burma, whose literary and religious traditions helped to mold early Pagan civilization.[7] More recently, Michael Aung-Thwin has argued forcefully that Anaw-rahta's conquest of Thaton is a post-Pagan legend without contemporary evidence, that Lower Burma in fact lacked a substantial independent polity prior to Pagan's expansion, and that Mon influence on the interior is greatly exaggerated. Possibly in this period delta sedimentation – which now extends the coastline by three miles a century – remained insufficient, and the sea still reached too far inland, to support a population even as large as the modest population of the late precolonial era.[8] Yet whatever the condition of the coast, all scholars accept that during the 11th century Pagan established its authority over Lower Burma and that this conquest facilitated growing cultural exchange, if not with local Mons, then with India and with the Theravada stronghold of Sri Lanka. Anaw-rahta's successors extended their influence farther south into the upper Malay peninsula, while to the east by

[6] On growing evidence of Pyu-Pagan continuites, see Hudson, "Origins of Bagan"; Bob Hudson, "Archaeological Survey, Sampling and Excavation in the Eastern Hinterland of Bagan, Myanmar. Report to the Director-General of Archaeology, Myanmar, May 2000" (ms); Stargardt, *Ancient Pyu;* Paul Strachan, *Imperial Pagan* (Honolulu, 1989), 8–9, 37; and Aung-Thwin, "Legend." Curiously, 18th/19th century Burmese chronicles also emphasized Pagan's links to pre-Pagan civilization.

[7] See summary at Luce, *Old Burma*, I, 6–27, 299–309; and early references in *The Kalyani Inscriptions Erected by King Dhammaceti at Pegu in 1476 A.D.* (Rangoon, 1892), 49.

[8] See *supra* nn. 2, 4, and H. L. Chhibber, *The Geology of Burma* (London, 1934), 15–16; R. Kay Gresswell and Anthony Huxley, eds., *Standard Encyclopedia of the World's Rivers and Lakes* (New York, 1965), 126. For a conjectural reconstruction of the late first millennium coastline, G. E. Harvey, *History of Burma* (rpt., London, 1967), first map.

the late 12th century the crown claimed authority at least to the Salween River. In the far north, Pagan held fortresses below the current China border. Effective authority in the west stopped at the Arakan Mountains, notwithstanding claims in later sources that Pagan controlled Arakan itself (see Figure 1.3).[9]

In and around the capital sprouted a rich Buddhist civilization whose most spectacular feature was a dense forest of pagodas, monasteries, and temples, totaling perhaps 10,000 brick structures of which the remains of over 3,000 survive. Starting on a modest scale in the 10th and 11th centuries and reaching their peak in numbers and architectural brilliance during the late 12th and 13th centuries, these edifices reflected Pyu temple traditions, north and south Indian decorative and architectural currents, Mon and Sinhalese literary motifs, all wedded to an original Burman aesthetic.[10] Word of Pagan's architectural splendor and Buddhist scholarship spread throughout Asia. Within an 80–100 mile radius, albeit concentrated in wet-rice districts like Kyaukse rather than in the immediate vicinity of Pagan itself, lived several hundred thousand cultivators and service people who sustained the Buddhist establishment and the lay elite at the capital.

What dynamics – economic, social, political – underlay this rather dramatic florescence? Insofar as Pyus had built Indianized centers for centuries prior to Pagan, while Burmans had entered the lowlands in force as early as the 830s, why did Pagan's authority expand only in the 10th and more especially in the 11th centuries? And how did Pagan's development relate to economic/political booms elsewhere in Eurasia? As Chapter 1 suggested, we find a remarkable burst of economic and political energy in northwestern Europe between c. 950 and 1300, in Kiev between 950 and 1240, in Angkor between 950 and 1250, and in Dai Viet between 1000 and 1300, while the so-called first Chinese commercial

---

[9] On Pagan's imperial sphere, Michael Charney, "Arakan and Ava (Upper Burma) in the 14th and 15th Centuries" (ms); Luce, *Old Burma*, I, 20–27, 29, 34, 91; Than Tun, *Hkit-haung*, 139; Michael Aung-Thwin, *Myth and History in the Historiography of Early Burma* (Athens, OH, 1998), 37–38, 76; idem, *Pagan*, 104–105; Frasch, "Coastal Peripheries," 61, 71–73; Michel Jacq-Hergoualc'h, "The Mergui-Tenasserim Region in the Context of the Maritime Silk Road," in Gommans and Leider, *Maritime Frontier*, 88–91.

[10] See Michael Aung-Thwin, "The Nature of State and Society in Pagan" (Univ. of Michigan PhD diss., 1976), 52, which gives larger figures for brick structures than Hudson, "Origins of Bagan"; plus Strachan, *Imperial Pagan*; Luce, *Old Burma*; and the detailed site survey by U Bo-Kei, *Pagan thu-tei-thana lan-hnyun* (Yangon, 1981), esp. 199–457.

revolution focusing on the Yangzi region and south China occurred between c. 800 and 1300. In several of these areas, including Pagan, agricultural extension, demographic growth, and commercial activity reached a temporary plateau in the 1200s.[11]

In each case pacification fed on itself insofar as a reduction in domestic warfare encouraged population growth, which expanded the base for conscription and corvees. Chapter 1 cited Southeast Asian evidence that endemic warfare was normally one of the most serious depressants of rural population growth. Yet what triggered the initial pacification? If accidents of personality played a role, Pagan's loose synchronization with other charter states also points to larger factors. I see five possible explanations, or some combination thereof, for the timing of Pagan's expansion.

The most obvious candidate for those interested in Eurasian synchrony is international trade. Janice Stargardt has suggested that by blocking the Irrawaddy basin's overland links to China, 10th-century disorders in the Nanzhao region in present-day Yunnan induced Pagan to turn for commercial revenues toward the increasingly prosperous coast.[12] According to Kenneth Hall and John Whitmore, this orientation was reinforced in the 11th century when raids by the Chola empire of south India created a power vacuum in the upper Malay peninsula which Pagan, Angkor, Sri Lanka, and Malay rulers all sought to fill.[13] More basically, such competition reflected a commercial upsurge across Eurasia. Scandinavian, Italian, and Muslim traders strengthened routes from northern Europe to the eastern Mediterranean to India.[14] In southern India itself between 900 and 1300, overseas demand encouraged new merchant associations and larger textile exports to the

---

[11] On Angkor and Dai Viet, see this volume, Chs. 3–4; on western Europe and Kiev, Vol. 2, Ch. 2, relying *inter alia* on N. J. G. Pounds, *An Historical Geography of Europe* (Cambridge, 1990), pt. 2; Simon Franklin and Jonathan Shepard, *The Emergence of Rus 750–1200* (London, 1996). On Song expansion, William T. Rowe, "Approaches to Modern Chinese Social History," in Olivier Zunz, ed., *Reliving the Past* (Chapel Hill, NC: 1985); and Vol. 2 of this study. Cf. Janet Abu-Lughod, *Before European Hegemony: The World System A.D. 1250–1350* (New York, 1989), 357.

[12] Stargardt, "Burma's Economic and Diplomatic Relations with India and China from Early Medieval Sources," *JESHO* 14 (1971): 38–62.

[13] Kenneth Hall and John Whitmore, "Southeast Asian Trade and the Isthmian Struggle, 1000–1200 A.D.," in Hall and Whitmore, eds., *Explorations in Early Southeast Asian History* (Ann Arbor, 1976), 303–40. Also Aung-Thwin, *Myth and History*, ch. 1; Burton Stein, "South India," in *CEHI*, 20; and David Wyatt, "Relics, Oaths and Politics in Thirteenth-Century Siam," *JSEAS* 32 (2001): 3, 23, 48.

[14] Abu-Lughod, *Before Hegemony*, esp. pts. I, II.

Mideast and Southeast Asia,[15] while in South China a rise in population and urban purchasing power nourished the eastern leg of this pan-Eurasian network.[16] From the 11th through the 13th centuries inscriptions and votive tablets testify to Burmese royal interest in peninsular ports, which were transit points between the Indian Ocean and China.[17] The *Culavamsa* also mentions an 1160s dispute over trade in elephants between Burma and Sri Lanka, and in the 12th and 13th centuries Pagan dispatched governors to supervise more closely ports in Lower Burma and the peninsula.[18]

Yet if growing commerce dominated Pagan's southern strategy and furnished the court with revenues and prestige goods (coral, pearls, textiles) valued for political redistribution, one would be hard pressed, on present evidence, to claim that such trade was fundamental to Pagan's political economy or provided the main motor of economic growth, least of all in the early or mid-Pagan era. Although lithic records of religious land donations (our chief contemporary sources) probably minimized maritime inputs, the fact remains that in Pagan – in contrast to early Java – inscriptional references to trade were rare and incidental.[19] Pagan funneled upland forest products, gems, and perhaps metals to the coast,

---

[15] Stein, "South India," 19, 36–42; Simon Digby, "Northern India under the Sultanate," *CEHI*, 45–47; Jan Wisseman Christie, "The Medieval Tamil-language Inscriptions in Southeast Asia and China," *JSEAS* 29 (1998): 239–68; idem, "Asian Trade between the 10th and 13th Centuries and Its Impact on the States of Java and Bali," in Himanshu Prabha Ray, ed., *Archaeology of Seafaring* (Delhi, 1999), 221–270; idem, "Trade and Value in Pre-Majapahit Java," *Indonesian Circle* 59–60 (1992–93): 3–17.

[16] John Miksic, "Archaeology, Ceramics, and Coins," *JESHO* 39 (1996): 287–97; Wang Gungwu, *China and the Chinese Overseas* (Singapore, 1992), 102–106, 123–25; Billy K. L. So, *Prosperity, Region, and Institutions in Maritime China* (Cambridge, MA: 2000), chs. 2–5; Angela Schottenhammer, "The Maritime Trade of Quanzhou (Zaitun) from the Ninth through the Thirteenth Century," in Ray, *Archaeology*, 271–90. Christie, in n. 15 *supra*, argues that Javanese state development, internal trade, even agricultural depended heavily on the Chinese-led maritime trade boom of c. 900–1250.

[17] Luce, *Old Burma*, 26–27; Frasch, "Coastal Peripheries," 60–67; Jacq-Hergoualc'h, "Mergui-Tenasserim Region," 79–92.

[18] *Culavamsa, Pt. II*, Wilhelm Geiger, tr. (rpt., London, 1973), 64–70; Aung-Thwin, *Myth and History*, ch. 1; idem, *Pagan*, 113–14; Hermann Kulke, "Rivalry and Competition in the Bay of Bengal in the Eleventh Century..." in Om Prakash and Denys Lombard, eds., *Commerce and Culture in the Bay of Bengal 1500–1800* (New Delhi, 1999), 17–35; and previous note.

[19] On Pagan source materials, Aung-Thwin, *Pagan*, 8–12. Although early Angkorian inscriptions, like their Pagan counterparts, had little to say on the subject, those from east Java, esp. from the 10th century when the area became more oriented to maritime trade, reflect a widespread concern with market activity and taxation. See Michael Vickery, *Society, Economics, and Politics in Pre-Angkor Cambodia* (Tokyo, 1998), 314.

but there are no archeological, textual, or inscriptional indications that such exports supported large numbers of producers or middlemen in Upper Burma itself. Fukui Hayao has suggested that in parts of Southeast Asia, cast iron maritime imports from Song China aided the spread of iron-socketed plows, which helped to control weeds and aided irrigation, but for Burma at least, again evidence is lacking.[20] Although a steady trickle of slaves from India reached Upper Burma through the delta ports,[21] their numbers relative to the interior population were always insignificant. Nor, compared to the defense of Upper Burma's eastern and northern fringes, was the throne willing to devote major resources to southern campaigns. Likewise, coastal apanage grants constituted a fraction of aristocratic patronage, which focused on grants of land and manpower in the dry zone. In short – as I shall also suggest was true for Angkor, Dai Viet, and much of Western Europe (though less clearly for Kiev) in this period – growing international ties appear to have been more symptom than cause of internal prosperity. According to Aung-Thwin, the leading scholar of Pagan's political economy, it was the 10th and 11th-century development of the Kyaukse agricultural basin northeast of the capital, some 400 miles from the coast, "that enabled the kingdom of Pagan to expand beyond the dry zone of Upper Burma in the first place" and to dominate the maritime south. Pagan "had little need for external trade."[22] The other chief Pagan researchers, G. H. Luce, Than Tun, and Tilman Frasch, concur fully with this judgment.[23]

As reconstructed by Aung-Thwin, Luce, and Than Tun, economic expansion centered on the endowment of Buddhist temples. Eager to acquire religious merit that would benefit them and their dependents in both this and future reincarnations, wealthy laymen, principally officials and members of the royal family, donated to the monkhood enormous acreages of agricultural land, typically in productive districts at some distance from Pagan itself, along with hereditary tied cultivators.

[20] Fukui, "Historical Cities"; idem, personal communication, Aug., 2001. Insofar as it has any validity, this hypothesis makes most sense for the islands.
[21] G. H. Luce, "Economic Life of the Early Burman," *JBRS* 30 (1940): 296; idem, "Note on the Peoples of Burma in the 12th–13th Century A.D.," *JBRS* 42 (1959): 70–73.
[22] Aung-Thwin, *Myth and History*, 96; idem, *Pagan*, 113–14; supported by personal communication, June, 1998.
[23] Luce, "Economic Life," 283–301 devotes some five sentences of text (296, plus n. 73) to maritime contacts, religious and commercial. Than Tun, *Hkit-haung*, 173–83, virtually ignores it. Frasch, "Coastal Peripheries," 59, 63, 66 emphasizes repeatedly that trade was marginal to Pagan's economy.

Both religious lands and cultivators were permanently tax-exempt. Yet religious merit aside, during the early phase of Pagan's growth the throne actually benefited from such tax-free endowments, first, because monastery-temple complexes helped to concentrate in accessible locales not only religious bondsmen (*hpaya-kyun*), but also lay cultivators who remained liable for royal service and taxation; and second, because such institutions stimulated an array of artisanal, commercial, and agricultural activities critical to the general economy. To accumulate land for endowments, as well as for awards to soldiers and servicemen, the throne joined local lay and monastic leaders in supporting reclamation work.[24]

The earliest projects focused on Kyaukse, where Burmans built a large number of new weirs and diversionary canals, followed by Minbu, a similarly well-watered district south of Pagan.[25] After these "hubs" or "heartlands" (*hkayaings*) had been developed, with population pressing on available resources, in the mid- and late 12th century Burmans moved into as yet undeveloped frontier areas (*taiks*) west of the Irrawaddy and south of Minbu. These new lands included both irrigable wet-rice areas and non-irrigable areas suitable for rain-fed rice, pulses, sesamum, and millet. Although we lack census figures, there is no doubt that together *hkayaing* intensification and *taik* extension permitted and reflected significant population growth,[26] perhaps too at least a temporary increase in per capita productivity and wealth. Agricultural expansion and temple construction in turn sustained a market in land and certain types of labor and materials, with lump coinages in silver (from domestic mines and Yunnan), copper, and gold providing the most common instruments of exchange.[27] According to Aung-Thwin, Bob Hudson, Nyein Lwin, and Win Maung, land reclamation, religious donations, and building

[24] On agricultural expansion and the role of temple endowments, Aung-Thwin, *Pagan*, chs. 2, 5, 8, 9; idem, "Nature of State," 52–56; idem, *Myth and History*, 96, 114; Luce, *Old Burma*, I, 29–38, 84–92; idem, "The Career of Htilaing Min (Kyanzittha)," JRAS 1966: 55; idem, "Geography of Burma"; idem, "Economic Life," esp. 286–88; Than Tun, *Hkit-haung*, chs. 15, 16; idem, "History of Buddhism in Burma, A.D. 1000–1300" (Univ. of London Ph.D. diss., 1956), chs. 7–10.

[25] Luce, *Old Burma*, I, 31–33. Cf. U Ba Thein, comp., *Ko-hkayaing thamaing* (Mandalay, 1910); U Maung Maung Tin, *Myit-tha taze-ywa kwin-zin-lei-la chet-hmat zu* (Mandalay, 2000).

[26] Previous notes, esp. Aung-Thwin, *Pagan*, 101–103, 186–92; Luce, *Old Burma*, I, 29–38, 84–92; idem, "Economic Life," 286–88.

[27] Ko U, *Myan-ma dinga-mya* (Rangoon, 1974), 56–57; Aung-Thwin, *Pagan*, 113–14, 169–82; Toe Hla, "Money Lending and Contractual *Thet-kayits*: A Socio-Economic Pattern of the Later Kon-baung Period, 1819–1885" (Northern Illinois Univ. Ph.D. diss., 1987), 5–7.

projects expanded slowly before 1050, increased to 1100, accelerated sharply with the opening of *taik* lands between c. 1140 and 1210, and continued at a lower level from 1220 to 1300 (see Figure 2.2).[28]

But if we are thus inclined to downplay foreign trade in favor of agrarian-based explanations of economic growth, the questions of timing and Eurasian correlation obviously remain. In varying degrees the remaining theories are speculative and their relative contributions, uncertain.

Perhaps one could smuggle in maritime influences by focusing on their immunological impact, to which Chapter 1 alluded. William McNeill, supported by historians of China and Japan, has argued that populations in the oldest, most densely settled, most commercialized Eurasian centers, including India, the Mideast, and north China, were first to develop limited immunities to certain diseases (measles, smallpox, and enteric fevers) that once had been uniformly lethal. By contrast, smaller, more isolated populations in western and northern Europe, Japan, rural south China, and mainland Southeast Asia in the mid–first millennium had yet to gain the regular exposure or internal densities that would support comparable resistances. When contagion did occur, these latter groups suffered high mortalities analogous to those which Amerindians and Oceanic peoples experienced on first contact with Europeans. If we follow this hypothesis, during the late first millennium the gradual strengthening and reticulation of east–west trade networks, by land as well as by sea, overcame that deficit, so that by the end of the first or the start of the second millennium epidemic diseases in many rimland areas had become merely endemic, killing chiefly children and old people rather than productive adults and thus permitting more rapid increases in population and cultivation. Hence, in part, the crudely synchronized demographic-cum-economic florescence of northwestern Europe, Kiev, south China, Pagan, Angkor, and Japan, and the rising importance of these areas vis-a-vis older cores. According to this, the second theory, external trade was important less for its direct economic benefits than for its immunizing effects. One thinks of Pagan's expanding coastal involvement and, in particular, the epidemiological implications of transporting Indian slaves to Upper Burma. By 1350 it appears that smallpox, which may have arrived

---

[28] Aung-Thwin's inventory of donations of land and silver reveals a pattern smoother and more long-lasting than the quantification of 89 religious construction projects by Hudson et al. But basic patterns are similar.

from India, had become merely endemic in Upper Burma. But the bald truth is that we have no idea when this first occurred in the Irrawaddy basin, nor do we yet have even rudimentary chronologies for other diseases.[29]

Third, one can focus on the cultural, as opposed to the commercial or epidemiological, value of strengthened Eurasian contacts. Pagan clearly benefited from trade with India and Sri Lanka insofar as such contacts provided a host of architectural, artistic, literary, ceremonial, and monastic models. David Wyatt has argued that in the 12th and 13th centuries closer trade links across the Bay of Bengal facilitated the spread of Sinhalese Theravada texts and rituals across the mainland.[30] Particularly after 1164, the reunification of the Sinhalese *sangha* and the development of an extensive Pali exegetical literature magnified the appeal of Theravada orthodoxy.[31] In Upper Burma, although contacts with

---

[29] William McNeill, *Plagues and Peoples* (Garden City, NY: 1976), ch. 3, and idem, *The Global Condition* (Princeton, 1992), 18–19 uses China and northern Europe as examples of trade-mediated disease acculturation, but says little about SE Asia. For coastal China starting in the 8th century, see Denis Twitchett, "Population and Pestilence in T'ang China," *Studia Sino-Mongolica* (Wiesbaden, 1979), 35–68. In Japan, which was farther removed from the main sealanes, William Wayne Farris, *Population, Disease, and Land in Early Japan, 645–900* (Cambridge, MA: 1995), 71; Ann Bowman Janetta, *Epidemics and Mortality in Early Modern Japan* (Princeton, 1987), 65–70; and Conrad Totman, *A History of Japan* (Malden, MA: 2000), 109–110 date the epidemiologically-based demographic transition to the late 11th century. Alfred Crosby, *The Columbian Exchange* (Westport, CT, 1972), ch. 2 offers a classic account of European diseases in the New World. On general Eurasian patterns, see too Donald R. Hopkins, *Princes and Peasants: Smallpox in History* (Chicago, 1983), esp. 13–21; Andrew Cliff, Peter Haggett, and Matthew Smallman-Raynor, *Measles: An Historical Geography of a Major Human Viral Disease* (Oxford, 1993), esp. 45–54. For SE Asia itself, we have speculative references to the introduction of malaria to Pagan and Angkor in the 13th or 14th centuries [Rhoads Murphey, "The Ruin of Ancient Ceylon," *JAS* 16 (1957): 181–200], and of smallpox to Siam in the 14th century [B. J. Terwiel, "Asiatic Cholera in Siam," in Norman Owen, ed., *Death and Disease in Southeast Asia*, Singapore, 1987, ch. 7]. See too Anthony Reid, *Southeast Asia in the Age of Commerce*, 2 vols. (New Haven, 1988, 1993), I, 57–61; David Arnold, "The Indian Ocean as a Disease Zone, 1500–1950," *South Asia* 14 (1991): 1–21; Frank Fenner, "Smallpox in Southeast Asia," *Crossroads* 3 (1987): 34–48; and *UK*, I, 358, which refers explicitly to smallpox in 14th-century Burma. According to Barbara Watson Andaya, personal communication, June 1991, in Sumatra and other areas "there is little doubt that the more isolated interior groups were more susceptible than coastal inhbitants" to smallpox and other epidemics.

[30] Wyatt, "Relics, Oaths," 3, 23, 48; idem, "Mainland Powers on the Malay Peninsula," in Wyatt, *Studies in Thai History* (Chiang Mai, 1994), 22–48.

[31] On the early growth of property-owning monasteries in medieval Sri Lanka and the post-1165 revival of Sinhalese Buddhism, see R. A. L. H. Gunawardana, *Robe and Plough* (Tucson, 1979), esp. chs. 2, 7, 9, 10.

Sri Lanka had widened following the 11th century conquest of the coast, Sinhalese artistic, architectural, and textual influence grew markedly from 1174, and missions to Sri Lanka inspired reformist sectors of the Pagan monkhood (*sangha*).[32] Conceivably – no one has researched the issue – such ties modified Pagan's system of religious endowments by: a) providing more cogent doctrinal rationales for donations, and b) strengthening the normative appeal of large monasteries, such as those in Sri Lanka, which depended for income not on daily alms, but on their own landed estates. As noted, monastic donations and associated *taik* reclamations accelerated in the late 1100s, at roughly the same time as Sinhalese influence increased. One could try to link such developments to civilizational brilliance elsewhere in mainland Southeast Asia, northwestern Europe, the Dnieper basin, and interior China south of the Yangzi by pointing out that all these areas in the mid- or late first millennium were still underpopulated, weakly urbanized frontier zones whose development required an intensified flow of administrative, religious, and literary technologies from longer-settled zones, namely South Asia, the Mediterranean, and north China.

But this approach too has its problems. The link between Sinhalese culture and larger monastic land holdings in Burma is not only institutionally uncertain, but actually contravenes evidence that the late Pagan throne sought to pit austere Sinhalese monks against more acquisitive indigenous sects in an express effort to limit the latter's landholding.[33] Moreover, given the disorder and weakness of the Sinhalese *sangha* prior to 1164 (in the late 11th and early 12th centuries Sinhalese monks turned to Burma for guidance, rather than vice versa) and the fact that the system of Burmese temple-building and endowments already was established by 1100, how transformative or necessary are post-1174 Sinhalese contacts likely to have been?[34] One also may ask why Angkor, which supported a non-Theravadin, predominantly Hindu/Mahayana cult, entered a phase of rapid temple construction and ecclesiastical colonization in the 11th and 12th centuries at roughly the same time as Pagan.

---

[32] On Sinhalese influence at Pagan, *Kalyani Inscriptions*, 50–59; Luce, *Old Burma*, I, 38–40, 90–94, 120–28; E. Michael Mendelson, *Sangha and State in Burma* (Ithaca, 1975), 38–42; Strachan, *Imperial Pagan*, 10, 15, 45–56, 66–126 passim; Kanai Lal Harza, *History of Theravada Buddhism in South-East Asia* (New Delhi, 1982), ch. 5.

[33] Than Tun, "Religion in Burma, A.D. 1000–1300," *JBRS* 42 (1959): 67; idem, "Maha-kathapa gaing," *JBRS* 42 (1959): 97.

[34] Gunawardana, *Robe and Plough*, 271–77, 313–37.

At Angkor too we shall find centuries-old ties to South Asia, but scant evidence of suddenly transformative external cultural contacts, least of all with Sri Lanka.[35]

After maritime-based commercial, epidemiological, and cultural influences, a fourth potential explanation of Pagan's prosperity is more local: perhaps Burmans brought with them in the mid-9th century novel agricultural expertise that by the early 11th century began to have a cumulative, transformative impact. Richard O'Connor, to whose imaginative work Chapter 1 referred, argued that Burmans arrived in the plains with new water-control techniques that they had developed in their putative homeland in the steeply graded hills of south Yunnan and Laos. In O'Connor's view, these techniques allowed them to open an ecological niche suitable for wet-rice production that their predecessors, the Pyus and Mons, both of whom he termed "flood-managing garden-farmers," had been unable to exploit. Pyus and Mons had relied on a combination of natural flooding, river-extending canals, river-filled tanks, and run-off-collecting tanks built in natural depressions. These techniques left untouched potentially fertile but higher elevation lands where rivers could not be extended and topography did not suit tanks. But these areas, with shallow perennial streams, were precisely where weirs worked best. According to O'Connor, Burmans, who were expert in weir-building, developed extensive rice acreages on upstream lands that had been neglected, originally in *hkayaing* and later in *taik* areas. Hence both the rapid Burman-led agricultural expansion throughout the lowlands and the long-term, largely peaceful Burmanization of other peoples eager to acquire Burman economic and social techniques.[36]

Yet the dating of pre-Burman irrigation works is too uncertain to allow easy acceptance of O'Connor's argument. Stargardt, a Pyu scholar, claimed that Burman migrants merely extended an already ancient

---

[35] Ian Mabbett and David Chandler, *The Khmers* (Oxford, 1995), 101–102. See Ch. 2 *infra*.
[36] Richard O'Connor, "Agricultural Change and Ethnic Succession in Southeast Asian States," *JAS* 54 (1995): 968–996, esp. 972–76, 983. On the Burman homeland hypothesis, see too Tadayo Watabe and Koji Tanaka, "Ancient Rice Grains Recovered from Ruins in Burma," in Watabe, ed., *Preliminary Report of the Kyoto University Scientific Survey To Burma, 1974* (Kyoto, 1976), 17. Fukui, "Historical Cities," 30, 34–36 implicitly supports O'Connor's chronology by arguing that in Upper Burma and other SE Asian dry zones, the late first millennium introduced a more productive stage of rice cultivation, characterized by transplanting, animal-drawn plows, and continuous cropping in lieu of alternating fallow regimes. But rather than explain this transition by pointing to new ethnically-linked techniques, Fukui, as noted, credits unexplained prior increases in population along with the sudden availability of Chinese cast iron suitable for iron-socketed plows.

and sophisticated Pyu system of weirs, dams, sluices, and diversionary barricades, with little novel technical input.[37] Her emphasis on agricultural continuity gains indirect support from Tadayo Watabe and Koji Tanaka, whose analysis of rice husks in Upper Burma bricks shows that *japonica*-type "round type rice" remained the preferred variety from the 5th through the late 13th centuries,[38] after which "slender type rice" associated with new irrigation systems began to take over. Moreover, even if O'Connor's theory can be substantiated, it would say nothing in particular about correlations between agricultural growth in Upper Burma and other sectors of Eurasia.

A fifth and final line of inquiry focuses on climate change, whose potential importance to Eurasian history both here and in future chapters justifies a brief excursion.

Geophysicists and paleoclimatologists have long sought to explain changes in temperature and precipitation that lasted for periods ranging from decades to millennia and that affected broad areas of the globe. Before the post-1850 onset of anthropogenic change, three principal forcing agents are thought to have dominated sub-millennial climatic modification, namely, variations in solar activity, in volcanism, and in ocean currents. Some studies claim that prior to 1850 fluctuations in solar brightness accounted for 70 percent of the earth's temperature shifts, with each 1 percent drop in radiation depressing global temperatures by at least one degree C. As determined by ice cores, tree rings, lake sediment, and sun spots, solar radiation was particularly strong from the 10th to 13th centuries, and particularly weak during the 14th century, the Sporer Minimum (1416–1534), and the Maunder Minimum (1654–1714).[39] There is increasing evidence that by injecting into the

---

[37] Stargardt, *Ancient Pyu*, ch. 2, esp. 54–55. However, Bennett Bronson, in his review of Stargardt's book, *JSEAS* 23: 435–38, suggests that she projected Burmese patterns onto the Pyu.

[38] Watabe and Tanaka, "Ancient Rice Grains," 1–18. See discussion *infra*.

[39] Current evidence is that *average global* temperature variations over the past millennium have been less than 1 degree C., but that some regional variations, as in Europe, have been significantly larger. For overviews of a vast literature on paleoclimatic change and forcing mechanisms, see T. Mikami, ed., *Proceedings of the International Symposium on the Little Ice Age Climate* (Tokyo, 1992); Raymond S. Bradley, *Paleoclimatology*, 2nd ed. (San Diego, 1999); idem and Philip D. Jones, *Climate Since A.D. 1500* (London, 1995); Michael E. Mann, "Lessons for a New Millenium," *Science* 289 (2000): 253–54; Michael E. Mann et al., "Global-Scale Temperature Patterns and Climate Forcing Over the Past Six Centuries," *Nature* 392 (1998): 779–87; Thomas Crowley, "Causes of Climate Change Over the Past 1000 Years," *Science* 289 (2000): 270–77; Melissa Free and Alan Robock, "Global Warming in the Context of the Little Ice Age," *Jl. Of Geophysical Research* 104,

atmosphere sulfate aerosols that deflect the sun's radiation back into space, volcanism has reinforced the cooling impact of lower radiation and has moderated the warming effects of radiation increases. Between 1200 and 1699 William Atwell calculated that volcanism helped to lower surface temperatures in at least 160 years, including dramatic episodes in 1225–1233, 1256–1262, 1444–1465, 1584–1610, and 1636–1644.[40] Finally, propelled by changes in solar energy and/or by internal rhythms, decade- to centuries-long oscillations in the heat economy and circulation of ocean currents also have influenced terrestial temperature and precipitation. By far the most powerful of the world's regional heat engines, and the oceanic system most relevant to Southeast Asia, is the El Niño Southern Oscillation (ENSO).[41] Note that despite their hemispheric reach, the impact of radiation, volcanism, and oceanic systems varies with altitude, latitude, and geomorphology, so that at any given time we find regional differences in the rate of climate change. Even in a given region, long-term trends coexisted with annual and decadal fluctuations.

The combined impact of these forcing agents has been most carefully documented in Europe, where starting as early as the 9th or 10th century a warming trend affected areas from the north Atlantic to Russia. Accordingly, the years c. 900/1000 to 1250/1300 are known as the Medieval Warm Period or, in a global context often, the Medieval Climate Anomaly. Most scholars accept that warm, relatively dry summers and autumns made a significant, if difficult to quantify, contribution to the rapid demographic and agricultural growth characteristic of the European high middle ages. In much of northern and western Europe the mid-1200s or early 1300s initiated a colder era with pluvial

D16 (1999): 19,057–19,070; C. K. Folland and T. R. Karl, "Observed Climate Variability and Change," in J. T. Houghton et al., eds., *Climate Change 2001* (Cambridge, 2001), 99–181.

[40] William Atwell, "Volcanism and Short-Term Climatic Change in East Asian and World History, c. 1200–1699," *JWH* 12 (2001): 29–98; Alan Robock and Melissa Free, "The Volcanic Record in Ice Cores for the Past 2000 Years," in Philip D. Jones et al., eds., *Climatic Variations and Forcing Mechanisms of the Last 2000 Years* (Heidelberg, 1996), 533–45.

[41] See Mike Davis, *Late Victorian Holocausts* (London, 2001), pt. 3, offering a lucid overview; B. G. Hunt, "Natural Climatic Variability as an Explanation for Historical Climatic Fluctuations," *CC* 38 (1998): 133–57; Henry F. Diaz and Vera Markgraf, eds., *El Niño: Historical and Paleoclimatic Aspects of the Southern Oscillation* (Cambridge, 1992); Diaz and Markgraf, eds., *El Niño and the Southern Oscillation* (Cambridge, 2000), esp. 465–88; and Richard H. Grove and John Chappell, eds., *El Niño: History and Crisis* (Cambridge, 2000).

summers markedly less favorable to cereal production and population growth. This cooling trend was partially reversed c. 1470–1560. Thereafter it resumed, intensifying in the mid and late 17th century – the height of the so-called Little Ice Age – only to yield to another mild, agriculturally propitious period c. 1710/1720–1805.[42]

What, if anything, does all this tell us about dry zone Burma, where water was the key variable and where the last thing cultivators needed was more heat? If the period c. 900–1300 brought heat and summer dryness to Europe, and if climate was loosely synchronized across the northern hemisphere, would not conditions around Pagan have been disastrous? Quite the contrary, because in Burma the Medieval Climate Anomaly seems to have yielded higher summer rainfall, and by implication more reliable rice crops.

As early as 1913 J. C. Mackenzie cited inscriptional evidence to argue that Pagan's early prosperity depended on a wetter climate than in modern times, while in 1932 Pagan U Tin used early literary evidence to reach the same conclusion.[43] Luce, however, debunked Mackenzie's interpretations, and the art historian Richard Cooler has analyzed Pagan architecture to suggest that rainfall has not changed substantially since the 14th century.[44] Nonetheless, a variety of recent theoretical and comparative materials do in fact point to a significantly wetter climate.

In terms of general models, scholars have shown that by heating the Central Asian landmass and by shifting to higher latitudes the intertropical discontinuity line (which governs seasonal wind patterns), Eurasian warming such as was associated with the Medieval Climate Anomaly magnifies the northern reach and intensity of Indian Ocean monsoon flows, to the benefit of northern India, mainland Southeast Asia, and

---

[42] On European climate phases, discussed more fully in Vol. 2, I rely on H. H. Lamb, *Climate, History and the Modern World*, 2nd ed. (London, 1995); Pierre Alexander, *Le climat en Europe au moyen age* (Paris, 1987), esp. 775–808; Thomas Crowley and Thomas Lowery, "How Warm Was the Medieval Warm Period?" *Ambio* 29 (2000): 51–54; C. Pfister et al., "Winter Severity in Europe: The Fourteenth Century," *CC* 34 (1996): 91–108; the special issue of *CC* 43 (1999) devoted to "Climatic Variability in Sixteenth-Century Europe and Its Social Dimensions"; Michael E. Mann, personal communication, Sept., 2001; and most recent, Jan Esper, Edward Cook, and Fritz Schweingruber, "Low-Frequency Signals in Long Tree-Ring Chronologies for Reconstructing Past Temperature Variability," *Science* 295 (March 22, 2002): 2,250–2,253, arguing that medieval warming was even more pronounced than was hitherto recognized.

[43] J. C. Mackenzie, "Climate in Burmese History," *JBRS* 3 (1913): 40–46; *MMOS*, II, 133–37.

[44] Luce, "Economic Life," 289–90 and n. 38; Richard Cooler, "Sacred Buildings for an Arid Climate: Architectural Evidence for Low Rainfall in Ancient Pagan," *The Jl. of Burma Studies* 1 (1997): 19–44.

parts of south China.[45] At the same time higher tropical temperatures increase water vapor in the atmosphere, strengthening monsoon rains and reducing evaporation.[46] Denser vegetation in turn magnifies convection.[47] Finally, recent work suggests that increased solar radiation contributes to a reduction in the power and frequency of El Niño events, which comprise one phase of the ENSO. Again, this tends to enhance Southeast Asian rainfall insofar as strong El Niño events, by shifting towards South America the so-called west Pacific Warm Pool with its incessant generation of cumulonimbus rain clouds, increase the likelihood of drought in the Ethiopian highlands, west and south India, eastern Indonesia, and mainland Southeast Asia.[48]

These theoretical and empirical studies pointing to increased Burmese rainfall during the Medieval Climate Anomaly gain added weight from the following historical correlations: a) According to reconstructions based on Nile flood data, during the entire era c. 700–1900, El Niño events, which as just noted tend to correlate with dry

---

[45] Increased heat over Central Asia also magnifies monsoon flows from the South China Sea to southern and central China. Reid Bryson and Thomas Murray, *Climates of Hunger* (Madison, WI, 1977), 101–110, 137–38; Jiacheng Zhang and Thomas Crowley, "Historical Climate Records in China and Reconstruction of Past Climates," *Jl. of Climate* 2 (1989): 833–49; Lamb, *Climate, History*, 236; Ka-Ming Lau and Mai-Tsun Li, "The Monsoon of East Asia and Its Global Associations – A Survey," *Bulletin American Metereological Society* 65 (1984): 114–25.

[46] J. Kutzbach et al., "Vegetation and Soil Feedbacks on the Response of the African Monsoon to Orbital Forcing in the Early to Middle Holocene," *Nature* 384 (1996): 623–26; Robert Marks, *Tigers, Rice, Silk, and Silt* (Cambridge, 1998), 220–21 n. 73; Zhang and Crowley, "Historical Climate Records," 833.

[47] Andrey Ganopolski et al., "The Influence of Vegetation-Atmosphere-Ocean Interaction on Climate During the Mid-Holocene," *Science* 280 (1998): 1916–19; Kutzbach, "Vegetation."

[48] See Davis, *Victorian Holocausts*, ch. 8; Roger Anderson, "Long-Term Changes in the Frequency of Occurrence of El Niño Events," in Diaz and Markgraf, *El Niño*, 193–200; Neville Nicholls, "Historical El Niño/Southern Oscillation Variability in the Australasian Region," ibid., esp. 167; Richard Grove and John Chappell, "El Niño Chronology and the History of Global Crises During the Little Ice Age," in Grove and Chappell, *El Niño*, 5–34; Peter Whetton et al., "Rainfall and River Flow Variability in Africa, Australia and East Asia Linked to El Niño-Southern Oscillation Events," *Geological Society of Australia Symposium Proceedings* (1990), 1, 71–82 (esp. graph on 73); R. Kane, "El Niño Timings and Rainfall Extremes in India, Southeast Asia, and China," *International Jl. of Climatology* 19 (1999): 653–72. Michael E. Mann, personal communication, Sept. 2001, has endorsed my linkage of European and SE Asian climate regimes via solar forcing and ENSO mechanisms. Of course, variables subsantially or completely independent of the ENSO, such as local volcanic effects and oceanic-atmospheric systems outside the ENSO, render imperfect correlations at any given time between SE Asia and other regions.

conditions in mainland Southeast Asia, were weakest between 1000 and 1300. Conversely, Nile flooding (which originates with rains in the Ethiopian highlands) was more severe between c. 1000 and 1290 than in any other period from the 7th century to the start of the 20th century.[49] b) At Sawankhalok in north-central Thailand, local stratigraphy and proxy Chinese climate records suggest that from the 6th to 10th centuries monsoon rains were weaker than the historical average, but from the 10th century to the mid- or late 13th century they were appreciably stronger.[50] c) The archeology of Satingpra in southern Thailand points to a major increase in cultivation and in the proportion of lands receiving irrigation water c. 850–1280.[51] d) An analysis, albeit not universally accepted, of the Great Lake in Cambodia argues that in Angkor's heyday, c. 1000–1300, it held considerably more water than in later periods.[52]

[49] William H. Quinn, "A Study of Southern Oscillation-Related Climatic Activity for A.D. 622–1900 Incorporating Nile River Flood Data," in Diaz and Markgraf, *El Niño*, 119–49; Anderson, "Long-term Changes," esp. 194, 198; Simon Haberle, "Vegetation Response to Climate Variability," in Grove and Chappell, *El Niño*, 66–68. For analysis of essentially post-1650 patterns, see also Michael E. Mann et al., "Long-Term Variability in the El Niño/Southern Oscillation and Associated Teleconnections," in Diaz and Markgraf, *El Niño*, 357–412.

[50] David Godley, "Flood Regimes in Northern Thailand" (Monash Univ. MA thesis, 1997), ch. 6 and Conclusion; Paul Bishop, Donald Hein, and David Godley, "Was Medieval Sawankhalok like Modern Bangkok, Flooded Every Few Years but an Economic Powerhouse Nonetheless?" *Asian Perspectives* 35 (1996): 119–53, suggesting that a drier regime began by the 13th century.

[51] Janice Stargardt, *Satingpra I: The Environmental and Economic Archaeology of South Thailand* (Oxford, 1983), 23–24, 82–84, 119–23, 181–83. As usual, political and climatic factors interacted.

[52] Robert Acker, "New Geographical Tests of the Hydraulic Thesis at Angkor," *SEAR* 6 (1998): 18, 37–38, argues that since the lake surface was roughly the same in the 11th–13th centuries as now, while sedimentation has been cumulative, formerly it must have had a larger volume, which again points to higher rainfall. Acker is supported, if indirectly, by claims in Ferenc Garami and Istvan Kertai, *Water Management in the Angkor Area* (Budapest, 1993), 27, 45 that recent sedimentation rates have been 2–4 mm a year and that medieval lake levels were 1–3 meters higher than at present; by Bernard P. Groslier, "La cite hydraulique Angorienne," *BEFEO* 66 (1979): 194; by Yoshino Masatoshi, "Monsoon and the Dry Areas in Southeast Asia," in Fukui Hayao, *Dry Areas*, 45; and by Roland Fletcher, "Seeing Angkor: New Views on an Old City," forthcoming in *Jl. of the Oriental Society of Australia*, 12, citing recent rises in sedimentation rates from 1–4 cm (sic) per year. However, Dan Penny, personal communication, Aug. 2001, calculated sedimentation rates during the Angkorian period itself of only .0640–.1064 mm per year; while Christophe Pottier, personal communication, Dec., 2001, claimed average annual sedimentation rates for the past 1,100 years were .45 mm. While these rates do not directly contradict Acker, both Penny and Pottier expressed reservations about his sedimentation thesis, nor were they convinced by his claims that the lake surface has remained unchanged.

e) Not only in Upper Burma, but in Angkor, Dong Kinh, and south-east China, the 10th to 13th centuries saw rapid agricultural growth to which Chinese (and less clearly, Vietnamese) materials suggest that climate contributed.[53] f) Local chronicles and/or climate proxies point to desiccation during much of the late 13th to early 15th centuries in South India, Kengtung (in eastern Burma), northern Thailand, Dong Kinh, and parts of south China. Southeast Asian desiccation in the 14th century thus correlated broadly to European cooling, reinforcing the view that prior to 1300 as well, Upper Burma participated in a larger hemispheric regime.[54] g) When after 1590 contemporary references to climate finally appear in lowland Burma itself, they too show strong, if imperfect, correlations. Thus in Burma as in Java, much of Europe, southeast China, and parts of India, harvests were exceptionally poor in the 1590s, much of the 1630s to 1670s, 1690–1710, and early 1800s, when Little Ice Age solar radiation, volcanism, and El Niños were in varying degrees adverse.[55]

[53] On Angkor and Dong Kinh, *infra* Chs. 3, 4. On south China, Marks, *Tigers, Rice,* 48–83; Rowe, "Approaches," 271; *Paleoclimate and Environmental Variability in Austral-Asian Transect during the Past 2000 Years* (Nagoya, Japan, 1995), 76–83; Zhang and Crowley, "Historical Climate Records"; Pao K. Wang and Zhang De'er, "Recent Studies of the Reconstruction of East Asian Monsoon Climate in the Past Using Historical Literature of China," *Jl. of the Meteorlogoical Society of Japan* 70 (1992): 423–46; Zhang De'er, "Evidence for the Existence of the Medieval Warm Period in China," *CC* 26 (1994): 289–97; Chen Jiaqi, "Historical Climatic Change and Little Ice Age in Changjiang Delta Area," in Mikami, *Proceedings,* 146–51; Davis, *Victorian Holocausts,* 248–51. Most of these sources argue that, contrary to pioneering work by Chu Ko-Chien, in China the 12th/13th centuries were not a cold era. The late 17th century saw colder weather in northern Europe and coordinated droughts in SE China, mainland and island SE Asia. On the other hand, medieval warming apparently began earlier in China than in northern Europe, i.e., by the 7th century, and tailed off earlier.

[54] On broadly, if incompletely, correlated climatic deterioration in parts of southern Asia and Europe in the 13th to 15th centuries, see Pfister, "Winter Severity"; Crowley, "Causes of Climate Change," 272; Grove and Chappell, "El Niño Chronology," 13; William Chester Jordan, *The Great Famine* (Princeton, 1996), 16–17; Sao Saimong Mangrai, *The Padaeng Chronicle and the Jengtung State Chronicle Translated* (Ann Arbor, 1981), 141–42, 237–38; Godley, "Flood Regimes"; Bishop et al., "Medieval Sawankhalok," 145–46; O. W. Wolters, *Two Essays on Dai Viet in the 14th Century* (New Haven, 1981), 16; John K. Whitmore, *Vietnam, Ho Quy Ly, and the Ming (1371–1421)* (New Haven, 1985), 33–34; previous entries on China; and Kathleen Morrison, "Naturalizing Disaster: From Drought to Famine in Southern India," in Garth Bawden and Richard Martin Reycraft, eds., *Naturalizing Disaster and the Archaeology of Human Response* (Chicago, 2000), 21–33.

[55] On Burmese famines, which invariably reflected combinations of climatic and administrative factors, see *UK,* III, 94–95, 269, 303, 306, 333, 337, 379; D. G. E. Hall, *Burma* (New York, 1950), 66; William Koenig, *The Burmese Polity, 1752–1819* (Ann Arbor, 1990),

The trick, of course, is to measure the impact of climate on Pagan, but without detailed local data, we must fall back on historic analogies elsewhere and on modern agrarian data. In Wales and England, H. H. Lamb calculated that between the height of the Medieval Climate Anomaly and of the Little Ice Age, summer rainfall changed by about 23 percent.[56] In the Changjiang delta of China, Chen Jiaqi claimed that cold-dry weather and natural disasters helped to depress Qing cereal yields by 17–33 percent below those of the Ming.[57] In 20th-century Sri Lanka and Thailand, rainfall was by far the single most important influence on rice yields and acreage. In Thailand from 1960 to 1975, for example, the correlation of yields to the monsoon index was +.64; while between 1907 and 1965 periodic droughts damaged the rice crop on as much as 32 percent of planted acreage.[58]

In the Upper Burma dry zone as well, where rainfall could double from one year to the next, correlations between rice harvests and monsoon levels were consistently strong.[59] According to the earliest British

33–36. On Little Ice Age, esp. 17th century, agricultural difficulties elsewhere, Davis, *Victorian Holocausts*, 216; Lamb, *Climate, History*, ch. 12; Marks, *Tigers, Rice*, ch. 6; Grove and Chappell, "El Niño Chronology," 14–22; Reid, *Age of Commerce*, II, 191–98; R. D. D'Arrigo et al., "Progress in Dendroclimatic Studies in Indonesia," *Terrestial, Atmospheric and Oceanic Sciences* 5 (1994): 349–63; J. Murphy and P. Whetton, "A Re-Analysis of a Tree Ring Chronology from Java," *Dendrochronology*, Proceedings B92: 3 (1989): 241–57.

[56] Lamb, *Climate, History*, 85, Fig. 31, showing increases in high summer, as opposed to annual, rainfall from 1290 to 1580, a pattern that contrasted with that of mainland SE Asia but whose impact on agriculture was no less negative. According to Quinn, "Study of Southern Oscillation," 142–44, between 622 and 999 weak Nile floods were 350 percent, and between 1291 and 1522, 270 percent more common than during the wet 1000–1291 era.

[57] Chen Jiaqi, "Historical Climate Change," 149–51. Although he claimed a fall of 17 percent and although he failed to disentangle properly social from climatic causes, his figures (334 and 225 kg. per mu) actually indicate a drop of 33 percent. Marks, *Tigers, Rice*, 220 concluded that "climatic changes were the single most important cause of harvest yield fluctuations" in 18th-century Lingnan, in south China, where a major drought in 1786–87 depressed yields by 14 percent. Ibid., 215–20, esp. Fig. 6.10

[58] Moreover, from 1960–1975 all four years of widespread poor harvests in Thailand occurred when the Seasonal Monsoon Index was at least one standard deviation below normal. M. Tanaka, "Synoptic Study on the Recent Climatic Change in Monsoon Asia and Its Influence on Agricultural Production," in Koichiro Takahashi and Masatoshi Yoshino, eds., *Climatic Change and Food Production* (Tokyo, 1978), 81–98, esp. Table 8.; E. Maruyama, "Fluctuation of Paddy Yield and Water Resources in Southeast Asia," ibid.,157–58. See too studies on Sri Lanka by M. Domros and Thailand by H. Tsujii, ibid., 101–110, 167–79.

[59] Tanaka, "Synoptic Study," 93, Table 8, showed correlations of only +.28 for Burma as a whole, but that included the well-watered delta where the vast bulk of the crop grew.

records, between 1888 and 1890 alone, weak monsoons compressed northern rice acreage by 16 percent in well irrigated districts and 75 percent in outlying areas like Shwebo.[60] If average annual rainfall in the 12th and 13th centuries rose over 10th-century levels by 25–30 percent – a plausible estimate – it would have permitted the opening of extensive *taik* acreages which relied on direct rainfall and irrigation (itself ultimately dependent on rainfall). All things being equal, this would have boosted Upper Burma's demographic carrying capacity (although the marginal productivity of most new lands must have been lower than that of established districts). This hypothesis is consistent with the aforementioned, well-documented spread of cultivation during the 12th and early 13th centuries from the *hkayaing* heartlands to *taik* areas like Mandalay, Shwebo, Lower Chindwin, Pakokku, and Thayetmyo. It is also compatible with O'Connor's theory insofar as improved rainfall, by creating and strengthening perennial streams, would have let Burmans deploy their water skills more widely. At the same time, *pace* Cooler, it is unlikely that even a 30 percent increase in average rainfall would have required modifications in basic Pagan architecture. Figures 2.2 to 2.4 set forth some of these correlations between Pagan reclamation as indicated by religious donations, on the one hand, and hemispheric climate change, on the other. This argument assumes, from analogies to other pre-industrial societies, that larger, more regular harvests favorably influenced nuptiality and fertility, while depressing child mortality.[61] Note finally that by boosting output, population, and urban demand in a wide band of Eurasian territories, including south India and south China, better climate c. 900–1300 may have contributed in some measure to that strengthening of multilateral long-distance exchange to which Janet

---

Ibid., 88 showed that in the dry zone the correlation between rice yields and rainfall was far higher, probably of the same order as in central and NE Thailand.

[60] *Reports on the Administration of Burma During 1888–89, 1889–90, 1890–91* (Rangoon, 1889, 1890, 1891), pt. III-E- Agriculture, No. 63. On close 19th/20th century correlations between rainfall and crop yields in Upper Burma, esp. marginal areas, see too J. P. Hardiman, comp., *Burma Gazeteer: Lower Chindwin District*, vol. A (Rangoon, 1912), 9, 141–50; H. F. Searle, *Burma Gazeteer: The Mandalay District*, vol. A (Rangoon, 1928), 5–7; A. Williamson, *Burma Gazeteer: Shwebo District*, vol. A (Rangoon, 1929), 7; R. S. Wilkie, *Burma Gazeteer: Yamethin District*, vol. A (Rangoon, 1934), 7–11; U Hla, "Synoptic Example and the Rainfall of Central Burma," *JBRS* 37, 2 (1954): 41–49.

[61] See essays by John Walter, Roger Schofield, and Jacques Dupaquier in Walter and Schofield, eds., *Famine, Disease and the Social Order in Early Modern Society* (Cambridge, 1989); Norman G. Owen, "The Paradox of Nineteenth-Century Population Growth in Southeast Asia," *JSEAS* 18 (1987): 45–57.

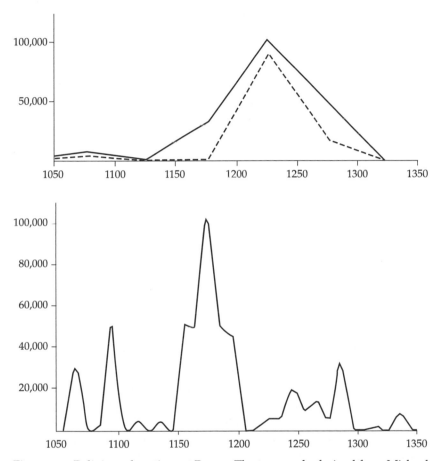

Figure 2.2. Religious donations at Pagan. The top graph, derived from Michael Aung-Thwin, *Pagan: The Origins of Modern Burma* (Honolulu, 1985), 187–88, shows donations to Buddhist institutions of rice land, represented by the solid line and measured in *pe* (here, 1 *pe* = c. 1.75 acres), and of silver, represented by the broken line and measured in *kyats* (1 *kyat* = .566 oz.). The bottom graph, based on a manuscript version of Bob Hudson, Nyein Lwin, and Win Maung, "The Origins of Bagan [sic]," *Asian Perspectives* 40 (2001), Fig. 1, shows cubic meters of building material used in a sample of 89 epigraphically or historically dated buildings at Pagan.

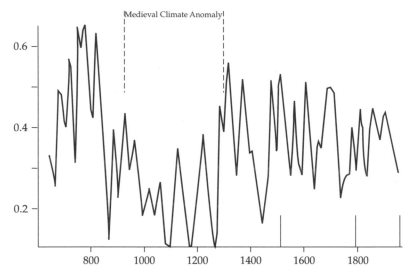

Figure 2.3. Composite time series for recurrence of EL Niño events since 622 c.e. Vertical axis represents events per year. Based on Roger Y. Anderson, "Long-Term Changes in the Frequency of Occurrence of El Niño Events," in Henry Diaz and Vera Markgraf, eds., *El Niño: Historical and Paleoclimatic Aspects of the Southern Oscillation* (Cambridge, 1992), Fig. 9.1, supplemented by Simon Haberle, "Vegetation Response to Climate Variability," in Richard Grove and John Chappell, eds., *El Niño: History and Crisis* (Cambridge, 2000), Fig. 1.

Abu-Lughod has drawn attention[62] – with diverse economic, epidemiological, and cultural benefits for each local society.

I hasten to emphasize that I am far from proposing a climatic interpretation of Burmese or Eurasian history for three reasons. First, although the raw materials for pollen and dendrological studies before c. 1400 probably exist, nowhere in mainland Southeast Asia, so far as I know, has anyone used them.[63] Thus we have no way to quantify long-term changes in rainfall with any precision, and the current argument is frankly provisional. Second, insofar as the other four theories in varying degrees remain plausible, we must look not to monocausal explanations for Pagan's growth, but to exceedingly complex, difficult to chart,

---

[62] Abu-Lughod, *Before Hegemony.*

[63] L. Kealhofer and D. Penny, "A Combined Pollen and Phytolith Record for Fourteen Thousand Years of Vegetation Change in Northeastern Thailand," *Review of Paleobotany and Palynology* 103 (1998): 83–93 offers little information on the second millennium C. E., while Thai dendrochronological studies by Rosanne D'Arrigo, Michael Barbetti, Manas Watanasak, and others start only in 1786.

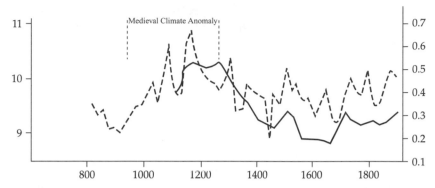

Figure 2.4. Long-term fluctuations in vegetation and temperature. The broken line shows average tree-line widths (20-year means), measured in millimeters (right vertical axis) in bristlecone pines at the upper tree line in the White Mountains, California, where increases in tree-ring width and in atmospheric temperature correlate strongly. Valmore LaMarche, Jr., "Paleoclimatic Inferences from Long Tree-Ring Records," *Science* 183 (1974): p. 1045, Fig. 4. The solid line shows reconstructed temperatures for central England in degrees C. (left vertical axis). Jiacheng Zhang and Thomas Crowley, "Historical Climate Records in China and Reconstruction of Past Climates," *Journal of Climate*, Aug., 1989, p. 847, Fig. 14, citing H. H. Lamb.

chronologically and geographically fluid interactions.[64] For example, even if climate change did aid agriculture, in some contexts new disease immunities or agronomic techniques may have provided a more critical spur. Moreover, as noted, Pagan inscriptions may have understated the role of foreign trade, which itself hardly can be reduced to a function of climate. Third and most obvious, to repeat a caveat from Chapter 1, whereas climate fluctuated or even deteriorated between 1300 and 1800, integration in Burma and across much of Eurasia grew ever more effective. After 1400 and more especially after 1600, weather conditions in northwest Europe, Russia, China, Japan, and mainland Southeast Asia were generally less propitious than before 1300, but these same areas saw sustained demographic growth and progressively higher levels of economic and political coordination. Not only can culture override climate,

[64] Even in early modern Europe, where climate data are available, climate's impact is much debated, precisely because it interacted with a host of social and political factors. See T. M. L. Wigley, M. J. Ingram, and G. Farmer, eds., *Climate and History* (Cambridge, 1981), esp. 3–50, 337–55; and essays by Christian Pfister, Rudolf Brazdil, et al., *CC* 43 (1999): 5–53, 55–109.

but adverse conditions can stimulate creative adaptation[65] – as, indeed, seems to have happened in Burma in the 15th and 16th centuries.

Nonetheless, here and subsequently I do suggest that unusually favorable climatic conditions c. 900/1000–1300 helped to "jump start" Pagan and other Eurasian charter civilizations, creating in each locale a richly innovative substratum – economic, cultural, institutional – on which subsequent generations would draw heavily to resume expansion in less favorable climates. Without minimizing the direct and indirect benefits of commerce, I also suspect that before c. 1500 long-distance trade was far less important, and climate more important, in promoting Eurasian coordination than would be true after 1500, with the spate of Japanese and New World silver, the worldwide diffusion of guns, and an accelerating shift from luxury to bulk goods.

POLITICAL AND CULTURAL INTEGRATION IN THE PAGAN EMPIRE

Let us turn from Pagan's genesis to examine the administrative and cultural systems that underpinned the empire.

Even in the 13th century Pagan exercised no substantive authority in the Chin, Kachin, or Shan hills. Although subject to greater central influence than these uplands, the lowland extremities – Lower Burma, Tenasserim, and the northernmost Irrawaddy valley – also were considered alien, forcibly held territories, as indicated by the generic description *naing-ngan*, "conquered [lands]." By the 13th century, certain towns in Lower Burma were awarded as apanages, while others on the northern frontier had resident governors from princely or ministerial families who were expected to pay regular tribute. But in these outlying areas Pagan seems to have been content with a largely ritual sovereignty. Frontier governors depended on local, rather than central, revenues and selected their own deputies. Nor in such areas is there evidence of royal censuses or direct contact between the Pagan court and headmen beneath the governors.[66]

Effective royal authority therefore was restricted to the dry zone, especially the environs of the capital and the irrigated "hubs" (*hkayaings*)

---

[65] Marks, *Tigers, Rice*, chs. 6–8 makes this point forcefully, as do contributors to the special issue on climatic history, *JIH* 10 (1980).

[66] On Pagan administration, I rely on Aung-Thwin, *Pagan*, ch. 5; Than Tun, *Hkit-haung*, 139–51; Luce, "Economic Life," 287–88; Paul J. Bennett, *Conference Under the Tamarind Tree* (New Haven, 1971), 5–6, 21; Than Tun, personal communications, Nov., 1987.

of Kyaukse and Minbu, the latter usually administered by governors drawn from the royal family. Newly settled dry zone *taik* areas on the west bank of the Irrawaddy were entrusted to men of lesser rank, perhaps from powerful local families, known as "*taik*-leaders" (*taik-thu-gyis*). Like distant frontier administrators, Upper Burma governors and *taik*-leaders lived off apanage grants and local gratuities, but the capital tended to exercise greater influence over these men because communications with the capital were easier, and because they had within their territories large concentrations of royal servicemen (*kyun-daw* or *ahmu-dans*). Such servicemen were responsible to royal agents whose authority crosscut the territorial jurisdictions of governors and *taik*-leaders.

Royal servicemen were one of four broad categories of commoners. Considered to be bondsmen (*kyun*) of the king but assigned to individual headmen and officials who acted as the king's representatives, royal servicemen received land grants from the crown and in return for regular military or labor service, were exempt from most personal taxes. By contrast, *athi* commoners lived not on royal land but on communally-held land and owed no regular royal service. But unlike servicemen, *athis* probably paid substantial head taxes. The third category, private bondsmen (*kyun*), owed labor only to their individual owner and thus lay outside the system of royal obligation. Finally, the aforementioned religious bondsmen (*hpaya-kyun*) resembled private bondsmen insofar as they too were obligated not to the crown but to private patrons, in this case, monasteries and temples.[67]

Although we do not know what proportion fell into each category, the latter two tax-exempt groups clearly constituted a significant segment of the general population. We can appreciate how circumscribed royal power was when we consider the prominence of these groups, as well as the cellular, self-sufficient nature even of service and *athi* units, the apparently rudimentary character of local written administration, the extensive autonomy of gubernatorial families, and most especially, the economic and political autonomy of Buddhist institutions in and around the capital city. Not only were religious bondsmen exempt from royal obligation, but by 1300, temples and monasteries had joined generations of donations with their own purchases to obtain somewhere between one- and two-thirds of Upper Burma's total cultivable land – also

---

[67] Than Tun, *Hkit-haung*, 185–96; idem, "History of Buddhism," ch. 10; Aung-Thwin, *Pagan*, ch. 4.

tax-exempt.[68] Temple wealth financed large-scale agricultural reclamation projects and supported communities of *athi* artisans and laborers
separate from religious bondsmen. In turn, their wealth and spiritual authority let Buddhist institutions sponsor grand rituals which helped to
structure communal life. As Chapter 1 suggested was typical of administrative Pattern A, autonomous religious institutions thus constricted
royal administration and rendered it partially redundant.

Not surprisingly, administrative localism joined with economic au-
tarky, limited literacy, and ongoing migrations to inhibit cultural integration in Pagan's realm, both lateral and vertical.

In the late 11th century ethnic Burmans in the dry zone were still
a privileged but numerically limited population, concentrated in the
hkayaings, uncertain of their cultural credentials, dependent on the cultural tutelage of longer-established, more Indianized peoples. Although
scholars debate the degree to which Burmans were indebted to Mon,
Pyu, and direct Indian models for the development of their own script
and literary language, in inscriptions and perhaps court usages Burmese
did not become dominant until the early – some claim, the late – 12th
century.[69] The growth of Burmese writing, the concomitant decline of
Pyu (and perhaps Mon) culture, new trends in art and architecture, and
the expansion of Burman cultivators from *hkayaing* to *taik* all point to
the construction of Burman cultural hegemony – a process that would
continue into the 19th century and eventually would blanket the entire lowlands. In the late Pagan era as in later centuries, Burmanization
probably drew strength from voluntary assimilation by bilingual peoples eager to identify with the imperial elite. Yet by 1300, this process
was still in an early stage. Significantly perhaps, the first extant Burmese-
language reference to "Burmans" (*myan-ma*) appeared only in 1190, and

[68] Quantification of religious lands poses a variety of technical problems. See Michael
Aung-Thwin, "The Role of *Sasana* Reform in Burmese History," *JAS* 38 (1979): 671–
88; idem, *Pagan*, 186–92; and my "The Political Significance of Religious Wealth in
Burmese History," *JAS* 39 (1980): 753–69. On the economy and administration of religious institutions, Aung-Thwin, *Pagan*, chs. 4, 8; Than Tun, *Hkit-haung*, chs. 15, 16;
idem, "Maha-katha-pa gaing," 81–98.
[69] Sanskrit and Pali influences on Burmese orthography and grammar also were considerable. See Saw Lu, *Pagan hkit myan-ma sa*, 3 vols. (Rangoon, 1996), chs. 2–5; U Sein
Maung Oo, "The Development of Burmese Writing and Monastic Education in Pagan
Period," *Cultural Heritage in Asia, 4: Study on Pagan* (Tokyo, 1989), 138–44; "A History
of the Myanmar Alphabet," in *Myan-ma in-galeik abi-dan*, iv–viii; Than Hswei, ed., *Yaza-
ku-mar mon kyauk-sa lei-la chet* (Rangoon, 1971); Luce, "Peoples of Burma," 54, 62–67;
Strachan, *Imperial Pagan*, 79, 83, dating Burmanization to the so-called Middle Period,
c. 1120–1170; and Aung-Thwin's views cited in n. 4 *supra*.

the first reference to Upper Burma as "the land of the Burmans" (*myan-ma pyei*) in 1235.[70] By the 13th century, if not earlier, not only were Mons dominant in Lower Burma, but many could be found at Pagan and in the Burman heartland of Kyaukse. In other areas in and around the dry zone that eventually would become solidly Burman, inscriptions referred to a variety of ethnic groups (Thets, Kadus, Sgaws, Kanyans, Palaungs, Was, and Shans). In short, the lowlands remained an ethnic mosaic. As for the highland perimeter, where Shan immigrants were displacing Austroasiatic-speakers, despairing perhaps of precise classification, inscriptions referred simply to "hill-peoples" (*taung-thus*).[71]

At the great capital itself and some provincial centers, Buddhist temples supported an increasingly sophisticated Pali scholarship, part of an international tradition, which specialized in grammar and philosophical-psychological (*abhidhamma*) studies and which reportedly won the admiration of Sinhalese experts. Besides religious texts, Pagan's monks read works in a variety of languages on prosody, phonology, grammar, astrology, alchemy, and medicine, and developed an independent school of legal studies. Most students, and probably the leading monks and nuns, came from aristocratic families.[72]

Erudite and increasingly Theravadin though such scholarship was, the religion of Pagan also was fluid, syncretic, and by later definitions (though obviously not by those of Pagan people themselves) unorthodox. Now I hasten to emphasize that through the 19th century, indeed to the present, Burmese Buddhism has remained an amalgam of brahmanic, animist, Theravada, and (some argue) Mahayana practices.[73] In the Pagan era, however, Tantric, Saivite, and Vaishnava elements enjoyed greater elite influence than they would later do, reflecting both the relative immaturity of early Burmese literary culture and its indiscriminate receptivity to non-Burman traditions. In this period "heretical" did not mean non-Buddhist, merely unfaithful to one's own scriptures,

---

[70] Luce, "Peoples of Burma," 53.

[71] On ethnic patterns, Luce, "Peoples of Burma," 52–81; idem, *Phases*, I, chs. 1–7; Frasch, "Coastal Peripheries," 66–67; and n. 4 *supra*.

[72] The definitive study of Pagan scholarship is Saw Lu, *Pagan hkit* , see esp. II, 220–34, and III, 467–522. See too Mabel Haynes Bode, *The Pali Literature of Burma* (London, 1909), ch. 2; Than Tun, *Hkit-haung*, ch. 17; *SHDMA*, 1–18; Pe Maung Tin, *Myan-ma sa-pei-thamaing* (Rangoon, 1955), ch. 1; Pannassami, *Sasanavamsa*, tr. B.C. Law (London, 1952), 82.

[73] Melford E. Spiro, *Burmese Supernaturalism* (Englewood Cliffs, NJ, 1967); idem, *Buddhism and Society* (New York, 1970); Terence P. Day, *Great Tradition and Little Tradition in Theravada Buddhist Studies* (Lewiston, NY, 1988).

whether brahmanic, Buddhist, or whatever.[74] Royal religion also accommodated – or more accurately, recontextualized – powerful animist traditions, as shown in official spirit (*nat*) propitiation ceremonies and in the court's sponsorship of an elaborate *nat* pantheon that sought to assimilate local deities and deceased men of prowess to a more unified cultus.[75] The custom of propitiating *nats*, including spirits associated with trees, great rocks, fields, and waterfalls, Burman migrants probably brought from the hills, but equivalent practices flourished among their non-Burman neighbors, and in fact the Burmese may have derived the concept of an official pantheon from Mon tradition.[76] Likewise, the early Pagan court worshipped snakes (*nagas*), venerated in pre-Buddhist times.[77]

More indicative of Buddhism's peculiarities in this period were the so-called Forest Dweller monks, who enjoyed wide influence at the late Pagan court. Contemporary inscriptions show that Forest-Dwellers ate evening meals and presided over public ceremonies where they drank liquor and where cattle and other animals were sacrificed – activities scandalous by Burmese norms of the 18th and 19th centuries. Plausible sources of a later date claim that some members of the Forest Dwellers also enjoyed a form of *jus prima noctis*. Although Tantrism may have exerted some influence, at a deeper level public intoxication, extravagant feasting, and ritualized sexuality probably reflected an assumption found throughout Southeast Asia that entry into a liminal condition, at the interface between different states of consciousness, could somehow regenerate life and increase one's spiritual potency. Ceremonial animal slaughter and alcohol consumption long antedated the Burmans' arrival (cattle sacrifice, for example, had been characteristic of the Pyus) and continued in remote parts of mainland as well as island Southeast Asia until recent times.[78] Likewise, the greater prominence of nuns and

[74] Than Tun, "Religion in Burma," 47–69, esp. 48, plus Nihar-Ranjan Ray, *Sanskrit Buddhism in Burma* (Amsterdam, 1936); Luce, *Old Burma*, I, 184–228 and *passim*; Aung-Thwin, *Pagan*, ch. 2; Strachan, *Imperial Pagan*, 10, 25–34, and *passim*.
[75] Aung-Thwin, *Pagan*, 52–56, 192–93; E. M. Mendelson, "Observations on a Tour in the Region of Mount Popa, Central Burma," *France-Asie* 179 (1963): 784–85; Spiro, *Burmese Supernaturalism*, 131–38, 217–29; Richard Temple, *The Thirty Seven Nats* (London, 1906).
[76] H. L. Shorto, "The *Dewatau Sotapan*: A Mon Prototype of the 37 Nats," *BSOAS* 30 (1967): 127–41, esp. 140; idem, "The 32 Myos in the Medieval Mon Kingdom," *BSOAS* 26 (1963): 590.
[77] Than Tun, "Religion in Burma," 49, 69. Cf. Luce, *Old Burma*, I, 13, 18.
[78] Charles Duroiselle, "The Ari of Burma and Tantric Buddhism," *Annual Report of the Archaeological Survey of India, 1915–16*, 79–93, first investigated this sect. Their

female students in the Pagan era than in later periods may point to pre-Buddhist notions of female autonomy.[79]

Scholars have always assumed that popular Buddhism was the same in the Pagan period as in the 19th century, but given the nature of elite observance, popular practices must have been yet more syncretic. In the 19th century a network of monasteries in every village used Burmese-language manuscripts, as well as *nissaya* translations from Pali to Burmese, to provide youths from diverse backgrounds with basic Buddhist literacy. This was a reciprocal exchange: monks relied on villagers for their daily food, while villagers depended on monks for schooling, sermons, and an opportunity to gain merit by giving alms and inducting their young men into the community of monks, the *sangha*.[80] Such arrangements, we shall find, produced male literacy rates of over 50 percent and remarkable levels of textual Buddhist knowledge on the village level.

But in the Pagan period, key 19th-century elements were not yet in place. The vast landed holdings of major sects meant that they had no need for daily alms, which in turn may have inhibited close interaction with villagers. The Forest Dwellers, for example, lived in great self-sufficient establishments which fed hundreds of monks from their own lands.[81] Although some prosperous, well-situated villages must have had monasteries, most monasteries and libraries probably were located in Pagan and the chief towns, or else in wilderness areas. The notion that the peasantry remained marginal to the system of public merit accumulation is consistent with an analysis of recorded religious gifts between 1100 and 1250: at most 9 percent of the donors were peasants and rural headmen, the other 91 percent being royalty, aristocrats,

---

memory had been preserved in 18th-century chronicles, *UK*, I, 181–82; but Than Tun, "History of Buddhism," chs. 7, 8; idem, "Religion in Burma," idem, "Mahakassapa-gaing" provided the first inscription-based analysis. On Indian, pre-Burman, and later Southeast Asian analogues to animal sacrifice and other Forest Dweller practices, see John Strong, *The Legend and Cult of Upagupta* (Princeton 1992), 70, 176–77, 330 n. 30; Reid, *Age of Commerce*, I, 39–40; Stargardt, *Ancient Pyu*, 187–88, 297, 301–304; *UK*, II, 58; Luce, "Economic Life," 324 n. 94; M. L. Manich, *History of Laos* (Bangkok, 1967), 118.

[79] Saw Lu, *Pagan hkit*, 227; Than Tun, "Religion in Burma," 47, 60.

[80] On 19th century practices, Shway Yoe, *The Burman: His Life and Notions* (London, 1910), chs. 2, 3. On texts, John Okell, "Nissaya Burmese," *Lingua* 15 (1965): 186–227.

[81] Than Tun, "Religion in Burma," 67–68; idem, "Maha-katha-pa gaing," 81–98; idem, personal communication, 1987. Cf. a comparable economic insularity in early medieval Sinhalese monasticism, Gunawardana, *Robe and Plough*, chs. 3, 4.

military officers, and temple-dependent artisans.[82] Moreover, the relative novelty of Burmese writing – the language was first written only in the 11th century and, as noted, became dominant at court only in the 12th century – meant that for much of the Pagan period written materials needed to produce large numbers of literate monks and students in the villages simply did not exist. In the words of Than Tun, Burma's leading epigrapher, even in the 13th century "the art of writing was then still in its infancy with the Burmans."[83] Manuscripts were rare and extremely costly: as late as 1273 a complete set of the *Tipitaka* cost 3000 *kyats* of silver, enough to buy 5250 acres of riceland, whereas a slave cost only 20 *kyats* and a large monastery, 750.[84] Literacy in Burmese, not to mention Pali, must have been the effective monopoly of the aristocracy and their monastic peers, helping to ensure that most commoners retained nontextual, essentially local religious identities tied to the worship of particular *nat* spirits. To be sure, peasant horizons would have been broadened by visual contact with Buddhist paintings and plaques at the great temples, as well as by pageants, sermons, and folkloric versions of the Jataka stories of the Buddha's life.[85] Notions of *karma* and some Indic terminology must have been almost universal, along with a conviction that a potent leader could confer religious merit on his followers. Yet, to judge from 14th-century patterns, sacrifices to *nat* spirits, mediated by shamans, were still a central village ritual. As elsewhere in Southeast Asia, homosexuals or transvestites (who already inhabited two "incompatible" realms) as well as women provided a shamanic bridge from the human world to that of the spirits.[86] Note too that local illiteracy probably militated against the sort of detailed village censuses and legal rulings that became a hallmark of post-1550 administration.

In sum, while Pagan Buddhism at all social levels was promiscuously assimilative, it also appears to have been divided into a textual component accessible to capital-based elites and a largely pre-textual, oral, popular religion. These patterns have some bearing on an obvious

[82] In terms of cash value, as opposed to numbers, peasant contributions were far less than 9 percent. Aung-Thwin, "State and Society," 53–57. Of course, this does not preclude the possibility that villagers gave daily alms, but it suggests that the chief public rituals of merit accumulation were far more socially exclusive than in the Kon-baung or contemporary eras.
[83] Than Tun, "Religion in Burma," 55.
[84] Than Tun, "Religion in Burma," 55–56; idem, *Hkit-haung*, 183, which says 2000 *kyats*. Cf. Saw Lu, *Pagan hkit*, 231.
[85] Cf. Than Tun, "Religion in Burma," 57.
[86] Cf. Leonard Andaya, "The Bissu: Study of a Third Gender in Indonesia" (ms).

conundrum: If administration was as superficial and cultural integration as limited as I have suggested, why did the empire survive as long as it did? Even a minimalist definition must concede that as a valley-wide polity, Pagan lasted over two centuries, from 1057 to the 1280s, longer than any subsequent, ostensibly more powerful dynasty. Much the same longevity, I hasten to add, characterized other Eurasian charter polities, including Angkor, the Frankish kingdom, and Heian Japan. At Pagan at least, such longevity seems to have had three roots. First, by inhibiting the growth of intermediate social groups and new provincial powers, the concentration of Indic religious knowledge, literacy, and other technical skills in a small, capital-based aristocracy, while not preventing intra-elite factionalism, may have shielded the elite as a whole and its chief institutions against outside challenges. This seems to have been especially true during the early and middle Pagan period. Second and related to the previous point, the system of extensive landholding by powerful Pagan-based temples, and the concentration of reclamation in the hands of monastic and lay elites who were closely connected to one another by family and court ties, may have inhibited the rise of insurgent social or economic groups. Not until the 14th–16th centuries, we shall find, did the spread of textually-based Buddhism join with new commercial options, new landholding patterns, and Shan incursions to support provincial and social challenges to charter institutions. Third and most certain, because vast empty tracts still separated charter polities in mainland Southeast Asia, external threats were far less frequent and less sustained than in later periods. Between Nanzhao-Burman intrusions in the 9th century and Mongol-Shan challenges in the late 13th century, Upper Burma faced no credible external enemy.

THE COLLAPSE OF PAGAN AND UPPER BURMAN HEGEMONY, 13TH–14TH CENTURIES

In the late 1200s Pagan's insulation ended, and the empire began to unravel. Mongol invasions between 1277 and 1301 traditionally are said to have been responsible for Pagan's disintegration, but in fact the process was more prolonged and agonized. A revolt at Martaban in Lower Burma that preceded the main Mongol incursion provided one of the first signs of disorder, while recent research questions whether Mongol armies ever reached Pagan itself. Even if they did, the damage they inflicted was probably minimal. Arguably the most devastating political – as well as demographic and cultural – shock to Upper Burma was not the Mongol incursions at all, but highly destructive Shan invasions in 1359–1368.[87]

How, then, shall we explain this decay of Upper Burman power, which we shall find was part of a 14th-century crisis that spread across mainland Southeast Asia? Again we are obliged to consider several theories, by no means mutually exclusive, although these are less speculative than those for Pagan's rise.

The most carefully considered, well-documented explanation, that of Aung-Thwin, argues that Pagan's collapse derived from the continuous growth of tax-free religious wealth. At first, we have seen, such endowments strengthened the throne by helping to tie down an exiguous population and by stimulating frontier colonization, but by the mid-13th century the Upper Burma heartland over which Pagan exercised most effective political control had run out of easily reclaimed fresh irrigable tracts. The rate of reclamation therefore began to fall behind the rate at which such lands were dedicated to the monkhood. Their fervent desire to accumulate religious merit for happy reincarnations made it impossible for Pagan kings to halt entirely their own or other courtiers' donations. In the name of Buddhist purification, the throne did attempt periodically to purge the monkhood and in so doing to regain control over lands that it claimed had been "improperly" dedicated in the past. Although some of these confiscations proved successful and although the decay of old religious foundations may have recycled additional acreages into the taxable lay sector, ultimately royal economic power failed before its own soteriological imperatives, before hydrological limits on the extension of dry zone cultivation, and before the political might of local monasteries.[88] By 1280, as noted, between one- and two-thirds of Upper Burma's cultivable land had been alienated to the religion. Thus, the throne lost resources needed to retain the loyalty of courtiers and military servicemen, inviting a vicious circle of internal disorders and external challenges by Mons, Mongols, and Shans which culminated in the Shan raids of 1359–1368. Elsewhere I have suggested that ministers, exploiting succession disputes, accumulated their own lands and retainers at the expense of the throne in a movement that ran parallel to, but independent of, religious accumulation.[89]

---

[87] Bennett, *Conference Under the Tamarind Tree*, 3–53; Strachan, *Imperial Pagan*, 94; Hudson, "Origins of Bagan"; and esp. Aung-Thwin, *Myth and History*, chs. 3–4.
[88] Aung-Thwin, *Pagan*, ch. 9.
[89] Lieberman, "Religious Wealth," 756–57.

If my argument for Eurasian climatic correlations is valid, markedly drier weather during the late 13th and much of the 14th centuries – corresponding to the end of the Medieval Climate Anomaly and to well-documented droughts in Dong Kinh, Kengtung, northern Thailand, and South India – compounded Upper Burma's problems by lowering yields on established cultivation, by withdrawing from cultivation marginal *taik* lands, many newly opened; and by helping to shift the center of gravity to better watered districts farther south.[90] Besides threatening peasant living standards, such changes may have placed additional pressures on royal (as well as aristocratic and monastic) income, intensifying factionalism at court and perhaps in the countryside. In essence, then, I suggest that after 200–300 years of sustained demographic/agricultural expansion, Upper Burma society faced severe pressures whose origins were simultaneously institutional and ecological. Although Southeast Asia has long been regarded, justifiably, as a people-scarce, land-rich environment, in this context instability reflected less a shortage of people than of quality arable land. (We will find similar pressures in Dong Kinh, Angkor, and 19th-century Upper Burma.)

There was more to Upper Burma's decline than this, however. The waxing power of the coast – which led to the creation of an independent Mon kingdom by 1300[91] and which from the late 14th to 16th centuries allowed Lower Burma openly to challenge the north for regional supremacy – drew strength from another sustained economic trend, namely growing maritime trade. Insofar as Eurasian commerce and agricultural overextension in Upper Burma both benefited from generalized population growth to c. 1300, we may be dealing with two aspects of a more basic phenomenon. Notwithstanding late Song monetary difficulties and demographic losses that attended the Song-Yuan transition, generally favorable Yuan (1279–1368) and early Ming (1368–1644) policies fostered commercial ties that aided Burma indirectly via the Malay peninsula. Likewise, in southern India turmoil associated

---

[90] See *supra* n. 54. In Burma, I 686, *PPA*, 325, refers to a severe 1375 famine around Toungoo, but it is unclear to what extent this reflected drought. According to Godley, "Flood Regimes," 140–42 desiccation in the late 13th and 14th centuries represented a major change to regional climate. Fukui, "An Overview," in idem, *Dry Areas*, 7; and idem, "Historical Cities," 27–37 suggests that desiccation and overpopulation c. 1200–1400 also contributed to the collapse of charter states in other ecologically fragile dry zone areas, including Angkor (see *infra*, Ch. 3), east/central Java, and northern Sri Lanka.

[91] *UK*, I, 319–20 dates the successful revolt of Martaban and Pegu to c. 1287. *SMK*, III, 196–97 claims that Dala, south of Pegu, was recaptured in 1296, but this was at best temporary.

with the conquests of the Delhi sultanate failed to destroy lucrative eastern trading networks that had developed in the 12th and early 13th centuries.[92] An increase in Pagan's foreign commerce, both indirectly with the South China sea via the peninsula and directly with the Bay of Bengal, may have led to more frequent coastal apanage grants in the 13th century. But with Pagan and its heir Ava facing their own problems some four hundred miles upriver, coastal cities like Martaban and Pegu which depended for their livelihood on maritime exchange proved to be the ultimate beneficiaries. During the 14th and 15th centuries growing east–west exchange also helped to shift the political center of gravity from the interior to the coast in the central mainland and in Java.

Finally, Shan incursions from the eastern plateau into Upper Burma had their own dynamic. Throughout the western and central mainland, the growing political power during the 1200s and 1300s of various Tai populations (a category both social and linguistic), of whom the Tai-Shans were a great western branch, exemplifies the process described by Michael Mann whereby civilizations unwittingly upgrade the "power capacities" of "barbarian" neighbors by transmitting organizational, military, and religious techniques.[93] In general, those Tai populations most exposed to Pagan and Angkorian administrative and religious culture proved best able to profit from the crisis of the charter states.[94] Burman entry into the lowlands in the 9th century seems to have been

---

[92] On Chinese and Indian trade, nn. 15, 16 *supra*. Christie's articles in n. 15 *supra* argue that disturbances in China contributed to a maritime depression in SE Asia c. 1250–1400, a view consistent with population trends in Lingnan as recorded by Marks, *Tigers, Rice*, 65, 85 and, more tangentially, with discussion of late Song policy in Richard von Glahn, *Fountain of Fortune* (Berkeley, 1996), 55. Yet while accepting that political transitions could be commercially dislocative and that Chinese trade networks periodically shifted focus, recent archeological studies from Malaya and Indonesia, studies of Chinese records from south Fujian, and other local accounts suggest that in much of SE Asia trade with India and China remained vigorous, even expanded 1250–1400. See Miksic, "Archaeology Ceramics"; Jacq-Hergoualc'h, "Merqui-Tenasserim Region," 88; Roderich Ptak, "From Quanzhou to the Sulu Zone and Beyond," *JSEAS* 29 (1998): 269–94; Schottenhammer, "Maritime Trade," 286–87; So, *Prosperity, Region*, 117–27; Chou Ta-Kuan, *The Customs of Cambodia* (Bangkok, 1993), 41–43, 69; Charnvit Kasetsiri, *The Rise of Ayudhya* (Kuala Lumpur, 1976), 79–81.

[93] Michael Mann, *The Sources of Social Power*, vol. 1 (Cambridge, 1986), 539. The "Tai" linguistic group is far broader than its "Thai" (also called "Siamese Tai") sub-category. See Frank Lebar et al., *Ethnic Groups of Mainland Southeast Asia* (New Haven, 1964), pt. 3.

[94] On early Tai movements and culture, Wyatt, *Thailand*, 24–60; idem, "Relics, Oaths," esp. 38–51; Luce, "The Early Syam in Burma's History," *JSS* 46, 2 (1958): 123–214; O'Connor, "Agricultural Change," 982–83; Amphay Dore, "Aux Sources de la civilisation Lao" (Ph.D. diss., Metz, 1987), chs. 6, 10, 11, esp. pp. 169–85; Martin Stuart-Fox, *The Lao Kingdom of Lan Xang* (Bangkok, 1998), chs. 1–2.

an earlier version of the same story. Although Tai migrations south and west from the China–Vietnam border area may have started as early as the late first millennium, the increased activity of Tai warriors during the 13th century responded to: a) the pull of wealthy valleys, as the great empires of Pagan and Angkor weakened internally; b) the push out of what is now southern Yunnan, northern Burma, Vietnam, and Laos, responding perhaps to local demographic pressures, and more particularly to the 1253 Mongol conquest of the Nanzhao kingdom in Yunnan, which released some Tai rulers from Nanzhao's control; c) the related post-1270 consolidation in the Shweli valley of the Tai kingdom of Mong Mao, which launched some of the most devastating 14th-century incursions into Upper Burma.[95] The political significance of Tai intervention becomes obvious if we contrast the collapse of the Upper Burman state and of Angkor, both of which bore the brunt of Tai movements, with far milder 14th-century upheavals in the eastern mainland in Dai Viet and Champa, both of which largely escaped such inroads.

Ironically, the intensification of the same factors as had destroyed Pagan – uncontrolled monastic autonomy, maritime expansion, and Shan incursions – would facilitate reunification in the 16th century.

THE POST-CHARTER ERA OF FRAGMENTATION, c. 1300–1550: POLITICAL ASPECTS

For two and a half centuries after Pagan's decline, between c. 1300 and 1558, the western mainland remained divided into four more or less distinct geopolitical-cum-ethnic zones which ignored, brutalized, and allied with one another in bewildering fashion. At the same time each zone remained internally fragmented (see Figures 1.4 and 1.5).[96]

a) The **Shan realm** refers to a series of upland valleys northwest, north, and east of the Irrawaddy basin. Because they were suitable for wet-rice agriculture, these valleys eventually proved capable of supporting Buddhist monasticism and relatively complex political structures.

---

[95] Geoff Wade, "The Bai Yi Zhuan: A Chinese Account of a Tai Society in the 14th Century" (Paper presented at the 14th Conference of the IAHA, Bangkok, 1996); Sun Laichen, "Yuan's Invasion of Pagan in a Dai (Tai) Text" (ms).

[96] The earliest detailed chronicle account of the era 1300–1558 is *UK*, I, 348–457 and II, 1–318. On the chronicle's utility, see my "How Reliable Is U Kala's Burmese Chronicle? Some New Comparisons," *JSEAS* 17 (1986): 236–55. Many chronicle entries can be checked against the six elephant volumes indexed in Chas. Duroiselle, ed., *A List of Inscriptions Found in Upper Burma*, I (Rangoon, 1921), and against *SMK*, III (s. 622–699), IV (s. 700–797), and V (s. 800–998).

Upland Shan valleys were thus distinct from the extensive intervening hill tracts that sustained only thin, eternally illiterate, animist populations of swidden cultivators (ancestors of modern Chins, Kachins,
Karens, and so forth).

Although reliable information on early Tai movements is scanty, by
the 12th century, possibly even the 11th, Shan migrants from the east had
taken control of the chief valleys in what are now known as the Shan hills,
where their agricultural/irrigation skills apparently gave them an advantage over older Austroasiatic-speaking inhabitants.[97] As it evolved,
the typical Shan kingdom became a loose federation of valleys, each containing anywhere from several hundred to several thousand cultivators,
separated from one another by inhospitable terrain, but all acknowledging the suzerainty of the ruler in the largest and most powerful basin.

From an early date Shan elites sought to localize Burman culture,
patronizing Buddhist monks and adopting alphabets from Burmese, or
in some cases Mon, prototypes. Compared to their Upper Burma counterparts, monastic establishments in these nominally Buddhist valleys
remained economically and politically impotent. The limited authority of Buddhist establishments constituted a chief difference between
administrative Pattern A, which was characteristic of Pagan and its immediate heirs, and Pattern B, which we shall find not only in the Shan
hills, but on the outer fringes of the dry zone and in Lower Burma
(see Chapter 1 on these ideal administrative types). Yet, despite the potential advantage that monastic subservience offered central authority,
wretched communications throughout the Shan hills ensured that royal
power remained more tenuous than in the lowlands. Gubernatorial rotation was rare, and offices quickly became hereditary. Royal servicemen
were less common than in Upper Burma, and taxes more irregular. Apart
from ritual claims and punitive expeditions, each Shan federation was
held together by family and patronage ties, cemented by gifts of women
to the overlord's harem. But given the fluidity of such bonds, it is hardly
surprising that revolts and succession disputes were endemic.[98]

Shan warriors soon became a mainstay of lowland armies, and Shan
blood flowed in the veins of many a courtier at the chief post-Pagan
Burman capital of Ava. Thus whereas for most of the Pagan period the

[97] Variously said to include Lawas, Mons, and "Noras."
[98] On early Shan government, *ZOK* 22, 23, 31, 36, 37, 89; *Shei-haung hkit myan-ma naing-
ngan myo-ywa ne pe thamaing* (Rangoon, n.d.), 47; and Shan state histories *in GUBSS*,
pt. II.

northern uplands had been marginal to upper Burma affairs, now these two realms became closely joined. The most critical periods of Shan involvement were the mid-14th century, when Shan raids precipitated the founding of Ava; and the first half of the 16th century, when Shans from Mohnyin and Hsipaw dominated the north. Meanwhile, Shan migrants began to settle hitherto Burman-dominated districts on the northern and eastern fringes of the dry zone.[99] As we shall see, Shans profited not only from lowland debility, but from growing Chinese overland trade and the transfer of Ming military technology. During this same period, c. 1350–1550, similar dynamics favored Tai-speaking principalities throughout the northern mainland, including present-day Laos and Thailand.

In contrast to those 9th-century Burman newcomers who supplanted the Pyus, Shans never seriously threatened Burman cultural supremacy. With a few dramatic exceptions (like the 16th-century king Tho-han-bwa, who massacred monks), the Shans continued to emulate Burman Buddhist culture, and in fact Avan courtiers and cultivators of Shan ancestry often "became Burman" after one or two generations. Even the 16th century saw no systematic Shan settlement of the Upper Burma heartland, not least because Shan disunity precluded large-scale efforts.[100] Moreover, although Mohnyin Shans conquered Ava in 1527, by that time the principal Burman stronghold had shifted to Toungoo, beyond direct Shan influence.

b) **Upper Burma**, that is to say, the lowland dry zone extending to just below the 19th parallel, remained the most populous area within the western mainland. Despite post-Pagan disorders and lower rainfall, more easily cultivated soils and less widespread malaria continued to support a larger population – two to three times larger, according to the earliest extant censuses – than in Lower Burma.[101] Upper Burma retained a comparable demographic superiority over the Shan uplands.

In the heart of the dry zone, near the juncture of the Irrawaddy with the famed granary of Kyaukse, **Ava** was founded in 1365. As the strongest interior polity and principal heir to Pagan's territorial and

---

[99] On Shan incursions, which are recorded for 1359–1368, 1375, 1410–11, 1426–27, 1501–1506, 1517, and 1523–27, see, e.g., the following inscriptions: I 642, *PPA*, 321; I 679, *B* II, 921; I 682, *A*, 281–84; I 686, *PPA*, 326; I 691, *B* I, 357–58; I 774, *A*, 336; plus *ROB*, II, xiii; List 91, #11; List 78, #2; *UK*, I, 349 ff.; II, 1–144 *passim*; Sun Laichen, "Ming-Southeast Asian Overland Interactions, 1368–1644" (Univ. of Michigan Ph.D. diss., 2000), 34–44, 224–42.

[100] For a similar emphasis on the limited nature of Shan influence, see Aung-Thwin, *Myth and History*, ch. 5.

[101] See 1581 census at *ZOK*, 41.

administrative system, Ava remained the preeminent western mainland state until the late 1400s. Yet if Ava reincarnated Pagan, this poor infant entered the world sickly. Not only were Shan irruptions increasingly worrisome, not only did Ava fail to profit from overland trade with China as substantially as some interior Shan states, but Lower Burma's independence deprived her of growing maritime revenues. During bitter north–south wars from 1385 to 1425, Ava repeatedly attacked the ports of Bassein and Dala. In 1442 an Avan ruler claimed suzerainty over Lower Burma and Arakan. In truth, Ava's failure to hold the coast advertised her weakness vis-a-vis Pagan.[102]

Ava continued to suffer as well from tax-free religious estates which by 1300, we have seen, already had absorbed one- to two-thirds of Upper Burma's cultivable land. During the disorders of the 14th century some glebe lands were recycled into the taxable sector. Avan rulers required aristocrats to buy royal permission for further gifts, while in imitation of their Pagan predecessors, kings also tried to reclaim "improper" past donations.[103] Yet land alienation continued, even if donations were less frequent and smaller on average than in the Pagan period.[104] As their holdings grew through gifts, purchases, and reclamation, and as secular authority faltered, Forest Dweller abbots (*sangha-rajas*) assumed wider administrative, even military, responsibilities. Whereas in the late Pagan period such sects had been challenged by Sinhalese-oriented monks, now they had no true rivals.[105]

In part because agricultural opportunities in the heartland were constricted, in part because Shan pressures encouraged southward Burman migration, and in part perhaps because desiccation favored wetter districts along the fringes of the dry zone, the late Pagan movement of

---

[102] See 1442 boast at I 938, *B* I, 225–26; and a similar 1400 claim at *SMK*, IV, 220. On the north-south wars, *UK*, I, 389–457, and II, 1–88 *passim;* and "Ya-za-di-ya-za ayei-daw-bon" in Hsaya-gyi U Bi et al., eds., *Ayei-daw-bon nga-zaung-dwe* (Rangoon, n.d.).

[103] On payments to the crown, see, e.g., I 630, *UB* II, 146; I 545, *B* II, 744; I 600, *PPA*, 22; I695, *B* I, 372; I 820, *B* I, 213; I 934, *PPA*, 81; I 983, *UB* I, 118; I 981, *A*, 408. On inquests, Than Tun, "History of Burma, A.D.1300–1400," *JBRS* 42 (1959), 124; *MMOS*, V, 35–36.

[104] On Ava-era dedications, Duroiselle, *List of Inscriptions; SMK*, III and IV. My characterization of post-Ava patterns agrees with Aung-Thwin, *Myth and History*, 134, 198–99 n. 51; idem, "The Myth of the 'Three Shan Brothers' and the Ava Period in Burmese History," *JAS* 55 (1995): 892.

[105] On the Forest Dwellers, Than Tun, "Religion in Burma"; idem, "Maha-katha-pa gaing"; idem, personal communications, Dec., 1987; Tin Hla Thaw, "History of Burma, A.D. 1400–1500," *JBRS* 42 (1959): 135–52; and such inscriptions as I 695, *B* I, 372; I 718, *A*, 314; I 796, *A*, 279; I 840, *UB* I, 75–79; I 845, *PPA*, 348; I 889, *B* I, 211–12; I 939, *UB* I, 93; I 944, *A*, 399; I 1066, *UB* II, 158; I 1053, *PPA*, 351; I 1073, *A*, 364–65.

reclamation resumed in southern areas like Taungdwingyi, **Prome**, and **Toungoo**, which at first were dependencies of Ava. As was typical of administrative Patterns A and B, the autonomy of outlying governors ensured that any augmentation of provincial manpower aided the system as a whole less than the governors themselves. In 15th-century inscriptions, Upper Burma governors honored the Avan overlord (*min-gyi* or *eka-yaza-min-gyi*), to whom tribute and levies were due and to whom disputes might be referred. Simultaneously, however, and with no sense of contradiction, provincial rulers presented themselves as sovereigns (*min* or *min-gyi*), entitled to hereditary succession, who had queens and palaces of their own and who engaged in acts of religious patronage suitable to royalty.[106] By the mid-15th century not only had Prome and Toungoo become fully independent, but in 1503 Ava lost the Kyaukse granary to Toungoo, then arguably the strongest dry zone kingdom. The fact that Ava, Prome, and Toungoo all were predominantly Burman and all used Burmese for administration provided few practical incentives to cooperate. In each realm monastic ideologues fired local patriotism by stressing the antiquity of pagodas, the noble ancestry of dynasts, and local links to Gotama Buddha and the paradigmatic Buddhist ruler Asoka.[107] Thus new realms devolved from Ava, even as Ava had devolved from Pagan.

Like the Shan kingdoms, these domains on the southern fringe of the dry zone enjoyed what Alexander Gerschenkron in an economic context termed the "advantage of backwardness."[108] Lying outside the classical heartland where land had been alienated to religion for 300–400 years, these new domains faced fewer monastic claims to tax exemption and thus were typical of Pattern B administration. Possibly too they began to experiment with monetary, rather than landed donations, in an effort to forestall the problems of resource depletion faced by their Pagan predecessors and Avan contemporaries. Compared to Ava, Prome and

---

[106] For typical inscriptions by satellite rulers, I 657, *UB* II, 251; I 661, *B* II, 715; I 671, *UB* II, 155–56; I 679, *B* II, 921; I 718, *A*, 312; I 934, *PPA*, 78; I 935, *PPA*, 91; I 1065, *UB* II, 160–61; I 1066, *UB* II, 158–59; *List* 75, #3, NL 2240, *hkaw* recto. Avan kings often used the same terms in referring to vassals as did vassals themselves: I 943, *UB* I, 103. See too 1400–1550 appointments at *UK*, II, 1–252; and Toe Hla, "In-wa hkit ok-chok-yei," *Tegga-tho panya padei-tha sa-zaung* 14 (1980): 21–35.

[107] Previous note, plus local histories at *UK*, II, 92–168 *passim*, 203 ff.; *List* 91, #11, NL 62/2339; *List* 78, #2, NL 2241; *List* 85, #6; Tin, *Myan-ma sa-pei*, 92–97; Wilkie, *Yamethin Gazeteer*, 29–31; *Gazeteer of Burma*, 2 vols. (1880, rpt., Delhi, 1983), II, 817.

[108] Alexander Gerschenkron, *Economic Backwardness in Historical Perspective: A Book of Essays* (Cambridge, MA, 1962).

Toungoo also were more effectively insulated from Shan raids. Yet despite these assets, each of these newly independent realms maintained a fissiparous system of autonomous governors similar to that of Ava and Pagan. So too, references to numerous and powerful *athi* leaders suggest that throughout the lowlands the percentage of royal servicemen (*ahmu-dans*) remained modest by later standards, probably below 20 percent. As owners of communal rather than revocable royal lands, *athis* depended less directly on royal patronage than did royal servicemen.[109]

c) **Arakan** was the third chief geopolitical zone. Although Arakan's population spoke a dialect of Burmese and its primary cultural tradition was Theravada Buddhist, the region's long coastline and the barrier to east-west communications posed by the Arakan Mountains encouraged a maritime orientation, much influenced by Bengali Islam, very different from that of Upper Burma. From about 1430, following the failure of Mon and Avan interventions, a new polity centered at Mrauk-u began to assert an unprecedented, though still fragile authority over the Arakanese littoral, with its many islands and riverine pockets. Like contemporary kingdoms to the east, the new Mrauk-u dynasty established what was basically a Pattern B administration in which outlying leaders, often relatives of the high king, imitated the central court's system of queens, ministers, and regalia. The strengths of the reorganized kingdom were several: direct control of the two chief agricultural basins, those of the Kaladan and Lemro; growing revenues from entrepot trade and from the export of rice, slaves, and elephants; lavish use of Muslim and eventually Portuguese firearms and mercenaries; and an imaginative cultural policy that saw Mrauk-u rulers patronize Buddhist shrines while adopting trappings of Muslim sultanship. As early as 1454 Ava is said to have acknowledged Mrauk-u as its equal. In the late 1400s and early 1500s, an increasingly confident Mrauk-u launched campaigns east over the mountains against Prome and west into Bengal, where Chittagong, the chief port of the eastern Bay, fell to Arakanese forces in 1539–1540. At the close of the 16th century Arakan helped to destroy

[109] On the distinction between *athis* and *ahmu-dans*, see *supra* n. 67. In the 17th century we shall find *ahmu-dan* concentrations around the capital approaching 50 percent. Typical pre-1500 *athi* references are I 566, *UB* II, 247–48; I 581, *UB* I, 154; I 587, *A*, 243; I 593, *A*, 252; I 684, *UB* I, 30; I 726, *A*, 317–18; I 747, *A*, 324; I 1001, *UB* I, 130; I 1007, *B* II, 652. On Ava administration, see also Than Tun, "History 1300–1400;" Tin Hla Thaw, "History 1400–1500," 148–49; Toshikatsu Ito, "Pagan Pinya Ava-cho Biruma ni okeru shakaikosei no henka ni tsuite," *Seijo Daigaku Keizai Kenkyu* 55–56 (1976): 337–62, tr. Mariko Foulk; Toe Hla, "In-wa hkit ok-chok-yei," 21–35. On censuses, ZOK 41; NL 1944, Edict of 960 thadin-gyut 5 wax., *kei* v.

the tottering First Toungoo dynasty and temporarily occupied parts of Lower Burma. Nonetheless, the mountain barrier meant that Arakan would forever remain a marginal player in western mainland politics. Its eastern forays were of no lasting significance, and in the 17th century Arakan itself, with its inherently centrifugal geography, began to disintegrate.[110]

d) If Arakan was peripheral, the Irrawaddy artery ensured that the **Lower Burma**, the fourth major zone, remained indissolubly joined to the dry zone, and by extension, to the Shan country. Towards the close of the 13th century an independent kingdom arose below the 18th parallel and soon became a major military and commercial rival to interior principalities. This was the kingdom of Ra-manya, portrayed in inscriptions, chronicles, and foreign accounts from the 15th and 16th centuries as a preeminently Mon homeland.[111] Mons, large numbers of whom may have entered Lower Burma from the central mainland during the Pagan era, were distinguished from Burmans not only by mutually unintelligible languages, but by distinctive hairstyles (in early accounts, Mons grew their hair atop but shaved the sides and back part of their heads, whereas Burmans wound long hair into topknots), body adornment (Burmans alone tattooed legs and bellies), religious and village traditions.[112] Ra-manya encompassed the three great coastal provinces

---

[110] I follow *UK*, I, 371–77, 406–408; II, 8; "Danya-wadi ayei-daw-bon," in U Bi, *Ayei-daw bon*, 1–155; Shin Sanda-linka's late 18th-century *Mani-yadana-bon* (Rangoon, 1901), 134–36; essays by Jacques Leider, Stephen van Galen, Swapna Bhattacharya, and Pamela Gutman in Gommans and Leider, *Maritime Frontier*; and these works by Michael Charney: "Rise of a Mainland Trading State," *Jl. of Burma Studies* 3 (1998); 1–27; "A Reinvestigation of Konbaung-Era Historiography on the Beginnings of the Relationship between Arakan and Ava," *JAH* 34 (2001): 53–68; and "Where Jambudipa and Islamdom Converged" (Univ. of Michigan Ph.d. diss., 1999), chs. 3–5.

[111] On Mon ethnicity in Lower Burma, see Luce, "Peoples of Burma," 62–67; nn. 112–113, 115–116, *infra*, plus the following 16th-century references: unpublished translation by H. L. Shorto of Phra Candakantho, ed., *Nidana Ramadhipati-katha* (Pak Lat, Siam, 1912), 34–44, 61–122 [pp. refer to original printed text]; "Ya-za-di-yaza ayei-daw-bon" (Burmese translation of a work by Mon author Banya-dala) in U Bi, *Ayei-daw-bon*, 157–381; *Jahangir and the Jesuits*, C. H. Payne, tr. (New York, 1930), 192–93, 204; Antonio Bocarro, *Decada 13 da Historia da India*, 2 vols. (Lisbon, 1876), I, 121; Gaspar Correa, *Lendas da India*, 4 vols. (Lisbon, 1858–66), III, 851. Also *Mon ya-zawin* (Rangoon, 1922); and R. Halliday, ed. and tr., "Slapat Rajawan Datow Smin Ron," *JBRS* 13 (1923): 1–67 incorporate earlier material. The theory of 11th–14th century Mon migrations appears in Aung-Thwin, "Lower Burma and Bago," 45 ff.

[112] Burman tattoos were mentioned c. 1430 by Nicolo Conti, in R. H. Major, ed., *India in the Fifteenth Century* (London, 1857), 13. Distinctive Mon hairstyles and/or dress were described c. 1512 in Armando Cortesao, ed., *The Suma Oriental of Tome Pires*, 2 vols.

of Bassein, Martaban, and Pegu. Among these districts, Pegu supplanted Martaban as regional leader after 1369 in part, perhaps, because by connecting estuarial islands and extending the coast, post-1300 desiccation joined ongoing sedimentation to increase the agricultural and demographic potential of the once swampy eastern delta. (Similarly, silting would later help move the chief port from Pegu to Syriam to Rangoon, and in the Chaophraya basin would assist a shift southward from Ayudhya to Bangkok.) Between 1350 and 1550, as their northern rivals polished up local claims to sanctity, Ra-manyan rulers and monks began publicizing Gotama Buddha's associations with local pagodas, the legend of the Mon patron saint Gavampati, and the unification of local cults into a cosmologically-sanctioned, kingdom-wide pantheon of 37 nominally Buddhist spirits.[113] Claims to great antiquity notwithstanding, a sense of Ra-manyan regionalism, perhaps too the very notion of Mons as a coherent ethnicity, may have emerged only in the 14th and 15th centuries after the collapse of Upper Burman hegemony. Aung-Thwin, whose pioneering work we have encountered in other contexts, argues that the chief towns of Lower Burma in fact were founded under Pagan patronage, and that this legacy provided the "structural and political wherewithal" to build the first Mon polity after c. 1350 in partial imitation of Pagan and in open rivalry with Pagan's Upper Burma successors.[114]

As with Arakan, Ra-manya's chief material strength was its access to maritime trade. Commercial revenues and Indian Ocean mercenaries not only provided a major asset during grueling north–south wars in the 14th to 16th centuries, but allowed Ra-manya's rulers to supplement landed religious donations with cash and commercial gifts, an arrangement that provided religious merit without depleting nonrenewable resources. Like Toungoo and Prome, Ra-manya also remained insulated against major Shan incursions.

(London, 1944), I, 102–103; in 1545 in U Kala's chronicle (*UK*, II, 214–16), and in a 1677 Dutch account cited in Wil O. Dijk, "The VOC's Trade in Indian Textiles with Burma: 1634–1680" (ms), 9. These Mon-Burman markers appear to agree substantially with 1750s accounts in *Dal*, I, 99; *AA–L*, 28, *KBZ*, I, 104–105, 122.

[113] *Kalyani Inscriptions*; Nai Pan Hla, *Eleven Mon Dhammasat Texts* (Tokyo, 1992); Donald M. Stadtner, "King Dhammaceti's Pegu," *Orientations* 21 (1990): 53–60; and H. L. Shorto's articles: "32 *Myos*," 572–91; "*Dewatau Sotapa*," 127–41; "The Gavampati Tradition in Burma," in H. M. Sarkar, ed., *R. C. Majumdar Felicitation Volume* (Calcutta, 1970), 15–30; and "A Mon Genealogy of Kings," in D. G. E. Hall, ed., *Historians of South East Asia* (London, 1962), 63–72.

[114] Aung-Thwin, "Legend," 10 and *passim*; "Lower Burma and Bago," 37–49.

Notwithstanding these advantages, two handicaps prevented Ra-manya from subduing her dry zone rivals and reuniting the basin. First, despite continuous sedimentation, swamps and malaria still restricted rice cultivation to three or four relatively modest, dispersed bands of settlement. Along with trade, such low-density activities as fishing, salt-boiling, the gathering of forest items for export, and shifting cultivation remained critical to the local economy.[115] With military strength still correlated closely to manpower, thin population was a critical weakness for which Indian Ocean auxiliaries offered inadequate compensation. Second, although Pegu, located in the center of Ra-manya, controlled the chief port, significant entrepots also operated at Bassein, Martaban, and Tavoy, each of which retained its own courts, urban pagodas, and traditions of sovereignty. Absent an east–west riverine artery, the dispersion of these port cities favored a localism almost as pronounced as the dry zone split between Ava, Prome, and Toungoo. Here too provincial cities were entrusted to relatives of the Peguan overlord or to local dynasts, who appointed their own subordinates while maintaining an essentially tributary relation to Pegu.[116]

ETHNIC AND CULTURAL PATTERNS DURING THE ERA OF FRAGMENTATION, c. 1300–1550

In sum, if one were to graph the amount of territory in the western mainland subject to a paramount political center, the line would ascend from c. 1050 to the late 1200s, then fall sharply and – with the breakup of the Avan realm in the mid–15th century – continue to descend until Toungoo's conquests began to reverse the trend in the late 1400s and early 1500s. If one could measure cultural integration, however, the graph after c. 1150 would continue to rise fitfully after Pagan's fall. Burman ethnicity, for example, continued to push south. Burman literature grew more voluminous and diverse, while textually-oriented Theravada observances gradually spread throughout Lower Burma, Upper Burma, and the Shan world alike.

How can we explain this disjuncture between politics and culture, which has led some scholars to deny one or the other element, despite abundant evidence for both?[117] What common elements might explain

---

[115] See 16th/early 17th century descriptions at *ZOK* 41, 50–51, 55, 58, 59.
[116] See, e.g., U Chit Thein, ed., *Shei-haung mon kyauk-sa baung-gyok* (Rangoon, 1969), 69–75, 101–102; and Shorto, "32 *Myos*," 578–79.
[117] See, e.g., Bennett, *Conference*, 3–4.

both patterns? Political fragmentation itself spurred Theravada reform insofar as rulers eager to strengthen their tax base or to enhance their reputation for piety encouraged monastic "purification." By the same token, the Shans' growing involvement in Upper Burma, unfortunate though it was for the lowlanders, created a conduit by which Burman influence could enter the hills. Perhaps most important, the same southward agricultural and commercial expansion as weakened Pagan and later Ava promoted the spread of Burman ethnicity, while generating novel resources to support literacy and village monasticism.

Let us look first at changing ethnic patterns. Ra-manya's emergence as a "Mon kingdom" was emblematic of a fairly widespread sense of politicized ethnicity. Mon and Burman sources of the late 14th to early 16th centuries routinely distinguished between "the land of the Mons" (*talaing-pyei*), that is Ra-manya, and "the land of the Burmans" (*myan-ma-pyei*), which lay north of about 18 degrees, 30 minutes and was subject to most effective Pagan and Avan control. In the words of a chronicle of the 16th century, in the south "there are as many Mons as there are hairs on a bullock, but we Burmans are as few as the horns."[118] By the same token, the northeastern hills were the "Shan country" (*shan-pyei*). Sometimes these designations provided the basis for bitter cleavages and invidious distinctions. At Ava in the 1540s Mohynin Shan courtiers humiliated their Burman colleagues, taunting them and knocking off their distinctive headgear, until the exasperated Burmans massacred every Shan they could lay hold of.[119] A 16th-century Burman children's song prophesied: "Shans shall plough the fields, carry rations for us, while we Burmans fly overhead."[120] An embittered late 14th-century Mon prince reportedly prayed that he might be reborn as a Burman to ravage his perfidious fellow Mons, and contemporaries sometimes characterized the north–south conflicts of 1385–1425 as Burman–Mon wars.[121]

---

[118] *Hanthawaddy hsin-byu-shin ayei-daw-bon* (Rangoon, 1918), 8. For typical 14th–16th century references to the "Burman country," "Mon country," as well as the "Shan country," see Chit Thein, *Mon kyauk-sa*, 79–80, 93–94, 106; I 729, *UB* I, 63; I 619, *B* I, 193; I 667, *UB* I, 55; I 943, *UB* I, 106; Shin Thi-la-wuntha, *Ya-zawin-gyaw*, Pe Maung Tin, ed. (Rangoon, n.d.), 77; *SMK*, IV, 207, 220, 230, 233, 255. Cf. Than Tun, "Social Life in Burma in the 16th Century," *Tonan Ajia Kenkyu* 21, 3 (1983): 267–69; Tin Hla Thaw, "History 1400–1500," 146–47.

[119] *UK*, II, 141–42. Also 128.

[120] Phra Candakanto, *Nidana Ramadhipati*, 158–59.

[121] *UK*, II, 170; I 916, *B* II, 635; "Yaza-di-yaza ayei-daw-bon," 164, 220, 229, 230, 240, 242, and *passim*. Note too that 1590s disorders at Pegu prompted unmistakable Burman-Mon tensions. *UK*, II, 93–95; and Iberian sources in n. 111 *supra*.

Flattering themselves as the first to have adopted Buddhism and the people in closest contact with Sri Lankan orthodoxy, Mons tended to pillory Burmans as ignorant, half-pagan rustics. Some Burmans turned around and stigmatized Shans as "wild and uncivilized."[122]

Much of this tension was rooted in north-south population movements, which pitted newcomers against established populations and encouraged stereotyping both as an emotional response to an alien presence and as a (perhaps unconscious) strategy of group mobilization. Shan raids on Upper Burma, which bred bitter anti-Shan diatribes, offer the most dramatic example. But of greater long-term significance – especially in light of the fact that dry zone ethnicity remained heavily Burman – was the continuous movement of Burmans themselves into thinly populated areas in the upper delta and Lower Burma which since the 11th or 12th century, if not earlier, had been dominated by Mons. In a sense, this extended the pattern of Burman-led settlement that had transformed frontier (*taik*) areas during Pagan's heyday.

The spread of Burman ethnicity from the 14th century to the early 16th century can be traced in the eclipse of old Mon communities in the north, in growing Burman settlement of coastal cities, and most especially in the Burmanization of rural districts between the 19th and 18th parallels that once contained sizeable Mon populations. Although vestiges of Mon place names survived, by the mid-15th century there is little evidence of Mons living north of the latter line.[123] Linguistic flows tell much the same story. In the early Pagan era Mon was sufficiently prestigious for Burman rulers to employ that language frequently for inscriptions and perhaps court usages.[124] By the 13th century Burman had become the main language of northern inscriptions, but still seems to have exercised negligible direct influence on Mon usages in the south. In the 15th century, however, Mon inscriptions in the south began to adopt Burmese orthographic conventions and to incorporate, consciously or not, large numbers of Burmese loan words.[125] Ironically, the creation of

---

[122] E.g., Maha-dama-thin-gyan, *Tha-thana-lin-ga-ya sa-dan* (Rangoon, 1897), 93–94, 170–71, citing the *Pagan ya-zawin;* I 642, PPA, 321; I 1073, A, 364–66; and from a later date, BL OR 3464, 146–47.

[123] H. L. Shorto, personal communication, Nov., 1976. By the early 1500s, if not earlier, sizeable Burman communities also inhabited Pegu and other port cities.

[124] See n. 69 *supra.*

[125] Luce, "Peoples of Burma," 53–54, 63–64; Chas. Duroiselle, ed., *Archaeological Survey of Burma: Epigraphica Birmanica*, I, pt. 2 (rpt., Rangoon, 1960), 72; H. L. Shorto, personal communication, Nov., 1976; Aung-Thwin, "Legend," 9–10. Aung-Thwin's hypothesis

a more expressly Mon political identity, perhaps too, to follow Aung-Thwin, the legend of Thaton as a glorious pre-Pagan kingdom, may have responded to anxieties caused by Burman encroachment.

Note too that as Burman cultural influence spread, Burmese literature itself grew more confident, popular, and stylistically diverse, chiefly through the efforts of monks who chose to write in the vernacular rather than, or in addition to, Pali. This period saw the second generation of Burmese law codes, which critiqued earlier compilations, new poetic genres, and the perfection of older verse forms by such celebrated monastic poets as Shin Utta-magyaw and Shin Rahta-tha-ra. Both prose and verse exhibited a more elaborate grammar and vocabulary. In the 15th and early 16th centuries also appeared the first Burmese-language chronicles, of which Shin Thi-la-wun-tha's *Ya-zawin-gyaw* ("The Celebrated Chronicle") was best known. The closing section of this history portrayed Upper Burma as a coherent dynastic/territorial unit, referring repeatedly to "our land . . . our country of Burma (*nga-to aya . . . nga-to myan-ma pyei*)." There, Shin Thi-la-wun-tha explained, Buddhism was most firmly rooted, for whereas even Sri Lanka had obtained the religion only after the Buddha's death, Gotama Buddha himself had visited Upper Burma to implant the faith. Insofar as the Mon kingdom had recently completed a Sinhalese-inspired monastic reform, this may have been an implicit critique of Ra-manya as well as Sri Lanka.[126]

Yet despite Th-la-wun-tha's boast and the extension of Burman influence, it is obvious that by 18th- or 19th-century standards, ethnicity in the basin remained highly fragmented. Without strong, geographically inclusive political centers, ethnicity could provide only a weak, episodic basis for affiliation. By 1500 Burman inroads still had not altered the overwhelmingly Mon character of the Irrawaddy delta; while Kadus, Shans, Karens, Chins, and other minorities still occupied dry zone fringes that had once been Burman or that would become so after 1700. Moreover, within both the Burman and Mon ecumenes, subethnic loyalties and polyethnic clientage vitiated overarching identities

that the Mon script of Burma derived from Old Burmese suggests an earlier instance of this same cultural trend.

[126] Shin Thi-la-wun-tha, writing c. 1520, *Ya-zawin-gyaw*, esp. 75 ff. On Burmese literature in this period, Tin, *Myan-ma sapei*, 35–90; *SHDMA*, 26–104; Myin Hswei, ed., *Twin-thin-taik ya-zawin-thit*, vol. 1 (Rangoon, 1968), *ni-dan*; Htin Aung, *Burmese Drama* (London, 1937), 4–5; Aung-Thwin, *Myth and History*, 132–33, 197–98; Anna Allott, Patricia Herbert, and John Okell, "Burma," in Herbert and Anthony Milner, eds., *South-East Asia: Languages and Literatures* (London, 1989).

far more substantially than in later periods. On the one hand, as I have emphasized, the Burman world, like its Shan and Mon counterparts, was fragmented into rival centers, with distinctive historical traditions and perhaps dialects. This then was an obvious difference between the pre-1550 and post-1600 eras: only in the latter period did Toungoo centralization begin to fuse Burman ethnicity with a single political loyalty. On the other hand, at each local center the universalism of Buddhist appeals and the fluid, personalized bases of loyalty enabled individuals of quite diverse ethnicities to secure royal favor and to cooperate. Not surprisingly, we therefore find: a) significant minority ethnicities in all armies and courts; b) frequent cross-ethnic defections, which bore no particular stigma; c) shifting alliances between predominantly Shan, Burman, and Mon principalities. For example, although they sometimes exhibited an ethnic element, the epic north–south wars of 1385–1425 started when a dissatisfied Mon governor invited the Burmans and Shans of Ava to join him in attacking Mons at Pegu.[127] Toungoo later enthusiastically supported Pegu against fellow Burmans at Ava, while Shans joined Burmans against fellow Shans. And the same Burman courtiers who massacred Mohynin Shans in the 1540s promptly offered the crown to the Shan ruler of Hsipaw![128] We shall find a similar fluidity and indeterminacy of ethnic allegiance in this period in the Tai world, Vietnam, Russia, and France.

Religion exhibited much the same pattern as ethnicity: extensive localism alongside modest, tentative integrative trends. Consider first the evidence of parochialism. Unembarrassed contemporary sources show that devotional practices in the western mainland remained not only fragmented, but animist, substantially preliterate, and decidedly heterodox by 19th-century standards. In the chief Shan kingdoms as late as 1557, a lord's favorite servants and animals were customarily killed and buried with him.[129] In 1539 the aforementioned Shan ruler of Ava, Tho-han-bwa, committed a sacrilege inconceivable for a Burman or Mon when he murdered 360 prominent monks, pillaged pagodas, and burned religious manuscripts.[130] But even at Ava in 1426 the soldiers of a Burman ruler celebrated his accession by sacrificing horses and cattle

---

[127] *UK*, I, 378 ff. Aung-Thwin, *Myth and History*, 146–47 and *passim* also emphasizes the disjuncture between ethnicity and allegiance.

[128] *UK*, II, 143–44.

[129] Chit Thein, *Mon kyauk-sa*, 108; *UK*, II, 307.

[130] *UK*, II, 139–40 is supported by inscriptions, I 1073, A, 364–65; Chit Thein, *Mon Kyauk-sa*, 107–108; and by local chronicles, *List* 75, #3, NL 2240.

to the Mahagiri spirit in a rite clearly of pre-Buddhist origin.[131] In the Burman countryside Forest Dwellers retained their influence through the early 1500s, and land-transfer rituals in which beer (*thei*) and distilled liquor (*ayek*) were consumed and cattle, pigs, and fowls were slaughtered, grew larger and more numerous.[132] Princes and Buddhist abbots attended these ceremonies.[133] Although in Ra-manya the Buddhicization of local spirits may have proceeded further, there too monastic practices were deficient by later standards, and spirit propitiation was a dominant local concern.[134] Moreover, throughout the region literacy – synonymous with Buddhist textuality – seems to have remained socially and geographically restricted. Because scribal talent remained rare, the cost of *Tipitaka* transcriptions as late as 1509 may not have been much lower than in the 13th century.[135] Burmese orthography continued to follow the antique square format developed for aristocratic stone inscriptions, rather than the cursive format that took hold from the 17th century, when popular writing led to wider use of palmleaves and folded papers known as *parabaiks*.[136] All this suggests (one cannot argue dogmatically *ex silentio*) that the system of near-universal village monasteries and male education characteristic of later centuries was not fully developed. Significant too, whereas in the Kon-baung period (1752–1885) lay authors were central to the florescence of Burmese poetry, law, and historiography, from the 14th through the mid-16th centuries Burmese, not to mention Pali, literature remained primarily the preserve of monks, who perforce also staffed the modest royal secretariats.[137]

---

[131] *UK*, II, 58. See earlier references to hill tribe animal sacrifices, and the 1407/8 inscriptional reference to human sacrifices among hill peoples, Tin Hla Thaw, "History 1400–1500," 138. So too, I 952, *A*, 402 refers to a 1451 ceremony in which local *nats* received liquor and animals. By contrast, most 19th-century *nats* were vegetarian, presumably because they had been Buddhicized. The U-min-gyaw *nat* and the Taungbyon Brother *nats* got liquor and sometimes fried fish and fowls, but never beef.

[132] I have found 56 references to such ceremonies between 1365 and 1500 in SMK, IV and V and in the inscriptions indexed in Duroiselle, *List of Inscriptions*. See too Than Tun, "Maha-katha-pa gaing," 81–98.

[133] E.g., I 671, *UB* II, 155; I 770, *A*, 328; I 889, *B* I, 211; I 902, *A*, 382.

[134] See Shorto, "Dewatau sotapan"; and *Kalyani Inscriptions*, 99–103.

[135] A total of 3373 *kyats* of silver and 3333 *tin* of rice were expended on *Tipitaka* transcriptions, but it is unclear whether more than one set were donated. I 1045, *B* I, 336.

[136] Pagan-era palmleaves, not to mention inscriptions, used only square characters suitable for chiseling on stone, but the earliest extant post-Pagan palmleaves, c. 1680, used the new round orthograpy. On the orthographic transition, *ROB*, IV, 492; V, 874; Than Tun, personal communication, Nov., 1987.

[137] Tin, *Myan-ma sapei*, 35–90; SHDMA, 26–104.

Yet we also find textual, standardizing movements which built on religious developments in the late Pagan era and which, like the spread of Burman ethnicity, ultimately provided a cultural substratum for political integration. The vitality of vernacular Burmese literature testifies to a wider community of readers as well as authors, which in turn suggests a growth in the number of monasteries in secondary towns and villages. The 253 new monasteries, many in outlying areas, for which dedicatory records survive between 1300 and 1550[138] can have been only a fraction of total constructions: the more modest and rural the edifice, the less likely we are to find any record. In fact, several distinguished 15th- and early 16th-century authors either trained in humble monasteries, especially on the dry zone frontier, or later moved to such sites.[139] A basic Kon-baung moral treatise for schoolboys, the *Law-kathara hson-ma za*, was written in the late 15th century,[140] while in 1442 the ruler of Taungdwingyi, a secondary political center, donated no less than 295 manuscripts to a new monastery.[141] In other words, if illiteracy was still the norm in most rural areas and at many social levels, it may have become less widespread than in the Pagan era.

Particularly indicative of more orthodox textual sensibilities was the growth of a teetotal movement. In 1375 a pious Upper Burma village headmen and his wife prayed that their children would "not be people who want to drink liquor. May they have only proper thoughts, speak only proper words, and do only proper deeds. May they ... practice the [Buddhist] precepts (*thi-la*) [which prohibit intoxicants] day and night." Significantly, they omitted beer from the usual gifts to land measurers.[142] In similar inscriptions from 1368 to 1468, local figures swore they would never touch alcohol, or simply called themselves "Mr. Won't Drink Beer" (*thei-mathauk*).[143] Whether or not these individuals were inspired by such classic texts as the *Dhammika Sutta*, they provide early evidence of a local, scripturally-based Buddhist reform movement among monks and

---

[138] *SMK*, IV and V *pasim*, and I 413–1070.

[139] See biographies of Shin Thi-la-wun-tha, Shin Ohn-nyo, Shin Ekka-thamadi, Shin Utta-makyaw, and the Hnat-hmi-lin Hsaya-daw, *SHDMA* 40–54, 88–100.

[140] Written by the Kan-daw-min Kyaung Hsaya-daw (c. 1438–1513). *SHDMA*, 36–37; J. A. Stewart et al., comps., *A Burmese-English Dictionary* (London, 1940), xvii. Cf. Maung Maung Gyi, *Burmese Political Values* (Westport, CT, 1983), 15–16.

[141] I 935, *PPA*, 85–90; *Inscriptions of Pagan, Pinya and Ava* (Rangoon, 1899), 37–47.

[142] I 682, *A*, 281–84. The inscription is from Kinmun village, probably in Sagaing district.

[143] E.g., I 780, B I, 462; I 812, B II, 872; I 858, *A*, 361; I 977 B I, 245; I 982, *UB* I, 125. In the Pagan era a monk also called himself "The monk who wouldn't touch beer." Than Tun, personal communication, Oct., 1987.

leading laymen which by the late 16th or early 17th century had succeeded in suppressing entirely the consumption of alcohol at public
ceremonies in favor of eating pickled tea.[144] We can only speculate as to
the emotional root of these new sensibilities. Orthodox Buddhism's association with coastal commercial wealth and textual power must have
exercised some appeal. The conviction that meritorious acts would yield
karmic rewards, in a future if not the present existence, probably offered
a greater sense of predictability and control over life's uncertainties than
spirit propitiation. Conceivably too, as Barbara Watson Andaya has suggested was true of early modern Islam, identification with orthodoxy
was a sign of superior social status, setting orthodox adherents apart
from more ordinary folk.[145]

By its nature, textual Buddhism tended to favor royal authority: it devalued local sources of sacred power in favor of universal perspectives,
preached respect for court-defined social hierarchy, lauded even petty
kings as guardians of morality, and acknowledged each throne's critical role in resolving monastic disputes and patronizing the monkhood.
Not surprisingly, ambitious rulers took the lead in promoting orthodox
adherence, often by stressing their connections to the Mahavihara tradition of Sri Lanka, hearth of orthodoxy. (Ironically, whereas Burman
ethnic integration moved north to south, religious reforms tended to
flow in the opposite direction.) In Ra-manya the most ambitious such
movement was sponsored by King Dama-zei-di (r. 1472–92), a former
senior monk and authority on the monastic code (*vinaya*), who insisted
that a Sinhalese-based reordination of 15,666 monks throughout Lower
Burma was necessary to unify the sects and to eliminate a variety of
textually-impure practices that he enumerated in shocking detail.[146]
From 1439 to 1591 the court of Mrauk-U in Arakan promoted a series of religious exchanges with Sri Lanka.[147] Notwithstanding less direct coastal access, rulers at Ava, Toungoo, and Prome also welcomed
Sinhalese-oriented monks, relics, and architectural models, possibly in
the case of Ava to promote sectarian reform at the expense of the Forest

---

[144] Than Tun, "Social Life in Burma in the 16th Century," *Tonan Ajia Kenkyu* 21 (1983): 272.
Chronicle claims that the last Mon king Taka-yut-pi (r. 1526–1550) and Tabin-shwei-hti
(r. 1531–1550) lost power because of drunkenness reflect this sensibility.

[145] Andaya, ed., *Other Pasts* (Honolulu, 2000), 252–53. On the appeal of textual religions,
see too insightful comments at Reid, *Age of Commerce*, II, 150–61.

[146] See *Kalyani Inscriptions*, and discussion Mendelson, *Sangha and State*, 50–53.

[147] Catherine Raymond, "Etude des relations religieuses entre le Sri Lanka et l'Arakan du
XIIe au XVIIIe siecle," *Journal Asiatique* 282 (1995): 479–80.

Dwellers, and more generally to enhance each ruler's pious reputation. Ava expressly obliged local officials to listen to sermons by royally appointed monks, so that reform from above reinforced movements from below.[148] Yet farther inland some Shan rulers (*saw-bwas*) likewise began to welcome proselytizing Burman, Mon, and Tai monks. Organized into so-called Old and New Ceylon sects, these devouts moved along trade routes from Martaban, Ayudhya, and coastal towns into what is now northern Thailand, western Laos, and northeastern Burma, spreading Theravada rituals and texts, lowland alphabets, and calendars, along with broader notions of court-centered hierarchy.[149] The seasonal movement of Shan, Burman, and Mon pilgrims and merchants to urban pagoda fairs throughout the basin and the Shan hills had a similar diffusionary impact. In these ways, elite and perhaps popular Theravada practices became more regionally uniform, the Tai-speaking uplands were drawn into closer contact with the basin, and the way was prepared for standardizing Buddhist reforms in the mid-16th century under the First Toungoo dynasty.

ECONOMIC TRENDS DURING THE ERA OF FRAGMENTATION, c. 1300–1550

Discussion of trade-mediated proselytism invites a more general consideration of economic growth and its relation to cultural and political change during the era of fragmentation, c. 1300–1550. As just indicated, wider cultural circuits had commercial counterparts.

To be sure, compared to later periods, the economy of the western mainland labored under a variety of restrictions. While the Black Death apparently spared Burma,[150] recurrent warfare (if we may extrapolate from later patterns) magnified mortality and limited fertility. As chronicles and inscriptions attest, particularly in the 1360s to 1380s, the 1520s, and the 1540s, Shan raids ravaged key northern districts, forced the abandonment of newly cleared lands, and prompted large-scale migrations to Toungoo and other better protected southern areas. "The heretic

---

[148] I 835, *PPA*, 69. See too I 780, *B* I, 462; I 931, *B* II, 729; I 1014, *UB* I, 86–87; I 932, *B* II, 727; and I 686, *PPA* 326.

[149] *List* 75, #3, NL 2240, *hkaw* r. On sect proselytism, *ZOK*, 26; Mangrai, *Padaeng Chronicle*, esp. xiii-49; Liu Yan, *Nanchaung fojiao yu Daizu wenhua* (Kunming, China, 1993), 93, tr. Sun Laichen.

[150] Although, or perhaps because, plague was endemic in the Yunnan-Burma border region, according to McNeill, *Plagues*, 139–45.

Shans pulverized, ground to pieces, and utterly destroyed the Burma country," wailed a typical inscription.[151] Likewise, warfare, competing tolls, and localized systems of weights, measures, and private coinage impeded long-distance trade and market exchange.[152]

Although monetization gradually increased, by later standards it remained quite limited: of 114 land sales between 1350 and 1512 preserved in lithic inscriptions that I have read from northern and central Burma, 36 percent were exclusively in cash, 16 percent exclusively in-kind (oxen, horses, beer, textiles, bowls), and 48 percent in a combination of cash and in-kind goods. Since these figures chiefly involved political elites, barter must have been far more pronounced in outlying areas and among lower social strata. Compared to later centuries, the variety of domestic handicrafts, the array of commercial foodstuffs, and the volume of bulk exports also were modest. Likewise, whereas between 1752 and 1802, almost 70 percent of all taxes in the Irrawaddy basin were paid in cash, between 1350 and 1550, 79 percent were still in kind, with the percentage tending to rise away from the coast.[153] Although, particularly in the middle decades of the 15th century, bullion shortages in much of East Asia, indeed Eurasia, encouraged reliance on barter and thus impeded trade,[154] over the long term and more basically such patterns reflected still modest external demand for Burmese goods and conditions intrinsic to the western mainland, including predominantly subsistence production and historically low population densities.

---

[151] I 682, *A*, 281 from 1376. See also I 642, *PPA*, 321; I 1073, *A*, 364–65; *List* 78, #2, NL 2241, *ngi* v.; *List* 75, #3, NL 2240, *hkei* v.; *UK*, II, 118–141; Chit Thein, *Mon kyauk-sa*, 106–108. Cf. Than Tun, "History 1300–1400," 129–31; idem, "Social Life," 270–72.

[152] See Toe Hla, "Pyo kabya-twin htin-ha-thaw in-wa hkit si-pwa-yei," *Tegga-tho panya padei-tha sa-zaung* 13 (1979): 67.

[153] On trends in monetization, commercialization, and taxation, Victor Lieberman, "Secular Trends in Burmese Economic History, c. 1350–1830, and Their Implications for State Formation," *MAS* 25 (1991): 18–21, 24, relying *inter alia* on ZOK; *ROB*, IV–VI; I 559–1053; and *List* 11, 16, 35, 39, 52–54, 57, 62, 63, 84.

[154] On China's mid-15th-century silver famine, which had correlates in Japan, Korea, Vietnam, and parts of island SE Asia, see William Atwell, "Time, Money, and the Weather: Ming China and the 'Great Depression' of the Mid-Fifteenth Century," *JAS* 61 (2002), 96–99 and Fig. 2; John Day, *The Medieval Market Economy* (Oxford, 1987), esp. 1–54, 185–215; John Deyell, "The China Connection: Problems of Silver Supply in Medieval Bengal," in John Richards, ed., *Precious Metals in the Later Medieval and Early Modern Worlds* (Durham, NC, 1983), esp. 212–14, 226–27; von Glahn, *Fountain of Fortune*, 83–115. However, Sun, "Ming-Southeast Asian Interactions," 100 claims that in Yunnan silver production actually rose in the mid-15th century and that silver was far more readily available than in the interior of China. Presumably, the low price of Yunnanese silver would have benefited Upper Burma.

That said, it is also clear that during much of the period 1350–1550 the economy of the western mainland exhibited considerable dynamism, contributing to the spread of Theravada orthodoxy and Burman culture and anticipating more rapid economic growth in the late First Toungoo (1486–1599), Restored Toungoo (1597–1752), and Kon-baung eras. Agriculture, whose rhythms naturally dominated the economy, was static neither in extent nor internal structure. Inscriptions refer repeatedly to waste and "green jungle" (*taw-sein*) brought under cultivation. Allowing for uncertain readings and ambiguous evidence, I have shown elsewhere that between 1350 and 1550 such freshly cleared lands, particularly along the better-watered northern and southern fringes of the dry zone, totaled at least 300,000 acres, of which the bulk were planted in rice rather than pulses, millet, sorghum, sesame, or other dry crops.[155] To be sure, a modest if indeterminate portion was merely Pagan acreage abandoned in the mid-1300s and now reclaimed. Some of these lands were abandoned yet again during 16th-century Shan incursions. Especially in the northwestern and southern sectors, however, the bulk were virgin fields that remained under more or less permanent cultivation. By 1500 total rice acreage north of the 18th parallel was probably in the order of 900,000–1,000,000 acres, which apparently was larger than late Pagan figures.[156] More modest colonization probably occurred in the upper and lower delta. Reclamation projects were led by Forest Dwellers, local *athi* headmen, and most especially regional overlords, who felt obliged both to compensate for the growth of religious lands and to boost their military strength in a period of escalating warfare. In northern foothills wet rice expansion typically involved the construction of dams and weirs, but along the southern fringes of the dry zone, where colonization was particularly active, numerous new tanks (*kan*) and feeder canals were the chief investment. Older irrigation works in places like Kyaukse and Meiktila also were renovated and enlarged.[157]

---

[155] Lieberman, "Secular Trends," 7–8, relying chiefly on I 545 to 1070; *Myan-ma kyauk-sa* (Rangoon, n.d.), 86–97; Toe Hla, "Pyo kabya-twin," 61–71.

[156] Cf. Lieberman, "Secular Trends," 7–9; and Aung-Thwin, *Pagan*, 190, which estimates total irrigated acreage at the height of the Pagan period at 570,000. But insofar as some fields escaped inscriptional identification and other fields depended on rain, rather than irrigation, total Pagan rice acreage must have been somewhat larger.

[157] For examples of reclamation and new irrigation, see previous note, plus I 677, B I, 168; I 754, A, 325; I 768, UB I, 53 (all examples of headmen initiative), I 667, UB I, 55; I 682, A, 280–81; I 775, B II, 694; I 733, B II, 612; I 784, A, 325; I 820, B I, 213; I 842, A, 343; I 906, B II, 546; I 921, B I, 224; I 1027, B I, 333; *List* 91, #11, NL 62/2339; *List* 100, #4, NL 1493. Cf. Than Tun, "Maha-katha-pa gaing"; Toshikatsu

Expanded irrigation boosted production in two ways. First, it permitted more double- and triple-cropping, either of rice and noncereal crops, or of rice alone. Second, it facilitated the spread of higher-yielding rice strains. Watabe and Tanaka, to whose analysis of husks I already referred, have shown that from at least 500 to 1300 C.E., "round type rice" (named after the shape of the husk), a relatively low-yield, early maturing, *japonica*-like rice with modest water demands that entered the lowlands from the north, was far more common than "slender type," a higher-yield, more water-intensive, late maturing *indica*-type grain that entered along the coast from Bengal. Starting in the early 14th century, however, ratios began to change until by the early 1500s at many interior sites slender type represented 50–80 percent of the total. Thereafter slender type continued to gain ground, not least in Lower Burma.[158] Independently of Watabe and Tanaka, my study of Burmese lithic inscriptions has shown that from the mid-14th century late-maturing rice strains known generically as *kauk-gyi* (big [-season] rice) became increasingly popular, accounting for over half of all variety-specific references between 1350 and 1500, while earlier-maturing summer rices and winter rice (*mayin*), the most common Pagan-era varieties, grew proportionately scarce. Chronology, geography, and maturation time leave no doubt that *kauk-gyi* is the same as Watabe's slender type rice.[159]

Why, then, did *kauk-gyi*, known in the Irrawaddy basin for centuries, now expand? Given our very imperfect data on climate, demography, and productivity, the following comments are necessarily conjectural. By reducing per capita yields and increasing labor availability, two to

---

Ito, "Biruma zairai no kangai gijutsu to inasakunogyo no hatten," *Kagoshima Daigaku* 11 (1979): 39–80, tr., Mariko Foulk; idem, "Kami-Biruma Mcittira-ike kangaishisetsu no ijikanrisi," *Ajia Afurika Gengo Bunka Kenkyu* 20 (1980): 121–73, tr., Mariko Foulk; J. M. B. Stuart, *Old Burmese Irrigation Works* (Rangoon, 1913); Luce, *Old Burma*, I, 33; Lieberman, "Political Significance of Religious Wealth," 754–55; Michael Aung-Thwin, *Irrigation in the Heartland of Burma* (De Kalb, IL, 1990), 38–52; Toe Hla, "Pyo kabya-twin," 63.

[158] Watabe and Tanaka, "Ancient Rice Grains." See too Watabe, "The Development of Rice Cultivation," in Yoneo Ishii, ed., *Thailand: A Rice-Growing Society* (Honolulu, 1978), 3–14; idem, *Ajia Inasaku no Keihu* (Hosei, Japan, 1983), 93–94, tr. Atsuko Naono.

[159] Rarely mentioned in the late Pagan era, *kauk-gyi* appeared regularly in inscriptions starting in the mid-1300s, e.g., I 549, *A*, 216; I 592, *A*, 246; I 666, *A*, 280; I 709, *B* I, 319; I 814, *B* I, 63; I 989, *B* I, 331; I 1007, *B* II, 652; I 1037, *UB* I, 132, while those for Pagan-era *than* (summer rice) and *mayin* became less common. See too Lieberman, "Secular Trends," 10–11; Ito, "Biruma zairai," esp. 78–80; and Than Tun, *Hkit-haung*, 180–81. According to Watabe and Tanaka, *kauk-lat* ("medium[-season] rice") was also a form of "slender" rice.

three centuries of more or less continuous population growth under Pagan may have increased the utility gain from innovation and made possible more labor-intensive projects, of which expanded irrigation offers a prime example. Rather than inhibit the spread of water-intensive *kauk-gyi*, drier conditions after c. 1270 may have spurred the development of tanks, feeder canals, and other water control works along the southern fringes of the dry zone where water resources were less stretched and post-1350 population growth was concentrated.[160] Perhaps too, the return of somewhat wetter conditions c. 1470–1560 – the result of reduced volcanism and El Niño activity – spurred *kauk-gyi* cultivation without benefit of irrigation in rain-fed districts just south of the dry zone and in the upper delta.[161] This would help to explain Toungoo's growing colonization and manpower strength, which let it steal key districts from Ava and finally smash into the delta in the 1530s.[162] As O'Connor was first to point out, improved water control technique was preeminently associated with ethnic Burman frontier settlement, as at Toungoo, Prome, Taungdwingyi, and in the upper delta. Rivalries between these post-Pagan successor states – rivalries without parallel in the charter era – provided a major incentive to welcome migrants, to promote reclamation, and to encourage higher-yield rice strains like *kauk-gyi*.[163] Perhaps too the fact that post-1350 frontier settlement was preeminently the work of *athi* families, rather than religious bondsmen (*hpaya-kyun*) attached to large temple complexes, afforded private economic incentives insofar as *athi* (and *ahmu-dan*) smallholders retained a larger portion of the crop. More certainly, double-cropping and *kauk-gyi* supplied the wherewithal for more monasteries and manuscripts, and it can hardly be accidental that leading centers of post-Pagan agricultural expansion, including Yamethin, Prome, Toungoo, and especially

---

[160] Watabe, "Development of Rice Cultivation," 12. Cf. *supra* Ch. 1, n. 69, plus Ronald Demos Lee, "Malthus and Boserup: A Dynamic Synthesis," in David Coleman and Roger Schofield, eds., *The State of Population Theory* (Oxford, 1986), 96–130.

[161] On climate 1300–1550, see *supra* nn. 49–55, plus charts at Bradley and Jones, *Climate Since 1500*, 674–75; Mann, "Lessons for a New Millennium," 253; Atwell, "Time, Money, and Weather," 100–101.

[162] On Toungoo agriculture and expansion, *UK*, II, 92–96, 110–16, 125, 155–183; *List* 91, #11, NL 62–2339; BL OR 3416, *kaw* ff.; Wilkie, *Burma Gazeteer: Yamethin*, 29–32.

[163] The clearest statement of the superior productivity of "slender type" rice appears at Tanabe, *Ajia Inasaku no Keihu*, 93–94. Ito, "Biruma zairai," 52 says irrigated rice in central Burma produced yields 1.5 larger than non-irrigated rice, but it is unclear if these ratios apply to "slender"/"round" differentials. On yields and maturation time, see too Lieberman, "Secular Trends," 10–11.

Taungdwingyi, also became strongholds of the new monastic scholarship and Sinhalese-style reform.

Because Pagan inscriptions frequently mention the harrow (*htun*), used for wet soil, but not the plough (*hte*) for dry lands, it has been suggested that the latter implement appeared only after 1300, and that this in turn contributed to an expansion in dry cultivation. I am skeptical, because the *hte* was an exceedingly simple instrument, and dry cropping already was common in the Pagan era.[164]

A more critical change involving unirrigated land was the spread of cotton cultivation, together with new spinning and weaving techniques. Cultivated in Bengal since at least the early first millennium, some varieties of the cotton plant (*Gossypium herbaceum* and *arboreum*, Burmese: *wa*) may have been grown in Pyu Burma as well.[165] Nonetheless, Pagan inscriptions mention almost exclusively the cotton-tree (*Bombax insigne*, Burmese: *let-pan-pin*), whose fibers were poorly suited for spinning, and until the 14th century the most popular domestic textile may have remained hemp. But from the mid-1300s to the early 1500s we find increasing inscriptional references to the cotton plant (*wa*), which alone made possible large-scale production, as well as to undressed and dressed (*gyun*) cotton, cotton threads, and cloth. Cotton was grown on gravel or sandy soils unsuited for other crops in dry zone districts like Myingyan and Meiktila as well as in parts of Lower Burma. As with *kauk-gyi*, population increases may have joined with *athi* initiatives and post-1300 climate shifts to promote cultivation in marginal districts of this labor-intensive crop that had long been available but insufficiently feasible or attractive.[166] In fact, cotton's practical advantages over hemp were substantial: fiber yields per acre were greater, cotton was more easily processed, and the finished product was more comfortable. As cultivation

---

[164] Cf. Ito, "Pagan Pinya Ava-cho," 361; Luce, "Economic Life," 291.

[165] Toshikatsu Ito, "Cotton Production and the Dry Areas of Mainland Southeast Asia from the 6th to 9th Century," in Fukui, *Dry Areas*, 95–105 argues that along with Chenla, Dvaravati, and Funan, the Pyu kingdom produced and even exported cotton cloths. But his Chinese sources are unclear whether this fiber came from the cotton tree or the cotton plant. Cf. the distinction in Pagan inscriptions discussed in Luce, "Economic Life," 293, 311 n. 60; and U Hla Sein, *Myan-ma wa* (Rangoon, 1974), 3–5.

[166] On cotton, Lieberman, "Secular Trends," 9–10, and such references as I 545, *B* II, 744; I 616, *B* II, 773; I 830, *B* II, 930; I 934, *PPA*, 85; I 968, *B* I, 243; I 978, *UB* II, 183; *Shei-haung myan-ma naing-ngan myo-ywa ne-pe thamaing* (Rangoon, n.d.), 44. *Kalyani Inscriptions*, 100 refers in 1476 to monks visiting cotton fields and trading in cotton. See too Than Tun, *Hkit-haung*, 176–79; Toe Hla, "Pyo kabya-twin," 66; *GUBSS*, I, 2: 363–72; Sylvia Fraser-Lu, *Handwoven Textiles of Southeast Asia* (Oxford, 1992), 8–10; Laichen Sun, "The Spread of Old World Cotton from India to Southeast Asia" (ms).

spread, particularly from the 16th century, it spurred household hand-icrafts, regional specialization, and commerce between rice-deficit and rice-surplus areas both within Upper Burma and the western mainland generally. Note that this was part of a wider East Asian trend. In the Yangzi basin, where cotton lay at the heart of Ming-Qing commercial-ization, large-scale cotton cloth production began only in the 14th–15th centuries, after which it spread to Korea and Japan, again with major implications for handicrafts and domestic trade.[167]

Indeed, China's cotton hunger began to influence overland Sino-Burmese trade. Between the Mongol conquest of Yunnan in 1253 and the early 17th century, government-sponsored immigration helped to boost the population of Yunnan and other southwestern Chinese provinces by 70 percent.[168] As Yunnan itself produced inadequate textile fiber, it be-gan importing cloth from elsewhere in China as well as from Burma, which supplied finished Indian textiles and its own raw cotton for spinning and weaving. According to Sun Laichen's analysis of Chinese sources, exports to Yunnan of Burmese raw cotton may have started in the 1400s and by c. 1600 had reached 1,100 short tons annually – modest by 19th-century standards but perhaps a significant fraction of Upper Burma's late 16th-century production.[169] Finished Indian (and Burmese?) cottons swelled the total value. Along with spices, gems, and salt, these goods moved by boat to the upper Irrawaddy, whence they were transferred to north-bound trains of oxen and ponies. One 1580s report referred to 200 merchants and 30 ships headed upriver towards the China frontier.[170] In the opposite direction flowed Chinese iron and copper vessels, weapons, tea, and silk, plus copper and silver from Yunnanese mines.[171]

---

[167] Philip C. C. Huang, *The Peasant Family and Rural Development in the Yangzi Delta, 1350–1988* (Stanford, 1990), 44–46, 81 ff.; Lloyd Eastman, *Families, Fields, and Ancestors* (New York, 1988) 142; Chie Nakane and Shinzaburo Oishi, eds., *Tokugawa Japan* (Tokyo, 1991), 82–85.

[168] James Lee, "The Legacy of Immigration in Southwest China, 1250–1850," *Annales de demographie historique*, 1982: 279–304; idem, "Food Supply and Population Growth in Southwest China, 1250–1850," *JAS* 41 (1982): 711–46.

[169] Sun Laichen, "Ming-Burmese Trade (1368–1644) and Its Implications" (ms), 9–10, cal-culating from Chinese sources that 1,000,000 kilograms of cotton were exported annu-ally, most of which apparently was raw cleaned cotton.

[170] Qu Jiusi, *Wanli Wu Gong Lu*, cited in Laichen Sun, "Burmese Tributary and Trade Relations with China between the Late 13th and 18th centuries" (ms), 22, 23. See too discussion in idem, "Ming-Southeast Asian Interactions," ch. 5, esp. 130–31.

[171] Sun, "Burmese Tributary and Trade Relations," 27–33; Toe Hla, "Pyo kabya-twin," 67–69.

North and east of Upper Burma in the Shan hills, the Ming court used silver to purchase large quantities of rubies, amber, and jade, to the benefit of Shan rulers at Mong Mao, Mong Mit, Mogaung, and elsewhere. The great Bawdwin silver mine lay under Shan control but relied almost exclusively on Chinese labor. In addition, adventurers from Yunnan served as advisers to individual *saw-bwas*, while Chinese traders and renegade soldiers as early as 1397 introduced primitive handguns, cannon, and rockets, which Shans soon learned to replicate. Along with Chinese-derived military techniques, these weapons substantially strengthened 15th-century Mong Mao and other Shan kingdoms not only against Ava, but against Ming China itself. Sun argues that this was part of a wider movement whereby states across the northern tier of mainland Southeast Asia, extending to Laos and northern Vietnam, availed themselves of expanding Chinese technical and commercial contacts.[172]

Yet by more effectively integrating Shan areas into an economy centered on the Irrawaddy basin, over the long term trade increased the Shans' political vulnerability. The uplands relied on the valley for salt, salted fish, and Indian textiles, supplying in return tea, gems, forest exotica, and most importantly, bullion. The extraordinary cheapness of silver and copper in Yunnan, which alone produced 50–100 percent of Ming China's silver revenue,[173] and at Bawdwin ensured a constant flow of precious metals into the lowlands, including middle and Lower Burma, which had limited local production and as yet few other external sources of bullion with which to lubricate trade. Insofar as population and markets became far more concentrated in the basin than in the hills, we shall find that commercial expansion in the 15th and 16th centuries served ultimately to magnify the former's already considerable material advantage.

As the reference to Indian textiles moving into Yunnan suggests, maritime contacts also expanded. Extrapolating from European spice imports, Anthony Reid suggests that Indian Ocean–Southeast Asian trade doubled during the course of the 15th century, lost steam from 1500 to 1530, but grew with unprecedented rapidity from 1530 to 1620.[174]

---

[172] Sun, "Ming-Burmese Trade," 22–26; idem, "Ming-Southeast Asian Interactions," 224–81; idem, "The Transfer of Chinese Military Technology to Northern Mainland Southeast Asia, c. 1390–1526" (ms). See too Harvey, *History*, 101–102; *UK*, II, 79–80.

[173] Between 1458 and 1580. Sun, "Ming-Southeast Asian Interactions," 100. On silver-copper ratios and flows to lowland Southeast Asia and thence to the Indian Ocean, I follow ibid., 100–105, 176–82; Deyell, "China Connection," esp. 223.

[174] Reid, *Age of Commerce*, II, 13–23, incl. Fig. 3.

Farther east, Yunnan's vigor was part of a broad Chinese demographic recovery that also aided maritime traffic. China's total population rose from 75,000,000 in 1400 to 150,000,000 in 1600, with the east and southeast coast showing particular vigor from the late 15th century. Along with mainland Southeast Asia, China benefited from improved climate after c. 1470, which increased yields and encouraged agricultural extension. In turn, rising demand for bullion elicited improvements after 1530 in mining and smelting, at first in Japan and later Spanish America, which ended the silver shortages of the previous century and facilitated a sustained increase in Chinese domestic and Asian maritime trade. Despite Ming bans on private commerce, lax enforcement joined with sanctioned tribute to swell exchange across the South China Sea.[175]

All three lines of Lower Burma's trade benefited from this international upsurge. To the rising ports of Melaka and north Sumatra, Lower Burma provided ocean-going vessels of excellent local teak, rice and other foodstuffs, locally-produced ceramics,[176] plus gems, forest luxuries, and metals drawn from Upper Burma and interior locales as distant as Yunnan and Chiang Mai. A second avenue of trade was with India, which supplied the Irrawaddy basin with printed cloths and yarns in return for local products and Chinese goods and Indonesian spices originally imported from Melaka and Sumatra. Finally, to Martaban, Tavoy, and other peninsular ports Chinese and Indonesian goods could be brought across the upper Malay peninsula as an alternative to the searoute focusing on Melaka. Mons were active in all three lines of trade.[177]

We may assume a complex synergy between domestic economic expansion, on the one hand, and stimuli from Yunnan and the coast, on the

---

[175] On Chinese vitality, William Lavely and R. Bin Wong, "Revising the Malthusian Narrative," *JAS* 57 (1998): 717, 719; Marks, *Tigers, Rice*, 85; Anthony Reid, "Flows and Seepages in the Long-term Chinese Interaction with Southeast Asia," in Reid, ed., *Sojourners and Settlers* (St. Leonard's, Australia, 1996); Atwell, "Time, Money, and Weather," 98–103; Timothy Brook, *The Confusions of Pleasure* (Berkeley, 1998), 119–24; von Glahn, *Fountain of Fortune*, 97. On rising world bullion output and linkages, Dennis O. Flynn and Arturo Giraldez, "Born with a 'Silver Spoon,' " *JWH* 6 (1995): 201–21; Ward Barrett, "World Bullion Flows, 1450–1800," in James Tracy, ed., *The Rise of Merchant Empires* (Cambridge, 1990), 224–54.

[176] Myo Thant Tyn and Dawn Rooney, "Ancient Celadon in Myanmar," *Orientations* 32 (2001): 57–61.

[177] See Cortesao, *Suma Oriental*, I, 97–103; Om Prakash, "Coastal Burma and the Trading World of the Bay of Bengal, 1500–1680," in Gommans and Leider, *Maritime Frontier*, 96–97; and my "Europeans, Trade, and the Unification of Burma, c. 1540–1620," *Oriens Extremus* 27, 2 (1980): 203–26 and sources therein, incl. *UK*, III, 111; RUL 45235, Edict 63, 1000 1st waz., 8 wan., pp. 58–60.

other. To follow the Skinnerian model introduced in Chapter 1, population growth magnified the number of consumers and markets at which imports could be sold. Any increase in per capita income that *kaukgyi* and cotton generated would have further increased consumption of textiles and other luxuries. In the opposite direction, imported textiles and ceramics attracted local commodity producers, while as noted, Yunnanese (and after 1540 some Japanese) bullion became critical to local exchange.

From the mid-1300s to early 1500s inscriptions, poems, European accounts, and tax records portray a commercial system of modest, but growing complexity corresponding roughly by the latter date to Gilbert Rozman's Premodern Urban Development stage D.[178] Periodic (5- or 15-day) village markets (*pwes*) supplied more permanent township markets (*zeis*). These in turn fed urban marts and pagoda fairs with a valley-wide, even international character, at Ava, Prome, Toungoo, Pegu, and Martaban. Agents of each local ruler normally sought to monopolize luxury exports and imports. But designated items aside, foodstuffs, handicrafts, draft animals, and common textiles were freely bartered and sold. There was also a substantial land market, albeit subject to prohibitions on the alienation of religious lands, communal *athi* land, and certain categories of service land. Commercial contracts recorded mortgages, sales, and money-debts. As was true across much of Southeast Asia but especially in coastal and riverine areas, from the late 1400s wider use of lead- and copper-alloy lump coinage as well as silver lump coinage points to incremental monetization.[179]

Commercial revenues facilitated the hiring of mercenaries, better royal control over patronage, and a gradual movement away from landed religious donations to cash donations. This latter arrangement, we have seen, protected the tax base from erosion and, along with Theravada reform, was arguably a precondition for durable political reintegration.

[178] Gilbert Rozman, *Urban Networks in Russia, 1750–1800, and Premodern Periodization* (Princeton, 1976), esp. ch. 1. A modified variant of this stage, applicable to Burma, would include regional urban centers, subordinate administrative centers, and inferior intermediate and standard marketing settlements.

[179] On commercial activity, see, e.g., *List* 92, #1, 70; I 817, *UB* I, 155; I 840, *UB* I, 77; I 853, *PPA*, 74–75; I 966, *B* II, 855; I 995, *B* II, 857; I 1037, *UB* I, 132; I 1043, *B* I, 254; Toe Hla, "Pyo kabya-twin," 61–70; ZOK 41; M. Robinson, *The Lead and Tin Coins of Pegu and Tenasserim* (Sale, UK, 1986); Lieberman, "Europeans, Trade," 203–26; Robert S. Wicks, "A Survey of Native Southeast Asian Coinage c. 450–1850" (Cornell Univ. Ph.D. diss., 1983), ch. 3.

Far from being uniformly beneficial, however, I already have suggested that agricultural growth, domestic and foreign trade all tended to favor the southern lowlands and the coast over Upper Burma and the Shan hills. Recall that new irrigation systems and land reclamation were concentrated along the southern fringes of the dry zone as at Prome, Taungdwingyi, and Toungoo. Furthermore, the inherent difficulty of overland transport helped to ensure that maritime exceeded overland trade. Our earliest figures suggest that maritime exports were substantially larger by volume and at least moderately larger by value.[180] By their nature, moreover, maritime revenues were easier to collect than interior taxes. That is to say, controlling a handful of ports was inherently less difficult than monitoring upland bazaars and thousands of dispersed agricultural villages. Finally, for any given agricultural, mineral, or forest product, each port normally had multiple sources of supply, but only one port controlled each river mouth, and with it the provision of Indian textiles prized throughout the interior. In dealing with interior markets, coastal centers thus tended to dominate terms of trade for both maritime imports and local exports. As Ava's increasingly futile efforts to subdue Prome, Toungoo, and Ra-manya suggest, the southern dry zone and the coast therefore increased their weight in the political economy of the western mainland.

THE RISE OF TOUNGOO, c. 1490–1540, AND THE 16TH-CENTURY UNIFICATION

To summarize the history of the western mainland between c. 1300 and 1550, the region remained politically fragmented, and Upper Burma, normally the most populous and powerful sector, was unable to assert its traditional hegemony. Yet five trends, all apparent in some degree by the mid-14th century and all gaining strength from the late 15th century, anticipated an unprecedentedly broad and successful reintegration. First, Burman ethnicity expanded throughout the lowlands,

---

[180] Whereas Sun points to 1,100 tons of raw cotton exports in the 1580s, according to Cortesao, *Suma Oriental*, I, 98, c. 1510 Lower Burma was sending to Melaka and Sumatra alone 15–16 junks and 20–30 shallow draft boats, whose combined cargoes were probably in the order of 7,500 tons, chiefly rice, but including high value goods like lac, benzoin, musk, gems, and silver. Pulicat c. 1516 sent another 4–5 ships annually to Bassein. See too Sun, 'Burmese Tributary and Trade Relations," 43–45; John Crawford, *Journal of an Embassy to the Court of Ava*, 2 vols. (London, 1834), II, 191–95, reflecting maritime superiority after a century of vigorous overland trade growth.

while Burman culture grew more literate and confident. Second, religious practices throughout the western mainland grew more uniformly Theravadin and more sympathetic to royal regulation. Third, agricultural output rose in key lowland areas, especially along the southern fringe of the dry zone, while commercial links multiplied throughout the region. Fourth, the Shans became more closely involved in lowland political, cultural, and economic life. Finally, the political center of gravity shifted southward, within the basin as a whole towards the coast, and within the interior towards Prome and Toungoo. In assessing the weight of maritime and nonmaritime factors, note that if Indian Ocean trade assisted commercial integration and Theravada reform, it was not solely responsible for either of these trends and probably had only a marginal influence on basic demography.

In the late 15th and 16th centuries all five of these trends came to a head under the leadership of Toungoo, which was a logical, if not inevitable, spearhead of political reunification. Notwithstanding its commercial strength, Ra-manya was an unlikely candidate for regional preeminence because of its demographic weakness and its cultural isolation in an increasingly Burman basin. Prome, which had a large Burman population and which became effectively independent of Ava by 1450, benefited from the southward shift in economic activity, but in the face of Arakanese as well as Toungoo attacks, it showed a curious passivity. To what degree were local Burman-Mon tensions or weak leadership responsible? Occasional forays across the mountains notwithstanding, Arakan remained peripheral to basin politics. Despite Upper Burma's vast potential, Ava, as we have seen, was paralyzed by Shan incursions, factionalism, and the unchecked growth of religious lands.

But Toungoo, which had been founded in 1279 in the Sittang valley as part of late Pagan frontier expansion, was heavily Burman, protected against Shan raids, and home to relentlessly ambitious leaders. As early as the 1350s Toungoo raided Kyaukse, then controlled by Toungoo's nominal suzerain, Ava. In the late 14th century, as waves of Burmans fled Shan raids, Toungoo emerged as the principal refuge for displaced northerners and as a new center of Burman culture. Under Min-gyi-nyo (r. 1486–1531), a new dynasty launched an expansion that continued in essence to the close of the 16th century. Determined to compensate for the Sittang valley's modest agriculture and aided perhaps by wetter conditions c. 1460–1560, Min-gyi-nyo sponsored elaborate reclamation and irrigation projects. A master of opportunistic alliance with Mon as well as Burman principalities, in 1491 and then again in 1510 he advertised his rising status by building new capitals. "Now I know why the bees swarmed on the gate of Toungoo," he allegedly declared. "It meant that my city was to be populous."[181] As a frontier settlement that eventually came to overawe the metropole, we shall find that Toungoo resembled the contemporaneous upstart principalities of Ayudhya, Phnom Penh, and Moscow.

Min-gyi-nyo's son and successor Tabin-shwei-hti (r. 1531–1550) accelerated Toungoo's conquests, but whereas his father had focused his energies on the dry zone, Tabin-shwei-hti switched to Lower Burma, whose maritime wealth was the chief lure. On taking the throne, he advertised his intention by conducting a ceremony at Pegu's Shwei-maw-daw pagoda in defiance of local authorities. In 1539, after repeated failures, Tabin-shwei-hti finally captured the chief Mon city of Pegu, thanks to a more martial Toungoo tradition, larger forces, Muslim mercenaries, and splits in the enemy camp. He now entrusted his dynastic seat at Toungoo to a senior relative in order to take up residence at Pegu, from which he extended control over both Martaban and Prome. At Pegu the capital of the First Toungoo dynasty would remain until the end of the century. This was the first and only time that a capital with authority over the entire basin would be located near the coast.[182]

Having consolidated authority over much of the dry zone and Lower Burma, Tabin-shwei-hti's yet more celebrated successor Bayin-naung (r. 1551–1581) – known as Victor of the Ten Directions – then pushed up the Irrawaddy in an effort to join the north and Lower Burma for the first time since the days of Pagan. If his stated goal was to restore "pure" Sinhalese-style religion,[183] victory in the north also promised to strengthen control over interior gems and bullion and to supply additional levees. In 1555 Ava, heart of Upper Burma, fell to southern forces. Over the next four years breathtaking campaigns reduced parts of Manipur and the entire Shan world to tributary status, thus ending at a stroke over two centuries of Shan domination and extending lowland

---

[181] On early Toungoo history, *UK*, II, 95–96, 110–16, 125, 155–183; and Toungoo chronicles at *List* 91, #11, NL 62–2339; BL OR 3416, *kaw* ff. The quote comes from Harvey, *History*, 125, which does not cite a Burmese source. The earliest inscriptional references to Toungoo I have found are I 686 and I 687, *PPA*, 325, 290, both from 1375.

[182] Tabin-shwei-hti's career appears in *UK*, II, 164–251.

[183] See his 1557 inscription, Chit Thein, *Mon kyauk-sa*, 106. On Bayin-naung, *UK*, II, 273–451; III, 1–69; "Han-th-wadi hsin-byu-shin ayei-daw-bon," in U Bi, *Ayei-daw-bon*, 383–481.

control much farther than Pagan had dreamed possible. Such Shan bastions as Mogaung, Mong Mit, and Hsipaw were obliged not only to supply tribute and troops, but to adopt Peguan weights and measures, to stop human sacrifices, to listen to the preaching of resident monks from the lowlands, and thus, in the words of the chronicles, to "harken to the Buddhist law."[184] Finally in 1569, with the military manpower of the entire western mainland at his back, Bayin-naung conquered mighty Ayudhya, capital of Siam and Pegu's long-standing rival for commercial and religious preeminence. He also established a loose authority over much of modern-day Laos. Pegu now exercised suzerainty from Manipur to the Cambodian marches and from the borders of Arakan to Yunnan.[185] Notwithstanding its fragility, this was probably the largest empire in the history of Southeast Asia.

These historic victories benefited from: a) the Shans' failure to revive Avan social structures, a failure that created a power vacuum in the traditionally strongest sector of the western mainland; b) Pegu's systematic pyramiding of manpower from conquered areas to overwhelm isolated principalities, first in the dry zone, then in the Shan hills, and finally in the larger Tai world; c) Pegu's methodical exploitation of maritime trade through tolls, monopolies, and overseas expeditions, which together must have been the largest single source of royal income.

First Toungoo conquests benefited as well from a vast expansion in Indian Ocean mercenaries and European-style firearms. As we have seen, Chinese handguns and cannon had been known in the interior since at least the early 1400s. Chinese- and Muslim-style firearms were also used at the coast in this period. Yet cannon and matchlocks supplied by Portuguese mercenaries, which became available in quantity starting in the 1530s, proved superior in accuracy, safety, ballistic weight, and rapidity of fire. Had Toungoo attacked Pegu a generation later, it is conceivable that Portuguese guns could have given Pegu the victory, thus altering the course of mainland history. But Tabin-shwei-hti arrived at the coast on the cusp of this transformation, which he and his successor quickly turned to their own advantage. By the 1550s Portuguese – and to a lesser extent, Muslim – cannon had forced a shift from wood to brick and stone fortifications, while the Portuguese may have encouraged a new emphasis on inflicting casualties, rather than or in addition to taking prisoners. Alongside elite Portuguese and Muslim corps, indigenous

[184] *UK*, II, 307, 312.
[185] See list of tributary domains at *UK*, III, 66–67.

infantry and elephant units also began using guns, with 20–33 percent of the troops so equipped on some late 16th-century campaigns. While coastal guns and revenues afforded Pegu no particular advantage over Ayudhya, a major port in its own right, the new weapons had a devastating effect, psychological and tactical, on interior Tai populations and help explain the Shans' permanent subjugation after 1560.[186] We shall find that elsewhere in Southeast Asia, in Muscovy, Western Europe, and Japan, the introduction of more effective firearms also tended to favor the wealthiest, most cosmopolitan principalities and helped bring the first phase of post-charter territorial consolidation to a climax in the late 16th century.

What cultural memories, what imperial models inspired Tabin-shwei-hti, Bayin-naung, and their advisers? The 20th-century Burmese nationalist emphasis on lineal succession from Pagan to Ava to Toungoo exaggerates the 16th-century sense of continuity.[187] Admittedly, the First Toungoo dynasty, like its late Pagan and Avan predecessors, drew on Upper Burma administrative precedent (the *ahmu-dan, athi*, and territorial systems, for example, derived from Upper Burma), used Burmese as its primary written and oral language, and patronized Burman culture.[188] In both European and indigenous accounts from the 1500s, there is clear evidence that southerners resented northern "carpetbaggers" who flocked to Pegu and other coastal towns as soldiers and officials, and that this resentment was expressed in terms of Burman-Mon ethnic opposition.[189]

Yet as befit a polity outside the charter heartland, First Toungoo culture also was remarkably innovative, eclectic, and experimental, not least in its ethnic and territorial design. If Tabin-shwei-hti was crowned at Pagan, his primary coronation was at Pegu, where he took a Mon princess as his chief queen and where, in his eagerness to win favor, he cut off his Burman hair-knot in favor of a Mon hairstyle, thus "becoming

---

[186] On guns, Lieberman, "Europeans, Trade," 210–17, and sources therein. On 15th–16th century warfare, too Myan-sa-gun-gyaw-myin, *Myan-ma yo-yathaing-pannya thamaing* (Rangoon, 1964), 4–70.

[187] See, e.g., Maung Htin Aung, *A History of Burma* (New York, 1967) and *Achei-pya myan-ma naing-ngan-yei thamaing*.

[188] See, e.g., *List* 91, #11, NL 62/2339, 12; *UK*, II, 156; Arthur Phayre, *History of Burma* (rpt., New York, 1969), 99–100.

[189] *UK*, II, 255, 258–59; and III, 92–95; *Shei-hkit myan-ma naing-ngan myo-ywa-ne-pe thamaing* (Rangoon, n.d.), 35; Chit Thein, *Mon kyauk-sa*, 106; Peter Floris, *His Voyage to the East Indies in the Globe 1611–15* (London, 1934), 53; Saw Tun, "Bayinnaun in Burmese Literature" (ms), 1; and nn. 111, 112 *supra*.

a Mon."[190] This gesture had no precedent. Moreover, he sought to build not a north-south empire along the Irrawaddy axis like that which Pagan constructed and to which Ava aspired, but an east–west coastal empire from Arakan to Siam that bypassed the Burman heartland entirely. Although Bayin-naung annexed Upper Burma and seems to have been more self-consciously Burman in his sympathies, he presented himself as the *cakkavatti*, or World Ruler, par excellence and was content to continue the dynasty's coastal orientation.[191] "All [of us,] his chosen men, in fact, whether Shans, Mons, or Burmans . . . declared ourselves willing to lay down our lives [for him]," a memoir by a Mon general concluded.[192]

LATE 16TH-CENTURY COLLAPSE

Given their astounding territorial claims and the strength of subordinate local kingdoms – whose sense of sovereignty, in many cases, had taken root only after 1400 – First Toungoo kings had no choice but to retain a Pattern B administrative system no less, indeed possibly more, decentralized than in the far smaller empires of Pagan, Ava, or Pegu.[193] Annexation meant simply placing on the throne of conquered kingdoms new nominees who became tributary to Pegu. The High King at Pegu governed directly only the lower Irrawaddy basin. Here maritime revenues were most profitable, military *ahmu-dans* were concentrated, and headmen responded directly to court directives. Other lowland principalities such as Martaban, Toungoo, Prome, and Ava, some with populations at least as large as that of Pegu, were entrusted to senior royal

---

[190] *UK*, II, 214–16.

[191] See his self-presentation in Chit Thein, *Mon kyauk-sa*, 105–108; and Siamese acceptance of those images discussed in Sunait Chutintaranond, "King Bayinnaung in Thai Perception," in *Traditions in Current Perspective* (Yangon, 1996), 59–61. In "Connected Histories," in Victor Lieberman, ed., *Beyond Binary Histories: Re-imagining Eurasia to c. 1830* (Ann Arbor, 1999), 289–316, Sanjay Subrahmanyam suggests that the rise of expansive empires throughout the 16th-century Mediterranean and South Asia owed much to the cross-cultural exchange of millenarian symbols and expectations. While Burmese "political theology" may have been influenced by Muslim millennialism, I am reluctant to invoke this as a primary explanation, first, because there is simply no evidence, and second, because like germs, millennial myths were ever-present, needing only propitious conditions to flourish. Similar millennial impulses appeared in the 1750s.

[192] Banya-dala in Phra Candakantho, *Nidana-ramadhipati*, 152.

[193] The ensuing discussion of First Toungoo administration relies on Lieberman, *Cycles*, 32–46.

relatives called *bayins*, who enjoyed substantially the same ceremonial and practical prerogatives as their local predecessors, including the right to control their own armies, to monopolize taxes, and in some cases to appoint sons as heirs. The sources of *bayin* authority therefore were in some sense contradictory: on the one hand, *bayins* acknowledged that their power derived from investiture by the High King, but on the other, they claimed to be *dhamma-rajas* ("Kings of Righteousness"), with their own royal attributes.[194] Aside from punitive expeditions, each High King sought to maintain control through marriages, gifts, and regular homage ceremonies. But as soon as the overlord died, these bonds of personal obligation necessarily dissolved, with *bayins* either declaring independence or challenging the Pegu Heir-Apparent for the imperial throne, to which their exalted lineages usually afforded them some claim.

A second group of lowland rulers, known as *myo-zas*, consisted of junior princes and (Burman or Mon) officials entrusted with more modest districts. Like the *bayins*, they were required only to forward tribute, to supply troops, and to render homage. Although their claims to the Peguan throne were less credible, *myo-zas* too were tempted to withdraw their authority during interregna or other periods of central weakness.

Finally, outside the Irrawaddy basin in the vast Tai world, that is, the Shan hills, Lan Na, Siam, and Laos, central authority was yet less secure. Military supply to outlying garrisons was incomparably more difficult than along the Irrawaddy. Unlike *bayins* or *myo-zas*, Tai princes were related to the High King, if at all, only by gifts of women. And despite efforts to spread Irrawaddy-basin religious norms and to create a unified status hierarchy focusing on the Peguan court, cultural ties to the capital were far weaker than within the basin. Accordingly, Tai revolts were endemic. In short, the creation of the First Toungoo empire reflected explosive military and economic dynamics joined to a millennial vision – but the resultant system was absurdly overextended in the east and inherently unstable.

From 1584 to 1599 the empire disintegrated no less rapidly than it had been constructed. On Bayin-naung's death a succession war between his son and heir-apparent at Pegu and Bayin-naung's brother, the *bayin* of Ava, provided Ayudhya (Siam) with an opportunity to declare its independence. After vanquishing his uncle in single combat

---

[194] See, e.g. I 1084, *UB* II, 237–38; *UK*, III, 50–51, 80–81.

at Ava, Bayin-naung's son launched the first of five major punitive expeditions against Siam. All failed, both because logistical problems proved overwhelming and because, in response to Burmese conquest, that proud kingdom had strengthened its army and system of provincial controls. With each Siamese victory, other Shan and Lao vassals, as well as Burman and Mon *bayins* and *myo-zas*, grew more inclined to throw off allegiance and more reluctant to contribute military forces. The court at Pegu in the late 1580s and 1590s therefore had to lean ever more heavily on the modest population of Lower Burma. Already resentful of Burman domination, many Mons now fled military service to become monks, debt-slaves, private retainers, or refugees in nearby kingdoms. Bayin-naung's son reacted with manic fury, branding men to facilitate identification, executing deserters, and forcing monks into the army. Coercion proved self-defeating. With cultivators disappearing, rice prices in Lower Burma reached unheard-of levels. Seeing the paralysis at Pegu, armies from Siam, Toungoo, and Arakan now began to menace Lower Burma. In 1599 the *bayin* of Toungoo and the king of Arakan finally sacked and burned the imperial capital, once one of the wonders of Asia.

In essence, then, rapid economic growth c. 1450–1570 joined with European firearms to encourage stunning military conquests that were not matched by stable administrative controls in the Tai world or outlying areas of the Irrawaddy basin. Not unlike Dai Viet, Valois France, and Muscovy – all of which recovered from 14th-century disorders, enjoyed rapid economic growth and territorial expansion c. 1450–1550, and collapsed in the mid- to late 16th century – the First Toungoo empire "overheated," a victim of its own success. But, if Burma's fundamental problem was ill-regulated territorial expansion, two other factors deserve mention. First, intense volcanism and heightened El Niño activity produced a disastrous northern hemispheric climate between 1584 and 1610 – 1601 may have been the coldest summer in the past 600 years[195] – with a characteristic linkage between Southeast Asian aridity and north European cooling. Weak monsoons contributed to severe Lower Burma famines in the 1590s and may have nurtured a rare plague of rats that swarmed across the capital in 1596.[196] Drought yielded a major Indian

---

[195] Atwell, "Volcanism," 57.
[196] *UK*, III, 92–99. Cf. Mangrai, *Padaeng Chronicle*, 247. Phra Candakantho, *Nidana-ramadhipati*, 204 also refers to a 1565 famine.

famine in 1596 and contributed to recurrent shortages in Dong Kinh in the late 16th and early 17th centuries. Exceptionally cold, wet summers also produced appalling harvest failures in northwestern and central Europe from 1590–1600 and in Russia from 1601–1603.[197]

Second and more speculative, price inflation may have aggravated local disorders. Although Asian data are weaker than European, some historians have claimed that prices in China and other Asian locales rose between 1490 and 1650 in a pattern that paralleled, if weakly, inflationary trends in Europe. Perhaps the most common explanation is that China's rapid demographic and commercial growth joined with the silver-dependent Single-Whip tax reforms of the 1570s to drain silver at first from the mines of Yunnan and Japan and then from the thesauri of the New World and of Spain, where the silver-to-gold price ratio as late as 1600 was almost twice as high as in China. To the degree that silver imports in Asia exceeded increases in circulation velocity and real output, the value of silver relative to other goods fell, which is to say that prices rose.[198] Burma may have been implicated: whereas the Irrawaddy basin had been importing silver from Yunnan, at some point in the late 1500s New World silver entering via the Indian Ocean and the Philippines reversed this flow, so that coastal treasure began moving into Yunnan.[199] We lack price series for Burma, but if New World bullion did stoke inflation, it could have accelerated the movement of taxpayers and servicemen into debt-slavery, while whetting the predatory appetites of those inflation-vulnerable elites dependent on fixed taxes.

[197] On South Asia, Grove and Chappell, *El Niño*, 14, and Atwell, "Volcanism," 59. On Vietnam, where climate figures less certainly, Li Tana, *Nguyen Cochinchina* (Ithaca, 1998), 162–63. On western Europe, Emmanuel Le Roy Ladurie, *Times of Feast, Times of Famine* (New York, 1971), 58, 67, 140–43, 235, 238; Atwell, "Volcanism," 56–58. On Russia, Ye. P. Borisenkov, "Documentary Evidence from the USSR," in Bradley and Jones, *Climate Since 1500*, 174, and Atwell, "Volcanism," 58.

[198] For evidence and interpretation of putative price rises in China and other locales, Jack Goldstone, *Revolution and Rebellion in the Early Modern World* (Berkeley, 1991), 359–62; von Glahn, *Fountain of Fortune*, 127–28, 233–37; David Hackett Fischer, *The Great Wave* (Oxford, 1996), 70–91; Flynn and Giraldez, "Born with a Silver Spoon," 201–21; *CEHI*, ch. 12; Sevket Pamuk, "The Ottoman Empire in the Eighteenth Century," *Itinerario* 24 (2000): 108–110, and Sanjay Subrahmanyam, ed., *Money and the Market in India 1100–1700* (Delhi, 1994), 209–18, 253–54, taking a more skeptical view.

[199] Sun, "Ming-Southeast Asian Interactions," 182–87. By 1800, silver flows between Yunnan and Burma had reversed direction again.

CREATING THE EARLY MODERN POLITICAL SYSTEM:
RESTORED TOUNGOO INNOVATIONS

With the disintegration of the First Toungoo Empire, confused, many-sided wars again engulfed the basin. But in contrast to over two and a half centuries of polycentrism following Pagan's collapse, this interregnum proved brief indeed. By 1613 a branch of the fallen house known (retrospectively) as the Restored Toungoo dynasty (1597–1752) had succeeded in reuniting the valley and surrounding highlands. Over the next half century – at roughly the same time as the rulers of Late Ayudhya Siam, Bourbon France, Romanov Russia, and Tokugawa Japan embarked on their own restorative experiments – the new dynasty proceeded to create a political and legal system whose basic features would continue under the Kon-baung dynasty well into the 19th century. Why, then, this rapid and durable success compared to the long post-Pagan interregnum and the ephemeral First Toungoo empire?

The First Toungoo dynasty had created a fresh sense of possibility. Headmen, *myo-zas*, and *bayins* alike demanded new military glory, the restoration of patronage, an end to anarchy. Yet by themselves, such expectations may not have distinguished the early 17th from the early 14th century. More basically, the system that emerged by 1650 and that continued, amidst significant Kon-baung modifications, to the First Anglo-Burmese War in 1824, drew strength from the following factors: a) a more considered geopolitical design; b) Shan pacification; c) a reduction in monastic autonomy; d) ambitious secular administrative reform; e) expanded use of firearms; f) continued demographic growth and commercial integration; g) increasingly hegemonic Burman cultural norms. The remainder of this chapter considers these factors in seriatim for the entire Restored Toungoo/early Kon-baung era, c. 1600–1830, while pausing to consider the 18th century political crisis and the early Kon-baung response.

I have emphasized that Upper Burma's agricultural and demographic superiority made it the center of political gravity throughout most of Burmese history. The long era of fragmentation, c. 1300–1550, and the First Toungoo unification, 1555–1599, both reflected an unhappy marriage between an Upper Burma too crippled to assume its "natural" hegemony and a Lower Burma too weak to enforce its "unnatural" claims on the rest of the basin. Even had Pegu not embarked on suicidal invasions of Siam, over the long term it probably would have had difficulty controlling the north, but with Pegu's collapse, Toungoo leaders in the early 1600s had little choice but to return to Upper Burma. In that region – first at Ava, then at nearby Amarapura and Mandalay – the capital would remain until the British conquest.[200]

Although the north obviously lacked direct access to maritime trade, it profited from commerce with Yunnan, while a series of provincial reforms (see below) preserved direct control over the invaluable ports. In the event of rebellion, an interior capital always made more sense: one could go downriver up to seven times more quickly than one could ascend the Irrawaddy. Most critical, with refugees streaming up the Irrawaddy and with Upper Burma prospering from 80 years of more or less continuous peace, population in the north again rose markedly. Reinforced by deportations, in 1635 the dry zone contained over three times more people, hence potential soldiers, than Lower Burma. To control some 4,000 villages spread throughout this zone was a far more critical task, requiring on-site royal supervision, than to control a far smaller number of villages and two or three ports in the south. Unfavorable climate later in the 17th century may have hit Upper Burma harder than the coast, but of course, when the decision to change capitals was finalized in 1635, this problem lay well in the future. In any case, famines around the Bay of Bengal from 1630–1635 slammed Lower Burma no less savagely than the interior.[201]

Nor after 1555 did the Shans pose a credible threat to Upper Burma. Hammered by Bayin-naung, bereft of quality firearms, and subject to severe pressure from Ming and later Qing China, after c. 1550 the Shans were effectively partitioned into Burmese and Chinese spheres and pacified, independently, from both directions.

The perennial northern problem of tax-free monastic wealth also eased substantially through a combination of local turmoil, policy changes, and broad commercial currents. Amidst the disorders of the early 1500s, Shans expropriated some religious lands, while numerous lithic dedicatory markers disappeared. At the same time, many Burman monks abandoned their properties to move to Toungoo and other southern locales; the Forest Dweller sect virtually disappeared. Extensive glebe lands thus shifted, illegally but in effect permanently,

---

[200] Ava was capital c. 1635–1752, 1764–83, 1823–37; Amarapura, 1783–1823 and 1837–57; Mandalay, 1857–1885. Shwebo and Sagaing served more briefly.

[201] See my "The Transfer of the Burmese Capital from Pegu to Ava," *JRAS* 1980: 64–83; Grove and Chappell, *El Niño*, 15; D. G. E. Hall, "The Daghregister of Batavia and Dutch Trade with Burma in the Seventeenth Century," *JBRS* 29 (1939): 140–41.

from religious to lay ownership. As they established their authority over the north in the 17th century, Restored Toungoo kings severely restricted landed donations by laymen other than themselves, so that alms in cash or perishable goods and new monastery constructions became the chief means by which laymen accumulated religious merit. Following First Toungoo practice and aided by commercial expansion (see below), Restored Toungoo and Kon-baung kings also shifted their own primary patronage from land to cash. Thus the large-scale monastic accumulation of landed estates that had been a principal feature of the Pagan and post-Pagan eras ended. By drawing the monkhood closer to village society and rendering it more economically dependent, these changes – which were adumbrated elsewhere in the basin as early as the 15th century – transformed lay-*sangha* relations. Moreover, with the subsequent growth of an active land market, many extant glebe lands were openly sold and mortgaged like private property. Notwithstanding periodic bans on such alienations, the throne was either unable or unwilling to halt the process. To strengthen its control over such landed religious wealth as did remain, the Restored Toungoo court, in the name of purification, developed new administrative procedures that were perfected in the Kon-baung era. Ministers for Large Donations and for Glebe Lands (the *maha-dan-taik-wun* and the *wut-myei-wun*) received tithes from lands that lacked custodians or that had local officials as custodians. In practice these funds were often diverted to secular purposes, but even where this was not the case, the monkhood lost direct control. At the same time, privatization of religious lands joined with an officially sanctioned, radical decline in the social status of glebe-land cultivators (the aforementioned *hpaya-kyun*) to marginalize and severely to compress this once sizeable group of tax-exempt personnel. Finally, Toungoo and Kon-baung kings strengthened control over the professional monkhood itself by expanding Pali examinations, appointing bishops (*gaing-oks*) and sub-bishops (*gaing-dauks*), and tightening the registration of bona fide monks. Although these measures did not eliminate endemic sectarianism, they did remove the monkhood as a major factor in the political economy.[202]

Of course, the First Toungoo problems of overextension and weak provincial control remained to be addressed. Unable to reconquer Siam

---

[202] For discussion and documentation, see my "Religious Wealth," 757–69; and Teruko Saito, "Rural Monetization and Land-Mortgage *Thet-kayits*," in Anthony Reid, ed., *The Last Stand of Asian Autonomies* (New York, 1997), 153–84, esp. 165–68.

or Laos, and showing at least some retrospective insight, in the 1620s Restored Toungoo kings reluctantly abandoned 16th-century visions in favor of a zone of influence extending merely from the Arakan Mountains to Kenghung and Chiang Mai, and from Mogaung to Tavoy. With these 1620s campaigns, the post-First Toungoo interregnum finally ended, and the restored empire achieved its final shape. Unlike Bayin-naung's improbable domain, this was a realistic and organic unit, which had a primary axis in the Irrawaddy and which did not extend in any direction to a point where Burma's supply lines were more extended than those of her nearest lowland rival. The best testimony to the wisdom of these strategic goals is the fact that the essential spheres of influence of the mid-17th century (they were not frontiers in the modern sense) survived until the 1820s. Even Kon-baung kings, after their campaigns against Siam aborted, achieved limited alterations.

In order to reduce further the danger of provincial revolt, Toungoo leaders, in experiments between 1610 and 1660, made several broad changes in administrative structure, most of which also continued through the 19th century and which, in combination, moved Burma from administrative Pattern B to Pattern C.[203]

In the now compressed Tai/Shan tributary zone Restored Toungoo kings inaugurated a policy, extended in the Kon-baung era, of stationing more garrisons, cultivating closer patronage and family ties between Burmese courtiers and their Tai counterparts, and in certain cis-Salween states, eliminating the right of the ruler (*saw-bwa*) to hereditary succession. At the same time, they necessarily accepted that some of the most distant tributaries would continue to pay homage to China and/or Siam as well as to Burma.

In the lowlands, early Restored Toungoo rulers – much like their Siamese, Japanese, and French contemporaries – gradually mastered the problem of gubernatorial insubordination by obliging most senior princes (those who in the 16th century would have served as *bayins*) and many junior princes (*myo-zas*) to reside not in the provinces, but at the capital itself, in special palaces. Separated from their apanages and subject to diverse practical and ceremonial controls, these princes were politically emasculated. To direct administration at the former *bayin* centers of Prome, Toungoo, Pegu, and Martaban, the throne now appointed commoners and/or junior princes who lacked blood claims to the throne.

[203] Ensuing discussion derives from my *Cycles*, ch. 2, which in turn relies chiefly on RUL 45235, *ZOK*, *UK*, III, and *MMOS*.

The new governors, styled *myo-wuns*, lost the royal insignia of the *bayins* along with the right of hereditary succession. Nor in most cases could they appoint their own deputy officials (provincial spies, military commissioners, secretaries, treasurers, and so forth), whose numbers and duties expanded in the course of the 17th century.[204] Precisely because they owed their appointments not to the governor but to patrons at Ava, and indeed often considered themselves rivals to the governor, deputies could frustrate unauthorized gubernatorial initiatives. Thus at the same time as provincial rebellions declined, central control over provincial manpower improved markedly. The prestige of the old *bayin* centers was further diluted by extending the new gubernatorial system to formerly inferior towns, including what was now Burma's principal port, Syriam.

With the help of its new governors, the throne also moved to establish a more effective presence on the subprovincial level, that of townships (*myos*) and villages (*ywas*), where it sought to regulate succession among quasi-hereditary gentry headmen, to monitor taxes more closely, and to encourage judicial appeals to the royal courts at Ava.[205] In other words, arrangements long in force around the capital now extended throughout the basin. The chief monument to this policy was the census of 1635–1638 instituted by King Tha-lun (r. 1629–1648). Almost certainly the first to cover the entire basin, this celebrated inquest recorded gentry rights, population figures, tax and service obligations for every lowland district as far as Martaban and for a number of nearer Shan areas as well. And how was local penetration achieved? In part through coercion, of course, but more basically by strengthening individual headmen against local rivals so as to win clients beneath the governors, by opening more court and provincial posts to gentry youths, by ending that post-1590 anarchy that had threatened stable hierarchy in the countryside, by regulating local titles, and above all, by guaranteeing the gentry commissions on expanded tax collections. Such commissions often amounted to over a third of the total. Not surprisingly, local elites were generally eager to negotiate new tax and patronage arrangements with capital officials.

---

[204] On provincial establishments, including spies (*na-khans*), military commissioners (*sit-kes*), secretaries, (*sa-yei-gyis*), and treasurers (*taik-zos*), see BL OR 3464, *hka*; RUL 45235, Edict 16, 997 kahson 5 wax.; Edict 44, 999 nadaw 2 wax.; Edict 45, 999 nadaw 5 wax., Edict 77, 1000 tazaung-mon 3 wax.; *ZOK*, 65, 83, 98; *UK* III, 105, 275, 287, 384; *LBHK*, 42, 59, 194, 311; *HNY*, 275, 293–95, 301, 304, 380–84.
[205] On the legal system, Kaing-za Manu-ya-za, *Maha-ya-zathat-gyi* (Rangoon, 1970); *ZOK*, 65–66; RUL 45235, Edict 28, 997 nayon 10 wan.

In turn, self-interest led royal officials and headmen to cooperate in expanding the population of hereditary servicemen (*ahmu-dans*) around Ava. Whereas only 21 percent of residents within a 120-mile radius of Pegu in 1581 had been *ahmu-dans*, by 1650 the throne had achieved concentrations of over 40 percent within 120 miles of Ava by reorganizing old units and by forming numerous specialized military and civilian platoons de novo. This expansion tied nuclear zone populations more closely to the throne and its local agents, while increasing Ava's military advantage over the less *ahmu-dan* rich provinces. Service families received as a conditional grant from the crown three types of land, heritable but in theory inalienable to outsiders, which were carefully graded according to rank and generally irrigated. To accommodate new platoons, the throne reactivated and expanded irrigation works in Kyaukse, Salin, the Mu basin, and other centers. Through an elaborate program of tattoos, decennial censuses, specialized insignia, and written passes, officials also sought to minimize physical and social mobility among *ahmu-dan* units, which provided the backbone not only for the army, but for the entire system of palace service. Similar if less ambitious controls applied to *athis*, that is to say, tax-paying non-servicemen, whose status vis-a-vis *ahmu-dans* now declined as royal influence became more pervasive.[206] In the long term Ava benefited from commercial growth, which inherently favored social mobility. But in the early 1600s the Restored Toungoo court bent every effort to prohibit and circumscribe such mobility, even to discourage *ahmu-dan* exogamy, in part because recent events had created a dread of disorder, but more basically because labor scarcities and at best rudimentary labor markets meant that if the court were to obtain adequate resources, there was no alternative to hereditary obligation and tied service. Burma's situation thus contrasted with that of France, where by 1600 serfdom and hereditary service had become anachronistic, but in varying degrees resembled that of Japan, Late Ayudhya, and Russia, all of which inaugurated elaborate systems of peasant control and social segregation in the late 16th to mid-17th centuries. In these three realms as well as in Burma, the controls of the mid-1600s survived substantially into the mid-1800s.

Finally, the central apparatus itself expanded. To accommodate more members while emphasizing appropriate notions of hierarchy, the

---

[206] Broadly speaking, *athis* still dwelled on communal lands, paid heavier taxes than *ahmu-dans*, but did not have regular service duties. On popular organization, Lieberman, *Cycles*, 96–107.

Restored Toungoo royal court grew more stratified and ceremonially complex. To process a greater volume of written reports, secretariats developed more routinized procedures, even though ministerial jurisdictions themselves remained fluid and subject to pressures of personality. Law courts, headed by the Council of Ministers (*hlut-daw*) and the Eastern Court (*shei-yon*), expanded their authority. Above all, we find a heightened emphasis on the ruler's personal morality, benevolence, and pity; and on his officials' self-abasing obligation to honor their oaths of allegiance and to repay royal patronage (*kyei-zu-daw thit-sa-daw saung*). In truth, some Restored Toungoo and Kon-baung kings became creatures of powerful ministerial families, whose authority tended to grow at the expense of the princes, but the elevation of royal status provided a facade which cloaked, and also perhaps set limits, to ministerial factionalism.

In combination, these changes dramatically enhanced imperial stability. Whereas First Toungoo power rested almost entirely on Lower Burma, the Restored and Kon-baung empires walked on two legs. That is to say, relocation of the capital to the north, monastic curbs, and *ahmu-dan* expansion ensured effective control of the agricultural and demographic heartland of Upper Burma. But at the same time, the new port governorships and valley-wide censuses guaranteed continued access to the coast, with its indispensable trade revenues and firearms. Whereas every 16th-century royal succession precipitated destructive interprovincial warfare, from 1606 to 1819 succession disputes normally were resolved peacefully in the capital. Whereas the First Toungoo empire survived barely 60 years, the Restored empire endured 140 years; and if we consider Kon-baung continuities, the Restored system lasted over two and a half centuries in the teeth of an increasingly competitive international environment.

SPURS TO PRECOLONIAL INTEGRATION: FIREARMS, c. 1600–1830

Firearms remained a pillar of the new imperial order. Royal artisans produced gunpowder and matchlocks throughout the Toungoo period, while in 1787–1788 hundreds of rural metalsmiths were assembled at the capital to turn out guns for renewed attacks on Siam.[207] Guns were also

---

[207] *List* 80, #1, *gi*; "Shei khit myan-ma naing-ngan myo-ywa ne-pe thamaing, s. 999-hku si-tan-mya" (ms), 18; *ROB*, IV, 529, 531, and V, 424, 771, 867, 880.

secured from China and various Tai realms. Recognizing that these were generally inferior to maritime weapons, however, the court concentrated on procuring coastal imports, which – given the demands of campaigning and the guns' rapid deterioration in tropical conditions – became a Sisyphean task.[208] Thus a principal responsibility of coastal *myo-wuns* was to procure firearms through purchases and levies on incoming ships. Royal agents also purchased guns as far afield as India and Aceh; while diplomatic approaches to Europeans typically focused on this issue. In addition, Bo-daw-hpaya (r. 1782–1819) obliged Burmese merchants plying the Irrawaddy to supply specified quantities of foreign guns and powder in lieu of cash taxes.[209]

As Chapter 1 suggested, by comparison with Europe, in Burma the military arts remained conservative, not least in the period 1665–1724 when the level of interstate warfare waned. Burmese shared with other Southeast Asians a tendency to regard guns of imposing appearance as a source of spiritual power, regardless of how well they functioned. A motley assortment of local manufactures, Muslim imports, and French and English rejects defied standardized supply or training. Nor did European drill and tactical coordination have any clear echo, since field forces tended to fight in small groups under individual leaders. In sharp contrast to Europe as well, cannon were rarely used for frontal assaults on stone fortifications. Tellingly, from 1740 to 1757 Lower Burma rebels, having seized the ports, gained a monopoly on firearm imports, but still could not prevail against Upper Burma's manpower advantage.

Nonetheless, with expanding maritime trade after c. 1750 and with a coincident increase in the quality of European handguns and the frequency of warfare, firearms became both more common and more closely integrated into strategy. During the 16th century foreign mercenaries had been the most prominent gunners. But by the mid-1600s mercenaries, who had proven politically dangerous as well as expensive, virtually had disappeared in favor of cannoneers and matchlockmen in the regular *ahmu-dan* system. (Note, however, that these elite units

---

[208] On imported guns' high attrition rate, Henry Yule, *Narrative of a Mission to the Court of Ava in 1855* (rpt., Kuala Lumpur, 1968), 247–48.

[209] Through such quotas alone, during seven months in 1806 the crown obtained 1943 muskets. *ROB*, V, 788–1027. On gun procurement, see also *Dagh-Register gehouden int Casteel Batavia, 1664*, J. A. van der Chijs, ed. (Batavia, 1893), 155–56; *KBZ*, I, 111–12, 211, 225; G. M. Mantegazza, *La Birmania*, Renzo Carmignani, ed. (Rome, 1950), 103; *ROB*, IV, xi, xxviii, 590, 669, and VI, 323–653 *passim*; William Koenig, *The Burmese Polity, 1752–1819* (Ann Arbor, 1990), 25.

often were descended from Muslim or European captives.) In 1635, only 14–18 percent of royal troops used firearms.[210] But among Kon-baung field armies anywhere from 29–89 percent were so equipped, with 60 percent a reasonable average by 1824.[211] In the mid-18th century, two to three generations after a similar transition in Europe, the flint-lock began to replace the less efficient and less powerful matchlock. Burma also began to obtain cast-iron cannon. Late Restored Toungoo and Kon-baung tactics reflected the growing availability and effectiveness of firearms in three spheres: a) In controlling the Irrawaddy, teak warboats carrying up to 30 musketeers and armed with 6- or 12-pounder cannon dominated more conventional craft; b) during urban sieges, cannon mounted atop wooden platforms cleared defenders from the walls and shielded infantry attacks; c) particularly in jungle or hill terrain, Burmese infantry learned to use small arms to cover the building of stockades, which were then defended by firepower massed within.[212]

Although the gradual diffusion of guns into the countryside and the consequent likelihood that rebels would acquire them caused the crown no little distress, on balance these weapons and associated tactical innovations powerfully aided centralization. The value of guns became most obvious in the Shan hills and other interior districts, where firearms were slowest to penetrate and where guns repeatedly afforded royal garrisons a reliable advantage over numerically superior rebels and dacoits.[213] Not only was the 16th-century subjugation of the Shans systematically reinforced in this manner, but Kon-baung forces became better able to parry raids by Chins, Kachins, Karens, and other tribal peoples between the main Shan valleys. In the delta too, following the collapse

---

[210] *ROB*, I, 230; also RUL 45235, Edict 69, 1000 wa-gaung 10 wan.; *ZOK*, 66–67; Frank Trager and William Koenig, *Burmese Sit-tans 1764–1826* (Tucson, 1979), 73.

[211] Major Snodgrass, *Narrative of the Burmese War* (London, 1827), 94–95; *ROB*, IV, 165, 388–92, 557, 574–75; Cyril Skinner, "The Interrogation of Zeya Thuriya Kyaw," *JSS* 72 (1984): 59–95; List 11, #16, 8 ff.; List 78, #8, *gaw*; Father Sangermano, *A Description of the Burmese Empire* (rpt., New York, 1969), 97–98.

[212] See Snodgrass, *Narrative*; H. Lister Maw, *Memoir of the Early Operations of the Burmese War* (London, 1832); Harvey, *History*, 255–56; U Aung Thein, "Our Wars with the Burmese," *JBRS* 50, 2a (1958): 314–44; *HNY* 249–50, 268–69; *KBZ*, I, 328–32, 421–504 *passim*; Michael Symes, *An Account of an Embassy to the Kingdom of Ava* (rpt., Westmead, UK, 1969), 320; Cyril Skinner, ed., *The Battle for Junk Ceylon* (Dordrecht, Holland, 1985), 10–12; Thant Myint-U, *The Making of Modern Burma* (Cambridge, 2001), 19–20; Michael Charney, "Shallow-draft Boats, Guns, and the Aye-ra-wa-ti," *Oriens Extremus* 40 (1997): 16–63.

[213] Alexander Hamilton, *A New Account of the East Indies*, 2 vols. (Edinburgh, 1727), II, 48; Symes, *Embassy*, 276; List 79, #1, *nya, hsa*; *ROB*, V, 492, 816.

of a major Mon rebellion in 1757, the restoration of the royal monopoly on purchases of guns and gunpowder helped Burmese garrisons control restive Mon waterways and townships.[214] Meanwhile, on imperial frontiers guns became the *sine qua non* for success against forces whose military technology was broadly comparable to that of Burma. Wars against Siam from 1662–1665 and 1759–1811 and the Qing from 1765–1769 confirmed that only states enjoying easy access to guns could aspire to regional hegemony.[215]

ECONOMIC INTEGRATION C. 1600–1830: EXTERNAL AND DOMESTIC STIMULI

Economic growth resembled the importation of firearms insofar as both benefited from external trade, both had a destabilizing potential, yet in the long term both favored territorial and administrative centralization. The triumphs of the northern-based polity c. 1635–1824 testified not only to Shan pacification, firearms, monastic and administrative reforms, but also to the growing specialization of the basin economy. If climate was no more favorable than during the Pagan era, without doubt the economy had become considerably more complex and productive.

A venerable tradition, originating with the doyens of English scholarship and revived by Anthony Reid, argues that by cutting off Burma from world trade, the 17th-century initiated a period of economic isolation and retreat that was not reversed until the colonial conquest.[216] Now it is true that on returning to Ava, the throne began to divert a substantial portion of Lower Burma's rice from overseas export to dry zone granaries and that maritime affairs figured less prominently in court deliberations than during the First Toungoo era. So too from the early 1600s – less as a result of royal policy than of competition from larger, better armed Indian and European ships during a period of falling profits – Mons and coastal Burmans reduced their involvement in overseas trade.[217]

---

[214] *UK*, III, 280–83, 339; *ROB*, V, 100, 347, 836, 879 and VI, 331, 457, 650, 695, 724; Symes, *Embassy*, 81; B. R. Pearn, *A History of Rangoon* (rpt., Westmead, UK, 1971), 89–90.

[215] Qing commanders in 1768–1771 complained that foreign-made Burmese guns carried a heavier shot and were more effective than Chinese muskets. Jifa Zhuang, *Qing Gaozong shiquan wugong yanjiu* (Taipei, 1982), 305, tr. Sun Laichen.

[216] D. G. E. Hall, *Early English Intercourse with Burma 1587–1743* (London, 1968), 11; Harvey, *History*, 193, 248–49; Reid, *Age of Commerce*, II, 305–306, 309–11; *supra*, Ch. 1. n. 35.

[217] Victor Lieberman, "Was the Seventeenth Century a Watershed in Burmese History?" in Anthony Reid, ed., *Southeast Asia in the Early Modern Era* (Ithaca, 1993), 222–23;

Yet as Aracadius Kahan has argued for Russia, whose export trade in the 17th and 18th centuries was no less dominated by foreigners, insofar as alien exporters proved more efficient than local rivals, their triumph actually aided the economy by lowering transport costs and raising producer prices.[218] In any case, 17th-century maritime dislocations were less severe on the mainland than in the archipelago. During the mid- and late 1600s Dutch interference induced some Indian and West Asian traders to shift operations from the archipelago to Burma and the upper peninsula. Between c. 1660 and 1740 Mughal policies and European capital infusions in the Indian littoral also promoted small-scale ventures to Pegu and Tenasserim. Restored Toungoo imports were chiefly yarns, numerous types of finished Indian textiles, and New World silver, which flowed into Burma via both Pacific and Indian Ocean routes. In exchange Burma supplied *inter alia* Chinese copper coins, local metals, ceramics, timber, gems, animal and forest exotica.[219] Following disruptions associated with the Mon rebellion, between 1757 and 1825 Burma's coastal trade expanded, as Muslim and especially British private traders sought new markets for a growing array of Indian and European broadcloth, piece goods, hardware, and glassware, while satisfying external demand for Burmese teak logs, planks, and cutch. Thus bulk exports, especially lumber, substantially replaced luxuries.[220]

Extant, quite fragmentary trade statistics are as follows: In the 1510s, 15–16 three- to four-masted junks (probably 200–500 tons each) and 20–30 smaller ships with very limited cargo capacity sailed each year between Lower Burma and its chief southern trading partners, Melaka and north Sumatra; while Pulicat, the principal Coromandel port, sent at least another 4–5 ships of unspecified size. By 1560 Burmese-Malay trade may have grown, but in the 1590s we have records of only 2–3 ships a year leaving Masulipatam, which had replaced Pulicat, for

---

Pierre-Yves Manguin, "The Vanishing *Jong*," ibid., 197–213; Reid, *Age of Commerce*, II, ch. 5; Wil O. Dijk, "The VOC's Trade in Indian Textiles with Burma: 1634–1680" (ms), 8, n. 17.

[218] Arcadius Kahan, *The Plow, The Hammer, and the Knout* (Chicago, 1985), 264–65.

[219] Lieberman, *Cycles*, 117–24, 156–61, 277; idem, "Secular Trends," 14–17; Dijk, "VOC's Trade"; idem, "The VOC in Burma: 1634–1680" (ms); idem, "Burma in the 17th Century: What the VOC Archives Have Brought to Light" (ms); Sinnappah Arasaratnam, *Merchants, Companies, and Commerce on the Coromandel Coast, 1650–1740* (Delhi, 1986), 206–207, 347–52; Tapan Raychaudhuri, *Jan Company in Coromandel, 1605–1690* (The Hague, 1962), 119–29, 213–14; Hall, *English Intercourse*, chs. 8, 10; Prakash, "Coastal Burma," 100–105.

[220] Crawfurd, *Journal*, II, 195–99; Symes, *Embassy*, 214–19, 456–62.

Lower Burma.[221] Coromandel-Peguan trade for 1617–1644 appears to have been in the same order of magnitude as in the late 16th century.[222] From 1651 to 1680 the average annual number of Dutch voyages from India to Burma doubled over 1634–1651, but Dutch trade was probably a small portion of the total.[223] Between the decades 1679–1690 and 1700–1710 average annual voyages of all nationalities between Syriam, then Burma's chief port, and the Coromandel coast's new chief port of Madras tripled to 12; yet we lack tonnages and have no figures for secondary Burmese ports or for other Asian ports, including Aceh and Malay entrepots, trading with Burma.[224] In 1709 a British visitor reported that a total of about 20 large foreign vessels, of 600 tons maximum, visited Syriam.[225] Between 1788 and 1811, however, the annual number of square-rigged vessels leaving Rangoon, which had supplanted Syriam, ranged between 18 and 40. From 1811 to 1822, the annual number of such vessels, with tonnages from 200 to 700, rose to between 35 and 56. Smaller craft at Rangoon and diverse ships at Bassein and secondary ports would have swelled this figure to a significant, if uncertain, extent.[226] In sum, such data as we have suggest that the absolute volume

[221] On Burma's 16th-century trade, Cortesao, *Suma Oriental*, I, 98; M.A.P. Meilink-Roelofsz, *Asian Trade and European Influence* ... (The Hague, 1962), 69–70; Prakash, "Coastal Burma," 96–97. On tonnages, Pierre-Yves Manguin, "The Southeast Asian Ship," *JSEAS* 11 (1980): 268; Reid, *Age of Commerce*, II, 36–43.

[222] W. Ph. Coolhaas, ed., *General missiven van Gouverneurs-General en Raden aan Heren XVII der Verenidge Oostindische Compangnie*, Vol. 1 (The Hague, 1960), 297, 410; Prakash, "Coastal Burma," 100–103; Sanjay Subrahmanyam, *The Political Economy of Commerce: Southern India, 1500–1650* (Cambridge, 1990), 214, 311, 334.

[223] Dijk, "Burma in the 17th Century," 3.

[224] See sources in Lieberman, *Cycles*, 156. Cf. Denys Lombard, "The Indian World as Seen from Aceh in the Seventeenth Century," in Prakash and Lombard, *Commerce and Culture*, 190–91.

[225] Hamilton, *New Account*, II, 41.

[226] See Crawfurd, *Journal*, II, 195–99; Anne Bulley, ed., *Free Mariner* (London, 1992), 137, a 1788 memoir; Great Britain: Parliament: House of Commons: Sessional Papers, 1831–32, vol. 10, pp. 240 ff: "Papers Relative to Finance and Accounts – Trade," pp. 799, 821; ibid., Sessional Papers 1847–48, vol. 61, pp. 1 ff.: "Commercial Tariffs and Regulations, Resources and Trade of the Several States of Europe and America ... Part XXII: India, Ceylon, and Other Oriental Countries," pp. 194, 200, which cite c. 40 ships per annum from Burma to Calcutta and Madras for 1810–1820. (My thanks to Jörg Schendel for bringing the latter source to my attention.) Analyzing Burmese-Calcutta-Madras shipping 1795–1846, Schendel, "Upper Burma's External Trade, c. 1850–1890" (Univ. of Heidelberg Ph.D. diss., in progress), ch. 2 points to "steady, but moderate growth." In truth close comparisons are impossible not only because tonnages are rarely given, but because sources fail to distinguish between registered, measured, and cargo tonnage. See John McCusker, "The Tonnage of Ships Engaged in British Colonial Trade During the 18th Century," *Research in Economic History* 6 (1981): 73–105.

of Burma's maritime trade, though perhaps not its importance in the political economy, was no smaller – indeed, may well have been significantly larger – in the 1820s than in the 16th-century "heyday."[227] Note too that in the 18th and early 19th centuries, superb local teak and low labor costs rendered Burma's shipyards among the most important in Asia, with orders from as far as Oman.[228]

On the whole, Yunnan trade between 1600 and 1820 seems to have been more vigorous than maritime trade. Buoyed by New World crops, more specialized mining and handicrafts, and constant migration from eastern China, Yunnan's population, after recovering from a mid-17th century downturn, grew almost eight-fold between 1740 and 1850.[229] Exchanges with Burma expanded, to service both Yunnan itself and the Chinese interior. By the 1820s traders were estimated to be taking back to Yunnan some 7,000 short tons of Burmese cotton a year,[230] over six times the estimated annual figure at the turn of the 17th century. Employing caravans of 2,000 or more pack animals, Chinese traders also obtained Burmese forest exotica and gems, whose total worth was about one-third that of cotton exports, in exchange for Chinese handicrafts, foodstuffs, and large quantities of raw silk. In the early 1820s the annual value of Burma's overland exports and imports was said to range between 67 and 117 percent of the value of trade at Rangoon.[231] After c. 1720

[227] The Pegu-Melaka-Sumatra trade in n. 221 *supra* (the only 16th-century figures available) totalled roughly 8,000 tons. If we assume – very generously – that Pegu-India trade was comparable, the total would be c. 16,000 tons. More comprehensive 1820s figures for Rangoon alone cited in n. 226 *supra* were in the order of 20,000 tons. (In each case I have chosen the median number of tonnages and of vessels.) Yet, to continue the cautionary tone of the previous note, we have accurate information neither on tonnages nor the level of mid- and late-16th century trade.

[228] See n. 226 *supra* plus "Pegu" references in *Generale missiven van Gouverneurs-Generaal en Raden aan Heren XVII der Verenidge Oostindische Compangnie*, 9 vols. (The Hague, 1960–1988); India Office Records, London, Bengal Secret Consultations, 6/20/1805; Symes, *Embassy*, 457–61; Pearn, *History of Rangoon*, 65–79; ROB, V, 947.

[229] Lee, "Food Supply," esp. 720–23.

[230] That is, 14,000,000 lbs. Crawfurd, *Journal*, II, 194. Cf. Yule, *Narrative*, 148; Reid, *Last Stand*, 75, citing Teruko Saito. There is no evidence this increase was accompanied by improved ginning techniques, which relied on hand-worked wooden rollers. *GUBSS*, I, 2: 368 ff.

[231] According to Crawfurd, *Journal*, II, 195, 199, overland trade was 400–700,000 pounds sterling, or 4–7,000,000 ticals (*kyats*), compared to Rangoon trade of 600,000 pounds. Considerably smaller, but earlier, figures appear at William Francklin, *Tracts, Political, Geographical, and Commercial; on the Dominions of Ava* (London, 1811), 53–55, 99–102; and Symes, *Embassy*, 460 (referring to British imports), which may explain the Crawfurd, *Journal*, 199 claim for "a remarkable increase" in maritime trade of 5–600 percent in

the Bawdwin and Mawlong silver mines, employing "several tens of thousands" of Chinese workers, also expanded. Although tributary to Burma, these mines supplied part of their output to Chinese merchants who used it to help redress Burma's sizeable trade surplus.[232]

In combination, maritime and Chinese trade – plus smaller overland exchanges with Siam, Arakan, Khun, and Lao principalities – stimulated the Burmese economy in diverse ways. Some sectors, including teak, shipbuilding, and cotton, came to depend directly on foreign markets. In the opposite direction, domestic silk weaving, which by the early 19th century supplied virtually all classes, relied almost totally on Chinese raw silk.[233] By collecting local surpluses, supplying rural peddlers with textiles, and providing credit, Indian, Persian, Armenian, and Chinese merchants helped to join ports and frontier towns to interior producing areas. Once routes specializing in export-import trade had developed, handicrafts and other goods of a purely domestic character found easier distribution. As Wil O. Dijk has shown, Indian textile imports in the 17th century were largely of the coarser grades, intended for a popular market.[234] Supplemented in the 18th and early 19th centuries by Chinese and European consumer goods, such imports must have provided an attractive incentive for market producers in towns and hinterlands. By the same token, imported metals offered a major, possibly critical, commercial lubricant. Along with silver, copper (which was produced locally and imported from Japan and Yunnan) formed the basis for Burma's private lump-coinage through the late 1500s. But thereafter Japanese, Yunnanese, Bawdwin, and most notably New World silver encouraged a gradual shift to the white metal, which was inherently more practical than copper for large-value and long-distance transactions and which could be assayed more easily. *Pace* Andre Gunder Frank, who sees silver

12 years. Cf. Sun, "Burmese Tributary and Trade Relations," 43–44. A tical or *kyat* was 1/100 of a *viss*, which usually weighed 3.65 lbs.

[232] Francklin, *Tracts*, 102, c. 1810 put Burma's annual trade surplus with Yunnan at 400,000 ticals of silver, but it is unclear if this was true of the 17th–18th centuries. On Sino-Burmese trade and mines, see too Sun, "Burmese Tributary and Trade Relations," 37 ff., 44; *Dagh-Register 1664*, 156, 169; Crawfurd, *Journal*, II, 191–95; Symes, *Embassy*, 263, 325, 432; *ROB*, V, 14, 378, 711; VI, 473, 802; Chiranan Prasertkul, *Yunnan Trade in the Nineteenth Century* (Bangkok, 1989), ch. 2.

[233] By 1850 silk-weaving in the capital may have employed 4000 people. See Yule, *Narrative*, 144, 153; Symes, *Embassy*, 263, 432; *GUBSS*, I, 2: 372–99; Crawford, *Journal*, II, 193–94; G. W. Strettell, *The Ficus Elastica in Burma Proper, Or a Narrative of My Journey in Search of It* (Rangoon, 1876), 8–9, 41.

[234] Dijk, "VOC's Trade," esp. 7–8, 16.

inflows as testimony to Asia's economic superiority,[235] there is no reason to imagine that Burmese economic technique was particularly efficient. Nonetheless, by increasing bullion stocks in an economy that was imperfectly monetized and in which credit techniques were undeveloped, and by helping to make *ywet-ni* silver the 19th-century standard, imported metals encouraged commodity production, long-distance bulk trade, and labor mobility in the ports. Bullion imports thus help to explain not only Burmese commercial vitality, but as we shall see, Burma's economic coordination with other Eurasian sectors.[236] Yet more indirectly, guns and trade revenues aided reclamation and exchange by promoting state pacification.

But if foreign trade stimulated the economy, expansion retained strong domestic roots. To a considerable degree, the growth of Burma's foreign trade reflected larger aggregate (and per capita?) demand for imports in the Irrawaddy basin itself. Consider, moreover, the modest size of external trade within the overall economy. Eager to stock Upper Burma's granaries, the throne, as noted, curbed rice exports, which even in good years probably never equaled .5 percent of the crop and remained small even by Siamese and Vietnamese standards.[237] The chief exports were raw cotton and teak, but less than half of the cotton crop normally left Burma.[238] Given that cotton acreages in the first half of the

---

[235] Andre Gunder Frank, *Re-Orient* (Berkeley, 1998), esp. ch. 3.

[236] Cf. John Lee, "Trade and Economy in Preindustrial East Asia, c. 1500–1800," *JAS* 58 (1999): 16. But accurate assessment is impossible, because we lack reliable figures on bullion imports or domestic supplies. *Ywet-ni* was roughly 90 percent silver, 10 percent copper. Until 1857 Burmese currency was mainly privately-produced lump coinage, rather than royal coinage. Note that copper continued to be preferred for small-scale exchanges. On bullion flows and coinage, n. 219 *supra*, plus Schendel, "External Trade," ch. 2; Ko U, *Myan-ma dinga*, 56–57; Lieberman, *Cycles*, 32–33, 121–25, 156–63; M. Robinson and L. A. Shaw, *The Coins and Banknotes of Burma* (Manchester, UK; 1980); and Sun, "Ming-Southeast Asian Interactions, 176–87.

[237] See Crawfurd, *Journal*, II, 191–99; *ROB*, IV, 192, 650 and VI, 488; *Dal*, II, 375, 377; Michael Adas, *The Burma Delta* (Madison, WI, 1974), 20–26. Cf. James C. Ingram, *Economic Change in Thailand 1850–1970* (Stanford, 1971), 24; Li Tana, "The Late 18th Century Mekong Delta and the World of the Water Frontier" (ms).

[238] In the 1820s some 7,000 short tons of overwhelmingly ginned cotton went annually overland to Yunnan and 200 tons (600 unginned) by sea to Dacca. Crawfurd, *Journal*, II, 194, 196; Reid, *Last Stand*, 75. According to Myo Myint, "The Politics of Survival in Burma: Diplomacy and Statecraft in the Reign of King Mindon 1853–1878" (Cornell Univ. Ph.D. diss., 1987), 230–31, in the mid-19th century total production of ginned cotton was 7,770,000 "units" (viss), or 14,180 short tons. Acreage in Mindon's reign was probably little changed from the 1820s. But in fact, the ratio of exports to total production was probably below 1:2 because some districts underreported their cotton

19th century represented only 2–5 percent of total lowland cultivated acreage, and that other sectors reliant on overseas markets – forestry, shipbuilding, river haulage, and silk-weaving – employed only small numbers, it is difficult to see how much more than 3–4 percent of the lowland population depended primarily on foreign trade for their livelihood.[239] And if foreign trade in 1800 was worth in the neighborhood of 4,000,000 to 8,000,000 *ticals*,[240] the exchange of domestic textiles, handicrafts, timber, metals, petroleum, and above all, foodstuffs dwarfed it in value as well as volume.[241]

What, then, were the domestic sources of expansion? Pacification provided one obvious spur. In contrast to more or less continuous lowland warfare between 1300 and 1555 – which may have helped to keep the population of Upper Burma below its Pagan-era peak – Toungoo and early Kon-baung rule provided most of the basin with three centuries of substantial peace.[242] As Chapter 1 suggested, warfare, with its disruption of births and childrearing, normally provided a major impediment to population increase. Either on their own initiative or with

---

crop, and a small part of cotton exports to Yunnan apparently went with the seed, which increased their weight 3-fold. My thanks to Jörg Schendel for his help with these matters.

[239] *Reports on the Administration of Burma, 1888–91*, Tables III-E (No. 63) show cotton acreages of 91,000–145,000 acres out of total Upper Burma cultivated acreages of 2,849,000–3,249,000. According to Jörg Schendel, personal communication, July, 2001, cotton exports expanded little between 1830 and 1890. In 1830 Lower Burma's cultivated acreage was probably 650–750,000, of which a only a tiny portion was in cotton. *Gazeteer of Burma*, 1, 423; Adas, *Burma Delta*, 22. I estimate that fewer than 30,000 people (many of whom, of course, had dependents) out of 4,500,000 were employed in forestry, shipbuilding, silk-weaving, hauling, carting, and export ceramics. Of course, insofar as some industries catered to both domestic and foreign markets, and foreign trade conditioned domestic exchange in a thousand indirect ways, no simple line can be drawn between foreign and domestic sectors.

[240] As noted, in the early 1820s Crawfurd, *Journal*, II, 195, 199 put foreign trade, both via Rangoon and overland to China, at 10–13,000,000 *ticals*, but this came after a period of expansion and was appreciably (perhaps 2–3 times) larger than implicit and explicit estimates for the 1794–1810 period provided in Francklin, *Tracts*, 99–102, and Symes, *Embassy*, 460 (for the latter, total trade must be extrapolated from British imports).

[241] We have no estimate of the food or domestic textile trade, but in 1796–97 the wholesale (not retail) petroleum trade, a minor element in domestic commerce, was worth 1,082,000 *ticals*. Hiram Cox, *Journal of a Residence in the Burmahn Empire* (London, 1821), 44. In the opening years of the 19th century Francklin, *Tracts*, 53–55, 99–102 estimated total maritime imports and exports at only 2,320,000 ticals.

[242] The chief exceptions were the 1590s and 1740–1757.

encouragement from royal officials and gentry eager to increase their revenue, *athi* and *ahmu-dan* villagers with inadequate land opened new agricultural tracts in the dry zone, along its fringes, and most especially in Lower Burma. From the late 1600s the latter area provided the principal outlet for Upper Burma's surplus population.[243] In a repeat of 14th/15th century patterns, drier weather c. 1660–1710 may have increased dry zone emigration by pulling people to the fringes. Ironically, the return of more favorable rainfall during much of the period 1710–1805 seems to have had much the same effect by pushing people from overcrowded northern districts.[244]

Natural increase aside, the basin population also grew through immigration from surrounding areas. Part of this was voluntary, driven by a desire for basin land, as with Shan movements to c. 1550, and then more commonly with Karens, Chins, and Kachins.[245] Of greater significance were massive deportations of war captives to Upper Burma from outlying areas, chiefly Manipur, Lower Burma, and the Shan hills. Concentrated in the 1630s and 1760s–1780s, such movements were designed by the court both to strengthen the *ahmu-dan* system and to weaken refractory provinces and tributaries. By 1820 perhaps 350,000 people, roughly a sixth of Upper Burma's population, traced their origins to such deportations.[246]

All told, cultivated acreage in Upper Burma grew between 1600 and 1830 by at least a third, from 1.8 to 2.5 million acres, divided more or less evenly between rice and dry crops. By 1830, another 650,000 acres were under rice in Lower Burma. There the data base is too weak to estimate the percentage increase, but Pegu's devastation in 1600, frequent subsequent references to Karens and especially Burmans moving into the delta, the continuous extension of the delta coastline through sedimentation, and the unprecedented importance of delta rice in the

---

[243] On frontier settlement, see, e.g., "Shei-khit myan-ma naing-ngan," 28, 32–60; Symes, *Embassy*, 93, 183; *ZOK*, 15, 32, 66–98; Trager and Koenig, *Sit-tans*, 46, 63–189, 277, 280, 290, 343; *ROB*, II, 208, 292 and V, 471, 489, 660, 674, 678–79; *List* 69, #3; *List* 53, #7; NL 1950, Edict of 1041 2nd wa-zo 3 wax., *gei*.

[244] On climate's agricultural impact, see *UK*, III, 269, 303, 306, 333, 337; *Dal*, II, 375; Marks, *Tigers, Rice*, ch. 6; Godley, "Flood Regimes," chs. 6, 7. On northern population pressures, see too Thant, *Making of Modern Burma*, 43.

[245] See, e.g., Trager and Koenig, *Sittans*, 64, 77–86, 144–68; *ZOK*, 11, 14, 58, 101; *ROB*, I, 416, 446, 465; Wilkie, *Burma Gazeteer: Yamethin*, 26, 30–33, 45.

[246] *ROB*, IV, xxvii–xxviii, 569, 599, 607 and VI, 471; *List* 79, #1; Stuart, *Old Burmese Irrigation*, 5–14; Lieberman, "Secular Trends," 5–9, which assumed a somewhat smaller total population.

19th-century political economy all suggest that acreage in Lower Burma expanded more rapidly than in the dry zone.[247]

Rice extension was hardly the only agricultural change. To supply pickled tea to replace alcohol for ceremonial use among observant Buddhists, tea cultivation spread in the northern Shan states after 1500. Particularly in Upper Burma, New World peanuts, tobacco, and maize began to offer a significant source of supplementary nourishment and/or income on alluvial and hill tracts. On overpopulated dry zone lands ill-suited for rice, as in Meiktila, Yamethin, and Myingyan districts, cotton became a truly major crop, supplying not only Burma's principal export to China, but its chief handicraft industry and an extensive domestic trade. By 1830 probably over 90,000 acres in Upper Burma were regularly planted in cotton, which as noted, was labor intensive. At the same time cotton dressing, spinning, dyeing, and weaving engaged growing numbers of urban as well as village workers, generally women, whose jackets, shawls, and skirts, at least at the lower end of the market, competed successfully with imports.[248] Finally, in Lower and more especially Upper Burma *kauk-gyi* continued to advance at the expense of "round type rice." Throughout the 17th and 18th centuries pacification and new irrigation works encouraged both the dissemination of existing *kauk-gyi* strains and the development of scores of new *kauk-gyi* as well as *kauk-lat* sub-strains adapted to specific soils, aridity, disease, and insect threats.[249]

In combination, agricultural extension, intensification, and new commercial opportunities supported (and reflected) a population increase between 1600 and 1830 of c. 50 percent, that is from perhaps 3,000,000 to 4,500,000 in the empire as a whole, of whom perhaps 70 percent resided in the Irrawaddy basin.[250] Although, apart from the mid-18th century

[247] Lieberman, "Secular Trends," 8–9, plus Symes, *Embassy*, 233, 259, 325; Harvey, *History*, 350–51; Adas, *Burma Delta*, 15–28; *Dal*, I, 130–31, 174–75; Henry Gouger, *Personal Narrative of Two Years' Imprisonment in Burma* (London, 1860), 19–20.

[248] On cotton production, spinning, dyeing, and weaving, *supra* nn. 238, 239, plus *GUBSS*, I, 2: 363–99; *Dal*, I, 109–110; Crawfurd, *Journal*, II, 216; tax records in *Zam-bu kun-cha* (Rangoon, n.d.), 46–47; *ZOK*, 51; *ROB*, II, 239; IV, 47 and VI, 677; Trager and Koenig, *Sittans*, 341.

[249] *Kauk-lat* ripens in 150–170 days cf. *kauk-gyi's* 170–200. On new crops and rice strains, Toe Hla, "Kon-baung hkit let-ya thet-kayit-pa lu-hmu si-bwa-yei thamaing" (Rangoon Univ. Research Project, 1981), 104–105; Lieberman, "Secular Trends," 9–11; Watabe and Tanaka, "Ancient Rice Grains"; Cheng Siok-Hwa, *The Rice Industry of Burma 1852–1940* (Kuala Lumpur, 1968), 36–39.

[250] See discussion in Lieberman, "Secular Trends," 11–12. These estimates agree broadly with Reid, *Age of Commerce*, I, 14.

crisis, growth may have been more or less unbroken, the period of most rapid expansion seems to have been the climatically propitious 1710–1825 era. By the latter date – to judge from north-south emigration, periodic food shortages in the north, and large-scale imports of delta rice – pressure on dry zone lands had become serious, recalling 14th-century strains. Early 19th-century population densities almost certainly exceeded those in the Pagan period.

Such tensions notwithstanding, all levels of the marketing system stood to benefit from rural expansion. Larger aggregate demand for cotton and silk textiles, salt, dried fish, jaggery, cooking oil, petroleum, metal utensils, and earthenware made specialized enterprises more viable. Because their members relied heavily on the market for food and other supplies, the growth of urban, shipbuilding, and mining communities created additional incentives to expand output of rice, vegetables, dried fish, cattle, and handicrafts. At the same time, as recourse to poorer dry zone lands reduced productivity, peasants were tempted to shift from rice to more specialized crops or handicrafts, or to leave Upper Burma for the delta and the Shan hills either permanently or as seasonal workers.[251] Following Skinner, Elvin, and van Zanden, we would anticipate some or all of the following responses to such pressures: the velocity of commercial exchange would rise, the number and size of periodic markets would grow, older provincial and capital markets would accommodate more subordinate units, and complementarity would increase between regions with specialized endowments.[252]

The state's contribution to commercialization between c. 1600 and 1830 was ambiguous, but on balance, probably beneficial. On the one hand, impediments were obvious. Although handicrafts, many domestic textiles, cattle, and rice were freely traded, the most lucrative, easily policed branches of trade were monopolized by the king and senior princes, or what was more common in the Kon-baung period, by consortia of private merchants (Burmese and foreign) who purchased monopoly rights from the crown to sell in urban markets a range of

---

[251] On 18th/early 19th century economic migrations in the lowlands, see epistles in Saya Pwa, ed., *Kyi-gan shin-gyi myit-tasa* (Rangoon, 1932), nos. 2, 3, 7, 10, 12, 13, 15, 36, 37.

[252] G. William Skinner, "Marketing and Social Structure in Rural China," *JAS* 24 (1964–65): 3–43, 195–228; Mark Elvin, *The Pattern of the Chinese Past* (Stanford, 1973), chs. 10–12; Jan Luiten van Zanden, "Early Modern Economic Growth," in Maarten Prak, ed., *Early Modern Capitalism* (London, 2001), 69–87.

goods extending from diamonds, sticklac, and silk to peas, betel, and cooking oil.[253] Insofar as they could be enforced, such contracts obviously reduced competition. Ruinous military exactions, farmed tolls, and ill-restrained apanage demands had much the same dampening effect. Elite wealth was normally used for religious donations, money-lending, and conspicuous display, rather than investment. On the other hand, the throne promoted trade by welcoming foreign merchants, standardizing commercial measurements, encouraging bullion imports and mining, eliminating tolls levied by once-independent lowland rulers, and diverting Lower Burma's sizeable rice surplus to northern markets. Of more indirect economic benefit, Restored Toungoo and Kon-baung kings created a legal system with broader and more uniform reach, protected against Shan incursions and bandits, sponsored agricultural reclamation, and demanded cash taxes that, intentionally or not, forced peasants to expand commodity production.[254] If commercial considerations had little to do with the initial decision, the requirement that major princes transfer their residences to the capital also stimulated trade by promoting competitive display and concentrating market demand in a fashion reminiscent of the *sankin-kotai*, alternate attendance, system of Tokugawa Japan.[255]

But how much hard evidence supports these claims of economic expansion and stronger commodity production, that is to say, of both extensive and Smithian growth? From 1610 to 1783 the number of market towns (*myos*) in the lowlands and adjacent Shan areas grew from 145 to over 200, and the population and/or urban perimeter expanded for most provincial cities on which we have information (including Tabayin, Prome, Henzada, Kanaung, and, of course, the new port of Rangoon, founded in 1755). As for the capital area (the Ava-Amarapura-Sagaing complex), between 1783 and 1826 alone, it reportedly grew by 53 percent, to about 150,000.[256] As early as 1700 Burmese urbanization may

[253] See, e.g., *ROB*, V, 611, 737, 788, 805, 864–65, 874, 914–1010 *passim*; VI, 577, 579, 682, 803, 814, 849.

[254] See *UK*, II, 307; *AAm*, 275; *ROB*, IV, 223–25, 282, 405, and V, 461, 1031; *LBHK*, 162; Donald and Joan Gear, *Earth to Heaven* (Harrow, UK: 1992).

[255] Cf. Constantine Vaporis, *Breaking Barriers: Travel and the State in Early Modern Japan* (Cambridge, MA: 1994).

[256] Trager and Koenig, *Sit-tans*, 408, assuming the 1826 figures are reliable and 5 people per household. Of course, as Rangoon grew, Pegu and Syriam declined. For Burmese urban trends, Lieberman, "Secular Trends," 18 and sources therein; P. Gouye, 1692, cited in Reid, *Age of Commerce*, II, 71.

have approached Rozman's stage E, characterized by market as well as administrative linkages between a national capital, provincial centers, sub-provincial market towns, and local markets.[257] Between Upper and Lower Burma, and between the lowlands and the Shan hills, specialized bulk items like tea, raw cotton, domestic textiles, and possibly earth-oil were first traded in the 14th or 15th century, but by the 18th century had become staples. So too, only in the 17th and 18th centuries did the north come to depend on Lower Burma's rice, supplied through private trade as well as taxes. In the 1790s "several thousand" boats, ranging from 10–200 tons burden, carried rice (as well as salt and fishpaste) from Lower Burma to the capital.[258] Toungoo and early Kon-baung sources also refer to an unprecedented array of Upper Burma districts specializing in cotton, indigo, tobacco, sesame, fruits, and other cash crops as well as in the manufacture of diverse textiles, iron and brass implements, ceramics, paper, carts, lacquerware, religious objects, even fireworks, much of which was traded downriver and east to the Shan country.[259] In other words – much as in Russia in this same period – as the southern frontier became its reserve granary, the northern heartland grew more economically diversified and less self-sufficient. Specialized brokers, wholesalers, and retailers divided often along ethnic lines. The early Kon-baung era also saw a marked proliferation of commercial contracts (*thet-kayits*), which regulated land and commodity sales, mortgages, and loans. Along with late 17th-century edicts on *ahmu-dan* debt, these materials confirm that even the most humble rural strata had access to cash.[260]

---

[257] Cf. Rozman, *Urban Networks*, 34–35. Yet the population at a typical provincial center, level 3, was considerably smaller than in Rozman's schema.

[258] Symes, *Embassy* 233 (suggesting an average burden of 60 tons), 259, 325; *Dal*, I, 130–31, 174–75; Gouger, *Imprisonment*, 19–20 (claiming boats up to 200-tons); Crawfurd, *Journal*, II, 190 (citing tonnages of 10–100) and 187–212 *passim*; *ROB*, V, 952; VI, 577, 682, 803, 814, 849; VII, 273–75.

[259] Crawfurd, *Journal*, II, 187–91; Toe Hla, "Kon-baung hkit let-ya thet-kayit," ch. 5; Symes, *Embassy*, 230–83; ZOK, 50–51; Marilyn Longmuir, *Oil in Burma* (Bangkok, 2001), 5–49. For evidence of associated improvements in river and overland transport, see Symes, *Embassy*, 233, 259, 325; *Dal*, I, 130–31, 174–75; *ROB*, IV, 182–83; List 32, # 2, 69–71.

[260] I rely *inter alia* on NL 1950, Edict of 1041 kahson 12 wax., Edict of 1053 kahson 11 wax., Edict of 1054 wa-gaung 14 wax., Edict of 1051 thadin-gyut 4 wax.; U Toe Hla, ed., *Kon-baung hkit let-ya thet-kayit-pa lu-hmu si-bwa-yei thamaing thu-tei-thana si-man-kein atwet asi-yin khan-sa*, 2 vols. (Rangoon, 1977–79); a 222–page unpublished, untitled collection of *thet-kayits* collected by Dr. Toe Hla [hereafter Toe Hla's Collection]; and Toe Hla, "Kon-baung hkit let-ya thet-kayit," esp. chs. 1–4. Dijk, "VOC's Trade," 19–23 describes 17th-century urban wage labor.

Perhaps the most convincing evidence of monetization derives from land sales. Between 1350 and 1512, recall that in 64 percent of extant Upper Burma land sales the properties were exchanged for in-kind goods or for a combination of lump-coinage and in-kind goods. By contrast, from 1750 to 1830, 97 percent of lands were paid for exclusively in lump-silver coinage. Moreover, whereas early inscriptions involved capital elites with easy access to bullion, Kon-baung commercial actors were socially diverse and overwhelmingly rural. Land sale documents show finally that by comparison with the 15th century, when land transfers were encumbered by *athi* communal rights vested in local headmen, by the Kon-baung period such restrictions had lessened dramatically. Nor apparently did royal claims prevent de facto alienation of *ahmu-dan* land. In other words, a limited system of private, marketable land, with individual rights to ownership and alienation enforceable by contract (*thet-kayit*), had emerged.[261] The trend towards monetization of major transactions (barter still dominated petty exchanges) was also consistent with the shift from land to money in monastic patronage, as well as from in-kind to cash taxation.

POLITICAL BENEFITS

Economic change c. 1600–1830 aided centralization, at least in the long term, in four ways. (I focus here on the political economy, rather than on cultural integration, to be discussed later.)

First, foreign trade continued to strengthen central authorities vis-a-vis provincial leaders. Overland and perhaps maritime trade in this period grew more rapidly than agricultural output.[262] As in most pre-industrial societies, widely dispersed in-kind rural production was

---

[261] I have found 67 *thet-kayits* dated 1750–1830 that give the price of land sales in the following sources: Toe Hla, *Kon-baung hkit let-ya thet-kayit-pa lu-hmu si-bwa-yei* I, documents through May 25, 1827 and II, documents through April 13, 1829; Toe Hla's Collection, 1–34; Trager and Koenig, *Sit-tans*, 371–72; *List* 64, #4; *ROB*, V, 981 and VI, 330; Toe Hla, "Kon-baung hkit let-ya thet-kayit," 26–27. Moreover, 83 percent of 243 extant early Kon-baung commercial transactions of all types – mortages, indentureships, loans, as well as land sales – were in silver, a claim based on previous sources plus *List* 11, #10; 16, #9; 39, #4; 52, #5, 12; 53, #7, 9, 13, 21; 54, #10; 57, #8; 60, #7, 8, 13–15; 62, #14; 63, #2; 84, #7, most of which are *parabaik* records of loans and mortgages. See also Lieberman, "Secular Trends," 19–21; Saito, "Rural Monetization."

[262] Recall that the number of large ships visiting Syriam/Rangoon more than doubled between 1709 and 1824 (a more modest increase may have occurred between 1600 and 1824) and that Chinese trade rose more sharply. But we have seen that from 1600 to

more difficult to tax than commercial wealth concentrated at cities, ports, and riverine checkpoints, so each increment of foreign trade promised imperial authorities disproportionate benefits. I have argued that the genius of the 17th-century reforms, which continued into the Kon-baung era, derived from the fact that they allowed kings to reside in the agricultural/demographic heartland without surrendering control over the ports (or the China trade). Restored Toungoo and Kon-baung rulers used the proceeds from customs duties, trade monopolies, and overseas expeditions to patronize officials and monks, to glorify the capital, and to buy guns in a virtuous circle that left economically marginal districts ever weaker politically. Notwithstanding the modest size of exports in the overall economy, because maritime revenues were easy to collect, a plausible 1770s/1780s European account claimed that they often provided the largest single source of royal revenue.[263]

Second, much like foreign trade, expanding domestic output and population magnified the imbalance between lowland core and upland periphery. Even if the basin and more peripheral areas enjoyed comparable rates of growth, Chapter 1 has argued that the former's initial superiority would have ensured a constantly increasing absolute advantage in manpower and rice, two key indices of military strength. But in fact rates in the basin probably exceeded those in the hills, both because foreign stimuli were more concentrated and because voluntary and involuntary population transfers strengthened the lowland economy at the expense of outer zones. More indirectly, we shall find, Burman settlement in outlying areas aided administration by promoting psychological identification with the throne.

Third, whatever the level of rural production, as the countryside became more monetized, so did the facility with which the crown could extract resources. Notwithstanding the crown's determination to build rice stocks as a hedge against famine, over the long term agricultural, household, and market taxes tended to change from kind to cash: cash taxes constituted only 21 percent of extant local levies between 1350 and 1550, but some 42 percent from 1600 to 1752 and almost 70 percent from

---

1830 rice acreage increased by only about a third in Upper Burma, and probably by well under 50 percent in the basin as a whole.

[263] Mantegazza, *La Birmania*, 103. We have no Burmese-language trade figures, but on maritime revenues generally, see *UK*, III, 208; *ROB*, V, 378, 711, 805, 969 and VI, 473, 670, 681.

1752 to 1804.[264] In addition, we shall find that the Kon-baung court instituted new retail/wholesale monopolies, tax farms, and money-lending
schemes.

Finally, commercial growth nurtured forms of wealth more sympathetic to central influence. Recall that the dominant lay stratum in
Upper Burma c. 1300–1600 was hereditary *athi* headmen ruling self-
sufficient, subsistence-oriented *athi* communities. *Ahmu-dan* headmen
also depended on hereditary labor services. Gradually, money eroded
this self-sufficiency. Starting perhaps as early as the mid-1500s, and very
obviously in the 1700s and early 1800s, headmen became involved in
supra-local webs of contract and exchange. In Upper Burma and even
to some extent in the Shan hills, *athi* and *ahmu-dan* headmen supplemented their income with commodity production, tax farming, land
speculation, money-lending, and the accumulation via money-lending
of debt-slaves and dependents. Starting in the mid-1700s, ostensibly
hereditary headmanships themselves were mortgaged or sold to parv-
enues, including money-lenders from outside the locality.[265] Even the
wealthiest provincial families came to depend on capital patrons to secure tax farms and commercial monopolies, and to win legal cases involving property rights and commissions. At the same time the king,
his family, and leading ministers provided extensive loans to provincial clients. Thus, patronage chains based on debt and credit radiated
from the royal court to Shan rulers, junior officials, headmen, and big
traders, reinforcing and supplementing formal structures and bolster-
ing the court's practical authority.[266] The large-scale conversion of glebe
lands into private property, which benefited headmen and officials, and
the economic emasculation of the monkhood reflected these same commercial trends.

---

[264] Lieberman, "Secular Trends," 24.
[265] Saito, "Rural Monetization," 153–84; Toe Hla, "Kon-baung hkit let-ya thet-kayit,"
esp. chs. 3–6; Lieberman, "Secular Trends," 27–28, relying on *List* 24, 201; *List* 52,
#5; *List* 53, #13, 21; *List* 54, #10; Trager and Koenig, *Sit-tans*, 368–74; Crawfurd, *Journal*,
app. 49–50.
[266] Saito, "Rural Monetization," esp.168–71; Toe Hla, "Kon-baung hkit let-ya thet-kayit,"
44–60; idem, "Money-lending," 131–36; Lieberman, "Secular Trends," 26–28; *MMOS*,
III, 43 ff.; NL 1605, *hka*; and Kyaw-hmu Aung, "Kon-baung-hkit-hnaung salin-thu-
gaung thamaing" (Univ. of Rangoon MA thesis, 1992), esp. ch. 3. Cf. Thant, *Making
of Modern Burma*, 253–43 discussing the consolidation in the late Kon-baung era of a
"commercial and landholding class" composed largely of court nobles, their friends,
and clients.

POLITICAL COSTS: THE 18TH-CENTURY CRISIS AND ITS
LIMITED RESOLUTION IN THE KON-BAUNG ERA

Yet at the same time economic change was destabilizing insofar as involuntary pressures joined social and geographic mobility to threaten those hereditary obligations that underlay the royal service system. Even in the early 1600s *ahmu-dan* controls were inadequate to prevent service confusion and evasion for three reasons: a) the overly complex system of registers, natal residence, and platoon endogamy was subject to inherent entropy; b) overburdened low-status *ahmu-dans* were constantly tempted to move illegally into higher-status units whose work load was easier or to become private retainers of ministers and princes who promised reduced obligations;[267] c) for their part, and again often in defiance of royal prohibitions, officials were tempted to welcome absconders as a fresh source of wealth and influence. The search for factional advantage was endemic, but in a system without clear rules of royal succession, it became particularly intense when ministerial factions backed different candidates for the throne. Whereas in the First Toungoo era princely *bayins*, with secure provincial bases, had led their own armies, after c. 1640 princely immurement at Ava repeatedly allowed ministerial families to select the weakest, most pliant candidate for the throne. Royal debility in turn nourished factionalism. This was the downside of Restored Toungoo reforms.

But, if such problems had an institutional root, demographic and commercial growth in the late 1600s and 1700s aggravated them by increasing both popular evasion and intra-elite competition. Population pressure in Upper Burma, particularly in irrigated districts around the capital, gradually reduced the land allotments of *athi* tax-payers and low-ranking servicemen. Those hardpressed individuals who did not emigrate illegally to the south were tempted to borrow money from wealthy officials, and when unable to discharge their debt, to enter their creditors' households as debt-slaves or private retainers. Since work quotas were fixed per platoon (*asu*), any loss of members increased per capita burdens on remaining platoon members, who themselves became more tempted to abscond. The late 17th and early 18th centuries thus saw a sharp rise in evasion and debt-slavery, as well as in the illegal

---

[267] See, e.g., *UK*, III, 126; RUL 45235, Edicts 19, 26, 27, 34, 63, 65, 78; *ZOK*, 63–64; NL 1950, Edict of 1026 nayon 13 wan., Edict of 1027 tabo-dwe 6 wan., Edict of 1028 1st wa-zo 9 wan.; and Lieberman, *Cycles*, 96–105.

mortgaging of service plots and in the formation of estates cultivated by private retainers and bondsmen. Apparently much of the produce of those estates was sold at Ava.[268] The chief beneficiaries from such trends were ministers, especially those with access to market taxes, whose practical influence at court soon came to exceed nominal rank. Less favored officials sometimes sought to compensate by extorting funds from servicemen still in their charge and by stepping up their own recruitment of private dependents. Inflation in the price of imported textiles during the 18th century further threatened officials who depended on fixed cash taxes (*hkun-thei*).[269] In these ways popular evasion, court factionalism, and commercial expansion fed one another. The last two Toungoo kings repeatedly forbade servicemen to become retainers or debt-slaves, and tried to force absconders back into military support units. Yet neither they nor alliances of leading officials were able to establish a secure authority. In the 1730s and 1740s the military system dissolved into a welter of private ministerial and princely retinues, which began fighting one another in and around the capital of Ava. As the court's authority waned and as fighting disrupted agriculture, local headmen in Upper Burma withdrew into their own hastily fortified domains.

Peoples on the imperial periphery – Shans, Manipuris, Mons – were not slow to exploit this ill-disguised collapse. Entirely marginal to Burmese affairs until the 1730s, Manipuri leaders were suddenly inspired both by Avan weakness and by their own conversion to Vaishnavite Hinduism to spread their new religion to the banks of the Irrawaddy. Reports that Manipuri horsemen were galloping unchecked across Upper Burma in turn spurred a 1740 uprising at Pegu. The southern rebels nourished two chief grievances. First, they were embittered by extortionate Avan taxation, which reflected unchecked ministerial factionalism and perhaps too a northern perception that the coast had become unusually prosperous. Second, they resented Burman immigration to delta towns, where newcomers formed a privileged stratum; and in fact, the 1740 uprising sparked a general massacre of Burman migrants and garrisons. In the name of Ra-manyan independence, a new king now took power at Pegu. After moving up the basin in a see-saw ten-year campaign, the southern armies – primarily Mons, but with a

---

[268] See, e.g., NL 1950, Edict of 1041 kahson 12 wax.; Edict of 1043 tazaung-mon 5 wax.; Edict of 1053 kahson 11 wax.; Edict of 1056 wa-zo 12 wan.; Edict of 1054 wa-gaung 14 wax.

[269] Lieberman, *Cycles*, 159–60.

growing leaven of southern Burmans and Karens – finally seized Ava and overthrew the Restored Toungoo dynasty in 1752.[270] This collapse would prove to be the first of three such imperial disasters across mainland Southeast Asia in a mere 34 years.

Coming after the crises of the 13th/14th centuries and the late 16th century, this proved to be the shortest and least disruptive of Burma's three interregna, precisely because economic and cultural links throughout the western mainland had become ever more secure. Even more dramatically than in the early 1600s, imperial disintegration galvanized Upper Burma to exploit its underlying demographic superiority. The founder of the Kon-baung dynasty, a petty headman from the far north known posthumously as Alaung-hpaya ("Embryo Buddha"), rallied the panicked population of the dry zone in part by appealing to Burman racial solidarity against "Mon" invaders. Having revitalized the military service system with massive recruitment and forcible re-enrollment, he and his sons then launched a series of vengeful campaigns in all directions. By 1759 they had smashed the southern rebellion, reconquered the Shan uplands, and ravaged Manipur. By 1770 his heirs had temporarily dismembered the Siamese kingdom, subdued much of Laos, and defeated four major invasions from Qing China, no less. These near simultaneous victories over Ayudhya (1767) and China (1765–1769) testified to a truly astonishing elan unmatched since Bayin-naung.

To be sure, the strength of the new Kon-baung dynasty can be exaggerated. The Restored Toungoo problem of uncertain succession feeding ministerial-cum-princely factionalism was never fully resolved. More basic, because they attempted to protect fixed *ahmu-dan* tenures in the face of an active land market and growing emigration from Upper Burma, Kon-baung leaders soon faced pressures similar to those that had undermined their predecessors. Food shortages and continued emigration from the north suggest that the man/land ratio in the dry zone was growing less favorable. In the face of royal bans, needy *ahmu-dans* and *athis* continued to sell themselves to wealthy courtiers and headmen, to leave their villages, and to mortgage or sell service lands. Many glebe lands were also illegally sold as private property, so that as Teruko Saito has shown, the original status of lands became increasingly

[270] On southern revolts, including anti-Burman massacres, see India Office Records E/4/4 Coast and Bay Abstracts: Letters Received 31 Aug. 1734 to 19 Feb. 1744, p. 332; Madras Public Proceedings, 29 Dec. 1740; *Dal*, I, 101; BL OR 3464; *LFSG*, vol. 26 (1741), 8–9, 35–37; *HNY*, 380 ff.

problematic. Nominally fixed categories of official, communal/family, and glebe land collapsed into a de facto system of private, marketable land. Indeed, the proliferation of legally-enforceable land contracts (*thet-kayits*) gave the system greater security.[271] This incipient privatization of service lands joined growing economic hardship and excessive tax and service demands to reduce the registered population between 1783 and 1802 by 17 percent, a decline which accelerated with a severe drought and famine from 1805–1812.[272] The Kon-baung court's inability to resolve these problems – and its related failure to profit from maritime trade as fully as Siam – contributed to its declining military fortunes vis-a-vis Siam between 1775 and 1811.

That said, if we use as a yardstick not Siam but Restored Toungoo Burma, the new dynasty achieved impressive levels of internal control and external expansion. Kon-baung administrative reforms to 1824 fell into three categories.[273] First, early Kon-baung leaders sought to reinvigorate basic features of Toungoo government. As self-made military men, they assumed, with good reason, that they could force the system to work more effectively than their anemic predecessors. Accordingly, through marriages and personal ties to ministerial and gentry families, they forged new patronage chains radiating into the countryside. In their enthusiasm to secure recognition of prerogatives threatened during the recent disorders and to win posts under a triumphalist dynasty, the gentry of northern and central Burma were no less eager than Kon-baung princes to restore central authority. Secure patronage networks allowed Kon-baung leaders to organize a vast number of new *ahmu-dan* platoons and to fix popular tax and service contributions with countrywide censuses in 1783 and 1802 that were the most complete since Tha-lun's pioneering inquest of the 1630s. The post-1783 loss of servicemen must be set against this enormous antecedent increase.

Second, even as they sought to restore the Restored Toungoo *ahmu-dan* system, they modified military organization and territorial governance. So as to take advantage of demographic fluctuations, they shifted from fixed local military quotas to variable levies. They systematically expanded the procurement of firearms. They replaced some hereditary township headmen with appointed governors (*myo-wuns*), strengthened

[271] Saito, "Rural Monetization."

[272] Koenig, *Burmese Polity*, 58–59; Thant, *Making of Modern Burma*, 43, emphasizing the depressing effects of overpopulation on Upper Burma living standards.

[273] Discussion follows my "Political Consolidation under the Early Kon-baung Dynasty," *JAH* 30 (1996): 152–68.

marriages ties between Burmese and Shan aristocracies, and assimilated some of the nearer Shan states to the same system of *myo-wuns* and censuses as in lowland provinces.[274] Long-term centralization thus had an undeniable internal logic: the First Toungoo dynasty had unified a vast territory, but had preserved autonomous kingdoms within the basin. The Restored dynasty had extended direct rule throughout the lowlands, but had honored the hereditary privileges of Shan *saw-bwas*. Now Kon-baung kings tightened control in the lowlands and reduced the nearer Shan principalities.

Third, again building on Toungoo experiments, Kon-baung officials, particularly after 1780, began to tap commercial wealth more imaginatively. They commuted various in-kind taxes and converted fixed tolls, ferries, and brokerages into tax farms, actions that both increased government income and rendered it more predictable. Likewise, they sold retail/wholesale monopolies, expanded money-lending on behalf of the crown, launched novel trading ventures overseas and along the Irrawaddy, and experimented with royal coinage. Apparently for the first time, on-duty soldiers began receiving small cash payments.[275] It is unclear how these experiments intersected with hereditary service. Did paid units operate separately from *ahmu-dan* platoons, or within the shell of the old system? Were apanage grants devalued? How extensive was *ahmu-dan* commutation? Clearly the money economy continued to gain ground, for in 1857 the crown inaugurated a full-fledged system of cash taxes and salaries, both lubricated by Burma's first standardized silver coinage.[276]

These changes combined with new military leadership to permit territorial expansion unprecedented since the ephemeral conquests of the 16th century. Disadvantaged vis-a-vis the more commercially innovative Siamese kingdom, which by 1778 had expelled the Burmese not only from the Chaophraya basin but from Laos and Chiang Mai, Kon-baung armies nonetheless retained the peninsular ports in the southeast. They also strengthened their authority over Shan areas that had grown restive in the twilight of Toungoo rule. (Indeed, the Sino-Burmese wars of

---

[274] See., e.g., *List* 11, #16, p. 8; So So Aung, "Kon-baung hkit shan ne ok-chok-yei thamaing" (Mandalay Univ. MA thesis, 1992), chs. 1, 2.

[275] On commercial income and cash outlays, *ROB*, V, 570, 721, 788, 805, 864–65, 874, 914–23, 939, 960, 972, 978–1015, 1020–27 *passim*; VI, 577, 803, 814, 849; *List* 78, #8, NL 1605, *ku-hku*; Ko U, *Myana-ma din-ga*, 72–74; Toe Hla, "Kon-baung hkit let-ya thet-kayit," 167–68.

[276] Myo Myint, "Politics of Survival," 43–47.

1765–1769 grew partly out of Shan attempts to enlist Chinese support for their new-found autonomy.) Far more dramatic were Kon-baung gains to the west, in Arakan, Manipur, and Assam. Buffeted by internal revolts, the loss of Chittagong, and commercial inroads by European companies and private traders, Arakan had entered a trajectory curiously reminiscent of Reid's 17th-century crisis in the island world, and as such, was unable to resist a Burmese invasion in 1784–1785. Burma promptly sought to assimilate Arakan to its system of lowland provincial administration. In Manipur, north of Arakan, in 1819–1820 growing Kon-baung interference culminated in the installation of a puppet ruler backed by a Burmese garrison. Most astounding, from 1821–1823 Burmese armies crossed the snow-clad Himalayan passes to destroy the distant court of Assam, from whose territory they cast covetous eyes on Cachar, Jaintia, Bhutan, even Bengal. If Manipur and Assam were held more loosely and far more briefly than Arakan, their subjugation confirmed the escalating advantage that the Irrawaddy basin enjoyed over smaller principalities and more isolated areas (see Figure 1.6).[277] As we shall see, Kon-baung conquests paralleled the post-crisis military success of Chakri Siam, Nguyen Vietnam, and Napoleonic France. Yet the most fateful result of Burma's western expansion was this: by bringing the Burmese and British empires into closer contact, it precipitated the First Anglo-Burmese War of 1824–1826. With the British annexation of Arakan and the peninsula in 1826, followed by the loss of Lower Burma after a second war in 1852, the centuries-long process of Burmese expansion finally halted.

CULTURAL INTEGRATION, c. 1600–1830: CHANGES IN BURMAN AREAS

I turn finally to the dynamics and lineaments of cultural change in the Restored Toungoo and early Kon-baung eras. How did political and cultural integration influence one another? How did universal and empire-specific loyalties intersect? How could standardization coexist with growing cultural fracture? I consider first the Burman-dominated northern two-thirds of the basin.

---

[277] On western conquests, *KBZ*, II, 1–17, 189–207, 343–53; *ROB*, IV, 71–84, 152, 164, 441, 546, 621; Charney, "Jambudipa and Islamdom," chs. 7–9; Gangamumei Kabui, *History of Manipur, Vol. 1: Pre-Colonial Period* (New Delhi, 1991); S. L. Baruah, *A Comprehensive History of Assam* (New Delhi, 1985).

After 1555 the end to Shan raids eliminated a major source of instability and, by drying up fresh Shan movement into the basin, hastened
the Burmanization of lowland Shan communities. Conversely, stabilizing the Shan frontier allowed Burman colonists to resume their historic
advance around the northern and eastern fringes of the dry zone. The
basic situation may have been analogous to that of Western Europe after the 11th century, when an end to major folk migrations permitted an
expansion of regional ethnicities.[278]

Insofar as Shan raids had severely disrupted the Upper Burma
sangha, pacification of the Shan hills contributed as well to a proliferation of rural monasteries (*kyaungs*). Although such structures became
more numerous in the post-Pagan era, apparently only in the late 16th,
17th, and 18th centuries did they become truly universal on the village level. Evidence for this claim is indirect, but compelling.

On the one hand, the following social and economic factors created
preconditions favorable to the spread of village *kyaungs*, with their chests
of manuscripts and programs of systematic instruction. Rural pacification improved, not merely in the lowlands. More censuses, law cases,
and commercial contracts created a stronger popular need for literacy
and numeracy, which could be met only by monasteries; in circular
fashion, more monastic libraries required more copyists. With the disappearance of sects like the Forest Dwellers, whose landed estates had
made them economically independent, a central element in lay-*sangha*
relations now became the provision of religious instruction in exchange
for alms from the villagers.[279] By the 18th century at latest, the large majority of village males were learning to read and write during their years
as lay students (*kyaung-daw-thas*), novices (*ko-yins*), and/or ordained
monks (*rahans* and *hpon-gyis*). As once marginal lands were opened to
cotton and handicraft production, a larger surplus became available to
support economically unproductive monks.

On the other hand, the following evidence testifies to a substantial
growth between c. 1600 and 1830 of popular, monastically-supplied literacy. As writing became more common, the cost of *Tipitaka* transcription
declined sharply.[280] Square orthography based on elite lithic inscriptions
yielded to cursive orthography based on palmleaves, which were the

[278] Mann, *Sources of Social Power*, I, 380, Joseph Strayer, *On the Medieval Origins of the
Modern State* (Princeton, 1970), 16–17.

[279] Cf. Gunawardana, *Robe and Plough*, ch. 4, discussing a reverse change from alms dependence to self-sufficiency in early medieval Ceylon.

[280] Than Tun, *Hkit-haung*, 182, and personal communication, Nov. 1987; I 1045, B I, 336.

natural medium of monastic communication and popular literacy.[281] In the 15th Ava century scribal work normally had been reserved for monks, but by the late 18th century copying of the *Tipitaka* was routinely entrusted to laymen culled from common *athi* and *ahmu-dan* units.[282] The 18th century saw the appearance of the first Burmese spelling books[283] and (we shall see) an ever more copious and diverse vernacular literature. And whereas the 15th-century lay population was substantially illiterate, those who drafted Kon-baung commercial contracts came from diverse lay strata, with no sign of professional specialization.[284] In an observation confirmed by other visitors, an English officer in 1830 remarked, "I have not seen a single village on my way down[river] without these monasteries, and reading and writing are rendered so common by the universal custom of founding their village schools, that men following the most menial offices can both read and write, though, of course, not with considerable fluency."[285] Most tellingly, the first British censuses, faithfully reflecting precolonial patterns, showed that in Upper Burma adult male literacy, defined as the ability to read and write simple materials, exceeded 50 percent.[286]

---

[281] The earliest extant palmleaf, c. 1680, already used circular script, although square orthography for lithic inscriptions continued into the 19th century and is still used for monastic ordination books. *ROB*, IV, 492; V, 873–74; Than Tun, personal communication, Nov., 1987.

[282] *ROB*, IV, 358, 414, 482–83, 489 and V, 824.

[283] Allott et al., "Burma," 5.

[284] Saito, "Rural Monetization," 163.

[285] D. G. E. Hall, ed., "R. B. Pemberton's Journey from Munipoor to Ava, and from Thence Across the Yooma Mountains to Arracan," *JBRS* 43 (1960), 35. See too Symes' 1795 report in *Embassy*, 123 ("There are no mechanics, few of the peasantry, or even the common watermen [usually the most illiterate class], who cannot read and write in the vulgar tongue"); Sangermano, *Burmese Empire*, 180 ("There are few among the Burmese who do not know how to read and write; for the Talapoins, to whose care they are intrusted as soon as they attain the age of reason, always teach them to read, as also to write . . ."); and T. A. Trant, *Two Years in Ava, from May 1824 to May 1826* (London, 1827), 259.

[286] Government of India, *Census of 1891, Imperial Series*, Vol. IX (Rangoon, 1892), 137, 142–43 said 53.2 percent of Upper Burma males over age five were either literate or in school, compared to a mere 1.5 percent of females. But among males age 15–24, the ratio of literates or in school was 59.2 percent; and among males age 25 and over, 62.5 percent. Excluding non-Burmans would have raised these figures further. C. C. Lowis, *Census of India, 1901, Part 1: Report* (Rangoon, 1902), 61, 70, using modified criteria, put the ratio of specifically Burman male literates at 49 percent, and females at 5.5 percent for Burma *as a whole*, not merely Upper Burma as in the 1891 census. Precisely because *kyaung* instruction was more intact and illiterate immigrants were fewer in Upper than in Lower Burma, literacy levels were higher.

By facilitating tax collections and *ahmu-dan* controls, wider literacy and numeracy provided a foundation for administrative centralization. The post-1630 explosion of written exchanges between court and countryside dealing with everything from census and tax reports to military provision, religious organization, headmen succession, legal decisions, and *ahmu-dan* controls provides sufficient evidence. "It is a kingdom governed by the pen," an Italian traveler reported in the early 1700s, "for not a single person can go from one village into another without a paper or writing, whereby the government is made most easy."[287]

In a more subtle sense, monastic networks and their offshoot, expanded literacy, strengthened the crown by continuing to drive elite notions of religious and social regulation deeper into the countryside. In 1800 monks and novices constituted 1–3 percent of the male population. Not only were they drawn from a reasonable cross-section of society; not only did all monks, despite their sectarianism, memorize the same Theravada texts, but throughout the kingdom they instructed their young charges in similar materials, including the Pali formulae, the lives of the Buddha, and the *Loka-niti* and *Raja-niti* literature. Such works venerated royal authority.[288] By hearing monastic sermons and by employing monks for life-passage rituals, even illiterate men and women imbibed the notion that social rank was a function of unequally apportioned religious merit extending from "wild hill people" at the base to the king at the apex. Famous provincial scholars were invited to monastic colleges at the capital, whence some returned to their home communities. Many lesser monks loved traveling to fairs and distant monasteries, preaching as they went. "Mother" monasteries spawned "daughter" or branch monasteries, emphasizing particular textual approaches, throughout the countryside. Here, then, were mechanisms of horizontal as well as vertical acculturation.

Although far less numerous than monks, itinerant troupes of entertainers had a similar impact. The 18th century saw, if not the birth of theatre, its elaboration and commercialization. The first documented Burmese play, *Mani-ket*, was performed in the 1730s or 1740s, while from 1785 Bo-daw-hpaya's Heir-Apparent compiled records of foreign

---

[287] Niccolao Manucci, *Storia do Mogor, or Mogul India 1653–1708*, William Irvine, tr., 4 vols. (London, 1906), I, 373.

[288] *TL*, 206–207; James Gray, *Ancient Proverbs and Maxims from Burmese Sources* (London, 1886); Maung Gyi, *Political Values*, 15–16; Shway Yoe, *The Burman*, chs. 2, 4, 13, 20–21; Koenig, *Burmese Polity*, 89–90.

plays, dance, and music sufficient to fill 54 volumes.[289] Drama reached the countryside as governors and local nobles sought to imitate royal performances, and more particularly as professional troupes blended court conventions with village traditions of singing and dance to produce performances that were increasingly comic and action-oriented and directed specifically at rural audiences. The late 1700s and early 1800s saw a marked increase in the number of professional puppeteers, singers, musicians, and dancers, all of whom in theory became subject to ministerial regulation in 1776. Presenting stylized versions of the Ramayana, the Jatakas, and Burmese historical events, these performers disseminated knowledge of Buddhism, punctilio, and social hierarchy as conceived by the court and reconfigured by local imaginations. According to Ma Thanegi, "the theatre was the only means of knowing what went on in the city and keeping abreast of the times."[290]

Theatrical patronage was part of a multifaceted royal effort to standardize key cultural definitions and symbols. Here it is useful to distinguish between religious and secular policy, and between intentional and unintentional effects. As befit a throne whose self-proclaimed raison d'etre was to promote Buddhism and more specifically to maintain uniform monastic standards, post-1600 kings devoted the great bulk of their efforts to religious projects. Insofar as gifts to the monkhood were the chief means by which laymen accumulated merit necessary for happy reincarnations, and insofar as the benefits of any given donation were proportionate to the sanctity of the monastic recipient, royal supervision of the monkhood – which lacked adequate internal policing mechanisms – remained a matter of enormous practical import. During much of the 18th century the monkhood was embroiled in an acrimonious split between those who believed that novices should wear the monastic robe over one shoulder and those who favored covering both shoulders. Bo-daw-hpaya resolved the issue in favor of the two-shoulder (*a-yon*) sect, which went on to dominate capital monasteries and monastic councils well into the 19th century.[291] Besides convening councils to adjudicate issues of this sort, the crown appointed capital and provincial abbots, conducted regular monastic examinations,

---

[289] Noel Singer, *Burmese Dance and Theatre* (Kuala Lumpur, 1995), 9, 13.
[290] Ma Thanegi, *The Illusion of Life: Burmese Marionettes* (Bangkok, 1994), 15 and 1–45. See too "Thabin-wun" in *Myan-ma swe-zon kyan* (Rangoon, 1964); *ROB*, II, 124–25, 316; Htin Aung, *Burmese Drama* (Oxford, 1937), 6–75, 144–46; Noel Singer, *Burmese Puppets* (Singapore, 1992), chs. 1, 2; idem, *Dance and Theatre*, chs. 1–5.
[291] *TL*, 85–220; *MMOS*, III, 128–40.

disseminated "purified" copies of the *Tipitaka*, and again most notably under Bo-daw-hpaya, dispatched missionaries to outlying provinces.[292] In acts that were as much cosmological theatre as social control and that bespoke an increasingly textual, fundamentalist, even puritanical vision shared by lay leaders of the wider society, Kon-baung kings also issued more explicitly Buddhist law codes, harassed Muslims and heretics, outlawed liquor (hapless recidivists had to drink boiling lead), and forbade animal slaughter. Prohibitions on liquor and meat contradicted ancient customs which we saw had been ardently supported by courtiers and leading monks in the early 1500s and which still found grudging official tolerance in the late 1600s.[293] Like all Burmese, Toungoo and Kon-baung kings believed implicitly in the *nats*, but they prohibited animal sacrifices to these spirits and sought to gain better control over the cults by marginalizing female and transvestite shamans and by promoting a standard pantheon revolving around 37 approved *nat* spirits.

In the secular domain too, royal interventions provided a set of norms which Upper Burma elites, seeking emulatory prestige and practical patronage, readily imitated. The crown tried to standardize Burmese spelling and orthography, along with weights, measures, and calendars, at least in the towns where its writ ran strongest. It sponsored normative works of history, literature, and law that circulated widely in manuscript.[294] By obliging provincial officers and gentry to attend regular homage (*kadaw*) festivals, the crown promoted, unintentionally perhaps, normative styles of architecture, ritual, speech, poetry, drama, and dress which spread to provincial courts. The post-1635 requirement that apanage-holders and their retainers reside for long periods at the capital, and the induction of Upper Burma gentry youths into the corps of royal pages, had a similar impact. At a lower social level tens of thousands of military and non-military *ahmu-dans* served capital service rotas lasting from several months to three years. This too was a

[292] See the late 18th-century record of missions, Pathama Maung-taung Hsaya-daw, *Amei-daw-hpyei* (Mandalay, 1961), 457–61, plus *ROB*, IV, 44, 54–55, 316, 352–53.

[293] On 17th-century tolerance, *ZOK* 96; *ROB*, II, 66, 295–96. On Restored Toungoo and Kon-baung restrictions, Hpaya-byu Hsaya-daw, *Tha-thana ba-hu-thu-ta paka-thani* (Rangoon, 1928), 171–73; *ROB*, III, 229; IV, 12, 220, 425; 471–75; VI, 19–30, 240, 253, 260, 352–93; VII, 66–67, 411; Symes, *Embassy*, 51, 65–66, 166, 173–74, 246, 381; Sangermano, *Burmese Empire*, 159–60, 198–99; Gouger, *Imprisonment*, 52, 97; *TL* 162–250.

[294] *AAm*, 230; *ROB*, I, 70; III, 229; IV, xiv–xix, 5, 22–23, 71, 130–31, 220, 489, 492; V, 458, 572; *SHDMA*, 156–385 passim; Toe Hla, "Kon-baung hkit let-ya thet-kayit," 61.

marvelously efficient, if unintended and perhaps even unnoticed, device for homogenizing speech, dress, ritual, consumer tastes, and identities. Insofar as the great bulk of *ahmu-dans* lived in Upper Burma, it helps to explain why Burmanization was most pronounced in that zone.

Alongside new educational structures and royal interventions, by promoting colonization and spatial mobility, economic expansion itself eroded parochialism. A combination of migratory pressures and superior agronomic technique allowed Burmans to continue absorbing and displacing ethnic minorities throughout the dry zone and along its fringes. Early Kon-baung accounts point to an ill-regulated swell of peddlers, dockyard workers, seasonal laborers, tattooers, and pilgrims moving along trade routes to and from the chief towns and annual pagoda fairs.[295] Like monks, entertainers, and colonists, these itinerants bore with them the traditions of their home villages plus, in idiosyncratic recombinations, borrowings from urban centers.

Finally, I shall emphasize that intensifying warfare – both internal conflicts against predominantly Mon forces, and external contests with Siam, Manipur, China, and eventually Britain – stimulated Burman pride and social cohesion.

To be sure, one can overstate the ensuing uniformity. Even in Burman-speaking areas provincial identities retained much of their appeal. Legends and histories of Prome, Toungoo, and other major towns continued to claim unique associations with the Buddha and proudly to recall their days of independence and the glories of local tradition. Provincial and village communities, including royal officials, continued to honor specific protective spirits.[296] Moreover, especially around the capital, large-scale settlement of ethnically distinct, non-Burman *ahmu-dan* deportees – Manipuris, Mons, various Shan groups, Siamese, Laos, Portuguese, French – created a mosaic of inheritance, ritual, even linguistic practices that fed on service segregation and endogamy and that persisted for two, three, or more generations in direct opposition to the larger assimilative trend.

---

[295] Presumably these were *ahmu-dans* and *athis* who escaped headmen supervision or gained permission for temporary leave. Saya Pwa, *Kyi-gan shin-gyi*; Crawfurd, *Journal*, 187–91; Symes, *Embassy*, 230–77; Toe Hla, "Kon-baung hkit let-ya thet-kayit," ch. 5; *ROB*, IV, 182–83, 621; *List* 32, #2, 69–71; Thaung Blackmore, ed., *Catalogue of the Burney Parabaiks in the India Office Library* (London, 1985), 71.

[296] R. R. Langham-Carter, "Lower Chindwin Nats," *JBRS* 23 (1933): 97–105, and 24 (1934): 105–111.

In addition to such distinctions, which may be termed vertical insofar as they united people from different social stations on the basis of
geography or service affiliation, we find broad horizontal social cleavages. Htin Aung's social idylls notwithstanding, Burmese society was
deeply stratified.[297] Royalty and officials were divided into numerous
sub-grades, each with its own sumptuary insignia. In a broader sense,
princes, officials, service leaders, and local headmen – who were exempt
from taxes, attended royal homage festivals, and were known collec-
tively as "rulers" or *min* – were sharply distinguished from the servile,
tax-paying masses, the so-called *hsin-yei-tha* ("people of poverty"). Although gentry headmen, like monks and entertainers, served as cultural
brokers, high social barriers, reflected in sumptuary insignia and intermarriage bans, tended to inhibit elite-to-mass transmissions.

At the same time, try as they might, commoners could never quite
"catch up" with the latest elite usages insofar as greater leisure, a more
self-conscious interest in novelty, and broader foreign contacts rendered
elite culture unusually plastic and innovative. *Min* males, on balance,
were more likely to study for long periods in monasteries, to be knowledgeable in Pali, even Sanskrit; to wear Indian and Chinese textiles,
to be familiar (through adaptations and translations) with foreign conventions, in short, to think in supra-imperial contexts. In part to satisfy
intellectual curiosity, in part to make more universal the cultural authority of the court, Kon-baung missions to India, Siam, Cambodia, and Java
expressly sought to acquire scholarly manuscripts and to transmit foreign artistic and theatrical traditions. Along with Siamese entertainers
captured in 1767, such contacts transformed entertainment at capital
and provincial courts, as shown, for example, in the appeal of Malay
plays, Javanese epics, Khmer and Siamese dance and music.[298] Meanwhile within Upper Burma itself elite culture grew more specialized and
competitive through the multiplication of indigenous art styles, literary
schools, and religious interpretations, all of which fed on leisure, literacy, and elite prosperity. As patronage of theatre and music expanded,
court entertainers perfected rival styles. As religious inquiry became
more textual, learned laymen as well as monks questioned the accuracy

[297] Cf. Htin Aung, *Burmese Monk's Tales* (New York, 1966), 5–6. On social divisions, see
my *Cycles*, ch. 2.
[298] On foreign influences, *ROB*, IV, xxix, VII, xii–xiii; Thi-ri-zei-da-yat-kyaw, *Paw-tu-gi
ya-zawin* (Rangoon, 1918); Htin Aung, *Burmese Drama*, 43; Koenig, *Burmese Polity*, 92;
Singer, *Dance and Theatre*, 11–13, 23–24, 38.

of the calendar and the proper role of the *sangha*.[299] As historiography grew more robust, so did erudite debates on the reliability of sources and the value of legends.[300]

Such was the social divide that some commoners sought to satirize or to subvert *min* cultural pretensions. Clowns at village fairs, for example, voiced sentiments critical of monks and *min* leaders that would never be tolerated off stage. Thant Myint-U suggested that this sort of concealed protest grew more common as Kon-baung demands increased.[301] Likewise, although many humble laymen and monks were every bit as observant as their capital counterparts and although teetotalism had village roots, several sources agree that tolerance for alcohol and attachment to pre-Buddhist rites, including the more extravagant *nat* rituals, increased with social and physical distance from the court.[302] Among the most marginal social groups in Upper Burma, namely Karens, Chins, and other non-Burman migrants from the hills, what Marshall Sahlins terms "cultural defiance" – a determination to preserve self-respect in a separate hierarchy rather than enter the lowest rung of a dominant hierarchy – bred a steadfast rejection of Buddhism and Burman ethnicity altogether.[303]

In short, far from being uniform, basin culture remained vertically and horizontally fissured, while elite culture in particular became more variegated. But it is no less certain that between 1600 and 1830 geographic and social isolates grew less distinct as judged by objective markers and subjective expression alike. As Chapter One suggested, in its Janus-like attention to overarching unity and internal fracture,

[299] *ROB*, VI, 352–93; *TL*, 185–211. On the mysterious Zawdi heresy of Bo-daw-hpaya's reign, see Mendelson, *Sangha and State*, 73–77; Sangermano, *Burmese Empire*, 111–12, Yule, *Narrative*, 241–42.

[300] See Twin-thin-taik-wun Maha-si-thu, *Twin-thin myan-ma ya-zawin-thit*, 3 vols. (Rangoon, 1968), I, *ni-dan, ta-ha*, 1–2; *UK*, I, sects. 2–3; Pe Maung Tin and G. H. Luce, *The Glass Palace Chronicle of the Kings of Burma* (London, 1923), ix–xxiii, 8–11, 17, 29, 32–409; Mon-ywe Hsaya-daw, "Maha-ya-zawin-gyaw" in *List* 24, # 1.

[301] Thant Myint-U, "Crisis of the Burmese State and the Foundations of British Colonial Rule in Upper Burma (1853–1900)" (ms), 34, 58. On horizontal cleavages, see too J. S. Furnivall, *Report on the Settlement Operations in the Myingyan District, Season 1909–1913* (Rangoon, 1915), 37; Peter Vandergeest, "Hierarchy and Power in Pre-National Buddhist States," *MAS* 27, 4 (1993): 843–70; James C. Scott, *Weapons of the Weak* (New Haven, 1985).

[302] See, e.g., *Zam-bu kun-cha*, 47; *ROB*, II, 295; III, 229; *ZOK*, 96; Trager and Koenig, *Sit-tans*, 396; Symes, *Embassy*, 65–66; Crawfurd, *Journal*, II, 182; Thant Myint-U, "Crisis," 13.

[303] *ZOK* 11, 83, 98; RUL 45235, Edict 94, 1001 taw-thalin 10 wan. Cf. Marshall Sahlins, "Goodbye to *Tristes Tropes*," *Jl. of Modern History* 65 (1993): 1–25.

cultural change was analogous to administrative and commercial change. As administrative and commercial networks grew more encompassing and penetrating, they too engendered more complex hierarchies and more expert functions. In each sphere specialization required a grid of mutually-validated, empire-wide references – a hierarchy of offices, a system of markets, a shared set of intellectual and aesthetic assumptions – whereas by definition, geographic isolates, which tended to be more characteristic of an earlier era, lacked supra-local reference.

The erosion of encapsulated forms of knowledge, the rise of an overarching culture that was simultaneously more "orthodox" Theravadin, more self-consciously Burman, and more sympathetic to central regulation became apparent in four broad spheres. Most of these changes began in the First Toungoo period, if not earlier, but all intensified in the 18th and early 19th centuries.

First, local sources of sanctity were devalued in favor of universal textual norms endorsed by the crown and the monkhood. Kings outlawed animal sacrifices atop Mt. Popa and other sacred sites, while female and transvestite shamans lost status. Starting in the 1770s and gaining ground under Bo-daw-hpaya, essentially pre-Buddhist origin myths linking the monarchy to a solar spirit yielded to claims of royal descent from the clan of Gotama Buddha and thence the first Buddhist king of the world, Mahasammata.[304] Although continuing of course in private, alcohol consumption became frowned upon at all social levels, and ritualized public drinking, once exceedingly common, yielded to Buddhist-sanctioned rites that featured the eating of pickled tea. The public slaughter and sale of meat (though not fish) also ceased in the main towns, while edicts were passed (enforcement was a different matter) against opium, opium derivatives, gambling, and prostitution as well as alcohol and hunting.[305] Not only the crown, but reforming monks and common laymen exhibited a textually-justified, frequently intense hostility to monastic "corruptions" and religious/social deviance of all sorts. Public debates in the 18th and 19th centuries, like the robe-wrapping dispute and the Zawdi heresy, typically revolved around scriptural interpretation. Village ritual came to focus on standardized forms of monastery-based merit making. Monks, who were subject to a

[304] Tin, *Myan-ma sapei*, 197–99; Tin and Luce, *Glass Palace Chronicle*, 30–39. Cf. Michael Charney, "The Creation of Historical Tradition in Early Kon-baung Burma" (ms).
[305] See n. 293 *supra*, plus Hamilton, *New Account*, I, 34; Crawfurd, *Journal*, I, 47–48 and II, 182.

degree of central supervision and whose power derived from the universal code (*vinaya*), became objects of popular veneration, the roots of which were both instrumental (a desire by lay devotees to acquire "good karma") and expressive. At the same time popular culture became suffused with the Jatakas and Buddhist maxims, and Buddhism achieved an unqualified superiority – intellectual, aspirational, economic – over the *nat* cultus, notwithstanding the latter's ability to maintain a discrete mundane jurisdiction.[306]

A second index of cultural integration was the rise of a more popular, socially inclusive literature. Reflecting and stimulating wider literacy, composition was now dominated by laymen, including a few women, rather than monks. Readers and authors hailed from provincial towns as well as the capital, while in literature and legal studies, non-*min* usages exerted greater influence. From the early 1700s, and more especially in the early Kon-baung period, hoary conventions were liberalized, with humor and social satire becoming more prominent and with secular topics rivaling religious themes. Alongside the four classical verse forms appeared more experimental free verse and narrative poems. Public recitations of poetry became common. We also find a proliferation of popular prose works, including dramas and other forms of fiction, vernacular law codes, vernacular meditation manuals,[307] medical treatises,[308] collected legal precedents, and imperial histories.[309] In legal studies, for example, the first Burmese-language text, Kaing-za's *Maha-ya-zathat-gyi* c. 1640, sought to make Burmese legal norms, hitherto chiefly in Pali, available to a wider audience; but the vernacular *Manu-kye dhamma-that* of 1756 was far more influential and inaugurated a spate of legal compilations and commentaries that were accessible to headmen, village monks, and people of intermediate rank. By the late

---

[306] On the growing orthodoxy of popular observance, previous nn. plus Than Tun, "Social Life," 272; Harvey, *History*, 314–15; Koenig, *Burmese Polity*, ch. 3; Spiro, *Burmese Supernaturalism*, esp. 271–80; idem, *Buddhism and Society*, ch. 17. On the robe-wrapping dispute and Zawdi heresy, see *supra* n. 299. Note that Buddhist textual orthodoxy proved fully compatible with the importation of Sanskrit texts from India, the special preserve of court brahmins.

[307] Thus in 1754 the Taung-lei-lon Hsaya-daw wrote a popular meditation manual. See Daw On-hmi, ed., *Satu-giri shu-bwe kyan* (Rangoon, 1968), *ga*.

[308] E.g., the "Nara-thu-ki-pyo kyan" (1749), the "Datu-bo-daw kyan" (1794), and the "Dwa-daya-thi kyan" (1830), all in *RUL*. My thanks to Atsuko Naono for bringing these to my attention.

[309] For an overview of new literary genres and styles, *SHDMA*, 173–435; Tin, *Myan-ma sa-pei thamaing*, chs. 5–7; Htin Aung, *History*, 43, 151–52, 192–9; idem , *Burmese Drama*, 46–47; Allott et al., "Burma"; Sangermano, *Burmese Empire*, 180.

19th century no purely Pali *dhamma-thats* (legal codes) were composed in Burma, all new manuscripts being either Burmese or Pali equipped with *nissaya* translations into the vernacular.[310] As the first in a line of imperial histories disseminated throughout the realm, the *Maha-ya-zawin-gyi* ["Great Royal Chronicle"], which was written c. 1711 by U Kala, a private scholar outside the court, revolutionized historiography much as the *Manu-kye dhamma-that* promoted legal studies. So novel was U Kala's work that he had to begin with an apologia providing a religious justification for the study of secular history. After U Kala came a "rain of [imperial] chronicles," including both private and official histories, by laymen as well as monks.[311] Paralleling this popularization of legal and historical writing was the growing influence of rural conventions on court drama and perhaps painting.

Third, imperial and pan-Burman loyalties increasingly superseded local identities. One sign of this was the appearance of an unabashedly imperial/national vision in popular histories like that of U Kala. Although, as noted, Shin Thi-la-wun-tha's "Celebrated Chronicle" c. 1520 had referred to "our country of Burma," this book was little more than a king list linking Burmese rulers to ancient India. So far as we know, other chronicles remained resolutely focused on Pagan, Prome, Toungoo, Ava, and other provincial centers. However, by synthesizing local histories and adding new material, U Kala's three-volume work told the story of the western mainland as a whole from earliest times to his own day, complete with an origin myth for the Burman people.[312] This format became the norm for subsequent authors, including the Twin-thin-taik-wun, whose 1798 chronicle may have been the first to put "Burma" (*myan-ma*) in its title. Local chronicles were still written, of course, but they too usually referred to national/imperial events. This same

---

[310] On legal literature, see Kaing-za Manu-ya-za, *Maha-ya-zathat-gyi* (Rangoon, 1870); D. Richardson, ed., *The Damathat, or the Laws of Manoo* [the *Manu-kye*], 2nd ed. (Rangoon, 1874); J. S. Furnivall, "Manu in Burma," *JBRS* 30 (1940): 351–70; Ryuji Okudaira, "The Role of Kaingza Manuyaza, An Eminent Jurist of the 17th Century," *Jl. of Asian and African Studies* 27 (1984): 180–86; Andrew Huxley, "The Village Knows Best," *SEAR* 5 (1997): 21–39, emphasizing the impact of rural tradition on legal reform; idem, "The Importance of the Dhammathats in Burmese Law and Culture," *The Jl. of Burma Studies* 1 (1997): 1–18, esp. 6.

[311] Myin-hswei, in *Twin-thin myan-ma ya-zawin-thit, ni-dan.* On chronicles, Lieberman, "U Kala's Chronicle"; *SHDMA*, 47–54, 179–81, 210–321 *passim*; U Tet IItoot and Tin Ohn in D.G.E. Hall, ed., *Historians of South-East Asia* (London, 1961), 50–62, 85–93; Tin and Luce, *Glass Palace Chronicle*, ix–xxiii.

[312] *UK*, I, 141.

pan-Burman/imperial perspective infused the *Manu-kye dhamma-that*, as well as a 1790s history of religion by the Mehti Hsaya-daw, which for the first time blended the monastic lineages of Upper and Lower Burma into a hybrid tradition said to be superior in longevity and antiquity to that of Sri Lanka.[313]

More broadly indicative of changing popular identities was the disappearance of regional insurgencies within the dry zone. Through the 16th century, recall, Toungoo, Prome, and smaller towns had maintained independent courts, while in the 1590s *bayins* again had declared their independence. But during the great mid-18th century crisis – not to mention subsequent Kon-baung disorders – no effort was made to revive the independence of dry zone capitals. By the same token – consistent with new communications circuits, the first spelling books, and official efforts to standardize written and spoken Burmese – dialect differences eroded, and northern pockets of people speaking Mon, Pyu, Tai, Chin, and Kadu shrank.

Fourth and related to the strengthening of imperial loyalties, we find a sharpening of Burman/non-Burman boundaries and a stronger link at all social levels between Burman ethnicity and loyalty to the northern throne. Had the First Toungoo empire not overextended itself in Siam, had it thus avoided collapse within a few years of its greatest triumph, Pegu (despite Upper Burma's demographic strength) well might have remained the imperial capital, and Tabin-shwei-hti's vision of Mon-Burman synthesis might have moved ethnic relations within the basin along a very different path. Possibly this was one of the great turning points of mainland history. But in the event, the post-1600 transfer of the capital far upriver, the consequent marginalization of Mon families in imperial councils, and the growth of imperial culture based on dry zone Burman norms increased the potential for exclusivity.

Critical to realizing that potential, however, was intensified warfare, including the peculiar stresses of the mid-18th century. Although in fact Ra-manyan forces came to include significant numbers of Burmans, the devastation that these predominantly Mon armies inflicted on the north during the rebellion of the 1740s and 1750s inspired bitter anti-Mon stereotypes among panicked northern peasants desperate to restore a sense of control over a chaotic world. By appealing explicitly to Burman ethnicity, by artificially exaggerating out-group differences, the Kon-baung resistance answered this yearning for renewed social

[313] Mehti Hsaya-daw, *Wun-tha-dipani* (Rangoon, 1966), 68–77.

cohesion. Early Kon-baung fighters unfurled their topknots to show Burmans at a distance that they were comrades. They massacred Mon prisoners, but carefully spared fellow Burmans, while spreading rumors of anti-Burman pogroms in the south. Any Burman, they boasted, could defeat ten "Talaings" – a pejorative racial epithet for Mons. Burmans supporting Pegu were pilloried as traitors to "the Burman people" (*myan-ma lu-myo*).[314] An omen at Pegu was interpreted to mean that although the head of the fish (the last Toungoo king) had grown putrid, the tail of the fish – the Burman people – was yet vital and would flap about.[315]

The bloody Kon-baung reconquest of the south in the 1750s, followed by a series of failed Mon revolts, continuous warfare against Siam, and historic victories over Arakan, Manipur, Assam, and China strengthened Burman triumphalism. Campaigns melded conscripts from separate districts for long periods, fostered a sense of shared dependence on the new dynasty, and created a stock of heroic tales and self-serving stereotypes. One cannot dismiss the common report of British prisoners during the First Anglo-Burmese War that in Burman eyes, all other ethnic groups should be slaves to their king.[316] Such reports tallied with popular songs and poems about Burman conquests,[317] and with prophecies touted by Kon-baung soldiers that a Burman king was destined to rule over Shans, Mons, Manipuris, Chinese, Siamese, Indians, and Arakanese.[318]

Two questions arise: How was ethnic chauvinism compatible with imperial polyethnicity and religious universalism? How was the sense of community implicit in the appeal to Burman ethnicity reconciled with an inflexibly hierarchic social ethic?

As regards ethnicity, bear in mind that the northern throne readily honored loyal minority leaders. Not only was ethnic standardization outside the basin physically impossible, but without a theory of popular

---

[314] *AA-L*, 29. See too *KBZ*, I, 104–105, 122; *AA-T*, 170–1, 186. Contemporary European accounts present a similar picture of ethnic polarization, e.g., *Dal*, I, 164; William Hunter, *A Concise Account of the Kingdom of Pegu* (Calcutta, 1785), 29–30; *LFSG*, vol. 26 (1741), 9.

[315] *AA-T*, 183–84; *KBZ*, 104–105; BL OR 3464, 142–43.

[316] Crawfurd, *Journal*, II, app., 71, 123; Gouger, *Imprisonment*, 103, 329; Harvey, *History*, 363.

[317] Khin Hla Than, "Function of History in Myanmar's Society," in *Comparative Studies on Literature and History of Thailand and Myanmar* (Bangkok, 1997), 69.

[318] *KBZ*, I, 237; *AAm*, 28. They conformed too to patriotic self-justifications of common bandits who killed an Armenian merchant in 1831. Blackmore, *Catalogue of Parabaiks*, 33.

sovereignty, there was no intellectual impulse for such a policy. The world was divided into 101 more or less discrete "peoples" (*lu-myo*).[319] Lists of dependent "countries" (*taing* or *pyei*), some ethnically-defined, implied that these realms had a permanent character that Burmese kings, as aspirant World-Rulers (*cakkavattis*) with ever more expansive visions, were proud to protect.[320]

Yet as a practical matter, because Burmans after 1635 completely dominated the court, the throne and its supporters tended to identify Burmans with Theravada purity and, whenever conflict arose, instinctively sought to ensure the ritual subordination of minority cultures. In attacking Manipur, Alaung-hpaya explained that he sought to crush the religious errors of the Hindus.[321] Although Arakanese, Shans, and Siamese were also Theravadin, on invading their realms, Burman leaders explained that they had come to reform "corrupt" practices so that the Lord Buddha's Religion might shine once again.[322] In the case of the Mons – perhaps because of the Mons' reputation for scholarship or perhaps because Burman-Mon religious differences were modest – hairstyle, tattoos, and language tended to be the most prominent boundary markers.[323] But even in these campaigns, invaders claimed that the faith shone most brightly in Upper Burma and that as Kings of Righteousness (*dhamma-rajas*) and World-Rulers (*cakkavattis*), Burman kings were obliged to spread True Doctrine in the south.[324] A hundred years later anti-British resistance leaders championed the same fusion of religion and ethnicity, as in the oft-stated claim that they fought to defend the "Buddha's religion and Burmese tradition" (*Buddha batha, myan-ma dalei-hton-san*).

In opposing the hierarchic dynastic realm organized around the high royal center to the nation-state, Benedict Anderson and Ernest Gellner contrasted the categories of dependent subject and autonomous, juridically equal citizen; the latter alone, they argued, has a sense of

[319] U Hla Tin, ed., *Za-ta-daw-bon ya-zawin* (Rangoon, 1960), 99; "Shei khit myan-ma naing-ngan myo-ywa ne-pe thamaing," 25; *ROB*, II, 219. But *ZOK* 72 says 75 peoples. Cf. Thant, *Making of Modern Burma*, 83–90.
[320] The throne often required ethnic identifications in censuses and tattoos, e.g., *ZOK*, 46, 55–58; Trager and Koenig, *Sit-tans*, 79, 83–88.
[321] *KBZ*, I, 295–99; *AA-T*, 226–27; *AAm*, 106–107.
[322] *KBZ*, I, 311, 313; *AAm*, 175–84, 212–13; *ROB* IV, 75, 83, 388 and V, 433. Cf. Chit Thein, *Mon kyauk-sa*, 105–108.
[323] *AAm*, 12, 16–17, 28–34, 75–76, 85.
[324] Lieberman, *Cycles*, 244–47. Mons replied that a Burman king could never win, because he championed "false doctrine." BL OR 3463, 146–47.

political community.[325] But for an 18th-century Burman, the most prized psychological state was not personal autonomy, which carried associations of exposure, isolation, and vulnerability. Rather, he prized the shelter of a powerful patron. Social order was inconceivable without inequality. Ultimately, all Burmans depended on their king, because as principal patron, he not only authorized subordinate hierarchies, but like the first king Mahasammata, transmitted those principles of order inherent in the cosmos. Burmese records and European accounts show that such images, far from being a conceit of royal ideologues, were deeply rooted in popular consciousness.[326] The chaos of the 1740s nourished a yearning for more effective royal leadership and a firmer, necessarily inegalitarian ordering of society at the same time as it sharpened ethnic boundaries. Hence, joint abject dependence on the throne not only was compatible with a sense of politico-ethnic community, but provided a critical foundation for such an identification. Absent popular political institutions, however, one also would expect that a reduction in external danger would weaken communal sentiments and open the way to more visible polyethnicity.

Note finally that the insecurity of interregna, followed by a renewed sense of mastery, also may have encouraged a deeper commitment to Buddhist teachings. According to Theravada understanding, all misfortune derives from one's karma, and the Buddha's teachings provide the only guide to kammatically-correct behavior. Possibly such thinking inspired the collecting of religious manuscripts, the growing hostility to alcohol and *nat* sacrifices, the desperate compilation of law codes, and other acts of purification, royal and local, that marked the Kon-baung restoration (and to a lesser extent, the Toungoo renewal of the early 1600s).[327]

THE ECLIPSE OF MON CIVILIZATION

Nowhere was the sharpening of ethnic boundaries more apparent than in the accelerated destruction of Mon civilization in the delta.

---

[325] Benedict Anderson, *Imagined Communities* (rev. ed., London, 1991), 19 ff. and *passim*; Ernest Gellner, *Nations and Nationalism* (Ithaca, 1983).

[326] See, e.g., *UK*, III, 113–14; Yi Yi, *Myan-ma naing-ngan achei-anei 1714–52* (Rangoon, 1973), apps. 17, 22, 23; *AAm*, 28–30, 32, 33; Gouger, *Imprisonment*, 11, Sangermano, *Burmese Empire*, 152–53. Cf. Manning Nash, *The Golden Road to Modernity* (rpt. Chicago, 1973), chs. 3, 7.

[327] Cf. David Wyatt's work on Siam, discussed in Ch. 3 *infra*.

Whereas in the mid-16th century Mons solidly dominated Lower Burma, by 1740, H.L. Shorto estimated, they were only 60 percent of the population south of Henzada, while of the remaining 40 percent, Burmans were the chief element. (Various Karens, a non-Buddhist people who had migrated from the hills, were the third principal group.) Burmans served in the towns as officials, garrison soldiers, and traders. In the northern and western delta they increasingly established themselves as cultivators.[328] Less through official policy perhaps than family and personal ties, urban newcomers, we have seen, enjoyed disproportionate advantages.

Mon responses to Burman immigration varied. Long before 1740 much Burmanization of the south probably represented a voluntary or partial shift in self-identification by bilingual "Mons" seeking patronage and prestige. Anthropologists of Southeast Asia have shown that ethnicity can profitably be regarded as a role vis-a-vis other groups. Like Tabin-shwei-hti, who "became a Mon," people wishing to change their role within the larger society can adopt, temporarily or permanently, symbols of recognized significance.[329] Avan patronage, the circulation of Burman manuscripts, pilgrims, monks, and traders along the Irrawaddy corridor, the growing Burman presence in delta towns, the spread of bilingualism in frontier areas, the concomitant decline of Mon literary production – all worked to strengthen the appeal of partial or full assimilation. No doubt various situationally-specific identities arose in the cultural "middle ground."[330]

Yet other southerners not only refused accommodation, but in self-conscious reaction to Burman encroachment, strengthened their Mon identity. Their bitterness is suggested by an anti-Avan, anti-Burman uprising that broke out in the southeast from 1660–1664,[331] and by the observations of Dutch residents in the port of Syriam in the 1670s. The Dutch distinguished readily between Mons (*Peguwers*) and Burmans

---

[328] Shorto, personal communication, 1974. See southern ethnic profiles in *ZOK*, pt. 2; *Dal*, I, 99, 133–42; *KBZ*, I, 104–105; BL OR 3464, 139–40.

[329] F. K. Lehman, "Ethnic Categories in Burma and the Theory of Social Systems," in Peter Kunstadter, ed., *Southeast Asian Tribes, Minorities, and Nations*, 2 vols. (Princeton, 1967), I, 93–124; E. R. Leach, *Political Systems of Highland Burma* (London, 1964); Michael Moerman, "Ethnic Identification in a Complex Civilization," *American Anthropologist* 67 (1965): 1215–30.

[330] Cf. Richard White, *The Middle Ground: Indians, Empires, and Republics in the Great Lakes Region 1650–1815* (Cambridge, 1991), describing the North American frontier as an arena of constant cultural negotiation.

[331] Lieberman, *Cycles*, 200–201.

(*Bramanen*), with the latter described by one writer as "an extraordinarily proud and conceited people" who originated from the area around Ava. Each ethnic group had quite distinctive hairstyles, tattoos, housing, and clothing. In the early 17th century, Joris van Coulster explained, "the Peguan nation (*Peguse natie*) ... had to submit to the yoke and bondage of the Burman ... [and] at present are tormented above all others."[332] However, observed two of his colleagues in 1677, "the Peguers ... are just looking for a suitable opportunity to rid themselves of the Burman domination and at the same time to take revenge on them for their tyrannical behavior." With the slightest encouragement from Siam, "everyone is of the opinion that ... the Peguers would in all probability put to death the Burmans, who are far fewer than they, here in Syriam, in the city of Pegu, as well as in the surrounding villages."[333]

This is more or less what happened in 1740–1757. It is true that during the opening phase of the great Peguan revolt, local leaders welcomed not only Karens, but southern Burmans who shared their hostility to the Avan court. Indeed, the first king of newly independent Ra-manya won support by claiming to be a fugitive prince of the Toungoo dynasty, which was a notable source of prestige. Yet at the same time, Ra-manya was portrayed in contemporary histories as a quintessentially Mon kingdom, ordained by prophecy, wherein Mon language and cultural symbols would enjoy pride of place and to which the Burman north would become tributary. Not only was the 1740 rising accompanied by anti-Burman massacres, with 7000–8,000 victims according to contemporary accounts,[334] not only were Burmans serving in Peguan garrisons in the north expected to adopt Mon hairstyles as early as 1752, but in reaction to Alaung-hpaya's movement, ethnic relations in the south grew ever more polarized. After executing scores of Avan captives, in 1754 Mons obliged all Burmans remaining at Pegu to wear an earring with a stamp of the Pegu heir-apparent and to cut their hair in Mon fashion as a sign of loyalty to the southern kingdom.[335] Insofar as self-identified Mons

---

[332] Joris van Coulster, Algemeen Rijsarchief, The Hague, "Overgekomen brieven en papieren," Codex 1313, FF. 170–171 (Feb., 1675).

[333] Cornelis Mersman and Joannes Verkerck, in ibid., Codex 1323, 1835–37 (Jan., 1677). My thanks to Wil O. Dijk for bringing these passages to my attention.

[334] See n. 270 *supra*, esp. first source.

[335] BL OR 3464, 139–40; *AA-T*, 183–84; *KBZ*, I, 104–105; "Memoires sur le Pegou," *REO* 2 (1883): 507; and my "Ethnic Politics in Eighteenth-Century Burma," *MAS* 12 (1978): 455–82.

remained a minority within the lowlands as a whole, this acquiescence in ethnic polarization proved dismally self-defeating.

Rejectionist and assimilationist responses continued to vie with one another after the Kon-baung reconquest of 1757, but henceforth both led in the same direction: Burmanization. In keeping with the polyethnic theory of Buddhist empire, Kon-baung officials had no principled objection to Mons' enjoying a degree of cultural, even administrative autonomy: some self-declared Mons held local office, and Bo-daw-hpaya in 1782 married a Mon princess. But Mon rejectionists, often aided by Karens and on rare occasion by local Burmans, staged fresh uprisings in 1758, 1762, 1774, 1783, 1792, and 1824–1826. Each revolt typically was followed by fresh deportations, Mon flight to Siam, and punitive cultural proscriptions. The last Mon king was publicly humiliated and executed in 1774, and a Burman finial placed atop the chief Mon pagoda in Pegu. In the aftermath of revolts, Burman language was encouraged at the expense of Mon; while Burman earrings and tattoos became a "badge" of superiority proudly displayed by those "descended from the conquerors," in the words of a British surgeon c. 1785.[336] Chronicles by Mon monks in the late 1700s and early 1800s portrayed Ra-manya's recent history as a tale of unrelenting northern encroachment and persecution, which they too interpreted in unmistakably ethnic terms.[337]

Undergirding the northern assault was accelerated colonization, which the Kon-baung court – in contrast to its Restored Toungoo predecessor – self-consciously encouraged through military colonies and civilian resettlement, but which seems to have been primarily a matter of private migration from the more densely settled dry zone towards the shipyards, cities, and open lands of the delta.[338] Assimilation, intermarriage, and displacement in Lower Burma proceeded apace. In the early 1790s another Briton observed, "Those [Mons] that remain have intermixed so much with the Burmas [sic], and conceal themselves so

---

[336] Hunter, *Concise Account*, 28–30: "The Birmahs . . . who pique [sic] themselves on being descended from the conquerors and wish to be distinguished from the nation they subdued, use [tattooing as] a badge for that purpose . . . the accidental circumstance of its preserving a separation between them and the original natives of the country, has undoubtedly enhanced its value . . ." Hunter referred also to specifically Burman earrings. Cf. *KBZ*, I, 493–99; Symes, *Embassy*, 75–85, 101–102, 183.

[337] *BL OR* 3462, 3463, 3464 by the monk of Athwa; and "Phongsawadan Mon Phama," in *Prachum phongsawadan phak thi* 1 (rpt., Bangkok, 1963), vol. 2, 1–133, tr. Ken Breazeale, which was probably compiled c. 1793.

[338] Adas, *Burma Delta*, 16–19, 57, 231–32; Trager and Koenig, *Sit-tans*, ch. 7; Saya Pwa, *Kyi-gan shin-gyi*, Letters 2, 3, 12, 15, 13, 36.

much by adopting their language and dress, that it is difficult to distinguish them." Those who have not "taken refuge with the Siamese... have assumed the Burma dress and language in order to avoid extortion."[339] In 1813 a Baptist missionary added, "The Peguers no longer exist as a nation; they are nearly become extinct, or are incorporated with the Burman."[340] These accounts overstated the case for parts of the delta and especially in the trans-Sittang littoral, where Burmans remained chiefly urban. Fluid and intermediate categories also bedeviled any simple accounting. Nonetheless, Burmese and Western accounts agree that between 1770 and 1860 extensive tracts once solidly Mon in Prome, Tharawaddy, Henzada, Bassein, and Rangoon districts became substantially or completely Burman.[341] If in 1400, something like 60 percent of the basin population identified themselves in most contexts as Burman, as early as 1830 the figure must have been close to 90 percent. These changes were accompanied by the virtual cessation of Mon literary production.

CULTURAL PATTERNS OUTSIDE THE IRRAWADDY BASIN

Outside the lowlands Burman cultural influence also expanded during the Restored Toungoo and Kon-baung eras, albeit far less dramatically than in the Irrawaddy delta.

Given Arakan's long-standing religious ties to the basin and the status of Arakanese as a Burmese dialect, one might have thought that the 1784 conquest would have led to extensive Burman cultural penetration. If this did not happen, it was not for lack of royal interest, practical and symbolic. Bo-daw-hpaya ordered that Arakanese monks and rituals be supervised by Burmese monks, that local measurements conform to Burmese standards, and that administration in each of Arakan's four new jurisdictions conform to Burmese provincial norms. Significantly, these years also engendered a Burman-sponsored

---

[339] "[Francis] Buchanan's Journal," cited in Koenig, *Burmese Polity*, 61; and India Office Records, Home Miscellaneous Series 388, f. 599, Dr. Francis Buchanan, "Account of Burma and Pegu." So too Cox, *Journal*, 426–28 reported in 1796 that Mon villagers all along the river below Prome had moved away "to avoid the oppressive government of their Burmhan conquerors" and had been replaced by Burmans.

[340] F. Carey to W. Carey, 10 March 1813, in *Periodical Accounts Relative to the Baptist Missionary Society* 5 (1813): 257. Cf. Duroiselle, *Epigraphica Birmanica*, I, 71–72.

[341] Previous notes, esp. Adas, *Burma Delta*, 16–19, 231–32; plus 1145, 1164 Han-tha-wadi *sit-tans*, 1145 Martaban *sit-tans*, 1145 Bassein *sit-tan*, 1145 Prome *sit-tan*, 1145 Toungoo *sit-tan*, all in private collection of Yi Yi.

chronicle tradition portraying Arakan's founder as a junior offshoot of a Burman royal family. Yet a variety of factors impeded Burman penetration. The number of missionaries remained modest. Trans-montane trade and Burmese settlement were meager. Arakanese Buddhism at the outset was deeply idiosyncratic. New tax demands proved extremely unpopular, and above all, effective Burmese rule lasted little more than a generation, to 1824. Not surprisingly, although the foundation was laid for a Burman Buddhist identity that would deepen later in the 19th century, in 1824 Burmese influence remained limited even in the chief towns.[342]

Moving around the periphery in clockwise fashion, we find that imperial influence grew more substantially in the northwestern and northern Shan world than in Arakan. Although the former areas – including the upper and middle Chindwin basin, northern Shwebo, Wuntho, Katha, and western Mong Mit – had been largely Shan in the early 1500s, they lay adjacent to the Burman heartland. Trade and Toungoo military campaigns enhanced the prestige and accessibility of Burman culture, which was further bolstered in the 18th and early 19th centuries by Burman settlement. By 1830, not only had some hereditary Shan *saw-bwa*s in this zone yielded to appointed Burman governors, but the population itself had become substantially Burman in speech, body adornment, religious practices, and self-identification. In dynamics and chronology, Burmanization along the northwestern and northern fringes of the dry zone thus paralleled ethnic change in the delta. Yet, because this area was more sparsely settled and more politically fragmented, Mon resistance to Burmanization found no counterpart.[343]

In the great Tai-speaking uplands northeast and east of the basin, stretching from cis-Salween kingdoms like Hsenwi, Mong Nai, and Mong Pai to the trans-Salween realms of Kenghung, Kengtung, and Chiang Mai, Burman influence also advanced, albeit at more restricted social levels and without hint of ethnic change. From the 16th century, if not earlier, Burman and Mon traders were circulating as far east as Kengtung, while their Shan counterparts were supplying the plains with

---

[342] On Burmese-Arakanese relations, *List* 79, #1, NL 1605, *ne* v.; *ROB*, IV, 61–62, 180, 352–53, 548, 614 and V, 332; Charney, "Reinvestigation of Kon-baung-Era Historiography," 53–68; idem, "Beyond State-Centered Histories in Western Burma," in Gommans and Leider, *Maritime Frontier*, 213–24.

[343] *GUBSS*, I, 1: 198–208, 281; II, 1: 48, 59, 233, 280, 326; II, 3: 14–15, 360; *UK*, III, 288, 290; Sao Saimong Mangrai, *The Shan States and the British Annexation* (Ithaca, 1965), 33–34; Leach, *Political Systems*, 34.

forest products and specialized foodstuffs. In cis-Salween states, recall, Bayin-naung suppressed animist rites, reformed the *sangha* along lowland lines, and obliged rulers to listen to sermons by lowland monks. Such patronage continued in the Restored Toungoo and Kon-baung eras. Bo-daw-hpaya, for one, targeted the Shan hills for proselytizing missions. Beyond that, Toungoo and Kon-baung kings widened access to lowland culture by enrolling *saw-bwas'* sons as pages at the capital, increasing *saw-bwa* attendance at imperial ceremonies, and arranging marriages between Tai and Burman aristocrats.[344] Through such channels court ceremonies, scripts, calendars, weights, measures, architecture, and monastic observances in varying degrees came to mimic Burman models.[345] Even in distant Kengtung such models overshadowed Chinese and Siamese influences, and events at Ava figured in Kengtung chronicles written for local consumption.[346] Yet it is likely that lowland affairs impinged only intermittently on the consciousness of Shan rulers, who were as absorbed in intra-Tai as in imperial diplomacy and some of whom paid tribute to China and Siam as well as to Burma. Moreover, if Burman norms gained a growing cachet, imitation almost never extended to changes in ethnicity. Many Shans resented the arrogance of Burman garrisons, while below the level of *saw-bwa* courts, knowledge of Burman customs remained more limited. As hinges between imperial and local cultures, Tai rulers who identified too closely with Ava faced a potentially fatal loss of local support.[347] In selecting administrators in the Shan realm, Burmese rulers themselves therefore had to restrain their oft-expressed preference for Burmans and for heavily Burmanized Shans.

Finally, between Shan valleys the mountain tracts inhabited by illiterate Chins, Kachins, Karens, Palaungs, and so forth escaped Burman political control entirely by virtue of their poverty, inaccessibility, and the fragility of their supra-village organizations. Here commoners were yet less receptive to Irrawaddy basin norms. Nonetheless, in somewhat the same way as Shan *saw-bwas* looked to Ava, the Tai-Shan politico-social

---

[344] On Burman-Shan intercourse in the 1700s and early 1800s, Saya Pwa, *Kyi-gan shin-gyi*, Letters 7, 10; *LBHK*, chs. 4, 7–9; *ROB*, IV, 316, 352–53.

[345] Previous note, plus *MMOS*, IV, 120 ff.; *ROB*, V, 396–97; *GUBSS* I, 1: 198–212, 280–88, 320, 326; I, 2: 399; Lieberman, *Cycles*, 133–34; idem, "Seventeenth-Century Watershed," 244–47; Donald Gear, "The Ancient Royal Animal Weights of Burma" (ms), 185–86; List 78, #11, *ga* v.

[346] Mangrai, *Padaeng Chronicle*, 245–70.

[347] As at Hsenwi, in *UK*, III, 314–15, 327–28.

order served as a model for Kachin, Palaung, and Karen chiefs who, as early as the late 16th century, sought to use revenues from the mineral, tea, or timber trade to construct proto-statelets and to magnify internal stratification. South of the Shan plateau, for example, between c. 1700 and 1840 Red Karen (Kayah) chiefs who profited from the teak trade tried to imitate Shan political organization, while sponsoring a new animist cult whose sacred flagstaffs and ritual paraphernalia copied Shan (and in some cases, Burman) Buddhist usages.[348] Likewise some Lawa hillsmen came to Kengtung as early as the 15th century to learn about Buddhism, elements of which they transmitted back into the hills.[349] In these indirect ways, hill peoples also came to participate in a loose system of intergroup relations whose major reference was the Irrawaddy basin.

CONCLUSIONS

Burman ethnicity and Theravada orthodoxy gained ground during most of the period under review. During the early and mid-Pagan era lowland ethnicity was relatively fragmented, and popular religion seems to have been localized and substantially pre-textual. In the late 13th and 14th centuries Shan incursions and the rise of an independent Mon kingdom further complicated the ethnic map. Yet starting in the mid-Pagan era and continuing throughout the era of division, the elaboration of a specifically Burman culture and the expansion of Burman settlement laid the foundation for a long-term unification of lowland ethnicity. Likewise, wider literacy and coastal-interior links encouraged more orthodox Theravada identities, and not only among Burmans. Under Toungoo and Kon-baung rule, economic and demographic expansion joined royal patronage and massive warfare to accelerate both forms of cultural change. By 1820, with the eclipse of Mon culture, Burman ethnicity no longer faced a lowland rival. Within and outside the central basin court-defined Theravada orthodoxy – if not Burman ethnicity – also exercised unprecedented influence.

Compared to cultural integration, political change was more episodic, but again the decreasing length and trauma of successive breakdowns

---

[348] F. K. Lehman, "Burma: Kayah Society as a Function of the Shan-Burma-Karen Context," in Julian H. Steward, ed., *Contemporary Change in Traditional Societies*, vol. 2 (Urbana, IL, 1967), esp. 14–41; Lieberman, *Cycles*, 134–36.

[349] Liu Yan, *Nanchaung fojiao yu Daizu*, 93.

betrayed a progressive tendency. The first interregnum, following Pagan's collapse, lasted over 250 years. During this long era the relation between Upper and Lower Burma shifted, the Pagan system of temple landholdings came under severe strain, and independent polities proliferated. In the mid-16th century the First Toungoo dynasty suddenly reunited the western mainland – only to collapse within two generations through absurd overextension. Yet not only was the second interregnum (from the early 1590s to the mid-1620s) relatively short-lived, it inaugurated a far more secure integration. Through a combination of Pattern C administrative changes and a more intelligent geopolitical design, the Restored Toungoo dynasty succeeded in tapping – and stimulating – the wealth of both Upper and Lower Burma under more or less secure northern hegemony. The Restored empire itself disintegrated c. 1740–1752, but the system was quickly resurrected in its essential features, and substantially strengthened, by Kon-baung rulers. Thus, by 1824 on the eve of the First Anglo-Burmese War, a region extending from Assam to Mergui and from Arakan to Kenghung owed some degree of allegiance to a single center. By comparison with administrative Patterns A and B, the Restored Toungoo-Kon-baung system reduced the autonomy of monastic estates, provincial governors, township headmen, and Tai tributaries alike. If these changes affected most directly officials and monks, they also modified the social structure, the linguistic and religious patterns, the very self-images and life choices of peasants throughout the western mainland.

Integration ultimately rested on an increase in aggregate (and for limited periods perhaps, per capita) wealth, which simultaneously enhanced the material superiority of the central basin over outlying areas and nourished more ramified economic, cultural, and political networks. Concentrated in the lowlands but extending throughout the western mainland, these networks included market links between increasingly specialized producers, an expanded infrastructure of village monasteries, a wider circulation of texts and entertainers, new service rotas at the capital, and more elaborate patronage, tax, and ceremonial connections between local leaders and the imperial center. All such structures served to erode local autonomy and to foster an assumption that Irrawaddy-based unification was normative and inevitable.

To the development of new linkages after c. 1400, maritime and Yunnanese trade made critical contributions, more vital certainly than during the Pagan era, when foreign trade seems to have been quite limited and when economic florescence is most readily explained by a combination of unusually propitious climate and new forms of temple-led land reclamation. Post-1400 external inputs included firearms, bullion, new crops, wider religious contacts, and market stimuli. But, even after 1400 external trade can take us only so far, both because the vigor of Burma's external commerce itself was to some extent a function of local growth, and because some local dynamics remained partly or substantially independent of external stimuli. For example, although it is true that trade and guns powerfully aided pacification and thus spurred population growth, Burma's basic demographic rhythms, the spread of *kauk-gyi* cultivation, the peopling of the Lower Burma frontier, and ethnic unification depended more heavily on domestic processes.

If we compress the role of foreign commerce, how can we explain political and cultural parallels between mainland Southeast Asia and other regions of Eurasia? This is the task of subsequent chapters, but for now I would observe simply that parallel integrations reflected the combined impact of climate, firearms, and growing international trade, on the one hand, and a cumulative growth within each region of population, market efficiency, and political-military technique, on the other hand.

Lest one exaggerate integration in the western mainland, note finally how limited it remained by, say, West European standards. The Konbaung realm was still a solar polity whose outer tributaries owed a fluid, contested allegiance. Within the basin relations between the king, ministers, and provincial lords remained personalized and ill-defined, while royal patronage still relied substantially on apanages and nonmonetary rewards. On the eve of the First Anglo-Burmese War the service system was again under severe strain. Moreover, in 1820 self-identified Burmans still were probably no more than 60 percent of the imperial, as opposed to the basin, population.

CHAPTER 3

A Stable, Maritime Consolidation

The Central Mainland

The histories of western and central mainland Southeast Asia were closely joined and reasonably comparable. The central mainland is here defined as present-day Thailand, Laos, Cambodia, and more peripherally, the Mekong delta. Although in fact communications between this region and China were at least as easy as with South Asia, from an early date India and Sri Lanka provided the central, no less than the western, mainland with its chief high cultural inspiration. The broad similarities between the western and central mainland in art, literature, law, kingship, and Theravada affiliation that grew from this common South Asian exposure were reinforced by a constant west-central exchange. Monks, diplomats, traders, soldiers, and migrants showed that upland barriers between the Irrawaddy, Chaophraya, and Mekong river systems were relatively porous. Thus a unique Theravada civilization embracing virtually all wet-rice areas in the western and central mainland cohered and diverged from the ever more Sinic eastern sector.

To these shared cultural traditions must be added the unifying effects of demography and geography, particularly in what became the two chief Theravada kingdoms, Burma and Siam. In both kingdoms a semicircle of highlands surrounded a great alluvial plain whose chief river, the Irrawaddy or Chaophraya, provided the main avenue of communication. In both sectors a maritime coastal region competed with a less commercially privileged interior zone. Whether because of comparable soils, agronomic technique, or social structures, all of the western and central mainland also had low demographic densities (about a quarter those of northern and central Vietnam, for example) and modest total

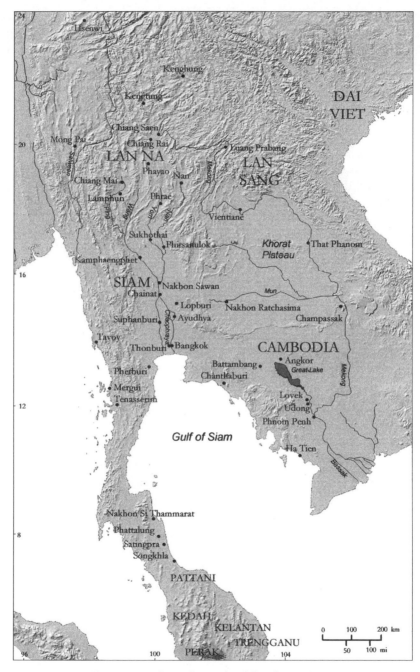

Figure 3.1. Central mainland Southeast Asia.

populations.[1] Moreover, again in contrast to the Red River delta, in the 13th and 14th centuries both sectors were severely disrupted by the large-scale settlement of Tai-speakers from the northern hills, of whom the Burmese Shans were one branch.

The resultant similarities between the western and central mainland were minute and gross, affecting the rhythms of political integration and the texture of society. In both sectors, charter civilizations expanded their authority in the 10th or 11th centuries and fragmented in the 13th and 14th centuries. Both areas then experienced centuries of rivalry among numerous post-charter successor states whose ranks contracted, especially from the late 15th century. By the mid-1500s consolidation had proceeded farther in the western than in the central mainland, but basic processes were analogous. Following the collapse of virtually every Theravada state in Southeast Asia between c. 1550 and 1600 – a collapse that reflected the interplay of Pattern B administrative weaknesses, intensifying warfare, and commercial growth – both the western and central sectors followed a series of synchronized gyrations to the end of the period under consideration: successful late 16th–early 17th century reforms, renewed economic growth and territorial consolidation halted by another breakdown in the third quarter of the 18th century, which in turn inaugurated an unprecedented burst of imperial military vigor and cultural patronage. In both realms not only did successive interregna become less disruptive, but both sectors by 1820 were more effectively knit together – administratively, commercially, culturally – than in any previous era. Throughout these centuries Theravada societies across the mainland – in Cambodia, the Shan and Lao kingdoms, as well as in lowland Burma and Siam – developed similar strategies of manpower control and kindred administrative, literary, and artistic traditions. In lowland areas in particular, wider literacy and denser cultural circuits pressed elite conventions deeper into the peasantry, while modifying those norms in the direction of Theravada textual orthodoxy. Surely among the Eurasian regions examined in this two-volume study, none resembled one another more closely than the western and central mainland, and in particular the victorious kingdoms of Burma and Siam that lay at the core of each sector.

---

[1] Anthony Reid, *Southeast Asia in the Age of Commerce*, 2 vols. (New Haven, 1988, 1993), I, 14. In both sectors, moreover, low average densities co-existed with reasonably heavy concentrations in the capital zone.

If these regions were twins, however, they were fraternal rather than identical. One obvious difference: the central sector, as I have defined it, was roughly a third larger, and its geography far more fragmented. In the west, notwithstanding the highland perimeter's irreducible autonomy, the Irrawaddy represented the only viable axis, but in the central sector the Chaophraya and Mekong provided competing axes separated by only modest uplands. Moreover, major tributaries of the Chaophraya were more ramified than their Irrawaddy counterparts, while rapids segmented the Mekong. Not surprisingly, the chief charter polity Angkor, rooted in the Great Lake/lower Mekong area, exercised an uncertain, often shadowy authority over the western Chaophraya basin and its tributary rivers. Subsequently, the situation reversed itself. Siam (Ayudhya), based on the lower Chaophraya, failed to control all Chaophraya tributaries and the middle Mekong until the early 19th century. Compare this to the Toungoo reunification of the entire western mainland as early 1558.

Besides being more fragmented, the central mainland lay more exposed to Tai migrations. Shans never threatened to submerge Burman, much less Mon, ethnicity in the Irrawaddy basin. But in great stretches of the central mainland ethnicity and language, at first among elites and eventually among the lowland population at large, gradually changed from Mon and Khmer to Tai. Notwithstanding substantial continuities between Ayudhya, on the one hand, and Angkor and local Mon kingdoms, on the other, these ethnic and linguistic changes joined with widespread political fragmentation and the post-1250 spread of Theravada Buddhism at the expense of Angkorian Hinduism to engender what was arguably a deeper sense of post-charter rupture than in the west. By extension, Siamese, north Tai, and Lao religious culture and literature tended to evolve later than their Burmese equivalents. Indeed, in severity and duration, post-charter dislocations in the central mainland exceeded those in any Eurasian region we shall consider, including western Russia.

And yet if the central mainland as a whole proved more politically fragmented and culturally labile than the western mainland, in the Chaophraya basin itself political integration was more stable and continuous. In the Irrawaddy lowlands, recall, the center of gravity swung violently between the agricultural north and the maritime coast for centuries until 1635 (with a repeat performance in the 1740s–1750s). But Ayudhya's combination of agricultural and maritime superiority over interior rivals made it preeminent in the area drained by the Chaophraya and its triburaries – indeed, I would argue, in the entire central mainland – as early as 1480 or 1515. Given Siam's easy access to the coast, it is not surprising that elite culture was more cosmopolitan than its Burmese counterpart, and the political economy more dependent on maritime trade. In the late 18th and early 19th centuries rapid Chinese-led economic growth allowed Siam to redress her historic military inferiority to Burma. Precisely because Siam, its capital first at Ayudhya and then at Bangkok near the coast, expanded its sectoral dominance more or less constantly from the late 1400s to the late 1800s, I refer to a "stable, maritime consolidation."

Finally and somewhat ironically in view of Siam's political continuity, because secular culture fused with Theravada themes less thoroughly than in Burma, the link between ethnicity and political loyalty was weaker. Several factors were at work. A distinctive Siamese culture arose later than its Burmese counterpart. Frontier colonization, north–south rivalry, and the associated spur to ethnic competition were less pronounced. External cultural options and foreign traders were more influential. Repeated Siamese defeats required unusually large deportations of ethnic minorities to the heartland, while bitterly anti-Burman Mon refugees further loosened the fit between political loyalty and Siamese ethnicity. Thus an insistent commercial and political centripetalism lacked an equally powerful ethnic counterpart.

THE CHARTER STATE OF ANGKOR: GENESIS AND INTERNAL ORGANIZATION

If not in all the particulars of its chronology, then surely in the broad features of its genesis, internal organization, and devolutionary fate, the most influential charter principality in the central mainland, Angkor, resembled Pagan.

As in the Irrawaddy basin, so in the central mainland local units coalesced, gradually and fitfully, into an overarching system – what Hermann Kulke termed the "imperial kingdom."[2] The earliest documented polities arose from the 2nd to 6th centuries C.E. in the lower reaches of the Mekong and along the southern coasts of what are now Cambodia and Vietnam, where they profited from Indian

---

[2] Hermann Kulke, "The Early and the Imperial Kingdom," in David G. Marr and A. C. Milner, eds., *Southeast Asia in the 9th to 14th Centuries* (Singapore, 1986), 1–22.

Ocean-Chinese trade moving along the coast. Chinese sources awarded this area, known as "Funan," an exaggerated political solidity, for in truth what Chinese writers, eager to flatter their emperor, described as a substantial tributary kingdom seems to have been no more than an unstable network of superficially Indianized ports and small principalities.[3] During the 6th and early 7th centuries new sailing routes from Indonesia to southern China bypassed, and in effect starved, the entrepots of Funan, encouraging a shift in the political center of gravity from the coast towards what is now southeastern and central Cambodia, where Khmer-speakers dominated[4] and where wealth rested on control not of maritime trade, but of land, people, and overland exchange. Thereafter authority in the Khmer world gravitated yet farther inland, in part perhaps because the interior offered better access to metals needed for weapons and artistic production and in part because it was more agriculturally attractive.[5]

P. Dupont, O. W. Wolters, and Claude Jacques argued that in the 7th and 8th centuries, Khmer principalities remained as ephemeral as they were numerous, fragile testimonies to the prowess of individual rulers.[6] More recently, Michael Vickery has seen during this period a gradual consolidation of authority,[7] culminating in 802 in the so-called unification of the Khmer realm by Jayavarman II, who had himself consecrated

[3] See Claude Jacques, "'Funan,' 'Zhenla,' and the Reality Concealed by These Chinese Views of Indochina," in R. B. Smith and W. Watson, eds., *Early South East Asia* (Oxford, 1979), 371–79; Michael Vickery, *Society, Economics, and Politics in Pre-Angkor Cambodia: The 7th–8th Centuries* (Tokyo, 1998), 18–19, 61–71; Charles Higham, *The Civilization of Angkor* (London, 2001), 23–35.

[4] The linguistic and ethnic affiliations of Funan are less certain. Vickery, *Society, Economics*, 63–65.

[5] Also the northeast around Sambhupura probably offered access to export products. Vickery, *Society, Economics*, 315–18. On Funan and the pre-Angkorian era, see too idem, "Some Remarks on Early State Formation in Cambodia," in Marr and Milner, *9th to 14th Centuries*, 95–116; Ian Mabbett and David Chandler, *The Khmers* (Oxford, 1995), chs. 6–8; Robert L. Brown, *The Dvaravati Wheels of Law and the Indianization of South East Asia* (Leiden, 1996); Charles Higham, *The Archaeology of Mainland Southeast Asia* (Cambridge, 1989), chs. 5, 6; Elizabeth Moore, "Water Enclosed Sites," in Jonathan Rigg, ed., *The Gift of Water* (London, 1992), 26–46.

[6] P. Dupont, "Etudes sur l'Indochine ancienne, I: La dislocation du Tchen-la et la formation du Cambodge Angkorien," *BEFEO* 43 (1943): 17–55; O. W. Wolters, "Khmer Hinduism in the Seventh Century," in Smith and Watson, *Early South East Asia*, 427–42; Wolters, "North-Western Cambodia in the Seventh Century," *BSOAS* 37 (1974): 355–84; Jacques, "Funan, Zhenla," 371–79.

[7] Vickery, *Society, Economics*, 25–29, 321–93. Cf. Claude Jacques, *Angkor: Cities and Temples* (Thailand, 1997), 56–60.

"lord over the earth who [is] absolutely unique."[8] In fact, Jayavarman II continued to struggle against local rulers, and his career did not mark a decisive break; but he articulated an ideal of unity that subsequent rulers would invoke periodically and with increasing practical effect. Two generations later, Yasovarman (r. 889?–910?) centered the realm on Angkor (or as it was called until the 14th century, Yasodharapura), at a site north of the Great Lake distinguished for its fine riverine and lacustrine communications, rich fisheries, and lakeshore suitable for receding flood farming. With command over extensive manpower, Yasovarman built an urban embankment some four kilometers square and a reservoir eight times larger than that of his predecessor. His inscriptions have been found in the south of present-day Cambodia, in Laos, and as far west as Chanthaburi, but there is little or no evidence for Angkorian political control in the Chaophraya basin to the west or in the broad ricelands of the Mun and Chi valleys to the north. In other words, the realm ("Kambuja-desa" in inscriptions) was still confined to the riverine and lacustrine lowlands of Cambodia, especially the area north of the Great Lake and the Mekong valley.[9] Even within this area, some scholars argue that royal authority over the outer provinces contracted sharply under Yasovarman's immediate successors.[10]

Not until the mid-10th century – at roughly the same time as Pagan apparently began to extend its power in Upper Burma – did the notion of a single Khmer kingdom gain stable expression. Starting with Rajendravarman (r. 944–968), we encounter what Ian Mabbett termed "one of the major discontinuities" of Khmer history, arguably more significant than that represented by Jayavarman's 802 consecration or the establishment of a long-lived capital at Yasodharapura.[11] From

---

[8] Sdok Kak Thom inscription quoted in Mabbett and Chandler, *Khmers*, 89. On Jayavarman II, Claude Jacques, "La carriere de Jayavarman II," *BEFEO* 59 (1972): 205–20; idem, *Angkor*, 61–64; O. W. Wolters, "Jayavarman II's Military Power," *JRAS* 1973, no. 1: 21–30; Vickery, *Society, Economics*, 27–29, 392–408.

[9] On Yasovarman, Chandler, *History*, 39; Mabbett and Chandler, *Khmers*, 98–99, 262; Higham, *Civilization*, 84; Christophe Pottier, "A la recherche de Goloupura," *BEFEO* 87 (2000): 79–107; Jacques, *Angkor*, ch. 3.

[10] Claude Jacques, "Sur les donees de la stele de Tuol Ta Pec, K. 834," *BEFEO* 58 (1971): 163–75, esp. 172–73; idem, *Angkor*, 83–95; Mabbett and Chandler, *Khmers*, 97–99, 262.

[11] Mabbett and Chandler, *Khmers*, 100. Michael Vickery, "The Reign of Suryavarman I and Royal Factionalism at Angkor," *JSEAS* 16 (1985): 231 makes a similar claim. The following discussion relies on Mabbett and Chandler, *Khmers*, 100–106, 165, 170–82; Hubert de Mestier du Bourg, "La premiere moitie du xi siecle au Cambodge," *Journal Asiatique* 258 (1970): 281–314; Jacques, *Angkor*, ch. 4; and sources on agricultural expansion, *infra*.

the mid-10th through the 11th centuries, the following developments point to a truly novel phase. Local dynasts of ancient principalities were increasingly absorbed into a central apparatus, more officials were dispatched to the provinces, and administrative divisions were to some extent standardized. The core population around Angkor expanded markedly, facilitating the construction of unprecedentedly grand hydraulic projects and religious buildings. Shortly before Pagan expanded from Upper Burma to conquer the coast, the Khmer empire itself expanded from the Mekong and around the Great Lake to incorporate the Mun and Chi valleys to the north and the rich region around Lopburi to the west. A more shadowy authority extended over the upper peninsula.[12] Ecclesiastical foundations spearheaded frontier colonization, particularly west and northwest of Angkor in what is now eastern and central Thailand, where Khmer culture and language exercised growing influence.[13] As the economy grew more complex, it has been suggested that the number of urban sites in the empire more than doubled.[14] By the reign of Suryavarman II (r. 1113–1145/1150), builder of Angkor Wat, the empire was arguably at its height, with varying degrees of authority over the Chaophraya basin, Champa, and much of what is now northern and southern Thailand and Laos. Representing a quantum increase in the scale of construction, Angkor Wat itself is not only the most spectacular of all Angkorian temples but, according to one authority, the world's largest known religious monument.[15] Outside the capital the area from the Great Lake northward to the Kulen Hills, roughly a thousand square kilometers, supported a dense network of villages set amidst a mycelium of fields, roads, canals, reservoirs, and embankments.[16] At its peak, the population of the imperial core may have exceeded 1.5 million.[17] After a devastating Cham

[12] Higham, *Civilization*, 99; David Wyatt, "Relics, Oaths, and Politics in Thirteenth-Century Siam," *JSEAS* 32 (2001): 13; Mabbett and Chandler, *Khmers*, 262; Kenneth Hall, "Khmer Commercial Development and Foreign Contacts under Suryavarman I," *JESHO* 18 (1975): 318–36.

[13] Mabbett and Chandler, *Khmers*, 103.

[14] Bourg, "Premiere moitie," 308, pointing to 47 *-pura* locations under Suryavarman I compared to 12–24 in the previous century. But Christophe Pottier, personal communication, Dec., 2001, cautions that many of these later "urban sites" probably predated the use of the *-pura* suffix.

[15] Higham, *Archaeology*, 332. Cf. Eleanor Mannikka, *Angkor Wat* (Honolulu, 1996).

[16] Leigh Dayton, "The Lost City," *New Scientist*, Jan. 13, 2001, 30–33, summarizing research by Roland Fletcher, Christophe Pottier, and Dan Penny.

[17] Bernard P. Groslier, "La cite hydraulique angkorienne," *BEFEO* 66 (1979): 190–91 estimated population of the six capital-region *sruk* at 1,900,000, while Robert Acker, "New

counter-invasion in the 1170s, Angkor under Jayavarman VII (r. 1181–1219?) entered a final phase of military and architectural vigor: Champa and other outlying areas were again subdued, albeit temporarily, and the throne again sponsored massive, if relatively shoddy, temple construction projects, including Angkor Thom.[18]

In sum, we see a long-term increase in territorial authority and a progressive expansion in the scale of royal constructions and legitimation by display, until the apogee was reached in the early 1200s. Thereafter, although the city of Angkor continued to prosper into the 14th century, the regular production of inscriptions and monumental architecture ceased, and its territories steadily contracted.[19] So far as I know, scholars have yet to observe that this chronology anticipated but also coincided very substantially with that of the western mainland. In both regions during the second half of the first millennium, the scale of urban and political organization increased. Although continuities once seemed more pronounced in Cambodia than in the Irrawaddy basin, where the coming of the Burmans in the 830s was long interpreted as a disruptive element, recent research, summarized in Chapter 2, has emphasized the strong links between late Pyu and early Burman settlement and culture.[20] Moreover, if Angkor's frontier colonization and its imperial ambitions were precocious by Pagan standards, during the 11th century both realms experienced an expansion in population, temple-led land reclamations, and territorial control. In both areas the 1100s and early 1200s saw a further dramatic increase in temple construction – Jayavarman VII reportedly moved and shaped more stone than all his predecessors combined[21] – which declined sharply later in the 13th and 14th centuries. Although I know of no scholar who has attempted it,

Geographical Tests of the Hydraulic Thesis at Angkor," *SEAR* 6 (1998): 22 estimated 1,588,000.

[18] Mabbett and Chandler, *Khmers*, ch. 15; Donnatella Mazzeo and Chiara Silvi Antonini, *Monuments of Civilization: Ancient Cambodia* (New York, 1973), 133–67; David Chandler, *A History of Cambodia* (Boulder, CO: 1992), ch. 4.

[19] See the 1296–97 account by the Chinese envoy Chou Ta-Kuan (Zhou Daguan), *The Customs of Cambodia* (Bangkok, 1993). The last known Angkorian monument, dedicated in 1295, was the small Mangalartha temple.

[20] See discussion and n. 6 in Ch. 2 *supra*.

[21] Higham, *Archaeology*, 355. Angkor Wat, the largest single Angkorian monument, began within 10–20 years of the start of the peak period for large monuments at Pagan, 1140–1205. Yet Pottier, personal communication, Dec. 2001, notes that some works attributed to Jayavarman VII may turn out to have been later.

if one were to chart cubic meters of building material used at Angkor between c. 1000 and 1300, the graph might look much like that for Pagan in Fig. 2.2.

How, then, shall we explain Angkorian genesis and growth in comparative context? Angkor and Pagan had indirect cultural, perhaps even military and commercial contacts, but these were far too spasmodic and tenuous to yield common internal rhythms.[22] What about broader maritime-based cultural currents to which both Pagan and Angkor may have been exposed? Obviously in Cambodia as in the Irrawaddy basin, contacts with India (and with Indic cultures elsewhere in Southeast Asia) provided the high cultural inspiration for royal and temple organizations, which in turn conditioned social and economic growth. Specifically, Wolters argues that the 7th-century arrival of *bhakti*-intoxicated brahmins known as Pasupatas inspired the Saivite royal cult on which Khmer kingship came to rest.[23] In the 12th century Kulke suggests that the Vaishnava displacement of Saivisim in Orissa which led to the building of the great Jagannatha temple paralleled the Vaishnava orientation of Angkor Wat.[24] In the early 1200s Jean Filliozat argues that the Muslim conquest of Bengal displaced Buddhist scholars to Cambodia, where they are said to have inspired Jayavarman VII, as well as to Pagan and other Southeast Asian locales.[25] But relating specific foreign inputs of this sort to long-term local development is problematic. The truth is that most Hindu and Buddhist elements during Angkor's expansion in the 10th and 11th centuries had been an integral part of elite Khmer culture since the 7th century. Rather than invoke fresh Indian inspiration, it is more reasonable, on present evidence, to assume that

---

[22] See Kenneth Hall and John K. Whitmore, "Southeast Asian Trade and the Isthmian Struggle, 1000–1200 A.D.," in idem, *Explorations in Early Southeast Asian History* (Ann Arbor, 1976); and G. H. Luce, *Old Burma – Early Pagan*, 3 vols. (Locust Valley, NY: 1969), I, 21–23, offering an account of Pagan-Angkor warfare that strikes me as improbable.

[23] O. W. Wolters, "Khmer Hinduism"; idem, *History, Culture, and Region in Southeast Asian Perspectives* (rev. ed., Ithaca, 1999), 110–12.

[24] Hermann Kulke, *The Devaraja Cult* (Ithaca, 1978), 39–40.

[25] Jean Filliozat, "Sur le civaisme et le bouddhisme du Cambodge, a propos de deux livres recents," *BEFEO* 70 (1981): 59–99; "Emigration of Indian Buddhists to Indo-China c. A.D. 1200," *Studies in Asian History* (New Delhi, 1969), 45–48; "New Researches on the Relations between India and Cambodia," *Indica* 3 (1966): 95–106. On Indian influence in Cambodia, Mazzeo and Antonini, *Monuments*; Mannikka, *Angkor* Wat; Helen Ibbitson Jessup and Thierry Zephir, eds., *Sculpture of Angkor and Ancient Cambodia* (Washington, D.C., 1997).

changing local needs from the 10th century inspired people to redeploy and reinterpret long familiar motifs.[26] Filliozat notwithstanding, it
is also difficult to attribute Pagan and Angkorian cultural rhythms to
a common Indian source, because whereas Pagan turned increasingly
to Sinhalese, Theravadin, and Pali models, Angkor retained a Sanskrit-
based mix of Saivite, Vaishnava, and Mahayana cults, with virtually no
Sinhalese component.[27]

What about maritime trade's more narrowly economic contribution
to Angkor's vitality? From the 7th to 9th centuries a desire for prestigious
foreign goods that could attract clients led rival Khmer lords to expand
control over trade routes leading from the Cambodian plain west to the
Gulf of Siam, east to the Cham coast, and south to the Mekong delta.[28]
Their success probably strengthened emergent principalities, while in-
spiring competitive experiments in administration and ritual display.
Then from the early 10th through the 13th centuries, as Chapter 2 has
shown, commercial innovations and population growth in south China
and India contributed to an expansion of maritime trade along an arc
from the Mideast to the South China Sea. Like Pagan, Angkor not only
benefited, but according to Kenneth Hall, made a determined effort
in the 11th century to strengthen access to traffic on the Malay peninsula.[29] Through the agency of Cham, Vietnamese, Indian, as well as
Chinese traders, Angkor exported diverse forest exotica, while importing Chinese and Indian Ocean handicrafts. With the growth of Southern
Song and Yuan seafaring, the Chinese community at Angkor became
particularly prominent, as shown in illustrations of Chinese junks on
the bas reliefs of Angkor Thom, in extensive finds of Chinese porce-
lains, and in the graphic, often amusing description of Chinese immigrants provided by Zhou Daguan, a Chinese envoy to Angkor, in
1296–1297.[30]

---

[26] In emphasizing that the Khmers engaged in "self-Hinduization" ("Khmer Hinduism,"
440) and thus retained the initiative, Wolters makes somewhat the same point.

[27] As North Indian Mahayanists, Filliozat's Bengali monks represented a minority current
within Pagan Buddhism. Andrew Qintman, "The Weikza and the Mahasiddha: Toward
a Paradigm for the Transmission of Esoteric Buddhism at Pagan" (ms).

[28] Higham, *Archaeology*, 314–19; Vickery, *Society, Economics,*, 307, 316, 405–406.

[29] Hall, "Commercial Development," 318–36; idem, *Maritime Trade and State Development
in Early Southeast Asia* (Honolulu, 1985), 177–78; Luce, *Old Burma*, I, 21–23.

[30] Chou Ta-Kuan, *Customs*, 37–45, 66, 69; Bernard P. Groslier, "Pour une geographie historique du Cambodge," *Les Cahiers d'Outre-Mer* 104 (1973), 362–63. On Angkorian trade,
see also idem, "Our Knowledge of Khmer Civilization: A Re-Appraisal," *JSS* 48 (1960):
17–18; Mabbett and Chandler, *Khmers*, 175–82.

Yet if foreign trade provided the Khmer elite with revenues and prestige items and if (as also seems to have been true at Pagan) royal interest in trade increased in the late charter era, there is no indication
that maritime commerce was central to patronage structures or to the
general economy, certainly not in the critical period 950–1150. As at
Pagan, awards to courtiers and temples normally focused on land and
cultivators, not imported textiles or bazaar taxation. Angkor did export
some locally-produced cotton fabrics and raw silk,[31] but the exports
Zhou Daguan identified were overwhelmingly luxury products from
the forests – rare woods, elephant tusks, bird feathers, wild pepper,
wax, cardamom – involving hill tribes and small networks of lowland
distributors.[32] Although silver or gold ingots served as units of value
alongside copperware, clothes, and cattle, through at least the late 1200s
market transactions were not monetized and taxes were all in-kind.
Vickery emphasizes the utter neglect of money and markets in Khmer inscriptions, which contrasts with frequent commercial references in near-
contemporary inscriptions from Java and with references to coinage
at Funan. After the 7th and more especially the 9th centuries, Vickery
claims, the Khmer "economy was almost entirely agrarian." Concentrating on land and labor, post-870 inscriptions show an "almost total
disinterest" in coastal Cambodia.[33] Even under Suryavarman I (r. 1002–
1050), Hall concedes that trade was entirely secondary to developing
his agrarian base.[34] Claude Jacques concludes succinctly, "Everybody
agrees that the Angkorean [sic] economy was based only upon agriculture."[35] Given that Angkor – like Pagan – arose not at the coast, but in an
interior rice zone, and that after Angkor fell Cambodia's commercially-
oriented rulers turned towards the coast, can anyone be surprised by
this scholarly consensus?

---

[31] Mabbett and Chandler, *Khmers*, 177.

[32] Chou Ta-Kuan, *Customs*, 41–43.

[33] Vickery, *Society, Economics*, 300, 405–406; on Java and Funan, ibid., 314. See too 257 ff.,
317. Cf. Sachchidanand Sahai, *Les institutions politiques et l'organisation administrative
du Cambodge ancien (VI–XIII siecles)* (Paris, 1970), 113–28, 143; Claude Jacques, "Sources
on Economic Activities in Khmer and Cham Lands," in Marr and Milner, *9th to 14th
Centuries*, 331–32; Robert S. Wicks, *Money, Markets, and Trade in Early Southeast Asia*
(Ithaca, 1992), 183–209.

[34] Hall, *Maritime Trade*, 177–78.

[35] Jacques, "Economic Activities," 330; also 332. Nor is there any more archeological or
textual support here than in Burma for Fukui Hayao's suggestion, noted in Chapter 2,
n. 20, that Song cast-iron imports facilitated the spread of animal-drawn iron-socketed
plows.

Chapter 2 raised the possibility that in the upper Irrawaddy basin foreign contacts bred immunity to trade-borne diseases that once had been uniformly lethal. In Cambodia the 7th–8th century demographic shift from the Mekong delta, which presumably had the earliest exposure to trade-borne diseases, to more protected inland sites is consistent with such an hypothesis, as is evidence that Indian Ocean diseases in the 8th century moved along the seaways to coastal China.[36] But again, Southeast Asian disease patterns for this period remain entirely conjectural. In any case, if immunities did increase, they probably did so in combination with agricultural changes that permitted self-sufficient regional populations to cross the size threshold needed to convert epidemic diseases like smallpox and measles to endemicity.[37]

What, then, were the roots of Angkor's agrarian expansion c. 900–1300? At the outset, we can dismiss for Cambodia Richard O'Connor's hypothesis that new ethnic groups introduced new agricultural regimes, because inscriptions show that people of Khmer ethnicity and language dominated the Cambodian plain since the 7th century, and probably much earlier.[38] Rather, I believe that Angkor's agrarian upturn, like that of Pagan, reflected a synergy – as yet unquantified and poorly charted – between improved climate and novel forms of agricultural organization and religious patronage, reconfigured in some contexts by maritime influences.

Recall the studies that point to a wetter climate in mainland Southeast Asia during the Medieval Climate Anomaly. Specifically, composite time-series for El Niño events raise the possibility that annual rainfall in central mainland Southeast Asia increased in the mid-800s, fell off in the early 900s, but again rose sharply c. 950 and, despite two interludes of modest desiccation, remained at unusually high levels until about 1280.[39] Independent climate reconstructions from north-central

---

[36] William Wayne Farris, *Population, Disease and Land in Early Japan, 645–900* (Cambridge, MA: 1995), 71. See *supra*, Ch. 2, n. 29.

[37] According to Frank Fenner, "Smallpox in Southeast Asia," *Crossroads* 3 (1988): 34–35, an interactive population of 100,000–200,000 is needed before smallpox can become endemic. Measles requires a yet larger population.

[38] Vickery, *Society, Economics*, 20; cf. ibid., 64–65. Cf. O'Connor, "Agricultural Change and Ethnic Succession in Southeast Asian Societies," *JAS* 54 (1995): 968–96, and *supra*, Chs. 1, 2.

[39] See studies cited *supra* in Ch. 2, esp. Roger Y. Anderson, "Long-Term Changes in the Frequency of Occurrence of El Niño Events," in Henry F. Diaz and Vera Markgraf, eds., *El Niño: Historical and Paleoclimatic Aspects of the Southern Oscillation* (Cambridge, 1992), 193–200, esp. Fig. 9.1; William H. Quinn, "A Study of Southern Oscillation-related

Thailand suggest that the climate became wetter for brief periods in the 7th century and then again c. 800–860, dried out somewhat c. 860–950, and then became substantially wetter c. 950–1280, with a modest reversal c. 1030–1100.[40] Southwest of Angkor in the peninsula, archeology also shows that between c. 850 and 1280 the percentage of lands receiving regular irrigation water increased sharply, only to fall thereafter.[41] In north-central Cambodia itself in this period, Robert Acker has speculated that the Great Lake held more water than in later periods, again suggesting higher rainfall in the drainage area.[42]

To appreciate the potential significance of such climate shifts, consider that the Angkorian heartland, like Pagan, lies in a rain shadow where annual precipitation now averages less than 40 inches and where crops are highly vulnerable to shortfalls.[43] Even without a change in agricultural technique, improved rainfall would have boosted yields. But in fact, archeology, epigraphy, and hydrology raise the possibility that higher rainfall encouraged more productive cultivation regimes. Starting in the 8th century, and more vigorously during the 9th and 10th centuries – the period of Angkor's genesis – farmers moved from easily cleared but comparatively unproductive sites in the Mekong delta and the Mun-Chi river floodplains towards more wooded lowlands in the same river basins and around the Great Lake. After clearing the forest cover, they dug new ponds, constructed flood-retarding and perhaps flood spreading earthworks, and enclosed what eventually became millions of small bunded rice fields. Whereas the original farming regime depended on natural flooding and thus had limited scope, the alluvial plains and low terraces on which the new system relied were more extensive and ecologically diverse, capable of supporting more specialized rice types. Whereas the floodwaters on which their ancestors depended had been available only during the rainy season, in many locales new flood-retarding systems and reservoirs could release water during the early dry season. And whereas their ancestors had been

Climatic Activity for A.D. 622–190 Incorporating Nile River Flood Data," ibid., 119–49; Richard Grove and John Chappell, "El Niño Chronology and the History of Global Crises During the Little Ice Age," in Grove and Chappell, El Niño – History and Crisis (Cambridge, 2000), 5–34; Simon Haberle, ibid., 66–78, esp. Fig. 1.

[40] See supra, Ch. 2. n. 50. These rely not on palynology or dendrology, but on local stratigraphy and Chinese records.

[41] See supra, Ch. 2. n. 51.

[42] See supra Ch. 2, n. 52 for Acker's somewhat controversial thesis.

[43] Charles Fisher, South-East Asia (London, 1964), 35; M. Nuttonson, Climatological Data of Vietnam, Laos, and Cambodia (Washington, D.C, 1963).

content to broadcast seeds, post-9th century farmers broadcast seeds in some areas, but in others engaged in the labor-intensive, high-yield transplantation of germinated crops from nursery beds to bunded fields. For these reasons, and also because dry-season irrigation usually provides better yields than inundation, the new regime almost certainly produced higher yields per acre as well as larger, more reliable overall harvests.[44] (However, to anticipate later discussion, I hasten to add that insofar as it still concentrated on the floodland edge, this new agricultural pattern failed to exploit areas at both higher and lower elevations that Tai newcomers would later develop.)

Extrapolating from the work of Vickery, W. J. van Liere, Charles Higham, Hubert de Mestier du Bourg, and Christophe Pottier, I theorize three *in seriatim* links between this post-9th century Khmer agricultural regime and possible climatic changes[45] – links which will have to be confirmed, rejected, or modified by later research: a) By helping to increase population under the original broadcast regime, improved rainfall – along with new epidemiological patterns? – provided the extra labor needed to clear forests, build bunds and reservoirs, and begin transplantation; b) once bunded fields and flood-retarding systems were in place, better rainfall ensured the success of the new regime on lowland terraces where moisture is normally insecure. Likewise during the 11th century improved climate aided the extension of Khmer settlement into eastern areas of modern Thailand, where annual rainfall also averages less than forty inches; c) across the Cambodian plain population growth under the new agricultural regime encouraged political consolidation, hence rivalry, among petty chiefs. In circular fashion, competition for followers and rice led chiefs to sponsor fresh reclamation.[46] Prestigious

---

[44] On agricultural evolution, Vickery, *Society, Economics*, 315–18; Elizabeth Moore, "Enclosed Sites," in Rigg, *Gift of Water*, 26–46; W. J. van Liere, "Traditional Water Management in the Lower Mekong Basin," *World Archeology* 11 (1980): 265–80; Higham, *Civilization*, 15, 33, 48–49, 154–55; Christophe Pottier, "Some Evidence of an Interrelationship between Hydraulic Features and Rice Field Patterns at Angkor during Ancient Times," *Jl. of Sophia Asian Studies* 18 (2000): 99–119; idem, personal communication, Dec., 2001.

[45] Van Liere, "Water Management," esp. 271–73, suggests that the transition to a new regime reflected "a change in the flood pattern of the major streams," which in turn probably was caused by changing rainfall. On agricultural intensification and frontier reclamation, previous nn. plus Bourg, "Premiere moitie," 281–314; Mabbett and Chandler, *Khmers*, 263–64.

[46] Analyses of rice husks by Tadayo Watabe and other agronomists suggest that at Angkor as early as the 9th century more productive slender-type *indica* rice had begun to replace round-type *japonica* strains. We have seen that a similar transition started in Upper

foreign trade goods would have reinforced such competition, while Indian religious doctrines gradually re-contextualized indigenous notions of political authority.[47]

Khmer lords in the late first and early second millennia expended much energy in constructing stone temples and endowing them with land, livestock, and bonded cultivators (*khnum*). Besides providing religious merit and public statements of each donor's spiritual power, temple networks spearheaded agricultural expansion, while strengthening ritual and economic links between emergent political centers and their outlying dependencies. Admittedly, as at Pagan, temples were not the only agency promoting land reclamation: small landowners initiated frontier clearings, while some lords may have promoted reclamation independent of temple foundations.[48] Yet surviving inscriptions focus overwhelmingly on temple endowments, which grew dramatically in organizational complexity and number, totaling perhaps 3,000–3,500 in Angkor's extended core by 1200.[49] Such temples fulfilled three economic functions: a) They were centers of investment, distributing seeds, livestock, and land to bondsmen and free cultivators; b) by supporting artisans and scholars whose expertise cultivators could draw upon, temples served as repositories of technical knowledge; c) temples absorbed the costs and risks of reclamation and water projects that were beyond the ability of small groups. As on the northern and western frontiers, temples often received virgin lands, with new temples emerging as hubs of whole communities.[50] The ensuing increase in population,

Burma only in the 14th century, about the same time as in the northern Chaophraya basin. Note, however, that in contrast to these two areas, in Cambodia slender rice seems to have been restricted to areas watered by runoff and waterway floods, rather than by irrigation. Tadayo Watabe, Tomoya Akihama, and Osamu Kinoshita, "The Alteration of Cultivated Rice in Thailand and Cambodia," *Tonan Ajia Kenkyu* 8 (1970): 39–40; Watabe, "The Development of Rice Cultivation," in Yoneo Ishii, ed., *Thailand: A Rice Growing Society* (Honolulu, 1978), 12; Watabe and Akihama, "Morphology of Rice Grains Recovered from Ruins in Thailand," *Tonan Ajia Kenkyu* 6 (1968): 89–92.

[47] Wolters, "Khmer Hinduism"; Vickery, *Society, Economics*, ch. 5; Hiram Woodward, Jr., "Practice and Belief in Ancient Cambodia," *JSEAS* 32 (2001): 249–61.

[48] Sahai, *Institutions*, 124; Jacques, "Economic Activities," 330–31; idem, *Angkor*, 21.

[49] Kulke, "Early and Imperial Kingdom," 16.

[50] Hall, *Maritime Trade*, ch. 6, esp. 161–62; Mabbett and Chandler, *Khmers*, 97, 171–72; G. Coedes and P. Dupont, "Les steles de Sdok Kak Thom, Phnom Sandak et Prah Vihar," *BEFEO* 43 (1943–46): 56–134, esp. 69 ff.; Sahai, *Institutions*, 123–24; Jacques, "Economic Activities," 330–32; Bourg, "Premiere moitie"; Srisakra Vallibhotama, "The Dry Areas in the Archaeology of Southeast Asia" and "The Decline of *Barai*," in Fukui Hayao, ed., *Dry Areas in Southeast Asia* (Kyoto, 1999), 17–25, 107–113.

wealth, and patronage provided a principal incentive for royal as well as aristocratic endowments. Recall that in the 10th and 11th centuries Pagan improved cultivation in the *hkayaing* heartlands, while from the 12th century Pagan's temples also spearheaded reclamation on the *taik* frontier. Given the distinct religious traditions of Pagan and Angkor and the lack of direct contact, temple projects in both places appear to have been independent responses to similar opportunities. The creation of such networks, we shall see, was by no means typical even of the central mainland. Insofar as Angkor was more precocious than Pagan, that precocity, one may speculate, reflected some combination of greater ethnic continuity, slightly earlier pluvial conditions, stronger external stimuli, and accidents of local leadership.

Let us turn from the question of Angkor's genesis to consider how the realm was held together. A long-running debate concerns the system of water control. Contemplating the great royal reservoirs, some of which held over 50,000,000 cubic meters of water, a generation of French scholars led by Bernard Groslier concluded that the prosperity of the realm depended on a centralized hydraulic bureaucracy capable of penetrating to the lowest levels of society.[51] From the late 1970s a revisionist school started by van Liere and eventually including Elizabeth Moore and Acker argued, first, that the great reservoirs lacked a distribution system by which water actually could enter the fields, and second, that even with such a system, the reservoirs could support no more than a very small percentage of the realm's population. In their view, the great reservoirs, like the royal temples, served not a practical agrarian, but a primarily cosmological function, namely, to advertise royal claims to control the fructifying waters of the world.[52] Recently, Roland Fletcher and Pottier again have shifted the terms of the debate. Painstakingly, they demonstrated that a network of collecting and distribution canals did in fact join the great West Baray reservoir (and presumably other reservoirs) to bunded fields. Furthermore, by doubling rice production

[51] Bernard P. Groslier, *Indochina* (London, 1966); idem, "Agriculture et religion dans l'Empire angkorien," *Etudes Rurales* 53–56 (1974): 95–117; idem, "La cite hydraulique"; Jacques Dumarcay, "Khmer Hydraulics," in Jessup and Zephir, *Sculpture*, 93–101.

[52] Van Liere, "Water Management"; E. Moore, "Water Management in Early Cambodia," *The Geographical Journal* 155 (1989): 204–14; idem, "The Waters of Angkor," *Asian Art and Culture* 8 (1995); 37–51; Acker, "New Geographical Tests"; supported by Philip Stott, "Angkor: Shifting the Hydraulic Paradigm," in Rigg, *Gift of Water*, 47–58; Higham, *Civilization*, 156–65; and Fukui Hayao, "Groslier's Hydraulic Society Theory of Angkor in the Eyes of an Agroecologist," *Southeast Asian Studies* 36 (1999): 546–54.

on surrounding lands, Pottier calculated that royal reservoirs made it possible to feed an additional 148,000 people, who provided an invaluable reserve for those construction and military activities on which capital superiority rested.[53] At the same time, it seems clear that across most of the empire, both laborers tied to aristocratic families and smallholders produced rain-fed and locally-irrigated rice without any sort of central supervision. Moroever, even at Angkor (as indeed, in Upper Burma) at the local level water control probably remained in the hands of autonomous temples, villages, and family groups.

Two administrative networks – those of temple officials and of secular officials – linked the court to the countryside.[54] Angkorian temple lands were not automatically tax exempt like Pagan lands, but the autonomy of Angkorian religious institutions was typical of administrative Pattern A. Powerful families endowed local temples, dedicated to ancestral spirits, whose priests entered into reciprocal relations with officials at large central temples, of which in the year 1000 there were about ten. In exchange for religious merit, local shrines made modest gifts to the central shrines, which in turn funneled goods to the royal court. The king sanctioned each family's control over local temples, often exempting new ones from taxation. The second network focused on non-temple peasant communities which were liable for specified in-kind levies, royal corvees, and ad hoc military service. Within each territorial unit or province (*visaya*) various grades of inspectors and officials worked with hereditary leaders at the level of the village and district (*sruk*) to meet these obligations and to ensure that land was properly demarcated and registered. The king himself seems to have served essentially as umpire among priestly and aristocratic families, awarding titles and immunities and confirming earlier grants of patronage. Even within the core (roughly 80 miles around Angkor), royal influence seems to have rested less on sustained supervision than on a combination of ritual attraction, family ties, and patronage.

---

[53] Pottier, "Evidence of an Inter-relationship"; idem, personal communication, Dec., 2001; Roland Fletcher, "Seeing Angkor: New Views on an Old City," forthcoming in *Jl. of the Oriented Society of Australia*; idem, personal communications, Oct., 2001.

[54] On administration, previous nn. on temples, plus Sahai, *Institutions*, chs. 2–8; I. W. Mabbett, "Kingship in Angkor," *JSS* 66 (1978): 1–58; idem, "*Varnas* in Angkor and the Indian Caste System," *JAS* 36 (1977): 429–42; Vickery, "Reign of Suryavarman I"; Leonid A. Sedov, "Angkor: State and Society," in Henri Claessen and Peter Slalnik, eds., *The Early State* (The Hague, 1978), 111–30; Yoshiaki Ishizawa, "The Preservation of Law and Order in Cambodia," *Jl. of Sophia Asian Studies* 2 (1984): 11–31.

Beyond the core, Rajendravarman (r. 944–c. 968) began the work of standardizing provincial administration and absorbing once independent kingdoms by replacing or supplementing local dynasts with central appointees, and by drawing members of powerful families to court.[55] By the 11th century royally-sanctioned temples, garrisons, and officials were in place well beyond the Angkorian plain. In the 1200s, if not earlier, a system of raised highways linked Angkor to Phimai and other key towns. Yet the court never sought to divest powerful provincial families, nor could it prevent princes from developing autonomous provincial bases that they used in repeated military bids for the throne. The possibility that succession could pass laterally among brothers as well as vertically through generations bred endemic uncertainties. Of 26 Angkorian rulers, only eight were sons or brothers of their predecessors, and one of these had to fight his way to the throne in a conflict that may have destroyed the royal city.[56] "In the previous reign, the land, though shaded by many parasols [symbols of royalty], suffered from extremes of heat; under [the present ruler] there remained but one parasol, and . . . the land . . . was delivered from suffering," boasted one inscription after an extended period of disorder.[57]

In yet more distant areas, in the upper Malay peninsula and Chaophraya basin, tributary rulers exploited the first evidence of central weakness to attempt to break away entirely. Angkor's position outside both the Chaophraya and Mekong valleys and the uncertainty of royal succession rendered central authority more unstable than in Pagan, which lay astride a single riverine axis and where father-son, if not primogeniturial, succession was standard. Yet much as at Pagan, the absence, at least until the 12th-century, of serious external threats, the concentration of Indic literacy and technical skills within a small aristocracy, and the very dispersion of authority among self-sufficient institutions all served to afford the system as a whole, the civilization itself, an extraordinary longevity, in this case nearly half a millennium, and a gelatinous resilience against the disruption of its individual parts.

Cultural integration, horizontal and vertical, was comparably modest. The extension of Khmer settlement and authority into northern,

---

[55] Sahai, *Institutions*, 71–86, 141–45; Mabbett and Chandler, *Khmers*, 100, 164–69; Chou Ta-Kuan, *Customs*, 63; Claude Jacques, "Sur l'emplacement du royaume d'Aninditapura," *BEFEO* 59 (1972): 193–205.

[56] Mabbett and Chandler, *Khmers*, 97, 161; Jacques, "Sur les donnees."

[57] By Jayavarman VII's wife, quoted in Chandler, *History*, 59.

eastern and southern Thailand as well as Laos encouraged the spread of Saivite and Mahayana cults such as were found at Angkor, accompanied in some cases by Khmer language and ethnicity. In northeast Thailand, for example, most Hinayana Buddhist *stupas* yielded to the standardized *prasat* structures of Angkorian Hinduism or Mahayana Buddhism.[58] In 1200 people who spoke Khmer as their primary tongue probably formed a majority in the Cambodian plain, the Mekong basin as far north as That Phanom, much of the Chi and Mun river valleys, and the area immediately north and east of present-day Bangkok.[59] But the lowlands also contained very substantial non-Khmer populations. Those parts of the Chaophraya basin subject to Angkor, for example, were dominated by Mon- and later by Tai-speakers, both of whom tended to be more attached to Hinayana Buddhism than to Hinduism. The basin also included people who in later times might be labeled Malay, Cham, or Karen.[60] Angkor itself by 1297, according to Zhou Daguan, had Siamese (Tai) settlers as well as a large population of enslaved hill peoples, who were treated as a race apart. Each city and village in Cambodia, he added, had its own Khmer dialect.[61]

Even more clearly than at Pagan, popular illiteracy and poor communications substantially separated aristocratic and popular culture. Villagers' visions were preeminently local, but according to O. W. Wolters, Khmer courtiers and priests saw themselves living in a Hindu universe. The elite focused on universal gods, chiefly Siva and Vishnu, whereas the mass of smallholders and bondsmen normally propitiated local spirits, the *nak ta*, including departed ancestors, village tutelary deities, and guardians of trees, caves, and fields, the generic equivalent of the Burmese *nats* or the Siamese *phi*.[62] Aristocrats and brahmins used Sanskrit for votive and aesthetic expression, while the vernacular was restricted to mundane records. From the earliest period Sanskrit

[58] Vallibhotama, "Dry Areas," 20. Also Wyatt, "Relics, Oaths," 8–9, 13, 39–44.

[59] Wyatt, *Thailand: A Short History* (New Haven, 1984), 25; Martin Stuart-Fox, *The Lao Kingdom of Lan Xang: Rise and Decline* (Bangkok, 1998), 18–29.

[60] H. G. Quaritch Wales, *Dvaravati* (London, 1969), 18, 30, 92–93, 109–110; G.Coedes, *The Indianized States of Southeast Asia* (Honolulu, 1968), 122; Wyatt, *Thailand*, 25–28, 64; idem, "Relics, Oaths," 6–7; Brown, *Dvaravati Wheels*, Ch. 2, esp. 37–41.

[61] Chou Ta-Kuan, *Customs*, 21, 23, 58. Cf. Vickery, *Economics, Society*, 63–65.

[62] See discussion at Wolters, "Khmer Hinduism" 441; Alain Forest, "Cambodge: Pouvoir de roi et puissance de genie," in Forest et al., eds., *Cultes populaires et societies asiatiques* (Paris, 1991), 185–222; Nidhi Aeusrivongse, "The *Devaraja* Cult and Khmer Kingship at Angkor," in Hall and Whitmore, eds., *Explorations*, 114; Vickery, *Economics, Society*, 139–71.

massively invaded Khmer, but there was no reverse influence, and literate poetry remained exclusively Sanskrit; before the 15th century, in fact, literate literary production in Khmer does not seem to have existed.[63] "Mandarins" and "men of letters," Zhou Daguan noted, had their own speech.[64] Excruciatingly detailed symbolism made temples like Angkor Wat into architectural codes about the fate of the cosmos – but only the initiated could decipher these codes.[65] Now it is true that indigenous beliefs and Indian concepts often interrogated one another: local spirits acquired Hindu names or statues, Siva lingas entered village shrines, and lower spirits did homage to higher Indic ones.[66] Yet, within this loosely unified world view, the powers and territorial responsibilities of Indic guardian spirits, no less than the language used to address them, remained separate from the realm of *nak ta* spirits to which popular strata owed primary allegiance. If propitiation of village spirits and court divinities reflected a common psychology and similar rules, each ritual sphere was autonomous.[67] Precisely for this reason – in contrast to later Theravada practice but in common with Pagan custom – the court made no effort to influence, much less control village rituals or religious personnel. Without normative texts or a unified monastic structure, how could one conceive of local orthodoxy?

The assumption that multiple spiritual forces had legitimate, yet discrete realms also explains the remarkable fluidity and tolerance of elite religion. Even where the central shrine was dedicated to a particular deity or *bodhisattva*, surrounding galleries and shrines normally held images of divinities of other sects. Although Saivism normally dominated, the relationship between Saivite, Vaishnava, and Buddhist cults was labile, and (apart from the reign of Jayavarman VIII, said to be a fierce opponent of Buddhism) all traditions were assured of some royal patronage.

To recapitulate: In the 9th century, but more especially in the 10th and 11th centuries, Khmers initiated an unprecedented phase of temple

[63] Sheldon Pollock, "The Cosmopolitan Vernacular," *JAS* 57 (1998): 12.
[64] Chou Ta-Kuan, *Customs*, 23.
[65] Manikka, *Angkor Wat*.
[66] Likewise kings sought to tap the powers of departed ancestors in peculiarly Southeast Asian fashion. On unifying religious themes, Pollock, "Cosmopolitan Vernacular," 33–34; Aeusrivongse, "*Devaraja* Cult," esp. 123–27; Forest, "Cambodge," 195, 208; Chou Ta-Kuan, *Customs*, 5; Vickery, *Economics, Society*, 207, 251, 398, and *passim*; Kamaleswar Bhattacharya, "The Religions of Ancient Cambodia," in Jessup and Zephir, *Sculpture*, 34–52.
[67] Mabbett and Chandler, *Khmers*, 112.

construction and political consolidation that lasted to the 13th century. Corresponding roughly to Pagan's heyday, this vigor reflected the combined effects of improved rainfall, agrarian intensification, new forms of temple patronage, plus modest economic and perhaps epidemiological influences from the sea. Like Pagan, Angkor was an unstable solar polity. So too, despite differences between the increasingly Theravada culture of Pagan and the Hindu tradition of Angkor, in both realms textual knowledge and detailed Indic ritual remained an elite monopoly, while religious observance at all levels was syncretic and fluid.

OTHER CHARTER PRINCIPALITIES IN THE CENTRAL
MAINLAND TO c. 1250

Angkor had no military rival in the central mainland, but her armies' limited reach meant that Angkor was not the only polity in this region to provide a charter for later peoples. Of particular importance were independent and quasi-independent kingdoms in the Chaophraya and middle Mekong basins that were influenced by earlier Mon civilizations, including that of Dvaravati (loosely dated from the 6th or 7th to the 9th or 10th centuries).[68] Indeed, judged solely in terms of long-term religious influence, in the central mainland the Buddhist culture of Mon-speaking peoples was arguably more seminal than the culture of Angkor itself.

If they were so culturally seductive, why did pre-14th century Mon-influenced states fail to challenge Angkor? In particular, why prior to 1300 did the Chaophraya basin – which later became the focal point of the entire central mainland – not produce a polity or a temple complex comparable to that of Angkor or Pagan? Like the problem of Pagan's and Angkor's genesis, these questions are worth asking, but present evidence does not permit confident answers. The military weakness of Mon kingdoms is all the more puzzling both because Dvaravati and early Angkor shared artistic features and elite connections, and because archeology reveals an expansion after c. 900 of urban sites and polities in the Chaophraya basin as well as the Cambodian plain.[69] Moreover,

---

[68] Not unlike Pyu Burma, Dvaravati was never a unified political entity, according to Brown, *Dvaravati Wheels*, and Wyatt, "Relics, Oaths," 6–8. Cf. Wales' older interpretation in *Dvaravati*.

[69] Brown, *Dvaravati Wheels*, 19 ff., 193; Srisak Vallibhotama et al., "Siam Before the 14th Century," in Varunyupha Snidvongs, ed., *Essays in Thai History* (Singapore, 1991), 43–45; Moore, "Water Enclosed Sites."

the same post-900 improvement in rainfall as aided Angkor affected the Chaophraya basin.[70] What, then, was lacking?

The contrast between the Mons' Theravada affiliation and Angkor's Hinduism is unlikely to have been significant: Pagan, Ayudhya, and Toungoo Burma were all Theravadin and all militarily successful. On the other hand, pre-1300 populations in Lower Burma and the Chaophraya basin were predominantly Mon and in political terms, comparatively weak. Should we search for some essentialist deficiency in Mon culture? Considering that temples at Angkor and Pagan provided the economic and ritual sinews for early centralization, Robert L. Brown has argued that the disinclination of Mons in Dvaravati to build large temples was less symptom than cause of political weakness.[71] Mon Lower Burma also failed to erect large brick or stone edifices. But how shall we explain this predilection – and why should it have been particularly Mon?

What about material differences? Although to 1200 slender rice was present at Angkor but extremely rare in the Chaophraya basin, this hardly can have been fatal: slender rice apparently was not Angkor's dominant strain, and in any case Pagan flourished without a slender rice base. On the other hand, during this rainy 900–1280 era, Mon areas in both Lower Burma and the lower Chaophraya plain may have been ecologically disadvantaged vis-a-vis interior dry zones like Pagan and Angkor. If the potential productivity of coastal/deltaic areas exceeded that of dry zone lands, in both the central and western mainland bringing the latter under the plough presented a less formidable task than taming malarial swamps and swirling floodwaters.[72] As David Wyatt has emphasized, before 1300 the southern part of the central plain of Thailand was far wetter than today – and in some places was still open sea. Similar conditions, we have seen, obtained along the Irrawaddy coast. Besides limiting each region's agricultural potential, in Thailand such conditions would have impeded political and military coordination between the eastern and western shores of what was still an enormous, if continuously sedimenting swamp.[73]

[70] David Godley, "Flood Regimes in Northern Thailand" (Monash Univ. MA thesis, 1997), chs. 5–7.

[71] Brown, *Dvaravati Wheels*, 193–97.

[72] Fisher, *South-East Asia*, 433–35, 486–87; Michael Adas, *The Burma Delta* (Madison, WI: 1974), 22–27.

[73] I follow Wyatt, "Relics, Oaths," 7–9, 19, citing Yoshikazu Takaya; plus P. Pramojanee and T. Jarupongsakul, "Evolution of Land Forms and the Site of Ancient Cities and Communities in Lower Chao-Phraya Plain," in Kajit Jittasevi, ed., *Proceedings for the*

Yet if they were unable to duplicate Angkorian grandeur, between c. 900 and 1250 all along Angkor's northern and western periphery a number of modest states succeeded in preserving distinctive cultural and political forms. All were critical to post-1250 evolution. In counter-clockwise direction, starting with modern Laos, let us quickly survey these polities (see Figs. 1.3 and 3.1).

Along the middle Mekong, from Champassak to Sai Fong (Vientiane), small Austroasiatic and Tai-speaking principalities adopted elements of Mon Buddhist culture entering from the Chaophraya basin and Haripunjaya. Inscriptions and Buddhist images suggest that Mon culture, albeit more attenuated and syncretic, also extended up the Mekong as far as modern Luang Prabang, where it helped to lay the foundations for the first Lao kingdom in the 14th century. Such influences continued throughout the charter era, but with the extension of Angkorian military power from the 11th to 13th centuries, Khmer ritual and artistic conventions began to rival Mon, especially in the south around Champassak and That Phanom.[74]

Farther west in the Ping and adjacent river valleys, the old kingdom of Haripunjaya, in existence since the 7th or 8th century, steadfastly maintained its independence from both Angkor and Angkor's western tributaries. Although Haripunjaya was Mon in language and presumably ethnicity and became a renowned center of Theravada Buddhism, the kingdom seems to have been less a cultural/political offshoot of Mon Dvaravati than an independently evolved entity whose links to Mon Lower Burma were at least as important as to the Chaophraya basin.[75]

In the central and southern Chaophraya basin, the chief powers between c. 1000 and 1250 were Lopburi east of the central swamp and Suphanburi and allied towns in the west. Originally a center of Dvaravati culture, Lopburi was incorporated into Angkor's domain under Suryavarman I (r. 1002–1050) and became a major Khmer garrison site, an Angkorian provincial hub whose administrative language was Khmer, and a noted center of Hindu as well as Buddhist learning. As we shall see, Lopburi, which was more urbanized than regions farther west,

International Workshop: Ayudhya and Asia (Bangkok, 1995), 24–25. Compare the situation in the Irrawaddy delta, *supra*, Ch. 2, nn. 4, 8.

[74] Stuart-Fox, *Lao Kingdom*, 1, 17–32; Brown, *Dvaravati Wheels*, Ch. 2; Betty Gosling, *Old Luang Prabang* (Kuala Lumpur, 1996), 26; Vallibhotama, "Siam," 68–69.

[75] Hans Penth, *A Brief History of Lan Na* (Chiengmai, 1994), 3–9; Brown, *Dvaravati Wheels*, 62–64; Donald Swearer, *Wat Haripunjaya* (Missoula, 1976), 1–22; Vallibhotama, "Siam," 62–63.

later provided a principal conduit for the transmission of Khmer traditions to Ayudhya. However, when Angkor seemed weak, as between
c. 1150 and 1180, this affiliation did not preclude Lopburi's attempting
to carve out an independent political role by sending its own diplomatic
missions to China and extending its authority over neighboring areas.[76]
On the western side of the basin the Mon Buddhist kingdom of
Suphanburi and coastal towns like Phetburi farther south seem to have
been subject to Angkor only nominally and intermittently. The strength
of Suphanburi and nearby towns rested on a combination of intensive
rice agriculture and international trade, the latter spurred by Chinese
merchants and immigrants.[77] From the union of these western towns
and Lopburi eventually would emerge Ayudhya, or Siam. Finally, in the
Malay peninsula principalities like Nakhon Si Thammarat were subject
to periodic Khmer control.

Our information on these polities' internal life is far more fragmentary than for Angkor, but outside Lopburi the limited role of Hindu
temples may have rendered administration closer to Pattern B than to
Pattern A. Within each principality autonomous princes or local dynasts ruled towns outside the capital. If Mon-speakers dominated in
western and southern areas, ethnicities everywhere were heterogeneous
and became more so with Tai infiltration. As at Pagan and Angkor, multiple Indic cults were perfectly compatible with one another and with
strong animist currents. Textually-transmitted elite rituals differed substantially from popular customs, although this gap may have been less
pronounced in Mon-oriented than in Khmer-oriented areas.

THE PASSING OF THE CHARTER ERA, 13TH–14TH CENTURIES

In the 13th and 14th centuries the central mainland suffered dislocations even more wrenching than those in the Irrawaddy basin. These
upheavals were four-fold. First and most dramatic, Angkor's empire
fell apart. During the second quarter of the 13th century Angkorian
forces were withdrawn from Champa. By mid-century most of the
peninsula, areas west of the Chaophraya river, and northern Thailand
had broken away, to be followed shortly by Lopburi and other states

[76] Charnvit Kasetsiri, *The Rise of Ayudhya* (Kuala Lumpur, 1976), 20–22; Sahai, *Institutions*,
78–79; O. W. Wolters, "The Khmer King at Basan (1371–73)," *Asia Major*, n.s. 12 (1966):
83–85; Wyatt, "Relics, Oaths," 8–9, 12–14, 55; Coedes, *Indianized States*, 162–63.
[77] Kasetsiri, *Ayudhya*, 22–25; Vallibhotama, "Siam," 53–59; Wyatt, "Relics, Oaths," 8, 19–22,
44–59.

in the Chaophraya plain. By 1297 Angkor was defending against Tai attacks from the west. After new Tai pressure forced what some historians claim was a temporary withdrawal from Angkor during the mid- to late 14th century (various dates between 1350 and 1389 have been proposed), Khmer rulers may have abandoned the great capital in the 1430s or 1440s in favor of Phnom Penh in the southeast. It is equally plausible that Angkor was never actually abandoned, but that a more powerful royal lineage established itself at Phnom Penh in rivalry with the old Angkorian family.[78] In either case, the 14th century enfeebled central power. Thus Angkor's disintegration began somewhat earlier but overlapped substantially with that of the Upper Burma state, whose problems began in the 1280s, which suffered a major military-political crisis in the 1360s, and which also limped along into the 15th century.

Second, Angkor's collapse permitted, as it reflected, the founding of new kingdoms on the imperial frontiers, especially in the upper and middle Mekong, the Phnom Penh area, central and northern Thailand. In the Irrawaddy basin as well, power fragmented and shifted to the periphery, but whereas Ava maintained Upper Burman political preeminence until the 1420s or 1440s, Angkor yielded pride of place to the lower Chaophraya basin as early as the third quarter of the 14th century.

Third, in Khmer-dominated areas after the mid-1200s, the nature of Indic civilization changed far more drastically than in the western mainland, where Theravada Buddhism and Burman culture not only maintained but strengthened the position they had enjoyed in the charter era. The Cambodian elite shifted its primary allegiance from Hindu to Theravada cults. The erection of large reservoirs ceased, inscriptions became rare, and the last traditional-style temple was dedicated in 1295. Pali replaced Sanskrit, and Theravada monks supplanted brahmins. The richness of Indian literature and iconography, reflected in Angkorian bas-reliefs, sculpture, and architecture, was recast to satisfy the more

---

[78] On the uncertain chronology of Angkor's decline, Wolters, "Khmer King at Basan," esp. 78–87; Mabbett and Chandler, *Khmers*, 212–13; Stuart-Fox, *Lao Kingdom*, 38; Tatsuo Hoshino, *Pour une histoire medievale du moyen Mekong* (Bangkok, 1986), 125–27; Ralph Smith, " 'Cambodia' and 'Vietnam' in Regional Perspective," in Nguyen The Anh and Alain Forest, eds., *Guerre et paix en Asie du sud-est* (Paris, 1998), 247; Charnvit Kasetsiri, "Ayudhya: Capital-Port of Siam and Its 'Chinese Connection' in the 14th and 15th Centuries," *JSS* 80, 1 (1992): 76; Coedes, *Indianized States*, chs. 12–14; Jacques, *Angkor*, 291–95; Wyatt, "Relics, Oaths," 44, 52–56, incl. n. 130. On 13/14th century dislocations, see too Betty Gosling, *Sukhothai: Its History, Culture, and Art* (Singapore, 1991), chs. 2–4; Chandler, *History*, ch. 5; Wyatt, *Thailand*, chs. 3, 4.

austere demands of Theravada Buddhism.[79] Even while Khmer kings remained at Angkor, therefore, Khmer culture was becoming post-Angkorian.

Fourth, everywhere outside the Cambodian plain Tais began to displace Khmer, Mon, and other elites, eventually transforming the ethnic identity of entire populations. The fact that new states in the upper and middle Mekong, the central plain, and northern Thailand were all preeminently Tai creations challenged cultural and ethnic conventions not only at Angkor, but also at predominantly Mon kingdoms like Haripunjaya and Suphanburi. In the Irrawaddy basin, recall, Shan incursions never threatened Burman or Mon supremacy.

Why, then, these upheavals? In part, obviously, Angkor succumbed to internal strains. Yet there are several variants of this theory. One approach – which parallels Aung-Thwin's Pagan hypothesis but lacks his careful documentation – argues that over time politically indebted kings alienated excessive tax-exempt acreages to aristocratic supporters, who were able to pursue power through religious munificence in competition with the king himself. This in turn obliged the crown to attempt more lavish projects of its own, which ultimately exhausted the realm.[80] But in the absence of external coordination, why should these internal processes have climaxed at roughly the same time in both Upper Burma and Angkor?

Groslier drew attention to ecological pressures when he speculated that demands by a growing population for land, fuel, and construction materials caused deforestation and soil erosion. He suggested further that by drying the ground and bringing ferrous-oxide bearing subsoil water to the surface, sedimentation of irrigation works sterilized the soil.[81] If the "soil sterilization" hypothesis is controversial, more recently the archeologists Pottier and Fletcher and the paleo-ecologist Dan Penny have begun to refine and to document the argument that Angkor suffered from cumulative resource constraints. To these scholars we owe the aforementioned discovery that a vast zone outside the

---

[79] Chandler, *History*, 70–71; Ashley Thompson, "Changing Perspectives: Cambodia After Angkor," in Jessup and Zephir, *Sculpture*, 23–24; Jacques, *Angkor*, ch. 8.
[80] This is my synthetic reading of Lawrence Palmer Briggs, *The Ancient Khmer Empire* (Philadelphia, 1951), 257–61; Mabbett, "Kingship," 9; Sahai, *Institutions*, 123–24, 145–48; and Higham, *Archeology*, 355.
[81] Groslier, "Agriculture et religion," 105–106; idem, "La cite hydraulique," 191–94. This thesis of soil sterilization is dismissed by Fukui, "Groslier's Hydraulic Society Theory."

capital of roughly 1,000 square kilometers supported an expanding, relatively thick network of village settlements. As land-scarce farmers within this zone pushed ever farther north to clear the lower slopes of the Kulen hills, they accelerated soil erosion and sedimentation along rivers flowing south to the Great Lake. Not only did the productivity of marginal lands therefore begin to fall, but the complex of transport canals and agricultural waterworks on which Angkor's economy rested became clogged. At the same time, Fletcher speculates, sedimentation may have joined phosphates from human and animal waste to modify the ecology of the Great Lake, a principal source of Angkor's animal and even vegetable food.[82] Presumably, such pressures translated into popular distress, declining rents, more intense intra-elite dissension, and eventually, growing external challenges.

Pagan-Angkor synchronization therefore makes sense if we consider that: a) aided in some measure by improved climate, both civilizations entered a period of intense development in the 10th and 11th centuries; b) reclamation in both areas continued through the 13th century; c) in both areas growing desiccation after c. 1280 aggravated resource constraints that three hundred years of rapid development had engendered. According to David Godley, "a major and striking change to the climatological regimes of the region," namely a "general desiccation of Indochina," began c. 1280 and continued to the late 15th or 16th century.[83] This is not to claim that reserves of good cultivable land became exhausted at precisely the same time in both areas, merely that both experienced some combination of ecological and climatic stress. Shortages of good land in the core probably combined with drier weather to encourage that shift to fertile, less populated, somewhat wetter regions southeast (as well as west) of Angkor which became a principal feature of post-charter history.[84] We shall find that in the 13th and 14th centuries

---

[82] *Supra* n. 53, plus Dayton, "Lost City"; Dan Penny, personal communications, July and Aug., 2001. Elsewhere in Asia, dry areas flourished under limited population pressure, but rapidly deteriorated once a certain ecological threshold was breached. See Fukui, "An Overview," in Fukui, *Dry Areas*, 7; idem, "Historical Cities and Agriculture in Tropical Asia," *Jl. of Sophia Asian Studies* 18 (2000): 27–37, citing parallels in Burma, Java, Vietnam, and Sri Lanka.

[83] Godley, "Flood Regimes," 140; 142: "The most dramatic change in the data occurs in the 14th century and lasts until the 16th century." For additional evidence of 13th–15/16th century mainland desiccation, see *supra* Ch. 2, nn. 54, 90.

[84] Renewed interest in Angkor during the next pluvial phase in the mid-1500s is consistent with this hypothesis. Jacques, *Angkor*, 295–97; Chandler, *History*, 29, 83–84. However, the rain differential between Angkor, on the one hand, and the Cambodian and Thai

after generations of unprecedented growth land shortages joined deteriorating climate and institutional strains to undermine not only Pagan and Angkor, but Dai Viet and Capetian France. In 13th-century Kiev too, although land shortages per se were not a problem, some 300 years of rapid economic growth created severe centrifugal strains.

Yet at Angkor as in the Irrawaddy basin, evaluating the impact of climate is complicated by the fact that the same coastal districts as may have benefited from the interior's agricultural difficulties certainly profited from a long-term growth in maritime trade. Such exchange drew strength from the continuing vitality of Indian Ocean demand[85] and from the southward movement in China's economic center of gravity. Although the Mongol conquest helped to depress the population of south China and although early leaders of the ensuing Ming dynasty (1368–1644) were hostile to private overseas trade, in the late 14th and 15th centuries Ming support for official tributary trade created valuable openings for Southeast Asian coastal rulers.[86] Facing a relative, if not absolute, loss in wealth and manpower, interior capitals found it ever more difficult to control coastal dependencies. Angkor and Upper Burma became the principal victims of this shift, while Suphanburi, Ayudhya, Phnom Penh, and perhaps Champa were among the chief beneficiaries. In a belated effort to woo Chinese trade, between 1371 and 1419 Angkor sent more tribute missions to China than in the previous 500 years, but the subsequent effective transfer of the capital to the more commercially viable site of Phnom Penh marked the eclipse of pro-Angkor elements within the Khmer elite.[87]

In combination with climatic change and a long-term expansion in maritime trade, Tai infiltration revolutionized the political map. As Chapter 2 indicated, bands of Tai-speakers – from whom Assamese, Burmese Shans, Khuns, Lus, Laos, Yuans, and Siamese all evolved – apparently began migrating from the modern Vietnam-China border area to Burma, Thailand, and Laos in the late first or early second millennium.

coasts, on the other, is less than that between Upper and Lower Burma. Fisher, *South-East Asia*, 35; Nuttonson, *Climatological Data*, Tables 47, 48.

[85] See *supra* Ch. 2, n. 15, esp. Christie, "Medieval Tamil-Language Inscriptions," 261.

[86] *Supra* Ch. 2, nn. 16, 92, plus Anthony Reid, ed., *Sojourners and Settlers* (St. Leonards, Australia, 1996), 15–27; Chang Pin-tsun, "The Rise of Chinese Mercantile Power in Maritime Southeast Asia, c. 1400–1700" (ms).

[87] Vickery, "Cambodia After Angkor: The Chronicular Evidence for the Fourteenth to Sixteenth Centuries" (Yale Univ. Ph.D. diss., 1978), 491–522; idem, "The 2/K.125 Fragment, a Lost Chronicle of Ayutthaya," *JSS* 65, 1 (1977): 78–80; Mabbett and Chandler, *Khmers*, 179–82, 215–16; Vallibhotama, "Siam," 88, 104.

The newcomers' success reflected both their martial ability and their irrigation skills, to which we shall return. As Tai migrants settled among
inhabitants in lightly populated northern valleys and then eventually in
the great plains, some non-Tais began to adopt the newcomers' language
and social conventions – even as Theravada Buddhism and other elements of Indic culture flowed in the other direction. Tai-speakers per se
had no collective identity, but a separate language and religious and
social organization often permitted individual Tai groups to maintain
their distinctiveness vis-a-vis Mons, Khmers, and hill peoples.[88] Between c. 1250 and 1310 the Mongols – who destroyed Kiev and pressured
Japan in this period – assisted the Tai advance in two ways: a) By col-
lapsing or weakening the great empires of Nanzhao (1253) and Pagan,
Mongols removed the chief military barriers to the southward movement of Tai warriors and settlers. b) In the upper Mekong, the Mongols
encouraged the creation of Tai client states, most notably Lan Sang,
while providing Tais with new military and administrative models.[89]
Wyatt argues that production of ceramics and other exports also pulled
Tai migrants southward.[90] By the early 1300s, Tais dominated the upper
and middle Mekong, Haripunjaya, and most of the Chaophraya plain.

Having established themselves along Angkor's periphery, Tai newcomers proceeded to enfeeble the imperial heartland at roughly the same
time as they began to raid Upper Burma. As early as 1297 Tai-led forces,
perhaps from Lopburi, laid waste villages on the Cambodian plain.[91]

---

[88] On early Tai migrations, see *supra* ch. 2, n. 94, plus Richard O'Connor, "A Regional
Explanation of the Tai *Muang* as a City-State," in *A Comparative Study of Thirty City-
State Cultures* (Copenhagen, 2000), 431–44; Vallibhotama, "Siam," 52–74; Kasetsiri,
Ayudhya, ch. 3; Betty Gosling, *A Chronology of Religious Architecture at Sukhothai* (Ann
Arbor, 1996), 4; Michael Vickery, "A New Tamnan About Ayudhya," *JSS* 67, 2 (1979):
136–43; James Chamberlain, "The Efficacy of the P/PH Distinction for Tai Lan-
guages," in Chamberlain, ed., *The Ram Khamhaeng Controversy* (Bangkok, 1991), 453–86;
Hiram Woodward, Jr., "The Movement of Thai Speakers from the 10th through the
14th Century," in Robert Bickner et al., *Papers from a Conference on Thai Studies in Honor
of William J. Gedney* (Ann Arbor, 1986), 247–56. For Tai taxonomy, Frank M. Lebar et al.,
Ethnic Groups of Mainland Southeast Asia (New Haven, 1964), pt. 3.

[89] Mongol pressures on Angkor in the 1280s were less serious. On the Mongols' regional impact, Jacques, *Angkor*, 284; Hoshino, *Histoire*, 64–66, 154–57; Stuart-Fox, *Lao
Kingdom*, 9, 32–37; G.H. Luce, *Phases of Pre-Pagan Burma*, 2 vols. (Oxford, 1985), I, 43,
103; Nidhi Aeusrivongse [Eiosrivongs] et al., "Early Ayudhya," in Snidvongs, *Essays*,
116–17.

[90] Wyatt, "Relics, Oaths," 22–25.

[91] Chou Ta-Kuan, *Customs*, 65; Wicks, *Money, Markets*, 178–79. B. J. Terwiel, "Burma in
Early Thai Sources," in Jos Gommans and Jacques, eds., *The Maritime Frontier of Burma*
(Amsterdam, 2002), 17 suggests that the attacks came from pre-1351 Ayudhya.

After its founding c. 1351, the Tai center of Ayudhya escalated these attacks, contributing to the shift from Angkor to sites that were not only economically privileged, but better insulated from Tai attacks. More-over, as Khmer royal power waned, the southeastward movement of Tai and Mon settlers, as well as Mon and perhaps Tai monks, provided a conduit for destabilizing Theravada doctrines to enter Cambodia. By diverting patronage from Saivite temples towards more self-sufficient Theravada monasteries, Theravada Buddhism may have weakened the economic bases of the Angkorian monarchy along with the monarchy's central ideological claims.[92]

In sum, I submit that both Pagan and Angkor succumbed to a combi-nation of ecological strains in the core, climatic deterioration, maritime shifts, and Mongol-assisted Tai incursions. This mix was sufficiently uni-form to explain correlations between Pagan and Angkor, but sufficiently complex to allow for differences in local chronologies.

NEW STATES, NEW ELITES, C. 1250–1440

The large number of warring *muang* – which is the Tai term for a town or group of towns owing allegiance to a single "lord" (*chao*) – between c. 1250 and 1440 led Charnvit Kasetsiri to characterize this era as one of "*muang* pluralism." Their kaleidoscopic fortunes, he noted, "gives the present-day historian a sense of fragmentation and of many things hap-pening disconnectedly in neighbouring places."[93] During the first phase of post-charter fragmentation, approximately 13 kingdoms in the central mainland were independent in the sense that they paid regular tribute to no other regional power.[94] They drew inspiration from Angkorian, Mon, and Tai traditions, with those farthest from the old Indianized centers tending to exhibit the greatest plasticity and the strongest Tai admixture. In their basic chronology and incessant competition, these states thus resembled Ava, Prome, Toungoo, Pegu, Martaban, and other post-Pagan kingdoms in the Irrawaddy basin. What, then, did the post-charter map of the central mainland look like?

---

[92] See Chandler, *History*, 68–71; Briggs, *Khmer Empire*, 242, 259; Higham, *Archaeology*, 355, employing the work of R. Hagesteijn.

[93] Kasetsiri, *Ayudhya*, 13, 25.

[94] Including in 1340 Luang Prabang, Vientiane, Kenghung, Kengtung, Lan Na, Phayao, Nan, Sukhothai, Lopburi, Suphanburi, Angkor, That Phanom, and Nakhon Si Thammarat.

As the Khmer polity contracted, its center of gravity, we have seen, shifted towards more maritime, secure areas in the southeast. In order to tap Chinese trade during the late 1300s, more and more Mekong river ports arose in the region of the future Phnom Penh, even as Hindu culture mutated in the face of growing Theravada influence. Still, well into the 15th century Khmer leaders continued to draw heavily on classical ritual, dance, and aesthetic standards and to regard Angkor as a model realm.[95]

Along the upper and middle Mekong, then dominated by Mon- and other Austroasiatic-speakers, Tai newcomers in the 13th century seized or founded a number of small principalities, including Luang Prabang and Vientiane. In the third quarter of the 14th century a ruler from Luang Prabang drew together some of these scattered *muang* to form the confederation of Lan Sang – "A Million Elephants," a title redolent of military strength. This consolidation apparently gained support not only from the Mongols, but from Angkor, which sought help against the rising power of Ayudhya.[96] Although still influential, Khmer and Mon cultural elements became subordinate to specifically Tai legends of royal descent, to Tai visions of a three-class social order, and to the communal worship of powerful Tai spirits. Lan Sang would later become a major regional power, but for much of the 15th century its authority was severely tested by succession disputes and external attacks.[97]

Farther north and west Tais founded or reinvigorated such scattered principalities as Kenghung in the Sipsongpanna, Chiang Saen in the Yonok country; and Phayao, Nan, and Chiang Mai along northern tributaries of the Chaophraya. The most influential of these new principalities, Chiang Mai, was created in 1292–1296 by a Tai prince who had moved south from Chiang Saen into the ancient Mon-dominated realm of Haripunjaya. Although a substantial portion of the population remained Mon and although local script, legal codes, and literature continued to reflect Mon tradition, the end of Mon inscriptions at Haripunjaya suggests a rather sudden elite displacement. Like their peers at Lan Sang, Chiang Mai's rulers sought to advertise their power with the name of their new confederation – Lan Na, "A Million Ricefields." Also as at

[95] Vickery, "Cambodia After Angkor," 491–522; idem, "2/K. 125 Fragment," 56, 61, 78–80; Aeusrivongse, "Ayudhya," 129; Mabett and Chandler, *Khmers*, ch. 16; Thompson, "Changing Perspectives," esp. 23–28.

[96] Hoshino, *Histoire*, esp. ch. 2; Stuart-Fox, *Lao Kingdom*, 35–39; Dore, "Aux sources," 574–692. Luang Prabang was known earlier as Muang Swa or Siang Dong Siang Thong.

[97] Stuart-Fox, *Lao Kingdom*, ch. 2; Wyatt, *Thailand*, 82–84; Vallibhotama, "Siam," 67–70.

Lan Sang the momentum of early consolidation ebbed, in this case in the early 14th century.[98]

Southeast of Chiang Mai at Sukhothai, in an area whose agriculture and ceramics attracted a stream of northern migrants, sometime between 1219 and 1243 Tai chiefs defeated a Khmer garrison to establish another independent kingdom. From the late 1200s to the mid-1300s, Sukhothai extended its influence to the east, and south into the upper peninsula. Twentieth-century Thai patriots lauded this state as progenitor of the "Thai Buddhist nation" because they believed they saw a number of ur-Thai features: Sukhothai "liberated the Tai from the Khmer yoke," it was the first kingdom to use Tai as its official language, its Khmer-based alphabet evolved via Ayudhya into that of modern Thailand, and it was more Buddhist and less Hindu than Ayudhya. But recent scholarship has dismissed as wildly anachronistic any idea of pan-Tai loyalties, while noting that Tai writing did not originate at Sukhothai and that the kingdom's era of maximum power did not coincide with strong Buddhist influence.[99]

Far more important to the long-term fortunes of the central mainland than Sukhothai was the lower Chaophraya basin, which in the early 1300s remained divided among small towns and principalities, most of them also increasingly Tai in language and social custom. Still preeminent were Suphanburi to the west of the river and its swampy delta, and Lopburi to the east. About 1351 a leader with connections to the ruling houses of both of these principalities established a new capital at Ayudhya roughly midway between the two older sites.

---

[98] On early Tai kingdoms in the Ping, Nan, and Yom basins and the Sipsongpanna, see *The Nan Chronicle*, Prasoet Churatana, tr. (Ithaca, 1966), sects. 1–2; *The Laws of King Mangrai*, Aroonrut Wichienkeeo and Gehan Wijeyewardene, eds. and trs. (Canberra, 1986); *The Chiang Mai Chronicle*, David Wyatt and Aroonrut Wichienkeeo, trs. (Chiang Mai, 1995), Intro. and chs. 1–3; Wyatt, *Thailand*, 44–50, 74–76; idem, "Relics, Oaths," 9, 13, 39–49. On the relation of Lan Na to Mon culture, John Hartmann, "The Spread of South Indic Scripts in Southeast Asia," *Crossroads* 3 (1988): 6–20; Anatole-Roger Peltier, "Les litteratures Lao du Lan Na, du Lan Xang, de Keng Tung et des Sip Song Panna," *Paeninsule* 1990: 29–44.

[99] In the extensive Sukhothai literature, see esp. Gosling, *Sukhothai*; idem, *Chronology*; Wyatt, "Relics, Oaths," 4, 22–31, 38–55; Srisakra Vallibhotama, "The Ancient Settlements of Sukhothai," in Bickner, *Papers*, 231–38; idem, "Siam," 70–74; A. B. Griswold and Prasert na Nagara, "On Kingship and Society at Sukhodaya," in *Change and Persistence in Thai Society*, G. William Skinner and A. Thomas Kirsch, eds. (Ithaca, 1975), 29–92; Michael Vickery, "A Guide Throgh Some Recent Sukhothai Historiography," *JSS* 66 (1978): 182–246; Dhida Saraya, "Rice Cultivation and Politics in the Sukhothai State," *East Asian Cultural Studies* 24 (1985): 99–107; Chamberlain, *Ram Khamhaeng Controversy*.

Although rivalry between Suphanburi and Lopburi would continue into the 15th century, gradually both ruling houses came to accept Ayudhya as a paramount center whose throne became the ultimate prize. At least three factors explain the timing of this pregnant alliance: a) the growth of private Chinese trade increased the appeal of coordinated commercial and diplomatic strategies; b) the military decline of Sukhothai and Angkor created a new space for local initiatives; c) sedimentation reduced Suphanburi's capacity for independent action by silting up its river link to the Gulf. In a broader sense, sedimentation (and post-1280 desiccation?) may have joined land reclamation to extend the shoreline, to connect estuarial islands, and to fill in swampy districts. This would have facilitated contact between the eastern and western shores of the ancient swamp, while providing a more attractive settlement site between the older towns. In a locale that had enjoyed some prominence even before 1351, Ayudhya eventually proved suitable for extensive rice cultivation, while its position astride the chief north-south river channels afforded access both to the sea and to hinterland supplies of forest exotica and ceramic exports.[100] Through natural sedimentation and human reclamation, the development of more southerly areas would continue into the 18th century and beyond, as shown by the agricultural shift from the old to the young delta below Ayudhya and by the change of Siam's commercial/political center from Ayudhya to Bangkok.[101]

Benefiting from the same movement of Angkorian people, ideas, and texts as later enriched Phnom Penh, Ayudhya owed a heavier debt to Khmer culture than did most of its interior Tai-led competitors. The new court awarded itself the classical name for Angkor (Yasodhara), spoke Khmer as well as Tai, used Khmer in official documents well into the 15th century, and thereafter retained Khmer script for religious writings. Notwithstanding the growing prestige of Theravada Buddhism, court etiquette, poetry, drama, dance, and art also remained for a time substantially Angkorian. Much of this influence was transmitted via the former Khmer outpost of Lopburi, but deportations that followed Ayudhya's

---

[100] On early Ayudhya, Kasetsiri, *Ayudhya*, esp. chs. 4–5; Vallibhotama, "Siam," 53–56; Aeusrivongse, "Ayudhya;" Wyatt, *Thailand*, 63–72; idem, "Relics, Oaths," 58–61; Vickery, "New Tamnan"; B. J. Terwiel, "Early Ayutthaya and Foreign Trade, Some Questions," in Nguyen The Anh and Yoshiaki Ishizawa, eds., *Commerce et navigation en Asie du Sud-Est* (Paris, 1999), 78–90. On ecological changes and sedimentation, *supra* n. 73.

[101] Ishii, *Thailand*, chs. 1–3, 7; Yoshikazu Takaya, *Agricultural Development of a Tropical Delta* (Honolulu, 1987), ch. 4.

invasions of Angkor and later Lovek provided another channel.[102] The subsequent territorial division into "Thailand" and "Cambodia" therefore should not obscure the fact that by 1450 the leaders of both Ayudhya and Phnom Penh participated in a hybrid culture and regarded themselves as heirs to Angkor's classical brilliance. Perhaps the closest Eurasian analogy to this triangular post-charter relation, we shall see, arose in Russia, where Muscovy and Lithuania emerged as rival heirs to a physically distant Kiev. At the same time Ayudhya inherited directly the Mon culture of the western basin ("Dvaravati" also appeared in Ayudhya's official title), which contributed to Ayudhya's increasing Theravada commitment.[103] Ethnicity was correspondingly complex, with large residual Mon and Khmer populations, growing numbers of Tai immigrants and assimilated Tais, as well as Chinese traders.

How were these post-charter kingdoms organized? If some Chaophraya basin rulers, in the style of Angkor, used temples to ensure an accessible supply of manpower,[104] religious foundations generally played a more modest role than at Angkor, and administration in all these small polities (as in Middle and Lower Burma after 1300) was closer to Pattern B than to Pattern A. No doubt this reflected conscious policy less than local traditions outside the Pagan and Angkorian heartlands.

Like their Irrawaddy basin counterparts, even the strongest of the new timber-palisaded capital cities governed directly only a modest region at a distance of two or three days' journey.[105] Almost by definition,

[102] On Ayudhya's relation to Angkor and Phnom Penh, I rely on David Wyatt, personal communication, June 1995; Michael Vickery, personal communication, September, 1992; idem, "Cambodia After Angkor," 517; idem, "The Khmer Inscriptions of Tenasserim," *JSS* 61 (1973): 51–70; Kasetsiri, *Ayudhya*, 100–102; Chandler, *History*, 79–80; Aeusrivongse, "Ayudhya," 187 ff.; Hans Penth, *Brief History*, 12 n.; John F. Hartmann et al., "Lexical Puzzles and Proto-Tai Remnants in an Old Thai Text," *Crossroads* 4 (1989): 71; William J. Gedney, "Siamese Verse Forms in Historical Perspective," in Gedney, *Selected Papers on Comparative Tai Studies*, Robert J. Bickner et al., eds. (Ann Arbor, 1989), 513–18; Wyatt, "Relics, Oaths," n. 188.

[103] Brown, *Dvaravati Wheels*, xxi, citing Jean Boisselier.

[104] Kasetsiri, *Ayudhya*, 42–43, 101–102; Srisakra Vallibhotama, "Political and Cultural Continuities at Dvaravati Sites," in Marr and Milner, *9th to 14th Centuries*, 232.

[105] On early political organization, Aeusrivongse, "Ayudhya," 147–72; Wales, *Ancient Siamese Government and Administration* (rpt., New York, 1965), esp. chs. 1–4, 8; Vallibhotama, "Siam," 74–86; Kasetsiri, *Ayudhya*, ch. 6; Takashi Tomosugi, *A Structural Analysis of Thai Economic History* (Tokyo, 1980), ch. 4; Wyatt, *Thailand*, ch. 4; Lorraine

each nuclear zone boasted the kingdom's largest population, perhaps in the range of 20,000–50,000. In the case of Ayudhya, whose organization has been studied most closely, Nidhi Aeusrivongse and his colleagues have argued that even around the capital, the great bulk of non-noble freemen were *phrai som*, that is, peasants who were private dependents of various lords, rather than *phrai luang*, who owed service to the king. The king, in other words, had access to the peasantry through quasi-hereditary local lords, the so-called *munnai*, who received no salary from the crown but whose right to collect *phrai som* services and gifts enjoyed royal sanction.[106]

Outside the nuclear zone lay a zone of formerly independent cities entrusted to relatives of the king and thus known as "princely cities" (*muang luk luang*). Typically these were located in secondary commercial or agricultural districts with their own satellite communities. Thus, for example, Sukhothai's ruler appointed members of his family to rule Kamphaengphet, Phitsanulok, and Si Satchanalai, while Lopburi and Suphanburi were among Ayudhya's original princely cities. Prince-governors had to send tribute, pay homage, and provide troops, but collecting taxes for the capital was not required, nor did the central overlord normally take censuses of *phrai* in the provinces. Governors took wives from influential local families, and gubernatorial succession was often hereditary. Although Ayudhya's early kings may have appointed spies (*yokkrabat*),[107] other local officials were chosen by the prince-governor himself. As in the Irrawaddy basin in this period, if the overlord seemed vulnerable, governors were tempted to attack the capital to seize the throne.

At a yet greater distance lay tributary states (*muang prathetsarat*), invariably ruled by hereditary dynasts. Such areas owed at best a nominal allegiance, which they themselves were likely to interpret as a gesture of friendship between equals. Insofar as they sometimes paid tribute to more than one ruler, imperial borders were largely meaningless.

Gesick, "Kingship and Political Integration in Traditional Siam, 1767–1824" (Cornell Univ. Ph.D. diss., 1976), ch. 1.

[106] Aeusrivongse, "Ayudhya," 166–70. Cf. Akin Rabibhadana, *The Organization of Thai Society in the Early Bangkok Period, 1782–1873* (Ithaca,1969), 19 ff.

[107] Rabibhadana, *Thai Society* 28, 75 says the capital appointed *yokkrabat* only after 1569, but Aeusrivongse, "Ayudhya," 159–60 sees such appointments in the Early Ayudhya period.

RICE, TEXTILES, SILVER, AND GUNS: MATERIAL SPURS TO CONSOLIDATION c. 1400–1560

During the 15th and more especially the 16th centuries these modest early efforts at consolidation grew more sustained and successful. In the central as in the western mainland, the centrifugal thrust of the late charter and early post-charter eras now yielded to a great countermovement. By 1540 an insistent cannibalism had reduced the 13 or so independent kingdoms of 1340 to a mere four – Cambodia, Lan Sang, Lan Na, and Ayudhya – among which Ayudhya and Lan Sang fought one another, as well as Burma, for the privilege of devouring Lan Na. Consolidation in the center would continue into the 19th century until only Ayudhya's heir – Bangkok – survived.

Before chronicling the emergence of the big four states, I shall discuss general integrative dynamics in the 15th and 16th centuries, beginning with agricultural and demographic change.

To recall O'Connor's hypothesis, the ease with which Tai "valley-wanderers" gained an economic foothold and the rapidity with which Mons and Khmers assimilated to a Tai identity owed much to the Tais' water management skills, which they had developed in their upland home territories. Mon and Khmer rice-growers depended not on irrigation, but on the management of runoff and waterway floods; the latter techniques necessarily neglected large areas suitable for wet rice cultivation at elevations that were both higher and lower than the floodland edge. Thus early Tai chronicles and archeology suggest that along the tributaries of the Chaophraya and in the northern central plain, Tais occupied empty or under-utilized lands, much of it high quality soil, at levels above the floodland edge.[108] O'Connor's reconstruction receives support from Tadayo Watabe, Yoneo Ishii, Yoshikazu Takaya, and other Japanese scholars whose analysis of rice husks shows that from the 12th to 15th or 16th centuries, wet-rice expanded wherever Tais settled, first in small upland enclaves, then in larger valleys.[109] Meanwhile around

---

[108] O'Connor, "Agricultural Change," esp. 972–73, 981–83.

[109] I rely on four essays – Tadayo Watabe, "The Development of Rice Cultivation," Yoneo Ishii, "History and Rice-Growing," Shigeharu Tanabe, "Land Reclamation in the Chao Phraya Delta," and Toru Yano, "Political Stucture of a 'Rice-Growing State,' " – in Ishii, *Thailand*; plus Watabe, "The Glutinous Rice Zone in Thailand," in Shinichi Ichimura, ed., *Southeast Asia: Nature, Society, and Development* (Honolulu, 1976), 96–113; idem, *Ajia Inasaku no Keihu* (Hosei, Japan), 1983, 93–94, tr. Atsjuko Naono; Yoshikazu Takaya, "An Ecological Interpretation of Thai History," *JSEAS* 6 (1975): 190–95; Watabe and Akihama, "Morphology of Rice Grains"; Watabe, "Alteration of Cultivated Rice,"

Ayudhya and other low elevations along the Chaophraya floodplain, by building a system of levee-breaching slits and local distributary channels to direct floodwaters into the fields, Tai cultivators may have turned hitherto neglected backswamps into paddy land.[110]

As they introduced new hydrological techniques, Tais promoted two types of lowland rice – round and slender – at the expense of upland rice. This was significant because the upland variety, cultivated on dry land or land with limited flooding, produces lower and less stable yields than either lowland type. Watabe suggests that Tai migrants brought with them round type rice, the early-ripening cereal mentioned in Chapter 2, as they descended down the Mekong and Chaophraya systems.[111] By contrast, late-ripening slender type rice probably entered along the coast from the Bay of Bengal as early as the 6th century, and was grown in naturally flooded areas in northeast Thailand and Cambodia subject to Khmer influence. Tais thus encountered slender rice when they entered the plains. However, by turning uncultivated lower Chaophraya floodplains and backswamps into paddy land, and by constructing irrigation facilities on hitherto neglected lands in northern valleys, Tais pushed slender rice into new niches in areas where it was already grown, and extended its use farther north and west.

Watabe has traced the progress of cultivation in the changing ratio between husk types preserved in ancient bricks. Until the 13th century both upland and lowland rice were equally common in the central plain, but between c. 1250 and 1500 the former lost out and within another century disappeared completely from the plain. Thereafter it retreated in more isolated northern regions as well. Furthermore, in those areas specializing in lowland rice, slender gradually displaced round (see Fig. 3.2). From the 11th to 15th centuries the two varieties were grown with roughly equal frequency in both the central plain (at Suphanburi, Lopburi, Ayudhya) and along its northern tributaries (as at Chiang Mai).

36–45; Vallibhotama, "Siam," 65; and personal communications from T. T. Chang, David Feeney, and R. D. Hill. On the link between Tai migration and rice techniques, see too Amalendu Guha, *Medieval and Early Colonial Assam* (Calcuta, 1991), 161–78; and Louis Golomb, "The Origin, Spread and Persistence of Glutinous Rice as a Staple Crop in Mainland Southeast Asia," *JSEAS* 7 (1976): 1–15, which, *pace* O'Connor, sees Tais borrowing from Khmers.

[110] Esp. O'Connor, "Agricultural Change," 972, 981–83; Tanabe, "Land Reclamation," 49–52.

[111] See n. 109 *supra*. Conceivably, Tais also introduced more individualized and secure, hence more productive, landholding systems than their Khmer and Mon predecessors, but we have no information on this early period.

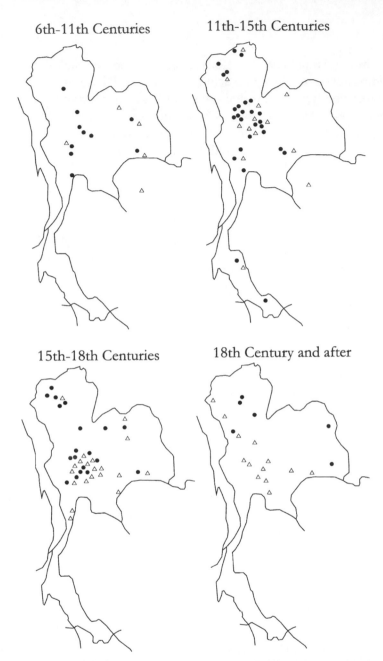

Figure 3.2. Distribution of rice husk types by period in Thailand and Cambodia. Triangles identify historic finds of "slender type rice"; circles identify finds of "round type." Tadayo Watabe, "The Development of Rice Cultivation," in Yonei Ishii, ed., *Thailand: A Rice-Growing Society* (Honolulu, 1978), Fig. 3.

But in the 15th century late-ripening slender rice became dominant in the plain and began to push northward wherever Tai irrigation works allowed fields to be flooded for an adequate period. A return to wetter conditions c. 1470–1560 may have aided this process. By the 18th century slender rice had become standard in northern valleys as well as the central plain. As we have seen, this transformation – which paralleled the triumph of slender *kauk-gyi* in the Irrawaddy basin – had significant nutritive implications, because slender rice normally was more productive than round.[112] Nor was slender rice genetically static: in response to local problems of water level, salinity, soil quality, and insects, trial and error created specialized strains. The deep-water belt below Ayudhya, for example, saw the refinement, if not the creation, of so-called floating rice, much noted by foreign visitors, which kept pace with the rapidly rising water level of the summer delta.[113] "Without doubt," Watabe concluded, "the thirteenth to fifteenth centuries witnessed a remarkable change in rice cultivation in Thailand, particularly in the Central Plain near the Chao Phraya river."[114]

Although not new, cotton cultivation probably also expanded. If we extend the crop chronology of southeastern Burma, with which peasants and traders in north Thailand were in regular contact, this fiber critical to the cultivation of marginal lands and to local handicrafts alike was first grown on a significant scale along Chaophraya tributaries during the 14th or 15th centuries. By the early Chakri period if not earlier, raw cotton and cotton manufactures represented a modest portion of Siam's total exports, although far less than from Burma.[115]

In turn, agricultural refinements and associated population increases may have reduced epidemic susceptibility. For smallpox an interactive population of 100,000–200,000 is generally the minimum needed to maintain endemic status, and for measles, a somewhat larger figure. Tai settlement of the hitherto lightly populated Ping, Wang, Yom, and Nan

---

[112] See Watabe citations in n. 109 *supra*, and Dao The Tuan, "Types of Rice Cultivation and Its Related Civilizations in Vietnam," *East Asian Cultural Studies* 24 (1985): 48.

[113] Ishii, *Thailand*, 26–27, 42; O'Connor, "Agricultural Change," 983; *The Ship of Sulaiman*, John O'Kane, tr., (London, 1972), 153–54; Nicolas Gervaise, *The Natural and Political History of the Kingdom of Siam*, John Villiers, tr. (Bangkok, 1989), 10–11.

[114] Watabe, "Development of Rice Cultivation," 9.

[115] See cotton discussion, Ch. 2 *supra*. On 16th-century Cambodian cotton, Bernard P. Groslier, *Angkor et le Cambodge au XVIe siecle* (Paris, 1958), 152. On early Chakri cotton, James C. Ingram, *Economic Change in Thailand 1850–1970* (Stanford, 1971), 10; B.J. Terwiel, *Through Travellers' Eyes* (Bangkok, 1989), 94–97, 113–28 *passim*. By the mid-14th century cotton also was grown in the northern Malay peninsula.

basins, as well as tributaries of the upper Mekong, may have crossed those thresholds.[116] In this scenario, the benefits of endemicity that more southerly, exposed areas like the Great Lake region achieved at the start of the second millennium now extended farther into the interior.

How did agricultural and demographic expansion influence political consolidation? In Laos, north Thailand, and the Chaophraya plain, larger aggregate (and perhaps per capita) surpluses – which courts tapped directly through land taxes and indirectly through corvees and military levies – facilitated royal patronage, building projects, monastic establishments, and warfare. To enhance their military position, Tai courts in the central mainland, like their counterparts in the Shan hills and the Irrawaddy basin, promoted pacification and agricultural extension with an enthusiasm that may have had no precedent in the less intensely competitive charter era. Royal documents referred frequently to reclamation and land taxes.[117] At the same time, as in Burma, larger aggregate demand for salt, fishpaste, ceramics, textiles, and other handicrafts promoted market exchange, which in turn aided fiscal extraction. One sign of commercial activity throughout the region was the proliferation of silver taxes and fines. Another index – although, as we shall see, external as well as domestic stimuli were at work – was the standardization of weights and the introduction c. 1430–1450 of so-called bullet coinage at Ayudhya, where previously the only media of exchange were cowrie shells and locally produced lumps of metal. So too in 15th-century Sukhothai and Chiang Mai, silver media, coming from local mines, Yunnan, and perhaps the coast, replaced cowries; while in Cambodia, where coinage had been unknown in the Angkor period, the first flat coins, in gold and silver, were minted in the 1510s. Thus in terms of monetary systems, for most of the central mainland the 15th century seems to have been seminal.[118]

---

[116] A 1376 Lao census claimed 300,000 Tai males eligible for military service. Stuart-Fox, *Lao Kingdom*, 60–61. Cf. Fenner, "Smallpox"; O'Connor, "Agricultural Change," 982. On post-1500 smallpox outbreaks consistent with background endemicity, see *Chiang Mai Chronicle*, 105; Dhiravat na Pombejra, "A Political History of Siam under the Prasatthong Dynasty 1629–1688" (Univ. of London Ph.D. diss., 1984), 225, 359; Wyatt, *Thailand*, 65; Stuart-Fox, *Lao Kindom*, 95.

[117] Aeusrivongse, "Ayudhya," 215; Vallibhotama, "Siam," 81; Gesick, "Kingship," 16, n. 4. Cf. *Crystal Sands*, David Wyatt, tr., (Ithaca, 1975), 112–14, referring to the peninsula.

[118] On taxes, Aeusrivongse, "Ayudhya," 155, 166–72; Ishii, *Thailand*, 32; Wales, *Siamese Government*, ch. 9. On coinage, Robert S. Wicks, "A Survey of Native Southeast Asian Coinage c. 450–1850" (Cornell Univ. Ph.D. diss., 1983), 117–31, 154–58, 167–73, 188, 451; idem, *Money, Markets*, 168–82; Sun Laichen, "Ming-Southeast Asian Overland

Yet if internal growth whet political ambition throughout this region, the lower Chaophraya basin enjoyed major advantages over constricted, irrigation-dependent valleys to the north. Measuring some 15,000 square miles, the Chaophraya plain is many times broader than the largest northern Thai valley; in the southern sector, whose alluvial fertility is renewed through annual floods, excess, not dearth is the chief hydrological problem. Given the development of floating rice in the deep-water belt below Ayudhya and the suitability of the old delta north of Ayudhya for more conventional wet rice, cultivation in the floodplain was capable of considerable extension. Already in the late 1300s, A. B. Griswold and Prasert na Nagara estimate that the population of Ayudhya was "several times" larger than that of Sukhothai, its chief interior rival.[119] Thereafter, as in the Irrawaddy basin, even if lowland and upland populations grew at the same rate, the former's absolute advantage was bound to increase. But in fact (notwithstanding what may have been more dramatic immunological improvements in the interior) a combination of better water resources, deportations, and new commercial openings probably yielded more rapid growth in the lower Chaophraya basin. We can detect a similar pattern within Laos, where the demographic center moved steadily south from the narrow valleys of northern Laos into more level and fertile regions of the central Mekong and the Khorat plateau, contributing to a shift in Lan Sang's royal residence from Luang Prabang to Vientiane in the mid-1500s.[120]

Desiccation for much of the period 1280–1470, not least the late 14th and early 15th centuries, may have offered an additional advantage to Ayudhya in its competition with Sukhothai and Lan Na, where rainfall averages 20–40 percent less than in the floodplain. Here again, Ayudhya may have been comparable to Pegu, and Sukhothai and Lan Na to Ava. Wetter, more propitious conditions c. 1470–1560 did not alter the essential equation, both because Ayudhya's agricultural base continued to provide a cumulative demographic advantage, and because by 1530 maritime factors had joined agriculture to shift the balance of power irrevocably in favor of the coast.

Interactions, 1368–1644" (Univ. of Michigan Ph.D. diss., 2000), 176–77; Ashin Das Gupta and M. N. Pearson, eds., *India and the Indian Ocean 1500–1800* (Calcutta, 1987), 66–67; Reid, *Age of Commerce*, II, 93–107; Jeremias van Vliet, *The Short History of the Kings of Siam*, Leonard Andaya, tr. (Bangkok, 1971), 71.

[119] Griswold and Prasert, "Kingship and Society," 70.

[120] Stuart-Fox, *Kingdom of Laos*, 76; Wyatt, *History*, 85.

How did Cambodia fit these patterns? Although the lower Mekong suffered no climatic disadvantage vis-a-vis Ayudhya, O'Connor argues that there and in the Cambodian plain inertia led Khmer farmers to retain their strategy of manipulating runoff and waterway floods, which tapped a smaller area than Tai-style cultivation. If true, this would help to explain why Ayudhya's domain in the late 1500s was two to three times more populous than the comparably sized Cambodian realm.[121]

Alongside agricultural growth, in the central as in the western mainland, external commerce began to shape the economy more profoundly than during the charter era. Responding to growing demand in Europe, the Mideast, India, and the central mainland itself, Siamese trade with the Indian Ocean grew briskly during the 15th century, especially perhaps during the first and last thirds, only to double or triple again between 1520 and 1560. Through all-water routes and isthmian portages, contact with Bengal, the Coromandel coast, Pattani, Banten, and Aceh grew accordingly, and 16th-century Ayudhya boasted significant communities of Bengalis, Arabs, and Persians. Phnom Penh and its successor Lovek were no less cosmopolitan. One factor in this expansion was a post-1460 increase in western Eurasia's stock of precious metals. As bullion prices rose, technical improvements in European mining and larger shipments of African gold to the Mediterranean helped end the so-called bullion famine of the mid-15th century, to which Chapter 2 referred. From 1525 to 1575 a five-fold increase in New World silver imports to Europe further increased liquidity.[122] Meanwhile, as noted, East Asian trade between 1370 and 1550 exhibited a similar dynamism. Early Ming invitations to renew tributary trade elicited a particularly enthusiastic response from Ayudhya, whose founder was probably of Chinese background.[123] Thereafter, China's post-1460 Malthusian

---

[121] O'Connor, "Agricultural Change," 976–83; van Liere, "Water Management," 265–80; Reid, *Age of Commerce*, I, 14, lumping Khmer and Cham populations together.

[122] On expanding Indian Ocean-SE Asian trade, see Reid, *Age of Commerce*, II, 10–23; Siamese trade estimates at Wyatt, *Thailand*, 88; Lieberman, "Europeans, Trade," 209–10; Armando Cortesao, ed., *The Suma Oriental of Tome Pires*, 2 vols., (London, 1944), I, 104. On growing West Eurasian bullion stocks, see supra Ch. 2, nn. 154, 175, plus Harry Miskimin, *The Economy of Later Renaissance Europe, 1460–1600* (Cambridge, 1977), 28–35; Halil Inalcik, *An Economic and Social History of the Ottoman Empire*, Vol. 1: 1300–1600 (Cambridge, 1994), 58–61.

[123] Kasetsiri, *Ayudhya*, 66–72; "Translation of Jeremias van Vliet's Description of the Kingdom of Siam," R. F. van Ravenswaay, tr., *JSS* 7 (1910): 6–8. Puzzling, however, is the mid-15th-century contrast between bullion and specie shortages in China and much of Eurasia, on the one hand, and indications of adequate supplies at Ayudhya (*supra* n. 118).

upturn, which roughly paralleled that of Europe, joined the post-1520 Japanese and New World silver booms to transform China's monetary regime and to precipitate what has been termed China's "second commercial revolution," with obvious potential benefits for Southeast Asia.[124] Early Ming bans on private trade with the Nan-yang (Southern Ocean) were circumvented by indirect contacts through the Ryukyus, and more especially by surreptitious voyages from Fujian and Guangdong directly to the Gulf. Portuguese visitors to 16th-century Siam noted that Chinese traders and immigrants were "everywhere established."[125]

As with agricultural expansion in the central mainland, the economic and political benefits of foreign trade were by no means restricted to the coast. For one thing, many of those mainland products most in demand overseas – rare woods, benzoin, gems, deerskins, copper – derived from the interior, where local rulers operated monopolies and customs posts. Beyond that, the same expansion in overland trade with Yunnan (and Guangxi) as aided Shan kingdoms helped principalities in what is now north Thailand and Laos. Thus "many merchants out of China" flocked to 16th-century Chiang Mai to exchange gold, silver, and Chinese handicrafts for Indian textiles, copper, and benzoin,[126] while from Luang Prabang, Lower Burma, and Ayudhya other caravans converged on Chiang Mai and Sukhothai. Vientiane superseded Luang Prabang due to its agricultural attractions, no doubt, but also because it was better served by commercial routes linking the middle Mekong to Vietnam, Cambodia, and Ayudhya.[127] In substantial measure, the

---

[124] William Rowe, "Approaches to Modern Chinese Social History," in Olivier Zunz, ed., *Reliving the Past* (Chapel Hill, 1985), 272 ff.; William Atwell, "Time, Money, and the Weather: Ming China and the 'Great Depression' of the Mid-Fifteenth Century," *JAS* 61 (2002), esp. 97–103 See *supra* Ch. 2, nn. 92, 154, 175.

[125] Joaquim de Campos, "Early Portuguese Accounts of Thailand," *JSS* 32 (1940): 22–25. On Chinese trade, private and tributary, c. 1400–1560, see too Chang, "Chinese Mercantile Power"; G. William Skinner, *Chinese Society in Thailand* (Ithaca, NY: 1957), 3–7; Suebsang Promboon, "Sino-Siamese Tributary Relations, 1282–1853," (Univ. of Wisconsin Ph.D. diss., 1971), 105–17; Kasetsiri, *Ayudhya*, 66–82; Yoneo Ishii, "Some Aspects of the 15th Century Ayuthayan Port-Polity as Seen from a Ryukyuan Source," *SEAR* 2 (1994): 43–53; A. Kobata and M. Matsuda, *Ryukyuan Relations with Korea and South Sea Countries* (Kyoto, 1969), 53–100; David Wyatt, "Ayudhya 1409–1424," in Jittasevi, *Proceedings*, 191–95.

[126] Ralph Fitch in Samuel Purchas, ed., *Hakluytus Posthumus or Purchas His Pilgrimes*, IX (Glasgow, 1905), 194–95. Cf. Sun, "Ming-Southeast Asian Interactions," 154–67, 176–82.

[127] Stuart-Fox, *Lao Kingdom*, 76; Wyatt, *Thailand*, 85; *The Kalyani Inscriptions* (Rangoon, 1892), 73–74; Skinner, *Chinese Society*, 86.

renewed military-cum-political vigor of Lan Na and Lan Sang in the 15th and 16th centuries reflected quickening long-distance trade and cheaper bullion along an arc from Yunnan and Guangxi down the chief river valleys to the coast.

But as with agricultural expansion, the principal benefits of maritime commerce went not to inland states, but to lowland and coastal polities, particularly Ayudhya, which had access to multiple sources of interior products. Situated at the confluence of three rivers, Ayudhya could restrict maritime access to Sukhothai, Lan Na, and other interior states, manipulating terms of trade in much the same way as Pegu dominated Ava. Phnom Penh and later Lovek enjoyed similar advantages vis-a-vis the interior, although rapids along the middle Mekong meant that Cambodia's main avenue into the interior offered a less serviceable route.

Alongside local forest, mineral, and agricultural products, coastal entrepots sold Indian textiles, peninsular tin, archipelagic spices, Chinese porcelain and silk. International (as opposed to petty domestic) trade in Siam and Cambodia was embedded in systems of official sale and official purchase, which gave the royal family and its clients an effective monopoly over the most lucrative goods. Cash revenues, whose collection benefited from rising imports of specie and bullion and the production of local coins, were used for pious works, patronage, and to hire mercenaries. The importance the Siamese crown attached to such income is suggested by the prominence of export goods in the tax system and by the fact that commercial goals frequently inspired territorial expansion (see below). Likewise, from at least the late 1400s Ayudhya devoted enormous corvee resources to dig short-cut and transverse canals to the Gulf so as to facilitate both military transport and commercial access to the coast. Ishii concluded (with some exaggeration perhaps) that "the outstanding characteristic of the 'medieval' state is probably its commercial nature."[128]

Finally, here as in Burma foreign firearms and mercenaries provided another spur to integration. Sun Laichen has shown that 15th-century

[128] Ishii, *Thailand*, 33. On canals and trade, idem, "Religious Patterns and Economic Change in Siam in the Sixteenth and Seventeenth Centuries," in Anthony Reid, ed., *Southeast Asia in the Early Modern Era* (Ithaca, 1993), 181–84; Aeusrivongse, "Ayudhya," 199–208; van Vliet, *Short History*, 68–69; Robert V. Hubbard, *The History of Inland Waterway Development in Thailand* (Ann Arbor, 1977), 10–21; Shigeharu Tanabe, "Historical Geography of the Canal System in the Chao Phraya River Delta," *JSS* 65 (1972): 23–72.

Ming deserters introduced gunpowder technology and firearms not only to Shan states, but to Lan Na and other central interior principalities, which benefited in contests with southern rivals.[129] Such an advantage, however, may have been short-lived, both because Chinese-cast cannon and Muslim firearms were also known at Ayudhya in the 15th century,[130] and because after 1517 the Portuguese began supplying not only Lower Burma but Ayudhya with European-style firearms that were superior in range and accuracy to anything hitherto available. King Chairacha (r. 1533–1547) of Ayudhya reportedly had 120 Portuguese bodyguards and firearms instructors, whom he employed in increasingly successful campaigns against Lan Na. During the epic Burmese-Siamese wars of the second half of the century, Portuguese matchlocks and cannon proved indispensable for sieges and naval warfare alike. Although disciplined Portuguese and Muslim mercenaries continued to comprise elite corps, Siamese also produced and employed their own handguns and cannon, including pieces made along European lines.[131] In response to the threat of Burmese cannonades, between 1549 and 1584 the walls of Ayudhya and of at least one frontier fortress, originally earth-and-post, were rebuilt in brick or laterite, with angled bastions capable of withstanding artillery and with projecting gun-towers. The walls of Vientiane and Chiang Mai also were rebuilt in brick.

Again, however, Lan Na and the Lao principalities were disadvantaged vis-a-vis Ayudhya because they could obtain European firearms and experts only through the ports. In the late 1500s Pegu's king "subjected [Laos] into obeying him through the use of firearms, which were still unknown here," reported an Italian missionary either ignorant or contemptuous of Chinese firearms.[132] Likewise, perhaps because of its

---

[129] In 1457/8 a Lan Na musketeer reportedly killed the "prince of Ayudhya." Sun, "Ming-Southeast Asian Interactions," ch. 3; idem, "The Transfer of Chinese Military Technology to Northern Mainland Southeast Asia, c. 1390–1526" (ms); and *Chiang Mai Chronicle*, 69–70, 80–81, 86, 89, 97 referring to handguns and cannons, the latter designated by what Sun believes is a Chinese-derived term (*pu cao*).

[130] *CHSEA*, 381; and C. A. Seymour Sewell, "Notes on Some Old Siamese Guns," *JSS* 15 (1922): 39–43. Intharacha (r. 1409–1424) sent "junks to other countries to buy weapons." van Vliet, *Short History*, 62–63.

[131] Indicative of indigenous interest in military manufacture, a Siamese treatise of 1580 explained how to produce incendiary rockets and various strengths of gunpowder. *CHSEA*, 382.

[132] Based on 1640s reports about events in the 1570s, G. F. Marini, *A New and Interesting Description of the Lao Kingdom*, Walter E. J. Tips and Claudio Bertuccio, trs.(Bangkok, 1998), 26.

lesser commercial stature, Cambodia apparently did not obtain large quantities of Iberian firearms until the 1590s.[133]

In short, after 1400 and more especially between 1450 and 1570, three material factors encouraged a new phase of political consolidation: agricultural extension, maritime commercial expansion, and European-style firearms. These dynamics resembled those in the western mainland, yet there was a critical difference. In the Irrawaddy basin, the agricultural center remained in Upper Burma, while maritime trade and firearms favored the coast. Not surprisingly, authority oscillated between the two zones, with Upper Burma dominant through the early 1400s and again from the early 1600s. But in the central mainland, the lower Chaophraya basin, that is to say, Ayudhya, had a clear advantage on every score and therefore enjoyed a more stable sectoral hegemony.

Can we go further and weigh the relative contribution to Ayudhya's success of agricultural and maritime factors? I suspect that foreign commerce grew more rapidly than agriculture after 1400 or 1450 but here as in the western mainland, without statistics on rice acreage, population, or shipping, it is impossible to prove this or to dissect external-internal synergies. One might argue that Lower Burma, which despite its inferior agricultural base defeated Upper Burma in the 16th century, proves the primacy of maritime factors in regional politics, but this is hardly persuasive because: a) The interior-based Toungoo dynasty originally conquered the coast, rather than vice versa; b) Upper Burma suffered from debilitating Shan raids, from which Ayudhya was exempt; c) Upper Burma was weakened by enormous glebe land holdings, which again had no Ayudhyan counterpart. We shall find too that Vietnam's dramatic territorial expansion at the expense of the Chams after 1470 depended almost entirely on non-maritime factors.

BUDDHIST PROSELYTISM, c. 1400–1560

Along with economic growth, in the central mainland as in the west the spread of Buddhist norms favored long-term consolidation.

---

[133] On guns and fortifications in the central mainland to c. 1600, Damrong Rajanubhab, "Our Wars with the Burmese," *JBRS* 38, 2 (1955): 138–96; Larry Sternstein, "Krung Kao," *JSS* 53, 1 (1965): 97–98; Chandler, *Cambodia*, 86; *CHSEA*, I, 381–82; Sunait Chutintaranond, "The Origins of Siamese-Burmese Warfare," in Jittasevi, *Proceedings*, 99–100.

In rejecting Sukhothai as embodying an ur-Thai identity, revisionist scholarship has also denigrated the once-hallowed claim that early Tai migrants were quintessentially Buddhist.[134] It is true that Tai migrations concentrated on Mon areas where Theravada-oriented Buddhism had long assumed a popular character, and that as early as the 13th century a Buddhist identity informed many community rituals.[135] Nonetheless in this early period the mix of animism, folk brahmanism, court brahmanism, and Pali Buddhism that A.Thomas Kirsch described for later Tai religious practice[136] tilted rather heavily towards animism, more so perhaps than when the same areas had been ruled by Mon-oriented elites. In early Sukhothai, for example, the largest building was not a monastery, but a shrine dedicated to the realm's spirit protector (*phi muang*), whose worship required the slaughter of buffaloes, pigs, ducks, and chickens, the smearing of blood on ritual objects, and the drinking of animal blood or rice wine in ceremonies reminiscent of those in 14th and 15th-century Burma.[137] In 14th-century Lan Sang as well, the chief ritual involved blood sacrifices to the *phi thaen*, the ancestral spirits of the capital.[138] Ayudhya's "Golden Mount" (Phu Khao Thong) was originally built to house the *phi muang*, the royal tutelary spirit, and only later was converted to a Buddhist stupa.[139] As late as the second quarter of the 15th century a king of Chiang Mai, to the scandal of monastic chroniclers, revered shamans while sacrificing cattle to the spirits of trees, rocks, and mounds.[140] In chronicle accounts of early Lan Na and even in early law codes, Buddhist references were incidental, but spirit

---

[134] Gosling, *Chronology*, esp. 3–6, 239–43. Cf. Charnvit Kasetsiri, "Preliminary Observations on Thai Historiography," in *Comparative Studies on Literature and History of Thailand and Myanmar* (Bangkok, 1997), 111–19.

[135] Wyatt, "Relics, Oaths," esp. 18, 28, 35–63.

[136] A. Thomas Kirsch, "Complexity in the Thai Religious System: An Interpretation," *JAS* 36 (1977): 241–66.

[137] Gosling, *Sukhothai*, 23–26.

[138] Stuart-Fox, *Lao Kingdom*, 45; also 50–58.

[139] Gosling, *Sukhothai*, 26; Prasert na Nagara and A.B. Griswold, "The Pact Between Sukhodaya and Nan," in *Epigraphic and Historical Studies* (Bangkok, 1992), 78, 84–85. Cf. Constance Wilson, "The Holy Man in the History of Thailand and Laos," *JSEAS* 28 (1997): 349 n. 16.

[140] *The Sheaf of Garlands of the Epochs of the Conqueror*, N.A. Jayawickrama, tr. (London, 1968), 128. Cf. Donald Swearer and Sommai Premchit, "The Relationship Between the Religious and Political Orders in Northern Thailand (14th–16th Centuries)," in Bardwell Smith, ed., *Religion and Legitimation of Power in Thailand, Laos, and Burma* (Chambersburg, PA: 1978), 28.

guardians of places and people were omnipresent.[141] All this is familiar from post-Pagan Upper Burma.

However, in the 13th century and then in greater numbers from the mid-14th to 16th centuries, Tai as well as Burmese, Mon, and Khmer monks studied at monasteries within Southeast Asia and in Sri Lanka. On their own initiative or at the invitation of Tai rulers, coastal-based monks then journeyed into the interior to spread "true doctrine" at Shan kingdoms, Sukhothai, Chiang Mai, Lan Sang, Kengtung, and smaller principalities.[142] If Tai aristocrats, not to mention peasants, remained emotionally wedded to spirit cults, why were they also attracted to these itinerants, many of whom were as stiff-necked as they were learned?[143] And why the upsurge in Buddhist proselytism?

Here, as in the western mainland, a variety of social and psychological mechanisms deserve consideration. Economic expansion was an enabling factor both because it extended interior-coastal trade links, and because wealth made possible the building of more monasteries and the laborious transcription of texts. Although monks usually did not engage in trade, interior peoples may have identified them with the prosperity of the coast. To those who through trade or migration had lost the protection of natal spirits, or simply to those of anxious temperament, the place-neutral predictability of karmic reward must have been psychologically reassuring.[144] More broadly, many Tai newcomers saw in Buddhism that cosmopolitan power and esoteric knowledge that had always been preeminent attributes of valley civilization. To interior zones where literacy was still rare, missionary monks brought sacred texts and all-purpose scripts.[145] We sense something of the awe texts could inspire in 15th-century accounts from Kengtung that *suttas*

---

[141] David Wyatt, "Southeast Asia, 'Inside Out,' 1300–1800," *MAS* 31 (1997): 689–709; Mayoury Nagosyvathn, "An Introduction to the Laws of Khun Borom," in Andrew Huxley, ed., *Thai Law: Buddhist Law* (Bangkok, 1996), 76.

[142] On monastic networks in this period, Kasetsiri, *Ayudhya*, 85–86, 139–40; Sao Saimong Mangrai, *The Padaeng Chronicle and the Jenglung State Chronicle Translated* (Ann Arbor, 1981), 40–42, 101–25; Swearer and Premchit, "Relationship," 20–33; Dore, "Aux sources," 765–70; A. B. Griswold and Prasert na Nagara, "Epigraphic and Historical Studies No. 4," *JSS* 57, 1 (1969): 109–48; Vallibhotama, "Siam," 93–101; Aeusrivongse, "Ayudhya," 187–208.

[143] See revealing anecdotes at Mangrai, *Padaeng Chronicle*, 40, 123, 125, 138.

[144] Mangrai, *Padaeng Chronicle*, 126 ff. Cf. Reid, *Age of Commerce*, II, 150–61.

[145] On legal, orthographic, and artistic exchange, Diller, "Extra 'Y'"; Hartmann, "Spread of South Indic Scripts"; Andrew Huxley, "Introduction," and "Thai, Mon, and Burmese Dhammathats – Who Influenced Whom?" in Huxley, ed., *Thai Law*; Stuart-Fox, *Lao Kingdom*, 68; Vallibhotama, "Siam," 100–101; Peltier, "Litteratures Lao," 29–44.

vanquished demons and quelled fires, and in a later north Tai report that a worried abbot gathered all the religious manuscripts in his district, burned them, and used the ashes in amulets.[146] No less potent were Buddha images and saint relics from the coast, which precipitated earthquakes and miracles.[147] Association with these prestigious objects undoubtedly had a certain social cachet. Meanwhile, through a concept of compensatory social power known in local guises across Southeast Asia, asceticism brought Buddhist monks extraordinary authority with which laymen of all ranks were eager to identify. Khmer monks, in the words of a 16th-century Portuguese visitor, were "exceedingly proud and vain, and alive they are worshipped for gods ... [with devotees] praying unto them and prostrating themselves before them: and so the common people [treat them] with a great reverence and worship: in sort that there is no person that dare contradict them in anything ..."[148]

Here too, Buddhism's all-encompassing social vision and its capacity for cooptation attracted would-be centralizers, who normally became its chief patrons. Buddhism came equipped with an explicitly universal, text-based ideology that portrayed even petty dynasts as "World Rulers" (*cakkavattis*) and "Kings of Righteousness" (*dhamma-rajas*). As set forth in the 14th-century Sukhothai treatise *Three Worlds According to King Ruang*, by postulating a perfect vertical fit between social rank and religious merit, Buddhism fused power with morality and made kings the link between mankind and cosmos.[149] Horizontally too, the doctrine promised an attack on particularism more withering than anything rulers could achieve by manipulating spirit hierarchies. Because the *Tipitaka* were standardized texts, they automatically privileged central over local notions of sacred power. Likewise, monks, in contrast to shamans, followed uniform criteria of ordination and training subject to royal enforcement.

---

[146] Mangrai, *Padaeng Chronicle*, 113–17; James Chamberlain, "The Literature of Laos," in John Whitmore, ed., *An Introduction to Indochinese History, Culture, Language and Life* (Ann Arbor, 1979), 59, citing anecdote of uncertain date. On textual magic, also Lorraine Gesick, *In the Land of Lady White Blood* (Ithaca, 1995), 32.

[147] *Sheaf of Garlands* (an early 16th-century account), 117–20, 130–31, 140–46, 175–76; Wyatt, "Relics, Oaths," 37.

[148] Fr. Gaspar da Cruz in C. R. Boxer, ed., *South China in the Sixteenth Century* (London, 1953), 61. For similar accounts of Lao and Siamese monks, Marini, *New and Interesting*, chs. 4–6; Donald Lach, *Southeast Asia in the Eyes of Europe* (Chicago, 1965), 528–29.

[149] *Three Worlds According to King Ruang*, Frank and Mani Reynolds, trs. (Berkeley, 1982); Craig Reynolds, "Buddhist Cosmography in Thai History, with Special Reference to Nineteenth-Century Culture Change," *JAS* 35 (1976): 203–10.

These intellectual/emotional departures created two sets of tensions, both familiar from the Irrawaddy basin. First was that between Theravada Buddhism and animism. To be sure, Buddhism freely acknowledged the power of local spirits by incorporating them into the lower levels of its own cosmography in a process Kirsch calls "religious upgrading,"[150] and over the long term this helped to smooth transitions. Yet where entrenched Tai spirit cults and shamans resisted "true doctrine," the latter's partisans sometimes took forceful measures. We saw this with Bayin-naung's attack on Shan religious practices, and we shall find further instances in Lan Sang.[151]

Second was a tension between universal religious identities and local political allegiances. The circulation of texts and monks across Southeast Asia and between Southeast Asia and Sri Lanka encouraged lay elites as well as monks to think of themselves as participants in a vast Theravada community. Buddhist art, sacra, architecture, scripts, and legal codes were eminently mobile, as shown by the closely linked literary traditions of Lao, Yuan, Khun, and Lu Tai communities in the interior, and by the spread of Sinhalese-style Buddha sculptures from coast to interior.[152] At the same time, however, with no sense of contradiction, Buddhist piety could become intensely local. Through a combination of royal patronage and popular pride, as in the Irrawaddy basin so at Lan Na, Lan Sang, Ayudhya, Cambodia, and smaller principalities, the conceit took hold that Buddhism flourished most brilliantly in one's own kingdom, and that rival states supported traditions that were correspondingly deficient – even in need of external correction. Like the Emerald Buddha, said to embody "the heart of Laos," or the statue whose destruction led to a Cambodian defeat in the 1580s, Buddha images became palladia of particular kingdoms.[153]

Within each kingdom ethnicity, dialect, dress, and architecture (at least among local elites) often showed a similar specificity. Mother-daughter monasteries and pilgrimage sites intensified cultural exchange

---

[150] Kirsch, "Complexity," 263.

[151] See Stuart-Fox, *Lao Kingdom*, 52, 74–75; *supra* Ch. 2, nn. 183, 184; and discussion *infra*.

[152] Diller, "Extra 'Y' "; Hartmann, "Spread of South Indic Scripts"; Huxley, "Introduction," and "Thai, Mon, and Burmese Dhammathats"; Peltier, "Litteratures Laos," 29–44; Philip Rawson, *The Art of Southeast Asia* (London, 1967), chs. 5, 6; Vallibhotama, "Siam," 100–101.

[153] Mayoury and Pheuiphanh Ngaosyvathn, *Paths to Conflagration* (Ithaca, 1998), 151; Peltier, "Litteratures Laos," 38; Reid, *Age of Commerce*, II, 196. See too Stuart-Fox, *Lao Kingdom*, 50, 52, 79 on the Pra Bang image; and Gesick, *Lady White Blood*, 50–51, on universalist/particularist tensions.

within particular river systems. Networks involving the collection of export goods strengthened links among local elite families, as did royal-local marriages. Through ceremonial display and artistic and literary patronage, each capital defined local norms, sometimes in self-conscious opposition to external communities. So too, with its emphasis on state-specific in-group mobilization, warfare sharpened (or created *de novo*) boundaries that may be termed "ethnic" insofar as they posited a common name, history, and cultural symbols. Such distinctions provided a poorly theorized, but at times emotionally significant source of cohesion that could fuse with claims to superior Buddhist virtue.

THE BIG FOUR EMERGE, C. 1440–C. 1560

Without lapsing into a tale of kings and battles, let us trace the fortunes of the four chief kingdoms to benefit from economic change, firearms, and new Buddhist currents. A military free-for-all began rather earlier in the central mainland than in the Irrawaddy basin, where Ava kept a lid on dry zone rivalries until the mid-1400s and where Toungoo's triumphs started only towards the end of that century. Nonetheless, both regions saw a marked increase in political and cultural consolidation, hence too in the scale of warfare, between 1440 and 1560 (see Figure 1.5).

Cambodia. The shift to Phnom Penh, we have seen, signaled a victory for those Khmer leaders who sought to develop trade with China and the archipelago. Located at the confluence of the Mekong and the Tonle Sap – a point known in Khmer as the "four faces" – Phnom Penh could tap the export of Lao gold, silk, and forest products and the domestic trade in pottery, fish sauce, and dried fish from the Great Lake area. It was also in a position to control the distribution of Chinese and Indian goods coming up the Mekong, while providing an entrepot for archipelagic items. Phnom Penh in the 1540s was said to have had 3,000 Chinese, while later Lovek had separate quarters for Chinese, Japanese, Arabs, Portuguese, and Malays. By marrying into the Khmer elite, Chinese and Malays reinforced its commercial orientation.[154] What is more, the Phnom Penh area – which may have served as one of Angkor's original granaries – was fertile and capable of supporting a reasonably large population.[155] When, starting in the second half of the 16th century,

---

[154] Chandler, *History*, 79–80, 86; Mabbett and Chandler, *Khmers*, 220–21; Cortesao, *Suma Oriental* I, 112.

[155] Previous n. plus F. Grunewald, "A propos de l'agriculture dans le Cambodge medieval," *Asie du Sud-est et Monde Insulindien* 13, 1–4 (1982): 23–38.

the royal seat shifted northward to Lovek and Udong, these capitals remained in the same vicinity.

During the 16th century the hitherto hybrid cultural practices of Siamese and Cambodian elites grew more distinct, a development that owed much to the still unsettled rivalry between the two courts. Although Siamese influence may be detected in some spheres, a uniquely Khmer Theravada tradition now took form, not by abandoning, but by reanimating the heritage of Angkor, by evolving brahmanic temples into stupas, and by incorporating ancestral cults into a new Theravada ritual and architectural complex. With Sanskrit composition now abandoned, more populist Theravada practices encouraged the emergence of a Khmer vernacular literature. At the same time, European accounts suggest that brahmins retained extensive influence at court.[156]

Notwithstanding signs of cultural vitality, in military terms Cambodia remained on the defensive. A highly decentralized version of Pattern B administration left the kingdom prone to provincial revolts, which in turn repeatedly opened the door to foreign interference. Wolters has argued that feuds within the royal family, manipulated by Ayudhya, provided the immediate cause for Khmer withdrawal from Angkor.[157] In the late 15th century conflict between Phnom Penh and southeastern districts let Ayudhyan armies intervene successfully on behalf of a royal claimant from Phnom Penh. In the 1590s some Khmer leaders again looked beyond Cambodia's borders for help, this time to Spanish Manila in a forlorn effort to halt Ayudhyan attacks.[158] In the face of steady Lao encroachments, Cambodia also lost ground in the Khorat plateau and the middle Mekong, retaining secure control only over the Cambodian plain and the Mekong delta. Although still able to exploit Ayudhya's late 16th-century troubles with Burma, Cambodia (along with Lan Na) had become one of the two most feeble of the four surviving kingdoms.

Lan Sang (Laos). In part because its interior position left it less vulnerable to Ayudhyan pressure, the kingdom of "A Million Elephants" proved more competitive than Cambodia.

[156] On post-Angkorean Khmer culture and religion, Thompson, "Changing Perspectives"; ibid., "Introductory Remarks Between the Lines," in Barbara Watson Andaya, ed., *Other Pasts* (Honolulu, 200), 47–68; ibid., "The Ancestral Cult in Transition," *Southeast Asian Archaeology*, 1996; Cortesao, *Suma Oriental* I, 112, referring to *suttee*; Boxer, *South China*, 60–63; Groslier, *Angkor et le Cambodge*, chs. 1, 4, 6 *passim*.
[157] Wolters, "Khmer King," 85–86.
[158] Chandler, *History*, 81–86; Vickery, "2/K.125 Fragment," 60–61.

Lan Sang's late 15th and 16th-century success was all the more strik-
ing when set against her lackluster fortunes during much of the 1400s,
when aristocratic feuds and provincial revolts had been endemic. With
a modest agricultural potential and rugged terrain, Lan Sang, even at
its height, was no more than a Pattern B confederation of self-sufficient
muang held together by force and by the desire of local leaders to find
a wider arena for their ambition and to avail themselves periodically
of Luang Prabang's protection.[159] The aforementioned division of the
Mekong by two sets of rapids further limited central control.

Despite enduring weakness, from 1486 to 1571, Lan Sang became
somewhat more cohesive, temporarily in response to a Vietnamese invasion in 1479 as smaller *muang* turned to Luang Prabang for help,
but more fundamentally a result of economic opportunities to which
a string of forceful leaders – including Phothisarat (r. 1520–1547) and
Setthathirat (r. 1547–1571) – responded creatively. Growing coastal, that
is, foreign, demand for Lao luxury goods (gold, benzoin, sticklac, musk,
ivory) led to an expansion of trade with Ayuhdya and Phnom Penh and,
to a lesser extent, Vietnam and Burma. In this same period, aided perhaps by more pluvial post-1470 conditions and experimenting with new
agricultural and irrigation techniques, Lao peasants accelerated their
historic movement down the valley of the Mekong and onto the Khorat
plateau. Limited though their population remained by Chaophraya
standards, the Vientiane plain and the plateau as far south as the Chi
basin supported far more people than the narrow valleys of northern
Laos. As agriculturalists moved south and as commerce with Ayudhya,
Vietnam, and Phnom Penh grew more lively, Vientiane became the logical site for the capital. Accordingly, Phothisarat not only shifted his
residence south from Luang Prabang, but patronized a relic shrine at
the southern site of That Phanom, which henceforth assumed a central
role in the religious life of the Mekong below Vientiane.[160]

Lan Sang's expansion led to conflict with polities engaged in similar consolidations to the west and south. Trade ties notwithstanding,
Ayudhya and Lan Sang fought over the Khorat region in the 1530s, a
rivalry that may have added a strategic rationale to Phothisarat's move

---

[159] Hoshino, *Histoire*, 202; Stuart-Fox, *Lao Kingdom*, 60–65; Peter and Sanda Simms, *The
Kingdoms of Laos* (Richmond, UK: 199), 55, 126.

[160] Wyatt, *Thailand*, 85; Stuart-Fox, *Lao Kingdom*, 76, 79. In 1533 Phothisarat moved
his court to Vientiane but Vientiane formally replaced Luang Prabang only
c. 1560.

to Vientiane.[161] Lao-Siamese rivalry then shifted to Lan Na, where Lan Sang in 1546 succeeded in installing its own prince.[162] Yet this potentially historic annexation proved short-lived in the face of fresh upheavals in Lan Na and massive invasions from Burma that menaced the entire central mainland.

Largely in order to mobilize resources for warfare, administration grew more complex. Capital officials became responsible for specific services, such as defense, land taxes, foreign trade, and popular registration. The capital area was divided into districts and sub-districts, each with a headman charged with keeping tax and census records. The court also attempted to forge a more unified sumptuary and service hierarchy. In the provinces kings sought to assert their influence less by punitive expeditions than by appointing relatives to key *muang*, marrying into influential *muang* families, supporting a network of spies, and developing paradigmatic religious rituals.[163]

Interstate rivalries combined with expanding Buddhist contacts and greater wealth to generate a more textual, orthodox culture that supported a moderately distinct Lan Sang political identity. Monastic exchanges with Ayudhya and more especially Lan Na in the late 1400s and 1500s contributed to the development of Pali scholarship, along with a Lao/northeast Tai script and a novel Lao-language literature that included the first royal prose chronicles. Distributed to all major monasteries where they were recited on holidays, these histories lent a Buddhist gloss to the origin myths of the Lao and of the ruling dynasty.[164] An increasingly close throne-*sangha* alliance led post-1450 rulers to grant senior monks extensive privileges and to attack the spirit worship that had once been a central element of the state cult. Hence Phothisarat's celebrated decision to prohibit sacrifices to *phi* spirits (a decision that anticipated Bayin-naung's proscription in the Shan states), to destroy spirit shrines, and to build a Buddhist monastery on the site. The 16th century also saw promulgation of self-consciously Buddhist law codes,

---

[161] This was later reinforced by the need to protect against Burmese invasions. Saveng Phinith, *Contribution a l'Historie de Royaume de Luang Prabang* (Paris, 1987), 213, n. 542; Paul Le Boulanger, *Histoire du Laos Francais* (rpt., Westmead, UK, 1969), 74.

[162] Stuart-Fox, *Lao Kingdom*, 75–83, 85; M. L. Manich, *History of Laos* (Bangkok, 1967), 130–46.

[163] Stuart-Fox, *Lao Kingdom*, 72–73; Manich, *History*, 129–34; Dore, "Aux sources," 750–64.

[164] On Lao culture and literature, Dore, "Aux sources," 765–810; Hoshino, *Histoire*, ch. 4; Diller, "Extra 'Y' "; Stuart-Fox, *Lao Kingdom*, xii–xiii, 64–87; Peltier, "Litteratures Lao"; idem, *Le Roman Classique Lao* (Paris, 1988); H. Saddhatissa, "Pali Literature from Laos," in A. K. Narain, ed., *Studies in Pali and Buddhism* (New Delhi, 1979), 327–40.

the building of provincial monasteries, and elaborate public veneration of the Pra Bang Buddha image at Luang Prabang and the Emerald
Buddha at Vientiane as palladia of the dynasty and realm. Wyatt and
Martin Stuart-Fox both suggest that the elevation of these images reflected a self-conscious effort to nurture a separate Lao identity partly
in opposition to Ayudhyan inroads.[165] Phothisarat and Setthathirat consistently portrayed themselves as exemplary Buddhist monarchs, fully
equal to their great neighbors in piety and splendor.

What limited information we have on popular belief suggests that
monastic missions spread Buddhist teachings into more remote lowland villages, but that well into the 17th century, if not later, illiteracy
and a barely diluted animism remained the norm. A yawning cultural
gap therefore separated nobility from free commoners (*phrai*) and slaves
(*kha*), which suggests that not only Lao identity and religious textuality, but an associated decline in female legal status remained preeminently elite phenomena. Note finally that although they traded actively
with lowlanders, the vast population of non-Tai hill peoples – illiterate,
unreservedly animist, dismissed as "savages" by Tai valley-dwellers –
remained yet more marginal to cultural currents in the valleys.[166]

Lan Na. Lan Na, the kingdom of "A Million Ricefields" whose capital was Chiang Mai, resembled Lan Sang in its fragmented geography,
modest population, territorial ambition, and distinctive Tai identity, in
this case that of the Yuan. Lan Na differed from its eastern neighbor
because it lay closer to the coast, which permitted a relatively precocious Buddhist florescence but which also exposed her earlier than Lan
Sang to southern military pressure. In the end, of the four chief central
mainland kingdoms, Lan Na was first to collapse.

Chiang Mai lay in an area of large-scale irrigated agriculture, the Ping
basin, some 36 miles long by 12 miles wide.[167] In part perhaps because
climate in this already dry region was unfavorable, in part because of dynastic splits, Lan Na languished through the early 15th century, accom-
plishing little with desultory campaigns against Nan, Phrae, Phayao, and
Sukhothai. But from about 1440 Chiang Mai pursued a more aggressive
policy that benefited from agricultural expansion and growing foreign
demand for interior products, and more particularly from the energy
of Lan Na's longest-reigning ruler, Tilokaracha (r. 1441–1487), unifier of

---

[165] Wyatt, *Thailand*, 84; Stuart-Fox, *Lao Kingdom*, 71–72, 79.
[166] Stuart-Fox, *Lao Kingdom*, 25, 47, 51–64, 75.
[167] On agriculture in this zone, Ishii, *Thailand*, 19–26.

north Thailand. His consistent strategic goal, and that of his successors, was to accumulate men and war elephants from smaller northern Tai principalities and then to push south into the market centers and population clusters on the northern fringe of the central plain. He thus ran up against Ayudhya, which was simultaneously pushing north. Intense from 1451 to 1486, fighting between Lan Na and Ayudhya continued more sporadically until the 1540s. In its grand sweep and its conclusion unfavorable to the north, this hundred years war resembled contemporary struggles between Upper and Lower Burma. So too, north-south conflict – in this case, between linguistically distinct Tai groups, the Yuan and the "Southerners" (as the Yuan called the Siamese) – strengthened the northerners' sense of cultural alterity. To enhance its prospects, Chiang Mai's court reorganized the army, standardized ranks, taxed commerce more effectively, and used the resultant income to win support among influential *muang* families. Chinese-style firearms figured conspicuously in several engagements.[168]

Yet in the long run Lan Na could not counter Ayudhya's demographic and maritime advantages. By the early 1500s – even before Ayudhya obtained Portuguese guns – the military balance had begun to shift. Beset with internal feuds that reflected and fed external reverses, with its intermontane basins still supporting an unusually fractious aristocratic autonomy, Lan Na in the 1540s collapsed into civil war and chaos. This opened the way to fresh invasions from Ayudhya, Lan Sang, and various Shan kingdoms – and ultimately, to a 200-year Burmese occupation.[169]

Lan Na's attempt to build an exemplary Buddhist realm antedated its period of military glory and continued after that phase ended. As elsewhere, local pride and claims of unequaled Buddhist fidelity fed one another. In 1370 the throne welcomed monks from Martaban who claimed to follow pure Sinhalese tradition. Although Chiang Mai remained home to a number of independent monastic lineages, the Old Ceylon sect, as it became known, sought to integrate the Buddhist legacy of Haripunjaya, the Mon kingdom that preceded Chiang Mai, into a tradition more closely identified with the new Tai-Yuan dynasty. Some seventy years later the New Ceylon sect, through its missionary work and its unflinching support for Tilokaracha, encouraged a yet more

---

[168] *Chiang Mai Chronicle*, 80–81, 86, 97 (also 69–70); *The Nan Chronicle*, David Wyatt, ed. and tr. (Ithaca, 1994), 52–53; Sun, "Ming-Southeast Asian Interactions," 49 51.

[169] On Lan Na political history, Wyatt, *Thailand*, 75–81; idem, "Presidential Address," *JAS* 53, 4 (1994): 1076–91; *Chiang Mai Chronicle*, chs. 4, 5; Penth, *Brief History*; Manich, *History*, 43–85.

distinctive and socially inclusive Tai-Yuan identity. Tilokaracha's patronage of this sect, his convocation of the eighth world Buddhist Council, and his promulgation of more explicitly Buddhist laws advertised Lan Na's claims to Theravada leadership. His successors sponsored vernacular works as well as Pali commentaries and Pali chronicles of widely recognized literary merit.[170] As at Lan Sang and Ayudhya in this period, however, there are indications that a supra-local identity, together with Buddhist literacy, remained preeminently the preserve of *muang* aristocrats, exerting a more marginal impact on commoners and slaves, not to mention hill peoples.[171]

Ayudhya (Siam). As the most populous, geographically favored kingdom, Ayudhya not surprisingly was the most expansive.

To the south, Ayudhya's interest in pepper and tin for export to China, as well as in Indian textiles, led her in the mid-1400s to threaten the famed Malay entrepot of Mclaka. With the failure of that effort and in the face of Chinese diplomatic support for Melaka, Ayudhya contented itself with periodic tribute from north Malay states and with the seizure of Tavoy and Tenasserim on the west peninsular coast.[172]

To its east, after contributing to Angkor's abandonment, Ayudhya menaced Phnom Penh. Siamese-Cambodian rivalry reflected competition for manpower and Chinese trade, as well perhaps as a desire by each of Angkor's successors to claim its legacy.

Ayudhya directed her chief energies, however, towards the headwaters of the Chaophraya in an effort to obtain fresh manpower and export staples. Sukhothai, on the edge of the basin, first fell victim, accepting Ayudhyan overlordship in 1378. A rebellion in 1400–1412 failed, and in 1438 Sukhothai was converted into an Ayudhyan province under a princely viceroy. It was this advance that helped to precipitate the hundred years war with Lan Na.

---

[170] On Lan Na cultural history, Swearer and Premchit, "Relationship"; idem, "A Translation of Tamnan Mulasana Wat Pa Daeng," *JSS* 65 (1977): 73–110; Mangrai, *Padaeng Chronicle*, 31; *Chiang Mai Chronicle*, Intro.; Aroonrut Wichienkeeo, "Lanna Customary Law," in Huxley, ed., *Thai Law*, 31–42; A. B. Griswold and Prasert na Nagara, "Epigraphic and Historical Studies No. 19," *JSS* 66 (1978): 66–88; Kamala Tiyanavich, *Forest Recollections* (Honolulu, 1997), 5.

[171] Cf. the split between cultural levels in the Sipsongpanna. Lebar, *Ethnic Groups*, 211.

[172] Ayudhya also strengthened (some accounts say, inaugurated) control over Nakhon Si Thammarat. Barbara Watson Andaya and Leonard Andaya, *A History of Malaysia* (London, 1982), 62–65; Wyatt, *History*, 86; Cortesao, *Suma Oriental*, I, 97–98, 108; Anthony Reid, "Documenting the Rise and Fall of Ayudhya as a Regional Trade Center," in Jittasevi, *Proceedings*, 5–7.

During this drawn-out contest, a series of reforms sought to improve control over officials who provided military manpower and supplies.[173] In particular, Tilokaracha's arch-rival King Trailok (1448–1488) issued two Khmer-influenced pieces of legislation, the Law of the Civil Hierarchy and the Law of Military and Provincial Hierarchies. Although it is unclear how effectively these laws were implemented, they attempted to establish a unified system of ranks and to divide central administration into military and civilian ministries, each organized into specialized departments (*krom*) and sub-units with quasi-functional jurisdictions. Ayudhya also strengthened its authority over four grades of dependent provinces, including hitherto autonomous "princely cities," which became part of the capital region (*wang ratchathani*), while former vassal kingdoms now became "princely cities." Neither Lan Na nor Lan Sang exhibited a comparable administrative dynamism. By 1500 the entire Chaophraya plain was under Ayudhyan control, and rather than seek independence, once restive Sukhothai elites were content to advance their interests within patronage networks centered on Ayudhya.[174] The link between warfare and reform continued under Ramathipodi II (r. 1491–1529), who reportedly undertook a grand registration of adult males for compulsory military service.[175]

Ayudhya's economic strength is suggested by its ability to attract 56 percent of all Ryukyuan trade to Southeast Asia between 1511 and 1543; Ayudhya's only serious regional competitor, Pattani, attracted less than half as many ships. Indeed, until the late 16th century (when Burmese attacks and competition from Melaka, Banten, and Cambodia took their toll), Ayudhya may have been the single most active Southeast Asian port.[176] Maritime contacts not only provided revenues and firearms, but supported an elaborate system of in-kind taxes in export goods (*suai*) that succeeded in "squeezing dry every one of [Ayudhya's] minor cities."[177]

---

[173] Discussion of administration follows Aeusrivongse, "Ayudhya," 158–66; Kasetsiri, *Ayudhya*, ch. 7; Wales, *Siamese Government*, chs. 4, 5, and *passim*; Wyatt, *Thailand*, 72–74; Lailert Busakorn, "The Ban Phlu Luang Dynasty" (Univ. of London Ph.D. diss., 1972), 164–66; S. J. Tambiah, *World Conqueror and World Renouncer* (Cambridge, 1976), 133–36.

[174] Kasetsiri, *Ayudhya*, 137–42.

[175] However, Junko Koizumi, "King's Manpower Reconsidered" (ms) questions the both the antiquity and extent of allegedly universal military service.

[176] Reid, "Documenting the Rise," 7–8; Ishii, "Ayuthayan Port-Polity."

[177] Aeusrivongse, "Ayudhya," 160.

Yet if 16th-century Ayudhya became the strongest power in the central mainland, by later standards it remained fissiparous. Under Pattern B administration, viceroys in the new "princely cities" retained the right to appoint subordinates, with the possible exception of "royal inspectors" (*yokkrabat*). As senior princes with their own troops, viceroys – like their *bayin* counterparts in Toungoo Burma – were in a position to attack weak incumbents at the capital and to fight among themselves for the throne. To cite the most famous of several such revolts, in the 1560s the viceroy of Phitsanulok supported the Burmese against Ayudhya.[178] Moreover, registration of *phrai* still did not extend to the provinces, and even within the capital region private dependents with no regular obligation to the throne (*phrai som*) continued vastly to outnumber royal servicemen (*phrai luang*), who worked a specified period each year (possibly six months) for the crown.

As usual, elite cultural integration both aided and drew strength from political consolidation. By the mid-15th century if not earlier, Mon, Khmer, and Tai elements had joined to produce a distinctively Siamese dialect, script, literature, and architecture. The vernacular language that gave birth to Siamese (Central Thai) was a mixture of a more northerly Tai dialect with Khmerized Tai from the Ayudhya area itself. Siamese script underwent several modifications, achieving its final form at Ayudhya by about 1600.[179] Here as in northern areas, insofar as Tai scripts facilitated the expression of Pali concepts and made tonal Tai accessible to speakers of non-tonal Mon-Khmer languages, they probably facilitated assimilation to a Tai identity. Ayudhya – known to outsiders as Hsien, Anseam, hence Siam[180] – had its own Buddhist palladia and myths that nourished self-serving alterities. One of the earliest and most famous Ayudhyan epics, *Yuan Phai* ("The Vanquished Yuan"), commemorated Trailok's victory over the soldiers of Lan Na.[181]

---

[178] Rabibhadana, *Organization*, 26–27, nn. 59–60.

[179] On early Siamese language, script, and culture, J. Marvin Brown, *From Ancient Thai to Modern Dialects* (Bangkok, 1965); Hartmann, "Lexical Puzzles," Patricia Herbert and Anthony Milner, eds., *South-East Asia Languages and Literatures* (Honolulu, 1989), chs. 2–4; J. Burnay and G. Coedes, "The Origins of the Sukhodaya Script," *JSS* 21, 2 (1927); Wyatt, *Thailand*, 89; P. Schweisguth, *Etude sur la litterature Siamoise* (Paris, 1951), chs. 2, 3; Klaus Wenk, *Thai Literature: An Introduction* (Bangkok, 1995), 6–7; Thomas Hudak, "Thai Poetry" (ms); Gedney, *Selected Papers*, 207–28, 489–544.

[180] On the origin of "Siam" and related terms, L. P. Briggs, "The Appearance and Historical Usage of the Terms Tai, Thai, Siamese and Lao," *JAOS* 69 (1949): 60–73.

[181] Schweisguth, *Etude*, 49–51; A. B. Griswold and Prasert Na Nagara, "A Fifteenth-Century Siamese Historical Poem," in C. D. Cowan and O. W. Wolters, eds., *Southeast Asian History and Historiography* (Ithaca, NY: 1976), 123–63.

Combining Khmer genres and Theravada themes, monks and lay writers began to produce distinctive works of law and poetry. Notwithstanding Theravada Buddhism's prominence, brahmanic and Hindu-Mahayana concepts still exercised a major influence on political thought and public ritual, and the religious tolerance characteristic of charter civilizations remained much in evidence.[182]

How much vertical – as opposed to lateral – standardization occurred? The only scholars, so far as I know, to have investigated this question for Ayudhya – Nidhi Aeusrivongse (Eiosrivongs), Akom Pattiya, Kobkua Suvanthat-Pien, and Nanthawan Poosawang – have argued that the emergent Siamese culture was preeminently the preserve of the *munnai*, the tax-exempt administrative elite in the capital and provincial centers.[183] As noted, sharply stratified cultural patterns seem to have been characteristic of other Tai societies as well as charter polities, but we have far more information for 15th- and 16th-century Ayudhya. *Munnai* alone participated in court ceremonies, foreign trade, and supra-local political marriages. They alone bought luxuries, wore imported textiles, and ate with foreign utensils. Only *munnai* males attended Buddhist monastery schools for extended periods, had access to the cultural treasures of Khmer and Pali civilization, and participated in a world of texts. Elaborate forms of speech, replete with abstruse expressions of Pali or Sanskrit origin, sought to ritualize and sanctify government affairs, while separating them from common parlance.[184] From diction and dress to drama, religious doctrine, poetry, and architecture, the capital set the standard for *munnai* throughout the kingdom.

But for *phrai* in this period, culture was preeminently local, and monastic education beyond the most rudimentary level was, in Nidhi Aeusrivongse's words, "quite a luxury."[185] Oral court procedures for commoners, the *phrai's* use of personal stamps or marks rather than signatures in legal cases, and exclusively oral forms of popular poetry and literature all point to an essentially illiterate popular universe in the 15th and early 16th centuries, a situation comparable to that in the Irrawaddy basin. By extension, animism, black magic, and non-textual pre-Buddhist rituals remained more entrenched among the *phrai*.

---

[182] Kasetsiri, *Ayudhya*, 85–86, 100–102, 135–37.
[183] Aeusrivongse, "Ayudhya" (written by Aeusrivongse and his three collaborators), 173–91, 206–209.
[184] B. J. Terwiel, "The Introduction of Indian Prosody among the Thais," in Jan Houben, ed., *Ideology and Status of Sanskrit* (Leiden, 1996), 321–22.
[185] Aeusrivongse, "Ayudhya," 173.

In contrast to *munnai* mobility in government service, *phrai* were normally prevented from leaving their villages except to perform corvees or military service. Thus, whereas *munnai* culture and language grew increasingly standardized according to capital norms and texts, *phrai* idiom, dialect, intonation, and cultural genres varied by district, if not by village. As late as 1515 the Portuguese Tome Pires claimed that most commoners in Ayudhya still spoke Mon dialects rather than Tai, and cut their hair like the Mons of Pegu.[186] No doubt, there were also sizeable *phrai* populations speaking Khmer, Lao, and other Tai dialects. In effect, the *munnai* (like aristocrats at Lan Sang and Lan Na) were a kind of caste, and what subsequently became known as Siamese language, culture, and ethnicity were in this period their more or less exclusive preserve. Marriage between provincial and capital *munnai* was feasible, but between social classes, out of the question. Indeed, *munnai* distinctiveness actually may have increased after c. 1450 through Theravada and Khmer acculturation and foreign mercantile contacts.

Nonetheless, by comparison with Hindu Angkor, Theravada monasticism probably reduced the cultural gulf between classes. Without large-scale land endowments, in the central mainland as in post-1500 Burma the rural monkhood must have relied on village support, an arrangement that favored enrolling some village youths as novices, if only briefly. Although we lack geographic or social profiles for the Siamese monkhood in this period, indigenous and foreign records suggest that a rudimentary rural network was in place. The fact that most monasteries used a similar curriculum favored a common world view among students from *phrai* and elite backgrounds. Moreover, even if the vast majority of *phrai* men, not to mention women, failed to acquire literacy, the illiterate were exposed to monastic sermons on such topics as *karma* and the Mahajati or Mahanibat Jatakas, to religious festivals at the beginning and end of Lent, to communal merit-making activities, and to artistic portrayals within the temples of Jataka stories and Buddhist cosmography. The temple and the monkhood thus became channels by which elements of *munnai* culture passed into *phrai* circles.[187] Such

---

[186] Cortesao, *Suma Oriental*, I, 103: "The kingdom of Siam is heathen. The people, and almost the language, are like those of Pegu. . . . They are tall, swarthy men, shorn like those of Pegu." In this early period it is very unlikely that he was referring to Mon refugees. Aeusrivongse, "Ayudhya," 179 makes the same point.

[187] Vallibhotama, "Siam," 96–101; Aeusrivongse, "Ayudhya," 183–84; *Asia de Joao de Barros, Terceira Decada*, Hernani Cidade, ed. (Lisbon, 1946), 80–82; Lach, *Southeast Asia in the Eyes of Europe*, 528–29; Stuart-Fox, *Lao Kingdom*, 54–56.

activities created a fund of shared symbols and the basis for a common outlook that deepened in the late Ayudhya and Bangkok periods.

THE 16TH-CENTURY CRISIS

In sum, between c. 1440 and 1550 agricultural vitality joined international trade and new Buddhist currents to reduce the number of warring polities in the central mainland and to foster among the elites of each of the four chief survivors a more expressly Buddhist identity that was at the same time supportive of local political claims. In the second half of the 16th century, this pyramiding of resources reached its first great watershed. Much has been written about the 17th-century "crisis."[188] But in the central as in the western mainland, if we employ the standard definition of that popular term – a culmination, a turning point, a decisive moment – the crisis of the mid and late 1500s was far more momentous than anything in the relatively placid 1600s.

Insofar as First Toungoo armies crippled Lan Na, Ayudhya, and Lan Sang, one might imagine that the central mainland's 16th-century transformation was basically external in origin. Yet I have argued that across the western and central mainland post-1450 consolidation was a reasonably uniform process, driven by substantially the same economic, religious, and interstate pressures. In the 1540s, well before Toungoo armies appeared on the scene, competition between Ayudhya and Lan Sang to devour emaciated Lan Na already presaged a new stage of consolidation in the center. Coming in 1548, a mere two years after Lan Sang's temporary annexation of Lan Na, the first Burmese invasion of southern Siam differed in scale, but not in kind, from these other contests.

If both sectors were subject to substantially the same dynamics, why did Toungoo Burma go on to conquer the central mainland rather than vice versa? As a small frontier outpost embroiled in more or less constant war, Toungoo nurtured a more martial culture and a more aggressive leadership than far larger, more secure Ayudhya, the chief polity in the center. After 1759, similar advantages aided the self-made Kon-baung dynasty in its attacks on Siam. In both periods, Siam could revive only after collapse had bred more competent military leaders. Also crucial to First Toungoo success were different strategic equations in the western and central sectors: by opposing Ayudhyan expansion, Lan Sang and Cambodia prevented a rapid aggregation of resources. But Upper

---

[188] See discussion in Ch. 1 of Reid's "Age of Commerce" thesis.

Burma's sudden collapse in the second quarter of the 16th century – the result of Shan raids and monastic excesses that had no equivalent farther east – invited an extraordinarily dramatic, virtually unopposed unification of the entire western mainland.

The First Toungoo dynasty could thus begin leveraging victories. Shan forces helped Bayin-naung to subdue Lan Na, which in turn let him isolate Ayudhya. Possibly the largest in the history of the region, the army that conquered Ayudhya was drawn from throughout the Irrawaddy basin and the Tai world.[189] This momentous victory reflected, in addition to Burmese numbers and strategic brilliance, the fatal autonomy of Siamese princely governors: as noted, the viceroy of Phitsanulok joined the Burmese attack, after which Bayin-naung made him vassal ruler of Ayudhya. With Siam submissive, in 1574–1575 Burma occupied Vientiane and dethroned the ruler of that supposedly inaccessible kingdom.[190]

But if Burmese-led armies carried all before them, in the long term Ayudhya, not Burma, emerged as the big winner in the central mainland. As we have seen, Bayin-naung's goal of controlling virtually the entire mainland from Pegu proved utterly mad, and the First Toungoo Empire disintegrated soon after his death. The renaissance of Ayudhyan power that followed the debacle of 1569 allowed Ayudhya to throw off Burmese suzerainty by 1584 – indeed, by 1599 to invade Lower Burma itself – and to strengthen control over a wide circle of dependencies. As soon as they had secured their western and northern frontiers, the Siamese turned with a vengeance on Cambodia, which had exploited Ayudhya's difficulties to attack from the east. In 1594, with the help of cannon, Siam sacked the new Khmer capital of Lovek. Although Cambodia in the early 17th century would reassert its independence and would exhibit bursts of resilience even into the 18th, Ian Mabbett and David Chandler argue that this defeat foreshadowed an era of Thai influence over the Cambodian court that would last, with some interruptions, until the arrival of the French in the 1860s.[191] Through a combination of external

---

[189] *UK*, II, 407–13 claims 546,000 men, while "Extracts of Master Caesar Frederick ...," in Samuel Purchas, ed., *Hakluytus Posthumus or Purchas His Pilgrimes*, vol. X (Glasgow, 1905), 111 claims 1,400,000. But since Louis XIV, with a population of 20,000,000, marshalled no more than 360,000, both claims seem absurd.

[190] Victor Lieberman, *Burmese Administrative Cycles* (Princeton, 1984), 65–76.

[191] Mabbett and Chandler, *Khmers*, 222–23; Chandler, *History*, 84–85. Popular legend also regarded the fall of Lovek as a sign of Cambodia's permanently reduced status. Michael Vickery, "Review Article," *JSEAS* 27 (1996), 402, and Mak Phoeun, *Histoire du Cambodge*

pressures and intrinsic weakness, in the 1590s Lan Sang, like Cambodia, entered a period of vulnerability from which it would gain but temporary respite in the 17th century. As for Lan Na, her 16th-century loss of independence proved permanent: after 1558 she remained a Burmese province for the better part of over two centuries, whereupon Lan Na entered the Siamese empire. Thus by 1600 Ayudhya no longer had a credible rival in the central mainland. To be sure, this transformation was less complete than in the west: whereas in the west only Arakan – tiny and marginal – escaped Toungoo annexation, in the center Cambodia and Lan Sang both remained viable kingdoms long after 1600. But the accelerated thrust towards regional hegemony was comparable. Having compressed history in the Irrawaddy basin, Toungoo did the same farther east.

Insofar as sustained economic growth had overwhelmed political institutions in the 14th century, one could argue that the 16th century crisis, fueled by agricultural and demographic expansion and maritime trade, repeated familiar themes. Beyond such grand abstractions, the two transitions differed in key respects. First, in the 14th century lightly inhabited zones separating Pagan from Angkor kept contact to a minimum. By the 16th century, the novel power of lowland systems, their close interaction with new Tai interior states, as well as the fact that Ayudhya lay far closer to the Irrawaddy basin than Angkor – all joined to ensure that weaknesses in one empire quickly invited outside intervention. Second, whereas desiccation in the late 13th and 14th centuries almost certainly aggravated problems at Angkor and Pagan, there is no evidence that dryness in the second half of the 16th century was sufficiently early or potent to have had a major effect on Lan Na or Ayudhya.[192] Third, price inflation played no demonstrable role in the poorly monetized economies of the 14th century, but in the early to mid-16th century, inflation caused strains even in far-off Lan Na, where a 40 percent rise in prices over 30 years led people to wonder what had happened "to the value of their money."[193] Presumably such strains reflected a combination of excess demand for marginally increasing supplies of foodstuffs and textiles and growing inflows of Yunnanese

---

de la fin du XVIe siecle au debut du XVIIIe (Paris, 1995), 61, 413–23 see 1594 as rather less of a turning point.

[192] Recall that Pegu's most severe crop failures came in the 1590s, while in Dai Viet chronicle accounts of famine and rural distress also were concentrated between 1570 and 1597. But Lan Na fell in 1558 and Ayudhya, 1569.

[193] Penth, *Brief History*, 23, which does not give precise years.

and Japanese silver, to which Chapter 2 referred. Conceivably too, in keeping with Jack Goldstone's model of demographically-driven rivalries, the wild internecine feuds that weakened Lan Na and Ayudhya even before the Burmese arrived reflected a disproportionate growth in marginal elites.[194] According to Goldstone, if population doubled while officials posts increased by 50 percent, the number of marginal elites – in the case of Siam, men from official families without posts – would have grown by 650 percent.[195] In this scenario, then, inflation would have eroded royal income just as elite demands for royal patronage were increasing.

However, the most obvious difference between the collapse of the 14th century and that of the 16th century was their duration. The former inaugurated centuries of severe fragmentation and cultural disruption. But because economic, political, and cultural ties had grown far more secure, the disorders of the late 1500s proved to be brief – Ayudhya remained subordinate to Pegu a mere 15 years – culturally benign, and conducive to a yet more durable order.

THE LATE AYUDHYA PERIOD, 1570–1767: INTERNAL CONSOLIDATION

The Late Ayudhya period, 1570–1767, is defined at both ends by successful Burmese invasions. During these two centuries, most especially during the decades following the first Burmese victory, Siamese government evolved from Pattern B, decentralized Indic administration, to Pattern C, centralized Indic administration. As in Burma, many of the basic administrative and cultural features of this period would continue well into the 19th century.

Ayudhya's collapse precipitated some thirty years of warfare on her western and eastern flanks. During this difficult era, capital and provincial leaders apparently concluded – we have no record of their deliberations – that their common survival demanded far-reaching changes. In any case, the ability of princes and local *munnai* to resist centralization after 1569 declined due to the death and capture of many prominent leaders. Those inner *muang* disorganized by war that were reconstructed

---

[194] On those feuds, see Wyatt, *Thailand*, 81–82, 92–95.
[195] Jack A. Goldstone, *Revolution and Rebellion in the Early Modern World* (Berkeley, 1991), ch. 1, esp. 32–33. Such demographic pressures would have affected 16th-century Pegu less severely insofar as its conquests generated military and apanage awards that less successful states in the central mainland could not match.

under Ayudhyan direction necessarily fell under closer royal control. At the same time many private retainers who lost their lords became available for inscription as royal servicemen (*phrai luang*), which further tipped the balance towards the throne. These reforms benefited from the energy of the famed warrior kings Naresuan (r. 1590–1605) and Ekathotsarot (r. 1605–1610/1611). Subsequent warfare with Burma, especially from 1660 to 1665, domestic conflicts, and maritime wealth combined to encourage further experiments. In short, the reforms of the late 16th and 17th centuries had both a cyclic compensatory character and a genuinely innovative dimension.

Similarities between Siamese and Burmese reforms reflected, in part, independent responses to similar challenges. But they also suggest a degree of squint-eyed mutual borrowing. Prisoners, envoys, and monks provided up to date accounts of activities at rival courts, which must have found eager audiences on both sides of the upland divide.[196]

In Siam as in Restored Toungoo Burma, the most significant change was the court's determination, expressed as early as Naresuan, to halt or to restrict the dangerous appointment of senior princes to provincial towns, and to oblige them to reside at the capital in special palaces where they could more easily be monitored. In their stead went relatively humble commoners who perforce lacked claims to the throne. Four provincial grades were reorganized so as to reduce their territories and balance first-class provinces against smaller units.[197] Writing c. 1636, the Dutch factor Jeremias van Vliet described a further tightening of control. According to van Vliet, before King Prasat Thong (r. 1629–1656) all governors resided in their provinces. But this king, himself a usurper, was so suspicious that he forced most of them to stay at Ayudhya, while entrusting actual administration to yet more humble officials who were frequently summoned to the capital. What is more, governors were rotated in office every few months.[198] In 1687 the French envoy Simon de la Loubere summarized provincial history: "The Kings of Siam have ruin'd and destroy'd the most potent [hereditary princely governors], as much as they could, and have substituted in their place some Triennial

---

[196] On Burmese/Siamese administrative borrowing, Lieberman, "Provincial Reforms in Taung-ngu Burma," *BSOAS* 43, 3 (1980): 548–69. On Burmese-Siamese legal exchanges, Huxley, "Thai, Mon & Burmese Dhammathats."

[197] Wales, *Siamese Government*, 108; Rabibhadana, *Organization*, 27–28; and Tambiah, *World Conqueror*, 136 date these changes to Naresuan's reign. Cf. Gesick, "Kingship," 31–32; Wyatt, *Thailand*, 107.

[198] "Van Vliet's Description," 60–61.

Governors by Commission."[199] His compatriot Nicolas Gervaise, while confirming that governors were subject to visiting commissioners with plenary powers, related how a governor of the northern province of Phitsanulok, whom commissioners judged guilty of malfeasance, had been executed on the spot.[200]

Despite such testimonies – influenced no doubt by an image of royal omnipotence that Siamese informants fed the Europeans – it is clear from these same accounts and from Siamese sources that governors, especially in the north, in the east at Nakhon Ratchasima, and in the peninsula, not only retained enormous autonomy, but in some cases enjoyed de facto hereditary succession. Although no longer able to threaten Ayudhya militarily, heads of major provinces were "worshipped by [their] subjects with more than human honour, they can bend and change all laws as they please," van Vliet noted.[201] "[I]t is no difficult matter for some of these Governors, and especially the most powerful, and for the most remote from Court, to withdraw themselves wholly or in part from the Royal Authority," la Loubere added.[202] Foreign powers negotiated trade concessions directly with peninsular governors – whom they frequently referred to as "kings." During the 17th and early 18th centuries rebellions at Nakhon Ratchasima, Nakhon Si Thammarat, and Songkhla could be suppressed only with difficulty and great expense. In short, early 17th-century reforms strengthened the empire's centripetal pull without destroying its basic solar structure, which in fact endured to the late 19th century.[203]

Where they were most effective, namely in the second- to fourth-class provinces of the basin, the new centralizing efforts paid particular attention to sub-gubernatorial provincial officials. We have seen that with the possible exception of royal inspectors (*yokkrabat*), Early Ayudhya provincial deputies had been appointed by the prince-governor himself. During the Late Ayudhya period, not only the *yokkrabat*, but the

[199] Simon de la Loubere, *The Kingdom of Siam* (rpt., Singapore, 1986), 83.
[200] Gervaise, *Natural History*, 72–73.
[201] "Van Vliet's Description," 60.
[202] La Loubere, *Kingdom*, 82.
[203] Gesick, "Kingship," 33–37; Wyatt, *Thailand*, 125; Dhiravat na Pombejra, "Princes, Pretenders, and the Chinese Phrakhlang," in Leonard Blusse and Femme Gaastra, eds., *On the Eighteenth Century as a Category of Asian History* (Aldershot, UK: 1998), 109–14. On limits to centralization in Ayudhya, see also Tej Bunnag, *The Provincial Administration of Siam 1892–1915* (Kuala Lumpur, 1977), ch. 1; Sunait Chutintaranond, "Mandala, 'Segmentary State,' and Politics of Centralization in Medievel Ayudhya," *JSS* 78 (1990): 89–100.

deputy governor (*palat*), provincial military commander (*phon*), and provincial secretary (*mahatthai*) received their posts from the capital. (Note that these deputy posts corresponded closely to Restored Toungoo positions.) Although as in Burma, governors still sought appointments for their own clients, in theory, and sometimes in practice, the sense of obligation that deputies incurred to capital patrons inclined them to counter unauthorized gubernatorial actions.[204] At the same time capital departments (*krom*) extended their authority so as to dilute gubernatorial control over local manpower. During the Early Ayudhya period, departments responsible for organizing and monitoring royal servicemen (*phrai luang*) apparently were quite modest, but during the late 16th and 17th centuries, they expanded their provincial enrollments and recruited more petty provincial officials.[205]

These measures benefited from a substantial increase, absolute and proportional, in the number of royal servicemen. Before 1569 the vast majority of *phrai* were private retainers (*phrai som*), but as noted, the death and capture in battle of *munnai* lords joined with widespread social disorder to create a large body of unattached men whom officials could enroll as royal servicemen. Ekathotsarot further swelled this category when, after demanding that *munnai* list their *phrai som*, he punished recalcitrants by seizing all unlisted dependents and inscribing them on royal registers. To appreciate the significance of these developments, consider that *phrai som* – like Burmese private retainers – served their lords as laborers or soldiers, but had no obligation to the throne. By contrast, *phrai luang* (functionally equivalent to, if less prestigious than, Burmese *ahmu-dans*) had to work six months a year for the crown, building fortifications, palaces, and public works, or serving in ad hoc military forces. Much as in Restored Toungoo Burma, the expansion in royal manpower offered the throne two principal benefits: a) It tended to crosscut territorial jurisdictions, especially in areas with easy corvee access to the capital; and b) it increased the security of the king by reducing the power of the princes, who had been the chief owners of *phrai som*.[206]

The capital city enhanced its preeminence. The relocation of major princes at Ayudhya, the growing size of *krom* departments, the larger

[204] Rabibhadana, *Organization*, 28–29, 71.
[205] Rabibhadana, *Organization*, 29–30; van Vliet, *Short History*, 87–88; Aeusrivongse, "Ayudhya," 168–69. Cf. discussion of deliberate jurisdictional fragmentation in Gesick, "Kingship," 33–35.
[206] Rabibhadana, *Organization*, 32–34; van Vliet, *Short History*, 88; la Loubere, *Kingdom*, 78; Gervaise, *Natural History*, 115.

number of servicemen, more regular communications with provincial officials, expanded homage requirements – all fed Ayudhya's grandeur and self-importance. With a population in 1650 probably exceeding 150,000, the city and its suburbs included some 400 temples, many of great size and architectural grandeur.[207] To emphasize royal superiority over princes and courtiers, the king's ceremonial persona grew more remote and court discipline, more severe. There are also indications that procedures for *phrai* registration and provincial-capital communication became more routinized, that capital courts extended appellate jurisdictions, and that the size of officialdom grew substantially.[208]

Apart from the king himself, the chief beneficiaries of these changes were senior officials (upper levels of the *khunnang*), who had often competed with princes in a zero sum game for manpower and whose control over *phrai luang* now gave them a novel advantage. As in Restored Toungoo Burma, which underwent similar reorganization, the most obvious result was a modification in the dynamics of royal succession. Whereas before 1569 princely viceroys in the provinces frequently fought one another for the throne, from 1590 to 1758 provincial armies were neutralized, and succession was normally settled at Ayudhya itself through factional contests in which ministers exercised a major influence. While in theory appointments were at royal pleasure, in practice ministerial families colonized the administration, with some departments remaining in the hands of the same family for generations.[209]

Ministerial autonomy, however, carried its own price, as steep as it was unintended. Notwithstanding my suggestion that external dangers encouraged a degree of corporate unity after 1569, the absence of any clear law of succession meant that virtually every Late Ayudhya succession was contested. On two occasions (in 1628–1629 and 1688) high officials displaced princely candidates to seize the throne themselves. (Such

---

[207] On urban population, Reid, *Age of Commerce*, II, 70–71. On architecture and ceremony, Gervaise, *Natural History*, ch. 10; "van Vliet's Description," 69–76; Jeremy Kemp, *Aspects of Siamese Kingship in the Seventeenth Century* (Bangkok, 1969), 8–40; Forrest McGill, "The Art and Architecture of the Reign of King Prasatthong of Ayutthaya" (Univ. of Mich. Ph.D. diss., 1977).

[208] On changes in capital administration, see la Loubere, *Kingdom*, 85–89; Gervaise, *Natural History*, 75–78; Pombejra, "Political History," Sect. 1, esp. 49–62; B. J. Terwiel, "The Battle of Nong Sarai (1593) and the Relationship between the Largest Political Units in Mainland Southeast Asia," in *Guerre et paix en Asie du sud-est* (Paris, 1998), 53–54.

[209] Pombejra, "Political History," esp. Sect. II; idem, "Princes, Pretenders," 107–30; Busakorn Lailert, "Ban Phlu Luang Dynasty," esp. chs. 2–6.

developments had no parallel in Burma, where the indispensability of royal blood led powerful ministers to prefer *rois faineants* over usurpation.[210]) By enriching a group of extended families in departments concerned with overseas affairs, maritime trade reinforced ministerial autonomy. Late Ayudhyan kings, including the two usurpers who knew the danger all too well, tried various solutions. They balanced ministries against one another and set those in control of maritime wealth against those in control of manpower. After 1688 they also built up a handful of senior princes at Ayudhya by giving them departments with large manpower enrollments. But when this led to princely battles in Ayudhya during the succession struggle of 1733, Borommakot (r. 1733–1758) fragmented princely manpower among thirteen small departments. In the event, by inhibiting military coordination, this arrangement contributed to Ayudhya's final collapse.

In short, during its last two centuries Ayudhya, like Restored Toungoo Burma, strengthened its control over manpower, dramatically reduced territorially-based princely challenges, and expanded its central apparatus. Yet, again as in Burma, the system engendered fresh instabilities.

SECONDARY KINGDOMS IN AN AGE OF GREAT POWER HEGEMONY

While post-1570 Ayudhya was strengthening its position, its former rivals Cambodia, Lan Sang, and Lan Na began to disintegrate.

After the Siamese sacked Lovek in 1594, not only Siamese and Vietnamese, but at various points Portuguese, Spaniards, Malays, Chams, Chinese, Japanese, and Dutch played a prominent role in Cambodian politics. Most influential until 1658 was a Muslim faction, including Malay shippers and Cham mercenaries, on whom the Khmer court, in the absence of its own naval forces, relied to preserve maritime access along the Mekong. In fact, Persians and Indian Shi'ites in this period also enjoyed considerable influence at Ayudhya, where they helped King Narai (r. 1656–1688) seize the throne. But Cambodia's military and cultural fragility presented outsiders with wider openings. After Dutch threats drove him closer to his Muslim backers, a Khmer

---

[210] Note, however, that Siamese usurpers had close ties to the throne: Prasat Thong (r. 1629–1656) was a first cousin of Song Tham (r. 1610–1628), while the 1688 usurper, Phetracha, was son of the wet-nurse of Narai (r. 1656–1688) and Narai's effective foster brother.

king in 1643/44 introduced Malay usages at court and embraced Islam –
to the utter dismay of the Buddhist *sangha*.[211]

By later standards, Cambodia's vulnerabilities in the 17th century
were still limited. Elite literary traditions, enshrined for example in local
versions of the Hindu *Ramayana*, continued to exhibit considerable vitality. The country still traded freely with the outside world. Early 17th-
century provincial reforms, probably modeled on those of Ayudhya,
sought to replace princely viceroys with more reliable appointive officials (*sdach-tranh*). And although paying occasional tribute to Ayudhya,
Cambodia was strong enough to decimate a Siamese expeditionary force
in 1622 and on occasion to menace Siamese territory.[212]

Without pressures on its eastern flank, Cambodia might have retained room for maneuver. But during the course of the 1600s and especially from 1658, the Nguyen regime of southern Vietnam, seeking
resources to resist their Trinh foes in northern Vietnam, increased pressure on Cambodia. By the 1680s the Nguyen had taken over the port of
Prey Nokor – now Saigon. This acquisition, followed by the occupation
of smaller ports along the Gulf of Siam by Vietnamese troops, Ming
refugees, and Sino-Vietnamese entrepreneurs, began to seal Cambodia
off from the sea, with obvious implications for royal revenues. Although
Khmer elites apparently still regarded their kingdom as a distinctive
cultural and ethnic space, in practice this did not prevent courtiers and
governors from splitting into pro-Siamese and pro-Vietnamese camps,
with the losing faction only too eager to invite foreign help.[213] Much as
in 18th-century Poland (Europe's Cambodia) – which was also wedged
between predatory great powers – factionalism and external aggression
fed one another. As much of western Cambodia slid under Siamese influence, and as the east fell under Vietnamese control, the country's post-
1700 history became, in Chandler's words, "one of almost continuous

---

[211] Muslim ascendancy in Cambodia ended c. 1659. See Reid, *Age of Commerce*, II, 186–92
and n. 213 *infra*.

[212] On culture, Saveros Pou, *Etudes sur le Ramakerti* (Paris, 1977), esp. 41–50, 77–99; Phoeun,
Histoire, 215–16; Thompson, "Changing Perspectives"; Chandler, *History*, 89–94. On
17th/18th century commercial vitality, Yoneo Ishii, *The Junk Trade from Southeast Asia*
(Singapore, 1998), ch. 5. On 17th-century military/political history, Phoeun, *Histoire*,
164–75, 207–15, 258–67; Pombejra, "Political History," 223–25; van Vliet, *Short History*,
90; "van Vliet's Description," 35–36; Ahdemard Leclere, *Recherches sur le droit public
des Cambodgiens* (Paris, 1894), 189–90.

[213] Phoeun, *Histoire*, 416–22. On Cambodia's 17th–18th century decline, ibid, chs. 4–10,
and Conclusion; Dhiravat, "Political History," 285–86, 334–35, 433; Gervaise, *Natural
History*, 195–205, 233; Wyatt, *Thailand*, 110–111, 126, 130.

invasions from Vietnam and Siam, preceded and followed by ruinous civil wars."[214] On the whole, especially under King Borommakot, Ayudhya was more successful in setting clients on the throne. These incursions, we shall find, joined with a common Theravada sensibility to expose Khmer culture to growing Siamese influence.

Lan Sang's political devolution began some two generations after that of Cambodia, but once underway, proved yet more dramatic. The long reign of Surinyavongsa (r. c. 1637–1694) is usually seen as the Indian summer of Lan Sang history, the calm before the storm of the 18th century. After decades of internal strife, he restored to Vientiane some authority over a vast area from Champassak in the south to the frontiers of Kenghung in the north. According to 1640s accounts by an Italian missionary and a Dutch merchant, Surinyavongsa required his seven chief governors to reside at the capital and to entrust administration of their provinces to their deputies.[215] Comparable to provincial reforms in Cambodia and Ayudhya, these efforts to move from Pattern B to Pattern C administration, although ultimately unsuccessful, again suggest an easy exchange of intelligence between Theravada courts. As a center of Buddhist studies, Vientiane attracted monks from north Thailand, Siam, Cambodia, even Burma. Nonetheless, the Lao monks' sexual indulgence – vaguely reminiscent of the Forest Dwellers of Upper Burma – and their refusal to beg alms set them apart from more orthodox *sanghas* and suggest a still very limited Buddhist textuality among Lao aristocrats, not to mention commoners. According to the Dutchman Gerrit van Wuysthoff, Lao Buddhists regarded their monks' peculiar customs with pride, condemning Khmer monastic asceticism as a disgrace to the religion! They boasted too that because Gotama Buddha had visited Laos, his visage was captured most faithfully in their sculptures. "They are very stuck-up and claim that, in consequence, their God is superior to that of Siam, Cambodia, and other countries."[216] "The king and the chief men of the realm have no great affection for the Siamese," van Wuysthoff added.[217]

[214] Chandler, *History*, 95.
[215] Marini, *New and Interesting Description*, 21, relying chiefly on G. M. Leria; and Jean-Claude Lejosne, ed., *Le Journal de Voyage de G. van Wuysthoff et de ses Assistants au Laos (1641–1642)*, (Metz, France, 1987), 165–66.
[216] Lejosne, *Le Journal*, 167, including the references to sexual habits, and for which some later corroboration appears at 170 n. 26. Cf. Marini, *New and Interesting Description*, 60–61; Peltier, "Litteratures Lao," 38–39; and the sexual overtones of provincial Tai monastic customs, Kamala, *Forest Recollections*, 26–30.
[217] Lejosne, *Le Journal*, 215.

In part, elite Lao resentment of Siam and Cambodia reflected the landlocked kingdom's weakening commercial position. By blocking Lan Sang's access to coastal markets, Cambodia and more especially Siam were able to set terms for the export of gold and forest products and for the import of Indian cottons and other luxuries prized by Lao notables.[218] By the same token, Ayudhya controlled Lao access to Indian Ocean firearms, which reduced the value of Laos' traditional military asset, elephants. Nor, given difficult routes and restricted volume, did trade with Yunnan and Guangxi offer adequate compensation.

If these economic changes belied the surface glitter of Surinyavongsa's reign and formed the background to a long-term deterioration in Lan Sang's position, succession disputes on his death provided the critical wedge for Lan Sang's neighbors. In 1698 the Trinh Vietnamese helped to install at Vientiane one of Surinyavonga's nephews, who soon faced a challenge from a relative at Luang Prabang. Rather than allow either prince to reunite the kingdom, a Siamese army c. 1707 reinforced the division between Luang Prabang and Vientiane, both of whose rulers became more beholden to Ayudhya than to Vietnam. Some six years later the southern realm of Champassak also broke away. Thus the once formidable kingdom of Lan Sang split into three small, mutually antagonistic realms, corresponding to natural geographic regions and all in some degree subject to Siamese influence. Each local ruling house sought legitimacy by emphasizing links to the old Lan Sang dynasty and by elevating a Buddha image as a palladium of the successor state.[219]

To the west Chiang Mai had even less room for maneuver. During most of the period 1558 to 1727, Chiang Mai remained a tributary/province of the Toungoo empire, ruled by Tai clients and then more commonly by Burman appointees. No longer a major Buddhist center in its own right, Chiang Mai absorbed extensive Burmese influence in religion, architecture, art, cuisine, and literature. The better to exercise control, Burma split the old kingdom of Lan Na into northern and southern sectors. In 1727 Chiang Mai and the south revolted, but even then Burma, with a strong force at Chiang Saen, succeeded in

---

[218] For references to trade-cum-political tensions, *Records of the Relations between Siam and Foreign Countries in the 17th Century*, 5 vols. (Bangkok, 1915), I, 27; "van Vliet's Description," 34–35; Stuart-Fox, *Lao Kingdom*, 89–90, 97–100; Lejosne, *Le Journal*, 157–59, 165, 176, 180–81, 215. On Lao trade generally, ibid., 102–105, 130–60, 212–20.

[219] Stuart-Fox, *Lao Kingdom*, 99–106; Simms, *Kingdoms*, 107–16; Manich, *History*, 158–83.

confining rebel authority to the Ping valley. Accounts from the 1700s point to depopulation, agricultural decline, and chronic disorder.[220]

In the peninsula Ayudhya sought to enforce a more effective suzerainty over Pattani, Kedah, and Kelantan. When enough pressure was applied, these Malay states – like Cambodia – paid tribute, provided military levies, and sheltered under Ayudhyan protection. Yet Siamese interference often was resented, and Pattani, for one, rebelled repeatedly.[221] By Bangkok standards, Ayudhyan influence also remained uncertain over Nakhon Si Thammarat, which served as Ayudhya's forward base in the peninsula.[222]

During this period when Ayudhya was moving towards regional hegemony but Lan Sang and Cambodia remained independent, we get our first glimpse of mainland diplomacy. Conventions governing the treatment of envoys may have arisen in the 15th century, when for the first time states of comparable power had to negotiate. Although permanent ambassadors were unknown, in the 17th century kingdoms recognizing one another's independence (for example, Burma and Ayudhya or Ayudhya and Lan Sang) regularly exchanged envoys to handle ad hoc military and commercial issues. On the basis of this experience, 17th-century Siam moved effortlessly into diplomatic exchanges with Persia, the Mughals, Japan, France, Portugal, and the Dutch East India Company.[223]

ECONOMIC TRENDS TO c. 1760: CHINESE TRADE AND DOMESTIC EXPANSION

A complex synergy continued to link political consolidation to economic growth, domestic and foreign. Because Siamese records suffered wholesale destruction during the 1767 sack of Ayudhya, most of our economic evidence derives from maritime accounts. Let us examine this

---

[220] Penth, *Brief History*, 24–29; Wyatt, *Thailand*, 123–24; *Chiang Mai Chronicle*, 125–55; Lieberman, *Cycles*, ch. 4.

[221] David Wyatt, "Chiang Mai and Ayudhya," Jittasevi, *Proceedings*, 182 suggests that after c. 1600 Ayudhya's interest shifted from the interior to the coast.

[222] On peninsular relations, Kobkua Suwannathat-Pian, *Thai-Malay Relations* (Singapore, 1988), 5–8; A. Teeuw and D. K. Wyatt, *The Story of Patani* (The Hague, 1970), 270, 292–96; R. Bonney, *Kedah 1771–1821* (Kuala Lumpur, 1971), 11–23; Gervaise, *Natural History*, 233.

[223] Gervaise, *Natural History*, 227 ff.; Guy Tachard, *A Relation of the Voyage to Siam* (rpt. Bangkok, 1981), 153–97; Han ten Brummelhuis, *Merchant, Courtier and Diplomat: A History of the Contacts between the Netherlands and Thailand* (Gent, 1987), 9–51.

information before trying to say something about agrarian and domestic commercial trends.

From the 1570s until the 1630s or 1640s demographic growth and expanded market networks in Europe, the Ottoman empire, China, Japan, and Southeast Asia joined with dramatic increases in the production of New World silver to stimulate trade across Eurasia. Southeast Asia exchanged unprecedented quantities of spices and other primary products for European bullion, Indian textiles, Japanese and Chinese metals and manufactures.[224] On recovering from the Burmese wars, Ayudhya faced stiff regional competition for this traffic less from Burma than from Batavia and Manila (which by the 1630s had replaced Ayudhya as the chief regional entrepots), Pattani, a revived Cambodia, and the Vietnamese port of Hoi An. Siam survived commercially by concentrating on the China trade and by drawing to itself both the Dutch and a variety of merchant communities who had been harmed by Dutch monopolies in the archipelago. The Dutch East India Company became the largest single foreign trading organization at Ayudhya, buying deer hides, tin, lac, and rare woods for sale in China, Japan, and South Asia, and providing somewhat below 20 percent of Siam's imports from 1633 to 1694.[225] In total volume, however, European trade probably remained inferior to that of Indian Muslim and more especially Persian merchants.[226] Meanwhile the lifting in 1567 of the Ming ban on Chinese private trade allowed junks to supply porcelain and raw and finished silk. These goods, and to a lesser extent Siamese forest products, provided the chief draw for silver-laden Japanese ships, which Ming authorities

[224] Colin McEvedy and Richard Jones, *Atlas of World Population History* (London, 1978); William Lavely and R. Bin Wong, "Revising the Malthusian Narrative," *JAS* 57 (1998) 716–20; Ward Barrett, "World Bullion Flows, 1450–1830," in James Tracy, ed., *The Rise of Merchant Empires* (Cambridge, 1990), 224–54, esp. Fig. 7.1; Reid, *Age of Commerce*, II, 16–31.

[225] George Vinal Smith, *The Dutch in Seventeenth-Century Siam* (DeKalb, IL: 1977), 111 and *passim*. On 17th-century Siamese trade, also Ishii, *Junk Trade*, 1–102; "van Vliet's Description," 89–96; la Loubere, *Kingdom*, 71–73, 93–94, 112–13; Joost Schouten in Francois Caron and Schouten, *A True Description of the Mighty Kingdoms of Japan and Siam*, Roger Manley, tr. (Bangkok, 1986), 147–49; Reid, "Documenting the Rise," 8–13; and other essays in Jittasevi, *Proceedings*.

[226] Smith, *The Dutch*, 58–68, 85–87, 110. On Muslim trade, see *Ship of Sulaiman*; Sanjay Subrahmanyam, "Iranians Abroad," *JAS* 51, 2 (1992): 340–63; Leonard Andaya, "Ayudhya and the Persian and Indian Muslim Connection," in Jittasevi, *Proceedings*, 133–42; Dhiravat na Pombejra, "Crown Trade and Court Politics in Ayutthaya during the Reign of King Narai (1656–88)," in J. Kathirithamby-Wells and John Villiers, eds., *The Southeast Asian Port and Polity* (Singapore, 1990), 127–42.

prohibited from trading directly with China.[227] Siamese kings themselves sent junks throughout Asia, and in fact, in both volume and value, royal ventures probably outclassed the Dutch.[228] Periodic turmoil at court and the fickle nature of the entrepot trade contributed to a certain instability in Ayudhya's fortunes – trade was strong in the 1610s and 1620s, weaker in the 1630s and 1640s, exceptionally vigorous under Narai (1656–1688) – but on the whole Ayudhya remained one of the most active ports in Southeast Asia.

It is against this background of periodic fluctuations that we must assess the Age of Commerce thesis that the late 17th century saw a transformative decline in Siamese trade and foreign contacts.[229] Admittedly, after a 1688 coup directed in part against French and English interests, trading companies from those nations withdrew from Siam and cultural intercourse with Europe diminished. In this same period Cambodia seems to have become a more serious commercial competitor. But to speak of a general post-1688 Siamese retreat from external involvement is misleading insofar as a wider employment at court of Indians, Malays, Persians, and Chinese easily compensated for a decline in European specialists.[230] Although trade with the Indian Ocean apparently declined from 1688 to 1703 – we lack overall figures – royal factors and private merchants, both Muslim and European, continued to sail between Indian ports, Siamese Mergui, and Ayudhya. Indeed, declining interest by European companies, including the Dutch, during the 1690s and the first half of the 18th century reflected limited market opportunities in Siam less than competition from private Asian and European merchants, including British country traders, with smaller overheads.[231]

[227] Yoneo Ishii, "Seventeenth-Century Japanese Documents About Siam," *JSS* 59, 2 (1971): 161–74; Yoko Nagazumi, "Ayutthaya and Japan," in Jittasevi, *Proceedings*, 43–48; Sarasin Viraphol, *Tribute and Profit* (Cambridge, MA: 1977), chs. 1, 3, 4; Richard von Glahn, *Fountain of Fortune* (Berkeley, 1996), 113–25.

[228] Smith, *The Dutch*, 111 and *passim*; idem, "Princes, Nobles, and Traders," *Contributions to Asian Studies* 15 (1980): 6–13.

[229] See Reid, *Age of Commerce*, II, ch. 5, esp. 306–309, 311, 325; and discussion in Ch. 1 *supra*. Cf. a similar emphasis on 17th-century commercial decline in Alain Forest, "Le Siam dans le movement de la navigation et du commerce a la fin du XVIIe siecle," *Jl. of Sophia Asian Studies* 7 (1989): 42–81.

[230] Dhiravat na Pombejra, "Ayutthaya at the End of the Seventeenth Century: Was There a Shift to Isolation?" in Anthony Reid, ed., *Southeast Asia in the Early Modern Era* (Ithaca, 1993), esp. 258–60, 267–69. On Narai's European relations, Constantine Phaulkon, and the events of 1688, Wyatt, *History*, 112–18; E .W. Hutchinson, *Adventurers in Siam in the 17th Century* (London, 1940). On Cambodia's post-1690 trade vitality, n. 212 *supra*.

[231] Pombejra, "Princes, Pretenders," 115, 126; idem, "Ayutthaya at the End of the Seventeenth Century," 263–70; Smith, *The Dutch*, chs. 3, 6.

Most critical, as Dhiravat na Pombejra, Sarasin Viraphol, and G. William Skinner have emphasized, if Indian Ocean trade lost some of its luster, Siamese-Chinese trade entered a period of sustained expansion. Although the latter exchange showed no strong trend during the reign of Phetracha (1688–1703), it grew under Thai Sa (1709–1733) and most especially under Borommakot (1733–1758).[232] Several factors were at work. Overland contacts with Yunnan and Guangxi widened, as did maritime sales to China of sappanwood and other forest products. Siam also exported increasing quantities of peninsular tin to satisfy an "almost insatiable" Chinese demand for spirit money and tin-lined chests.[233] After the Tokugawa forbade Japanese to go overseas, Chinese vessels developed a Nagasaki-China-Siam triangular trade of which Siamese "crown ships," exporting tin, sappanwood, and deerskins, had the major share well into the 18th century.[234] But what basically drove Sino-Siamese commercial expansion was the seaborne trade in Siamese rice, and for obvious reasons: between 1650 and 1780 China's population more than doubled, while market specialization encouraged a shift from rice to nonfood commercial crops, especially on the south Chinese coast. The resultant rice deficit forced the Qing in 1683 and again in 1727/29 to rescind decrees (never fully effective) banning trade with the Nan-yang. From 1722 to the late 1740s trade was conducted under the guise of the tributary system through consortia between the king of Siam and Fujian merchants, but thereafter the Qing government encouraged private Chinese traders to import rice on their own account as well. Whereas Siamese rice exports to China prior to 1722 had been negligible, by the 1750s Fujian merchants were importing at least 6,000–8,000 tons

---

[232] Pace Reid, *Age of Commerce*, II, 308 (incl. n. 5), Pombejra, the leading authority, sees no decline, and possibly a modest rise, in Chinese shipping under Phetracha. See Pombejra, "Ayutthaya at the End of the Seventeenth Century," 263 ("It was therefore already apparent, from the 1680s onward, that Chinese trade with Siam would become more extensive and lucrative than before. It is no surprise that King Phetracha and Prince Sorasak seized this opportunity to increase their revenues through participation in international trade."). See also n. 278 *infra* and Sarasin, *Tribute*, 54–55 for problems with Reid's analysis of these figures. From 1703 to the early 1720s, and again from the 1720s to 1760s, the growth in Chinese shipping is well documented in Viraphol, *Tribute*, 46–107, esp. 85–107 (note misprint on 85); Skinner, *Chinese Society*, 12–18; Ishii, *Junk Trade*, 53–101; Sucheta Mazumdar, *Sugar and Society in China* (Cambridge, MA: 1998), 110–112; Adisorn Muakpimai, "Chantaburi," in Jittasevi, *Proceedings*, 163–71.

[233] Pombejra, "Princes, Pretenders," 119.

[234] Nagazumi, "Ayutthaya and Japan," 43–48; Sarasin, *Tribute*, 58–69, 246–47, 251; Pombejra, "Ayutthaya at the End of the Seventeenth Century," 262–63; and esp. Ishii, *Junk Trade*, ch. 1.

a year, but this was separate from imports by Guangdong and Zhejiang merchants and presumably from tributary trade. In all, annual Siamese rice exports to China from 1740 to 1765 must have averaged well over 10,000 tons.[235] By the mid-1700s Chinese miners and cash-crop cultivators who had settled around the Gulf and the Malay peninsula in order to supply the China market were generating substantial additional, if as yet unquantifiable demand for Siamese rice. These linkages depended on yet wider global networks insofar as China absorbed substantial quantities of Indian raw cotton and 33–50 percent of New World silver, while selling tea, porcelain, and textiles to the Nan-yang and more especially to Europe.[236]

As commercial ties with China and with overseas Chinese settlements strengthened, between 1680 and 1767 the Chinese community in Siam itself may have tripled to 30,000, while becoming more occupationally diverse.[237] From the early 1700s well into the 19th century Chinese not only dominated Siam's external trade, but (excepting a partial hiatus in the 1730s and 1740s) outclassed other foreign communities at court, in provincial government, and in collecting provincial tribute. Ayudhya's 1767 collapse was arguably more of a political than an economic or social watershed. It was hardly accidental that a half-Chinese general reunified the kingdom and that the mother of the Chakri dynastic founder, in King Mongkut's charming words, was "a beautiful daughter of a very rich Chinese family" in Ayudhya.[238]

---

[235] Viraphol, *Tribute*, 100–101, cites annual rice imports in 1754, 1755, and 1758 by Fujian merchants of 90,000–120,000 piculs (c. 6,000–8,000 tons). The Kangxi emperor as early as 1722 (ibid., 90) requested 300,000 piculs (c. 20,000 tons), while on the basis of 19th-century figures, ibid., 90–91 suggests a theoretical ceiling of "several hundred thousand piculs" (perhaps 40,000 tons). But we do not know if these figures were realized. See too Robert Marks, *Tigers, Rice, Silk, and Silt* (Cambridge, 1998), 163–94; and n. 232 *supra*.

[236] On Siamese trade with Chinese settlements elsewhere in SE Asia, Li Tana, "The 18th Century Mekong Delta and the World of the Water Frontier" (ms); Carl Trocki, "Chinese Pioneering in 18th-Century Southeast Asia," in Anthony Reid, ed., *The Last Stand of Asian Autonomies* (New York, 1997), 83–101. On China and the international economy, Marks, *Tigers, Rice*, ch. 5; Mazumdar, *Sugar and Society*, 109–119, 387–409; Kenneth Pomeranz, *The Great Divergence* (Princeton, 2000), chs. 3, 4, 6; and *supra* Ch. 1., n. 61, Ch. 2, n. 175.

[237] Skinner, *Chinese Society*, 13, 19 says all of Siam had at least 10,000 Chinese in the latter half of the 17th century, with a third or less at the capital. He also cites 6,000 Chinese fighters at the capital in 1767, but this can only have been a fraction of the total Chinese population at Ayudhya, not to mention the realm. Pombejra, "Princes, Pretenders," 122 cites a missionary estimate of 20,000 in the kingdom as early as 1734. Cf. Viraphol, *Tribute*, 46.

[238] Pombejra, "Princes, Pretenders," 126–27; Chang, "Chinese Mercantile Power."

In short, instead of a late 17th-century retreat from foreign trade, we find a change in emphasis from Indian Ocean to Chinese networks and a general intensification after c. 1710.[239] We also see a shift from entrepot functions to the supply of local produce, as well as a continuation of the same movement from high value, low bulk trade to the opposite mix as began in Siam, Burma, and other parts of Southeast Asia in the 16th or 17th century.[240]

Insofar as economic change did contribute to Ayudhya's 1760s collapse, we shall find that the problem was less one of commercial contraction, than of destabilizing growth. During most of the Ayudhya period, there is little question that trade strengthened the crown internally and contributed to Siam's waxing influence over Cambodia, Lan Sang, and peninsular states. The direct benefits were four-fold. Most obvious was increased central revenues. Although lumber, foodstuffs, and cheap exports were freely bought and sold, the crown continued to monopolize the most valuable exports. Royal agents obtained such goods (as well as non-monopoly items like rice) through tribute, taxes, domestic purchase, and in-kind payments (*suai*) in lieu of corvee. These materials were then sold to foreign visitors or taken directly to other Asian ports in royal vessels. Foreign imports the crown used itself, sold at Ayudhya, or sent upcountry to exchange for fresh exports. In all, the Late Ayudhya court obtained from a quarter to a third of its revenues from monopoly sales, overseas trade, and port dues.[241]

Second, kings employed foreign traders and mercenaries with specialized skills whose weak local ties rendered them unusually dependent on the throne. Of a prominent Japanese courtier a Japanese account from the 1620s said, "There were some [Siamese] who were jealous of

---

[239] This conclusion is consistent with the views of Thai specialists, e.g., Viraphol, *Tribute*, 46–48 and *passim*; Wyatt, *Thailand*, 126–27; Pombejra, "Ayutthaya at the End of the Seventeenth Century"; ibid., "Princes, Pretenders"; Yoneo Ishii, personal communication, July, 2001.

[240] Cf. David Wyatt, "The Eighteenth Century in Southeast Asia," in Blusse and Gaastra, *Eighteenth Century*, esp. 46; Reid, "Documenting the Rise," 11–13. By extension, if Ayudhya's share of SE Asia's total entrepot trade was smaller in 1760 than in 1630, this change speaks more to the dynamism of regional trade than to any absolute decline in Siamese involvement.

[241] Kasetsiri, "Ayudhya: Capital-Port of Siam," 75, citing the *Khamhaikan Chao Krungkao*, says 27% of revenues came from overseas trade by the 18th century. Viraphol, *Tribute*, 18–19, following Damrong Rajanubhab, claims Narai got one-third of his income from monopolies and port taxes; while David Wyatt in David J. Steinberg, ed., *In Search of Southeast Asia* (rev. ed., Honolulu, 1987), 53 says roughly one-quarter of Ayudhya's revenues came from royal monopolies.

[him] and there were also many who kissed his ass."[242] In the 1680s a Greek became Siam's highest civil official.[243] Muslims and Japanese tended to dominate to c. 1630, followed by Muslims and Europeans to 1688, followed, we have seen, by Chinese. Although families of foreign descent assimilated to Siamese elite culture, each group gained an initial foothold through external trade.[244] This cosmopolitanism, which distinguished Ayudhya from interior Tai rivals as well as Burma but which found parallels in Cambodia, had major cultural as well as political implications.

Third, as noted, Ayudhya was able to dominate landlocked states that sought a wider outlet for their products. Siamese nobles obliged Lao traders to sell at artificially low prices, while periodically discouraging foreign traders from visiting Laos.

Finally, the coast still afforded unique access to guns and strategic metals. Although two 17th-century Siamese-made cannon sent as gifts to France were used in the storming of the Bastille in 1789, and although European- and Chinese-style firearms were also manufactured in interior Tai states, European visitors repeatedly noted that the best guns came from the coast, and that Japanese, Portuguese, Mon, and Malay warriors were more useful than conscripted *phrai luang*. Firearms were among the goods that royal vessels sought most eagerly, while the import of arms, ammunition, and gunpowder remained a strict royal monopoly. In 1767 Ayudhya's armory reportedly contained cannon for dismantling city walls, 10,000 muskets, and 50,000 shells manufactured in Siam, China, Laos, Europe, and India.[245]

As it transformed royal finances, foreign trade powerfully influenced the domestic economy. Coastal-based networks run by foreigners and mestizos (Muslim-Thais, Mon-Thais, Sino-Thais) drew rural *phrai* and *munnai* to interior market towns by supplying cash and textiles in return

---

[242] Chihara Goro, *Sham Koku Yamada shi Kobouki*, 5, cited in Atsuko Naono, "The Japanese Trading Community in Ayudhya and Its Role in Thai Trade and Politics" (ms), 9.

[243] The famed Constantine Phaulkon. See Luang Sitsayamkan, *The Greek Favourite of the King of Siam* (Singapore, 1967).

[244] Engelbert Kaempfer, *A Description of the Kingdom of Siam 1690* (rpt., Bangkok, 1987), 28, 38; David Wyatt, "Family Politics in Seventeenth- and Eighteenth-Century Siam," in Bickner, *Papers*, 257–65; Pombejra, "Princes, Pretenders"; idem, *Court, Company, and Campong* (Bangkok, 1992).

[245] *CHSEA*, 381–83; "van Vliet's Description," 10, 28–30; van Vliet, *Short History*, 62–63; Gervaise, *Natural History*, 111; la Loubere, *Kingdom*, 90–95; Pombejra, "Political History," 38, 77–78; Sewell, "Notes on Siamese Guns"; Schouten, *True Description*, 134–35.

for specialized exports.[246] Although other mestizo networks dealt solely in domestic goods like lumber and rice, they too encouraged rural money use. In the provinces – whose Chinese population far exceeded that of the capital – as well as in Ayudhya, Chinese worked as ship-builders, miners, artisans, pig-breeders, vegetable gardeners, and ped-dlers. Because they relied on the market for raw materials and food more than did the average peasant, here as in Burma such specialists offered a disproportionate stimulus to commercial production.[247] Here too, moreover, imported metals lubricated domestic exchange. Bullion imports to East Asia grew at least four-fold from 1580 to 1640, leveled off or declined c. 1640 to 1680, then rose steadily to 1770 and beyond. Although we lack figures on net bullion flows, cargo lists suggest that Late Ayudhya Siam maintained a favorable balance with European companies and, at least to 1730, with China. By introducing foreign coins, including Chinese cash, and by facilitating the local minting of silver *baht*, foreign trade thus encouraged commodification, bulk trade, and labor mobility.[248]

All this suggests that by comparison with the pre-1500 era and certainly with the charter era, maritime economic influences were particularly potent. Nonetheless, agricultural extension and domestic commerce retained their own dynamic. In what is now north Thailand, southern Laos, and the Khorat plateau, as Tai-speaking wet-rice cultivators converted ever more acreage to lowland rice, upland rice contracted until by 1800 it was confined to mountain fields tilled chiefly by slash-and-burn cultivators. Between 1600 and 1800, the balance between late-ripening slender type rice, which depended on long-term flooding and which we have seen was normally more productive than round type rice, also continued to shift in favor of the former. Meanwhile slender rice extended into virgin lands ever farther south. Traditionally rice cultivation was concentrated in the floodplain north of Ayudhya, where new acreages were brought under the plough in the late 17th century.

---

[246] Smith, "Princes, Nobles, and Traders," 9–10; idem, *The Dutch*, 74–77.

[247] Skinner, *Chinese Society*, 12–20; G. E. Gerini, "Historical Retrospect of Junkceylon Island," *JSS* 2 (1905): 31–32; la Loubere, *Kingdom*, 112; "van Vliet's Description," 69.

[248] On Asian flows, Artur Attman, *American Bullion in the European World Trade 1600–1800* (Goteborg, Sweden, 1986), chs. 4, 5, esp. Tables IV.2, IV.3, V.1; Reid, *Age of Commerce*, II, 25–27 (Table 3), 93–110, 286–88; Barrett, "World Bullion Flows," 224–54, esp. Tables 7.4, 7.6, 7.7; and Andre Gunder Frank, *Re-Orient* (Berkeley, 1998), 142–49. On copper and silver imports to Siam, Smith, *The Dutch*, 62–70 (esp. Table 4), 92–95; Viraphol, *Tribute*, 13, 22, 45, 64–65, 99, 200; Pombejra, "Princes, Pretenders," 112.

But in Ayudhya's last years as reclamation to the north began to lose impetus, interest shifted to the young delta, a vast swampy tract subject to progressive sedimentation between Ayudhya and the sea that originally specialized in that type of broadcast slender rice known as floating rice. Destined to accelerate dramatically in the Bangkok period, cultivation of the young delta opened extensive new acreages and promoted the continuous refinement of local strains.[249]

Agricultural expansion benefited from familiar stimuli: natural population growth, domestic pacification, state incentives (see below), large-scale deportations in the late 1500s and early 1600s, and perhaps more favorable rainfall between c. 1720 and c. 1805 (although this impact may have been ambiguous[250]). Overseas markets also were a factor, absorbing Siamese sugar, pepper, indigo, and coconut oil, not to mention rice. Yet although foreign demand was influential in some southern districts, especially around the capital, such demand seems to have remained marginal to the agrarian economy as a whole: even with the spurt in purchases by coastal China and by Chinese settlements in Southeast Asia, on present evidence it is difficult to see how Late Ayudhya rice exports exceeded 2–3 percent of the crop.[251] Sugar was more substantially

[249] On changing rice types and locales, Watabe, "Development of Rice Cultivation" and Tanabe, "Land Reclamation," in Ishii, *Thailand*, esp. 41–42; Watabe, "Glutinous Rice Zone," 96–113; Yoshikazu Takaya, *Agricultural Development of a Tropical Delta* (Honolulu, 1987), esp. 186–88; la Loubere, *Kingdom*, 19; *Ship of Sulaiman*, 153–54; Ishii, *Junk Trade*, 55–56; O'Connor, "Agricultural Change," 982–83; Fukui Hayao, personal communication, Aug., 2001; Dhiravat na Pombejra, personal communication, Sept. 2000. Cf. Lao agriculture, Stuart-Fox, *Lao Kingdom*, 113.

[250] On the one hand, excessive rains may have created problems of flood control and rendered inaccessible for cultivation some swamp and deep-water areas, much as c. 900–1300. But it is also possible that increased rainfall extended the area on the margins of the delta in which floating rice could be grown, while enhancing the security of transplanted rice in bunded fields farther north. Moreover, despite or perhaps because of increased rainfall, sedimentation joined with levee-breaching techniques to encourage southward reclamation. On dry climatic conditions, to which references ebb after 1716, see *infra* n. 254.

[251] As n. 235 observed, maximum known authorized annual exports to China totalled 300,000 piculs, but on average probably were far less. Before 1750 rice exports within SE Asia still must have been a fraction of that figure. Since Siam's population may have increased 50 percent from 1750 to 1850 (Skinner, *Chinese Society*, 70; Reid, *Age of Commerce*, I, 14) and since the rice crop 1850 was c. 23,000,000 piculs (Ingram, *Economic Change*, 8), the 1750 crop may have been c. 15,400,000 piculs, or 51 times the maximum known requested exports to China. As late as 1850, after a sustained period of export expansion, D. E. Malloch, a knowledgeable informant, estimated that on average only 2–3 percent of the crop went overseas. Jennifer Wayne Cushman, "Fields from the Sea" (Cornell Univ. Ph.D. diss., 1975), 128–32. Cf. Ingram, *Economic Change*, 23–24.

for export, but required only a tiny portion of the land and labor devoted to rice.[252]

Siam's population may have increased from c. 2,500,000 in 1600 to 4,000,000 in 1800.[253] On the assumption that agricultural technique was stable and that slender rice yields advanced only modestly, cultivated acreage also must have expanded by 50–60 percent. Although we lack diachronic mortality or acreage figures, population and acreages probably grew most rapidly 1570–1630, when Ayudhya was recovering from Burmese invasions, and after c. 1720, when cultivators began moving into the young delta. By contrast, indigenous and foreign records from Siam, Burma, and South China alike point to deficient rainfall and poor harvests in many years between c. 1630 and 1716. Whether because food shortages weakened resistance or because dry conditions bred disease, several drought years were also years of smallpox and other epidemics.[254]

Over the long term, by increasing aggregate demand, here as in Burma demographic and agricultural growth encouraged the proliferation, upgrading, and integration of local markets. Late Ayudhya-era materials portray a network of commercial sites that may have approximated Rozman's Premodern Urban Development stage E ("standard marketing"), with a national administrative center, 18 or 19 (in the 1630s) provincial capitals-cum-major market towns, which in turn served as hubs for standard marketing centers and periodic rural markets. Provincial cities redistributed a wide array of local goods, chiefly foodstuffs, timber, dyes, cotton textiles, iron goods, and handicrafts. Timber aside, the lower Chaophraya basin was the principal source of domestic commodities, some of which circulated as far as the Khorat plateau and Lan Sang.[255]

---

[252] Ishii, *Junk Trade*, 23, 56; Mazumdar, *Sugar and Society*, 81, 85, 112.

[253] These are quite rough figures. Reid, *Age of Commerce*, I, 14 estimates the 1800 population at 3,500,000, but this is well below the estimate of 4,750,000 for 1825 at Skinner, *Chinese Society*, 68, 70 and raises the possibility that Reid's 1600 figure of 2,200,000 also is too low.

[254] For references to epidemics and drought, often linked, between 1645 and 1716, but chiefly to 1691, see Pombejra, "Poltical History," 225, 307, 334, 359; idem, "Ayutthaya at the End of the Seventeenth Century," 257, idem, "Princes and Pretenders," 116; Smith, *The Dutch*, 61; Stuart-Fox, *Lao Kingdom*, 95; Godley, "Flood Regimes," chs. 5, 6. Massimo Livi-Bacci, *Population and Nutrition* (Cambridge, 1991) argues that early modern mortality was governed more by epidemiological cycles than by nutrition.

[255] Gervaise, *Natural History*, 114–15, 119; "van Vliet's Description," 66–69, 89–96; Smith, *The Dutch*, 72–75; Reid, *Age of Commerce*, I, 71; la Loubere, *Kingdom*, 71, 95; Schouten,

Demographic and domestic commercial expansion strengthened Siam's international trade in four ways: a) It boosted the supply of potential exports like rice and sugar. b) It increased the number and possibly the per capita purchasing power of Siamese commoners as well as nobles eager to buy foreign textiles and other imports. The crown itself sought silver for reminting, copper for construction, and textiles for diplomacy and patronage. c) It nourished a market network along which imports and exports could circulate more easily. d) It provided corvees needed to excavate fresh canals linking Ayudhya to the sea. Expanding Southeast Asian trade is normally seen as a function of external demand, but this perspective restores a degree of local agency by suggesting that some of the same demographic/internal economic trends as affected China and Europe influenced Siam.

By the same token, military superiority still required agricultural and demographic superiority. In the 18th century, recall, Siam's domestic revenues (taxes on fishing, agriculture, and market transactions; the produce of royal estates, profits from domestic trade, and tribute) remained two to three times larger than maritime income.[256] Although between 1720 and 1767 overseas trade almost certainly grew more rapidly than land reclamation, during the entire 1570–1767 era the difference may have been much less.[257] Pombejra has noted that the wealth of most 17th-century high officials (*khunnang*) rested not on trade per se, but on land, that is, family estates and more especially non-hereditable estates given them by the crown, which they worked with bondsmen and *phrai som* and the produce of which they sold on the domestic market. These officials still considered overseas trade beneath their dignity, and although in fact some traded through agents, only a minority, chiefly of Moorish or Chinese origin, did so openly.[258] To the end of the dynasty, the critical factor in succession disputes at Ayudhya remained control not of foreign trade, but of manpower.[259]

True Description, 147–48. Cf. Gilbert Rozman, *Urban Networks in Russia, 1750–1800, and Premodern Periodization* (Princeton, 1976).

[256] *Supra* n. 241. On domestic taxes, "van Vliet's Description," 26–27; Smith, *The Dutch*, 74; la Loubere, *Kingdom*, 93–94; Wales, *Siamese Government*, ch. 9.

[257] Cf. discussion of 17th-century trade *supra*.

[258] Pombejra, "Political History," 51–53, and personal communication, Sept., 2000: "I still see [late Ayudhya] Siam as overwhelmingly agricultural, but with an increasingly commercially aware elite."

[259] Wyatt, *Thailand*, 131.

In these ways, agricultural/demographic change joined maritime trade to strengthen central authorities. But again, the relation between state power and economic growth was reciprocal. Unintentionally, pacification encouraged population growth and exchange. Quite intentionally, the Late Ayudhya court spurred agriculture by promoting irrigation north of Ayudhya, levying punitive taxes on fallow land, and settling refugees and prisoners around the capital. "[T]he present King of Siam, to force his Subjects to work, has [imposed unprecedented taxes on] those that have possessed Lands for a certain time, although they omit to cultivate them.... He loved nothing so much, as to see Strangers come to settle in his States, there to manure those great uncultivated Spaces," wrote la Loubere.[260] By requiring princes to move from the provinces to the capital and by expanding the court, Late Ayudhya kings encouraged competitive display ("the great mandarins [build temples and monasteries in the capital] in emulation of each other and spare nothing to surpass each other in the richness and magnificence of their buildings"[261]). Courtiers sought to enhance their income primarily through clientage and usury, but also, as noted, through commodity production. By stimulating urban growth, the court – like its counterparts in Edo, Paris, St. Petersburg, and Ava – concentrated market demand, and not only among elites, for textiles, foodstuffs, and raw materials of all sorts. Finally, in pursuit of commercial and military advantage, the Late Ayudhya crown cultivated contacts with South Asian and European powers and excavated at least eight more canals, three of them in the 18th century, to straighten river courses between the capital and the gulf.[262]

The combined impact of overseas trade, domestic economic growth, and state action became apparent in several domains:

 • To counteract recurrent monetary shortages caused by more domestic transactions and by intensified silver demand in China, new media were introduced c. 1730–1760 to supplement royal flat silver coins, silver bullet coins, Chinese copper cash, Japanese gold coins, and cowries. Produced by Chinese merchants and perhaps local officials,

---

[260] La Loubere, *Kingdom*, 93; see also 94. Cf. Gesick, "Kingship," 16; *Crystal Sands*, 112–14; Tanabe, "Land Reclamation," 51–52; R. Halliday, "Immigration of the Mons into Siam," *JSS* 10, 3 (1913): 1–13.

[261] Gervaise, *Natural History*, 165.

[262] Hubbard, *Inland Waterway*, 21–27; Tanabe, "Land Reclamation," 44–52; idem, "Historical Geography of the Canal System."

these new media included clay seals (*prakab*) and gambling counters of brass, bronze, and porcelain for small transactions, as well as brass and bronze coins.[263]

• The legal system began to sanction land as something close to private property, and an active land market arose around the chief urban centers, again with particular vigor from the late 1600s and early 1700s. Little research has been done on pre-1600 Ayudhya landholding, but Takashi Tomosugi believes it was characterized more by de facto access and occupancy than by formal property rights; land rights vested in village headmen or community leaders impeded private transfer. According to Tomosugi, however, in the late 17th and 18th centuries growing demand for foodstuffs increased the value of land around Ayudhya and provincial towns, while the issuance by the government of land holding certificates (*chanot*), though originally designed merely to facilitate tax collections, served to make occupancy more stable, publicly apparent, and legally secure than earlier verbal agreements. Accordingly, from at least the 1720s we see an increase in legally-sanctioned sales (*sukhai thidin*) and in the mortgaging/pledging (*khai fak thidin*) of land. Thus by the end of the Ayudhya period land ownership had been systematically documented and reinforced to the benefit, Tomosugi suggests, of individual cultivators as well as local and central officials.[264] As seems to have been true in Burma, these developments encouraged litigation and judicial appeals to the capital. Conceivably too, more secure property rights joined market opportunities to encourage peasants to experiment with new agricultural techniques.

• Late Ayudhya officials introduced a series of tax changes designed to tap market activity. These included: a) imposts from the early 1600s on orchards, inland transit, and market sales; b) more precise classifications of taxable land quality, starting in the early 18th century; and c) tax farms, usually administered by Chinese, on liquor, markets, fishing, royal agricultural estates, and gambling, several of which arose between 1730 and 1760. Also indicative of growing monetization was the practice, in vogue by the late 1680s and destined to expand thereafter, whereby local officials allowed *phrai luang* to commute service obligations in return for specified payments of cash or export commodities.

---

[263] "Van Vliet's Description," 95–96; la Loubere, *Kingdom*, 72–73; Wicks, "Survey of Coinage," 173–76.

[264] Tomosugi, *Structural Analysis*, 109–114. Cf. Loubere, *Kingdom*, 71, discussing the weakness of land ownership; Wales, *Siamese Government*, 202.

Most likely to seek commutation were *phrai* laborers or artisans near the cities, where a modest labor market seems to have developed.[265]

• Although diachronic claims about occupational profiles are difficult, the 17th and 18th centuries offer evidence of substantial specialization in handicrafts, construction, artisanry, domestic transport, and commercial agriculture.[266]

To summarize developments in the central mainland between 1570 and 1767: As Lan Na receded to provincial status, as Lan Sang fragmented, and as Cambodia was whipsawed between its neighbors, Ayudhya became the only viable polity. Ayudhya's success reflected a combination of administrative reforms, which recall contemporary changes in Burma; expanding maritime contacts, particularly with China after 1685; and agricultural and demographic growth. If maritime influences on Ayudhya were indisputably greater than on Angkor, Pagan, or Ava, without reliable statistics it is impossible to separate external from domestic stimuli. Clearly, however, the late 1600s and especially the early 1700s inaugurated a period not of sustained decline, but of Chinese-assisted economic vitality that would continue into the 19th century.

18TH-CENTURY DRAMA: AYUDHYA'S FINAL DEFEAT

Chapter 2 explained how the new Kon-baung dynasty, mimicking its First Toungoo predecessor, launched a series of eastern invasions. By 1765 Chiang Mai and Luang Prabang had fallen. Two years later a massive Burmese army burned and sacked famed Ayudhya.

Once again, therefore, as in the 16th century, Siam's collapse was an artifact of Burmese aggression. Yet by itself, such pressure cannot explain why Siam proved so humiliatingly vulnerable, a failure all the more puzzling in that a mere seven years after Ayudhya's final defeat, the Siamese general Taksin, with no more resources than his Ayudhyan predecessors, had succeeded not only in reconstituting the kingdom and driving out the Burmese, but in seizing Lan Na and dominating Laos. Nor can Burmese pressure alone explain why Ayudhya's failure

---

[265] Van Vliet, *Short History*, 88; Wales, *Ancient Siamese*, 55–56, 202, 209; Hong Lysa, *Thailand in the Nineteenth Century* (Singapore, 1984), 76; Gervaise, *Natural History*, 114–16; la Loubere, *Kingdom*, 94; Wyatt, *Thailand*, 131–32; Ishii, *Thailand*, 32; Koizumi, "King's Manpower," 4, 15.

[266] "Van Vliet's Description," 66–69, 91, la Loubere, *Kingdom*, 71, 95; Smith, *The Dutch*, 72–73.

occurred within a few years of comparable collapses in Restored Toungoo Burma, Nguyen Vietnam, and Trinh Vietnam.

If we restrict our comparison to Burma, in both countries by the mid-18th century we find that long standing weaknesses, particularly in the system of manpower control, had become acute. In much the same fashion as low-ranking Burmese *ahmu-dans* were tempted to become private servicemen or debt-slaves so as to escape hereditary labor obligations, so in Siam the fact that *phrai luang* (royal servicemen) bore heavier obligations than *phrai som* (private retainers) encouraged a steady flow from royal to private service, including various forms of debt-bondage and unauthorized clientage. Ministers, princes, and governors were the chief beneficiaries, in many cases the instigators, of these transfers, which augmented their supply of laborers and armed retainers. As in Burma, succession conflicts encouraged rival factions to enlarge their followings. On the whole, new registration procedures, concessions to heavily indebted *phrai luang*, and royal prohibitions proved ineffective in staunching the flow.[267]

In part, then, these problems reflected structural tensions between royal and private work routines, and between loyalty to the king and to factional leaders. One cannot reject entirely the notion that the Restored Toungoo and Late Ayudhya systems, having been founded at roughly the same on similar principles, exhausted their supply of servicemen at roughly the same time because of comparable internal rhythms.

Yet there is evidence that economic growth and commercial intensification in the late 17th and 18th centuries aggravated long-standing weaknesses in three ways broadly familiar from Burma. First, wider money use and market activity created more opportunities for ministerial and princely usury and for peasant borrowing, which in turn increased the incidence of *phrai luang* becoming debt-slaves. Second, commercial opportunities induced officials, princes, and local *munnai* to accumulate lands and to recruit servicemen for cash crop cultivation, especially around Ayudhya, where water resources were good and domestic and foreign markets beckoned.[268] By the same token, in return for gifts of salable commodities or cash, officials allowed *phrai luang* to

---

[267] My analysis of Late Ayudhya decline derives from Rabibhadana, *Organization*, esp. 34–39, 151, 174–76; Wyatt, *Thailand*, 128–38; idem, "Eighteenth Century," 39–56; letter from Nidhi Aeusrivongse to Anthony Reid, May 4, 1991; Busakorn, "Ban Phlu Luang," esp. chs. 2, 8; and Tomosugi, *Structural Analysis*, 111–14.

[268] Tanabe, "Land Reclamation," 71–72; "van Vliet's Decription," 26–27, 64–65; Dhiravat, "Political History," 51–53.

reduce their service obligations or escape them entirely. This could occur by formal arrangement with the government or by informal agreement with individual patrons (official commutation may have sought to fore-stall the latter, more politically dangerous, option). Third, the growth of commercial wealth, accompanied conceivably by price inflation (we have few figures), undermined the system of official ranks which rested on allocations of agricultural manpower. This in turn bred compensatory efforts by downwardly mobile officials to recruit *phrai som* illegally, to permit illegal commutations, and to demand more bribes and cash gra-tuities from their *phrai luang*. As the Ayudhyan elite changed to include more families who had Chinese connections and whose wealth derived from commerce, insecure older members of the court sought to protect themselves: in 1740 they obtained a royal decree (which may not have been well enforced) that henceforth no one could enter the administra-tive elite (*khunnang*, technically defined as men with a *sakdina* rank of 400 or above) who lacked *trakun* (good, noble family), who made money by gambling, or who bribed nobles to present him to the king in order to become a royal page.[269] Social tensions of this sort became intertwined with princely and factional rivalries. In short, in Siam as elsewhere that universal solvent – money – was eroding ascriptive status.

If aspirants for official posts increased more rapidly than the posts themselves, Goldstone's theory about the destabilizing effects of a dis-proportionate expansion of marginal elites would provide an explana-tion for late-18th century tensions distinct from theories of institutional weakness and commercial intensification. We lack prosopographic data, but demographic growth, renewed factionalism (reminiscent of the mid-1500s), and Chinese entry into the lower levels of the Siamese elite are consistent with Goldstone's model.[270]

Ayudhya's last years saw intense rivalries between princes allied to ministerial families, each with an extensive clientele. Borommakot ascended the throne in 1733 only after pitched battles in the capital be-tween his retainers and those of two rival princes. His death in 1758 led to more princely executions and the abdication of his short-lived successor under threat of renewed civil war. As retinues of *phrai som* expanded along with commutation and evasion, growing per capita burdens on the remaining *phrai luang* fed a cumulative decline in royal

---

[269] Rabibhadana, *Organization*, 155–56; Wyatt, "Eighteenth Century," 51–52, 55 n. 32. On Chinese penetration of the elite, see too Dhiravat, "Princes, Pretenders," 127.

[270] Goldstone, *Revolution and Rebellion*, 32–34 and *passim*.

ranks.[271] Moreover, during the 1750s, a period of limited external danger, factional intrigue placed a higher premium on political than military skills. Preoccupied and ill-prepared, Ayudhya's elite thus failed to mount an effective defense against Burma either in the outer provinces or the capital. This combination of proliferating retinues and external vulnerability recalls Upper Burma in the 1740s and 1750s.

To be sure, significant differences separated Restored Toungoo and Late Ayudhya collapse. Either because population densities were lower or access to land less circumscribed, around the Siamese capital there is little evidence of politically-destabilizing land shortages such as distressed Upper Burma cultivators. Whereas in Burma many *ahmu-dans* sought refuge by entering illegally into higher royal service units, in Siam enrollment as private retainers (*phrai som*) remained the preferred mode of escape, perhaps because *phrai luang* were of uniformly lower status than *ahmu-dans*. In Burma, township and village leaders became the main beneficiaries of royal collapse, but in Siam their role was generally filled at a higher territorial level by provincial governors. Chinese traders in Siam were far more influential than their foreign counterparts in Burma, and ministerial involvement in trade, more obvious.[272] But surely the principal discrepancy was that Ayudhya required an external invasion to break open the system, whereas Ava, because of peculiar north–south tensions, fell to rebels within the Irrawaddy basin itself. In effect the Burmese empire self-destructed and then, having revived, went on to destroy – and in that very process – to revitalize the Siamese state.

APOGEE: THE EXTRAORDINARY VIGOR OF THE EARLY BANGKOK EMPIRE

In Siam as in Burma, therefore, collapse was a precondition for a political revival more rapid and complete than either the western or the central mainland had experienced after the crises of the 14th century, if not also the 16th century. But in Siam in the late 1700s the sense of possibility and innovation seems to have been more pronounced than in Burma. I shall sketch political and economic vitality through the first three reigns (1782–1851) of the new Chakri dynasty, when Siam became, arguably, the preeminent mainland state.

---

[271] Rabibhadana, *Organization*, 34–39, 151, 176.
[272] Lieberman, *Cycles*, 289–91.

Once again, defeat summoned a more competent leadership. Although strongmen in four outlying provinces tried to set up their own regimes, the material advantages of the central plain and the memory of Ayudhya's achievement doomed their efforts. Within three years the famed warrior Taksin had reunited Ayudya's domain. This new king's parvenue status – his father was a Teochiu Chinese immigrant and he lacked close ties to the Ayudhyan court – and his religious eccentricity – Taksin discovered physical similarities between himself and the Buddha and reportedly sought to fly through the air – led to his dethronement by aristocratic families headed by the founder of the Chakri dynasty, Rama I (r. 1782–1809). Thereafter Rama I's remarkable personal abilities and his family networks joined with fresh external dangers to forge a more durable elite consensus reminiscent of that in the late 16th century after Ayudhya's first collapse.[273]

The restoration of central authority benefited from another cyclic phenomenon, namely a sudden increase in war prisoners and in *phrai som* and debt-slaves whose lords (*munnai*) had disappeared during the fighting and all of whom now became available for registration as *phrai luang*. Determined to prevent fresh manpower flight, early Chakri leaders continued the practice, initiated apparently by Taksin, of marking *phrai luang* with identifying tattoos, while requiring both *phrai som* and *phrai luang* to do royal corvees and reducing the length of *phrai luang* service. By and large these measures succeeded in halting the flight of *phrai luang* to *phrai som* status.[274]

Providing much of the wealth on which military and administrative reform depended was a rapid growth in overseas commerce. Exports to China, already the mainstay of Ayudhyan trade, were bound to increase, given the cheapness of Siamese rice and other products and a 30 percent jump in the population of Guangdong and Fujian from 1787 to 1812 alone.[275] With economic pressures in south China spurring emigration, and with Chinese in Siam creating labor-intensive enterprises that sucked in fresh compatriots, the Chinese population in Siam soared

---

[273] Gesick, "Kingship," chs. 3, 4; David Wyatt, "Family Politics in Nineteenth Century Thailand," *JSEAH* 9, 2 (1968): 208–28; idem, "The 'Subtle Revolution' of King Ram I of Siam," in Wyatt and Alexander Woodside, eds., *Moral Order and the Question of Change* (New Haven, 1982), 9–52; Klaus Wenk, *The Restoration of Thailand under Rama I 1782–1809* (Tucson, 1968).

[274] Rabibhadana, *Organization*, 56–59. Cf. B. J. Terwiel, "Tattooing in Thailand's History," *JRAS* 1979: 156–66.

[275] Viraphol, *Tribute*, 112.

from perhaps 30,000 in 1767 to 230,000 by 1825.[276] Faced with economic devastation and fresh Burmese invasions, Taksin and Rama I – both with strong ties to the Chinese community – were only too eager, indeed desperate to strengthen the China connection. They therefore increased substantially trade/tribute missions to China, and with Chinese crews developed state trade and royal monopolies to an unprecedented level. Apart from China, which absorbed about a third of Siam's foreign trade, Vietnam, Malaya, Borneo, Sumatra, Java, and (after 1819) Singapore, all with their own vibrant Chinese diasporas, were the most frequent ports of call for Siam-based ships. The southward shift of capital, first to Thonburi and then to Bangkok, symbolized and facilitated this orientation. Whereas maritime trade supplied Late Ayudhya with a fourth to a third of its cash revenues, it provided Taksin and Rama I with over half. In Hong Lysa's view, after the disaster of 1767 the China connection essentially saved the kingdom.[277]

By the 1820s, continued maritime growth had outstripped the system of administered trade. Siamese officials and mushrooming numbers of resident Chinese sent their own junks to sea with rice, sugar, cotton, wood, tin, and other products over which the king claimed no monopoly. Chinese in the countryside also began negotiating directly with producers to secure goods in larger volume and at lower prices than were available to the king's factors. Thus the crown found it more difficult to secure cargoes, and the king's share of overseas trade dwindled. In 1825 some 265 junks visited Bangkok, which had replaced Batavia as the busiest Southeast Asian port; but the crown and Siamese officials as a whole owned only twenty-odd junks. Although Reid's claim of a ten-fold jump in Chinese trade to Siam between 1720 and 1820 cannot easily withstand scrutiny, a two- or three-fold increase in total volume is probable. By 1850, the number of junks entering the port had risen to 331.[278]

---

[276] See n. 237 *supra* and Skinner, *Chinese Society*, 25, 79.

[277] Hong, *Thailand*, ch. 3, esp. pp. 38–43; *The Dynastic Chronicles, Bangkok Era, The First Reign*, Thadeus and Chadin Flood, trs. (Bangkok, 1978), 303; Viraphol, *Tribute*, 152, 181. See too Cushman, "Fields from the Sea," 118 ff.; Yumio Sakurai, "Vietnam and the Fall of Ayudhya," in Jittasevi, *Proceedings*: 143–62.

[278] Shipping figures at Hong, *Thailand*, 52, citing D.E. Malloch; John Crawfurd, *Journal of an Embassy to the Courts of Siam and Cochin China* (rpt., Singapore, 1987), 383, 410, 415; Viraphol, *Tribute*, 55, 72, 186, 188, 194, 239 The claim of a ten-fold increase appears at Reid, *Last Stand*, 12, 71, setting Crawfurd's 1822 claim of 140 Chinese junks against Viraphol's alleged figure of 14–15 junks a century earlier. In fact, the figure of 14–15 at

How did Chakri leaders respond to the new economic climate? Basically they abandoned overseas trading in favor of heavier taxes on the Chinese-stimulated domestic economy, whose vigor kept pace with maritime commerce but which was easier to tap.

As Teochiu, Hainanese, and other Chinese newcomers fanned out along the coast, in the central plain, and the peninsula, they started or expanded tobacco, cotton, pepper, and sugar cultivation, commercial fisheries, poultry-raising, alcohol distilleries, ironworks, shipyards, tin mines, and sugar refineries. Everywhere Chinese entrepreneurs hired indigenes, lured producers to the market, widened credit. At a lower social level, Chinese laborers did the rough work in sugar factories, distilleries, and canal projects. With c. 65,000 Chinese in 1840, the capital became a majority or near-majority Chinese city.[279] Bangkok was not only the basin's chief source of specie and credit, but the most concentrated market for foodstuffs and materiel and a major handicrafts center.

Yet, again it would be wrong to attribute exclusive agency to the Chinese. Between 1780 and 1850 the indigenous Siamese population expanded by perhaps a quarter, and rice acreage by at least that amount.[280] Although foreign demand became increasingly influential around the capital and in coastal districts, between 1780 and 1850 the shift in reclamation from the old delta north of Ayudhya to lands farther south responded substantially to domestic pressures: As late as 1850 annual rice exports rarely equaled 5 percent of the crop and usually were less than

Viraphol, *Tribute*, 55 is only a partial list ("Some Chinese Ships Trading to Siam . . .") – and for 1689, not 1720. Ibid., 72 cited a figure of 110 Chinese junks a year trading to Southeast Asia from Fujian and Guangdong alone c. 1740, of which 70–80 percent went to Siam and Malaya. Smith, "Princes, Nobles," 11, seems to suggest that 200 ships from all sources visited Ayudhya annually during much of the 17th century. Moreover, Crawfurd, *Journal of an Embassy*, 410 claims that in volume – a more useful indicator than ships – "the whole trade between Siam and China" c. 1820 was 561,500 piculs. But in 1722, we have seen that the Kangxi emperor authorized 300,000 piculs of rice from Siam.

[279] On Bangkok's total and Chinese populations, Skinner, *Chinese Society*, 81–83; Larry Sternstein, "The Growth of the Population of the World's Pre-eminent 'Primate City,'" *JSEAS* 15 (1984): 43–68. On Chinese enterprise, Viraphol, *Tribute*, ch. 8; Terwiel, *Travellers' Eyes*, 55–254 *passim*; Skinner, *Chinese Society*, 20–90; Hong, *Thailand*, ch. 3; Jennifer Cushman, "Siamese State Trade and the Chinese Go-Between, 1767–1855," *JSEAS* 12 (1981): 46–61.

[280] See *supra* n. 253, plus Sternstein, "Growth of the Population," Fig. 1. Skinner, *Chinese Society*, 79 estimates 5,200,000 for 1850. All these figures include Chinese. Viraphol, *Tribute*, 86 suggests that total rice cultivation doubled from 1720 to 1850, but offers no breakdown for 1780–1850.

half that.[281] Likewise, the virtual disappearance of round type rice in the basin after 1780, and its retreat at the expense of slender rice in more northerly locales, continued long-standing domestic trends.[282] Starting from an artificially low level in 1767, population growth seems to have reflected most basically the restoration of peace and large-scale deportations to the basin, reinforced perhaps by favorable rainfall. The court itself aided economic expansion by encouraging Chinese immigration and enterprise, widening Khmer and Lao access to the markets of Bangkok, expanding the system of land holding certificates (*chanot*), and building at least five more canals between 1782 and 1840, some of which (although military in origin) facilitated movement to the agricultural frontier.[283]

Above all, Siamese and Lao commoners, responding to domestic as well as foreign demand, undertook new commodity and wage-labor activities on their own initiative or at the urging of their *munnai*. Many *phrai* made a living cutting firewood, boiling sugar, growing yams, quarrying ore, fishing, or producing sea salt.[284] This was obvious in central Siam, but even in the north where Chinese involvement was far more limited, Michael Moerman and Katherine Bowie have pointed to growing specialization, sharper class divisions, labor specialization, and monetization. Yunnanese contributions to northern textile production, for example, were no more significant than Lao or Siamese, and most traders were Tais, rather than Chinese. Junko Koizumi has shown how in the Khorat plateau, where Chinese activity was minimal and which was always regarded as a backwater, peasants by the 1830s had learned to take advantage of changing commodity prices, paying *suai* taxes in kind when the price in Bangkok was low and in cash when the price

---

[281] Ingram, *Economic Change*, 8–9, 24, 29, 41, citing maximum exports of 5 percent and ordinary exports of "less than 2 or 3 percent" (p. 29); and Cushman, "Fields from the Sea," esp. 128, 131–32, citing 2.5 percent. On the other hand, it is unclear if these figures paid sufficient attention to rice exports to Chinese communities in coastal SE Asia. In Vietnam, Li Tana, personal communication, April 6, 2002, suggests such exports were larger than was hitherto appreciated. Note too that if we assume a population of 150,000 and per capita annual paddy consumption of 3.4 piculs, rice purchases to feed the predominantly Chinese city of Bangkok would have been another 2 percent. On the transition to the young delta, see Tanabe, "Land Reclamation," 41 ff.
[282] Watabe, "Development of Rice Cultivation," 10–14.
[283] Tomosugi, *Structural Analysis*, 115–21; Tanabe "Land Reclamation," 41–52; Hubbard, *Inland Waterway*, 28–37; Crawfurd, *Journal of an Embassy*, 380–81; Terwiel, *Travellers' Eyes*, 240–41; Ishii, *Thailand*, 38.
[284] Terwiel, *Travellers' Eyes*, 244 and *passim*.

rose.[285] As in the Irrawaddy basin, regional specialization increased, with the lower Chaophraya basin supplying metals goods and other handicrafts to interior markets as distant as Cambodia.[286] The growing market involvement of commoners – and the lure of consumer goods – appeared too in the changing mix of Chinese imports. Whereas for most of the Late Ayudhya period the chief goods had been luxuries, by the early 1800s they were mass consumption items – ceramics, textiles, food specialties, diverse metal goods – intended not only for the Siamese elite or Chinese, but for broad sectors of Siamese society.[287]

Chakri kings began to exploit internal trade with novel expedients, in effect substituting taxation for direct management. By the time Rama III announced the end of royal trading in 1824, Chinese-run tax farms had demonstrated their value in tapping hitherto inaccessible sources and in stabilizing government income without imposing additional costs. After 1824 tax farms mushroomed to cover a wide array of new commercial activities and products, as well as fresh geographic areas. In this same period, rice taxes were increasingly levied in specie, more services and *suai* payments were commuted, and triennial Chinese poll taxes yielded major additional funds. All told, these changes allowed average annual royal income to rise over ten-fold during 1824 to 1851 compared to the period 1809 to 1824.[288] While much of this went on warfare, it was also used to provide more regular cash gifts to officials and peacetime troops, and to expand the system – begun under Rama II – whereby Chinese wage-laborers built canals and public works once entrusted exclusively to less efficient *phrai luang*. In other words, the shift in the political economy from hereditary service to cash, adumbrated in the early 1700s, now became more pronounced, while some *phrai* became

[285] Michael Moerman, "Chiangkham's Trade in the 'Old Days,'" in Skinner and Kirsch, *Change*, 151–71; Katherine Bowie, "Unraveling the Myth of the Subsistence Economy," *JAS* 51, 4 (1992): 797–823; Junko Koizumi, "The Commutation of *Suai* from Northeast Siam in the Middle of the 19th Century," *JSEAS* 23, 2 (1992): 276–307. See also Constance Wilson, "The Northeast and the Middle Mekong Valley in the Thai Economy: 1830–1870," in *Proceedings of Thai Studies Conference* (Canberra, 1987), 169–90.

[286] Puangthong Rungswasdisab, "War and Trade: Siamese Interventions in Cambodia, 1767–1851" (Univ. of Wollongong Ph.D. diss., 1995), 78.

[287] Cushman, "Fields," 115–12; Terwiel, *Traveller's Eyes*, 94, 213, 235–44; Hong, *Thailand*, 51–56, 135; Crawfurd, *Journal of an Embassy*, 406–407; John Bowring, *The Kingdom and Peoples of Siam*, 2 vols., (London, 1857), I, chs. 6–8.

[288] Hong, *Thailand*, 77. Cf. essays by John Butcher, Anthony Reid, and Constance Wilson in Butcher and Howard Dick, eds., *The Rise and Fall of Revenue Farming* (New York, 1993).

valuable less as a source of corvee than as producers and taxpayers. Thus corvees, already whittled from six to four months, fell to three months in 1810.[289]

In broad terms this tension between fiscal/social categories inherited from the 1600s, on the one hand, and subsequent economic expansion, on the other hand, recalls problems in Kon-baung Burma (or, in varying degrees, Vietnam, Russia, France, and Japan). Tax-farming and commerce enriched ministers who dealt with the Chinese, but it weakened others whose income depended on traditional labor services. Although tattoos now prevented *phrai luang* from becoming *phrai som*, they sought to become informal clients of wealthy ministers through a variety of illegal subterfuges. At the same time, commercially-based ministers took needy officials in other departments under their wing. Thus by mid-century ministerial families again were circumscribing royal authority, and substantial tax revenues were being diverted to private hands.[290]

Why then did the Chakri dynasty not weaken like its predecessor? How was it able to defeat repeated Burmese invasions, to seize the strategic advantage in the northern Tai world, and then to best a reunified and powerful Vietnam in contests for Cambodia and Laos?

However troublesome Siam's problems were, they were no worse, and probably far less serious, than those facing the Kon-baung service system, as discussed in the previous chapter. Furthermore, the trauma of Ayudhya's fall and of continued Burmese threats, followed by competition with Vietnam and after 1826 the danger of British intrusions, may have moderated elite loyalty to family and faction. In reaction to Ayudhya's fall, we shall find that Siam also experienced a movement of Buddhist renewal and cultural exploration that enhanced the symbolic authority of the throne, if not its actual power. Whereas virtually every Late Ayudhya succession had been irregular, tensions

---

[289] On tax changes 1767–1850, Rabibhadana, *Organization*, 57–58, 143; Hong, *Thailand*, 49–55; 75–107; Terwiel, *Travellers' Eyes*, 85, 112–133, 138, 150, 169, 242–54; Wenk, *Restoration*, 27–35. On Bangkok-era property rights, Tomosugi, *Structural Analysis*, 115 ff. However, rather than posit a unilinear decay of the *phrai luang* system, Junko Koizumi, "The Pattern of the *Phrai Luang Khao Duan*, 1830–1850" (ms), and personal communication, July 2001, argues that for some *krom* in the 1830s and 1840s the enrollment of prisoners, a reduction in annual service, and the growing commercial value of services actually increased *phrai luang* rolls.

[290] Rabibhadana, *Organization*, chs. 5–8, esp. 167–70; Wyatt, "Family Politics in Nineteenth Century Thailand," 208–28; Hong, *Thailand*, 94–107; Tomosugi, *Structural Analysis*, 115–16.

surrounding the successions of 1809, 1824, and 1851 did not erupt into violence.[291]

Beyond this, Bangkok's commercial vitality continued to enhance its political influence. Booming revenues let the court expand infrastructural projects, support more officials, and broaden religious patronage. In Laos and the northeast, *muang* leaders seeking access to Bangkok markets for cotton and forest products became more docile, while forest products from northwest Cambodia also found a primary outlet in Bangkok. In the peninsula, Chinese tin-mining licensees became not merely revenue-collectors but investors who assumed the costs of local government.[292] Economic expansion was no less critical to military finance and supply. While we cannot compare gross domestic products, in the early 1820s when maritime statistics first become available, Bangkok's shipping was some five times greater than that of Rangoon and twice that of Vietnamese ports.[293]

In this connection consider again the role of firearms. Here as in the western mainland, insofar as local manufacture and purchase enhanced the possibility of provincial resistance, the effects were not uniformly centripetal.[294] Yet, on balance, Bangkok remained in an enviable position not only because access to foreign technicians and Chinese metals let it manufacture cannon and rifles on a unique scale,[295] but because as in Burma, the best guns still came from overseas. With the expansion of British and American trade and with the founding of British settlements at Penang (1786) and Singapore (1819), Bangkok found it easier to buy quality Western flintlocks (which had replaced the more cumbersome matchlock) as well as cast-iron cannon, ammunition, and shot. In 1777 from one peninsular port alone Siam imported over 2,300 flintlocks. Revealingly, two years earlier the landlocked ruler of Vientiane had asked

---

[291] I follow Wyatt, "Subtle Revolution"; idem, " History and Directionality in the Early Nineteenth-Century Tai World," in Reid, *Last Stand*, 425–43; and Rabibhadana, *Organization*. Yet Thongchai Winichakul, personal communication, Aug. 2001, calls attention to continuing intra-elite conflicts, to the fact that succession was not institutionalized until the 1880s, and to the fortuitous element in some peaceful transitions.

[292] Bunnag, *Provincial Administration*, 20; Jennifer W. Cushman, *Family and State* (Singapore, 1991), 11; Hong, *Thailand*, 92–93; Ngaosyvathn, *Paths*, 50–55; Puangthong Rungswasdisab, "Siam and Control of the Trans-Mekong Trading Networks" (ms).

[293] Victor Lieberman, "Secular Trends in Burmese Economic History c. 1350–1830," *MAS* 25, 1 (1991): 14–15, n. 39; Hong, *Thailand*, 52; and Crawfurd, *Journal of an Embassy*, 513, comparing Chinese trade. Yet ibid., 520, n. seems to offer a considerably higher Vietnamese figure.

[294] Wyatt, personal communication, June 1995.

[295] *CHSEA*, I, 382; Sewell, "Old Siamese Guns"; Hong, *Thailand*, 43.

Taksin not only for 2,000 rifles, but gunnery instructors.[296] Although cannon could not demolish reinforced stone fortifications (mining and scaling were needed for that), during the Burmese wars of 1760–1811 brass and iron artillery and massed rifles proved critical to siege operations, field encounters, and naval warfare. In the 1770s the Siamese developed tactics to coordinate cannon and rifle fire.[297] Whereas only one out of three conscripts in Bangkok's early armies had firearms, by 1827 each soldier sent to suppress a Lao rebellion carried a flintlock. By contrast, the Laos had only a few unreliable muskets, from which they were reduced to shooting pebbles. Lao corpses soon "pile[d] up to form an embankment."[298] To some degree, European and American guns after 1800 also helped to shift the Burman-Siamese strategic balance in favor of Bangkok.

In combination, these developments produced an empire considerably larger, more complex, stable, and powerful than that of either Ayudhya or Angkor. In this same period, of course, the Burmese and Vietnamese empires also reached their apogee before the onset of heavy European involvement (see Figure 1.6).

In the imperial core, as noted, factionalism declined over the Late Ayudhya period. In the third- and fourth-class provinces of the central plains, the upper peninsula, and the Gulf coast, Bangkok sought to supervise more closely gubernatorial deputies (*krommakan*) and to widen the authority of specialized capital departments. Tej Bunnag and Constance Wilson remind us how limited was Bangkok's success, how disordered and dependent on personal ties provincial administration remained even in the late 19th century.[299] Yet by comparison with Ayudhya, capital officials did strengthen control over registration of *phrai* – now tattooed for the first time – land assessments, taxes, and judicial appeals. Contributing to this trend were more generous rewards to provincial officials.[300]

---

[296] E.H.S. Simmonds, "The Thalang Letters, 1773–94," *BSOAS* 26, 3 (1963): 612; Wyatt, *Studies in Thai History* (Chiang Mai, 1994), 191; Junko Koizumi, personal communication, July 2001; Stuart-Fox, *Lao Kingdom*, 122; Crawfurd, *Journal of an Embassy*, 89, 91.

[297] *Chiang Mai Chronicle*, 145. See too Damrong, "Our Wars," *JBRS* 40, 2a; Cyril Skinner, ed., *The Battle for Junk Ceylon* (Dordrecht, Holland, 1985);Viraphol, *Tribute*, 143–45.

[298] Ngaosyvathn, *Paths*, 119; also 168, 174, 194–206. On Burman-Siamese warfare, ibid., esp. 174, n. 61, and *supra* Ch. 2.

[299] Bunnag, *Provincial Administration*, esp. 17–39; articles by Constance Wilson in *Contributions to Asian Studies* 15 (1980).

[300] Terwiel, *Travellers' Eyes*, 198–99, 238–43, 251; Constance Wilson, personal communication, March 31, 1998.

Farther afield, in large quasi-independent provinces like Nakhon Si Thammarat, Songkhla, and Nakhon Ratchasima, governors from influential families jealously guarded their right to appoint subordinates, levy taxes, in some cases even to negotiate with foreigners. Yet here too Bangkok's military superiority and commercial attractions allowed it to integrate local families more effectively into capital patronage networks and for the first time to send commissioners who organized cadastral surveys and tattooed able-bodied men. Whereas in the Late Ayudhya period Nakhon Si Thammarat and Nakon Ratchasima had rebelled repeatedly, in the early Bangkok era governors of these provinces sought to build their fortunes by acting as Bangkok's loyal agents in the drive to absorb, respectively, the northern Malay area and the Khorat plateau. For these governors, revolt had become unthinkable.[301]

At yet greater distances, in Malay areas, Cambodia, and what is now northern Thailand and Laos, the relation between Bangkok and tributary kings remained more ambiguous – comparable in some ways to that of Nakhon Si Thammarat and Nakon Ratchasima in the early 17th century – and force remained a key factor in everyone's calculus. In the peninsula, for example, Bangkok wanted a strategic buffer, while Malay rulers sought to minimize Siamese interference while retaining Siamese protection. Ever rebellious Pattani paid gravely for underestimating Rama I, who split the kingdom into seven jurisdictions and reduced it to provincial status. In 1841 Kedah also was divided. In Kelantan, Trengganu, and Perak as well, military pressure joined local instabilities to accord Bangkok greater influence than Ayudhya had enjoyed.[302]

To the east, Bangkok in 1794 placed under direct Siamese administration the provinces of Battambang and Siem Reap – roughly a third of the Cambodian realm, whose population fell to about a seventh of that of Siam. After Vietnam revived in the early 1800s, Siam faced stiff competition, battening as usual on Khmer factionalism. In 1835 the central and eastern parts of Cambodia passed into the Vietnamese

---

[301] Gesick, "Kingship," ch. 5, esp. 153–175; Bunnag, *Provincial Administration*, 17–31; Ngaosyvathn, *Paths*, 53–55 and *passim*; Suwannathat-Pian, *Thai-Malay Relations*, 6–7, 66–72; Andayas, *Malaysia*, 116–22.

[302] Suwannathat-Pian, *Thai-Malay Relations*, chs. 2–6; Bonney, *Kedah*, ch. 7; Thongchai Winichakul, *Siam Mapped* (Honolulu, 1994), 81–88; Andayas, *Malaysia*, 106–108; *Rama III and the Siamese Expedition to Kedah in 1839*, Syril Skinner, tr. (Clayton, Australia, 1993).

sphere. But after an anti-Vietnamese uprising, Bangkok gained the upper hand and by 1848 again had become dominant at the Khmer court.[303]

In the Lao world Siam achieved a yet more convincing hegemony. After driving out the Burmese, Taksin and Rama I pressured rulers of smaller *muang* on the west bank of the Mekong to transfer allegiance to Siam from Vientiane, Luang Prabang, and Champassak. Bangkok then proceeded to reduce the newly annexed *muangs'* autonomy by changing boundaries, raising corvee demands, tattooing tax-payers (the "red-iron policy"), and countenancing or promoting wholesale enslavement of upland tribal peoples. Resistance followed. In 1791 and 1817 millenarian "holy men" uprisings among upland peoples in southern Laos were savagely suppressed by Siamese garrisons assisted on the latter occasion by Vientiane.[304] Far more ominous, in 1827 the ruler of Vientiane himself, Anuvong, exasperated by Siamese slights, declared his independence and with help from rulers in Khorat and his son at Champassak, sent armies to within three days march of Bangkok. Thus Anuvong sought to reconstitute the once mighty realm of Lan Sang. In timing and inspiration, his revolt recalls the anti-Vietnamese Khmer revolt of 1840 and Mon uprisings against Upper Burma from 1740–1826 – but like the latter anti-centralizing efforts, it proved deeply counterproductive. Captured, Anuvong was tortured to death. Vientiane was utterly destroyed, its population deported to the west bank. Although some western Lao *muang* retained considerable autonomy, Lan Sang's royal legacy was preserved only at impoverished Luang Prabang, which tried to keep its balance by paying tribute to Hue and Beijing as well as to Bangkok.[305]

Lan Na, once the third great Tai contender, escaped Burmese control only to enter Bangkok's orbit as well after 1776. In return for defending the north and providing substantial tribute and trade goods, Bangkok allowed Chiang Mai's ruler to expand his regional authority and to repopulate the old Lan Na kingdom, not least by raiding the Burmese

[303] Wyatt, *Thailand*, 173–73; Chandler, *History*, chs. 6, 7 (population estimate, p. 100); Puangthong, "War and Trade," chs. 4–7.
[304] Constance Wilson, "The Holy Man in the History of Thailand and Laos," *JSEAS* 28 (1997): 345–64, esp. 357–59; Ngaosyvathan, *Paths*, 47–49.
[305] Stuart-Fox, *Lao Kingdom*, 106–37, Ngaosyvathn, *Paths*. On Vietnamese influence in NE Laos, Snit Smuckarn and Kennon Breazeale, *A Culture in Search of Survival: The Phuan of Thailand and Laos* (New Haven, 1988), 11, 32–38.

Shan states.[306] Farther west Bangkok began incorporating Karen leaders into the lower ranks of the imperial hierarchy.[307]

Thus virtually all of the central mainland came under some degree of Siamese authority. Far from having reached a natural conclusion, the centuries-long division of the mainland into Burmese, Siamese, and Vietnamese spheres still was still in full spate when the British, and more especially the French froze it in the third quarter of the 19th century. Predictably, in the early 1820s as the tripartition progressed, Kon-baung Burma asked Vietnam to join in a pincers attack on Siam, albeit without success.[308]

CULTURAL INTEGRATION IN THE IMPERIAL CORE,
c. 1600–1830

During this era of sustained consolidation, c. 1600 and 1830, what was happening to Siamese religious expression, literature, and ethnicity? At first sight, here as in Burma many such changes were contradictory. Siamese culture grew more cosmopolitan and religiously orthodox even as it became more distinct within the Tai world. Elite culture grew more complex even as the gap between elite and popular usages diminished. Political theory provided little or no space for proto-nationalism, and deportations magnified ethnic diversity at the same time as capital norms of language, ritual, and self-identification pervaded provincial society. How could such contrary trends proceed simultaneously? To repeat, in culture no less than in economics and administration, more inclusive and complex systems automatically engendered more specialized sub-functions.

This section focuses on the imperial heartland, that is to say, the Chaophraya basin, the southeast coast, the western Khorat plateau, and the upper peninsula. I will first consider processes governing cultural change and then the contours of that change (although, in practice, so neat a division is not always possible).

In Siam as in the western mainland, arguably the most critical spur to vertical and horizontal acculturation was the spread of monastic schools

---

[306] *Chiang Mai Chronicle*, chs. 7, 8; Wyatt, *Thailand*, 155–56. With Bangkok's blessing Nan also revived.
[307] Ronald Renard, "The Role of the Karens in Thai Society During the Early Bangkok Period, 1782–1873," *Contributions to Asian Studies* 15 (1980): 15–27.
[308] List 93, #4, NL 747, pp. 1–5; Ngaosyvathn, *Paths*, 96–100.

and libraries and the concomitant growth in Buddhist literacy. Recall the evidence that from the 14th to the early 16th centuries, *phrai* culture was intensely local and fundamentally illiterate, with monastic education – and by implication, monastic ordination – an unusual luxury. But 19th-century accounts indicate that monasteries were widely distributed and ordination, normally for one season at the onset of adulthood, extremely common, if not quite universal. Boys could acquire basic Tai literacy in six months, and usually studied for at least a couple years from age five or six. Those about to undergo ordination generally underwent a second period of instruction. As a result of this system, reinforced by practical opportunities for the exercise of adult literacy (see below), even among lower class rural males – agriculturalists, fishermen, woodcutters – vernacular literacy was widespread, though perhaps less so than in Burma. We lack Burmese-style censuses, but Europeans claimed that male literacy (depending on locale and definition) ranged from 20 percent to well over 50 percent.[309] Notwithstanding the functional autonomy and the wide ritual variety of rural monasteries,[310] a venerable Theravada tradition of textual purification joined with monastic exchanges and royal patronage to ensure that syllabaries, Tai and Pali texts, and instruction were reasonably uniform. Here as in Burma, monasteries thus tended to promote a common outlook that instinctively favored textual norms over local notions of sanctity.[311] Nor, as a result of folklore, annual festivals, bi-weekly monastic sermons, and other informal channels, were illiterates insulated from such currents.

The question is: When and why did the network of rural monasteries expand? Statistics and chronological markers are pitifully few. Seventeenth-century European accounts described what may have been a transitional phase when monasteries were more widely distributed than in the Early Ayudhya period, but when, by Chakri standards, access

---

[309] On literacy among Siamese, as well as among Siamese Mons (said to be 2/3 male literate), see D. E. Malloch in *The Burney Papers*, 5 vols. (rpt., Westmead, UK, 1971), II, iv, 230 ("there are but few amongst the Coolies who cannot read and write"); J.B. Pallegoix, *Description du royaume Thai ou Siam*, 2 vols. (Paris, 1854), I, 226; Terwiel, *Travellers' Eyes*, 41, 59, 157–58, 179, 221–24, 251–52; Gesick, *Lady White Blood*, 57–58 and *passim*. On pre-1850 monastic education and ordination, also David Wyatt, *The Politics of Reform in Thailand* (New Haven, 1969), ch. 1; Bowring, *Kingdom and People*, I, ch. 11; Crawfurd, *Journal of an Embassy*, 338–42, 350–72; B. J. Terwiel, *Window on Thai History* (Bangkok, 1989), 99–104.

[310] Kamala, *Forest Recollections*, 5–7, 18–40.

[311] Aeusrivongse, "Ayudhya," 183–84; Wyatt, *Reform*, 17–23; la Loubere, *Kingdom*, 115–17; Kamala, *Forest Recollections*, 23–38.

to education remained geographically and socially restricted. Thus, on the one hand, European visitors commented favorably on the degree of literacy in Siam, and la Loubere, in describing monks who stayed in the fields following the rice harvest, apparently referred to village monks.[312] Van Vliet's claim that some 60,000 monks lived outside the capital also suggests an extensive provincial network. On the other hand, van Vliet noted that that monastic education was restricted to "the children of decent people," meaning presumably the *munnai* elite, rather than the peasantry. And if provincial cities duplicated the capital's hugely disproportionate share of the *sangha*, the number of monks available to village communities may have been limited.[313]

During the Late Ayudhya period, we may assume that the proliferation of monasteries benefited from internal pacification, Tai migrants' cumulative familiarity with Buddhist culture, population growth, and commercial intensification. Larger aggregate and possibly per capita wealth allowed villagers to pay for monasteries, libraries, and manuscripts, and to support larger numbers of economically unproductive monks and students. Between 1760 and 1810, moreover, Wyatt has argued that military disasters induced many Tai communities to improve their karma lest those catastrophes be repeated. This yearning for the comfort of eternal verities, he argues, underlay astonishingly vigorous local movements to build monasteries and to amass libraries of sacred texts.[314]

State demands and commerce promoted literacy for non-religious functions as well. The growing volume of tax records and legal documents gave clerk-trainees and ambitious *phrai* a practical incentive to acquire or upgrade literacy and numeracy skills in local monasteries.[315] Likewise, headmen and low-level officials had to register *phrai* on a regular basis, ex-soldiers had to carry exemption papers, and traders received receipts for transport taxes that self-interest demanded they be able to read. Written contracts for land sales and mortgages, the issuance

---

[312] La Loubere, *Kingdom*, 114–16. See too Schouten, *True Description*, 147; Wyatt, *Reform*, 9–10, esp. n. 23; Siamese references in Marcelo de Ribadeneira, *History of the Philippines and Other Kingdoms* (Manila, 1970), I, 429–30.

[313] "Van Vliet's Description," 76, 87–88. Roughly 25 percent of the kingdom's more than 80,000 monks lived in the city of Ayudhya, which had only about 5 percent of the kingdom's population.

[314] David Wyatt, "History and Directionality."

[315] Note the functionalist emphasis in "van Vliet's Description," 88: "When they have learned enough to fill government positions, they are glad to put off the yellow robes."

of certificates (*chanot*) to certify land tax payments, the provision of tax-farming receipts, and the production of commercial ephemera provided similar literacy incentives for common cultivators and tax-payers. Even slave sales required written contracts, which in the case of resale, were entrusted to the slave himself or his guarantor.[316]

Nor was wider literacy the only mechanism of cultural exchange. As in Burma, colonists disseminated central norms of dialect, dress, ritual, and social organization, while professional entertainers, moving along trade and pilgrimage routes, spread dramatic and poetic conventions. By the 1680s at least five types of popular entertainment were performed by such troupes at funerals, temple dedications, marriages, and tonsures. Drawing on the Ramayana, Jatakas, and royal histories, these performances idealized a Buddhist social order centered on the throne.[317] In the towns commercial intensification joined with the 1760s decimation of *khunnang* families to weaken the status regime of Ayudhya, and by implication, to promote cross-class communication. Rama I complained that his pages included men from humble commercial backgrounds who lacked "proper" connections with the former ruling elite and who had no sense of "shame" or "right and wrong." To his dismay and that of older officials, insignia once reserved for the very highest ministers (such as silk gowns embroidered with gold thread and certain kinds of parasols) now had become popular among lowly officials and wealthy merchants.[318] As we shall see, the cultural counterpart to social mobility was closer popular embrace of Buddhist orthodoxy and greater elite interest in popular literary and linguistic conventions.

As in Burma, the courts of Ayudhya and Bangkok self-consciously sought to exert a normative influence by convening Buddhist councils, purifying the *Tipitaka*, supporting Pali examinations and honoring

---

[316] La Loubere, *Kingdom*, 11; Terwiel, *Window on Thai History*, 104; Tomosugi, *Structural Analysis*, 112–14; Hong, *Thailand*, 98; Wenk, *Thai Literature*, 56–57; "van Vliet's Description," 87–88; Rabibhadana, *Organization*, 105–106.

[317] These entertainments were masked drama (*khon*), dance-drama without masks (*lakhon*), shadow-puppet theater, marionette theater, and sing-song recitation (*sepha*). It is unclear how professional rural entertainers were in the late 17th-century. See Schweisguth, *Litterature*, 59–65, 144–45; James Brandon, *Theatre in Southeast Asia* (Cambridge, MA, 1967), 61–66; la Loubere, *Kingdom*, 47–49, 68–69; Mattani Rutnin, ed., *The Siamese Theatre* (Bangkok, 1975), 1–8, 115–20; Terry Miller and Jarernchai Chonpairot, "A History of Siamese Music Reconstructed from Western Documents, 1505–1932," *Crossroads* 8 (1994); E. H. S. Simmonds, "Thai Narrative Poetry," *Asia Major* n.s. 10 (1964): 279–99.

[318] Junko Koizumi, "Women and Marriage in Premodern Siam" (ms), 13–14. Cf. Rabibhadana *Organization*, chs. 7, 8.

monks who excelled in these tests. On at least one occasion in the 17th century, the crown defrocked "several thousand" monks who failed their examinations.[319] The king and leading courtiers also patronized monasteries in the capital which served as imperial universities and which attracted from throughout the kingdom laymen as well as monks eager to study medicine, astrology, law, literature, as well as religion.

Less intentional in their cultural effects but no less significant were public rituals and service rotas. Youths from influential families who trained as court pages, and provincial officials and their entourages who visited the capital for homage festivals, transmitted to their home districts capital patterns of architecture, dress, poetry, ritual, and speech. Increasingly, Central Thai became the lingua franca for communications between the capital and provincial officials and monks. Anthony Diller argues that from at least the 1700s, exchanges of this sort facilitated both the spread of Central Thai among elites in the peninsula and the mixing of Central Thai vocabulary with Southern-Tai tones.[320] In the central plain, presumably, linguistic and cultural exchanges were yet more intensive. Certainly, the constant movement of royal servicemen to and from the capital, for corvees as well as trade, exposed vast numbers of commoners from central provinces to the dialect and customs of the capital. The observations of Christian missionaries in 1841 applied no less forcefully to earlier periods: "The Siamese are almost . . . as much in the habit of coming several times a year to Bangkok, as the Jews were of going up to Jerusalem to worship." "[T]here is an immense influx and efflux of people at Bangkok, entirely disconnected from commercial transactions. Every male may be brought into the service of government every fourth month. Many avoid actual service by the payment of a sum of money . . . Still it is certain that vast numbers do spend their three months yearly at Bangkok, in performing various kinds of government service. . . . It may well be doubted whether there is another country in the world, of equal magnitude with this, every part of which

---

[319] Loubere, *Kingdom*, 115. On monastic organization and patronage, too idem, 113–19; "van Vliet's Description," 88; Gervaise, *Natural History*, 145–52; Yoneo Ishii, *Sangha, State, and Society* (Honolulu, 1986), 59–66; idem, "Religious Patterns and Economic Change in Siam in the Sixteenth and Seventeenth Centuries," in Reid, *Early Modern Era*, 180–94; Wyatt, *Reform*, 17–18; Craig Reynolds, "The Buddhist Monkhood in Nineteenth Century Thailand" (Cornell Univ. Ph.D. diss., 1972), 1–62, 155–59.

[320] Anthony Diller, "Reflections on Tai Diglossic Mixing," *Orbis* 32, 1–2 (1987): 147–66; idem, letter of March 2, 1988. On provincial-capital exchanges, also Simmonds, "Thai Narrative Poetry."

can be so easily and effectually reached by a missionary stationed at one point."[321] Mixing laborers from different *krom*, as for example, in the royal shipyards, had a similar potential impact.[322]

Finally, we shall see that warfare encouraged emotive popular identification with the capital. This it did by generating anti-Burmese stereotypes, by mixing local units in imperial armies, and by encouraging psychological dependence on the throne.

To be sure, in central Thailand as in the Irrawaddy basin, both the weakness and the strength of these impulses set limits to cultural uniformity. These impulses were too anemic insofar as poor communications, still limited commodification, and the continuing remoteness of capital administration and ceremony failed to rupture local cacoons. In the 1960s Tai-speakers in modern Thailand spoke over 50 local dialects, which was surely a substantial reduction from the early 19th century.[323] Even in the central basin, when remnants of the Ayudhya court moved a mere fifty miles to Bangkok, speech differences between social classes were aggravated by dialect differences between districts. What was true of language applied as well to dress, social custom, and ritual. Nineteenth-century provincial monks traveled on horseback, performed heavy labor, delivered sermons in a theatrical manner, and followed other customs that Bangkok authorities considered deeply unworthy.[324] Lorraine Gesick and Kamala Tiyavanich's emphasis on idiosyncratic pre-modern local sensibilities is therefore entirely salutary.[325] In this sense, integration did not go far enough.

Political and commercial integration went too far, that is to say, it crosscut homogeneity, by constantly promoting fresh distinctions in ethnicity and class behavior. As the crown deported prisoners from outlying areas to the central basin, it created ethnically distinct settlements. In the 1680s Gervaise claimed that over a third of the people in central Siam were "foreigners," descended chiefly from Lao and Mon war

---

[321] Quotes from *The Missionary Herald*, 37 (1841), 200, 434, both cited in Sternstein, "Pre-eminent Primate City," 49.

[322] Koizumi, "Pattern of *Phrai Luang*," 8.

[323] Anthony Diller, "What Makes Central Thai a National Language?" in Craig Reynolds, ed., *National Identity and Its Defenders* (Clayton, Australia, 1991), 97, citing J. Marvin Brown. On Tai linguistic classification and history, see ibid., 87–132; Brown, *Ancient Thai to Modern Dialects*; William A. Smalley, *Linguistic Diversity and National Unity* (Chicago, 1994).

[324] Kamala, *Forest Recollections*, ch. 1.

[325] Gesick, *Lady White Blood*, 12, 14, 48–51, 61, 70 and *passim*; Kamala, *Forest Recollections*.

captives.[326] In the early 19th century massive deportations designed to remedy depopulation caused by the Burmese wars joined with voluntary Mon migrations to raise the proportion yet higher. All told, Laos, Mons, Khmers, Burmese, and Malays may have equaled the number of self-identified Siamese in the central basin.[327] Phuan, Lao, Cham, and Khmer peasant units formed the backbone of the standing army and navy around Bangkok.[328] On the Khorat plateau after Anuvong's revolt of 1827 so many Lao deportees were resettled that they may have become as numerous as Siamese-speakers within the kingdom as a whole. Sheer numbers, as among the Lao, or endogamous service roles, as among Mons and Phuan, set strict barriers to assimilation. Mons, for example, tended to retain their own spirit hierarchies, writing system, festivals, and ecclesiastic jurisdictions.[329] The massive influx of Chinese created yet another distinctive group whose concentration in trade and tax farming engendered hostility – and occasional violence – from Siamese and Lao peasants.[330]

Commercialization and growing tax burdens also may have encouraged a sharper sense of opposition between many commoners and the *munnai* elite. In 1581, 1694, and 1698 *phrai* resentment of government demands coincided with poor harvests and disorders in the capital to inspire rural uprisings led by miracle-working "holy men" whose visions of local autonomy and social equality challenged Ayudhyan hierarchy. During the early Bangkok period, as noted, antigovernment "holy men" revolts shifted from the lowlands towards the imperial periphery, where slave hunts and massacres were devastating hill communities.[331] But if Siamese *phrai* themselves no longer resisted physically, Peter Vandergeest suggests that through shadowplays and folk-brahmanical practices they continued to mock *munnai* and monastic

---

[326] Gervaise, *Natural History*, 57.

[327] David Wyatt, personal communication, June, 1995; Terwiel, *Travellers' Eyes*, 253–54 *et passim*.

[328] Smuckarn and Breazeale, *Culture in Search*, 125–26.

[329] Terwiel, *Travellers' Eyes*, 59–254 *passim*; Brian Foster, "Ethnic Identity of the Mons in Thailand," *JSS* 61 (1973): 203–23; idem, *Commerce and Ethnic Differences* (Athens, OH: 1982); Dhiravat, "Political History," 76; Rabibhadana, *Organization*, 17 nn.; Smuckarn and Breazeale, *Culture in Search*, 125–28.

[330] Terwiel, *Travellers' Eyes*, 80, 170, 175, 254.

[331] Wilson, "Holy Man," esp. 352–64; Chatthip Nartsupha, "The Ideology of 'Holy Men' Revolts in North East Thailand," in Andrew Turton and Shigeharu Tanabe, eds., *History and Peasant Consciousness in South East Asia* (Osaka, 1984), 111–34;" Ngaosyvathn, *Paths*, 46–49.

pretensions and to champion an alternative society in which peasants and "holy men" enjoyed pride of place.[332] On the other side of the social divide, verbal and written codes at Ayudhya continued to use recondite vocabulary of Pali or Sanskrit origin that expressly sought to separate the business of government from common speech. Such perspectives were enshrined in the enormously influential 17th-century *Chindamani* (*Gems of Thought*) textbook for scribes and officials.[333] Rama I and his heirs proscribed cockfighting, linga-worship, and animal sacrifices, and repeated Ayudhyan bans on alcohol. If these reforms, which paralleled Kon-baung measures, reflected a sincere textualist current, they also said something about the disdain with which many elite writers in the early Bangkok era treated peasant customs.[334]

As the number of authors and readers grew in the 18th and early 19th centuries, elite culture itself exhibited a remarkable penchant for novelty and specialization, hence also for fracture. As we shall see shortly, new poetic meters and literary styles vied for attention among litterateurs. From the late 1600s a southern-based tradition of royal chronicles (*phongsawadan*) written by officials and focusing on the history of the monarchy, expanded alongside a northern-derived genre of local histories (*tamnan*) and universal Buddhist histories.[335] Visions of textually-pure Buddhism inspired not only attacks on peasant custom, but reformist currents within the circle of the court itself, most notably the future king Mongkut's Thammayut movement of the 1830s, which at first met bitter resentment from the ecclesiastical hierarchy.[336]

Uneven exposure to foreign contacts, which were concentrated among officials and senior monks, provided a final source of tension.

---

[332] Peter Vandergeest, "Hierarchy and Power in Pre-National Buddhist States," *MAS* 27, 4 (1993): 843–70, focusing not on the basin, but 19th century Songkhla. Cf. Mary Grow, "Tarnishing the Golden Era," in E. Paul Durrenberger, ed., *State Power and Culture in Thailand* (New Haven, 1996), 47–67.

[333] Terwiel, "Introduction of Indian Prosody," 307–23. See too Thomas Hudak, "Poetic Conventions in Thai *Chan* Meters," *JAOS* 105 (1985): 107–17.

[334] Nidhi Aeusrivongse, "The Early Bangkok Period: Literary Change and Its Social Causes," *Asian Studies Review* 18 (1994): 71–74, esp. n. 8; Wenk, *Restoration*, 35–42; Rabibhadana, *Organization*, 44; "van Vliet's Description," 20–21; la Loubere, *Kingdom*, 22–23, 93–94.

[335] Thongchai Winichakul, personal communication, Aug., 2001 has kindly updated Charnvit Kasetsiri, "Thai Historiography from Ancient Times to the Modern Period," in Anthony Reid and David Marr, eds., *Perceptions of the Past in Southeast Asia* (Singapore, 1979), 156–60, and David Wyatt, "Chronicle Traditions in Thai Historiography," in Cowan and Wolters, *History and Historiography*, 107–22.

[336] Reynolds, "Buddhist Monkhood," Ch. 3, esp. p. 65; Kamala, *Forest Recollections*, 5–7.

During the 17th-century height of Muslim influence, Narai is said to have modeled his harem, architecture, dress, and cuisine on Persian practices. Shortly thereafter, the *Chindamani* textbook may have been influenced by French missionary pedagogy.[337] From the late 1700s, the court encouraged adaptations and translations from a wide range of Asian literatures, including Malay/Javanese Panji stories, the Chinese historical novel *Romance of the Three Kingdoms*, a 16th-century Mon royal epic, the *Mahabharata* of India, the Sinhalese *Mahavamsa*, and Persian tales. More than mere entertainment, many such works were regarded by literati and *khunnang* – their main audience – as embodying political and martial wisdom and appropriate modes of behavior.[338]

In sum, the very growth of the state, wider literacy, and burgeoning foreign contacts ensured that Siamese culture, especially in the core and especially among the elite, became more variegated and experimental. My main point, however, is that these very processes also ensured a more rapid circulation of basic symbols and ideas. As vertical and horizontal exchange accelerated, local ethnicities, class-specific behaviors, new high culture variants, and foreign-derived conventions all tended to function as sub-specialties within an increasingly coherent, interdependent, mutually-referent system. I shall sketch integrative trends in three spheres: a growing cross-class exchange of literary and artistic conventions, a wider acceptance of Buddhist textual norms, and a stronger ethnic and political identification with the Siamese throne.

Compared to that of Ayudhya, Bangkok court literature was more lively, colorful, and heavily influenced by both village tradition and the urban milieu. At Ayudhya the metrical patterns of court poetry were elaborate, flowery, stilted, and far removed from the everyday language and word-play of the villages. Court literature served primarily didactic and ritual purposes, while folk poetry was recited but not written. In the closing decades of the Ayudhya period, much as in Kon-baung Burma, these two traditions began to converge, culminating in a truly novel literature in the early 19th century. In Siam a principal characteristic of these new works was the triumph of the simpler *klon* meter, ultimately derived from vernacular folk sources. At the same time

---

337 Sanjay Subrahmanyam, "Iranians Abroad," *JAS* 51 (1992): 349, citing J. Aubin; Wyatt, *Reform*, 21–22; Wenk, *Thai Literature*, 11.
338 Schweisguth, *Litterature*, 157–59, 179–238; Wenk, *Thai Literature*, 28–64; Wyatt, "Subtle Revolution," 36, 42. Chinese, and to a lesser extent Mon and Malay, models inspired elite drama and music. Miller and Chonpairot, "Siamese Music," 33–48; Tachard, *Relation* 186.

the public ritual functions of Ayudhya court poetry atrophied in favor of a greater emphasis on private reading for sheer entertainment and personal edification. Significantly perhaps, the early Bangkok period produced the first popular textbook for learning to read Thai.[339] Prose, chiefly of a fictional character, now became far more prevalent, comprising about half of total writings after 1780 and again reflecting more plebeian narrative traditions and presumably a wider readership. Likewise, *lakhon* drama, probably of popular origins, penetrated the court in the early 18th century (although court and popular forms subsequently diverged). Most revealing, as Nidhi Aeusrivongse and Junko Koizumi have pointed out, were changes in subject matter and tone. Much poetry and prose in the early Bangkok period abandoned the fanciful domain of supra-mortals for familiar social settings. Personal emotions tended to replace stereotyped expression, and stylized scenes yielded to closely textured observation. Towns were no longer sites permeated by the mystical might of kings, but mundane places of enjoyment and eccentricity where diverse peoples and occupations mingled. Whereas commerce in the Ayudhya period was a low-status calling unsuitable for kings, trade and traders appeared frequently in Bangkok literature, often as part of the eulogy of the king or his realm. Heroes' success reflected high birth less than education and self-mastery, so that literature became more humanistic and characterization, more complex. In keeping with this interest in subjectivity, women began to figure as actors with independent emotional needs.[340] Similarly, Bangkok religious literature placed a novel emphasis on people's capacity for change, on their ability to measure the rules by which they lived against a rational understanding of Buddhism. This outlook, along with a corresponding devaluation of animism and Hinduism, infused the massive literary corpus sponsored by Rama I that included a new edition of the Three Worlds cosmology, a completely new recension of the Scriptures, a new verse rendition of the Ramayana epic, a codification of Siamese law, and a new royal history.[341]

---

[339] Aeusrivongse, "Early Bangkok Period," 70.

[340] Discussion follows Aeusrivongse, "Early Bangkok Period," 69–76; Aeusrivongse's Thai-language work summarized by Wyatt, "Subtle Revolution," 36–38; Junko Koizumi, "Women and Marriage in Pre-Modern Siam" (ms); idem, "From a Water Buffalo to a Human Being," in Andaya, *Other Pasts*, 254–68; Wenk, *Literature*, chs. 3–5, esp. p. 30–64; Schweisguth, *Litterature*, chs. 6–13; Manas Chitakasem, "The Emergence and Development of the Nirat Genre in Thai Poetry," *JSS* 60 (1972): 135–68; Brandon, *Theatre*, 62, 64.

[341] Wyatt, "Subtle Revolution," 16, 20–40, and *passim*. On Buddhist rationalism, also Wenk, *Thai Literature*, 36; Aeusrivongse, "Early Bangkok Period," 73–74.

In these ways broader social currents influenced elite literature. But at the same time, royal patronage, wider literacy, commercialization, and so forth worked to spread court and capital norms down the social scale and into the countryside. Thus village monastic libraries commonly included alongside religious texts a substantial number of works of law, literature, medicine, mathematics, and history that became available to educated laymen as well as monks. We must assume from their rapid and costly proliferation that these manuscripts had a significance that was not purely symbolic. E. H. S. Simmonds, for example, has shown how the dissemination of texts helped to spread court styles of narrative poetry in the countryside to the detriment of country compositions.[342] Although originally centered at court, the new *phongsawadan* histories also influenced writing at provincial monasteries. Similarly, Chinese theatre and other dramatic forms moved from the court to lower urban and rural strata.[343]

In this connection I see the aforementioned growth among the Bangkok elite of Buddhist rationalism as a precocious, articulate expression of a reorientation found in some degree throughout society. Admittedly, the court's social vision remained suspicious of popular religion and extravagantly hierarchical. Yet by themselves, hostility to "corrupt" practices (including linga-worship and animal sacrifices) and a conviction that pure texts provided the best guarantee of moral order did not distinguish Rama I from those itinerant monks and local lay leaders who rebuilt monasteries and amassed libraries in the countryside. If religious reform was not a mass movement, neither was it the exclusive conceit of a few individuals in the capital. If we compare the early Bangkok to the early Ayudhya period, changing rural sensibilities appear in the spread of village monasteries, the wider distribution of religious texts, and the acceptance of near-universal peasant ordination. More orthodox sensibilities also seem to have inspired local chroniclers, laymen as well as monks. Thus Wyatt has shown that whereas 15th-century north Thai chroniclers viewed the world in primarily animist terms, their early-19th century successors saw Buddhism as central to their ritual complex and to their understanding of the

---

[342] Simmonds, "Thai Narrative Poetry," esp. 290. On the dissemination of secular texts, also Wyatt, "History and Directionality," 433–35; idem, "Subtle Revolution," 37–38.

[343] Miller and Chonpairot, "Siamese Music," 36–37; Simmonds, "Thai Narrative Poetry," 281, 289, 291.

moral order.[344] In short, both elite and popular religion grew more self-consciously orthodox, textual, and intolerant of syncretism. In timing and substance these steps therefore paralleled changes in Kon-baung Burma.

Finally, again as in Burma, cultural standardization fostered a closer ethnic and political identification with the throne. Limited data has joined with nationalist assumptions about the primordial character of Thai "nationality" to preclude serious consideration of how the medley of Mon-, Khmer-, and Tai-speakers who inhabited the lower Chaophraya basin in the mid-1300s became "Siamese." Recall Tome Pires' claim that in early 16th-century Siam the hairstyle and customs of the common "people, and almost the language, are like those of [Mon] Pegu."[345] If Pires' account is credible – and I hasten to recall that it concurs with Nidhi Aeusrivongse's research – it suggests that as late as 1515, many or most *phrai* still did not identify with the Tai-language "Siamese" culture of the *munnai* elite. Why and when did "Siamese" features penetrate to lower strata? And what subjective political significance – if any – did adoption of a "Siamese" identity entail?

Sixteenth-century Burmese sources referred to inhabitants of the lower Chaophraya basin as the "people" or "soldiers of Ayudhya" (*yo-daya-tha, yo-daya si-tha*);[346] while Europeans, following Malay or Peguan usage, called the kingdom "Anseam," "Siam," and the people "Siames."[347] But these accounts say nothing about how far elite ethnicity had penetrated into the peasantry. How much should we read into this 1630s account by van Vliet?: "In general the Siamese are . . . cowardly soldiers, but cruel towards the subdued enemy, or to those who are rejected by the king . . . Also they are proud and fancy that no other nation can be compared with them, and that their laws, customs, and learning are better than anywhere else on earth."[348] In the 1680s Gervaise was

---

[344] Wyatt, "History and Directionality," 432–36; idem, "Southeast Asia 'Inside Out,'" 689–709; idem, "Presidential Address," 1080–81. Of course, Chiang Mai and Nan sensibilities cannot be transferred automatically to the central plain.

[345] See *supra* n. 186.

[346] E.g., "Han-tha-wadi hsin-byu-shin ayei-daw-bon" in Hsaya U Bi et al., eds., *Ayei-daw-bon nga-zaung-dwe* (Rangoon, n.d.), 433, 475 *et passim*.

[347] Henry Yule and A. C. Burnell, *Hobson-Jobson* (London, 1903), 833–34; Mansel Longworth Dames, ed., *The Book of Duarte Barbosa*, 2 vols. (rpt., New Delhi, 1989), II, 162–63; la Loubere, *Kingdom*, 6–7.

[348] "Van Vliet's Description," 82. Cf. the late 16th-century account in Ribadeneira, *History of the Philippines*, I, 423: "They love their country loyally, and would give anything to prove Siam is better than any other kingdom, or nation."

more sociologically instructive. Having declared that over a third of the population in basin was descended from Mon, Lao, and other war-captives, Gervaise went on to observe, "Today they have merged so completely with the Siamese that it is quite difficult to tell them apart." Only vestigial differences in body adornment and dress remained between indigenous peasants and descendants of deportees.[349] Accounts by French missionaries c. 1730 suggest that religion was a key determinant of inclusion: descendants of Catholic Portuguese and Muslims long remained distinct, but Khmers, Laos, and Peguans – all fellow Theravadins – readily became Siamese.[350] If the host peasant population was capable of such effective absorption, it is reasonable to assume that by the late 17th century, at latest: a) local *phrai* had adopted many "Siamese" traits in religious ritual, adornment, and speech which in the 1400s had been associated preeminently with the *munnai*; and b) in consequence of these changes, when dealing with people who originated outside the basin, local *phrai* had come to regard themselves as "Siamese." Whereas in Lower Burma warfare and lateral displacement accelerated assimilation of the original population of Mon-speakers to elite imperial culture, in the Chaophraya basin a similar result apparently occurred through peaceful vertical exchange.

By the early Bangkok period, even common cultivators exhibited the national vanity of which van Vliet wrote, if we follow John Crawfurd's 1822 account: "The lowest [Siamese] peasant considers himself superior to the proudest and most elevated subject of any other country. They speak openly of themselves and their country as models of perfection; and the dress, manners, customs, features, and gait of strangers, are to them objects of ridicule. . . . [T]here can be no question but that the Siamese . . . half naked and enslaved, are yet the vainest people in the East."[351] Of course, Siamese continued to speak a variety of dialects and to define themselves in most contexts in local terms. Boundaries between so-called Siamese, Laos, and other groups remained situationally fluid. Nor when distinctions *were* made, is it always clear what criteria – language, dress, hairstyle, religion, self-description – told most heavily. Nonetheless, Bangkok-era censuses identified people in particular areas by ethnicity ("Siamese," "Lao," "Chinese," "Peguers," "Khmer,"

---

[349] Gervaise, *Natural History*, 57–58.
[350] Alain Forest, *Les missionnaires francais au Tonkin et au Siam XVIIe–XVIIIe siecles*, 3 vols. (Paris, 1998), III, 412.
[351] Crawfurd, *Journal of an Embassy*, 345–46. Cf. 488.

"Malay," etc.). Along with European references to Siamese as a distinct category, such references reinforce the supposition that acculturation between *munnai* and their *phrai* retainers had blurred once powerful horizontal cleavages.[352] In short, I am suggesting that here as in Burma (and, we will later find, in France) an ethnic marker that originally served to distinguish a political elite from the subordinate peasantry came to be adopted by wide sectors of that peasantry. At the same time, although we lack concrete data, it is reasonable to assume that the zone within which peasants spoke Central Thai dialects and exhibited other "Siamese" traits extended outward between c. 1500 and 1840 to include new areas in the upper peninsula, the Khorat plateau, and the upper Chaophraya basin.

Moreover, despite massive alien settlements in their midst, during the Bangkok era the Siamese peasantry continued to absorb the more socially mobile and prestigious of these aliens. If some Mon refugees long retained distinctive cultural features, others in more regular contact with the Siamese adopted the language, hairstyle, and dress of their neighbors and assumed a situationally-ambiguous, bilingual status whose long term trajectory pushed them towards a more complete Siamese identification.[353] The fact that Lao deportees and Mon refugees learned to read Central Thai by attending Siamese monasteries suggests that the spread of textual Buddhism and of Siamese ethnicity were mutually reinforcing.[354] Not surprisingly, the most commonly mentioned non-Siamese communities in the central region c. 1830 were relatively recent. Likewise, if not the children, then the grandchildren of Chinese-born fathers and Siamese mothers tended to adopt Siamese Buddhist practices, cremation, hairstyle, and dress. These adjustments allowed the overwhelming majority of third-generation descendants to become "Siamese" in external traits and self-proclaimed ethnicity. In the words of an 1830s European observer: "Within two or three generations, all the distinguishing marks of the Chinese character dwindle entirely away,

---

[352] Implicitly the ethnic censuses at Bowring, *Kingdom and People*, I, 81; Rabibhadana, *Thai Society*, 17 nn., and explicitly those at *The Burney Papers*, III, ii, 354–58; and Mayoury and Pheuiphanh Ngaosyvathn, "160 Years Ago: Lao Chronicles and Annals on Siam and the Lao," in *Procedings of the International Conference on Thai Studies, Australian National University, July 1987* (Canberra, 1987), 469–70, derive from official Siamese sources of the early 19th century.

[353] Terwiel, *Travellers' Eyes*, 40–41, 47–48, 52, 59, 71, 85, 122, 151, 253–54. Cf. the emphasis in Brian Foster, "Ethnic Identity of the Mons in Thailand," *JSS* 61 (1973), 203–26.

[354] Terwiel, *Travellers' Eyes*, 59.

and a nation which adheres so obstinately to its national customs becomes wholly changed to Siamese."[355] If an absence of females from their own community made cultural isolation more difficult for Chinese than for Laos or Mons, their trajectory nonetheless confirms the normative appeal of Siamese traits at different social levels. In sum, along with *munnai* and *phrai*, deportees and immigrants in various stages of assimilation constituted sub-categories within an overarching Siamese identity.

But we have yet to determine the political import of adopting Siamese traits. What, if anything, did a Siamese identity say about a person's political relation to the court of Ayudhya or Bangkok? Again, the evidence is complex, and not necessarily amenable to 20th-century categories.

Absent organs of popular political involvement, absent a persistent external threat, scattered villages had few opportunities to develop a sense of common interest. Yet as in Burma, warfare against a minatory, alien foe could create the psychological drive and social channels for such sentiments. Whether because records have been lost, because the 1569 conquest was not particularly destructive, or because the preliminary sense of Siamese ethnicity was inadequate, there is no evidence that the first Burmese conquest had this effect. But the Burmese campaigns of the 1760s – in which hundreds of thousands may have died – were deeply transformative. Like Burmese records after the Mon invasions, indigenous and foreign accounts of post-1767 Siam emphasize utter chaos and popular misery.[356] Sunait Chutintaranond has shown that these events, followed by a half century of continued Burmese attacks, nourished stereotypes of the Burmese as dehumanized devils and foes of Buddhism, in opposition to whom the Siamese and all who sheltered under the protective umbrella of the Bangkok king constituted a category of orthodoxy. "[T]he sinful Burmese ravaged our villages and cities. . . . Our peaceful kingdom was abandoned and turned into forest. The Burmese showed no mercy to the Thai [Siamese] and felt no shame for all sins they had committed," wailed a typical history, from 1793.[357]

---

[355] Charles Gutzlaff quoted in Skinner, *Chinese Society*, 132. Also, ibid., 126–34. Perpetuation of local Chinese society thus came to rely on continuous male immigration.

[356] See Wyatt, "Subtle Revolution," 11–12; and early accounts preserved in M. L. Manich Jumsai, *Popular History of Thailand* (Bangkok, 1976), 337–54.

[357] Sunait Chutintaranond, "The Image of the Burmese Enemy Through History," *JSS* 80, 1 (1992): 5–6. See ibid., 1–32; idem, " 'Cakravartin': The Ideology of Traditional Warfare in Siam and Burma, 1548–1605" (Cornell Univ. Ph.D. diss, 1990), esp. ch. 2; Wenk, *Thai Literature*, 55.

Not content to stigmatize the Burmese of their own day, early Chakri officials and monks rewrote accounts of earlier wars so as to give those struggles a primordial ethnic character.

Even in northern Thailand, outside the imperial core, these events encouraged the construction of over-arching cultural categories that facilitated coordination with the "Great King" of the south, in Bangkok. Thus some north Thai chronicles began to write about the unity of "Tais," that is to say, all who fought together under the Bangkok ruler, vis-a-vis Burmese and Vietnamese.[358] Besides encouraging such categories, the upheavals of the late 18th century resettled people from divergent areas in new districts and mixed local units in imperial armies. Under the circumstances, Wyatt argues, it is not surprising that localism weakened and that people identified more readily with the Chakri king as an idealized protector on whom the salvation of countless thousands depended. By the same token, these upheavals may have strengthened popular belief that Buddhist doctrine, to whose orthodox revival the Chakri throne devoted itself unstintingly, offered the surest guide to human happiness.[359]

We again sense the importance of political conflict in nourishing wider allegiances during and after Anuvong's aforementioned Lao-based revolt of 1827. Envisioning a hierarchy of peoples with Siamese at the top, non-Buddhist hill peoples at the bottom, and Laos and Khmers in intermediate roles, Bangkok officials reportedly ridiculed Lao customs and regarded as "idiots" their Lao subjects, whose resentments formed the background for the Vientiane uprising.[360] If we can accept Lao chronicles written after the event, Anuvong's heir-apparent declared, "I do not want to be a slave to the Thai [Siamese] any more."[361] According to an 1828 Vietnamese dispatch, supported by American missionary accounts, Siamese princes plotted to humiliate Anuvong "for the simple reason that he was Lao."[362] In disputed districts, Siamese documents claimed that Lao rebels bluntly asked, "Lao or Thai [Siamese]?" to determine whether people would live or die (Alaung-hpaya's men,

---

358 Wyatt, "Southeast Asia 'Inside Out,'" 701.
359 Wyatt, "History and Directionality," 435–36; ibid., "Subtle Revolution," 12 ff.
360 Charles Archaimbault, *Contribution a l'etude d'un cycle de legendes Lao* (Paris, 1980), 132; Ngaosyvathn, *Paths*, 144. Of course, the Ngaosyvathn's work is permeated by Lao nationalist bias.
361 Ngaosyvathn, *Paths*, 140, 144; idem, "160 Years Ago," 472–73.
362 Ngaosyvathn, "160 Years Ago," 472; Ngaosyvathn, *Paths*, 138, incl. n. 38.

recall, made a similar distinction between Mons and Burmans).[363] Long after 1827 popular poetry and song on the Khorat plateau expressed Lao resentment of Siamese control.[364]

To sum up, in the Siamese as in the Burmese realm, nuclear zone ethnicity was privileged, and the fit between ethnicity and political loyalty grew closer. Yet this is hardly to claim that ethnicity became the operative principle of imperial organization. How could such a principle have been implemented? Ayudhya/Bangkok controlled, and aspired to control, ever more heterogeneous populations, while as noted, within the basin post-1770 deportations may have reduced self-identified Siamese to a minority. Given this numerical weakness, given the state's utter incapacity to promote Siamese ethnicity on the village level, as a practical matter a strategy of ethnic exclusiveness would have been monumentally self-defeating. Moreover, here as in Burma there was no theoretical reason, no conceptual foundation to support such a policy. The realm was expressly conceived as a polyglot dynastic entity dedicated to the promotion of universal doctrine. If Siamese ethnicity was privileged, loyal non-Siamese could enjoy a secure and honorable status.[365] Thus the throne welcomed talented officials of diverse origins and freely recruited Mon, and Malay, as well as Lao (!) soldiers. If some combatants in 1827 invoked ethnic stereotypes, more fundamentally Anuvong's revolt was a dynastic conflict in which self-interest led Lao rulers at Luang Prabang and elsewhere either to stay neutral or to support Bangkok rather than their "fellow Lao" Anuvong.[366] In contrast to Kon-baung treatment of the Mons, in the aftermath of this rising there is no evidence that Bangkok sought to suppress Lao culture.

Indeed, four factors encouraged a looser tie between ethnicity and loyalty in Siam than in Burma. Most basic, in the early 19th century and probably in the 17th century as well, the ratio of Siamese to non-Siamese was lower than that of Burmans to non-Burmans. Whereas

[363] Ngaosyvathn, *Paths*, 157; also 140, n. 52.
[364] Stuart-Fox, *Lao Kingdom*, 127.
[365] Cf. Winichakul, *Siam Mapped*, Ch. 1; Gehan Wijeyewardene, "The Frontiers of Thailand," in Craig Reynolds, ed., *National Identity and its Defenders* (Victoria, Australia, 1991), ch. 6; Charles Keyes, "Who Are the Tai?" in Lola Romanucci-Ross and George Vos, eds., *Ethnic Identity* (Walcut Creek, CA, 1995), 136–60.
[366] Wyatt, "History and Directionality," 437–38 makes the same point, but sees Lao support for Bangkok as symptomatic of a new pan-Tai outlook. In fact, Phnom Penh's inclusion suggests it was as much a Bangkok-centered supra-ethnic alignment as a pan-Tai movement.

Chapter 2 suggested that Burmans in 1830 constituted some 60 percent of the imperial population, in the Bangkok empire as a whole Siamese may not have been much more than a third.[367] These discrepant ratios in turn reflected the following factors: a) The Siamese empire was larger, but its central riverine corridor was more modest and its geography more fragmented; b) the fact that Siamese culture as a distinct complex of practices and dialects crystallized only in the 15th or 16th century, some three hundred years after its Burmese counterpart, may have retarded both vertical and lateral diffusion; c) because Burma repeatedly devastated Siam, rather than vice versa, Siam required more deportees and immigrants from outlying areas to make good the damage. Whereas only a fifth or a sixth of Upper Burma's population in 1820 consisted of deportees and their offspring, in central Siam, as noted, such categories may have been as much as half.

Second and related to the issue of resettlement, in Siam strategically important communities of Mon refugees from Lower Burma, whose anti-Burman prejudice attached them firmly to the Ayudhyan and Bangkok thrones, weakened the link between political loyalty and ethnicity. In 1820 Siam hosted at least 40,000 unassimilated Mons, who occupied key military and clerical posts. Even including Shans, Burma had no comparably strategic minority.

Third, notwithstanding Chinese assimilation, the unique size and influence of foreign mercantile communities likewise served to depoliticize Siamese ethnicity. By 1825 Indians, Armenians, and Chinese must have been less than 1 percent of the population of Burma, whose capital remained inland, but in Siam unassimilated Chinese alone comprised almost 5 percent, concentrated along the Gulf coast and in the basin. No leading Burmese ministerial family descended from foreign traders, but most prominent Ayudhya/Bangkok families had such ancestry.

Fourth, in the west centuries of north–south conflict assumed a Burman-Mon coloration that planted ethnic stereotypes firmly in Burman folklore and psychology. But Siamese colonization was limited; and despite 15th-century contests and 18th-century invasions, Siamese wars with Yuans, Burmans, and Laos were briefer and less critical to local imaginations than Irrawaddy basin struggles.

---

[367] John Crawfurd, *The Crawfurd Papers* (Bangkok, 1915), 102 put the Siamese at 41 percent of the imperial population; while Jean-Baptiste Pallegoix, reproduced in Bowring, *Kingdom and People*, I, 81–82 and in Rabibhadana, *Thai Society*, 17, put them at 32 percent.

AFFILIATIONS IN THE TRIBUTARY ZONE

Capital influences obviously tended to be less potent in the outer zones of empire – Cambodia, northern Thailand, the Mekong valley, the mid-peninsula – than in the center. Yet in varying degrees Siamese conventions also began to distinguish tributaries of Ayudhya/Bangkok from areas primarily subject to Ava, Beijing, or Hue.

The dynamics of imperial acculturation are familiar. Monks, traders, and settlers introduced Siamese scripts, dress, music, and religious traditions to outlying areas – although as the popularity of Lao, Mon, and Malay entertainment in central Siam attests, exchange was hardly one-way.[368] At a higher social level, young Lao, Malay, and Khmer aristocrats, whether as hostages or pages, acquired an intimate knowledge of court culture at Ayudhya/Bangkok. Family ties to Siamese courtiers flowed from such contacts, as from the formal exchange of women between dependent rulers and the Siamese ruling house. Tributary missions to the capital offered a more irregular avenue of instruction. To help tributaries purify their *sanghas*, kings sent senior Siamese monks to outlying courts and trained non-Siamese monks at the capital. Eager to share in reflected glory, tributaries themselves often took the initiative in inviting Siamese specialists.[369]

Naturally the longer the association and the shorter the cultural and physical distance between capital and dependency, the more powerful Siamese influence was likely to be. Consider first the Theravada zone, within which Cambodia developed arguably the closest tie to Ayudhya/Bangkok. Although some linguistic usages still moved from east to west as late as the 17th or even the 18th century,[370] high culture increasingly mimicked politics. "It is fitting for large countries to take care of smaller ones," a Siamese diplomatic letter explained, taking as axiomatic the barbarity of the Khmers (whose king was described as "an unruly child") and the need for a Siamese civilizing mission. Sometimes this was envisioned in cooperation with Vietnam, but more often as a duty to uplift fellow Theravadins and protect them from Vietnamese heretics.[371] Following what Saveros Pou terms a "Siamese invasion" in

---

[368] Teeuw and Wyatt, *Patani*, 261–62; Miller and Chonpairot, "Siamese Music," 34, 115.
[369] Gesick, "Kingship," 124, 153–56; Suwannathat-Pian, *Thai-Malay Relations*, ch. 2; Ngaosyvathn, *Paths*, 217–18; *Nan Chronicle*, Churatana, tr., 52 and *passim*.
[370] Gedney, "Verse Forms," 515–16; Judith Jacob, "Some Features of Khmer Versification," in C. E. Bazell, ed., *In Memory of J.R. Firth* (London, 1966), 232.
[371] Chandler, *History*, 114, 96–97; Wyatt, "History and Directionality," 438.

vocabulary, thought, and art that reached its peak in the first half of the 1800s, Phnom Penh palace dances, architecture, royal language, temple painting, and Buddhist sculpture all became virtually indistinguishable from Siamese models. Several Cambodian princes grew up in Bangkok, and King Norodom required his children to learn Siamese.[372] Nor was Khmer popular culture unaffected. Notwithstanding the fact that Khmer and Tai come from different language families and are mutually unintelligible, Franklin Huffman has shown that from the 16th to 19th centuries Tai syntax replaced its Angkorian counterpart and Tai influence virtually transformed both spoken and written Khmer.[373] Huffman does not specify the mechanisms, but they may have included Tai settlement and wider monastic exchanges. Thus whereas the second millennium began with Angkor exporting its culture to the Chaophraya basin, in the second half of the millennium the flow between component parts of what had once been a hybrid Khmer-Tai civilization was reversed.

In the Tai-speaking peninsula as far as Nakhon Si Thammarat, I have called attention to the spread of Central Thai and the mixture of Central Thai vocabulary with southern tones. Diller attributes these changes to monastic mobility, perhaps to military movements, and certainly to the practice of training southern youths at Ayudhya/Bangkok before returning them to serve as provincial officials in the south.[374] Presumably the court at Nakhon Si Thammarat, like that at Phnom Penh, was indebted to Siam for ceremonial and artistic models (note, however, that Ayudhya's *lakhon nok* drama originated in the south[375]). At Phattalung, south of Nakhon Si Thammarat, Gesick has shown that as early as the 17th century, treasured local manuscripts, while expressing an unshakable regional identity, viewed the king in the "Great Capital of Ayuddhya" as a nonpareil source of authority.[376]

In the northern Tai-speaking zone, Chiang Mai, Nan, Luang Prabang, Vientiane, and the eastern Khorat *muang* came under Ayudhyan/Bangkok suzerainty 200 to 400 years later than Cambodia or the Tai mid-peninsula. Particularly in areas like Chiang Mai that had been

---

[372] Pou, *Etudes*, 117; Gedney, "Verse Forms," 514–16; Mabbett and Chandler, *Khmers*, 223–24.

[373] Franklin Huffman, "Thai and Cambodian – A Case of Syntactic Borrowing," *JAOS* 93, 4 (1973): 488–503. Gedney, "Verse Forms," 514–15; and Pou, *Etudes*, 114–17 broadly concur.

[374] See *supra* n. 320.

[375] Brandon, *Theatre*, 62.

[376] Gesick, *Lady White Blood*, 32, 39, 48, 86 and *passim*.

incorporated into the Burmese cultural sphere since the 16th century, this set obvious limits to the Siamese impact. Moreover, intermarriage and diplomacy between royal families in Lan Na, Laos, southern Yunnan, Kengtung, even the Shan states fostered traditions of literature, court ceremony, and female court dress that continued to distinguish this interior Tai region as a whole from central Siam.[377] On the other hand, even before its military conquest, Ayudhya had exerted some influence over north Tai ecclesiastic and artistic life. Thereafter, with the destruction of Vientiane, the systematic education of Lao and Yuan aristocratic youths at Bangkok, and closer coordination between the northern and Siamese *sanghas*, Siamese influence grew, facilitated perhaps by a common linguistic background.[378] Although we lack court studies comparable to those for Cambodia, a reading of Chiang Mai and Nan chronicles does suggest substantial post-1780 modifications in the self-image of north Tai elites. By definition, "Southerners," that is, Siamese, remained less civilized than Yuans. Yet, as noted, these chronicles evince a new interest in overarching ethnicities, including (Wyatt argues) an incipient pan-Tai identity, together with a novel acceptance of a hierarchy centered on the "Great King" of Siam. That monarch alone united leaders throughout the central mainland and, as Chiang Mai's ruler reminded his siblings in 1806, protected them from becoming "slaves" of the Burmese or Vietnamese. To most rulers, Anuvong's challenge to Bangkok therefore seemed as immoral as it was stupid.[379] In the northern hills, as Lawa, Karen, and Lao Thoeng tribal leaders developed closer political/commercial relations with Tai centers after c. 1770, they too gained more regular, if indirect, exposure to imperial culture.[380]

Finally, a limited degree of Siamese influence distinguished those north Malay kingdoms that paid tribute to Ayudhya/Bangkok from Malay kingdoms farther south. In the second quarter of the 19th century

---

377 Peltier, "Litteratures Lao"; Susan Conway, "Power Dressing: Female Court Dress and Marital Alliances in Lan Na, the Shan States and Siam," *Orientations*, April 2001: 42–49.

378 Ngaosyvathn, *Paths*, 217–18; Gesick, "Kingship," 123–24. On Siamese architectural influence, Gosling, *Old Luang Prabang*, 25.

379 Wyatt, "Southeast Asia 'Inside Out,'" esp. 700–701; idem, "History and Directionality," esp. 436–39; idem, "Presidential Address," esp. 1083; idem, "Chiang Mai and Ayudhya," 186–87; *Chiang Mai Chronicle*, chs. 7, 8; *Nan Chronicle*, Churatana, tr., 52–77.

380 Stuart-Fox, *Lao Kingdom*, 47–133 *passim*; Renard, "Role of Karens"; Charles Keyes, "The Karen in Thai History and the History of the Karen in Thailand," in Keyes, ed., *Ethnic Adaptation and Identity* (Philadelphia, 1979), 31–47; Hayashi Yukio, "How Thai-Lao Dominance Was Constructed in Northeast Thailand," in Fukui, *Dry Areas*, 187–214.

a noted Malay writer contrasted the Siamese-tinged dialect of Kedah, Kelantan, and Trengganu with the "pure" Malay language of Johor, and the Siamese-influenced dances of Kelantan with the "true" Malay dance of the south.[381] Northern Malays often expressed pride in their association with Ayudhya/Bangkok. With Siamese power looming larger, the lords of Phattalung, a largely Muslim domain, incorporated more and more Siamese rituals until in 1772 Phattalung officially rejected Islam in favor of Buddhism. In fact, this meant that the balance within what was still a syncretic faith had shifted.[382]

Yet as this story also suggests, in some contexts Islam and Buddhism were incompatible. With increasing central demands and with the growth during the late 18th and early 19th centuries of Buddhist textuality in Siam and of Wahabi fundamentalism in the Malay world, some restive Malay tributaries invoked Islam as a badge of defiance. One could see this as part of the same movement towards more encompassing religious and/or ethnic categories as bred tensions between Burmans and Mons, Vietnamese and Khmers. Thus Pattani sought to broaden its revolt against Rama I by projecting itself as a center of reformist Islam and Malay culture.[383] Some rebel Kedah princes, whose forces sacked Buddhist pagodas as they pushed north in 1838, portrayed their struggle as a holy war (*jihad*) against Siamese infidels (*kafir*). The Kelantan chronicle branded the king of Siam "an infidel [who] does not know correct behavior."[384] And Rama III himself concluded that Siamese and Malay customs were like "oil and water which cannot be made into one."[385]

In sum, Siamese imperial consolidation was accompanied by an extension into the tributary zone not of Siamese ethnicity – this was rare – but of more isolated, sometimes contested, religious, artistic, architectural, and other motifs, chiefly in the realm of high culture. In this respect, the situation resembled developments in the Burmese empire. Yet three considerations suggest that by 1830, imperial acculturation in the central mainland was less pronounced than in the west. First, as I have emphasized, Siamese demography was less dominant and ethnicity less important to the self-image and practical organization of the central

---

[381] Andayas, *Malaysia*, 118–19.
[382] Simmonds, "Thalang Letters," 613; Teeuw and Wyatt, *Patani*, 270.
[383] Suwannathat-Pian, *Thai-Malay Relations*, 160, 213, plus 65, 81–88, 212–13; Bonney, *Kedah*, 11–12, 14; Teeuw and Wyatt, *Patani*, 292–96.
[384] Andayas, *Malaysia*, 119, 120.
[385] Suwannathat-Pian, *Thai-Malay Relations*, 65 n. 81; 86.

government. Second, late 18th-century Siamese conquests, particularly in the north, were more extensive than early Kon-baung annexations. Because culture exchanges between the capital and northern tributaries were correspondingly more novel than in the Burmese empire, imperial motifs had less time to take hold. Third, with the very tardy exception of Manipur and Assam, virtually the entire lowland population in the Kon-baung empire was Theravada Buddhist. By contrast, Siam long had a significant, partly indigestible Malay Muslim component.

CONCLUSIONS

Territorial consolidation in the central mainland moved through four increasingly well-defined phases, the second and third of which both began and ended with region-wide political collapse. During the so-called charter era, Angkor exercised loose control over the Mekong basin, the upper peninsula, and parts of the Chaophraya basin, while to the west smaller Mon-oriented principalities maintained varying degrees of independence. This phase ended with the disruption of both the Angkorian solar polity and western principalities between c. 1240 and 1400 and with the simultaneous expansion of Tai influence. At the start of the second phase some 13 successor states contended, but in the course of the 14th and more especially the late 15th and 16th centuries, they collapsed into four – Lan Na, Cambodia, Lan Sang, and Ayudhya – among which Lan Sang and Ayudhya were preeminent by 1550. This second period of consolidation ended with the Burmese invasions and the regional crisis of 1558–1574. During the third phase, c. 1570/1584–1767, and particularly from the early 18th century, Ayudhya emerged as undisputed regional leader. Yet Malay and Lao states as well as Cambodia retained substantial authority. In the fourth period, c. 1770–1840, Thonburi-Bangkok, rising from Ayudhya's ashes, seized Lan Na and imposed unprecedentedly rigorous controls over Malay, Lao, and Khmer tributaries.

Over this long period administrative change had a linear quality. Thus although the area over which Bangkok enjoyed authority may have been only about a quarter larger than Angkor's empire at its peak, in practice the two imperial systems were substantially different. Angkor relied on autonomous temple networks in the core and exercised a notably unstable, quasi-ritual dominion over outlying areas (administrative Pattern A). In post-charter successor states like Early Ayudhya, Lan Na, and Lan Sang, although temples assumed a more modest

335

administrative role than at Angkor, powerful princes continued to rule outlying provinces, while *phrai* clustered in private patronage networks beyond direct royal control (Pattern B). However, the Late Ayudhya polity greatly expanded the number of *phrai luang*, together with the authority of capital ministries, at the expense of princes and provincial governors (Pattern C). Bangkok maintained these basic arrangements, while further strengthening *phrai luang* controls, dramatically enhancing commercial and monetary operations, importing more firearms, and subduing extensive outer regions. The power of the Ayudhya/Bangkok system appeared both in the growing extent and docility of outer zones and in the ease with which the system reconstituted itself after 1569 and, more remarkably, 1767.

Cultural integration in the central mainland paralleled political consolidation in a general sense, but the fit between political cycles and cultural change was not particularly close. Admittedly, the collapse of Angkor coincided more or less with the decline of Hindu civilization and the expansion of Tai ethnicity. Likewise, the Burmese wars of 1759–1811 nurtured popular identification with the Siamese court. Yet because it also reflected gradual local processes, much as in Burma the extension of imperial ethnicity and Buddhist literacy exhibited a stubborn gradualism. From the 10th through the 15th centuries the elite was heavily Indianized and literate, while the peasantry seems to have been substantially illiterate, animist, and localized. After c. 1600 and more especially after c. 1700, we find not exactly greater standardization – like administrative and economic functions, cultural production became more specialized – but more vigorous cross-class exchange, more socially inclusive trends in literature and entertainment, and greater provincial and tributary responsiveness to capital paradigms and, in some locales, ethnic claims. At the same time that fluidity, tolerance, and syncretism characteristic of both elite and popular religion in earlier periods diminished.

What dynamics governed political and cultural change? Insofar as techniques were rarely lost and successive crises bred fresh adjustments, administrative expertise had a cumulative character. As in the western mainland, warfare, including the bitter experiences of 1569 and 1767, spurred experiments. So too as in the west, royal power and cultural identification with the crown tended to reinforce one another. Yet given the superficiality of the early modern state, one is tempted to argue that the extension of political and communications networks rested primarily on economic growth – which in turn reflected an ever fluid synergy between agricultural/demographic rhythms and external trade. I have hypothesized that climatically-influenced agrarian/demographic cycles and new rice regimes governed the economy of the central mainland before c. 1500 more completely than after that date. Angkor's early vitality, in particular, seems to have been a function of agrarian expansion. Conversely, although historians have often underestimated Siamese agricultural and domestic commercial vitality, there is every indication that world bullion flows, firearms, and alien trade diasporas exercised a more decisive role after 1500 than before. Insofar as economic change both destabilized polities and lay the foundation for reintegration, such growth correlated poorly with dynastic change, as suggested by the Chinese-led trade boom lasting from the early 18th to the mid-19th century.

In basic trajectory, chronology, and dynamics, the political and cultural history of the central mainland clearly resembled that of the western mainland. Lest one exaggerate similarities, however, recall these major differences: The post-charter transition from Pagan to Ava was far less wrenching than that from Suphanburi and Angkor to Ayudhya, Phnom Penh, Lan Na, and Lan Sang. This was true whether one considers political geography (the shift from the Cambodian plain to the lower Chaophraya basin), ethnicity (the shift from Khmer to Siamese hegemony), religion (the transition from Hindu to Theravada dominance), architecture, or administration. Ironically, after 1350 only in the central mainland were primary agricultural and maritime resources concentrated in the same locale (around Ayudhya and Bangkok), so that the Chaophraya basin after that date enjoyed greater geopolitical stability than the Irrawaddy basin. Yet within the central mainland as a whole, poorer communications meant that political re-unification was not achieved until the late 1700s, compared to the mid-1500s in the west. Maritime trade and alien merchants were more consistently important to the Siamese than to the Burmese economy. Particularly after c. 1770 maritime growth encouraged greater military and administrative dynamism in Siam than in Burma. In turn the prominence of alien traders, an absence of sustained communal warfare, unusually large deportee populations, the novelty of Siamese culture itself, and the low ratio of Siamese to non-Siamese within the empire all joined to depoliticize ethnicity by comparison with the Irrawaddy basin.

CHAPTER 4

"The Least Coherent Territory in the World"

Vietnam and the Eastern Mainland

The eastern mainland exhibited a number of unique features whose interpretation became particularly embroiled in 19th and 20th century politics.

The eastern mainland is here defined as the Red River basin and surrounding uplands, the eastern half of the Annamite Chain, the coastal lowlands, and the Mekong delta. The most obvious difference between this region and the rest of the mainland was the east's unique exposure to Chinese culture, which began in systematic fashion with the incorporation of the Red River basin into the Chinese empire between 43 and 938 C.E. Encountering a monarchy that congratulated itself on fidelity to Confucian norms, Frenchmen in the late 1800s developed what has been termed "the little China fallacy": they assumed that Vietnam owed everything to Chinese tutelage, made few independent advances, and thus was no more able than its "stagnant" northern mentor to enter the modern world without European direction. That this endorsement of Europe's historic mission would appeal to many colonizers is hardly surprising.[1] Curiously, however, long after the French left Indochina, the notion that China provides the most appropriate template continued to grip even resolutely anticolonial Western historians who inherited the scholarly apparatus of colonial researchers, together with the Sinocentric bias inherent in Chinese-language records. So too the alliance c.1950–1978 between Vietnamese and Chinese Communism may

---

[1] Nola Cooke, "Colonial Political Myth and the Problem of the Other: French and Vietnamese in the Protectorate of Annam" (Australian National University Ph.D. diss., 1991); idem, "An Introduction to the Historiography of Late Traditional Vietnam" (ms).

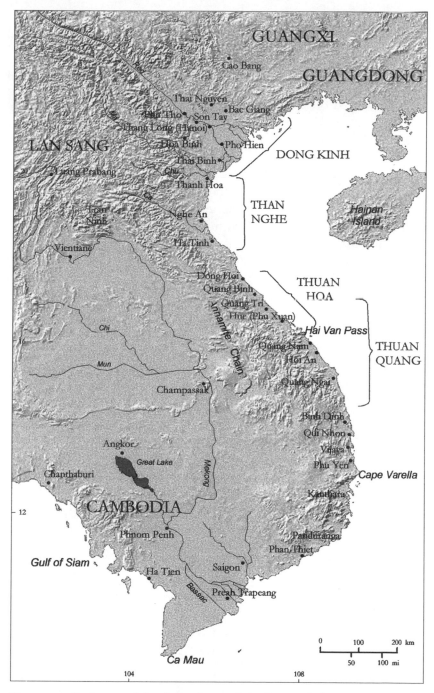

Figure 4.1. Eastern mainland Southeast Asia. Regional designations follow Keith Taylor, "Surface Orientations in Vietnam," *JAS* 57 (1998): map, p. 950.

have encouraged linkage in the minds of anti-Communist scholars and those sympathetic to Communism alike.

In recent years, this emphasis on Chinese influence has been criticized by writers tired of colonial and Cold War perspectives and eager to see Vietnam on "its own terms." Analyzing the social penetration of Confucianism, a number of scholars have confirmed Alexander Woodside's observation that even in the most Sinicized regions, Chinese norms were more important among the literati than the peasantry, who retained many habits similar to those elsewhere in Southeast Asia. Geographically too, Keith Taylor, John Whitmore, Li Tana, Nola Cooke, Insun Yu, and others have shown that Confucian influence tended to wane with distance from the Red River delta (although during the 18th and 19th centuries, the prominence in southern Vietnam of Chinese immigrant scholars complicated this picture). And chronologically, recent work has portrayed Sinicization even among the elite as a rather episodic project whose bursts of reforming zeal in the 15th, late 17th, and 19th centuries were by no means representative of all of Vietnamese history.[2]

Yet because it focuses on the relation between Vietnam and China rather than that between the eastern lowlands and the rest of the mainland, this scholarship leaves untouched the basic distinction: if Sinic influences varied by class and locale, in terms of social structure,

---

[2] On social, geographic, and temporal variations in Vietnamese culture, see Alexander Woodside, *Vietnam and the Chinese Model* (Cambridge, MA: 1971), ch. 1; idem, "Medieval Vietnam and Cambodia," *JSEAS* 15 (1984): 315–19; Keith Taylor, "Surface Orientations in Vietnam: Beyond Histories of Nation and Region," *JAS* 57 (1998): 949–78; idem, "Regional Conflicts among the Viet Peoples between the 13th and 19th Centuries," in Nguyen The Anh and Alain Forest, eds., *Guerre et Paix en Asie du Sud-est* (Paris, 1998), 109–34; idem, "The Literati Revival in Seventeenth-Century Vietnam," *JSEAS* 18 (1987): 1–23; idem, "Nguyen Hoang and the Beginning of Vietnam's Southward Expansion," in Anthony Reid, ed., *Southeast Asia in the Early Modern Era* (Ithaca, 1993), 42–65; John Whitmore, "The Development of Le Government in Fifteenth-Century Vietnam: (Cornell Univ. Ph.D. diss., 1968); idem, *Vietnam, Ho Quy Ly, and the Ming (1371–1421)* (New Haven, 1985), plus Whitmore's writings in nn. *infra*; Li Tana, *Nguyen Cochinchina* (Ithaca, 1999); idem, "An Alternative Vietnam?" *JSEAS* 29 (1998): 111–21; Nola Cooke, "Nineteenth-Century Vietnamese Confucianization in Historical Perspective," *JSEAS* 25 (1994): 270–312; idem, "The Composition of the Nineteenth-Century Political Elite of Pre-Colonial Nguyen Vietnam, *MAS* 29 (1995): 741–64; Insun Yu, "Law and Family in Seventeenth and Eighteenth-Century Vietnam" (Univ. of Michigan Ph.D. diss., 1978), published as *Law and Society in Seventeenth and Eighteenth Century Vietnam* (Seoul, 1990); O.W. Wolters, *Two Essays on Dai-Viet in the Fourteenth Century* (New Haven, 1988), plus nn. *infra*; Yang Baoyun, *Contribution a l'histoire de la principaute des Nguyen au Vietnam meridional (1600–1775)*, (Geneva, 1992), ch. 5; Esta Ungar, "Vietnamese Leadership and Order: Dai Viet under the Le Dynasty (1428–1459)" (Cornell Univ. Ph.D. diss., 1983).

administration, law, and religion, such influences increasingly did distinguish the eastern lowlands as a whole from the rest of mainland Southeast Asia. At virtually all levels and in virtually all regions, practices that derived ultimately from China were more pronounced in 1830 than in 930 because Vietnamese-speakers – attracted by the incomparable prestige and protean utility of northern civilization – embarked on a long-term, if spasmodic process of selecting and recombining elements of northern civilization to fit local needs and to reshape local identities. Here, one might argue, is one of the central ironies of Vietnamese history: as they struggled to maintain political independence from China, Vietnamese elites sought to localize Chinese culture and administration, which they like other East Asians saw as the common property of all civilized people and which they internalized to the point that their alien origins became irrelevant. To be sure, military pressures also influenced political reform. Yet whereas in Burma and Siam administrative change was normally a matter of trial-and-error precipitated by military crisis, Vietnamese reform, at least on paper, frequently followed Chinese models, antique and contemporary, and reflected shifting cultural paradigms more than military demands.

What was the significance of Sinic culture for our primary theme of integration? In some respects, it increased the potential for fracture. Differing Confucian sensibilities could symbolize, and in some measure inspire, conflicting regional loyalties, as between Dong Kinh in the north and Thuan Quang in the center, or between the latter area and the far south. The elitist nature of Chinese education contributed to a psychological/cultural distance between literati and peasantry, or court and peasantry, without close analogy in the more uniformly literate societies of Theravada Southeast Asia. The Confucian emphasis on lineage loyalty supplied uniquely effective tools of family organization to opponents of central authority. Likewise, the emphasis on Confucian lineage as an eternal corporation that persisted regardless of locale may have encouraged a higher degree of residential instability and religious experimentation than was possible in the more closely-monitored patron-client systems of Burma and Siam.[3]

On the whole, however, the integrative implications of Sinic culture appear to have been more formidable. From the 15th century the

---

[3] Alexander Woodside, personal communication, Sept. 14, 1999; Alain Forest, *Les missionaires francais au Tonkin et au Siam XVIIe–XVIIIe siecles*, 3 vols. (Paris, 1998), III, chs. 32–42.

Confucian distinction between civilized and barbarian favored, most obviously among the educated, a sharper cultural boundary between Vietnamese and their neighbors than was possible between peoples claiming the same Theravada allegiance.[4] This in turn reinforced a contextually-circumscribed sense of commonality that defied an exceptionally fissiparous physical environment. Vietnamese officials had access not only to Chinese military technology, but to Sinic administrative models that offered the possibility of a more horizontally uniform and vertically penetrating system than could be found in either Burma or Siam. Finally, Chinese agronomic and family traditions joined indigenous traditions to produce a marked Vietnamese demographic superiority over Chams and Khmers, as well perhaps as a stronger inclination toward both family and individual migration. These patterns in turn contributed to the southward-moving Vietnamization of the eastern corridor.

Alongside unique exposure to Chinese influence, a second major difference between the eastern littoral and the rest of the mainland was the east's persistent political centrifugalism. This issue, above all, has been politically fraught. Resentment of France's fragmentation of the kingdom joined with hostility to the American-backed division between North and South Vietnam to create among anti-colonial Vietnamese nationalists and sympathetic foreigners alike a fervent belief in the unshakable unity of the "Vietnamese people." Historians in this tradition, which is to say, the great majority, not only made "resistance to foreign aggression" the overriding principle for deciphering the past 2000 years, but placed Hanoi squarely at the center of "national" development.[5] Thus, as Keith Taylor observed, a "strangling obsession with identity and continuity mandated by the nationalist faith ... has animated virtually every twentieth-century historian who has written about Viet Nam."[6] Scholars long insisted on "a unified Vietnam, a village

---

[4] On these boundaries, see, e.g., John Whitmore, "A New View of the World" (ms), 70 ff.; Nguyen Ngoc Huy and Ta Van Tai, *The Le Code*, 3 vols. (Athens, OH: 1987), II, 185; Byung Wook Choi, "Southern Vietnam under the Reign of Minh Mang (1820–1841)" (Australian National Univ. Ph.D. diss., 1999), chs. 4, 5; and discussion *infra*. But on the possibility, even among literati, of fluid, nonethnic or supraethnic approaches, see Keith Taylor, "On Being Muonged," *Asian Ethnicity* 2 (2001): 25–34.

[5] Patricia Pelley, "The History of Resistance and the Resistance to History in Post-Colonial Constructions of the Past," in K. W. Taylor and John Whitmore, eds., *Essays into Vietnamese Pasts* (Ithaca, 1995), 232–45.

[6] Keith Taylor, "Preface," in Taylor and Whitmore, *Essays*, 6.

Vietnam, a Confucian Vietnam, and a revolutionary Vietnam."[7] However, in recent years scholarly research has focused ever more insistently on the polyphonic, localizing, fragmenting implications of post-1550 southern settlement in what Pierre Gourou as early as 1936 termed "the least coherent territory in the world."[8]

In one respect, Gourou overstated Vietnam's territorial misfortune: unlike the Burmese and Siamese lowlands, the Vietnamese lowlands were not ringed by great interior valleys inhabited by literate, wet rice Tai cultivators whose cultural sophistication and demographic densities allowed them to defy, even to occupy the imperial heartland. To be sure, Vietnam's western highlands did contain a plethora of minority peoples, but their numbers were relatively small and they formed localized, generally preliterate political units in no way comparable to the great Shan, Yuan, and Lao kingdoms farther west. Along with Chinese techniques and Dong Kinh's thick population, this geography helps to explain why within the Vietnamese empire as a whole in 1820 the percentage of the dominant ethnic/linguistic group was notably higher than in the Burmese, not to mention the Siamese, empire.[9]

But if we shift from overall imperial configurations in 1820 to compare only the lowland zones of Burmese, Siamese, and Vietnamese habitation, the aptness of Gourou's characterization is immediately obvious. Vietnamese-speakers occupied an extremely narrow coastal strip, wedged between sea and mountains and balanced at either end by an open delta, that of the Red River in the north and of the Mekong in the south. The eight-hundred mile corridor itself was cut up into narrow east–west basins, with no single center of gravity, no interior axis comparable to the Irrawaddy or Chaophraya. As Vietnamese-speakers pushed ever farther south – and I hasten to add that colonization from the 15th or 16th century was far more extensive than in Burma or Siam – culturally distinctive, frequently competitive political formations emerged within the wider Vietnamese-speaking world.[10] Such competition resembled that between principalities in the 14th/15th-century Chaophraya or Irrawaddy basins, but was less tied to urban centers and more capable of continuous geographic extension. During virtually the entire period

---

[7] Keith Taylor, "Vietnamese Studies in North America," keynote speech at the First International Conference on Vietnamese Studies, Hanoi, July, 1997, cited in Li Tana, "The Late 18th Century Mekong Delta and the World of the Water Frontier" (ms), 2.

[8] Pierre Gourou, *Les Paysans du Delta Tonkinois* (Paris, 1936), 8.

[9] See *infra* n. 280.

[10] This is the chief theme of Taylor, "Surface Orientations."

1540–1802, Vietnamese-speakers split into hostile north–south group-
ings, and it is by no means inconceivable that this could have yielded
a political division among people sharing the same language and culture comparable to that in German-speaking Europe. Even after 1802
"national" unity remained fragile. In this centrifugal tendency, therefore, Vietnam's precolonial history moved in a direction distinct from,
even opposite to the more or less continuous post-1550 integration of
Burma and Siam. In lieu of three sustained imperial integrations on
the mainland, one could argue that we have two and a fraction – and
that Vietnam's experience c. 1540–1802 fell somewhere between that of
western and central mainland Southeast Asia, on the one hand, and that
of the Malay/Indonesian world, on the other.

By the opening years of the 19th century why had all Vietnamese-
speaking areas again come together under a single dynasty? I suggest
that this reflected a series of political and military accidents, reinforced
by a shared political and cultural vocabulary and an assumption that
Vietnamese-speaking districts constituted a more or less coherent field
of political contestation (which was quite different from a unified polity).
Yet I am the first to admit that we know precious little about the sociol-
ogy and emotive appeal of pan-Vietnamese identities. Without a single
political center such as Ava or Ayudhya, how did dynastic/family ties
and common cultural symbols counter local entropy to the extent that
they did?

After Chinese influence and centrifugal geography, I would point to a
third major difference between the northern heartland of Vietnam (here
it is difficult to speak of the eastern littoral as a whole) and the other
chief sectors of mainland Southeast Asia: a longer, more continuous
political evolution and a correspondingly deeper sense of precedent.
Vietnam's incorporation into the Chinese empire during the first millennium provided not only a precocious political unification, but a more
direct and sustained transmission of alien high culture than was available to Pagan, Angkor, or Ayudhya. For these reasons, the Vietnamese
state of the 10th through 14th centuries was less seminal than its counterparts in the western and central mainland, and indeed, shared pride
of place with ancient Chinese dynasties. Moreover and of critical importance, between 1300 and 1450 Vietnamese areas – unlike the larger, more
heterogeneous empires of Pagan and Angkor – escaped sustained fragmentation and large-scale alien settlement, whether by Tais, Chams, or
Chinese. As a result, Vietnam's 14th-century crisis was relatively mild,
and the country's post-1350 transformation was less ethnic or territorial

than intellectual and institutional.[11] Ironically, in these respects Vietnam resembled its colonial partner, France – whose territory had been part of the Roman empire and whose 14th-century rupture was comparatively limited – more closely than it did any other sector of Eurasia examined in this two-volume study.

These then were distinctive features. Yet we also find sufficient similarities between the eastern littoral and the rest of the mainland to provide the entire mainland with a reasonable claim to coherence. Between c. 1000 and 1830 not only did each sector of the mainland grow more politically and culturally integrated, but each did so in a series of synchronized, already familiar cycles. From the 10th to 14th centuries, the so-called charter era, northern Vietnam, like the Irrawaddy basin and the central mainland, supported an eclectic religious system and a decentralized, yet expansive polity, known as Dai Viet, that benefited from vigorous agricultural and demographic growth. In the 14th century, Dai Viet, like other mainland charter principalities, collapsed through some combination of ecological/climatic pressures, institutional weakness, and external invasions. Aided by a more sustainable man/land ratio, novel external political stimuli, and improved climate, between c. 1400 and 1550 (and with particular vigor after 1450) political consolidation in the eastern littoral resumed – only to succumb again in the 16th century to the strains of over-rapid expansion in somewhat the same way as the First Toungoo empire collapsed. That is to say, in the mid- to late–16th century the entire mainland "overheated," producing a second generalized crisis less culturally disruptive than that of the 14th-century, but similar in its synchronicity and drama. The great difference between the eastern littoral and the rest of the mainland I have already emphasized: whereas Burma and Siam experienced only short-term dismemberment, in Vietnam a north–south split became ever more formal, lasting to 1802.

Yet this can also be seen as a variation on familiar themes of enhanced integration and antipodal tensions within a north–south corridor. Because both its agricultural and maritime assets were concentrated near the mouth of the chief river, the central mainland enjoyed the most precocious, continuous integration, which began under Ayudhya in the 1350s. Because the western mainland's agricultural and maritime

---

[11] For some 240 years after the height of the 14th century crisis, Dong Kinh – in sharp contrast to 14th/15th century Pagan/Ava and Angkor – retained a secure regional preeminence. Even Cham lands conquered by Dai Viet in 1471 remained politically marginal until the early 1600s.

districts were located at opposite ends of the same valley, this zone struggled to determine sectoral hegemony until Upper Burma emerged victorious in 1613 or 1635. Because agricultural and maritime districts in the eastern lowlands were widely dispersed and because it also lacked a riverine axis, this zone failed to achieve even moderate political unity until 1802. But clearly, the east was on the far end of a continuum of experiences all leading to more effective integration. Even had the southern polity remained independent after 1802, the eastern lowlands as a whole would have been more unified than during the charter era: whereas in the early second millennium the lowlands had been divided among Vietnam, Champa, and Angkor, as early as 1770 the Nguyen polity of southern Vietnam had devoured Champa and southeastern Cambodia and had helped to enfeeble the Khmer court. Precisely because the early Nguyen polity was more powerful and expansive than Champa, its rivalry with Siam to absorb Cambodia lacked local precedent, but paralleled contemporary east-west contests between Burma and Siam for control of vulnerable principalities along their interface.

Moreover, if we set aside the preoccupation with political boundaries and regard Vietnamese-speakers as an ethnic/cultural category (with both subjective and externally observable features), throughout the entire period c. 1400–1830 the basic pattern of culture change in the eastern lowlands resembled that in the Irrawaddy, and to a lesser extent the Chaophraya, corridors. Buoyed by greater numbers and superior military and political organization, Vietnamese-speakers displaced and assimilated Chams and Khmers at roughly the same time as Burmans overwhelmed Mons, and Siamese elites assimilated Mon- and Khmer-speakers. Whereas in 1400, two major language-cum-cultural systems (Burman and Mon) in the Irrawaddy basin, three (Tai, Mon, and Khmer) in the central mainland, and three (Vietnamese, Cham, and Khmer) in the eastern lowlands had co-existed, in each zone by 1830 one broad system was indisputably dominant. In Vietnam as in Burma and (less dramatically) Siam, particularly during the late 16th century and again in the late 17th to 19th centuries, a southward shift in settlement and commerce strengthened this dominant complex. As an explanation of cultural change, the concept of a thousand-year-long *nam tien* or "southern advance" of Vietnamese-speakers is suspect insofar as it gives a movement that took off only after c. 1500 a speciously early starting date, elides complex local dynamics into a single demographically-driven model, and exaggerates notions of common identity. Yet it is also undeniable that ethnic and cultural diversity in the eastern lowlands was far less pronounced in 1830 than in 900 and that in ever more southern districts both elites and peasantry derived norms from northern traditions (both Dong Kinhese and Chinese). As with Burmanization, this interpretation posits neither cultural homogeneity nor self-conscious affinity, merely a higher degree of objective similarity than could be found throughout the same region in earlier centuries.

Likewise, as in the western and central mainland, cultural standardization and specialization drew strength not only from frontier reclamation, but from foreign trade, stronger urban-rural links, a wider circulation of texts, and express government patronage. Notwithstanding major differences in social vision and claims to exclusivity, as a textual doctrine, dependent on new educational structures, that upheld central norms at the expense of local concepts of sanctity and that gained strength from the 15th century, Vietnamese Neo-Confucianism bears comparison to Theravada Buddhism.

Finally, as in Burma and Siam, so in the eastern lowlands in the second half of the 18th century, intensifying interstate competition, demographic expansion, and commercial change contributed to a third generalized collapse, which in turn stimulated a brilliant round of conquest, reform, and cultural patronage in the early 1800s. Much as Burmese invasions, in destroying Siam, provided the catalyst for Siam's renewal, Siamese threats to southern Vietnam helped to create preconditions for Nguyen revitalization. Nor was the formula for renewed success unfamiliar: cyclic compensations, new administrative experiments, imported European-style firearms, more monetized operations, and a major expansion in Chinese capital and trade.

The perennial query whether precolonial Vietnam should be studied in the context of Chinese or Southeast Asian civilization has no answer, precisely because it had properties of both. On the one hand, between c. 900 and 1830 as administration, high culture, and social structure in the eastern lowlands became more Sinic, the cultural fault line, still quite modest at the outset, between Vietnamese-speaking districts and the Indic mainland grew more pronounced. Vietnam's southern expansion also invites comparison with Chinese colonization and acculturation in Guangdong, Guangxi, Guizhou, and Yunnan. On the other hand, even in the early 19th century, as a result of Cham, Khmer, upland, and non-Sinic Vietnamese influences, social and even material culture retained a distinctive Southeast Asian flavor, including tattoos, cockfighting, betel-chewing, communal houses built on poles, multiform spirit cults, pronounced female autonomy, and a patrimonial ethos that tended to overawe bureaucratic norms.[12] Moreover, whether we consider Vietnam as a whole or the northern and southern polities separately, basic geopolitical patterns were distinct from those of China. That is to say, the modest overall size and population of both Vietnam and its sub-kingdoms, their insulation from nomadic conquest, the basic reconfiguration of lowland ethnicity between 1450 and 1850, endemic north-south tensions within a single corridor, the limited prestige of indigenous, as opposed to imported, literary traditions; the growing commercial importance of non-indigenous Asians, and deepening dependence on the South Sea economy – all these patterns linked Vietnam to mainland Southeast Asia, while in varying degrees distinguishing her from China. So too, the chronology of administrative cycles – with breakdowns in the 14th, 16th, and late 18th centuries – had a peculiarly Southeast Asian character, while Vietnam's drawn-out wars with Siam, whose fortunes hinged on Burmese threats, drew her into a specifically Southeast Asian military theater.

VIETNAM'S SOUTHERN RIVAL: CHAMPA TO c. 1350

As just indicated, until the 15th century, the Sino-Vietnamese state in the Red River delta shared the eastern littoral with two other realms, Angkor and Champa. The fortunes of Angkor, whose authority in the east focused on the Mekong delta region, Chapter 3 has chronicled. Before discussing the Sino-Vietnamese state, let us examine the third realm, Champa, which dominated the central coast until the 1470s and powerfully influenced Vietnamese-speakers both before and long after that period. At the outset, it must be said that epigraphic and foreign sources on Champa are comparatively limited, and that after a burst of French-led scholarship in the early 20th century, research languished. Thankfully, a modest recent revival offers fresh perspectives on the history of what is now central Vietnam.[13]

---

[12] See Samuel Baron, "A Description of the Kingdom of Tonqueen," in *A Collection of Voyages and Travels,* Awnsham Churchill, comp., vol. 6 (London, 1732), 19; John Whitmore, "Social Organization and Confucian Thought in Vietnam," *JSEAS* 15 (1984): 296–306; Anthony Reid, *Southeast Asia in the Age of Commerce, 1459–1680,* 2 vols. (New Haven, 1988, 1993), I, 77–80, 146–48, 164–70, 193–201 *passim;* Yu, "Law and Family," pt. 2.

[13] On recent Cham studies, *Actes du Seminaire sur le Campa Organise a l'Universite de Copenhague le 23 Mai 1987* (Paris, 1988); Momoki Shiro, "A Short Introduction to Champa Studies," in Fukui Hayao, ed., *The Dry Areas in Southeast Asia* (Kyoto, 1999), 65–74; *Le Campa et le Monde Malais* (Paris, 1991); Charles Wheeler, "Cross-Cultural Trade and Trans-Regional Networks in the Port of Hoi An" (Yale Univ. Ph.D. diss., 2002), ch. 2.

Inscriptions suggest that from an early date the vernacular tongue throughout the central coast was Cham, an Austronesian language entirely distinct from Vietnamese. Like the western and central mainland but in contrast to the Red River basin, this coast derived its high cultural inspiration from India, both directly from the subcontinent and indirectly through exchanges with Angkor, the peninsula, and Java. As early as the 4th century c.e., the founding of the Indian-style Bhadresvara temple at what became the great ritual center of Mi-son marked the beginning of a struggle to pull autonomous chiefdoms in local river valleys into the orbit of a religious-political core.[14] Although Siva generally was the chief deity and Siva's linga became the focus of royal ritual, in Champa as in Angkor and pre-1300 Java, Saivism blended with Vaishnava and Mahayana cults, and the king could be presented as a Siva-Buddha entity. So too as at Angkor, in conceptual if not iconographic terms, Indian deities fused with ancestral and chthonic spirits who protected designated territories. Indian influence was no less marked in Cham architecture, art, sculpture, and Sanskritic literature.[15]

The region in which these styles took root, stretching from modern Dong Hoi in the north to Phan Thiet in the south, may be divided into five major areas on the basis of geographic features and political criteria recognized by the Chams themselves (see Figure 1.3). Moving from north to south, these were: a) Indrapura, a zone of early contestation with the Sino-Vietnamese state; b) Amaravati, site of the Mi-son complex, with well-sheltered harbors and reasonable agricultural resources; c) Vijaya, with pockets of intensive cultivation; d) Kauthara, with limited agricultural potential, but a ritual center at Po Nagar; and e) Panduranga, a generally dry inhospitable zone, albeit with three small well-watered valleys, which became one of the Chams' final refuges from Vietnamese pressure.[16] Wet rice agriculture in the Cham alluvial plain and plateau was more productive, and less marginal to the overall economy, than earlier scholars assumed. Indeed, a substantial segment of the coastal

---

[14] Wheeler, "Cross-Cultural Trade," 111, 118–19; L. Finot, "Les inscriptions de Mi-son," *BEFEO* 4 (1904), 897–977.

[15] Paul Mus, "Cultes Indiens et indigenes au Champa," *BEFEO* 33 (1933): 367–410; Ian Mabbett, "Buddhism in Champa," in David G. Marr and A. C. Milner, eds., *Southeast Asia in the 9th to 14th Centuries* (Singapore, 1986), 289–31; Jean Boisselier, *Le Statuaire du Champa* (Paris, 1963); Claude Jacques, "Sources on Economic Activities in Khmer and Cham Lands," in Marr and Milner, *9th to 14th Centuries*, 333.

[16] Charles Higham, *The Archaeology of Mainland Southeast Asia* (Cambridge, 1989), 231, 297–301; T. Quach-Langlet, "Le cadre geographique de l'ancien Campa," in *Seminaire*, 27–48; and *Seminaire*, map.

population seems to have been tied to autonomous religious institutions, which were endowed by Cham rulers and aristocrats in a fashion that resembled, at least superficially, Pattern A administration in the great wet-rice states of Angkor and Pagan.[17] Yet, compared to those charter polities or to the Red River delta, Cham agriculture could support only a modest population, which necessarily combined rice farming with horticulture, fishing, piracy, and the export of rare woods, animal products, and minerals from the forested uplands. The lure of such exports joined with the development in the 5th–7th centuries of more direct sea routes between south China and Champa to draw more Chinese, Indian, and Malay traders to the Cham coast.[18]

Combining the assumptions of Chinese sources with their own bias in favor of consolidated states, early European scholars portrayed Champa as a unified kingdom, with a hierarchy of provincial functionaries and a centralized administration.[19] Recent research has substantially modified that view, preferring to see Champa (like neighboring Funan) even at its height as a loose confederation of local polities which might combine for longer or shorter periods under powerful leaders, but which retained a basic autonomy grounded in the self-sufficiency of small east–west river valleys and isolated coastal plains, and perhaps in an irreducibly polycentric world view. Not infrequently, Cham principalities fought one another. A hegemon became merely "king of the kings (*raja di raja*) of Champa," and the location of the preeminent center – when such a center existed – shifted: in the 8th century, which may have seen the first sustained coalescence, Panduranga dominated, in the late 9th century Indrapura, after c. 1000 Vijaya, and in the 16th century Kauthara and Panduranga.[20] It would be foolish to assume that Cham political structures remained frozen for centuries. The pre-1300 system

---

[17] Wheeler, "Cross-Cultural Trade," 112–14; Robert Wicks, *Money, Markets and Trade in Early Southeast Asia* (Ithaca, 1992), 210–14; Momoki, "Short Introduction," discussing Champa rice; idem, "Was Champa a Pure Maritime Polity?" (ms); David Griffiths Sox, "Resource-Use Systems of Ancient Champa" (Univ. of Hawaii MA thesis, 1972), esp. App. A; Mabbett, "Buddhism in Champa," 299–300; L. Finot, "La premiere stele de Dong Duong," *BEFEO* 4 (1904): 85 ff.

[18] Wheeler, "Cross-Cultural Trade," 121–22 argues that Champa's trade grew at Funan's expense. On Cham trade, ibid., 119–28; *CHSEA*, 252–60; P-B. Lafont, "Apercu sur les relations entre le Campa et l'Asie du Sud-East," in *Seminaire*, 71–81; Wicks, *Money, Markets*, 214–17.

[19] See Georges Maspero, *Le Royaume de Champa* (Paris, 1928), ch. 1 and *passim*.

[20] Po Dharma, "Etat des dernieres recherches sur la date de l'absorption du Campa par le Vietnam," in *Seminaire*, 61–62. Also Jacques, "Economic Activities," 333; Keith Taylor, "The Early Kingdoms," in *CHSEA*, 153–57.

of temple endowments, for example, seems to have waned or disappeared in later centuries.[21] Yet it is also clear that Cham principalities never advanced beyond a highly decentralized version of Pattern B administration. In this respect, they resembled interior Tai states and, more especially, states along the Malay coasts, where Chams in fact had important cultural ties and where the political economy also depended less on intensive wet-rice agriculture than on the flow of upstream trade goods to riverine ports.[22]

Recent research belies another early assumption, namely, that the population of Champa was synonymous with coastal Cham-speakers. Because Vietnamese elites distinguished between themselves, as "civilized" lowlanders, and "primitive" hill people to their west, it was assumed that Chams did the same. In fact, it now appears that Champa (*nagara Campa*) was conceived by its own people as a poly-ethnic domain extending into the Annamite chain and embracing besides lowland Chams, various Austroasiatic and Austronesian groups whose supply of forest goods was central to the political economy. All were identified as *"urang* [people of] *Campa."* Uplanders enjoyed a respected role, not only providing exports, but marrying lowland aristocrats and on occasion taking the throne themselves.[23] In some locales a political-religious center at a riverine midpoint served as fulcrum between the upstream population of hill peoples and the downstream population of traders, cultivators, and Indic specialists.[24]

Champa's position between the Khmer and Sino-Viet empires, both with stronger administrations and far larger populations, left her in an unenviable strategic position. When China controlled northern Vietnam, the rhythms of Chinese dynastic power tended to dominate relations along the fluid frontier. After the Vietnamese broke away from China, their interest in frontier security and the South Sea trade led them to sack Vijaya city with sea-borne forces in 1044 and 1069 and, at least according to the Vietnamese annals, to seize northern Indrapura. Not long thereafter, from 1145 to 1149 and 1190 to 1220, Khmer armies occupied much of Champa from the southwest. Although Angkor's subsequent decline

---

[21] See *supra* n. 17.
[22] Lafont, "Apercu," 77–78; idem, "Les grandes dates de l'histoire du Champa," in *Le Campa et le Monde Malais*, 8–14; H. Chambert-Loir, "Sur les relations historiques et litteraires entre Campa et monde malais," in *Seminaire*, 95–106; *CHSEA*, 253–54.
[23] Bernard Gay, "Vue novelle sur la composition ethnique du Campa," in *Seminaire*, 49–58; Quach-Langlet, "Le cadre geographique," esp. 27.
[24] Momoki, "Short Introduction," 70; Wheeler, "Cross-Cultural Trade," 112–18.

reduced pressure from that quarter, in the early 1300s the Vietnamese laid claim to new districts in Indrapura.[25] As we shall see, Cham efforts to reverse Vietnamese inroads helped to fuel the 14th-century regional crisis.

"CHARTER POLITIES" OF NORTHERN VIETNAM: THE LY AND TRAN DYNASTIES

While the peoples of what is now central Vietnam were developing their version of Indic civilization, China's conquest of northern Vietnam created a set of cultural options and political tensions without parallel elsewhere in the mainland.

At the start of the first millennium, in the foothills adjacent to the Red River plain and in less swampy parts of that plain, the ancestors of the Vietnamese grew wet rice, cast bronze and iron, and supported a network of chieftainships, the so-called Lac lords. It has been suggested that this culture emphasized hereditary privilege alongside charismatic authority, bilateral inheritance, and spirit propitiation in a manner not dissimilar to that of Chams and other Southeast Asians.[26] After what is now northern Vietnam was incorporated into the Late Han empire, and more especially under the T'ang dynasty (618–907), northern officials absorbed local leaders into the imperial hierarchy, and with the help of Chinese immigrants, introduced Chinese-style schools, law, clothing, marriage rites, and agriculture. Typically, Chinese influence receded with social distance from the great landowning families, often of mixed ancestry, who dominated the agricultural heartland of the Red River plain, and with physical distance from that plain, which was only a portion of the Protectorate of An Nam over which the T'ang claimed authority. As in Champa, the western foothills and uplands supported a mosaic of Austroasiatic-, Tai-, and Viet-speaking groups, while within the lowlands Cham and Indian Ocean contacts offered additional cultural currents. Thus T'ang efforts to transform non-elite society had limited success, and some provisions in the T'ang legal code may have applied only to immigrant Chinese. Even aristocratic Sino-Vietnamese families retained some local features – the Vietnamese

---

[25] On Cham relations with Angkor and the Sino-Viet state, Maspero, *Royaume*, chs. 6–9; George Coedes, *The Indianized States of Southeast Asia* (Honolulu, 1968); Lafont, "Les grandes dates," 7–25; Li, *Cochinchina*, 19–20.

[26] Higham, *Archaeology*, 190–203; Keith W. Taylor, *The Birth of Vietnam* (Berkeley, 1983), 2–13; O. W. Wolters, *History, Culture, and Region in Southeast Asian Perspectives* (Singapore, 1999), 15–26.

language itself for non-official communication, plus distinctive social customs and Buddhist traditions – which led them to develop their own perspective on Chinese civilization.[27]

T'ang decline in the 9th and early 10th centuries drew Vietnamese factions into a three-stage political evolution. In the first stage the relatively Sinicized landholding families declared their territory independent and defeated a Chinese attempt at reconquest, even as they preserved certain political features from the late T'ang era. In the second stage, from the 960s, rustic champions of more indigenous, less Sinic concepts of authority simultaneously infiltrated and challenged the aristocrats, shifted the capital from modern Hanoi to the southern edge of the Red River plain, and repelled another Chinese expeditionary force. But such military exploits were not matched by a political system capable of stabilizing relations with China or mobilizing fully the wealth and social authority of the plain. These were the achievements primarily of powerful Buddhist monks, who reconciled the two socio-cultural traditions and effected a relatively peaceful transfer of power to the Ly family, which if not the secular arm of the monkhood, was closely allied to it. This third stage saw a return to the T'ang-era capital (Hanoi), now renamed Thang Long, and the establishment of the Ly dynasty (1009–1225), which quickly surpassed its ephemeral 10th-century predecessors in power and longevity.[28]

Compared to Pagan, Suphanburi, or Angkor, Dai Viet ("Great Viet"), as the Ly named their polity in 1054, provided a weak charter for later generations. That is to say, because Dai Viet was heir to centuries of Chinese administrative precedents to which the more distant, religiously-oriented literature of India offered no equivalent, Dai Viet was less original, less politically seminal than contemporary Indic states on the mainland. After independence, O.W. Wolters argues that memories of the T'ang prevented the fracturing of Vietnam's territory, whose 10th-century warlords quickly adopted Chinese-style imperial titles, coinage, and ceremonies and tried to preserve the T'ang administrative framework.[29] Ly clan members, who hailed from an area of strong

[27] Taylor, *Birth*, chs. 7–9, esp. 220–21, 263–64; Jennifer Holmgren, *Chinese Colonisation of Northern Vietnam* (Canberra, 1980); Higham, *Archaeology*, 287–96.

[28] A somewhat similar three-stage evolution occurred in the 6th century. Taylor, *Birth*, 164, 250–301; idem, "Early Kingdoms," 137–40; idem, "The 'Twelve Lords' in Tenth-Century Vietnam," *JSEAS* 14 (1983): 46–62.

[29] Wolters, *Two Essays*, xxxii, following Keith Taylor; Wolters, "Le Van Huu's Treatment of Ly Than Ton's Reign (1127–1137)," in C.D. Cowan and Wolters, eds., *Southeast Asian*

Chinese influence with a high rate of literacy, proved yet more adept in employing T'ang institutions. In order to regulate internal family affairs and at the same time to set themselves apart from other families with whom they feared entangling alliances, the Ly built for themselves an Ancestral Temple, introduced a Chinese-style genealogy, and established each ruler's right to appoint his own heir without consulting his relatives. The latter step, in particular, encouraged patrilineal succession and reduced palace revolutions.[30] Also of great potential importance, men who could read and write Chinese were employed for diplomatic, ceremonial, and clerical chores. From 1075 to 1077, perhaps to strengthen itself during warfare with China, the Ly held examinations, loosely reminiscent of Chinese procedures, to select men with "classical learning."[31]

In addition to organizational precedents such as these, Chinese culture offered foundational myths that diminished the historic contribution of post-938 Vietnamese states and subjected them to potentially unflattering comparisons. Chinese antiquity provided idealized models of society and government to which Ly and then Tran rulers could only hope to aspire. The first Ly ruler himself affirmed his intention to restore the golden age of the Shang and Chou dynasties.[32] In 1272 the Vietnamese historian Le Van Huu praised a Chinese adventurer credited with founding the Vietnamese kingdom in the 3rd and 2nd centuries B.C.E., precisely because that adventurer retained the style of the Han emperors; but the 10th-century Vietnamese leader who actually won independence from China as well as several rulers of the Ly dynasty, Le Van Huu castigated for adhering to imperial norms that contravened the wisdom of antiquity as defined by Chinese texts.[33] As we shall see, Le Van Huu was first in a line of Sinophile critics who rejected Ly and Tran practices as unattractive, if not fundamentally immoral. Admittedly, Indic rulers invoked idealized precedents from the Indian

History and Historiography (Ithaca, 1976), 212; Taylor, "Twelve Lords," 61; Insun Yu, "The Changing Nature of the Red River Delta Villages during the Le Period (1428–1788)," *JSEAS* 32 (2001): 154–55.

[30] Wolters, "Le Van Huu," 212–15.

[31] Wolters, "Le Van Huu," 212–18; Taylor, "Early Kingdoms," 144, 147; idem, personal communication, Aug., 2001; idem, "Authority and Legitimacy in 11th Century Vietnam," in Marr and Milner, *9th to 14th Centuries*, 155; John Whitmore, "Elephants Can Actually Swim," ibid., 122–23, 128.

[32] Taylor, "Early Kingdoms," 140.

[33] Wolters, "Le Van Huu," 203–26, esp. 208, 215, 225; idem, "Historians and Emperors in Vietnam and China," in Anthony Reid and David Marr, eds., *Perceptions of the Past in Southeast Asia* (Singapore, 1979), esp. 72–77.

sub-continent (the Buddhist king Asoka, the kingdom of Ayodhya), but these models rarely, if ever, were used to devalue Pagan or Angkor, which for centuries inspired unalloyed admiration.

Such differences between what is now northern Vietnam and the rest of the mainland should not blind us to equally pregnant parallels which reflected some uncertain combination of pre-Sinic traditions, common non-Sinic external influences, and similar local exigencies.[34]

If we look at the organization of Ly government, for example, we find that beneath Chinese trappings, it resembled that of Pagan or Angkor more closely than it resembled the T'ang Protectorate of An Nam, not to mention the contemporary imperial government of Song China (960–1279). Although from the late 8th century T'ang control over An Nam's southern frontier weakened, Chinese rule in the Red River plain remained broadly similar to the closely administered prefecture-county system of metropolitan China.[35] In Song China itself, territorial administration grew more centralized than under the T'ang, while the civil service became more influential and bureaucratic, and an hereditary aristocracy faded into memory.[36] In independent Dai Viet the fiction of a unified government was necessary to avoid further Chinese interventions, and as we have seen, the Ly retained Sinic techniques to enhance its dignity for both domestic and external reasons. But in truth the Ly was merely a local dynasty, a *primus inter pares*, which controlled directly only one of several Vietnamese-speaking regions that had achieved a high degree of autonomy during the disorders of the 10th century. In typical solar polity fashion, the capital area provided virtually all the Ly's regular taxes and manpower, while autonomous leaders of outer administrative centers (*phu*) were tied to the throne through personal and family bonds in a system that was not only pre-bureaucratic, but substantially pre-literate. As elsewhere in Southeast Asia, a principal ritual involved oaths of personal allegiance, which meant imbibing sacralized animal blood before local spirits. After analyzing river embankments built before and during the Ly, Yumio Sakurai concluded that in contrast to the subsequent Tran era, no unified system of hydraulics provided the

---

[34] Perhaps one also could find similarities between Dai Viet and non-SE Asian polities such as the Yunnanese state of Nanzhao. Cf. Charles Backus, *The Nan-chao Kingdom and T'ang China's Southwestern Frontier* (New York, 1981), 59–63, 120, 159–61.

[35] Georges Maspero, "Le Protectorate general d'Annam sous les T'ang," *BEFEO* 10 (1910): esp. 551–84, 665–82; Taylor, *Birth*, 169–75, 201; Holmgren, *Chinese Colonisation*, ch. 6.

[36] Charles Hucker, *China's Imperial Past* (London, 1975), 154–55, 303–328; F. W. Mote, *Imperial China 900–1800* (Cambridge, MA: 1999), chs. 5–7, 14–15.

basis for centralized political power.[37] What can be gleaned about Ly court organization also points to a rudimentary set-up, with a handful of title-holding royal advisors and a few lower-level officers charged with specific duties in the capital or along the frontiers. To a surprising degree, kings themselves were the focus of official attention.[38] In recruiting officials, civil service examinations were marginal – the chief candidates in 1075–1077 were probably Buddhist monks, and there is little evidence of examinations after the 1080s – and all important posts were concentrated in the royal lineage, although favored courtiers could be enrolled into that family.[39] Despite their concern to designate each heir, Ly kings, like their Pagan and Angkorian counterparts, used polygamous marriages to cement ties to powerful regional families and failed to establish either hierarchical distinctions among legal wives or primogeniture. These practices, later pilloried by Confucian writers as profoundly unethical, unintentionally allowed maternal clans to introduce their rivalries at court. The custom of five queens may have had an Indic origin, and some royal women enjoyed a political role comparable to that elsewhere on the mainland.[40] So too, although Vietnamese law codes borrowed from the T'ang, the popular insistence, typical of Southeast Asia, on bilateral inheritance and relative female autonomy induced both Ly and post-Ly officials to reject or to modify substantially T'ang provisions on marriage and inheritance, while retaining more workable provisions on court etiquette and loyalty to the ruler.[41]

In short, the basic ethos and structure of Ly government were at best nominally Chinese. Just how bizarre post-imperial Vietnamese society must have appeared to educated Chinese is suggested in the late 10th-century ambassadorial account of a barefoot Vietnamese king who entertained his followers by fishing with a bamboo pole, but who asserted his equality to the Chinese emperor by tattooing "Army of the Son of

---

[37] Taylor, "Authority and Legitimacy," 140, citing Sakurai, whose approach is consistent with Gourou, *Les Paysans*, 83–85 and with Whitmore, "Elephants," 129–30. On Ly government, also Taylor, "Authority and Legitmacy;" Le Thanh Khoi, *Histoire du Vietnam des origines a 1858* (Paris, 1987), 144–51.
[38] Taylor, "Authority and Legitimacy," 150–51.
[39] Whitmore, "Elephants," 122.
[40] John Whitmore, "Gender, State, and History," in Barbara Watson Andaya, ed., *Other Pasts* (Honolulu, 2000), 217–18; Insun Yu, "Bilateral Social Pattern and the Status of Women in Traditional Vietnam," *SEAR* 7 (1999): 226–27; Taylor, "Authority and Legitimacy," 169–70; Wolters, "Le Van Huu," 215–16, 225.
[41] Nguyen and Ta, *Le Code*, I, 8–16; Taylor, *Birth*, 221; idem, "Early Kingdoms," 142; Whitmore, "Elephants," 124–25.

Heaven" in Chinese characters on his soldiers' foreheads. These people are "beyond civilization," the amused envoy concluded.[42]

As elsewhere on the mainland in this period, Ly dynasty religion was heavily animist, promiscuously eclectic, and non-exclusive. Now it is true that after the 10th century in China as well, the main trend in popular religion was toward the incorporation of Buddhist, Taoist, and Confucian elements into a "Three Doctrines" synthesis.[43] These patterns undoubtedly influenced Dai Viet, where in 1195 a "Three Doctrines" (tam-giao) examination tested knowledge of Confucianism, Buddhism, and Taoism/shamanism.[44] Note too that, although Indian and Southeast Asian influences on Vietnamese Buddhism were considerable,[45] the chief models for Vietnamese practitioners of Zen (thien) and for devotees of Amitabha and Avalokitesvara derived from China, and that Vietnamese Buddhism, like that of China, was Mahayanist rather than Theravadin.[46]

Nonetheless, Vietnamese religion in the Ly period differed from its Song counterpart in basic respects. For one, we find an unusual attention to Indian-style deities and cults. Indra, in particular, seems to have been the focus of a Hindu-Buddhist royal cult reminiscent of Pagan and Angkor, and the ruler Ly Cao Tong (r. 1175–1210), in identifying himself with the Buddha, may have imitated his Angkor contemporary Jayavarman VII.[47] In addition, Ly kings were far more preoccupied than their Song counterparts with placating local spirits. In part, Ly religion was eclectic because the very weakness of royal power necessitated accommodation with different local traditions, each with its own deities and cults. Ly kings strove, above all, to establish a personal relationship with the most powerful regional spirits, including

---

[42] Whitmore, "Elephants," 119, and earlier manuscript version of the same article; Gourou, *Les Paysans*, 134–35.

[43] Mote, *Imperial China*, 448–449, 499, 527–28; Hucker, *Imperial Past*, 357–78; Kenneth Ch'en, *Buddhism in China* (rpt., Princeton, 1973), 389–433, 439.

[44] Whitmore, "Foreign Influences and the Vietnamese Culture Core," in Truong Buu Lam, ed., *Borrowings and Adaptations in Vietnamese Culture* (Honolulu, 1987), 7; Taylor, "Authority and Legitimacy"; Cuong Tu Nguyen, *Zen in Medieval Vietnam* (Honolulu, 1997), ch. 3; Nguyen Thai Thu, ed., *History of Buddhism in Vietnam* (Hanoi, 1992), 194–95.

[45] Nguyen, *Zen*, 7, 19, 41, 71; Taylor, *Birth*, xix, 83–84.

[46] On the institutional, intellectual, and political history of Vietnamese Buddhism through the Ly, see Nguyen, *Zen*, pt. 1; Minh Chi, Ha Van Tan, and Nguyen Tai Thu, *Buddhism in Vietnam* (Hanoi, 1993), 71–85; Nguyen, *History of Buddhism*, chs. 1–8; Taylor, *Birth*, 80–230 *passim*; idem, "Authority and Legitimacy."

[47] Whitmore, "Elephants," 126; Nguyen The Anh, "Buddhism and Vietnamese Society throughout History," *SEAR* 1 (1993): 103.

nature gods and departed heroes, so as to create a kingdom-wide pantheon that would protect Buddhism and shelter the throne. Each king's
power depended substantially on his ability to rouse the spirits.[48] Recall
that in Pagan, Sukhothai, and early Lan Sang, kings also sought to incorporate pre-Indian local spirits into protective hierarchies. No less
revealing, whereas in Song China even at the local level elite literacy
was widespread, at the Ly court many high officials could not read,[49]
which suggests that as in other charter Southeast Asian states, textual
religious specialists employed by the court remained socially encapsulated. Whereas in Song China Buddhism retreated politically and culturally in the face of a dynamic Confucianism, which served as the creed
of a newly-dominant scholar official class, in Ly Vietnam Mahayana
Buddhism retained among the aristocracy the unrivalled influence it had
enjoyed during the imperial era. Finally, whereas in post-T'ang China
Buddhism's role in the political economy contracted, in Ly Vietnam we
find features reminiscent of Pattern A Indic administration. The Ly elite
gave lavishly to Buddhist institutions – one 11th-century king reportedly built almost 1,000 temples in five years[50] – while in turn temple
lands may have provided Ly kings with their first regular agrarian income outside the royal estates. As in Pagan and Angkor, temples were
concentrated in the capital region, where they helped compensate the
throne for the weakness of secular structures.[51] Yet it is unclear to what
extent Ly temple organization derived from local experiment, from contact with Champa and Angkor, or from the legacy of T'ang China, where
Buddhist temples also had played a major economic role.

The Tran dynasty (1225–1400), which acquired power after marrying
into the Ly, preserved the aristocratic Buddhist world of their predecessors, while achieving more effective political control, at least at the
outset. To regularize the succession and to prevent maternal family interference from which they themselves had benefited, Tran kings installed
a single empress, took queens only from their own family, insisted on
both primogeniture and patrilineality for themselves, and abdicated in

---

[48] Taylor, "Authority and Legitimacy," 143–50, 155–56, 161; Wolters, *Two Essays*, xvi–xx;
Nguyen, *Zen*, 17–19, 73–75.
[49] O. W. Wolters, "What Else May Ngo Si Lien Mean?" in Anthony Reid, ed., *Sojourners and
Settlers*, (St. Lucia, Australia, 1996), 108; Tran Quoc Vuong, "Traditions, Acculturation,
Renovation," in Marr and Milner, *9th to 14th Centuries*, 274.
[50] Nguyen The Anh, "Buddhism and Vietnamese Society," 100. Also Minh Chi et al.,
Buddhism, 85–89.
[51] Taylor, "Authority and Legitimacy," 151, 161; Nguyen, *History of Buddhism*, 117–29. On
temple lands under the protectorate, Taylor, *Birth*, 214.

favor of their eldest sons while retaining power behind the scenes.[52] In an effort to break the might of rival families in the Red River plain – something the Ly had never truly accomplished – the Tran at first experimented with bureaucratic Chinese procedures (see below) and then from the 1260s encouraged Tran princes to develop semi-hereditary estates with tied (serf and slave) labor and with the right to levy their own taxes, corvees, and soldiers. Apparently princely authority remained separate from that exercised by provincial "pacifiers" (*an-phu-su*), whom the throne appointed from other members of the royal can or court favorites. The armies that defeated Mongol invasions of Dai Viet in 1284 and 1287 were organized in princely domains without major help from the capital. In practice, therefore, the limits that some Tran princes set on royal power in the countryside may not have been appreciably less than the limits regional families had placed on the Ly kings. Yet so successful was the Tran clan as a whole in suppressing rival families, that when Tran dynastic power finally faded in the late 14th century, the clan that stepped forward to claim the throne came not from the Red River heartland, but for the first time from the Ma River area, farther south.[53]

Among the "three religions," Buddhism remained dominant. In the words of a later chronicler, the Tran, like the Ly, "venerated the Buddha as the source of everything."[54] Tran rulers, a majority of whom became patriarchs of a meditational school of Buddhism, left a considerable body of religious literature.[55] In combination with the temples' own economic activities, donations allowed these institutions to control what one critic claimed, perhaps polemically, was a fifth of Dai Viet's land.[56] Like their Ly predecessors, Tran kings and the Buddhist elite remained

[52] Whitmore, "Elephants," 132; Taylor, "Early Kingdoms," 148; O. W. Wolters, "On Telling a Story of Vietnam in the Thirteenth and Fourteenth Centuries," *JSEAS* 26 (1995): 64 ff.; idem, "Le Van Huu."
[53] On Tran administration, Nguyen and Ta, *Le Code*, I, 12–16; Whitmore, "Independent Vietnam: Indigenous Politics and Culture" (ms), 46–66; idem, *Ho Quy Ly*, 1–16; idem, personal communications, Jan., 2002; Wolters, *Two Essays*, 54–164 *passim*; idem, "Ngo Si Lien," 107–10; idem, "Telling a Story," 65–74; Taylor, "Early Kingdoms," 148–49; idem, personal communication, Aug., 2001; Nguyen Khac Vien, *Vietnam: A Long History* (Hanoi, 1987), 33–40.
[54] Wolters, "Ngo Si Lien," 107.
[55] Nguyen, *History of Buddhism*, 172–81. On Tran Buddhism, ibid., 171–228; Minh Chi et al., *Buddhism*, 89–122; Wolters, "Ngo Si Lien," 110; idem, "Telling a Story," 65; J. C. Cleary, "Buddhism and Popular Religion in Medieval Vietnam," *Jl. of the American Academy of Religion* 59 (1991): 93–118.
[56] Nguyen, *History of Buddhism*, 235.

intensely interested in local spirits: deities who helped Dai Viet prevail over the Mongols and Chams received imperial appointments and in 1329 were included in an official compilation to honor spirit protectors of Buddhism and the kingdom.[57]

Amidst these familiar elements, under the Tran Confucian models became more influential. In part, this was because economic growth favored an emerging class of modest private landowners – variously identified as "lower landlords" and "wealthy farming families" – who relied more heavily on tenants or hired labor than on serfs.[58] Far below Tran princes in wealth and status, these men instinctively favored government recruitment through civil service examinations over aristocratic ascription, and Confucian over Buddhist studies. From their ranks the Confucian literati emerged. No less important, some Tran princes proved more willing than the Ly to patronize Chinese culture, either because of a stronger cultural identification (the Tran may have been descended from Chinese immigrants) or because they recognized its utility. We must assume that through Chinese immigration, interstate diplomacy, and the circulation of texts, educated Vietnamese grew increasingly familiar with the details of Song and then Yuan (1279–1368) government and high culture.

Sinic influence became apparent in three areas. First, the Tran began using Chinese-style examinations to recruit literati into a somewhat larger, more formally structured administration. For the first time a handful of examination graduates obtained more than ornamental posts at the capital. After replacing Ly provinces with smaller units, the early Tran regime also sent some literati officials into the countryside and sought to set up Chinese-style population registers for each village, the better to improve tax collections, the military draft, and river diking. In the mid-13th century, when these experiments were still in vogue, most land apparently belonged to villages whose communal property bore tax obligations to the king and whose members were liable for corvee.[59] Second, the Tran's Sinic-inspired insistence on a single empress and royal primogeniture helped to produce a dynastic stability rare by

---

[57] Keith Taylor, "Notes on the *Viet Dien U Linh Tap*," *The Vietnam Forum* 8 (1986): 26–59; Nguyen, Zen, 73–75.

[58] Nguyen, *History of Buddhism*, 222–23; Taylor, "Early Kingdoms," 148; Wolters, *Two Essays*, 4, 122; Nguyen Khac Vien, *Vietnam*, 33–34, 57.

[59] Whitmore, "Elephants," 132; Nguyen Khac Vien, *Vietnam*, 33–34; Wolters, *Two Essays*, xxxv, 4, 5, 11; Taylor, "Early Kingdoms," 148; Gourou, *Les Paysans*, 84; Yu, "Changing Nature," 156.

Southeast Asian standards. (Note, however, that the Tran made no effort to push Chinese-style inheritance into society at large. That would occur only in the late 15th and 16th centuries.)[60] Third, classical scholars, like the aforementioned Le Van Huu, began to articulate a normative social vision that attacked Buddhist "superstitions," the Ly's non-Sinic family practices, and the willingness of both Ly and Tran courts to treat Chams and other "barbarians" as equal to Vietnamese.[61] These critiques anticipated a conflict between Chinese and indigenous modes that simultaneously bred tension between elite and village subcultures.

But if such Sinic innovations foreshadowed late 14th- and 15th-century transitions, in the Tran era Confucian literati never achieved a dominant voice. In this aristocratic world, personal favor, birth, and entourage still counted for everything. The blood oath remained a key ritual. Some courtiers who could not read a word still held key posts. Women continued to assume leadership roles, and courtiers still took their mother's family name in violation of the most basic Confucian precepts. After spearheading victory over the Mongols, high-ranking princes and officers drawn from local members of the Tran clan expanded their authority at the expense of the literati.[62] Indeed, in some contexts, Chinese norms favored by the literati came to be seen as unpatriotic. When Vietnamese scholars pressed the ruler Minh-tong (1320–1357) to adopt more Chinese-style reforms, he sternly rebuked them: "Our country has its own definite principles [of laws]. The Northern and Southern countries [China and Vietnam] are different. If we adopt the plan of the pale-faced [Confucian] students, disorder will immediately follow."[63] After another period of experimentation with Song laws and institutions, in the 1370s during what may have been an aristocratic reaction, the court again reverted to local ways. As Nghe-tong (1369–1394) explained, "When our former rulers founded the state, they did so with their own institutes. They did not follow the S[o]ng system, and the reason is that South and North each is ruled by its own emperor and

---

[60] Wolters, "Ngo Si Lien," 110; idem, *Two Essays*, 10; Whitmore, "Elephants," 131–33; idem and C. S. Chang, personal communications, March 2002; Nguyen and Ta, *Le Code*, I, 14. However, according to Tran, "Traditions, Acculturation," 274, the Tran cross-cousin marriage pattern was Malay, not Chinese.

[61] Wolters, "Le Van Huu"; idem, "Telling a Story," 63–74; Whitmore, "Independent Vietnam," 53–65.

[62] See nn. 53, 60 *supra*, plus Wolters, *History, Culture, and Region* 234, emphasizing the non-Sinic, often pivotal court role of Tran women.

[63] Nguyen and Ta, *Le Code*, I, 14. The scholars' pallor reflected their closeted lifestyle. See also Whitmore, *Ho Quy Ly*, 9–10, 16.

they are not to be confused."[64] In the same nativist spirit, the late Tran forbade Chinese dress at court, along with Lao and Cham speech.

Much the same combination of piecemeal innovation and structural continuity characterized pre-1400 relations with the Chams. In 1306, as noted, the Tran court claimed Cham lands in Indrapura down to the Hai Van Pass. But even if we take these claims at face value, Cham losses were but a fraction of the territory they would relinquish in the late 15th century. Chams, in fact, continued to launch lively incursions into Indrapura, while Vietnamese attacks, in typical Southeast Asian fashion, still sought booty and prisoners with only limited efforts at colonization.[65] Moreover, whereas in the late 15th century Vietnam's self-proclaimed civilizing mission would preclude any hint of Viet-Cham equality, the Tran continued to treat their powerful southern neighbors with respect, entering into marriage alliances and importing Cham music, choreography, and architecture, even in preference to those of China.

In sum, if Sinic elements grew more influential under the Tran, in terms of aristocratic leadership, decentralized, at best partially literate political organization, Buddhist-dominated religious syncretism, and external relations, the Tran and Ly together constituted a coherent period in Vietnamese history that exhibits intriguing similarities to Indic charter polities farther west.

What can be said about economic change during the Ly-Tran era? As elsewhere across the mainland and indeed many parts of Eurasia, such information as we have points to significant demographic growth and sustained land reclamation between c. 950 and 1300. Studies of Vietnamese village cults, family genealogies, and village traditions alike point to intensified movement after the 10th century from the higher, hillier areas of the Red River basin north and west of the capital into deltaic and coastal regions to the south and east. Taming the deltaic environment, which required laborious construction of small polders to establish footholds in the swamps, followed by drainage and irrigation works, was more taxing than cultivating the foothills, but potentially more rewarding insofar as fertile soil and abundant water guaranteed the rice harvest and facilitated multiple cropping.[66] During

---

[64] Wolters, *Two Essays*, 15. These royal dates follow ibid., 15.

[65] Nguyen The Anh, "Le Nam Tien dans les textes vietnamiens," in *Les Frontiers du Vietnam* (Paris, 1989), 121–23; Whitmore, *Ho Quy Ly*, 3–4; Li, *Cochinchina*, 20–21; *Seminaire*, map.

[66] Gourou, *Les Paysans*, 83–85, 113–21, 130–35; Yumio Sakurai, "Vietnam After the Age of Commerce" (ms); Taylor, "Authority and Legitimacy," 140, citing Sakurai; Whitmore, "Elephants," 129–30. See also the maps of early delta topography in Taylor, *Birth*, 2, 11.

the Ly era villages on the fringes of the delta tried to expand into the swamps via primitive polder construction. But under the Tran larger-scale engineering permitted a rapid expansion of the polder network and a corresponding growth in population.[67]

Why, then, this expansion from the 11th and more especially the 13th century? Chapters 2 and 3 have summarized dendrological, pollen, and historical evidence from areas near the Red River delta, including southeast China and northern Thailand, which point to stronger monsoons throughout much of the period c. 950–1300, not least the early to mid-1200s.[68] In so watery an environment as the Red River delta, would not increased rainfall have been a deeply unwelcome impediment? And would not extensive agricultural development in Dong Kinh discredit the suggestion that pluvial conditions c. 950–1300 favored dry zone sites like Pagan and Angkor over water-logged deltaic extremities?

Three factors may have privileged the early Red River delta over its Irrawaddy and Chaophraya counterparts. First, although annual rainfall at Hanoi and Bangkok is now similar (69 vs. 56 inches, respectively), Rangoon receives nearly 100 inches a year.[69] All things being equal, water control is therefore likely to have been a less daunting task in the Red River delta than in the Irrawaddy delta. Second, more obviously than in either the Irrawaddy or Chaophraya system, those who reclaimed the delta came from upland areas with limited agricultural potential that would have benefited from wetter conditions. Delta colonization in the Ly and Tran eras drew in part on communities at higher elevations in areas like Bac Giang, Thai Nguyen, Phu Tho, and Hoa Binh, where fifth-month and even tenth-month rice crops remain vulnerable to drought.[70] By reducing famine mortality and promoting early marriage and fertility, more reliable rain-fed harvests in hillier areas may have helped to create the demographic pressure that impelled delta reclamation in the first place, while providing the extra manpower needed for polder construction to succeed. Moreover, if we extrapolate from Robert Marks' recent study of Guangdong's Pearl River basin, whose hilly topography resembles that of the Red River far more closely than that of the Irrawaddy or Chaophraya, during the 12th–14th centuries population pressure and slash-and-burn agriculture in the hills aggravated erosion,

[67] Sakurai, "Age of Commerce," 1.
[68] See esp. Ch. 2, nn. 49–53.
[69] Charles Fisher, *South-East Asia* (London, 1964), 23, 486.
[70] Gourou, *Les Paysans*, 65–70.

thus increasing the downstream flow of fertile silt to support polder construction.[71]

Third, whereas in neither Lower Burma nor coastal Siam is there any evidence of centrally-coordinated river control, the Tran, relying to some extent on Chinese techniques, took responsibility for enlarging and maintaining dikes within a unified system of water distribution and flood prevention extending from the northwest delta all the way to the sea. Although the Ly period apparently saw some efforts at supra-local coordination, in that era dike construction and repairs depended chiefly on local initiatives, whether by villages, temples, or powerful local families. The Tran court, however, named a director-general and sub-director for water works under whom after 1255 a military official in each province marshaled troops to construct canals and dikes at the end of each agricultural season. Notwithstanding the subsequent retreat of literati influence, court-appointed administrators and military officials continued to coordinate water-control efforts. Through a combination of central and local initiatives, new dikes or major extensions arose along the Red, Thai Binh, Ma, and Chu Rivers. The Tran also built dikes along the coast to protect against tides and typhoons and to exploit new land formed by silt accumulating at river mouths. Thus, much of Thai Binh province at the Red River mouth was reclaimed from the sea and salt marsh.[72] Again, perhaps the closest analogy is neither the Irrawaddy nor the Chaophraya, but the nearby Pearl River basin, where some 62 dikes and embankments during the Song (960–1279) and Yuan (1279–1368) opened the floodplain to cultivation, reduced the habitat of malarial mosquitoes, and funneled silt to islands in the developing estuary.[73] The Irrawaddy and Chaophraya deltas would enjoy a similar agricultural florescence, but only at a somewhat later date and through primarily local, rather than central initiatives.

Although Tran diking projects had no close mainland counterpart, the growing scale of public works does call to mind the more or less contemporary increase in the scale of temple construction at Pagan and Angkor and the expansion of Angkorian reservoirs. Also familiar are the potential economic benefits of charter–era pacification. After almost a century of competition between the delta and other Viet-speaking areas,

[71] Robert Marks, *Tigers, Rice, Silk, and Silt* (Cambridge, 1998), chs. 1–2, esp. 29–33, 70.
[72] Taylor, "Authority and Legitimacy," 139–40, citing Sakurai; Nguyen Khac Vien, *Vietnam*, 35–36; Gourou, *Les Paysans*, 83–85; Keith Taylor, personal communication, Aug., 2001; John Whitmore, personal communication, Dec., 2001.
[73] Marks, *Tigers, Rice*, esp. 22–25, 66–83.

regional leaders' recognition of Ly primacy offered an umbrella under which local reclamation could proceed unhindered.[74] Tran pacification, yet more effective, continued well into the 14th century.

As at Pagan and Angkor, the contribution of foreign trade seems to have been modest. Momoki Shiro has argued that the Ly's limited agrarian authority encouraged a compensatory interest in maritime exchange both through the port of Vandon on the northeastern edge of the delta and farther south in Nghe An. The overland route from Nghe An to the Mekong valley rivaled long-established Cham routes farther south and probably contributed to Viet-Cham tensions. Under the Tran, Chinese techniques permitted the manufacture for export of Yuan-style brown underglaze ceramics, as well as silks. But there is no evidence before 1400 that such activities had more than a marginal impact on demography or rural production.[75]

EARLY COLLECTIVE IDENTITIES

Because political authority resided in the person of the ruler, to talk of collective identities is not to imply a sense of horizontal community, much less sanction for popular action. Yet under the Ly and Tran the notion became entrenched that the Vietnamese king ruled a culturally and historically distinct population. Given Dong Kinh's exposure to northern culture and the recurrent threat of northern reconquest – northern armies invaded at least five times between 981 and the final Mongol incursion in 1287 – it is hardly surprising that the local elite (at least the literate sector which left records) should have defined their ruler and his realm largely in terms of their relation to the great power to their north.

As the above references to the "Northern and Southern countries" suggest, the consistent strategy of early Vietnamese ideologues was to assert the equality of China and Dai Viet. But this equivalence could take two forms. On the one hand, some spokesmen – from Ly thinkers through the Tran emperors Minh-tong and Nghe-tong – emphasized the

[74] Taylor, "Twelve Lords," 61. Note, however, Taylor's comment that during the 10th century prior to the Ly accession, "there is little concrete evidence of any great disorder in Vietnam." See also idem, *Birth*, 271, 274, 278, 296.

[75] Momoki Shiro, "Dai Viet and the South China Sea Trade from the 10th to the 15th Century," *Crossroads* 12 (1998): 1–34; Whitmore, "Elephants," 130–31; John S. Guy, "Vietnamese Ceramics and Cultural Identity," in Marr and Milner, *9th to 14th Centuries*, 255–69; Le, *Histoire*, 150. A 13th-century Chinese account *Zhu Fan Zhi* claimed, "This kingdom [Dai Viet] does not trade [with foreigners]." Li, *Cochinchina*, 59.

separate heritage of the South, including its idiosyncratic terrain, which was protected by Heaven and by local guardian spirits, and its special customs (in one account, short hair, tattooing, and betel chewing), which Tran nativists proudly defended. In the late 13th century, in particular, Nguyen Ngoc Bich suggests that Mongol invasions helped to stimulate such distinctively Vietnamese cultural expressions as the first systematic recording of Vietnamese mythology, the first extant history of Dai Viet, the establishment of the distinctively Vietnamese Truc Lam sect of Mahayana Buddhism, perhaps too more systematized versions of demotic (*nom*) script.[76] On the other hand, Confucian writers also sought to use the Chinese' own criteria of civilization (proper social relations, rites, literature) to prove to themselves and to any Chinese who might be interested that Dai Viet was just as civilized as China, and therefore in no way in need of northern tutelage. Allied to this strategy was the attempt to demonstrate the equivalence of Vietnamese and Chinese antiquity by finding within Chinese history itself precedents for the existence of two Chinese-style emperors, two "Sons of Heaven." Gathering all Yueh (Viet) peoples under a mythic ruler who was descended from the same ancestor as the first Chinese, late 14th-century historians thus strove to place the Vietnamese and Chinese polities on equal footing.[77] Although in fact both intellectual approaches might appear in the same document, on the whole, given the growth of classical Chinese studies, the latter gradually became the strategy of choice.

As for the peasantry, preeminently local, at best dimly aware of Chinese cultural categories, mute as ever, it is difficult to know in what ways they may have been pulled by supra-local symbols and claims. Village subordination to the throne was reflected in tax and corvee obligations, and symbolically in shared Buddhist rituals and in what may have been the popular image of the ruler (*vua*) as virtuous protector.

[76] Nguyen Ngoc Bich, "Vietnamese Poetry," in Sara Robertson, ed., *Vietnam: Essays on History, Culture, and Society* (New York, 1985), 85. However, Keith Taylor, personal communication, Aug., 2001, emphasizes that *nom* may have originated as early as the 3rd century CE, and casts doubt on the claims for Tran systemization. On pre-1400 culture change and Viet identity, see too Wolters, *Two Essays*, 15, 30–31; Huynh Sanh Thong, *The Heritage of Vietnamese Poetry* (New Haven, 1979), xxviii–xxix, xl; John Whitmore, "Cartography in Vietnam," in J. B. Harley and David Woodward, eds., *The History of Cartography*, vol. 2, bk. 2 (Chicago, 1994), 481; Wolters, "Le Van Huu"; James Anderson, "The *ANCL* as Common Ground" (ms).

[77] E. S. Ungar, "From Myth to History," in Marr and Milner, *9th to 14th Centuries*, 177–86; Wolters, Two Essays, 22–26; idem, "Historians and Emperors," 69–89. Note, however, that "all Yueh peoples" probably included those of South China.

Some have argued that the Tran-era court and village both saw a landscape protected by fierce guardian genii, among which aquatic animal spirits (emblems of fertility and potency) were identified with the king. It has been suggested too that some of the earliest folktales mentioned danger from the north, that is, from China, and bespoke separate north/south destinies.[78] Be that as it may – and one must take care not to contaminate early materials with 20th-century nationalist biases – during the crisis of the 14th and 15th centuries, any notion of Vietnamese solidarity that did exist ran up against entrenched local allegiances. Pan-Vietnamese loyalties could not prevent many southern Vietnamese-speakers from joining Chams, or Dong Kinh literati from supporting a fresh Chinese invasion. Let us turn to the traumas of the 1300s and 1400s, which destroyed the aristocratic Buddhist world of Ly and Tran.

THE COLLAPSE OF THE 14TH CENTURY

Why Dai Viet suffered appalling disasters in the mid- and late 1300s is no more certain than why the empires of Upper Burma and Angkor disintegrated during roughly this same period. Surely, however, these transitions were related, directly and indirectly.

During the early 1300s the peasant population in the Red River delta began to outstrip available resources. In this same period, recall, Roland Fletcher and Christophe Pottier have suggested that sustained population growth and shortages of good land, accompanied by extensive deforestation and disturbance of irrigation channels and waterways, overwhelmed Angkor's fragile ecology; while in Upper Burma in the late 13th and 14th centuries, we examined evidence that by denying fresh income to a crown obliged to make continuous tax-free religious donations, a growing scarcity of irrigable land crippled central authority.[79] Monastic holdings in Vietnam were less dangerous to royal finances than at Pagan, but the general problem of land shortages in the agricultural core seems to have been at least as severe. In Dong Kinh as in much of the mainland (and indeed, Eurasia) in the 14th century, this was less a Malthusian problem per se – more equitable land

---

[78] On local-court relations in this period, Nguyen Ngoc Bich, "The Power and Relevance of Vietnamese Myths," in Robertson, *Vietnam: Essays*, 65–68; Trang Quoc Vuong, "The Legend of Ong Dong from the Text to the Field," in Taylor and Whitmore, *Essays*, 13–41; Taylor, "*Viet Dien U Linh Tap*," 26–59; Wolters, *Two Essays*, xxiv–xxxiv, 9–12.

[79] See discussion *supra* Chs. 2, 3.

distribution might have restored viability to sectors of the peasantry –
than a crisis brought on by the intersection of demographic growth with
institutional constraints. The aforementioned combination of beneficent climate, migration, water control projects, coastal reclamation, and
sustained pacification allowed the population of the Red River delta,
according to one estimate, to mushroom from c. 1,200,000 in 1200 to
c. 2,400,000 in 1340. By the latter date this created an average density
of 150–180 people and one to two villages per square kilometer.[80] But,
given a slowdown in reclamation efforts in the 14th century and the
tendency of Tran princes and temples to engross independent village
holdings, cultivators attached to those villages faced mounting difficulties. With more marginal lands under cultivation, productivity must
have fallen, along with the average size of holdings and the peasantry's
ability to pay rents. An expansion in trade and domestic handicrafts
could hardly compensate, nor is there any evidence of agronomic advance.[81] By 1350, no significant uncultivated delta tracts remained accessible to peasants attached to communal villages. Moreover, recently
founded villages were concentrated in those lowland areas most vulnerable to ruptures in the dikes. The fragility of the embankment and
irrigation system limited output to a modest 1–1.5 tons per hectare, and
in Sakurai's view, increased the instability of production insofar as it
created an involutionary, labor intensive structure easily disrupted by
political or social unrest.[82]

Such disruptions were not long in coming. As per capita welfare
fell, registered peasants began leaving village tax rolls either to seek
refuge with Tran princes and monasteries or to forage as vagabonds
and bandits. For their part, princes and other notables became ever
more eager to convert tax-paying village lands into untaxed private estates (*trang dien*) worked by servile laborers. Often the court itself, by
awarding large tracts to meritorious followers and temples, favored the
growth of such estates. Thus, much as in Pagan and post-Pagan Burma,

---

[80] Sakurai, "Age of Commerce" puts the late Tran delta population at c. 2,400,000 (in a
rather crude graph p. 3) and the total population for the delta and southern regions at
over 3,000,000 (p. 1). Esta Ungar, "Sources for Historical Demography: Vietnam from
the 15th Century" (ms) cites a Ly population figure, apparently for the entire kingdom,
of 3,300,000, and claims that the Tran figure was appreciably higher, but offers no
numbers. See too Sakurai, "Peasant Drain and Abandoned Villages in the Red River
Delta between 1750 and 1850," in Anthony Reid, *The Last Stand of Asian Autonomies*
(New York, 1997), 133–52; Gourou, *Les Paysans*, 114–21, 131–37.

[81] Nguyen, *History of Buddhism*, 171; Nguyen Khac Vien, *Vietnam*, 33–38.

[82] Sakurai, "Age of Commerce."

the weakening of royal authority and the expansion of private networks reinforced one another. Naturally, the loss of tax-paying lands
and cultivators increased fiscal and corvee burdens on those peasants
who remained on the royal registers, encouraging further flight and
weakening the labor-dependent dikes (some of which may not have
been properly repaired after Mongol damage in the 1280s). From 1343
onwards the annals referred repeatedly to rural uprisings that attracted
monks, princely dependents, and starving vagabonds. Under the ban-
ner "Relieve the impoverished people," one revolt lasted from 1343 to
1360. In 1389 an army of vagabonds led by a monk occupied the capital
for three days. These disturbances joined with drought, crumbling water
control, peasant flight, disease, and invasions to collapse the delta population, Sakurai estimates, from c. 2,400,000 in 1340 to perhaps 1,600,000
in 1400, although conceivably emigration to hilly areas and southern
districts reduced the demographic decline for Dai Viet as a whole.[83]

Of course, the question remains why these 14th-century disorders coincided broadly with growing difficulties in Upper Burma and Angkor,
both of which, we have seen, suffered severe setbacks in the 1350s and
1360s. Despite references to pestilence and a putative population fall in
the delta of a third, which was comparable to mortality rates in 14th-
century Europe during the Black Death, there is no evidence that the
Black Death hit Vietnam or any other part of mainland Southeast Asia.[84]
The Mongols may have been a marginal synchronizing factor insofar as
they sacked Pagan, encouraged Tai movements in the west and central
mainland, and weakened Dai Viet by impairing the hydraulic works
and magnifying the power of the Tran princes. Yet, Mongol incursions
in the 1280s hardly can explain Dai Viet's problems 60 years later, least
of all, overpopulation. One could posit for Dai Viet, Pagan, and perhaps Angkor, an inherent tendency toward dynastic cyclicity, whereby
an initially successful dynasty was obliged to tolerate the accumulation of resources by political or religious elites on whom it depended.

[83] Sakurai, "Age of Commerce," 3, offering delta figures somewhat larger than those
implied at Li, *Cochinchina*, 160, 171, which refers to the entire north. In the absence of
non-delta figures, Fig. 4.2 generalizes delta losses to other districts. The best descriptions
of 14th-century disorders appear at Wolters, *Two Essays*, 16 ff., 57; idem, "Telling a Story,"
68–74; Ungar, "Leadership," ch. 1; Yu, "Changing Nature," 160.
[84] B. J. Terwiel, "Early Ayutthaya, Trade, and Evidence of an Epidemic," *Tai Culture* 2
(1997): 72–73, speculates that the Black Death afflicted the lower Chaophraya in the mid-
14th century, but relies on flimsiest evidence. Population losses in 13th/14th century
Lingnan reflected primarily political disorders associated with dynastic transitions.
Marks, *Tigers, Rice*, 56–57, 85.

Wolters has called attention to the deteriorating caliber of Tran princes.[85] But such dynamics cannot tell us why under dynasties founded at very different times, "internal cycles" (to use a biological metaphor) should have climaxed at roughly the same time. (The Tran, for example, was founded about 180 years after Anaw-rahta took the throne, but growing difficulties in Dong Kinh and Upper Burma were more or less coordinated.)

How much synchronization can we attribute to climate? Evidence, some indirect, for Burma, north Thailand, and much of south China argues that a period of markedly drier weather began, depending on locale, between c. 1250 and 1350, and deepened into the 15th century. Early Vietnamese chronicles were more forthcoming about climate than those farther west. They too point to favorable agricultural conditions during most of the 12th and 13th centuries, followed by an era of pronounced instability dominated by drought. From the 1290s unseasonable droughts as well as occasional floods increased until by the mid-1300s such calamities had become almost annual. A general desiccation continued at least until 1392, perhaps 1407. Although floods may have been a function of poor dike maintenance, the same obviously cannot be said of droughts, which hit particularly hard the fringes of the delta and outlying areas. Inevitably these conditions precipitated famines, such as that associated with the summer drought of 1343, which marked the outbreak of violence by rural vagabonds. In turn, poor nutrition and roving bands of beggars and bandits helped to spread non-bubonic diseases (aggravated perhaps by climatic changes suitable to the dissemination of pathogens).[86] In short, I am hypothesizing – the data are too spotty to do more – that here as in much of mainland Southeast Asia, advantageous rainfall c. 1000–1290 joined with domestic pacification and beneficial foreign contacts to support sustained demographic expansion, but that after centuries of such growth, climatic downturn from c. 1290 joined with endemic political weaknesses to weaken the

[85] Wolters, "Telling a Story," 69–70.

[86] For accounts of climatic (and human) disaster, n. 83 *supra*, plus Whitmore, *Ho Quy Ly*, 34 and chs. 1–2 *passim*. Conceivably, chronicle accounts of climate were intended as moral statements about royal leadership, but their specificity and coincidence with external materials (the drought of 1392, for example, is confirmed by Sao Saimong Mangrai, *The Padaeng Chronicle and the Jengtung State Chronicle Translated* [Ann Arbor, 1981], 141) suggest otherwise. Note that increased climatic variability, juxtaposing drought and flood, was characteristic of the Little Ice Age generally. Jiacheng Zhang and Thomas Crowley, "Historical Climate Records in China and the Reconstruction of Past Climates," *Jl. of Climate* (1989): 843. See too *supra* Ch. 2, nn. 54, 90; Ch. 3, n. 83.

polity. Evidence of popular distress and land hunger is clearer for Dai Viet than for Pagan or Angkor, in part because records are more diverse, but more basically perhaps, because population densities in Dong Kinh must have been higher. Yet in all three zones by the mid-14th century, if not earlier, resource constraints had become severe. In Dai Viet, the rise of landowner-based literati who were severely critical of the Ly-Tran social order can be seen as another destabilizing factor rooted in part in sustained economic growth.

As in the Irrawaddy basin and the Cambodian plain, disorders in the heartland soon invited invasions, in this case by Chams eager to reverse Vietnamese advances. From 1361 to 1390 the Cham hero-king Che Bong Nga mounted a series of devastating raids into Dong Kinh, in 1377 killing the Tran ruler outside the Cham capital, followed by a new invasion of Dong Kinh and a sack of Thang Long (Hanoi). Here three possible connections to wider Southeast Asian developments deserve mention. First, Chinese and Southeast Asian trade in the 14th century may have aided Champa vis-a-vis Dai Viet in much the same way that it strengthened Pegu over Ava, and Ayudhya over Angkor. Insofar as the principal eastern shipping lanes bypassed Dong Kinh to run east of Hainan island between Champa and the south China coast, Champa would have been the chief beneficiary of late Yuan/early Ming trade expansion.[87] Second, Ayudhya's ferocious post-1350 attacks against Angkor, with which Champa had long been embroiled, allowed Champa to concentrate on the northern danger.[88] Insofar as Angkor's debility also reflected maritime trade expansion, the same factor was doubly injurious to Dai Viet's fortunes. Finally and more speculatively, Momoki Shiro has suggested that Champa in the 13th and 14th centuries experienced a population increase that was modest by Dai Viet standards but locally unsustainable, and that the ensuing agricultural over-exploitation helped inspire Che Bong Nga's northern forays.[89]

In the ensuing invasions not only did Dai Viet lose control over districts north of the Hai Van Pass, not only were long settled Vietnamese areas thrown into turmoil, but as noted, some disaffected courtiers and southern Vietnamese joined the Chams. At the same time, individual

[87] *Supra* Ch. 2, nn. 16, 92, Ch. 3, n. 86; Momoki, "South China Sea Trade"; idem, "Pure Maritime Polity," 6–8.

[88] Coedes, *Indianized States*, 152–71 *passim*, 229–30, 237–39; Whitmore, *Ho Quy Ly*, 16–23; Li, *Cochinchina*, 20–21.

[89] Momoki, "Pure Maritime Polity," 7. Improved 12th–13th century rainfall well may have aided Champa, but Mimoki provides little evidence of agricultural expansion.

Chams supported the Tran.[90] This fluidity of ethnic allegiance on the north-south interface recalls contemporary Mon-Burman crossovers.

Yet however serious Dai Viet's problems were, they proved far less crippling or sustained than those in either Upper Burma or Angkor. Compared to those sprawling, polyglot empires, Dai Viet was compact, easily monitored, and ethnically uniform. Unlike the Tais who settled in Upper Burma and along Angkor's northern and western perimeter, the Chams were too few to colonize densely populated Dong Kinh or even the southern borderlands. With the death of Che Bong Nga in battle in 1390, the tide began to turn, culminating in Champa's dismemberment by 1471. In effect, Champa became the final victim of the 14th/15th-century crisis. Nor did Dong Kinh suffer incursions by Tai-speakers, either because local population densities deterred settlement or because Tai migration routes had been pushed farther west.[91] Moreover, with its Sinic population registers, stable royal succession, and embryonic examinations, Dai Viet's educated elite had an exceptionally rich administrative technology on which to base recovery.

FROM THE 14TH CENTURY CRISIS TO THE FOUNDING OF THE LE DYNASTY

As in the western and more especially the central mainland, where Theravada Buddhism supplanted elite Hindu-Buddhist syntheses, the disasters of the 1300s generated transformative intellectual critiques that helped to make the late 14th and 15th centuries a period of extraordinary ferment.

To some extent perhaps, increased Tran patronage of the Truc-Lam Buddhist sect, with its harmonizing holistic views and its efforts to teach compassion and moral virtue to the common people, responded to the social crisis.[92] But the most influential response was that of literati steeped in Chinese classical scholarship, who with increasing vehemence and clarity condemned the entire system of Buddhist culture and aristocratic governance as responsible for the late Tran chaos. Although the literati came from a rising social class, it was this sudden, intense yearning for renewed order that gave classical studies their decisive

---

[90] Whitmore, *Ho Quy Ly*, 19, 29–32.

[91] John Whitmore, "Colliding Peoples: Tai/Viet Interactions in the 14th and 15th Centuries" (ms).

[92] Whitmore, "Chu Van An and the Rise of 'Antiquity' in 14th-Century Dai Viet," *The Vietnam Review* 1 (1996): 58; Wolters, *Two Essays*, 121.

appeal. Charging that Buddhism had made people insensitive to those obligations on which the social order rested, scholars began to demand the selection of more educated officials who would "love the people," as well as the establishment of Confucian-style schools in the country-side that would instill a stronger sense of social obligation. In the hands of these literati, stories about the legendary Vietnamese kingdom of Van Lang and Chinese stories of the ancient sage kings Yao and Shun were reworked to create specifically Vietnamese versions of Antiquity, a golden age, whose lessons in good governance promised an escape from the current impasse. The literati sought not to Sinicize Dai Viet – they were at pains to create separate genealogies for the Chinese and Vietnamese and, in some cases, to emphasize the superiority of indigenous custom – but to select from the classical canon such practical and miscellaneous prescriptions as could alleviate the crisis. Yet in pursuing this goal, they presaged a political and social order very different from the aristocratic, Buddhist society of Ly and Tran, a new order in which Confucian literati would act as architects of policy and as moral guardians of the relation between throne and society. For this reason, Wolters has argued that the 14th century constituted a true watershed in Vietnamese thought.[93]

The realization of the literati vision was a fragile, hesitant, extraordinarily complex transformation that proceeded between 1390 and 1509 in three major stages: that of the Ho dynasty to 1407, that of the Ming occupation to 1427, and that of the Le dynasty to 1509 (itself divisible into distinct sub-periods). Each stage promoted a peculiar version of Confucian teachings. Each also brought to the fore, in rather see-saw fashion, a political constituency with a more or less distinct regional base.

At the height of the Cham crisis, the minister Ho Quy Ly gained control over the Tran court, and went on to proclaim his own dynasty that lasted from 1400 to 1407. In seeking to justify his power not through Buddhism, but through an antique version of Chinese thought, the Ho regime testified to the growing power of Sinic norms. Ho Quy Ly sought to restore the power of the central apparatus, to destroy the retinues of Tran aristocrats, to curb the monkhood, and to promote Chinese learning. Yet the Ho regime failed to win substantial literati support. For

---

[93] Wolters, *Two Essays*, esp. vii, 3, 36, 22–39, 118–19, 124ff.; idem, "Telling A Story," 63–74; idem, "Phan Su Manh's Poems Written When Patrolling the Vietnamese Northern Border in the Middle of the Fourteenth Century," *Vietnam Forum* 4 (1984); idem, "Ngo Si Lien," 112. See also Ungar, "Leadership," 17–27; Whitmore, "Chu Van An," 50–61.

one thing, the Ho resembled the Tran in that major posts went to family members and proteges, while civil service examination graduates tended to receive honorific appointments. Moreover, whereas the delta literati naturally favored the retention of the capital in the delta city of Thang Long, Ho Quy Ly moved it to the southern frontier region of Thanh Nghe, where his family was based.[94]

At this point it is necessary to distinguish more clearly between the regional traditions of Dong Kinh, that it to say, the Red River plain, and Thanh Nghe. As a largely Vietnamese-speaking zone whose history was closely intertwined with that of the delta, from which many of its people in fact migrated, Thanh Nghe shared basic features with Dong Kinh. Its leaders – from Ho Quy Ly through the founders of the Le dynasty – focused unwaveringly on controlling the plain. We find no claims for independent Thanh Nghe sovereignty. As early as the Tran a handful of local men became known for their Confucian erudition, and as we shall see, by the 15th century, Thanh Nghe leaders were using Confucian family terminology to organize patrilineal clans. That said, Thanh Nghe was a poor, thinly populated frontier zone, whose Vietnamese-speaking lowlanders lived cheek by jowl with hill peoples and Chams and whose overall culture, by Dong Kinh standards, remained non-Sinic and primitive. Unlike the peasantry of the densely populated plain, Thanh Nghe men were famous as warriors, later providing the Le army with most of its officers. Dong Kinh accounts of the 15th century described southerners as fierce, overwhelmingly illiterate, devoted to blood oaths, magic, and animal sacrifices (monkey sacrifices, for example, were favored to ward off eclipses). No doubt they also spoke various local patois, which in the western hills probably shaded off into a related, but non-Vietnamese language spoken by people now known as Muong.[95] Notwithstanding literate traditions among some aristocratic families, most southern military leaders had little use for Chinese learning, emphasizing above all physical valor, charisma, and personal loyalty. Such values inclined many Thanh Nghe families to define their interests as distinct from those of Dong Kinh clans. The

[94] Whitmore, *Ho Quy Ly*, chs. 2–4. His base actually was in Thanh Hoa in northern Thanh Nghe.

[95] Thanh Nghe conventionally includes the provinces of Thanh Hoa, Nghe An, and Ha Tinh. Patois were spoken there in the 18th century, according to M. l'Abbe Richard, *Histoire naturelle, civile et politique du Tonquin*, 2 vols. (Paris, 1778), I, 97. On Thanh Nghe society and culture in the 14th/15th century, see Ungar, "Leadership," 50–60, 239, 244, 261; Whitmore, "New View." On the Muong, Taylor, "On Being Muonged"; Frank Lebar et al., *Ethnic Groups of Mainland Southeast Asia* (New Haven, 1964), 161, 171–75.

situation therefore was loosely analogous to that in late 14th-century Ayhudhya or Upper Burma, where families also maintained strong regional identities while competing within a nominally unified polity.

Such tensions are critical to understanding the transition from Ho to Ming to Le, as well as the long-term fate of Confucianization. In 1407 the new Ming dynasty in China took advantage of the Ho usurpation to invade Dai Viet. After at first claiming that they came merely to restore the Tran, the Ming announced the more ambitious goal of civilizing the region and reincorporating it within the empire. Notwithstanding 20th century assumptions about the sanctity of "national independence," in response to Ming calls for "men of talent," the Dong Kinh literati promptly split. Some scholars, motivated perhaps by pan-Vietnamese feeling or personal loyalty to the Ho or Tran, withdrew from public life. But others, probably a substantial majority, preferred the Ming to the Ho, precisely because they resented the Ho's regional bias and because the Ming now offered them unprecedented prestige and power.[96] In pursuit of their *mission civilisatrice*, the Ming encouraged a sensibility more Sinic and reformist than anything Ho Quy Ly had contemplated: the Ming promoted Chinese dress, founded Confucian schools in rural districts for the first time, and – of great intellectual import – promoted Neo-Confucian orthodoxy based on Zhu Xi's writings in preference to the antique Chinese classicism favored by Ho and 14th-century Vietnamese literati. The Chinese also went well beyond the Ho in breaking up private concentrations of land and manpower.

Ultimately, however, the Ming failed: in 1427 their armies were forced to withdraw after a series of humiliating defeats at the hands of Le Loi, the southern insurgent who went on to found the Le dynasty (1428–1788). Factors external to Vietnam were critical, including Ming financial difficulties, Ming worries about their northern frontier with the Mongols, and the fact that in the competition for military manpower, commanders in Vietnam fared worse than their counterparts in southwest China who had stronger connections to the Ming imperial family.[97] Had one or more of these factors altered, Vietnamese history

---

[96] On Vietnamese support for the Ming and the Ming occupation, Taylor, "Surface Orientations," 955–56; idem, "Regional Conflicts," 110–111; Yu, "Changing Nature," 156, 164; Whitmore, "Development," 3–10; idem, *Ho Quy Ly*, ch. 7, esp. 97–98, 115–16; Alexander Woodside, "Early Ming Expansionism (1406–1427)," *Papers on China* 17 (1963), esp. 17, 23, 29; Ungar, "Leadership," 48–49.

[97] James Lee, personal communication, July, 2001.

well might have gone in a very different direction. Yet within Vietnam itself it is also clear that Ming officials could neither defeat the guerrilla tactics of southern warriors nor extend their appeal beyond the Dong Kinh literati. Thanh Nghe warriors formed the core of Le Loi's movement whose victory, Taylor argues, represented something of a conquest of Dong Kinh by southern highland rustics.[98]

The question is, to what extent did Le Loi also tap wider pan-Vietnamese loyalties? Indeed, did such loyalties exist? The only ideological statement, the only conceptualization of political space, that Le Loi's movement has left are the writings of Nguyen Trai, a prominent anti-Ming scholar from Dong Kinh. Shocked at first by Le Loi's crude manner – Nguyen Trai met him carving a pig carcass and eating with his hands[99] – Nguyen Trai nonetheless crafted proclamations that sought to win over fellow literati to Le Loi's cause. Nguyen Trai envisioned a Confucian ecumene in which ethnically-neutral moral principles provided the only true yardstick of legitimacy. Yet alongside the emphasis on "humaneness" and "justice" as universal tenets, Nguyen Trai, in the tradition of 14th-century literati, referred to Dai Viet as a land unalterably distinct from the North, with its own customs and a geomantic terrain protected by Heaven and local spirits. Successive Dai Viet rulers had defeated Chinese invasions, precisely because Chinese incursions violated the natural order.[100] By reworking a trope from Han historiography so as to present himself, the loyal minister from Dong Kinh, and Le Loi, the man with kingly virtue from Thanh Nghe, as essential elements in a single leadership team, Nguyen Trai provided a metaphor for the unity of the kingdom.[101]

---

[98] Taylor, "Surface Orientations," 956–57.

[99] Ungar, "Leadership," 54–55.

[100] A 15th-century text celebrated the Ming defeat by noting, "The soil is again the soil of the Southern kingdom. The people are again the people of the Viet race." But when Le Loi asked why the Ming had been defeated, his ministers replied not because the Ming were foreigners, but because their harsh punishments had lost "the hearts of the people." Woodside, *Vietnam*, 21. On Nguyen Trai and Le Loi, Ungar, "Leadership," 15–20, 54–76, 96–97, 268; Truong Buu Lam, *Patterns of Vietnamese Response to Foreign Intervention: 1858–1900* (New Haven, 1967), 55–62; Nguyen Khac Vien, Huu Ngoc, et al., *Vietnamese Literature* (Hanoi, n.d.), 232–44; Stephen O'Harrow, "Nguyen Trai's Binh Ngo Dai Cao of 1428," *JSEAS* 10 (1979): 159–74; O. W. Wolters, "A Stranger in His Own Land," *Vietnam Forum* 8 (1986): 60–90; Le, *Histoire*, 201–18; Moto Furuta, *Betonamujin kyoshan shugisha no minzoku seisaku shi* (Tokyo, 1991), tr., Matthew Stavros, 46–62.

[101] At the same time, of course, he emphasized his own indispensability. Taylor, "Regional Conflicts," 111; idem, "Surface Orientations," 956–57.

It is difficult to determine how these edicts were received. Esta Ungar suggests that pre-Sinic notions of authority were sufficiently powerful, and intercourse among different sectors of the Vietnamese-speaking elite sufficiently regular, that leaders in both Dong Kinh and Thanh Nghe accepted this image of Dai Viet as a realm of supernatural terrain, entitled to its own Heaven-ordained ruler. Thanh Nghe warriors and many literati may have regarded the king (*vua*) as a father entitled to the same reverence as departed heroes.[102] Consistent with this interpretation, Tran loyalists in the north resisted the Ming, while other Dong Kinhese later joined Nguyen Trai and Le Loi in the south. On the other hand, there is little evidence that Le Loi's movement ever championed specific cultural attributes. Le Loi himself, one of the towering heroes of Vietnamese history, was in origin almost certainly not Vietnamese, but Muong, if we use 20th-century ethnic categories. In the 15th century, Taylor suggests that boundaries between these groups were indistinct and porous. Le Loi's decisive push against the Ming in 1424 relied on people from the Ca River basin, the bulk of whom were probably Muong by current usage.[103] Whether Vietnamese- or Muong-speaking, most rebel leaders in Thanh Nghe (probably including Le Loi himself) would have been unable to understand Nguyen Trai's Chinese-language edicts, which targeted a specifically literati audience. Conversely, insofar as they remained loyal to the Ming to the bitter end in 1427, many, perhaps most of Vietnamese-speakers who could understand Nguyen Trai refused to endorse his vision. While these Dong Kinh literati have left no apologia, we may assume that personal advantage and humane sensibility alike continued to demand their allegiance to the Ming court, epicenter of civilization.

THE NEO-CONFUCIAN REVOLUTION OF THE 15TH AND EARLY 16TH CENTURIES

Regionally-based family rivalries continued to influence early Le history – indeed much of early modern Vietnamese history – even as Neo-Confucian influence gradually increased. The Le dynasty, which the victorious Le Loi proclaimed in 1428, took steps to conciliate the Dong Kinh literati. To that end it kept Thang Long as its primary capital and preserved key features of Ming administration, including

[102] Ungar, "Leadership," 15–19, 266–67.
[103] Taylor, "On Being Muonged," 33–34.

the schools, a greater reliance on legal precedent, and from the 1440s, Dai Viet's first orthodox Chinese-style examinations. In this same period a new generation of modernist Neo-Confucian intellectuals who venerated Zhu Xi and the scholarship of Ming China triumphed over Vietnamese classicists who favored older writings. Nonetheless, through the mid-1400s not the literati, but Thanh Nghe military clans dominated the court. While honoring Confucian norms, when they selected officials southern soldiers favored not civil service exams, but family ties. Precisely because they had formed the backbone of Le Loi's army, and because Ming collaboration still tainted many Dong Kinh families, until 1460 southerners succeeded in maintaining an oligarchic structure basically similar to that of the Tran and Ho regimes.[104]

Under Le Thanh-tong (r. 1460–1497), whose conquests and whose pioneering embrace of the Neo-Confucian model arguably made him the most celebrated king in Vietnamese history, the pendulum shifted. Although Thanh Nghe clans, to whom the new king remained tied by blood and marriage, continued to dominate the army and benefited most directly from Le Thanh-tong's military expansion, scholar officials from Dong Kinh achieved undreamed of influence in royal councils. Why this new regional formula? To penetrate villages in the delta, whose resources were needed for domestic programs and a projected invasion of Champa, stronger literati support was essential. With a new literati generation, the stigma of collaboration wore thin. Most basic perhaps, Thanh-tong himself, who had been tutored by literati, shared their deeply moralizing vision that seems to have swept much of the countryside in this period.

Perhaps the most singular aspect of the Neo-Confucian reforms – which began under Thanh-tong, continued under his immediate 16th-century successors, and provided a model for literati into the 19th century – was their passionately transformative, almost soteriological raison d'etre. Responding to the traumas of the 14th century as well as to the Ming example, literati demands for fundamental political change, demands that had been pullulating for generations, now blossomed in a quasi-religious movement reminiscent in some ways of contemporary Theravada reform. Far more than mere social conventions, the "five relationships" as interpreted in Zhu Xi Neo-Confucian

---

[104] Whitmore, "Development," chs. 1–3; Ungar, "Leadership," chs. 3–6. Unless otherwise indicated, my discussion of early Le history relies on Whitmore, "Development," esp. chs. 4–6 and App.A; idem, "New View."

as well as in earlier classical texts embodied absolute cosmic principles (*ly*). To align one's self and one's society with these immanent forces, to give living expression to these "primal truths," was the highest responsibility of every cultivated man.[105]

This vision, this missionary zeal necessarily estranged the literati from the imperfect world in which they lived, even as it impelled them to colonize systematically the cultural space that now opened up. For one thing, Neo-Confucianism separated the literati from their own royal past. Whereas annalists as late as the 1440s had reported Ho Quy Ly's heterodox views without comment, the historian Ngo Si Lien, who was commissioned in 1479 to edit the royal Annals, not only branded Ho's thinking dangerously anti-Confucian, but went on to castigate a host of Tran practices – "incestuous" marriages, lapses in Confucian propriety, illiterate officials – as shockingly unethical. So shrill, so fundamental were these attacks that they underscore Wolters' argument for a "major discontinuity" between the Tran period and the later 15th century.[106] In response to these and similar critiques, the Tran emphasis on birth and personal charisma now gave way to more universal moral concerns and stylized bureaucratic structures. Closeness at court and the blood oath yielded to ceremonial distance. In iconography, an eel-like symbol of the throne was replaced by the Sinic dragon.[107] It is true that the 15th century saw an upsurge of poetry written in *nom* – quasi-phonetic scripts, derived from Chinese, but adapted for writing the Vietnamese language with Thanh-tong himself sponsoring one of the earliest anthologies of *nom* poetry. But this too was consistent with the basic Le project of localizing Sinic learning, all the more so as early *nom* closely reflected Chinese meters and themes. At the same time, Chinese still provided the medium for all official communications, and Chinese-character literature flourished under the early Le.[108]

As John Whitmore, the leading scholar of early Le history, has shown, Le literati became increasingly estranged not only from their own past, but from their non-Sinic neighbors, most notably the Chams. Despite or

---

[105] Woodside, "Medieval Vietnam," 315–19; Cooke, "Confucianization," 277, 292–93; and John Whitmore, "Text and Thought in the Hong Duc Era (1470–1497)" (ms), calling attention to the influence of "primordial," pre-Zhu Xi texts.

[106] Wolters, "Ngo Si Lien," 94–114, esp. 112. Cf. Cooke, "Confucianization," 292–93.

[107] Whitmore, "Foreign Influences," 10.

[108] Nguyen Khac Vien, Nguyen van Hoan, and Huu Ngoc, *Anthologie de la litterature Vietnamienne*, 3 vols. (Hanoi, 1972), I, 143–212; Nguyen et al., *Vietnamese Literature*, 232–55; Maurice M. Durand and Nguyen Tran Huan, *An Introduction to Vietnamese Literature* (New York, 1985), 58–69.

because of Cham raids in the late 1300s, Ho Quy Ly (and probably Le Loi himself) had continued to treat the Chams as legitimate competitors and potential allies. But Thanh-tong, echoing literati critiques of Tran policy and copying perhaps Ming treatment of Vietnam itself, denounced them as people insensitive to Heaven's dictates who had to be transformed. After a massive invasion in 1470–1471, Thanh-tong took some 30,000 prisoners and destroyed the Cham capital Vijaya, whose desolation he advertised by displaying on the prow of his returning ship the Cham king's severed head. The victor proceeded to annex the Cham territories of Amaravati and Vijaya as far as Cape Varella to form the new province of Quang Nam, while converting rump Champa into three tributary statelets. These annexations were over five times larger than all previously conquered Cham lands. Although in fact large-scale colonization did not begin until the late 16th century, by breaking the Cham hold on the plains of Quang Nam, the 1471 victory presaged their long-term assimilation and decline.[109] After upland Tais around Tran Ninh rebelled against Vietnamese interference, in 1479 Thanh-tong also launched a five-year punitive campaign that not only expanded his control over the western hills, but ravaged Lan Sang (which had aided the rebels) and Tai areas as far west as the upper Irrawaddy.[110]

Whereas non-Vietnamese defectors and deportees once had been welcomed without stricture, Thanh-tong ordered all Cham prisoners (as well as people of Lao and Chinese descent) to become Vietnamese, that is, to adopt Vietnamese names, to take Vietnamese wives, and to begin "correcting themselves."[111] If such demands embodied Thanh-tong's Neo-Confucian moralism, at a more visceral level they may have reflected a xenophobic reaction against repeated external attacks such as Burmese and Siamese exhibited at a later date. In 1499, for fear that Cham matriarchal traditions would interfere with Vietnamese inheritance, all Vietnamese "from princes down to commoners" were prohibited

---

[109] I simplify a complex narrative: Vietnamese took Vijaya in 1446, but Chams recaptured it. Likewise, in the 1500s Chams temporarily recovered parts of the territories lost in 1471. Maspero, *Royaume*, 226–41; Lafont, "Les grandes dates"; Po Dharma, "Le declin du Campa entre le XVIe et le XIXe siecle," in *Le Campa et le Monde Malais*, 47–63.

[110] Le, *Histoire*, 245; David Wyatt, tr., *The Nan Chronicle* (Ithaca, 1994), 57; Sun Laichen, "Ming-Southeast Asian Overland Interactions, 1368–1644" (Univ. of Michigan Ph.D. diss., 2000), 261–67. Cf. discussion of 15th-century Lan Sang *supra*, Ch. 3.

[111] Whitmore, "New View," 70. As early as the 1430s lowland literati wrote, "We Vietnamese cannot follow the languages and clothing styles of the Chinese, the Chams, the Lao, the Siamese, or the Cambodians and thereby create chaos among our own customs," idem, "Colliding Peoples," 7.

from marrying unassimilated Cham women. Ten years later, on discovery of a plot, anti-Cham discrimination reached its peak with orders to exterminate all Chams in the capital area. Whether such measures were actually implemented is less important than the distinction they sought to draw between a zone of increasingly Sinic norms in the heartland of Dai Viet and alien, non-Sinic, largely Indic cultures to the south and west.[112]

Arguably, however, the most pregnant divide separated the literati neither from earlier dynasties nor the Chams. Rather, it divided them from their own peasantry – from the peasants' "immoral" and "incestuous" family practices, their Buddhist rituals, witchcraft, and other "superstitions." Insofar as they sought to push textual orthodoxy into the countryside, these reforms recall those in Burma and Siam. Yet literati reforms were more ambitious, both because the Le could invoke Ming precedents, and more basically, because Neo-Confucianism had a social agenda far more comprehensive and intolerant than did Theravada Buddhism. To promote material welfare, the Le law code tried to regulate everything from land sales to debt interest to poor relief. But at the heart of the Neo-Confucian vision lay an insistence on proper family relations: mourning procedures, marriage rites, patrilineality and quasi-primogeniturial inheritance. The new code embodied these norms whose provisions district officals sought to honor while explaining laws and edicts to assembled villagers in words they could understand. Thus Sinic family norms began to influence the wider society, although the process was glacial and even the new code reflected extensive differences with China, especially as regards women.[113] The court likewise sought to curtail monks, Taoist adepts, and sorcerers, while sanitizing and centralizing cults of local deities dear to Ly and Tran monarchs.

Efforts to transform the countryside rested on two administrative structures characteristic of Pattern D: a rationalized system of local governance and an expanded program of examinations. Some 9,700 villages

[112] Nguyen The Anh, "The Vietnamization of the Cham Deity Po Nagar," in Taylor and Whitmore, *Essays*, 46; Nguyen and Ta, *Le Code*, II, 185; Ta Van Tai, "Ethnic Minorities and the Law in Traditional Vietnam," *Vietnam Forum* 5 (1985), 28. Did the continued fluidity of Viet-Muong boundaries reflect stronger linguistic/cultural affinities – or the Muong's failure to create a state system comparable to that of Champa that could threaten Dai Viet?

[113] Nguyen and Ta, *Le Code*, I, 60–68, 183–84, 189, and *passim*; Woodside, "Medieval Vietnam," 318; John Whitmore, "Administrative Control of the Spirits" (ms); idem, "New View;" Esta Ungar, "Sources for Historical Demography"; Nguyen, *Vietnam*, 76–77; Li Tana, personal communication, 1998.

in the Red River delta and Thanh Hoa were organized into a Chinese-style grid, exceptionally penetrating by Southeast Asian standards, of circuits (*dao*), prefectures (*phu*), and districts (*chau*). Whereas Theravada courts usually appointed but one level of provincial personnel, Thang Long appointed and rotated officers down to the district level, who in turn effectively appointed village (*xa*) leaders. Capping the system were six ministries, together with a Ming-style Communications Office to process the increased flow of written reports. Administrators were especially warned to protect peasant rights to communal land (*cong dien*), the only type then subject to taxation. On Sinic land registers (*dien bo*) and population registers (*dinh bo*), in theory collated every four to six years, rested the system of taxes, military conscription, and corvees. In fact, as Whitmore has emphasized, many of Thanh-tong's reforms were more a matter of style than substance, and authority at the highest levels continued to revolve around family networks in which royal women played a pivotal role. Yet their own desire to strengthen the state joined their new cultural orientation to make leading families, including some from Thanh Nghe, ever more willing to honor Chinese-style procedures.[114]

Accordingly, civil service examinations now became the chief means of government recruitment. From 1463 to 1509 the palace examinations, the highest of three levels, produced by far the highest number of graduates for any era of Vietnamese history. On a deeper level, the system of examinations – and preparation for the exams through private tuition and an expanded network of state schools – provided a reservoir of literate adepts who had no chance of ever holding office but who served as cultural models in the villages. The new insistence that village headmen be literate, maintain Chinese-style family structures, and serve as vanguards of moral transformation encouraged ambitious local families to pursue literacy and adhere to Confucian norms. Attested literacy also became necessary to gain exemption from corvees and to hold office on village councils. Thus landlords, rich and even middle peasants aspired to provide at least one son with sufficient literacy to pass local examinations every few years. Such was their enthusiasm that

[114] On early Le administration and examinations, previous nn. plus Whitmore, "Cartography," 478–508; idem, "Queen Mother: The Origin of Family Politics in Early Modern Vietnam" (ms); Yu, "Law and Family," 19–27; idem, "Changing Nature," 157, 164–66, 172; Yumio Sakurai "The Change in the Name and Number of Village[s] in Medieval Vietnam," *Social Sciences* 1 (1986): 124–45.

in the late 1400s and early 1500s up to 30,000 men took each low-level triennial regional examination. Notwithstanding Neo-Confucianism's greater ambition and secular elitism, this movement again resembled Theravada monasticism in its reliance on new educational structures and the incentive to literacy that tax exemptions provided.

To sum up, in the eastern as in the western and central mainland, the generalized collapse of the 1300s yielded in the latter half of the next century to a phase of vigorous territorial expansion, administrative experiment, and state-sponsored religious/moral reform. Beginning a generation before Toungoo Burma's first major conquests but roughly coterminous with Ayudhya's thrusts against Angkor and Lan Na, Dai Viet's southern victories benefited from the memory of earlier unity, competitive experiments, and receptivity to new cultural currents.

A GREAT UPSURGE: SOCIO-ECONOMIC CHANGE AND ITS POLITICAL IMPLICATIONS, C. 1400–1550

Although Vietnamese economic historiography remains the poor step-child of political studies, we know enough to see that here as in the rest of the mainland, political integration in the mid- and late 15th century also drew strength from rapid demographic and economic growth.

To begin with the most obvious potential agent of regional synchronization, international commerce was by no means unimportant to Dai Viet. It has been suggested that one goal of the Ming invasion was to gain control of Vietnamese emporia, and that Thanh-tong in expanding to the west and south, also sought, in part, to seize Champa's profitable trade with China and to forge a tributary trade system comparable to that of the Ming.[115] Taking advantage of post–1433 Ming curbs on Chinese

---

[115] Momoki Shiro, "Was Dai Viet a Rival of Ryukyu within the Tributary Trade System of the Ming during the Early Le Period?" (ms). On Dai Viet's foreign trade and bullion flows in this period, see too Sakurai, "Age of Commerce," 2; Abu Ridho, "The Meaning of Ceramics Found in the Sea of Tuban," in *Final Report: Consultative Report on Research on Maritime Shipping and Trade Networks in Southeast Asia* (Cisuara, Indonesia, 1984), 283–95; John Guy, *Oriental Trade Ceramics in South-East Asia 9th to 16th Centuries* (Singapore, 1986), ch. 6; Truong Huu Quynh, "The Birth and Development of Pho Hien," in *Pho Hien, the Centre of International Commerce in the XVII–XVIIIth Centuries* (Hanoi, 1994), 30–33; Woodside, "Ming Expansionism," 24–25; John Whitmore, "Vietnam and the Monetary Flow of Eastern Asia, 13th to 18th Centuries," in John Richards, ed., *Precious Metals in the Later Medieval and Early Modern Worlds* (Durham, NC, 1983), 363–93, esp. 369–70.

exports, Vietnamese kilns produced handsome Chinese-style blue-and-white wares and red Annamese ceramics that sold throughout Southeast Asia, China, and as far as Turkey, Persia, and Japan. Vietnamese raw silk and taffetas appeared in Melaka and Japan. Although Chinese and other foreigners handled most exchanges, some Vietnamese traded with south China and the Gulf of Siam, while traffic also went over the hills to Laos, Yunnan, and Guangxi. From its founding in the late 1400s, Thang Long's downriver port of Pho Hien grew rapidly, introducing significant, if as yet unquantified, amounts of copper cash from China and later Japan that aided commodity production.

Yet if we compare the economy of Dai Viet to that of Lower Burma or Ayudhya in the 15th and early 16th centuries, the balance between agricultural and maritime activities tilted far more heavily toward agriculture. This may have been a function in part of tepid Confucian enthusiasm for commerce, in part of Dong Kinh's weaker access to the main sea lanes. While dutifully listing Dai Viet's exports and imports c. 1515, Tome Pires argued that its power and wealth derived primarily from the land.[116] Some forty years later a Portuguese priest Fr. Gaspar da Cruz claimed that the people of Dong Kinh were quite prosperous but conducted virtually no trade with "other peoples outside of their own kingdom."[117] Not only did Le documents demonstrate a frequent disdain for commerce, but Thanh-tong is said to have discouraged visits by merchants from Siam, Malaya, and the islands, areas that in the Tran era had conducted a lively trade with Dai Viet.[118] Although in Guangxi and Guangdong foreign trade drove silk and other forms of agricultural specialization, which in turn spurred population growth, Dai Viet's silk exports were not on the same scale; moreover, even in south China these were essentially post-1550 phenomena.[119] In short, while conceding that Dong Kinh benefited from Chinese immigration and specie and that overseas demand provided ancillary employment, on current evidence one would be hard pressed to accord foreign trade primary responsibility for Dong Kinh's economic dynamism in the 15th and early 16th centuries.

---

[116] Armando Cortesao, ed., *The Suma Oriental of Tome Pires*, 2 vols. (London, 1944), I, 114–15.

[117] In C. R. Boxer, ed., *South China in the Sixteenth Century* (London, 1953), 73.

[118] Whitmore, "Monetary Flow" 378; Nguyen Thanh-Nha, *Tableau economique du Viet Nam aux XVII et XVIII siecles* (Paris, 1970), 188; Nguyen Khac Vien, *Vietnam*, 75; Le, *Histoire*, 240–41; Li, *Cochinchina*, 59.

[119] Marks, *Tigers, Rice*, ch. 3.

What then were the chief sources of renewed vitality? Proxy records of rainfall for north Thailand,[120] summer temperatures for China,[121] and the wetness index for Guangzhou[122] suggest that the Red River delta experienced stronger monsoons 1460/1480–1525 and 1545–1580. In Guangxi and Guangdong not only did rainfall aid yields, but warmer spring temperatures removed the twin dangers of delayed transplanting and damage to the early rice crop.[123] To an uncertain degree, by reducing mortality and enhancing nuptiality, climatic amelioration probably contributed to strong population growth in Dong Kinh c. 1400–1550 – an increase that, for whatever reasons, correlated with expansion in much of Europe as well as south China.[124]

There is no indication that recovery from disease played the central role it did in Europe's 15th-century demographic revival. On the other hand, in Dai Viet as in Europe, early Ming China, and other parts of Southeast Asia, renewed political consolidation, an associated reduction in strife, and government actions clearly spurred demographic and economic recovery. After the last serious Cham incursion in 1390 and the Ming withdrawal of 1427, Vietnam enjoyed almost a century of domestic peace that contrasted sharply with the turmoil of the three previous generations. The sharp population decline of the late Tran period and the concomitant abandonment of less productive, marginal lands suggests that per capita productivity for much of the 15th century was higher than in the 1300s. Villages in low-lying swampy areas outside the polder cores had been the first to empty out during the 14th-century troubles, but now with more settled conditions, peasants from older villages without adequate land quickly reoccupied these sites. Peasants also resumed the push into virgin lands, some of excellent quality, beyond the delta. The early Le strongly supported agriculture by confiscating

---

[120] David Godley, "Flood Regimes in Northern Thailand" (Monash Univ. MA thesis, 1997), chs. 5, 6, esp. 119–22, 139–42.
[121] Raymond Bradley and Philip Jones, eds., *Climate Since A.D. 1500* (London, 1995), Fig. 34.2, p. 674; Zhang and Crowley, "Historical Climate Records," 843; Zhang De'er, "Evidence for the Existence of the Medieval Warm Period in China," CC 26 (1994): 289–97; William Atwell, "Time, Money, and the Weather: Ming China and the 'Great Depression' of the Mid-Fifteenth Century," *JAS* 61 (2002): 100–101.
[122] Marks, *Tigers, Rice*, Fig. 6.3, p. 200. Also idem, "It Never Used To Snow," in Mark Elvin and Liu T'sui-jung, eds., *Sediments of Time* (Cambridge, 1998), 411–46, esp. 419–22.
[123] Previous note, plus Marks, *Tigers, Rice*, ch. 3, esp. 114, 126–27.
[124] Cf. this chapter Fig. 4.2; Marks, *Tigers, Rice*, 85; Colin McEvedy and Richard Jones, *Atlas of World Population History* (London, 1978), 18 and pt. I passim. However, it is unclear if Vietnam suffered a mid-15th-century economic/demographic slowdown comparable to that which Atwell, "Time, Money, and Weather," 83–113, posits for China.

uncultivated land, building new irrigation canals, creating special offices to manage delta dikes, and encouraging reclamation along the coast, the western foothills, and especially the southern frontier.[125]

Did new crops raise the area's carrying capacity? We have less information on post-1400 rice history than in Burma or Siam. Fast-ripening, drought-resistant southern strains known as Champa rice (probably varieties of *indica*) became popular in Dong Kinh, but this seems to have been underway by 1250. By 1770, three main types of rice – fifth-month concentrated in the floodplain, tenth-month on higher ground, and third-month along sandbanks – were subdivided into over 70 sub-varieties adapted to specific terrains.[126]

Although it is unclear when these adaptations occurred, population growth throughout most of the period 1400–1500 (and especially after 1470) is indicated not only by land reclamation, but by ecological strains: an early-16th century history claimed, with rhetorical exaggeration perhaps, that the demand for wood to build houses in the lowlands became so great as to denude nearby mountains, while coastal provinces could no longer store fish because of the enormous demand for salt.[127] Sakurai estimates that the delta population rose from its nadir of 1.6 million in 1400 to about 2.5 million in 1490, which was at or above its 14th century peak.[128] After analyzing chronicles, censuses, and village records for frontier areas as well as the delta, Li Tana has estimated that the population of northern Vietnam as a whole tripled during the early Le, from 1,862,000 in 1417, to 4,373,000 in 1490, to 5,625,000 in 1539. The number of villages (*xa*) rose proportionately (see Figure 4.2).[129]

In combination with Chinese trade and frontier colonization, renewed demographic growth boosted the volume and velocity of market exchange. By stimulating the production of armaments and military

---

[125] Nguyen The Anh, "Le Nam Tien," 122–23; Whitmore, "Development," 195–96; Nguyen, *Tableau*, 41, 61; Nguyen Khac Vien, *Vietnam*, 74. See discussion of colonization *infra*.

[126] Alexander Woodside, "The Relationship between Political Theory and Economic Growth in Vietnam, 1750–1840," in Reid, *Last Stand*, 254–57; Nguyen, *Tableau*, 50; Whitmore, "Elephants," 130; Sakurai, "Peasant Drain," 151, n. 2; Dao The Tuan, "Types of Rice Cultivation and Its Related Civilizations in Vietnam," *East Asian Cultural Studies* 24 (1985): 41–56.

[127] John Whitmore, "*Chung-hsing* and *Cheng-t'ung* in Texts of and on Sixteenth-Century Vietnam," in Taylor and Whitmore, *Essays*, 118. Perhaps demand for salt also reflected growing trade with hillpeoples.

[128] Sakurai, "Age of Commerce," 3.

[129] Li, *Cochinchina*, 159–72, esp. Table 4. Cf. Nguyen, *Tableau*, 40–41; Yu, "Law and Family," 191; Whitmore, *Ho Quy Ly*, 106.

supplies, Dai Viet's external campaigns and (to a lesser extent perhaps, insofar as they simultaneously bred disorder) her 16th-century civil wars reinforced that trend.[130] Growing demand for wood and salt point to stronger commercial demand, but the same conclusion derives from a look at market organization and monetary difficulties. In the early 1400s all Dai Viet had fewer than 90 recognized markets (*thi*), but during the late 15th century the court sanctioned and encouraged the opening of a large, if indeterminate number of additional sites. If we may extrapolate from somewhat later patterns, these included 7–day periodic markets which collected agricultural produce while supplying nearby villagers with cloth, fish-sauce, salt, hardware, and ritual goods; as well as seasonal fairs and permanent urban markets, concentrated in the delta and along the coast.[131] Although barter remained more common than it would become in the 17th century, a late Tran increase in demand for specie now accelerated, but could not be met from existing stocks. Aggravated by coin shortages throughout East Asia and especially China, where in the mid-1400s mine output plummeted even as the demand for silver media rose sharply, Vietnam's monetary difficulties led Nguyen Trai to declare. "Coin is the life's blood of the people; [they] cannot do without it."[132] Late 15th- and 16th-century Vietnamese rulers expanded the minting of copper cash, debased some denominations, experimented with zinc and iron coins as well as paper money, and after China's shortages eased in late 1400s, imported more cash from the north. Still, none of these responses satisfied the growing domestic demand for specie and bullion, nor did they eliminate monetary disturbances resulting from debasement and the spread of cheap private coins.[133]

---

[130] Keith Taylor, personal communication, Aug., 2001.

[131] Yu, "Law and Family," 188–89; Nguyen, *Tableau*, 153–54; Whitmore, "Social Organization," 301; Truong "Birth and Development of Pho Hien," 29–33. Cf. William Dampier's late 17th-century account, *Voyages and Discoveries* (rpt., London, 1931), 26–27.

[132] Ungar, "Leadership," 113 and 112. On Tran and Le monetary patterns, Wicks, *Money, Markets*, 54–65; Whitmore, "Monetary Flow," 366–89. On bullion shortages in mid–15th-century China, Korea, Japan, Europe, and India, see Richard von Glahn, *Fountain of Fortune* (Berkeley, 1996), 83–99; and *supra* Ch. 2, n. 154. Such shortages reflected local combinations of diminished mine output, restricted international bullion flows, and growing market demand.

[133] Previous note. Cf. 15th-century Chinese price series at von Glahn, *Fountain of Fortune*, 158–59. Although Vietnam did not use silver for state payments until the 17th century and for official currrency until 1740, 16th-century silver inflows to China from Japan and the New World may have aided Vietnam indirectly by reducing the use of copper coin in south China, thus releasing cash for export.

In sum, foreign trade, agricultural patterns, and market activity all point to an expansion in the size and complexity of the early Le economy, which certainly exceeded late 14th-century levels, and probably those of the mid-Tran era as well. The political repercussions were at least three fold.

Most basic perhaps, over the long term rising output strengthened a class of wealthy peasants and modest sized landowners from whom the literati tended to be recruited and whose support broadened the base of the monarchy. If the traumas of the era 1350–1430 were a psychological precondition for the Neo-Confucian revolution, this provided a social foundation. Here a brief retrospect is necessary. Starting as early as the late Ly era, in the most developed areas of the delta, market opportunities tended to favor tenants and owner-occupiers at the expense of large princely and monastic estates run by servile workers, who, Ngo Kim Chung argues, were inherently less efficient than family or contractual labor.[134] Although Mongol invasions and 14th-century traumas at first strengthened Tran princely estates, their advantage proved temporary both because Ho and Ming assaults decimated the Tran, and more basically, because demographic and commercial growth and Confucian norms continued to favor a more open, competitive social order. If we accept Ngo Kim Chung's thesis of enhanced productivity, the transition to a smallholder regime not only raised the demographic ceiling, but permitted new forms of elite acculturation. Even in outlying areas, prosperity allowed what might be termed the gentry to hire tutors for their sons in the hope of gaining entrée to government. Confucian ideology also may have strengthened this group by providing a familial gloss, real or fictive, to patron-client relations.[135] Whereas at first the literati were concentrated in the southern delta, by 1460 elites in formerly aristocratic Buddhist strongholds west

---

[134] Ngo Kim Chung, "Le developpement de la propriete privee dans le Vietnam d'autrefois," in Ngo Kim Chung and Nguyen Duc Nghinh, eds., *Propriete privee et propriete collective dans l'ancien Vietnam* (Paris, 1987), 97–99, 110. Also Georges Boudarel, "Un quantitativiste artisanal a l'oeuvre dans l'atelier de Hanoi," *ibid.*, 50–51; Ungar, "Leadership," 21–22.

[135] Wolters, *Two Essays*, 4, 19, 35–36, 122–23; Nguyen, *History of Buddhism*, 222–23; Keith Taylor, personal communication, Dec. 5, 1989; Charles Keyes, *The Golden Peninsula* (New York, 1977), 186–87; Nola Cooke, "Aspects of Nguyen Rule in 17th-Century Dang Trong" (ms), 5–6; Nola Cooke's commentary on an earlier version of this chapter [hereafter "Cooke Critique"], 10.

and north of the capital also were participating enthusiastically in examinations.[136]

These transformations resembled the evolution of aristocratic tenures toward more contractual landlord-tenant relations in late Song China.[137] More loosely, one might cite the post-1500 decay of monastic estates in Burma in favor of more individual – and perhaps efficient – *ahmu-dan* and *athi* tenures, and the simultaneous spread of rural literacy through village monasteries. Yet compared to Burma, where alms-dependent village monks began introducing literacy to most male peasants, in Dai Viet Confucian schools and private tuition were far more restricted.[138] Reinforcing institutional differences was the greater practical difficulty of learning thousands of Chinese ideographs compared to the phonetic alphabets of the Theravada world.[139]

A second, obvious consequence of economic growth was that more resources became available to royal authorities. Although with the occupation of more marginal lands involutionary strategies must have become more necessary and per capita productivity must have fallen, larger aggregate output expanded the tax base. The growth in state schools, civil service exams, central and provincial staffs, and army size (possibly from 120,000 campaign troops in 1377 to 260,000 in 1471[140]) provide sufficient testimony. At the same time, more efficient systems of village registration and curbs on untaxed private estates meant that whatever the size of the economy, central access to food and labor presumably improved.

Third, demographic and economic growth modified the relation between Vietnamese communities and Chams, as dramatized by Dai Viet's

---

[136] Cooke, "Confucianization," 288, 292–93; Whitmore, *Ho Quy Ly*, 3–26; idem, "Independent Vietnam," 51; R. B. Smith, "England and Vietnam in the 15th and 16th Centuries," in Cowan and Wolters, *Southeast Asian History*, 241.

[137] William Rowe, "Approaches to Modern Chinese Social History," in Olivier Zunz, ed., *Reliving the Past* (Chapel Hil, 1985), esp. 243–45; Mote, *Imperial China*, ch. 15.

[138] If we can project backwards 17th-century trends, Yu, "Law and Family," 196–97.

[139] Pali, of course, was no less alien, but: a) it was written in phonetic alphabets; b) it was immediately accessible through *nissaya* translations; and c) numerous phonetically-transcribed vernacular works appeared separate from Pali. In Vietnam even learning *nom*, the system of Chinese-derived characters to denote indigenous sounds, was more difficult than learning a phonetic syllabary with a mere 25–40 symbols. See Durand and Huan, *Introduction*, 15–16.

[140] Whitmore, *Ho Quy Ly*, 17 on 1377; "Cooke Critique," 10 on 1471. Cf. a 1467 figure of 200,000 in Thomas Hodgkin, *Vietnam: The Revolutionary Path* (London, 1981), 68; and Li, *Cochinchina*, 23–24, n. 31.

historic conquest of 1471 and by migratory pressures before and more especially after that conquest. Often poor members of the same family line were the first to leave their native village to "open the mountains and cut through the rocks" of the frontier, as the saying went.[141] In other cases charismatic leaders grouped together migrants from diverse origins. Le officials also organized war prisoners, retired soldiers, debtors, and landless peasants into military colonies (*don dien*) or civilian agricultural colonies (*dinh dien*). If the dynamics of Vietnamese expansion differed by time and place – armed attacks, diplomatic maneuvers, intermarriage and peaceful assimilation all played a role – ultimately southern colonization hinged on the Vietnamese ability to overwhelm Chams (and later Khmers) demographically and militarily. Why, then, were Vietnamese-speakers so much more successful? I propose four hypotheses which, with the partial exception of the first two, are mutually compatible. These apply both to the pre-1550 era and to later periods, when colonization became far more systematic.

Hypothesis #1. Perhaps the Vietnamese enjoyed no significant superiority in agricultural technique, but the soil and water resources of Dong Kinh and northern Thanh Nghe afforded local inhabitants an irresistible demographic superiority over people dwelling in more ecologically restricted basins farther south. In other words, the Chams through a mixture of agriculture, fishing, and trade may have exploited their environment with reasonable efficiency, but necessarily fell back in the face of continuous north-south migrations. In support of this view, I would note: a) Momoki Shiro, David Sox, and others claim that Cham cropping techniques, tools, and water-use systems, which relied on tanks and wells to capture streams and springs, were well suited to local conditions. Hence Vietnamese not only adopted early ripening Cham rice, which facilitated double and triple-cropping, but after entering Cham areas, retained local irrigation works as well as the Cham plow, which was better suited for the compact soils and thick grasses of that area than the plows of Dong Kinh.[142] b) Overpopulated Dong Kinh and Thanh

---

[141] Nguyen Tu Chi, "The Traditional Vietnamese Village in Bac Bo," *Vietnamese Studies* 61 (n.d.): 40–41. On early southern colonization, also essays by Nguyen The Anh and Po Dharma in P. B. Lafont, ed., *Les frontieres du Vietnam* (Paris, 1989), 119–35; Po Dharma, "Dernieres recherches," 59–70; Wheeler, "Cross-Cultural Trade," 78–87; Li, *Cochinchina*, 20–24, 161–63.

[142] Momoki, "Pure Maritime Polity"; Sox, "Resource-Use Systems," 75–117, 154–77; Nguyen Khac Vien, *Vietnam*, 119–20; Li, *Cochinchina*, 113; Quach-Langlet, "Le cadre geographique," 27–48; Richard O'Connor, "Agricultural Change and Ethnic Succession in Southeast Asian States," *JAS* 54 (1995): 973, 982; *CHSEA*, I, 252–60.

Nghe supplied significant numbers of southern migrants, not least in the 15th and 16th centuries.[143]

On the other hand, although Vietnamese expansion relied initially on northern settlers, by 1600, if not earlier, Vietnamese agriculture in former Cham districts sustained appreciably higher population densities than the Chams themselves had achieved. As a result, far more Vietnamese migrants to Thuan Hoa, Thuan Quang, and the far south eventually came from ex-Cham areas than from Dong Kinh and Thanh Nghe.[144]

Hypothesis #2. These problems with the first hypothesis naturally raise the possibility that superior agricultural techniques gave the Vietnamese, regardless of terrain, an advantage over Chams and, later, Khmers. This idea in turn has two variants. Richard O'Connor, whose research we encountered in Chapters 1–3, argues that along with the Burmese and Tais, the Vietnamese – quite independent of Chinese influence – developed the ability to harness fast-flowing perennial streams in their original home in mountain valleys or piedmonts. Although the Chams did employ streams and springs for water supplementation, wet-rice was only one element in a multi-niche, garden-based subsistence system that, according to O'Connor, was less productive than Vietnamese intensive, irrigation-based rice mono-cropping. So too, when later they entered the Mekong delta, the Vietnamese' ability to farm levees and to develop low-lying back swamps through flow-management techniques gave them a major advantage over Khmers, who restricted their flood-farming to upper delta terraces.[145] However, other authors argue that the China connection was decisive insofar as during the first millennium directly, and thereafter indirectly, China taught the Vietnamese methods of river diking and bureaucratic management, agricultural terracing, and tool manufacture more sophisticated than those available to other Southeast Asians. Presumably, Tran dikes illustrated this trend.[146] But, so far as I know, structured comparisons between south Chinese and Vietnamese, and more

---

[143] Note 141 *supra*.

[144] Li, *Cochinchina*, 24–31, 161–63; Nguyen, *Tableau*, 57; Gourou, *Les Paysans*, 130–37.

[145] O'Connor, "Agricultural Change," esp. 972–73, 975, 981–82. His notion of ethnically-tied agricultural niches gains support from Dao The Thuan, "Types of Rice," 41–56.

[146] Fisher, *South-East Asia*, 531–33; Keyes, *Golden Peninsula*, 182, 185; Paul Wheatley, *Nagara and Commandery* (Chicago, 1983), 67–77; Whitmore, "Elephants," 132; Hodgkin, *Vietnam*, 22, 29. On possible Chinese agricultural influences, see too Taylor, *Birth*, 34–36, 45–46; Nguyen, *Tableau*, 57.

important, between Vietnamese and Cham agriculture have never been attempted.

Hypothesis #3. Neo-Confucian family norms may have contributed to the Vietnamese demographic advantage. According to some social historians, China's internal and external colonization and its recurrent population crises owed much to peculiar family structures. Specifically, the equal partition of family assets among male heirs, the emphasis on early, near universal marriage, and patrilineal ancestor worship with its demand for male heirs combined to encourage the multiplication of patriarchal units eager to maximize their production potential.[147] But, if we accept this (not uncontested) interpretation of China, how closely did Vietnamese families conform? And how demographically distinct from Chams and Khmers would such practices have made them?

These issues are particularly opaque. On the one hand, the Le Code borrowed directly from Chinese law codes, and Le courts sought to enforce its rulings so as to promote Confucian family norms in the villages. Woodside has suggested that as Neo-Confucian influence rendered peasant society more family-centered, peasants became more likely to leave their natal villages, both because the family was conceived as an eternal corporation that could endure independent of place, and because impoverished sons were encouraged to seek opportunity in the south for the sake of the eternal lineage.[148] On the other hand, according to Insun Yu, in Vietnamese peasant families of the 17th and 18th centuries, patriarchal authority was typically weaker than in China, women were more economically independent before and during marriage, women maintained stronger links to their natal families, and male and female children shared more equally in inheritance. Presumably these patterns would have diminished pressures for the replication of patriarchal units, and may not have differed much from patterns among the Vietnamese' Indianized neighbors.[149] Consider too that Indic Southeast Asia could generate populations as dense as those of Dai Viet: whereas Dai Viet in 1600 had 18 people per square kilometer, Java had over 30, and Bali

[147] Judith Stacey, *Patriarchy and Socialist Revolution in China* (Berkeley, 1993), 62–63, 85; Albert Feuerwerker, "Handicraft Industry in Ming and Ching China" (ms). More recently, however, James Lee and Wang Feng, *One Quarter of Humanity* (Cambridge, MA: 1999), have emphasized the degree to which premodern Chinese families controlled fertility to meet the dictates of household economy.

[148] Yu, "Law and Family," ch. 1; Nguyen and Ta, *Le Code*, I, 191–206; Woodside, "Medieval Vietnam," 319; idem, personal communication, Sept., 1999.

[149] Yu, "Law and Family," 23–24, 193–98. See too Woodside, *Vietnam*, 25–26; Whitmore, "Social Organization," 299–300.

almost 80.[150] The key variable here was Java and Bali's rich volcanic soils. How much, then, did Sinic family influences distinguish Vietnamese-Cham relations from those between aggressive Burmans and wilting Mons, both Indianized?

Hypothesis #4. As Gourou emphasized over sixty years ago, Chinese administrative and social techniques aided southern settlement.[151] To be sure, a preoccupation with formal tables can obscure the new system's massive weaknesses: its superficiality, corruption, patrimonial subversions, and ruinous clan rivalries. Nonetheless, we have seen that Le Thanh-tong's reforms, not least his reliance on tax registers, codes, gazeteers, and exams (materials that were not only written but in some cases printed[152]) offered a novel possibility of permeative uniformity and finely-textured local knowledge. By contrast, Chams depended on royal personality and the most rudimentary administrative apparatus to coordinate autonomous, often mutually hostile principalities. Their peculiar habit of retreating to the mountains to join upland confreres must have further sapped Cham resolution. Consider too China's military contribution, which was both organizational – in 1466 Dai Viet's army was reorganized along Ming lines – and technological. From the Ming if not the Yuan, the Vietnamese learned the art of making hand-guns and artillery, to which Chams lacked comparable access. In 1390 Chinese-style handguns helped to demoralize the Cham army and cut down the great Cham king Che Bong Nga. By capturing and imitating Chinese prototypes during the Ming occupation, and by smuggling copper from Yunnan later in the 15th century, the Vietnamese further improved handgun and cannon manufacture.[153] In 1515 Dai Viet was said to have "countless musketeers and small bombards," based almost certainly on Chinese models, and to consume "a very great deal of powder" in war.[154] It cannot be entirely accidental that after centuries of indecisive competition, Dai Viet's most dramatic victory came on the heels of the Neo-Confucian revolution.

---

[150] Reid, *Age of Commerce*, I, 14. But if the Vietnamese mountainous zone, far larger than its Javanese or Balinese counterpart, were excluded, discrepancies would be smaller.

[151] Gourou, *Les Paysans*, 133. Cf. Woodside, *Vietnam*, 145–46, 163–64.

[152] Chinese woodblock printing entered in the mid-1400s. Woodside, "Medieval Vietnam," 316.

[153] Sun, "Ming-Southeast Asian Interactions," 259–67; idem, "The Transfer of Chinese Military Technology to Northern Mainland Southeast Asia, c. 1390–1526" (ms); Li, *Cochinchina*, 43–44. Cf. Geoffrey Parker, *The Military Revolution* (Cambridge, 1988), 83–84, 136–37.

[154] Cortesao, *Suma Oriental*, I, 115.

THE POISON FRUITS OF SUCCESS: SOCIAL AND REGIONAL
CONFLICTS IN THE 16TH CENTURY

In short, during the 1400s and early 1500s rapid demographic/economic growth joined with imported intellectual and organizational motifs to shift the balance in the eastern littoral decisively in favor of Vietnamese-speakers. As in the western and central mainland, however, the new order faced severe tensions that were in some measure a function of its very success. In the early and mid-16th century, roughly a generation before Toungoo Burma and Ayudhya suffered comparable disasters, groups alienated by the Le system succeeded in destroying the dynasty and in splitting the Le territory.

Within Dong Kinh itself the most exotic, embittered opposition came from hilly Vietnamese-speaking districts west, north, and northeast of the capital, which were traditionally areas of heavy Buddhist influence with links to the Ly or Tran dynasties. During the 15th century, al-though many upper-class men in this area had been won over to the Neo-Confucian system of education and examinations, local peasants remained deeply attached to non-Confucian, especially Buddhist cults. From 1511 to 1521 thousands of such people joined a series of rebellions some of whose miracle-working leaders claimed to be Tran descendants as well as incarnated Buddhist or Taoist deities. In one sense these were revolts by the periphery against the cultural impositions of the capital, but insofar as they drew on widespread popular traditions, they also re-vealed the danger of uneven acculturation between elite and peasantry. With the nativist and Buddhist bases of Ly and Tran kingship having crumbled, Dai Viet's political culture became more elitist and externally dependent, hence more fragile, than its Theravada counterparts.[155]

I believe that these uprisings also reflected renewed population pres-sures. Recall Li's estimate that the population of Dai Viet, concentrated in Dong Kinh, tripled between 1417 and 1539. Located on the immediate periphery of Vietnamese settlement, these rebellions were located pre-cisely where excess Dong Kinh peasants unwilling to head south were likely to migrate. The peasants' passionate commitment and the aston-ishing speed with which leaders attracted support suggest that these

---

[155] This is not to accept Marxist portrayals of these revolts as anti-landlord uprisings. On the rebellions and elite-mass cultural tensions, I rely on Cooke, "Confucianization," 288–93; "Cooke Critique," 12–14; Le, *Histoire*, 246–47; Taylor, "Early Kingdoms," 151; and Tran Quoc Vuong, "Popular Culture and High Culture in Vietnamese History," *Crossroads* 7 (1992), 5–37, esp. 21–23.

movements, more than a mere negative reaction to Le centralization, offered marginalized, uprooted people a sense of renewed community. Meanwhile, in densely settled areas of the plain itself the amount of communal land to which the lower peasantry had access, and the amount of private land they were likely to inherit, again became nonviable. Symptoms of late Tran rural distress now reappeared: peasants fled the tax-rolls to become vagabonds and migrants, bound themselves to wealthy patrons, or joined the Buddhist rebellions, one of which seized the capital before being dispersed by royal troops. In fact, the mid- and late 16th century became the second of three periods of severe disorder in Dong Kinh – along with the 1300s and mid-1700s – each shaped in substantial measure by overpopulation and politically restricted access to land. The aforementioned monetary disturbances of the 15th and early 16th centuries suggest inflationary pressures, which also reflected excessive demand within both Vietnam and adjacent regions. Chapter 3 referred to rising prices in the central mainland; for much of the 16th-century China too suffered from currency depreciation and an unbridled profusion of debased private coin.[156]

Monetary fluctuations, falling rents and taxes, and an expansion in the ranks of office-seekers fed elite factionalism even before the 1511 rebellion. Recall Jack Goldstone's argument that during periods of rapid population growth the ranks of marginal contenders for government posts expand more quickly than the number of such posts. Any decline in real incomes would have intensified competition. But sections of the elite also may have been disoriented psychologically insofar as Le Thanh-tong's bureaucratic norms conflicted with entrenched family and patrimonial loyalties. The fact that 16th-century politics revolved around family-led alliances much as in the 14th century suggests that the peasantry was not the only site of Confucian/pre-Confucian tensions.

A modified version of the Le political system survived the turmoil, but the dynasty itself collapsed. Profiting from the growing air of crisis, a Le general, Mac Dang Dung, seized power and in 1527 founded his own dynasty that was destined to keep power in Dong Kinh until 1592. The Mac were an eminent Dong Kinh literati family who, despite past political differences with the Le, were eager to associate themselves with the glory of their predecessors. To that end, they sought to preserve Le Thanh-tong's system, including his codes, Confucian schools,

---

[156] Von Glahn, *Fountain of Fortune*, 95–112, 142–43, 156–61, 233–37: Cf. n. 133 *supra*.

and triennial examinations. At least this is how John Whitmore and Insun Yu see the Mac.[157] Tran Quoc Vuong is less impressed by their Neo-Confucian commitment, pointing instead to the enhanced 16th-century visibility of traditions on which the Le had frowned, including Ly-Tran Buddhist practices and cults of matriarchal deities.[158] In fact, these views are not incompatible. From the outset, factionalism and rural distress probably prevented the Mac from reproducing Thanh-tong's penetration of the villages, whatever their ideological commitment. Then, with civil war intensifying from the mid-1550s (see below), they may have become yet more tolerant of heterodox practices and local autonomy so long as tax and military quotas were met. Thus in delta villages, family heads and local officials began to free themselves from close supervision so as to adjust land and tax allocations to their own benefit.[159]

In the long term, the most serious threat to Le Thanh-tong's political legacy stemmed neither from Buddhist rebels, nor Mac usurpers, nor Dong Kinh village leaders. Far more ominous was a revival of regional tension, from which Thanh-tong's remarkable personal leadership had produced a temporary and deceptive respite. Five years after the Mac founded their dynasty, military leaders from Thanh Hoa (the northern part of Thanh Nghe) proclaimed a Le figurehead as "legitimate" opponent to Mac "usurpers." Led at first by the Nguyen family, which had intermarried with the Le and which had played a critical, but ultimately unsuccessful role during prolonged court conflicts that began in 1509, the legitimists established a military base in Thanh Hoa and Nghe An in the south. Soon Dai Viet split, with the entire Thanh Nghe southern region under pro-Le forces, and with the delta and northern hills under the Mac. Most Dong Kinh literati supported the Mac, just as many, if not most, of their forebears had rallied to the Ming. Between 1539 and 1600 the two camps fought over forty major battles. In combination with unusually poor weather after 1580 and continued currency disorders, these contests further dislocated agriculture and depressed the late 16th century population by 10–15 percent. From 1561–1610, 14 years saw agricultural failure, accompanied frequently by severe pestilence.

---

[157] Whitmore, *Ho Quy Ly*, 115–16; idem, "Mac Dang Dung," in *Dictionary of Ming Biography* (New York, 1976), 1029–35; idem, "*Chung-hsing* and *Cheng-t'ung*," 116–36, Yu, "Law and Family," 33–35; idem, "Changing Nature," 161, 166. Cf. Cooke, "Confucianization," 284–88, 301.

[158] Tran, "Popular Culture and High Culture," esp. 23–30.

[159] "Cooke Critique," 14; Yu, "Changing Nature," 166.

According to Li Tana, this "was perhaps the longest period of disaster in Vietnamese history."[160]

The division ended with the Le restoration of 1592, when southern forces finally captured the capital and expelled the Mac. Yet even this unification proved extremely short-lived, for the victors themselves soon split along regional lines. The death of the Nguyen leader in 1545 had been followed by growing conflict between the Nguyen and their allies in the restorationist cause, the Trinh family, who also hailed from Thanh Hoa. The Nguyen avoided almost certain elimination at the hands of the Trinh by securing in 1558 governorship of the southern area of Thuan Hoa (not to be confused with Thanh Hoa; see Figure 4.1). Originally they had no intention of making this frontier area into a separate polity, but in the early 1600s Nguyen reluctance to accept Trinh domination produced that very result: Nguyen leaders began to develop the most southerly Le provinces, including areas captured from the Chams in 1471, into a family bastion for war against the Trinh.[161] Thus, even as both erstwhile allies, the Trinh in the north and the Nguyen in the south, continued to proclaim loyalty to the Le dynasty, Vietnamese-speaking peoples again collapsed into rival states, divided this time at Dong Hoi, some 200 miles below the divide between the Mac and their southern foes in the 16th century. At Dong Hoi, after prolonged and bitter north-south fighting, the frontier would stabilize until 1774.

This 16th-century experience resembled that of First Toungoo Burma in two respects. In both cases, an unprecedentedly successful, but overextended and inherently fragile polity succumbed to a mix of intensified capital factionalism and rebellions in outlying territories. In both cases, center-periphery warfare joined with food shortages in the core to produce an appalling social and economic collapse during the second half of the 16th century.

To be sure, land shortages were more evident in Dong Kinh than at either Pegu or Ayudhya, where social disorders were preeminently a function of military pressure. But the principal 16th-century difference between Vietnam and the rest of the mainland was this: whereas Toungoo Burma's collapse in 1599 and that of Ayudhya in 1569 each lasted less than a generation and served as prelude to a rapid, more

---

[160] Li, *Cochinchina*, 162, plus 159–63, 172, supported by Sakurai, "Age of Commerce," 1–2. The misery of this period was reflected in contemporary literature, e.g., Nguyen Khac Vien et al., *Anthologie de la litterature*, I, 247–65. On poor post-1580 weather, *supra* Ch. 2, nn. 195–97.

[161] Taylor, "Nguyen Hoang."

successful sector-wide integration, Vietnam's fragmentation proved more long-lasting and disruptive even than that of the 14th century. For almost two hundred years the Vietnamese-speaking lands remained split between Trinh and Nguyen.[162] To return to the problem raised at the outset of this chapter, why, then, was this division so uniquely persistent?

Clearly, the chief contrast was geographic. River links let Ava and Ayudhya monopolize the benefits of both burgeoning maritime contacts and agricultural extension, but in Vietnam, coastal commerce, guns, and land reclamation all proved relentlessly centrifugal. As we shall see, the southern Nguyen polity fended off the more populous Trinh in part because it exploited European guns more effectively and derived larger revenues from Chinese, Japanese, and European trade. No less basic, Nguyen-Trinh resistance to the Mac, followed especially by Nguyen resistance to the Trinh, drew strength from accelerating frontier colonization. Primarily through north-south immigration (reinforced by Cham-Viet intermarriages and local growth), Li estimates that the population in Thuan Hoa rose from some 64,000 in 1417 to 378,000 in 1555. This was a rate of increase almost twice as great as in northern Vietnam.[163] In Quang Nam farther south, a chronicle entry for 1602 said that "tax revenue greatly exceeded what could be collected in Thuan Hoa, and soldiers there were more than half the number of soldiers in Thuan Hoa."[164] Burmese colonization was more modest and more restricted to areas in easy riverine contact. Ayudhya was yet better placed to control reclamation. Thus, whereas in the western and central mainland economic expansion favored center over periphery, here the reverse was true.

One can therefore attribute much to geography – but not everything. Vietnamese unity was affected by another unusual factor, Sinic-style family loyalties. Over time Chinese influence tended to create family structures (*ho*) that were more stable, visible, and potentially competitive with the crown than were found in Indic Southeast Asia. Admittedly, insofar as Confucianism upheld the emperor as paterfamilias of

---

[162] Dating the onset of the split is a matter of definition. Nguyen Hoang, who secured the governorship of Thuan Hoa in 1558, did not depart permanently for the south until 1600 and continued thereafter to pay taxes to the Le-Trinh regime in the north. His son's refusal in 1620 to pay taxes formalized the split and precipitated Trinh punitive campaigns, but not until 1672 did the north abandon (until 1774) efforts to reconquer the south.

[163] Li, *Cochinchina*, 29–30, 171.

[164] Taylor, "Nguyen Hoang," 63.

all his subjects and facilitated social control in the villages, its family ethic provided a source of cohesion. Admittedly too, in contrast to Ming China and to 19th-century Vietnam, elite allegiances in this period were directed not to overarching clans, but to small, generationally limited groups that were by no means strictly patrilineal. Especially in Thanh Hoa, elite families retained much of the fluid entourage style that we find elsewhere in Southeast Asia, including loyalty to the most charismatic figure of the older generation whose authority depended as much on talent as on birth order. Nonetheless, by promoting identification with an organism whose members had a common ancestor (real or fictive), a common patronymic, and some sense of mutual obligation, Sinic notions made it relatively easy in periods of unrest to organize extended groups against established authority. Family-based rebellions by Tran, Ho, Mac, Trinh, and Nguyen – none with any clear analogue in the Indic mainland – showed this potential quite clearly. So too, even as family loyalties strengthened both regimes internally, they reinforced the division after c. 1600 between Trinh and Nguyen.[165]

THE NORTH DURING THE PERIOD OF DIVISION, C. 1600–1780

Having effectively declared its independence in 1620, the Nguyen secured that independence in 1672 with the failure of the seventh Trinh campaign to reconquer the breakaway territory. In basic respects both Vietnamese regimes that emerged from this split resembled Restored Toungoo Burma and Late Ayudhya Siam. All four arose in the aftermath of 16th-century political fragmentation. All four strove to re-stabilize society and to overhaul administration with largely ad hoc experiments. All four sought to expand territorially. And all four disintegrated in the mid- and late 18th century. (Except for 18th-century collapse in Russia and Japan, these same features, we shall find, characterized the Romanov, Bourbon, and Tokugawa regimes.) Let us divide our survey of Vietnamese-speaking lands after c. 1600 to consider developments within each regional state, starting with the more powerful and populous, that of the Trinh in the north.

Insofar as the southward advance of Vietnamese-speakers encouraged an oscillation in the political fortunes of Dong Kinh literati, that

---

[165] "Cooke Critique," 14–15, 18–19. On the political implications of family organization in later periods, Yu, "Law and Family," 79, 211, and *passim*; Woodside, *Vietnam*, 25–26; Nola Cooke, "Regionalism and the Nature of Nguyen Rule in Seventeenth-Century Dang Trong (Cochinchina)," *JSEAS* 29 (1998): esp. 131–42.

oscillation defied the linearity of southern colonization itself. To reca-pitulate (and over-schematize a bit), in the 1410s pro-Ming literati had replaced the Ho, only to be forced into a more limited role in 1427 by a coalition led by Thanh Nghe warriors. The latter in turn had yielded greater influence to scholar-officials under Le Thanh-tong and the Mac.

Now, with the Le restoration of 1592, the victors, who included a handful of Dong Kinh literati but who were overwhelmingly military leaders from Thanh Nghe, again were in a position to marginalize their literati enemies in the north. (These rivalries within the Trinh state, re-member, must be distinguished from simultaneous but far more seri-ous conflicts between the Trinh and Nguyen polities.) The victorious families were led by the Trinh *chua* ("lord," "military leader"), whose relation to the figurehead Le king superficially resembled that between the Japanese shogun and emperor.[166] After 1592 Thanh Nghe soldiers in effect organized a military occupation of the Dong Kinh plain, placing garrisons at potential trouble spots and restricting membership in the elite guards to men from Thanh Nghe. Administration was rough and ready, with generals collecting revenues which they split between their local commands and the capital. Although examinations were still held, upper level (*tien si*) graduates were confined to marginal posts, and their number fell dramatically.[167]

The influence of military commanders derived both from the Restora-tion victory of 1592 and from the need to complete that victory with two-front campaigning. Against the breakaway Nguyen regime in the south the Trinh hurled up to 180,000 land troops at a time in seven major offensives – all unsuccessful – from 1627 to 1672.[168] Meanwhile in the mountains of the north they fought Mac holdouts, who with Chinese protection maintained themselves until 1677. In this atmosphere, it was not surprising that the prestige of Neo-Confucian scholarship remained eclipsed by a more martial ethos.

In the mid-1600s, the wheel again began to turn much as under Le Thanh-tong some 200 years earlier. Trinh leaders may have found it politically expedient to reduce their dependence on their sometimes

---

[166] Without a legal status comparable to that of the Japanese *bushi*, Vietnamese warriors had few cultural defenses against literati claims that civil should prevail over military authority and that the Le emperor remained the only legitimate focus of loyalty. Cf. Forest, *Les missionnaires*, II, 68–69.

[167] See figures at Nguyen and Ta, *Le Code*, II, 90–91.

[168] M. L. Cadiere, "Le mur de Dong-hoi," *BEFEO* 6 (1906): 87–254. Troop figures ibid., 126–27; Yang, *Contribution*, 102.

unruly southern military allies, whose value now waned with an end
to active campaigning. In part too, the Trinh realized that more reliable
access to Dong Kinh's rice and manpower required a larger civil bureaucracy. At the same time, Alain Forest argues, Neo-Confucian education
again led cultured military leaders to internalize literati social and political ideals.[169] For their part, the impoverished Dong Kinh literati were
only too eager to renew their ancestors' tradition of service and, in the
process, to enrich themselves.

Having received a major boost under Trinh Tac (1657–1682), literati
influence expanded further in the early 18th century. All told, between
1682 and 1767, palace examinations were held with the same frequency
as during the height of the Le Neo-Confucian revolution (1463–1516),
and if the average number of graduates declined, it was still twice as
large as during the period of open military dominance from 1592 to
1620.[170] Accordingly, from the early 1700s the number of civil officials
multiplied, and military governors began to relinquish certain types
of judicial cases. Literati reformers sought, above all, to revive bureaucratic discipline and to strengthen control over the villages, to which
end they reorganized the work of the six ministries, systematized ranks
and reporting, and sought to transfer some village civil cases to district
courts. To stabilize income, in 1664 the government abolished the hoary
system of six-year village censuses in favor of fixed tax and manpower
quotas.[171] In the name of Confucian propriety, the capital also sought to
suppress unorthodox social customs, while sanctioning over 2500 village cults to approved spirits. As usual, these interventions drew on
detailed written codes and procedures.[172]

One might assume that this routinizing impulse, together with the
continued existence of three tiers of local appointees (compared to one
in most Indic areas) rendered the Trinh system more stable and penetrating than its Indic counterparts, and that of the four new 17th-century
regimes on the mainland, the Trinh was one of the more successful. Such
assumptions would be wrong. For one thing, because the population

---

[169] Forest, *Les missionaires*, II, 66, 68–69, 74, 441. On Trinh administration, ibid., chs. 13–
16; Dang Phu'ong-Nghi, *Les institutions publiques du Viet-nam au XVIIIe siecle* (Paris,
1969); Taylor, "Literati Revival"; Nguyen and Ta, *Le Code*, I, 19; Yu, "Changing Nature,"
166–72.

[170] Cooke, "Confucianization," 300; Yu, "Law and Family," 43 ff.

[171] Forest, *Les missionnaires*, II, 65–78; Dang, *Les institutions*, 77–121, esp. 112–14; Yu, "Law
and Family," 37–49, 185, 216–23; R. Deloustal, "Ressources financieres et economiques
de l'Etat dans l'ancien Annam," *Revue Indochinoise* 52 (1924), and 53 (1925).

[172] Yu, "Law and Family," 43, 47–48, 216–23; Whitmore, "Control of the Spirits."

of Dong Kinh and Thanh Nghe was at least twice as large as that of lowland Burma or Siam, the ratio of officials-to-subjects may not have been much different.[173] Beyond that, bureaucratic norms still coexisted with, or masked, patrimonial practices. Succession to the post of *chua* itself was no less conducive to factional struggle than royal succession in Theravada lands. Along with eunuchs and high officials, the *chua* and the Le imperial family awarded clients revenues from specified localities much as the Toungoo throne awarded apanages.[174] In 1658, as a revenue expedient, the government began selling posts; expanded and systematized in the 1730s, this practice eroded central control over regional officials and encouraged venality. The examination system itself became subject to recurrent scandal and in 1750 was thrown open to fee-paying entrants, regardless of qualification.[175]

On the village level too, literati projects stalled. Most basically perhaps, this reflected a long-term process, evident as early as the Mac, whereby the dissemination of Confucian learning allowed local officials and landlord families with a grounding in administrative procedures to manipulate the system to their own advantage. In contrast to earlier Le practice, the Trinh perforce allowed state land to shift to communal ownership and let local elites, rather than central officials, control the allocation of those lands and the selection of village officials (*xa truong*). Even in the 1800s the Nguyen regime could not replicate the control over delta villages that Le Thanh-tong had enjoyed in the late 1400s.[176] Reinforcing this long-term devolutionary trend were strains associated with chronic, largely unsuccessful warfare to 1677 and with mounting social and monetary disorders in the 18th century. Population pressure – the result of peace after 1677, reinforced by improved rainfall for much of the 18th century[177] – joined with unanticipated effects of the 1664 tax reform to overburden once again the most vulnerable villages and the

---

[173] Burmese provincial appointees in 1740 probably numbered about 120. Dang, *Les institutions*, 60, says Le-Trinh military and civilian officials totalled 300–500 at court and 200 in the provinces, while Nguyen and Ta, *Le Code*, II, 90–91 claims that at any given time, the total number of officials never exceeded 500.

[174] Forest, *Les missionaires*, II, 33–41, 65–78, 89–103; III, 438; Taylor, "Literati revival," 19–21.

[175] Yu, "Changing Nature," 167–68; idem, "Law and Family," 225; Dang, *Les institutions*, 64; Cooke, "Confucianization," 295. For a more favorable late 17th-century view of the exams, S. Baron, "A Description of the Kingdom of Tonqueen," in Churchill, ed., *A Collection of Voyages and Travels*, 6 vols. (London, 1732), VI, 15, 24.

[176] Yu, "Changing Nature," 167–72; idem, "Law and Family," 45–47, 222–23; Nguyen and Ta, *Le Code*, I, 19; Taylor, personal communication, Aug., 2001.

[177] Cf. Marks, *Tigers, Rice*, 200 and n. 299 *infra*.

weakest strata within each village. According to one source, as early as 1713 less than a third of the total population actually were paying taxes, a figure that certainly fell thereafter.[178] New mining taxes offset these losses to only a limited degree. At the same time, domestic demand joined unfavorable international bullion flows to create severe coin shortages that played havoc with mercantile and government operations alike.[179] As we shall see, in the 1730s and 1740s revolts flared across the northern provinces.

It is against this background of administrative and social disorder that one must consider the proliferation in the north of non-Confucian religious and cultural options. From the early 17th century, especially after the arrival of Jesuits expelled from Japan, Catholicism gained a following at the Trinh court itself, and more especially among men in dangerous occupations (fishermen, sailors, soldiers), women, and displaced strata. Despite or because of persecution by literati officials, who judged Christianity a threat to the social order, as early as the 1680s Dong Kinh may have had 200,000 Christians, some 4 percent of the total; a century later, one source claimed 300,000–400,000.[180] Why this modest success, which was duplicated elsewhere in East Asia but which contrasts with Catholicism's total failure in lowland Indic Southeast Asia? Catholicism succeeded, in part, because a tradition of compromising village differences by acknowledging minority rights allowed some hamlets to become "all Christian" in a way that the more unified patron-client hierarchies of Indic Southeast Asia could not tolerate. It succeeded in part because Vietnamese religious specialists competed less effectively with Catholic priests than did Theravada monks: Vietnamese shamans were uneducated and poorly organized, while the literati failed to address adequately the popular interest in miracle cures and the afterlife. Catholic soteriology was arguably closer to Mahayana than to Theravada tradition. Finally, the Neo-Confucian belief that lineage ties survived changes in residence joined demographic pressures to encourage greater

---

[178] Yu, "Law and Family," 45–46, citing the *Cuong Muc*. On 18th-century popular distress, also ibid., 222–29; Ngo Kim Chung, "La developpement," 81–91; Lydie Prin, "Les problemes agraires du Vietnam au XVIIIe siecle et les Tay Son," in Ngo and Nguyen, *Propriete privee*, 68–71; Dang, *Les Institutions*, 38, 121; Yumio Sakurai, "Peasant Drain," 133–52; Forest, *Les missionnaires*, II, 57–59, 83–106.

[179] Forest, *Les missionnaires*, II, 78–86, 89–106; Nguyen, *Tableau*, 28–32, 64–65.

[180] The first estimate appears in Cooke, "Confucianization," n. 120; the second, from a missionary account, appears in George Dutton, "The Tay Son Uprising: Society and Rebellion in Late Eighteenth-Century Viet Nam, 1771–1802" (Univ. of Washington Ph.D diss., 2001), 282–83. Dutton emphasizes the nominal status of many Christians.

physical mobility than in Indic lands. As during the severe disorders of the 1700s, Vietnamese Christians were drawn disproportionately from the most uprooted, mobile elements.[181]

Rural immiseration in the 18th century and the apparent failure of Neo-Confucian social ideals also enhanced the popular appeal in northern Vietnam of devotional Pure Land-style Buddhism, as well as a matriarchal, sexualized cult, probably derived from Cham traditions, devoted to the goddess Lieu-hanh.[182] At the court itself, Neo-Confucianism's inability to solve the social crisis and the personal predilections of some princes contributed to an extraordinary Buddhist renaissance. Individual Le and Trinh lords lavished resources on temples and pagodas, patronized monks, and with the aid of monks invited from China, helped to found new sects or to revive languishing ones, including the famed Truc Lam sect.[183]

Literary expression showed a comparable diversity. Not unlike Siamese literature in the 18th and early 19th centuries, we shall find that *nom* poetry, which was accessible to a wider audience than Chinese-character writing, adopted new genres and themes and became more attuned to individual emotion. Certain works exhibited a novel skepticism toward Confucian pieties. Also symptomatic perhaps of waning orthodoxy was the new pattern of examination results: from 1682 to 1786, the palace examinations showed a marked contraction in both geographic coverage and the average number of graduates, which suggests either that fewer men wanted to attend palace examinations or that fewer qualified at the prerequisite level.[184] To be sure, Neo-Confucianism not only retained its official preeminence, but in some social circles, showed fresh vitality. Convinced (not unlike 14th-century thinkers) that only intensive study of the classics offered a cure for the social and political turbulence of their times, 18th-century northern scholars developed new

---

[181] I rely on Samuel Popkin, *The Rational Peasant* (Berkeley, 1979), 125–31; Yu, "Law and Family," 202–204; Forest, *Les missionnaires*, III, chs. 35–42, esp. 438–47; and esp. Woodside, personal communication, Sept., 1999.

[182] Nguyen, "Vietnamization of Po Nagar," 47–48.

[183] Philipe Langlet, "La tradition Vietnamienne," *Bulletin de la societe des etudes Indochinoises*, n.s. 45 (1970): 71; Forest, *Les missionnaires*, II, 75–76, 88; III, 353; Le, *Histoire*, 291–93; Nguyen, *History of Buddhism*, 259–77; Cuong Tu Nguyen, "Rethinking Vietnamese Buddhist History," in Taylor and Whitmore, *Essays*, 81–115; Li Tana, "An Alternative Vietnam?", 114.

[184] From 1689–1729 palace examinations produced an average of 20 high graduates, but from 1730–1786 the figure fell to 9. Cooke, "Confucianization," 295–299; "Cooke Critique," 22.

approaches to textual interpretation, biography, and historiography. More important, they sought to popularize Confucian learning in the villages through abridgements and versification of the classics, "family admonitions" addressed to children, and translations of the classics into the vernacular script, *nom*.[185] Yet it is fair to say that social strains joined new communications circuits (see below) to encourage a more complex, competitive, and uncertain intellectual climate than in the confident days of Le Thanh-tong.

What, if any, political significance did ethnic or pan-Vietnamese identities have in the north in this period? Educated Vietnamese (we know far less about peasant usages) apparently referred to themselves as "Viet people" (*nguoi viet*) or "southern people" (*nguoi nam*). Notwithstanding the last term's implied territorial contrast to China, it sought to identify the Vietnamese with the sophistication of Chinese culture and to contrast them with various non-Sinic "barbarian" and upland peoples. As heirs to Sinic civilization and as nominal subjects of the Le kings, presumably the Nguyen and their Vietnamese-speaking followers were included within the category of "southern people." In periods of heightened insecurity and competition with border populations, such loyalties could engender ethnic polarization. We shall find this in the north during the 1788/89 Qing invasion of Dong Kinh and yet more persistently on the southern frontier with Chams and Khmers. Yet, by comparison with 20th-century Vietnamese identities or even 18th-century Burman usages, 18th-century Vietnamese/non-Vietnamese boundaries appear porous, while the pan-Vietnamese category itself was riven by powerful regionalisms and sub-regionalisms. Until 1788 Chinese threats were a matter of primarily historical interest to Dong Kinh literati, but hostility to the Nguyen, who had "betrayed" their Le lords, colored every aspect of Trinh ideology. Moreover, within the northern seigneury itself, certainly at the popular level and to some extent among elites, such areas as Thanh Nghe, Hai Duong, and Kinh Bac retained their own social personalities and, in some cases, their own political loyalties.[186]

---

[185] Woodside, "Medieval Vietnam," 316; Dutton, "Tay Son Uprising," 356–60; idem, "The Tay Son Uprising and the Response of Scholar Officials: Three Case Studies" (ms) [henceforth "Three Case Studies"], 6–11.

[186] *Nguoi kinh* ("metropolitan people") is apparently a colonial-era term for Vietnamese-speakers which was inserted anachronistically into *quoc ngu* translations of precolonial documents. However, literature on 18th-century ethnicity is thin. I rely on Alexander Woodside, letter of Jan. 5, 1996; Taylor, personal communication, Aug., 2001; Taylor, "On Being Muonged"; Li, *Cochinchina*, 31; Moto Furuta, *Betonamujin*,

THE NGUYEN POLITY IN THE SOUTH: "A NEW WAY OF BEING VIETNAMESE"[187]

We have seen that the southern polity faced repeated Trinh invasions to 1672. How did the Nguyen survive, and what cultural implications did the separation entail?

On paper the Trinh should have triumphed insofar as they controlled the Le monarch, whose legitimacy both sides accepted, and enjoyed a 17th-century population advantage of least 9:1 and a military superiority of between 2:1 and 4:1. But the Trinh had to worry about Mac remnants, struggled with longer supply lines, and fought on unfamiliar terrain. The Nguyen derived greater revenues from maritime trade, while developing exceptionally skilled naval forces. The Nguyen also magnified the defenders' usual advantage by building massive stone walls across a narrow neck of land between the mountains and the sea at Truong Duc and Dong Hoi. And the walls themselves bristled with cannon.[188]

Firearms, including European-style guns that superseded Chinese arms, were not a Nguyen monopoly. In 1643 the Trinh induced Dutch ships to fight on their behalf, and English visitors in the 1680s wrote admiringly of the dexterity with which Trinh soldiers deployed matchlocks, swivel guns, and cannon. Yet the Nguyen, because of their more enthusiastic maritime involvement, proved more adept at obtaining such weapons, at manufacturing firearms, and at integrating them into their overall strategy. From the Portuguese, in particular, they learned to deploy maritime cannon, which inhibited flanking movements around Dong Hoi. Thus, although within each of the two seigneuries, Trinh and Nguyen, a partial monopoly on guns strengthened central authorities, within the eastern littoral as a whole, in contrast to the western and central mainland, guns clearly encouraged fragmentation.[189]

46–62; Pelley, "History of Resistance," 238–39; David Henley, "Ethnogeographic integration and Exclusion in Anticolonial Nationalism," *CSSH* 37, 2 (1995): 300–301.

[187] Phrase is from the title of ch. 5 in Li's pathbreaking *Cochinchina*. The same theme is echoed in Taylor's "Nguyen Hoang" essay.

[188] Cadiere, "Mur," 131–40. On Nguyen forces, see too George Dutton, "Flaming Tiger, Burning Dragon: Elements of Early Modern Vietnamese Military Technology" (ms), and following note.

[189] On firearms, esp. in the south, Christoforo Borri, *Cochin-China* (London, 1633), ch. 7; Li, *Cochinchina*, 41–46, 176–79; Cadiere, "Mur," 151–58; Nguyen, *Tableau*, 39, 99, 123, 186–91, 206, 218; Pierre-Yves Manguin, *Les Portugais sur les cotes du Viet-Nam et du Campa*

For much of the 17th century southern leaders continued to define themselves in terms of the larger state of Dai Viet. Claiming to be the Le's only loyal subjects, even after the fighting stopped they committed themselves, at least rhetorically, to free the Le from Trinh "usurpers" and to complete the Restoration started by their 16th-century ancestors. At first, therefore, they valued the southern domain, known as Dang Trong, as a base from which to regain the north; and immigrants from Thanh Hoa (particularly those from the Nguyen family's home district within Thanh Hoa) maintained a virtual monopoly on high office in the south. Thus Cooke terms early Nguyen rule "a form of colonialism."[190] In some contexts, even educated southerners outside the ruling circle may have clung to the Le as a symbol of a wider unity. As late as 1775, sycophantic scholars in Thuan Hoa greeted invading Trinh troops by claiming, "After 200 years at last we see again the clothes and hats of the imperial [Le] court."[191]

If we consider cultural – as opposed to political – affiliations, several factors ensured that southern elites and, to a considerable extent, the wider society remained within a broad Viet-Sinic tradition. Because they sought both to preserve their family heritage and to demonstrate their equality to the Le-Trinh courts, early Nguyen leaders preserved certain cultural and ceremonial usages from the north.[192] At a lower social level, migration, both voluntary and involuntary, spread northern dialects and identities throughout Dang Trong. From the 1550s to 1631, when the Dong Hoi wall cut the coastal road, individuals and, more commonly, family groups fleeing famine and turmoil in the north aided rapid population growth in Thuan Hoa. In the mid-1600s the Nguyen resettled as far south as Phu Yen some 20,000–30,000 Trinh prisoners and civilian deportees from the north. Sakurai suggests additional northern refugees entered Dang Trong during the mid-18th century crisis.[193] We

(Paris, 1972), 204–209; Baron, "Description," 8, 24; Dampier, *Voyages*, 49–55; Li Tana and Anthony Reid, eds., *Southern Vietam under the Nguyen* (Singapore, 1993), 30–31, 70–71.

[190] Cooke, "Regionalism," esp. 125, 140–42, 146–49, 157–61. Cf. Taylor, "Surface Orientations," 958–64, emphasizing early 17th-century localization of Vietnamese culture within the south. The views of Cooke and Taylor may be less contrary than complementary, since she is concerned chiefly with political identities, and he, with emotional and aesthetic perspectives. Moreover, Cooke, ibid., and "Historicizing Vietnamese Christianity in the Late Traditional South (c.1680s–1740s)" (ms) agrees that the late 1600s saw a shift to a more southern sensibility. See discussion *infra*.

[191] Yang, *Contribution*, 179, citing Le Quy Don's northern-biased *Phu Bien Tap Luc*.

[192] Yang, *Contribution*, 144–48.

[193] Li, *Cochinchina*, 24–31, 163–65; Sakurai, "Age of Commerce," 3.

also find frequent secondary migration, whereby families from the north who had settled in Thuan Hoa in the 16th or 17th centuries later pushed farther south on their own or on state initiative. Insofar as migrants retained elements of their original speech and social practices, these various movements created pockets of modified northern culture all along the eastern littoral.[194] Finally, in a pattern that owed nothing to north–south diffusion, that actually tended to distinguish Dang Trong from the north, but that simultaneously emphasized Nguyen participation in a broad Han ecumene, southern elites looked for inspiration directly to China, without a Dong Kinh filter. Thus Nguyen rulers invited Chinese Buddhist monks to reform local practices and relied on Chinese emigres, the *minh huong* ("[Keepers of the] Ming Incense"), for administrative expertise. Nguyen leaders also regarded those emigres as exemplars of scholarship and good living whose "refined" Ming-style dress the court in 1744 mandated as a regional costume in preference to northern styles. Such contacts assisted not only the somewhat superficial Sinic changes in 18th-century government, but more substantive reforms in the early 1800s.[195]

Within a Southeast Asian context, Dang Trong's Sino-Vietnamese and Sinic affinities therefore remained palpable. Nguyen administrators necessarily retained the Sino-Vietnamese calendar and language, and in the 1700s began to support state Confucian schools. In a move that ran curiously parallel to the growth of literati influence in the north, between 1691 and 1740 the Nguyen expanded civil-service examinations and rewarded successful candidates with a few senior posts. As part of an effort to establish formal independence from the Le (see below), in 1744 the Nguyen created the six ministries that were traditional in China and Dong Kinh.[196] Japanese and European visitors commented on the Sinic attributes of Dang Trong elites – the modesty of women, the tendency of turbaned literati to grow long fingernails as a sign of status, chopsticks, Sinic architecture and painting, Chinese ideographs and literature – all

---

[194] Thus, for example, the Hue dialect is closer to that of Hanoi than of the geographically closer region of Nghe An. On northern migrations to and in the south, previous note, plus Cadiere, "Mur," 92–93, 103; Yang, *Contribution*, 63, 66, 70–79, 116–17; Nguyen, *Tableau*, 41, 43, 229; *Pho Hien*, 201; Wheeler, "Cross-Cultural Trade," 75–88; Taylor, personal communication, Aug., 2001.

[195] Charles Wheeler, "Patterns of Association in the *Haiwai jishi*" (ms); idem, "Cross-Cultural Trade," chs. 3, 4; Li, *Cochinchina*, 33–34, 46–48, 108; Brian Zottoli, "Roots of 19th-Century Vietnamese Confucianism" (ms); "Cooke Critique," 4–5, 26; Woodside, *Vietnam*, 115–18.

[196] Li, *Cochinchina*, 46–48.

of which obviously contrasted with usages in Cham, Khmer, and upland areas to the west and south.[197]

After episodic progress between 1471 and 1560, under the Nguyen southern settlement accelerated dramatically at the expense of Indic peoples. At least four factors were at work: a) In the late 17th and 18th centuries the Khmer court, which Mak Phoeun argues had a less proprietary sense of territory than the Vietnamese and which we have seen was subject to constant fissioning, repeatedly invited Vietnamese intervention.[198] b) Chinese immigration, although originally either politically autonomous or even pro-Khmer, worked ultimately to the advantage of the Nguyen by diluting Khmer cultural influence and by creating additional frontier settlements willing to accept Nguyen protection. Chinese developed the central port of Hoi An, the northeastern Mekong delta, and the southwestern port of Ha Tien, with the latter entering the Nguyen orbit after 1708. Especially from the 1740s and 1750s, the demand for foodstuffs in central Vietnam, in south China, and in Chinese settlements around Southeast Asia drew Fujianese and Cantonese to the Mekong delta to work, like their confreres in Siam, as growers, shipbuilders, and petty traders. By 1780 Chinese in Nguyen-controlled and Nguyen-allied districts probably totaled 40,000.[199] c) On their own initiative, families and individuals from overpopulated or disturbed Vietnamese-speaking areas sought opportunities in fertile Quang Nam, Quang Ngai, Qui Nhon, and finally the Mekong delta (which in 1700 was still a virtual wilderness). Whereas Thanh Nghe supplied the

---

[197] Borri, *Cochin-China*, chs. 5–6; the mid–18th-century "Voyage de Pierre Poivre en Cochinchine," *REO* 3 (1885): 105, 327–28, 384, 394, 508; Yang, *Contribution*, 42–50, 144–47; Woodside, "Medieval Vietnam," 316. For Japanese accounts, Li, *Cochinchina*, 65.

[198] See Mak Phoeun, *Histoire du Cambodge de la fin du XVIe siecle au debut du XVIIIe* (Paris, 1995), 420; as well as scathing late 17th-century views of Cambodian military and administrative ineptitude in Yoneo Ishii, ed., *The Junk Trade from Southeast Asia* (Singapore, 1998), 168, 170.

[199] On Chinese in the Nguyen zone, Wheeler, "Cross-Cultural Trade," chs. 3, 4; Jean Koffler, "Description historique de la Cochinchine," *Revue Indochinoise* 15 (1911): 460, claiming 30,000 c. 1740; Nguyen The Anh, "L'immigration chinoise et la colonisation du delta du Mekong," *The Vietnam Review* 1 (1996): 154–77; Nola Cooke, "Commerce and Catastrophe: Cochinchina, Cambodia, and the Chinese in Modern Southern Vietnam During the Later Nguyen Lords' Era (c. 1680–1770)" (ms), suggesting that Ha Tien was not founded until 1713/14; Yumio Sakurai and Takako Kitagawa, "Ha Tien or Banteay Meas in the Time of the Fall of Ayudhya" (ms); Li, *Cochinchina*, 33–34; idem, "An Alternative Vietnam?" 119, esp. n. 38; idem, "*Cang Hai Sang Tian*: Chinese Communities in the 18th Century Mekong Delta" (ms), claiming 30,000–40,000 Chinese in the early 1800s after a sharp post-1782 drop; Choi, "Southern Vietnam," 27–33, 64–69. Cf. *supra* Ch. 3, n. 236.

first colonists, after c. 1630 they hailed from increasingly populated districts in Thuan Hoa itself.[200] d) For its part, the Nguyen court vigorously supported immigration and colonization both to increase its resources during wars against the Trinh, the Chams, the Khmers, and Siam, and to provide cheap foodstuffs for Thuan Hoa and Quang Nam. By the mid-1700s roughly one-third of the entire Dang Trong population – including a large military/service class around the capital of Phu Xuan (Hue) as well as specialized producers who found it more profitable to buy than to grow food – depended on rice from the southern frontier.[201] Most reclamation was carried out by Nguyen and allied clansmen, officials, and family groups whom the court aided with tax relief, military protection, and help in obtaining labor, including permission to enslave upland ethnic minorities.[202] Without an independent southern Vietnamese polity whose fortunes hinged substantially on frontier colonization, it is unlikely that the conquest of Cham- and Khmer-speaking areas would have proceeded nearly as rapidly as it did. Together, Chinese immigration and, more especially, Vietnamese colonization and natural increase boosted the population of Thuan Hoa and Thuan Quang alone from less than 100,000 in 1417 to perhaps 900,000 in 1770.[203]

To summarize a complex series of territorial advances and retreats that southern expansion made possible: After unsuccessful Cham counterattacks in 1611, 1653, and 1692, the Nguyen annexed Kauthara. A yet more desperate Cham uprising in 1693, centered this time in Panduranga, succeeded in preserving a separate tributary status for that kinglet, but Cham power was broken, and over Cham objections Vietnamese settlers flocked to Panduranga and beyond. Meanwhile Nguyen authorities increased pressure on the anemic Khmer state, intervening in 1658 to impose their own choice on the throne, and in 1674 sponsoring two Khmer tributaries. One resided at the Khmer settlement of Prey Nokor – present-day Saigon or Ho Chi Minh City – whose territory subsequently became Vietnamese provinces. All told,

---

[200] *Supra*, nn. 193, 194.
[201] Li, *Cochinchina*, 144–45; idem, "Rice Trade in the 18th and 19th Century Mekong Delta and Its Implications" (ms), 2; Nguyen Dinh Dau, "Early Cochinese Domestic and Foreign Trade" (ms), 4; Choi, "Southern Vietnam," 64–67; Li and Reid, *Southern Vietnam*, 138; Dutton, "Tay Son Uprising," 199, 242.
[202] Nguyen, *Tableau*, 69–72; Ngo Kim Chung, "Le developpement," 92–93; Li, *Cochinchina*, 35, 125–29; Choi, "Southern Vietnam," 166–68.
[203] This is a conservative estimate because Li, *Cochinchina*, 29–30, 160 shows 789,800 in Thuan Hoa and 86,680 for a single prefecture in Thuan Quang. It is also likely that many Chinese were excluded from these figures.

between 1620 and 1772 during the "wars of the Cambodian succession," Nguyen armies, allied at times with Chinese forces from Ha Tien, intervened in Cambodia on some 13 occasions, usually to support a pro-Vietnamese prince against a rival favored by Siam. The way the Nguyen demanded territorial concessions after each intervention was likened by a Nguyen general to the way silkworms slowly devour mulberry leaves.[204] Judged in terms of territorial expansion between 1650 and 1760, of the four principal mainland states Nguyen Vietnam was undoubtedly most successful.

So long as Nguyen eyes were fixed on the struggle with the Trinh, their policy toward their southern neighbors remained opportunistic and relatively accommodating. Thus early Nguyen rulers married princesses to influential Cham and Khmer rulers.[205] But as the threat from the north ebbed, as they began to see non-Vietnamese communities as obstacles to expansion, and as the power differential between the Nguyen and non-Viet polities widened, cultural boundaries tended to harden and Sinic-style dichotomies between "civilized" and "barbarian" sometimes were pressed into service. In 1693, for example, Nguyen officials ordered captured Cham leaders to "change their clothes and to follow the customs of the Han [i.e., the Vietnamese] . . . in order to govern their people [properly]," while toward Cham, Lao, and Khmer envoys the court adopted a more arrogant tone.[206] Li suggests, further, that Mahayana Buddhism appealed to Nguyen leaders in part because it helped to preserve a distinctively Vietnamese identity in a multicultural environment.[207] Illiterate Vietnamese-speaking peasants surely cared less than courtiers for Sinic cultural labels, but it is worth noting that whereas Burmese and Siamese armies included diverse ethnicities, Nguyen armies routinely excluded non-Vietnamese.[208] Administration in 18th-century Panduranga assumed a leopard-spot pattern, with Vietnamese paying taxes to their own officials amidst a still self-sufficient population of Chams. As Vietnamese enclaves expanded through seizure,

---

[204] Woodside, *Vietnam*, 247. On territorial advances, ibid., 246–49; Po Dharma, "Dernieres recherches," 59–67; essays by Nguyen The Anh, Po Dharma, and Mak Phoeun in Lafont, *Les frontieres*, 119–55; Li, *Cochinchina*, 31–32; and esp. Phoeun, *Histoire*, chs. 7–10.

[205] Li, *Cochinchina*, 120; "Cooke Critique," 27.

[206] Yang, *Contribution*, 148, 153–54; Li and Reid, *Southern Vietnam*, 122; Li, *Cochinchina*, 120–21.

[207] Li, *Cochinchina*, 103; idem, "Alternative Vietnam," 113.

[208] Li, *Cochinchina*, 28, 40, esp. n. 14. Early Tayson regiments also were ethnically divided between Vietnamese, uplanders, and Chinese.

purchase, and assimilation, unassimilated Chams declined by 1800 to perhaps 50,000, many of whom sought to preserve their self-esteem by deepening ties to Malayan Islam.[209] Recall the contemporary eclipse of the Mons in Burma.

Ethnic divisions were no less apparent on the Khmer frontier. Vietnamese typically occupied river lands and backswamps; Khmers, the higher elevations. After a period of growing communal tension, Catholic missionaries reported that on at least three occasions – in 1730–1731, 1750–1751, and 1769 – Khmers on the Mekong delta frontier massacred every Vietnamese they could lay hands on, heedless of rank, age, or sex. Often Khmer courtiers supported these frontier outbreaks. The uprising of 1730–1731, which used religious symbols to define communal boundaries, alone killed an estimated 10,000 Vietnamese and reached Saigon.[210] Feeding on a sense of religious difference largely absent in Lower Burma, these slaughters were far bloodier and extended over a longer period than the anti-Burman massacres of 1740 and 1754. Yet the effort to halt accelerating immigration by a more populous, better organized northern ethnic group clearly paralleled Mon and Cham struggles. And again, such hostility was richly reciprocated and ultimately futile, with Nguyen authorities launching punitive campaigns and more intense settlement efforts. By 1775, although Khmers still dominated the Mekong banks and trans-Bassac and Preah Trapeang regions, to the east Vietnamese numbers were rising rapidly.[211]

In other words, if we focus on Vietnamese/non-Vietnamese dichotomies – if we essentialize the Vietnamese – we may conclude

---

[209] Richard Howland, "The Chams of Cambodia" (ms), 14; Po Dharma, "Les frontieres du Campa," in Lafont, *Les frontieres*, 133–34; H. Chambert-Loir, "Notes sur les relations historiques et litteraires entre Campa et monde malais," in *Seminaire*, 95–106; and Po Dharma, *Le Panduranga (Campa) 1802–1835: ses rappots avec le Vietnam*, 2 vols., (Paris, 1987), I, chs. 3–5, focusing on the 1800s.

[210] Adrien Launay, ed., *Histoire de la mission de Cochinchine 1658–1823: Documents historiques* (Paris, 1924), vol. II: 1728–1771, 365–73, esp. 366; Cooke, "Commerce and Catastrophe," 14, 19–24. Cf. Mak Phoen, "La frontiere entre le Cambodge et le Vietnam du XVIIe siecle a l'instauration du protectorat francais ... ," in Lafont, *Les frontieres*, 136–55; David Chandler,"Cambodia Before the French" (Univ. of Michigan Ph.D. diss., 1973), chs. 5–7; idem, "An Anti-Vienamese Rebellion in Early Nineteenth-Century Cambodia," *JSEAS* 6 (1975): 16–24; Dutton, "Tay Son Uprising," 334 ff.

[211] See map, Lafont, *Les frontieres*, 142; Louis Malleret, "La minorite cambodgienne de Cochinchine," *Bulletin de la Societe des Etudes Indochinoise* 21 (1946): 19–34; Choi, "Southern Vietnam," 134, 139. Post-1775 wars slashed Vietnamese population in the Mekong delta, but in the 19th century settlement resumed. Nola Cooke, "The Changing Nature of Persecution in Southern Vietnam from the Later 17th to the Early 19th Century" (ms), 3.

that southern colonization extended Vietnamese culture at the expense of Indic rivals. Yet the closer one looks at the ground, the more obvious it is that southern settlement also created novel political and social structures, perhaps too an ethnic/political consciousness, that distinguished Dang Trong (the "inner region," the south) from Dang Ngoai (the "outer region," the north) and gave it a more recognizably Southeast Asian coloration. More than a mere extension of northern patterns, as nationalist historians long assumed, in some ways this was a genuinely new society. Or perhaps we should say societies, insofar as within the south, Quang Ngai, Binh Dinh, Phu Yen, and various Mekong delta districts developed patterns quite distinct from Thuan Hoa.[212]

Revisiting Dang-trong administration, for example, we find that Confucian influence remained relatively shallow, as befit a "backward" frontier. As late as 1750, a French visitor claimed, rhetorically, that one would have difficulty finding ten scholars of Confucianism in the whole southern kingdom.[213] By comparison with the north, not only did civil-service examinations remain infrequent and intellectually undemanding, but they usually led only to clerical posts. Notwithstanding the 18th-century growth in civilian influence and Confucian trappings, Nguyen government remained essentially a military system which conscripted an astonishingly large (by Dong Kinh standards) percentage of taxpayers.[214] Of course, the Trinh also relied at first on Thanh Hoa officers, but in the north by the late 1600s Confucian influence had produced far more substantial civilian control than in Dang Trong three generations later.

As Li has shown, the flip-side of Confucianism's weakness was vigorous official support for Mahayana Buddhism and a pronounced openness, at both elite and popular levels, to religious syncretism. Although Confucianism could not provide this multiethnic, unlettered world with a dynamic ideology, the Nguyen, as noted, feared abandoning entirely a distinctly Vietnamese tradition. Mahayana Buddhism promised to solve this problem, while introducing a welcome degree of cultural flexibility and inclusion in areas where self-identified Chams remained numerous and Cham traditions, deeply influential. Mahayana Buddhism's many gods already echoed the polytheism of the Chams, with whose spirit

---

[212] Taylor, "Surface Orientations," 958–64; idem, "Regional Conflicts," 113 ff.; Choi, "Southern Vietnam," 106.

[213] "Voyage de Pierre Poivre," 87. From 1463–1600 only .3 percent of palace examination winners had hailed from what would become the Nguyen domain.

[214] Cooke, "Regionalism," 142–57; "Cooke Critique," 30–31; Li, *Cochinchina*, ch. 2, esp. 49–58, and 115–19.

cults the early Nguyen frequently sought to identify. Thus the Nguyen intentionally raised Buddhist pagodas on the sites of Cham temples, which in some cases were respectfully dismantled and rebuilt. Thus southerners fervently supported a Vietnamized version of the Cham earth goddess Po Nagar and claimed that the ruler was not merely Son of Heaven, on the Le-Trinh model, but part of Heaven itself, as Chams and Khmers had always believed.[215] So eclectic and localized a religious atmosphere also favored Catholic conversion rates in the 17th century said to be considerably higher than in Dong Kinh.[216]

Likewise, especially in long settled areas, peaceful intercourse with Chams, Khmers, and upland tribes encouraged a diversity of social practices unknown farther north. Serial female monogamy, for example, was unexceptional. Southern Vietnamese-speakers could be seen building houses on poles in Southeast Asian fashion, using Malay-type ships, Cham ploughs, Cham hairstyles, Cham female dress, Cham burial practices, and engaging in elephant fighting and slave trading along the frontier. In ethnically diverse districts marriage to Khmers, Chams, Chinese, even uplanders and foreign merchants, was not uncommon.[217] Indeed, later emperors complained that some Vietnamese were becoming Khmers in speech and dress.[218] Nor were economic relations necessarily competitive: Cambodia provided Vietnamese with large numbers of buffaloes crucial for the opening of the delta and the mass production of delta rice.[219] In short, as in Lower Burma, conflict along the frontier was hardly universal, probably not even typical.[220]

The very pattern of frontier settlement reinforced this openness. In Dong Kinh and some parts of Thuan Hoa, which were densely populated regions of elaborately organized villages, communal lands underpinned village cohesion. But, in districts south of Quang Ngai with

---

[215] Li, *Cochinchina*, 101–12, 124–25; idem, "Alternative Vietnam?" 112–17; Langlet, "La tradition," 70–71; Nguyen, "Vietnamization of Po Nagar," 48–50, emphasizing the greater power and durability of the Po Nagar cult in the south; Wheeler, "Cross-Cultural Trade," 72–93.

[216] Cooke, "Confucianization," n. 120; cf. Woodside, *Vietnam*, 285. On the appeals and subsequent vicissitudes of southern Christianity, Cooke, "Commerce and Catastrophe."

[217] Li, *Cochinchina*, 112–16, 132–33; Moto Furuta, *Betonamujin*, 46–62; Gerald Hickey, "The Village through Time and War," in Robertson, *Essays*, 54–55; Wheeler, "Cross-Cultural Trade," 72–93.

[218] O. W. Wolters, "Southeast Asia as a Field of Study," *Indonesia* 58 (1994): 11.

[219] Li, "Late 18th Century Mekong Delta," 7–8; idem, "The 18th and Early 19th Century Mekong Delta in the Regional Trade System" (ms), 11–12.

[220] Cf. *supra* Ch. 2, n. 330.

scanty population and enormous private holdings, communal lands were insignificant. Spread out in linear fashion along waterways or transport routes, villages, especially in the Mekong delta, were less cohesive, more atomizing, more open to the outside world. And because migrants were typically marginal to their original locales, they tended to be less knowledgeable about Confucianism than their northern peers, less tied by convention, more likely to dilute kinship ties, and to accord women a high role. Cham officials co-opted into the lower tiers of Vietnamese administration were yet less conventional.[221]

Southern experience differed in another respect critical to daily life and political fortune: through propitious geography and deliberate policy, Dang Trong became more heavily involved in maritime trade than the north. As noted, warfare provided the hard pressed Nguyen with a major incentive to welcome *minh huong* Chinese traders and to promote enterprises that fed Hoi An and other ports. Official patronage aside, the inherent dynamism of the local economy sucked in foreign bullion (Dang Trong had only gold), while enhancing the south's ability to absorb imports and to supply exotica from the western hills and local agricultural products. In effect, Charles Wheeler argues, Dang Trong inherited the commercial orientation and the upland-rivermouth symbiosis of the Chams.[222] For their part, foreign traders were only too eager to expand contacts with the old Cham coast. Because the late Ming banned direct trade with Japan, Japan's appetite for Chinese silks and China's appetite for Japanese silver could be satisfied only at third-country entrepots, among which Hoi An proved more convenient than Ayudhya. Insofar as Chinese supplied Hoi An with large quantities of New World silver via Manila, the growth of Chinese-Spanish exchange was another long-term enabling factor. Thus Hoi An became a powerhouse in the South China Sea economy, and early 17th-century Dang Trong became Japan's most important trading partner. Although from 1636 the Tokugawa banned Japanese overseas travel and reduced the number of Chinese vessels, this did little damage, because Cantonese merchants stepped up their purchase of Vietnamese goods for European ships and for the south China market, while restrictions at Japanese ports actually diverted Chinese junks to Vietnam. In effect, Chinese traders

---

[221] Yu, "Law and Family," 198–201; Li, *Cochinchina*, 55, 110–11; Gerald Hickey, "The Vietnamese Village Through Time and War," *The Vietnam Forum* 10 (1987): 1–25.

[222] Trade discussion follows Wheeler, "Cross-Cultural Trade," chs. 1–4; Li, *Cochinchina*, chs. 3, 4; Li and Reid, *Southern Vietnam*, 44–54; Borri, *Cochin-China*, ch. 8, and nn. 223, 224 *infra*.

replaced Japanese, and Hoi An, like Bangkok, became an essentially Chinese city. When later in the 18th century the rice trade began shifting the commercial center of gravity from Hoi An to Saigon, the Chinese pioneered that change as well.

In short, the late 17th century did not see a general commercial collapse in Dang Trong any more than in Burma or Siam. Li estimates the annual average value of Dang Trong maritime trade c. 1590–1640 at 600,000 *taels* of silver; 1640–1700, at 580,000 *taels*; and 1700–1750, at 400,000–450,000 *taels*. Focused on Hoi An, however, these pre-1750 figures failed to include ports farther south whose increasing importance compensated in part for problems at Hoi An.[223] Moreover, after 1767 disturbances in Siam joined with growing demand for foodstuffs in China and Chinese coastal settlement around Southeast Asia to encourage Vietnamese shipbuilding and exports.[224]

In the mid-1700s Chinese junks were still taking 40,000 casks of high-quality sugar per year from Quang Nam,[225] plus cotton, silk, gold, cinnamon, aquilaria, and other forest products. Dang Trong imported copper and silver bullion and a cornucopia of Chinese consumer goods, similar to those entering Siam: some 51 categories of textiles, medicines, paper, dyes, glass, ironware, crockery, and edibles were listed in the 1770s.[226] Accustomed to austere Dong Kinh standards, the visiting northern scholar Le Quy Don in 1776 found shocking the wealth of the south, which he viewed as a sort of Eldorado and which he described as "the world's most fertile land." Even commoners wore silk and satin, and

---

[223] Li, *Cochinchina*, 88–89 (not a problem in the 17th century, inflation became serious in the mid-18th; it is unclear if these figures are inflation-adjusted, but they correspond to changing tonnages), 97, 142–43; idem, "Rice Trade," esp. 5–6. Will Redfern, "Hoi An in the 17th and 18th Centuries" (ms), 27–31 calculates that whereas on average 12 ships per year visited Hoi An 1600–1650, in the 1690s the figure was 17–19, and in the 1740s, 60–80; in this view, Hoi-An did not reach its zenith until the 1750s. Wheeler, "Cross-Cultural Trade," 174–75 also argues that Dang Trong's prosperity continued at least to mid-century, as does Chen Chingho, *Historical Notes on Hoi-An* (Carbondale, IL, 1973). See too Alexander Woodside, "Central Vietnam's Trading World in the 18th Century as Seen in Le Quy Don's 'Frontier Chronicles,'" in Taylor and Whitmore, *Essays*, 162–63; Li and Reid, *Southern Vietnam*, 95, 115–17.

[224] Li, "Late 18th Century Mekong Delta," "*Cang Hai Sang Tian*," "Rice Trade," "18th and Early 19th Century Mekong Delta"; Sarasin Viraphol, *Tribute and Profit* (Cambridge, MA, 1977), 105–106; Cooke, "Commerce and Catastrophe." Whereas Li emphasizes overseas stimuli to late 18th-century rice production, Choi, "Southern Vietnam," 64–65 dates major exports only to the 19th century.

[225] Nguyen, *Tableau*, 54, citing P. Poivre. "Tonneaux" could also mean tons, but I take the more conservative interpretation.

[226] On consumer imports, Li, *Cochinchina*, 86; Woodside, "Trading World," 166.

"regard gold and silver as if it were sand, and rice paddy as if it were mud."[227] Maritime contacts supplied most of the bullion for market exchange. By the 18th century, so pervasive had monetization become that the government, like its Siamese counterpart, began paying for some hitherto obligatory labor services and accepting cash for certain in-kind taxes.[228]

All told, the southern state itself in the 1740s and 1750s obtained from a quarter to a third or more of its revenue from taxes on visiting junks,[229] which was comparable to Ayudhya but larger than in Trinh Vietnam. Trade revenues and contacts allowed the Nguyen to procure guns and strategic metals, and thus to deter Trinh assaults while intimidating Cambodia and keeping abreast of Siam. More broadly, Dang Trong's 40–odd ports provided a commercial link that compensated to some extent for the lack of a central river artery.[230] Li concludes that foreign trade not only underlay southern independence, but drove the region's economic development for over 150 years.[231] In truth, this judgment may require some modification. From 1600 to 1770, Li herself suggests that southern colonization was driven less by export demand than by local population pressures and by Hue's need for revenues and for rice to supply the capital region. Moreover, as just noted, even before Hoi An's decline, the bulk of government income came not from foreign trade, but domestic sources. Foreign trade was easier to tax, so it is fair to assume that the disproportionality between these sectors in the overall economy was yet greater. According to Wheeler, as the domestic economy grew more complex, the percentage of revenue that came from foreign trade declined.[232] Note finally that although foreign trade in Dong Kinh was

[227] Quotes from Woodside, "Trading World," 165–66. Cf. Li, *Cochinchina*, 86–87.
[228] Li, *Cochincina*, 86–88, 90–98 (esp. 94–95), and 145; Whitmore, "Monetary Flow," 386–88; Woodside, "Trading World."
[229] Li, *Cochinchina*, 97. It is unclear if profits from royal trade monopolies were separate, or subsumed in this category.
[230] Wheeler, "Cross-Cultural Trade," 42–44.
[231] Li, *Cochinchina*, 59, 67, 71, 77, 98, 119. Wheeler, "Cross-Cultural Trade" agrees substantially.
[232] Wheeler, "Cross-Cultural Trade," 33, 171–72. Cooke, "Commerce and Catastrophe," 2–4 notes that Nguyen maritime policy, although more receptive than that of the Trinh, was more short-sighted and exploitative than that of Ayudhya or Ha Tien. On domestic stimuli to frontier colonization, see too *supra* n. 201. On the other hand, Li, personal communication, April 6, 2002, indicates that Mekong delta rice exports via Ha Tien to Chinese communities in coastal SE Asia may have been substantially larger than hitherto appreciated. Clearly, to disentangle external and domestic stimuli, further research is needed.

less critical than in the south, the north experienced virtually the same trends to monetization and commutation. That said, no one would question Li's basic thesis that foreign trade allowed the Nguyen to survive, not least in the 17th century, and thus favored centrifugalism within the eastern lowlands.

This leads to a final distinction between Nguyen and Trinh experience: as the agricultural center of gravity moved farther south, as the southern capital Phu Xuan depended more heavily on Mekong delta rice, and as delta ports began to rival Hoi An, the Nguyen were drawn into a geopolitical world centered on the South China Sea and the Gulf of Siam that had virtually nothing to do with Dong Kinh. Prudence demanded that the bulk of Nguyen forces remain on the northern frontier. But with Trinh wars a fading memory, Nguyen energies focused ever more heavily on extending their influence over the open frontier of the delta and in parrying Siamese challenges in Cambodia, such as those of 1720, 1738, 1749, and during the 1770s. Originally autonomous, Chinese settlements in the Gulf at Ha Tien and Chanthaburi began to cooperate more closely with established regional powers. Thus by the 1760s a Siamese-Teochiu Chinese military alliance opposed a Nguyen-Cantonese alliance. Paralleling shifts in Burma as well as in Siam, this southern orientation would intensify under the Nguyen reunifier of Vietnam, Gia-long (r. 1802–1819), who represented a new force arising from the Mekong delta.[233]

Did this reorientation, in combination with the south's novel cultural and economic profile, finally overstrain Nguyen identification with Dai Viet and encourage a formal assertion of independence? In fact something like this happened – but the implications for Nguyen identity are ambiguous.

In a series of symbolic and diplomatic steps that began in 1687 but whose intellectual roots can be traced to the 1650s, Nguyen rulers hesitantly transformed themselves from regional warlords to independent monarchs.[234] As late as 1729, the realm over which they claimed

[233] Li, "Rice Trade"; idem, *Cochinchina*, 142–44; Cooke, "Regionalism," 157–61; Yumio Sakurai, "Vietnam and the Fall of Ayuthaya," in Kajit Jittasevi, ed., *Proceedings for the International Workshop: Ayudhya and Asia* (Bangkok, 1995), 143–62; Sakurai and Kitagawa, "Ha Tien."
[234] On ritual changes 1687–1744, see "Voyage de Pierre Poivre," 83–84; Koffler, "Description historique," *Revue Indochinoise* 15 : 448–575 and 16: 273–79, 582–607; Li, *Cochinchina*, 46–48, 101, 109; Leopold Cadiere, "Le changement de costume sous Vo-Vuong," *Bulletin des Amis du Vieux Hue* 4 (1915): 417–24; Yang, *Contribution,*

authority was still termed "Dai Viet" – if they had abandoned practical hope of displacing the Trinh, they still had not fully detached Dang Trong from the north psychologically. But in 1744, after awarding himself the same title as the Trinh lord enjoyed, the ruler Vo-vuong (r. 1738–1765) mounted the "kingly throne" in Phu Xuan and issued an enthronement edict that traced the development of the Nguyen realm as a political entity distinct from the north. He also employed a title (Duc Thanh Thuong) hitherto reserved for the Le sovereign, while expanding his court apparatus to fit the image of a proper Chinese-style polity. All this points to a new concept of Dang Trong as a genuinely independent state. Curiously, however, Vo-vuong chose to preserve Le regnal dates for internal documents, while maintaining symbolic subordination to the Le and using non-royal titles in communications with the Qing and Le courts. Should we conclude that an older Dai Viet and an emergent Dang Trong identity coexisted, neither fully formed, both available as circumstance demanded – somewhat as in Alabama in the 1850s loyalty to the United States wrestled with an emergent Southern national identity, or on Taiwan today Chinese and Taiwanese identities jostle one another? Or did Vo-vuong's hesitation reflect less lingering subordination than his fear that assuming full royal prerogatives without Beijing's recognition might antagonize China and disgrace his new kingdom in the eyes of *minh huong* and Sinic-educated literati?[235]

Whatever his intentions, relations among Vietnamese-speaking regions were utterly transformed by events of the late 18th century.

COLLAPSE AND (RE)UNIFICATION[236]

From 1771 to 1786 both the Nguyen and Trinh seigneuries collapsed. Obvious differences aside, in broad etiology and timing Vietnam's 18th-century trauma – and the subsequent brilliant creation of a new central apparatus – resembled contemporary developments in Burma and Siam.

20–24, 32, 156–57; Cooke, "Regionalism," 157–61; Nguyen Quoc Vinh, "The *Historical Romance about the Achievements of the Southern Court* [NTCNDC] in the Context of Official Historiography about 17th Century Vietnam" (ms), 4.

[235] An appeal for Beijing's recognition in 1702 had been denied. "Cooke Critique," 31, 42–43; Cooke, "Regionalism," 160–61, incl. n. 201. To some extent the Nguyen political ideal, as indicated by titles rulers gave themselves and their henchmen, was not Qing, but ancient Zhou China. Woodside, personal communications, Sept., 1999.

[236] The early 19th century reunified lands from the China border to Phu Yen over which Le Thanh-tong had claimed dominion, but areas below Phu Yen joined the north for the first time.

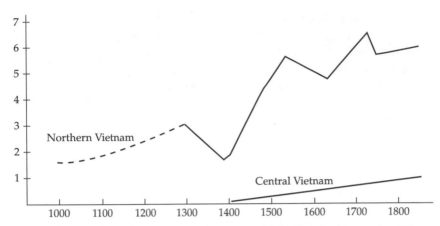

Figure 4.2. Estimated population of Vietnam. Vertical axis represents millions of people. Based on Li Tana, *Nguyen Cochinchina* (Ithaca, 1998), 159–72; Yumio Sakurai, "Vietnam After the Age of Commerce" (ms), 1, 3.

As in the western and central mainland, ill-regulated economic growth joined institutional weaknesses to cripple central administration. More obviously than in Burma or Siam, however, in the Trinh (and to some extent, in the northern Nguyen) domain a key element in that growth was renewed population pressure, which reintroduced social strains characteristic of Dai Viet's late 14th- and 16th-century crises. After falling to c. 4.8 million in the 1630s, the northern population expanded with the aid of renewed peace, New World crops, involutionary techniques, and commercial diversification to reach an unprecedented 6.5 million a century later (see Figure 4.2). This was despite epidemics and generally poor climate in the mid- and late 17th century. The number of landless peasants and those with inadequate land grew apace, along with tax evasion, vagabondage, and engrossment of abandoned lands by tax-avoiding elites.[237] By increasing per capita burdens in villages that suffered temporary population losses, the aforementioned fixed-tax reform of 1664, which could have succeeded only in a society with minimal mobility, intensified tax evasion and migration. Efforts to change the system in 1722–1725 foundered because of elite resistance and a loss of administrative memory on how to stage population censuses. As conditions in the countryside deteriorated, land-engrossing peasants fought

[237] On rural immiseration, n. 178 *supra*, plus Richard, *Histoire naturelle*, I, 27–28; Yu, "Changing Nature," 169–70. On epidemics, also Baron, "Description," 4. On climate, see *infra* n. 299.

land-poor peasants, and levee-sited villages battled low-lying villages. Most ominously, from 1737–1746 large-scale rural uprisings targeted the regime itself. The Trinh survived – barely – by pouring in elite troops from Thanh Nghe, and by addressing some peasant grievances. But lingering resentment joined Trinh succession disputes and poor weather in the 1770s and 1780s to spur a shift in popular sentiment away from the Trinh toward the Le. Similar, if less dramatic social tensions afflicted densely populated Thuan Hoa in the Nguyen domain.[238]

To a certain extent, market expansion reinforced the polarizing effects of overpopulation. We will return to this issue, but for now let it suffice to say that as the market for agricultural goods expanded in the environs of Thang Long, Phu Xuan, Hoi An, and other towns, land investments by Chinese traders, domestic merchants, and Vietnamese officials alike accelerated the privatization of communal property and the woes of land-poor strata.[239]

A growing shortage of specie throughout the eastern littoral – indeed in much of East Asia – was a symptom of region-wide demographic-cum-commercial growth, and in its own right a major cause of disorder in both Vietnamese domains. Population increase, market specialization, tax commutations, plus rising Nguyen expenditures for rice transport, palace construction, and war all placed heavy demands on available coinage. Unfortunately, Japan, a major supplier of copper to both Vietnams, began curbing exports in the 1710s; while in China – whose demographic vigor I have emphasized – the price of copper increased sharply to meet domestic demand. In essence, the South China Sea economy, on which both Vietnams depended for bullion and specie, was growing too rapidly for the available supply of precious metal, and China was both sucking money out of Vietnam and raising the cost of bullion imports. I have suggested that 18th-century price instability also affected Siam and Burma, but here the evidence of disorders is more detailed. The Trinh responded by debasing coins, promoting silver alongside copper coinage, turning a blind eye to counterfeiting, and encouraging a vast expansion of Chinese-run mines along its northern

---

[238] On Trinh problems, previous note, plus "Cooke Critique," 22; Cooke, "Confucianization," 297–98; Yu, "Law and Family," 44–48, 74–75, 174, 223; essays in Ngo and Nguyen, *Propriete privee*, 65–80, 90; Dutton, "Tay Son Uprising," 109–117; idem, "The Hoang Le Nhat Thong Chi and the Historiography of 18th Century Vietnam" (ms); Taylor, personal communication, Aug., 2001. On Thuan Hoa land pressures, Li and Reid, *Southern Vietnam*, 125–26; Yang, *Contribution*, 58, 99, 176–81.

[239] Previous note, plus Nguyen, *Tableau*, 134–42.

border. By the 1760s, mining taxes were actually supporting the Le-Trinh state. This coincided with a mining boom in China, where about half of all working Qing mines were developed between 1736 and 1786, as well as in northern Burma.[240] For their part, the Nguyen in the 1740s began to replace copper coins by minting debased zinc coins, which in turn encouraged large-scale private castings and counterfeiting.[241]

Not only were most of these expedients inadequate, but in the Nguyen domain Li has shown that debasement, private castings, and unslated market demand joined to stoke unprecedented price inflation. To compensate for a decline in real revenues to which inflation contributed, the Nguyen decided to increase customs duties on foreign ships. In fact, these increases, plus growing monetary disorders, the partial silting of Hoi An, and Mekong delta competition, eroded the commerce of Hoi An, long a mainstay of Nguyen finances, and impoverished much of central Vietnam.[242] Because its communications with and control over the Mekong were yet shaky, Phu Xuan could not easily compensate with fresh taxes in that region. Nor was it inclined to increase burdens on the Thuan Hoa heartland. Rather, the Nguyen boosted levies on politically impotent upland tribesmen, who by 1768 were paying an astounding 48.67 percent of all secondary taxes.[243]

The factionalized Phu Xuan regime – and its ill-regulated officials in their private capacity – also began squeezing more taxes and manpower from the Qui Nhon region, which was the pivot between the capital region and the increasingly vital, but still distant Mekong. Qui Nhon not only had to shoulder a disproportionate share of the burden of transporting delta rice over 500 miles to Thuan Hoa, but along with adjacent areas, provided much of the wealth and manpower to counter recurrent Siamese military threats to Vietnamese rice supplies and commercial interests in the Gulf. After the new Siamese king Taksin attacked Ha Tien and Cambodia in 1770–1771, that danger intensified dramatically. In other words, much as the revival of Burmese power under the

---

[240] On mines, *supra* Ch. 2, n. 232, and Woodside, "Political Theory," 258–60. On monetary problems and responses, ibid., 259–61; Woodside, "Trading World," 167–71; Baron, "Description," 7; Nguyen, *Tableau*, 86–90; Whitmore, "Monetary Flow," 369–70, 384–88; Li, *Cochinchina*, 94–95.

[241] Hitherto rarely used in the south, silver now became common as an exchange medium. Yang, *Contribution*, 180; "Voyage de Pierre Poivre," 108–13; and esp. Li, *Cochinchina*, 94–97; Dutton, "Tay Son Uprising," 194.

[242] Li, *Cochinchina*, 97, idem, "Rice Trade," 5; Li and Reid, *Southern Vietnam*, 114–17; Yang, *Contributon*, 87–90; Cooke, "Commerce and Catastrophe," 4.

[243] Li, *Cochinchina*, 136–37.

early Kon-baung kings destroyed Late Ayudhya and paved the way for Taksin, now the revival of Siam under Taksin increased the threat to its eastern rival. So interdependent had the mainland's interstate system become that for the first time events in the distant Irrawaddy basin were affecting the southeastern lowlands. But, instead of rallying behind the Nguyen, influential Vietnamese-speaking elements in Qui Nhon – not to mention nearby hillpeoples – deeply resented fresh military and fiscal demands from a distant capital with whose cultural traditions they did not readily identify and where they lacked all influence. As at Thang Long and Ayudhya in this period, succession conflicts increased the regime's vulnerability. The result was a political explosion centered around Qui Nhon – the famed Tayson revolt of 1771 – that not only destroyed the southern Nguyen regime, but went on to topple the Trinh and to reorganize the entire Vietnamese-speaking world.[244]

To recapitulate, a political and economic expansion that was simultaneously local and regional impinged on Vietnam in four ways to help precipitate the 18th-century collapse: a) As it moved ever farther south, Nguyen administration became overextended, a victim of its own success. Not unlike the Mon revolt of 1740 or the Vientiane uprising of 1826, the Tayson revolt started as a movement by the periphery against escalating demands from the center. b) Supplying new markets on the mainland, in island Southeast Asia, and in China itself, Chinese settlements along the Gulf of Siam stoked Siamese-Vietnamese interstate rivalry, thus increasing pressure on Nguyen administration. c) Domestic population growth and commercialization not only contributed to tax and monetary difficulties, but in Thuan Hoa underlay the dangerous dependence on delta rice. d) Currency demands in Japan and China aggravated Vietnam's monetary disorders. But if economic growth was the culprit, why did a decline in Hoi An's maritime trade from 70–80 junks per year in the late 1740s to eight in 1773 bring matters to a head? Precisely because it emphasized the weakness of Phu Xuan's tax base and its distance from the most dynamic sector of the economy, that of the Mekong delta.

Marxist and nationalist historians have tended to see the Tayson as anti-Confucian social revolutionaries with a national agenda – Communists *avant la lettre* – but this is dubious on all counts. It is true

---

[244] On the background to the Tayson, Sakurai and Kitagawa, "Ha Tien," 6–9; Sakurai, "Vietnam and the Fall of Ayudhya," 152–62; Cooke, "Commerce and Catastrophe," 20–21; Li, *Cochinchina*, 51–58, 94–98, 136–50; Taylor, "Surface Orientations," 964–65; Yang, *Contributon*, 175–86; Dutton, "Tay Son Uprising," 109–114, 150–54, 190–96.

that one of the three Tayson brothers, Nguyen Hue, proudly affirmed his humble origins as a man "of cotton cloth," opposed to the silk finery of the elites.[245] Yet, as George Dutton has shown, early efforts to champion the poor at the expense of the rich petered out before military exigency, and ultimately Tayson tax demands differed little from those of earlier and later regimes. Moreover, at first they were probably less hostile to elite Confucian scholarship, in the manner of the early Taiping in China, than they were untutored, coming as they did from the periphery of the Vietnamese periphery. Some Dong Kinh literati dismissed the Tayson as "barbarians" (*man di*), "dirty goats," or Chams,[246] and their early ranks in fact included Chams, Khmers, Laos, Bahnar and other minority peoples whose symbols – a sacred sword, the old Cham capital of Vijaya, the color red – they freely appropriated.[247] In its poly-ethnicity and frontier origins, the revolt may be compared to Le Loi's movement – or more especially, to the 1740 Mon revolt in Lower Burma insofar as both Mons and Tayson mobilized an ethnically diverse clientele whose initial goal seems to have been defense of regional autonomy.

Indeed, the Tayson's remarkable conquest of the north seems to have been fueled less by a national vision than by personal ambition, opportunism, and sheer good luck.[248] In 1774–1775, without a Trinh invasion that forced the Nguyen to fight on two fronts, the Nguyen might have strangled the Tayson at birth and the north-south division might have endured. Without the defection of a key Trinh general in 1786, the Tayson probably would not have entered the north at all. After occupying Dong Kinh, at first they treated it less as a recovered national territory than as a conquered province to be despoiled. The

---

[245] George Dutton, "Tay Son (Tyson, Taixones): Giving a Name to Rebellion in 18th Century Vietnam" (ms) 11, 13. On the composition, policies, and progress of the Tayson, I rely on idem, "Tay Son Uprising," chs. 2–5; which is destined to become the standard work on the Tayson; plus Li, *Cochinchina*, ch. 7; Dian Murray, *Pirates of the South China Coast 1790–1810* (Stanford, 1987), ch. 3; essays by Georges Boudarel, Lydie Prin, and Nguyen Duc Nghinh in Ngo and Nguyen, *Propriete privee*, 46–60, 72–78, 111–204; Viet Chung, "Recent Findings on the Tay Son Insurgency," *Vietnamese Studies* 1985: 30–62; L. Cadiere, "Documents relatifs a l'epoque de Gia-long," *BEFEO* 12, 7 (1912): 1–82; Forest, *Les missionnaires*, ch. 17.

[246] Dutton, "Tay Son (Tyson, Taixones)," 6–7; idem, "Tay Son Uprising," 160, 171.

[247] Cadiere, "Documents relatifs," 8; Li, *Cochinchina*, 150–53; Dutton, "Tay Son (Tyson, Taixones)," 5–7; idem, "Tay Son Uprising," 136–42, 158–61; and Nguyen Quoc Vinh, "Adrift at the Margins of National History: Relocating Nguyen Nhac and Local Ethnic Minorities in the Early Tay Son Rebellion" (ms).

[248] See esp. Dutton, "Tay Son Uprising," 164–76.

Tayson brothers' prompt redivision of Vietnamese-speaking lands into
autonomous realms separated at the Hai Van Pass also argues against
a pan-Vietnamese vision – as perhaps does Nguyen Hue's quixotic demand that China "return" Guangdong and Guangxi[249] and the fact that
resistance to the Chinese invasion of 1788/89 was confined north of the
Hai Van Pass.

On the other hand, it is clear that by breaking the century-old Nguyen-
Trinh stalemate, the Tayson suddenly rendered internal boundaries
within the entire Vietnamese-speaking lowlands exceptionally fluid.[250]
If the Tayson themselves failed to unify this area, they created preconditions for others to do so. It is also fair to suggest that linguistic, cultural,
and historical affinities let the Tayson move from south to north in the
1780s far more easily than if they had they tried to annex such genuinely
alien cultural entities as Cambodia or Laos. In private writings as well
as in late Trinh propaganda, some contemporary literati emphasized
north–south ties;[251] while the Tayson themselves, as they advanced on
Dong Kinh, sported the legitimist slogan "Destroy the Trinh, Restore
the Le."[252] After uniting Thuan Hoa and Dong Kinh in a single domain for the first time since the 16th century, Nguyen Hue, a man from
the south, emphasized his ties to the north by planning a new capital
at his ancestral site in Nghe An.[253] A man of some education as well
as pragmatic instinct, he also accorded literati far greater policy influence than they had enjoyed under the late Trinh; as one official wrote,
he "behaves toward scholars without differentiating between those of
South or North [Vietnam]."[254] In 1788/89 when Qing armies invaded
Dong Kinh on behalf of the now deposed Le ruler, an edict in Nguyen
Hue's name invoked the historic opposition between China and Dai

---

[249] Note, however, that Nguyen Hue claimed Guangdong and Guangxi as part of the
patrimony of the ancient Nam Yueh kingdom, to which literati attributed the origin
of the Southern Country.
[250] Whereas the Trinh-Nguyen border had been at Dong Hoi, the Tayson divided
their lands at the Hai Van Pass. By 1790 Nguyen-anh (Gia-long) controlled a third
zone, the Mekong delta. In response to that threat, in 1793 northern Tayson forces
moved into the southern Tayson zone of Qui Nhon. The post-1802 division represented yet another configuration, with Gia-long controlling a great central sector from Thanh Hoa to Binh Thuan, and autonomous viceroys at Thang Long and
Saigon.
[251] Dutton, personal communication, Sept. 2001; Yang, *Contribution*, 179.
[252] Dutton, "Tay Son (Tyson, Taixones)," 16; idem, "Tay Son Uprising," 167.
[253] Le, *Histoire*, 320, 329; Dutton, personal communication, Sept. 2001.
[254] See Dutton, "Three Case Studies," 2, 12 (source of quoted phrase), 38–39 and *passim*;
idem, "Tay Son Uprising," ch. 5.

Viet, while claiming that all Vietnamese shared a racial origin distinct from the Chinese.[255]

Between 1792 and 1802 the Tayson lost power to a scion of the Nguyen dynasty, the future Gia-long, who had escaped to build a new base in the Mekong delta. Were it not for the premature death of the brilliant Nguyen Hue in 1792 and the infighting that accompanied the reign of his young son, the outcome might have been different. The indefatigable Gia-long, scion of the old Nguyen seigneurial family, also triumphed because he developed a grand strategic vision unmatched by the Tayson and because he harnessed more effectively the wealth of the Mekong frontier, with whose large landholders and Chinese traders the Nguyen had long been allied.[256] With central Vietnam no longer able to requisition delta rice, he was able to sell some of the surplus overseas for war materiel, which gave him a critical advantage in ships and firearms. At various stages Gia-long received support from the Siamese court, from Khmer, Malay, and Cham warriors; from Chinese communities in the south, who were most militarily influential at least through the 1780s; and from French officers, who from 1789 transformed field artillery tactics and introduced new ship and citadel designs.[257] In effect, this was the latest in a series of rebellions that championed outlying regions against the center and that tended to move southward with Vietnamese settlement, starting with Le Loi's revolt in Thanh Nghe in the 1410s and 1420s, and continuing with Nguyen Kim's uprising against the Mac in Thanh Nghe in the 1530s, the Nguyen secession in Thuan Hoa in the early 1600s, the Tayson rising in Qui Nhon in 1771, and Gia-long's own movement in the Saigon area in the 1780s. Gia-long also resembled Taksin insofar as the latter's victories drew at first on Chinese coastal communities.

---

[255] I am not able to judge how appropriate the translated term "race" may be. See translated citations at Hodgkin, *Vietnam*, 88–89; Le, *Histoire*, 325; Lam, *Patterns of Vietnamese Response*, 63–65, Dutton, "Tay Son Uprising," 179. Similar themes appeared in Gia-long's early proclamations, quoted in Nola Cooke, "Peasant Rebellion and the Gia Long Reign" (ms), 5, 8.

[256] On late 18th century strategies, weapons, and battles, see esp. Dutton, "Flaming Tiger."

[257] On the pre-1802 career of Gia-long (Nguyen-anh), Choi, "Southern Vietnam," ch. 1; Cadiere, "Documents relatifs," 1–79; Woodside, *Vietnam*, 16–18; Taylor, "Surface Orientations," 965–69; Li, "Rice Trade;" idem, "*Cang Hai Sang Tian*," 6; idem, "Late 18th Century Mekong Delta," 8; Frederic Mantinne, "Military Technology Transfers from Europe to Lower Mainland Southeast Asia" (ms).

Like the Tayson, Gia-long initially invoked Le legitimist slogans to rally support outside the south. He also emphasized, no doubt sincerely, his family's ancestral ties to Thanh Hoa. But in driving him northward, military necessity and expediency again seem to have been more influential than nostalgia. After the Tayson, whom he was determined to extirpate, made Dong Kinh their last major redoubt, he had no choice but to invade the north. Having finally pacified that region in 1802, Gia-long could rethink the question to which the Tayson had no viable solution: How was so fissiparous a territory as the eastern mainland to be governed?

NGUYEN EXPERIMENTS WITH REGIONAL INTEGRATION AND FRONTIER SINICIZATION

In 1803, for purposes of diplomacy with China, the realm was officially renamed Vietnam.[258] To aid communications in this unusually elongated territory, Gia-long – whose imperial title emphasized his rule from *Gia*[-dinh] region in the far south to [Thang]-*long* in the north[259] – began to join existing road networks into the so-called Mandarin Road, with ten-mile rest-houses, all the way from Saigon to the China border. Vauban-type citadels, anchors of central power, sprouted at Hue, Saigon, Hanoi, and other provincial capitals. Gia-long began the most ambitious land measurement program in Vietnamese history, which by the late 1830s encompassed all 15,000–18,000 villages north to south. He also revived examinations after a fashion, patronized scholars, modeled his capital on Beijing, and promulgated a law code that reproduced most of the Qing code.[260]

Yet while taking these integrative measures and invoking sacramental Chinese terminology, Gia-long relied not on a national elite recruited via examinations, but on a new circle of southern military veterans (the Tayson had virtually eradicated the old Dang Trong aristocracy). In this reliance on his own entourage, he resembled the early Le and early Trinh, as well as his own Nguyen ancestors, whose post-1744 mix of military and Confucian elements he more or less resurrected. The new government had few fixed rules of tenure. Exams were of minor import.

---

[258] Woodside, *Vietnam*, 120–21; idem, "Political Theory," 248–49.

[259] I follow Choi, "Southern Vietnam," 36, n. 32.

[260] Woodside, *Vietnam*, 18, 77–86, 101–103, 136–42, 163–71; idem, "Political Theory," 265–66; Nguyen and Ta, *Le Code*, I, 29–31, 54–85.

Although he claimed sovereignty for the first time over everything from the Mekong delta to the China border, Gia-long saw himself not as founder of a new dynasty, but as heir to 200 years of Nguyen tradition rooted specifically in Dang Trong.[261] Thus he located his capital at Hue, near the old seat of Phu Xuan, and governed directly only the central sectors of the realm. A military governor-general in Hanoi, with his own army and seals of office, ruled the north, while a second semi-autonomous overlord ruled the Mekong delta from Saigon. Particularly in Dong Kinh, which had no tradition of Nguyen loyalty and which Gia-long (like the Tayson) treated as something of a captured area, his policies engendered bitter resentment. As late as 1822 the English envoy John Crawfurd referred to Dong Kinh as "a conquered country, and subject to almost yearly insurrections."[262]

Under his son Minh-mang (r. 1820–1841), the balance tilted from military rule and Dang Trong regionalism toward Sinic, nominally bureaucratic practices and more pan-Vietnamese loyalties. As in Dong Kinh in the 1460s and the 1660s, the original military oligarchy yielded to a faction (albeit, in this case, still a southern-led faction) with a stronger scholarly orientation. The Chinese model that these officials and their royal patron embraced offered three interrelated benefits. Most critical, it promised to bring the Mekong delta and Dong Kinh under closer control by eliminating local overlords. Regional uprisings, most especially a major revolt in the south from 1833 to 1835, drove home the need for such reform.[263] Besides reducing regional dangers, Sinic administration could mobilize military resources more efficiently against Siam, which challenged Vietnam after 1811 in Cambodia and 1827 in Laos. Finally, it promised to associate the dynasty more closely with the prestige of Chinese culture. Much as Rama I after the turmoil of the 1770s sought to strengthen royal authority by invoking orthodox texts, so Minh-mang (and, to a lesser extent, his father) bypassed Le traditions by turning directly to Chinese models.

---

[261] On the influence of the southern past and dynastic ancestralism, Cooke, "The Myth of the Restoration," in Reid, *Last Stand*, 269–95; and Philippe Langlet, *L'ancienne historiographie d'etat au Vietnam* (Paris, 1990). For a different emphasis, see Choi, "Southern Vietnam," 13 ff.

[262] John Crawfurd, *Journal of an Embassy to the Courts of Siam and Cochin China* (rpt., Singapore, 1987), 491. Cf. 495: "The subjugated countries of Kamboja [the Mekong delta and far south] and Tonquin lie at the two extremities of the empire, and being discontented, are peculiarly liable to insurrection." On southern autonomy, see esp. Choi, "Southern Vietnam," ch. 2.

[263] Choi, "Southern Vietnam," chs. 3, 4, 6; Woodside, *Vietnam*, 101–103, 284–85.

By reestablishing the three-tier Chinese-style examination system, Minh-mang signaled the dynasty's willingness to provide northern literati with far more than token roles. In fact, in the 1830s an unprecedented number of northerners entered the central administration.[264] At the same, largely in imitation of Qing models, the throne consolidated power in two executive organs, perfected a system of bureaucratic ratings, and replaced Gia-long's decentralized solar-polity with a Pattern D system of 31 provinces from the Chinese border to the Gulf of Siam. These controlled some 80 prefectures and 260 districts, with each district containing on average about 30,000 people.[265] Likewise Minh-mang's court expanded state schools, not least in the far south where Confucian influences were weakest, and patronized scholarship. In the villages it further bureaucratized the spirits, sought to enforce Confucian norms of female subordination and family organization, and combated heterodox religious groups, especially Christians, whose growing organizational and financial ties to Europe and whose involvement in the southern revolt of 1833–1835 rendered them ever more suspect.[266] To be sure, in the face of entrenched village elites Hue's rural penetration remained limited. Thus, in contrast to the late 15th century but in common with the Trinh era, prefecture and district officials in Dong Kinh imposed taxes not on individuals but on the village (*xa*), whose notables allocated burdens to their own satisfaction and the frequent discomfort of the poor.[267] Nonetheless, by welcoming literati from different regions, improving land cadastres and censuses, and encouraging social/intellectual orthodoxy, Hue by 1840 had better control over the chief Vietnamese-speaking lowlands than any regime since the early Trinh, and possibly the early Le.

Nor were administrative experiments confined to the lowlands. Although Hue declined to aid Anuvong's revolt against Bangkok, in 1827 in the aftermath of that conflict it seized the Laotian plateau of Tran Ninh and adjacent districts. In these area, as well as in the far

[264] On regional patterns of official recruitment, Woodside, *Vietnam*, 170–71, 194–223; Cooke, "Composition of Elite"; idem, "Confucianization"; Byung Wook Choi, "Nguyen Dynasty's Policy toward Chinese settlers during the First Half of the 19th Century" (ms); and idem, "Southern Vietnam," 107–108, which shows that among men with "key roles in central politics," northerners rose from 4.6 percent under Gia-long to 30.1 percent under Minh-mang.

[265] In the 1840s. Woodside, *Vietnam*, 143–44. On Nguyen administration, see Woodside's classic study, esp. chs. 2, 3.

[266] Woodside, *Vietnam*, 284–89; Choi, "Southern Vietnam," 54–60, 80–83, 91–94, 112–24.

[267] Yu, "Changing Nature," 165, 170; Woodside, *Vietnam*, 152–58.

north and the southwestern hills, the Nguyen court, rejecting the 18th-century status quo, pressured tribal leaders to accept Vietnamese social conventions – dress, hairstyle, marriage rites – and to incorporate local communes into Vietnamese-style administrative grids in which villages received Vietnamese names. In fact, in these inaccessible, malarial zones where Vietnamese settlement was minimal, such efforts had limited success and bred bitter revolts.[268]

More plausible were efforts directed against non-Vietnamese lowlanders – chiefly Chinese, Chams, Khmers. Notwithstanding Gia-long's close alliance with Mekong delta Chinese, both Minh-mang and Thieu-tri (r. 1841–1847) tended to distrust recent Chinese immigrants, *thanh-nhan*, as opposed to older communities of *minh huong*. Whereas the latter were substantially assimilated to Vietnamese culture and utterly loyal, *thanh-nhan* proved reluctant to adopt Vietnamese ways, became involved in rice smuggling, and played a prominent role in the 1833–1835 revolt. The Nguyen court therefore tried, with mixed results, to curb *thanh-nhan* trade and to naturalize them by registering new settlers with *minh huong* congregations rather than their own native-place congregations. By this time, Hue also had annexed the Chinese enclave of Ha Tien.[269] Likewise, whereas Gia-long had maintained Cham Panduranga as a tributary enclave poised uneasily between central Vietnam and the viceroyalty of the delta, Minh-mang incorporated it into the Vietnamese provincial system. After Muslim-led Cham revolts in 1833–1835 collapsed, the door was open to further colonization, further Cham assimilation, and the cultural and economic ghettoization of survivors.[270]

But as the largest non-Vietnamese population, Khmers bore the brunt of Nguyen policy, which was more activist but broadly reminiscent of

[268] Ta Van Tai, "Ethnic Minorities and the Law in Traditional Vietnam," *The Vietnam Forum* 5 (1985): 25; Woodside, *Vietnam*, 167, 237–40, 249; Choi, "Southern Vietnam," 133, 137, 141–42; Snit Smuckarn and Kennon Breazeale, *A Culture in Search of Survival* (New Haven, 1988), 25; Le Thi Thanh Hoa, "Doi net ve chinh sach su dung cac quan lai cua Minh Mang doi voi vung dan toc thieu so," D. N. Dang-vu, tr., *Tap Chi Dan Toc Hoc* 86, 2 (1995): 42–44. Moreover, as Taylor, "On Being Muonged" emphasizes, at the popular level Vietnamese-upland relations tended to be far more accommodating than official rhetoric.

[269] Choi, "Nguyen Dynasty's Policy," 13, 16; idem, "Southern Vietnam," 30–33, 64–78, 90–95, 137, 146–49; Wheeler, "Cross-Cultural Trade," ch. 3; Sakurai and Kitagawa, "Ha Tien."

[270] Po Dharma, "Dernieres recherches," 64–66; idem, *Le Panduranga*, I, 105–88, esp. 112–13, 122, 125, 144, 179.

Kon-baung Burmanization. Forsaking an earlier modus vivendi, the Nguyen pressured Khmer leaders in the delta and trans-Bassac region to adopt Vietnamese language and customs. Vietnamese settlements were planted in the midst of Khmer districts, Khmer villages disappeared in Vietnamese-dominated administrative units, and efforts were made to absorb Khmer ancestral cults into Vietnamese cults.[271] After parrying Siamese incursions, Hue in the mid-1830s annexed what is now eastern and central Cambodia, where it also promoted Vietnamese colonization and administrative norms along with Vietnamese speech, dress, and so-cial patterns. "The barbarians [in Cambodia] have become my children now, and you should help them, and teach them our customs . . . to use oxen . . . to grow more rice . . . to raise mulberry trees, pigs, and ducks. . . . As for language, they should be taught to speak Vietnamese. . . . If there is any out-dated or barbarous customs that can be simplified, or repressed, then do so." "[It is] like bringing the Cambodian people out of the mud onto a warm feather bed," Minh-mang told his officials.[272] Curiously ungrateful for this boon and determined to preserve their autonomy, Khmer district leaders and Buddhist monks organized a massive upris-ing in 1840–1841 that spread into what is now southern Vietnam. "All the ministers, local officials and common people of Cambodia agreed to join forces to kill the Vietnamese," a Cambodian chronicle claimed with hopeful exaggeration.[273] After Siamese troops intervened on be-half of the rebels, Hue in 1845–1847 was forced to accept a division of authority in Cambodia favorable to Siam. In contrast to the Mon rising of 1740 and Anuvong's revolt of 1827, here was an ethnically-based anti-centralizing revolt that succeeded thanks to outside help. Both in Cambodia and what is now southern Vietnam, the 1840 Khmer revolt – like the aforementioned 18th-century uprisings and another in 1820–1821 – triggered a lethal polarization in which Khmers, invoking distinctively Khmer religious symbols and magic spells, fought in the name of their king and of Theravada Buddhism.[274]

[271] Choi, "Southern Vietnam," 24–26, 136–41.
[272] Chandler, *A History of Cambodia* (Boulder, CO, 1992), 126, 130. On Nguyen policy and Khmer reactions, see too ibid., ch. 7; idem, "Cambodia Before the French," chs. 5–7; idem, "Anti-Vietnamese Rebellion," 16–24; Mak Phoeun, "La frontiere," 144–55; Woodside, *Vietnam*, 145–46, 167–68, 249–55; idem, "Territorial Order and Collective Identity Tensions in Confucian Asia: China, Vietnam, Korea," *Daedalus* 1998, esp. 208–212; Choi, "Southern Vietnam," 153–55.
[273] Chandler, "Cambodia Before the French," 150. It is unclear when the chronicle was written.
[274] Previous nn., esp. Choi, "Southern Vietnam," 154–55.

To be sure, Vietnamese-Khmer hostilities differed from modern nationalist mobilizations insofar as: a) vertical patronage systems militated against a theory of horizontal community, and in some cases permitted poly-ethnic followings; b) in border areas, ethnicity itself could be fluid; and c) the religious bases of authority remained nominally universal. Nonetheless, all parties seem to have understood that political allegiance had strong cultural correlates. In this polarized climate, Byung Wook Choi argues that a stronger psychological identification with Hue took root among Vietnamese-speakers in the far south, many of whom until then had maintained stubborn regional loyalties but among whom perhaps 30 percent of men aged 18–50 served in anti-Khmer suppression campaigns under Hue-sanctioned officers.[275] Recall that intense ethnically-colored warfare encouraged closer identification with the throne in early Kon-baung Burma and early Chakri Siam as well. Although forced to abandon its new Cambodian province in the 1840s, Hue continued to strengthen control over the far south, including Khmer enclaves in the Mekong delta. Specifically, it sponsored new settlements and garrisons, encouraged ethnic assimilation, and sought to advance Confucian scholars (*nho si*) and landlords (*dien chu*) allied to the throne at the expense of Vietnamese Christians, Khmers, and unassimilated Chinese.[276]

The border with China bred no antagonism comparable to that on the Khmer frontier, because highlands provided a natural buffer absent in the south and perhaps too because cultural differences were less pronounced. Literate Vietnamese dwelled in a civilized universe whose acknowledged center was China. Yet this outlook too was compatible with local pride and self-congratulatory memories, some quite recent, of resistance to Chinese invasion. A typical Sino-Vietnamese school primer emphasized Vietnam's high position within the Confucian world, while the aforementioned 18th-century scholar Le Quy Don invoked the superiority of local flora as a metaphor for Vietnamese difference from China.[277] "Decadent China and orthodox Vietnam" became a favorite trope of Nguyen courtiers eager to claim that their small country remained closer to Confucian ideals than their overly commercial,

---

[275] Choi, "Southern Vietnam," 87–95, 155–62, 199.
[276] Choi, "Southern Vietnam," 96–202, esp. 136–41, 153 62, 185–202.
[277] Woodside, *Vietnam*, 193; idem, "Political Theory," 256–57; idem, letter of Jan. 15, 1996; Forest, *Les missionnaires*, II, 11.

barbarian-ruled northern neighbor[278] – somewhat as Burmese prided themselves on being more orthodox than their great Theravadin rivals, the Siamese. In part perhaps, this assertion of identity sought to defend against destabilizing commercial influences, to which we shall return. Crawfurd in 1822 described Vietnamese ethnic consciousness as follows: "Like the Siamese, they are nationally very vain, and consider themselves the first people in the world, being hardly disposed to yield the palm even to the Chinese – the only strangers whom they are disposed to consider *respectable*. They consider the Kambojans ... as barbarians, and scarcely think the Siamese much better."[279]

In sum, the Nguyen after 1802 – like their Kon-baung and Chakri contemporaries – intensified expansionary and integrative trends apparent since at least the 15th century. In 1400 Vietnamese-speakers lacked authority south of the Hai Van pass, but by 1847 they had come to dominate the entire eastern littoral, the Mekong delta, and eastern districts in modern Laos. As cultural boundaries within the lowlands grew sharper, Chams and Khmers were absorbed, displaced, emasculated. In Hue's zone of control in 1847, consisting of modern Vietnam and the eastern fringes of Laos, at least 80 percent of the population regarded themselves as Vietnamese (*nguoi viet*), the rest being hill peoples and unassimilated Chams, Chinese, and Khmers.[280] By contrast, within the western empire in 1824 I suggested that self-identified Burmans (*myan-ma*) were about 60 percent, while in the Bangkok empire not much more than a third normally may have regarded themselves as Siamese. Moreover, despite rapid extension, political unity among Vietnamese-speakers obviously increased. Whereas for most of the period 1541–1802 Vietnamese regions split into two or more hostile states, and whereas even during Gia-long's reign, Dong Kinh and the Mekong delta had powerful overlords, by 1836 lowland provinces were uniformly organized and would remain so until the French annexation.

Lest we exaggerate this success or succumb to national essentialism, I hasten to add that by the standards of the Irrawaddy and Chaophraya basins, the integration of the eastern littoral not only was short-lived – a

---

[278] Woodside, *Vietnam*, 121; idem, "Political Theory," 248, 256.

[279] Crawfurd, *Journal of an Embassy*, 488. Italics in original.

[280] My estimate, which Keith Taylor, personal communication, Aug., 2001 accepts as reasonable. Even in the lowlands of the far south, Choi, "Southern Vietnam," 134, 199 suggests that as early as 1830 Vietnamese-speakers were 65–70 percent of the total population.

mere three generations – but fragile. On present evidence, 19th-century Dong Kinhese were no more interested in their fellow Vietnamese-speakers' anti-Khmer struggles in the south than the Nguyen had been supportive of anti-Chinese resistance in the north in 1788–1789.[281] According to Cooke, the effort to forge a unified imperial elite was basically a function of Minh-mang's personality. After he died, partisans from the old Dang Trong heartland, realizing that they could not compete honestly with far better qualified northerners, shamelessly manipulated the examinations system as well as mandarinal promotions to their own advantage.[282] Taylor takes a more geographically determinist viewpoint, arguing that from 1802 the attempt to control *both* the demographic center of Dong Kinh and the commercially dynamic Mekong from the weak central region was fatally flawed.[283] In either case, the resentment Dong Kinh literati felt at their renewed exclusion joined with rural distress to encourage a revival of pro-Le agitation in the north and a growing indifference to the fate of the dynasty. In the far south, Christians, *thanh-nhan* Chinese, and Khmers nursed their own grievances. Both sets of tensions, as well as rivalry between Thuan Quang and Thanh Nghe, contributed to Vietnam's ineffectual response to the French between 1858 and 1885.[284] To be sure, the Kon-baung and Chakri courts also had their share of factionalism, but those disputes reflected princely rivalries at the capital with no consistent geographic bases.

Noteworthy too is the failure of Sinic-style administration to pay Nguyen Vietnam larger dividends in its struggle with Siam over Cambodia. On paper, Vietnam's advantages were formidable: almost twice as many people and the prospect of organizing them effectively through more frequent censuses, more meritocratic recruitment, laws of avoidance, and more numerous levels of territorial appointees. Yet Vietnam could not overcome three handicaps: a) Her key population centers in Dong Kinh and Thuan Hoa lay farther from the theater of battle than Siam's key regions, and the most Sinicized administrative areas also were most distant; b) underneath the Sinic facade, patron-client ties

---

[281] But see Hue-Tam Ho Tai, *Millenarianism and Peasant Politics in Vietnam* (Cambridge, MA, 1983), 27.

[282] Cooke, "Composition," esp. 762–63; "Confucianization," 299–312; "The Nineteenth-Century Ruling Elite of Vietnam Revisited" (ms). Cf. Philippe Langlet, "L'historiographie d'ctat au siecle des Nguyen," *Vietnam Review* 1 (1996), 105–20.

[283] Taylor, "Surface Orientations," 969.

[284] Choi, "Southern Vietnam," 200–202; Taylor, "Surface Orientations," 969–70; Cooke, "Colonial Political Myth," ch. 3.

often remained more influential than bureaucratic norms, as a consideration of village autonomy and post–Minh-mang factionalism suggests; and c) with its pragmatic, cosmopolitan outlook, Siam harnessed growing maritime trade more effectively than did Vietnam.

ECONOMIC TRENDS C. 1650–1840

Let us approach the problem of imperial integration from a wider angle by moving from court politics to consider economic change during the two centuries prior to 1840. Increases in output, monetization, and Smithian specialization, particularly after 1750, had both centrifugal and centripetal implications, but on balance the latter were more influential.

What were the chief external stimuli? I have already discussed pre-1770 Hoi An. During the 17th century the same exchange of Japanese bullion for Chinese and Vietnamese silk as aided Hoi An benefited the chief northern port of Pho Hien.[285] After c. 1700 Tokugawa curbs, competition from Bengali silk, and diminished military needs blighted northern trade with Japan and with European companies; yet Chinese demand compensated, making the 18th century a "Chinese century" in Dong Kinh no less than in Nguyen Vietnam or Siam. By century's end, 50–60,000 Chinese lived in urban merchant settlements and more especially in the great mining communities in the northern hill country.[286]

Northern vitality notwithstanding, under the imperial Nguyen the center of foreign trade continued moving south, especially to the delta where Gia-long had been based. In the early 1800s, one source claimed that 300 Chinese junks a year visited the ports of the center and south, among which Saigon was clearly preeminent. This compared to 70–80 at Hoi An at its height.[287] The Chinese – "nothing equals the activity

---

[285] Nguyen, *Tableau*, ch. 3; *Pho Hien*; Nguyen-Long, "Vietnamese Ceramic Trade to the Philippines in the Seventeenth Century," *JSEAS* 30 (1999): 1–21.

[286] On Chinese in the north, Nguyen, *Tableau*, 183–227 (estimate p. 200); Nguyen The Anh, "L'immigration Chinoise," 160–61, citing Koffler's 1744 estimate; Richard, *Histoire naturelle*, I, 38–39, 287–97; Dampier, *Voyages*, 17–18, 47–49; Sun Laichen, "The 18th Century Sino-Vietnamese Overland Trade and Mining Industry in Northern Vietnam" (ms).

[287] These figures are not without problems. Li, "Rice Trade," 6 accepts the figure of 300 junks of 100–600 tons, which comes from Chaigneau's undated manuscript cited in Crawfurd, *Journal of an Embassy*, 520 n., and herself provides the Hoi An figure. Yet Crawfurd, *Journal of an Embassy*, 511–13 cites for the early 1820s only 78 junks at Saigon and other southern or central ports, and 38 in Dong Kinh, all averaging 172 tons. Assuming the discrepancy does not arise from an error in Chaigneau's manuscript or simple misinformation, it may reflect Crawfurd's imperfect attention to trade with: a) Phnom Penh and b) small Chinese settlements in coastal Siam, Malaya, and the

of this mercantile people," a Frenchman noted[288] – used their contacts with south China, the new English port of Singapore, and Chinese coastal settlements in the Gulf of Siam, Malaya, and Sumatra to integrate Vietnam into a Chinese-run South China Sea network. Saigon absorbed virtually all of Cambodia's commerce, further weakening that kingdom. Note, however, that Vietnam's total trade with China in 1822 may have been only half as large as Siam's trade with China, while anti-Chinese upheavals and government policy reportedly depressed the south's Chinese population to about 15 percent that of Siam.[289]

Multilateral maritime trade and overland contacts with China aided the Vietnamese economy in five familiar ways. First, as the discussion of 18th-century strains suggests, imported bullion and specie remained critical to domestic exchange. From 1633–1638 alone the Dutch shipped over 100,000,000 (sic) Japanese coins to Dang Trong, while in the 17th and 18th centuries New World silver flowed in via Manila, Batavia, China, and India.[290]

Second, created by the same bullion hunger as drew precious metals from overseas, Chinese-run copper and more especially silver mines in the Dong Kinh hill country became at one and the same time a fiscal mainstay of the Trinh regime, Vietnam's chief non-agricultural industry, and a major source of exchange media.[291] Note that in the late 17th and 18th centuries Burma, Siam, and Vietnam all suffered bullion shortages, benefited from the opening of mines along the Yunnan and Guangxi frontier, and accelerated the long-term shift from copper to silver-based media.

Foreign, chiefly New World, crops offered a third stimulus. Starting in the 1600s and accelerating in the 18th century, Dutch peas, New World

western archipelago, much of which involved smuggling at minor Vietnamese ports outside the purview of official statistics. Without providing any figures, Li, "Late 18th Century Mekong Delta," and "18th and Early 19th Century Mekong Delta" suggests that these latter branches were extensive.

[288] Chaigneau in Crawfurd, *Journal of an Embassy*, 519 n.

[289] Trade figures at Crawfurd, *Journal of an Embassy*, 513 (but see n. 287 on interpretive problems). Chinese figures at Li, "*Cang Hai Sang Tai*," 2–3; and G. William Skinner, *Chinese Society in Thailand* (Ithaca, 1957), 79. See too Woodside, *Vietnam*, 139–40, 261–76; Choi, "Southern Vietnam," 64–65.

[290] Unfortunately no one has attempted diachronic measurement of specie and bullion imports. Although impressionistic, by far the best overview is Whitmore, "Monetary Flow." Japanese coin imports 1633–1638 come from Li, *Cochinchina*, 92.

[291] Nguyen, *Tableau*, 86–91, 125, 162–64; Dang, *Institutions*, 102, 109, 114; Woodside, "Political Theory," 258–61; idem, *Vietnam*, 138, 268, 278; Whitmore, "Monetary Flow," 372, 369–89.

tobacco (which entered via Laos), and New World maize, sweet potatoes, and peanuts, as well as sesame, millet, and black-kidney beans
(all introduced via south China) boosted local agriculture. Peas and
beans enriched the soil, while maize and sweet potatoes were suitable
for marginal lands, as for example in the northern province of Son Tay
where within a century of its introduction c. 1670 maize reportedly had
replaced rice everywhere.[292]

Fourth, although a history of indigenous technology has yet to be
written, there is evidence of significant foreign influence. Europeans
transformed arms manufacture. Chinese techniques dominated mining,
printing, papermaking, sugar-processing, and some textile processes.
William Dampier c. 1690 reported that Ming refugee "artificers" had
introduced the Vietnamese to "many useful arts, of which they were
wholly ignorant before."[293]

Finally, as in Burma and Siam, foreign incentives continued to promote specialization. In the sugar industry, for example, which relied
at first on Japanese and then Chinese markets and capital, separate
Vietnamese households grew cane, processed juice, refined the juice,
and made containers. Insofar as export-oriented producers of silk, ceramics, dyes, and sugar in Thuan Hoa found it more profitable to buy
food from the delta than to grow it themselves, foreign trade encouraged
a regional division of labor comparable to that in the Irrawaddy basin,
or more especially Guangdong. The growing availability and variety of
consumer goods – many domestically produced but including European
and more especially Chinese textiles, metal goods, handicrafts, and specialty foods – encouraged producers in urban and coastal areas to expand output and to experiment with new techniques.[294] Chinese credit
lubricated both imports and exports.[295]

---

[292] Nguyen, *Tableau*, 51, 53; Pham Ai Phuong, "Tim hieu nghe trong trot Viet Nam the ky
XVIII nua dau XIX", *Nghien Cuu Lich Su* 224, 5 (1985): 48–54, 94, John Whitmore, tr.;
Woodside, "Political Theory," 254–57.

[293] Dampier, *Voyages*, 13; Nguyen, *Tableau*, 102–107; Woodside, "Medieval Vietnam," 316;
Richard, *Histoire naturelle*, I, 292.

[294] Cf. *supra* Ch. 3, n. 287, this chapter nn. 226, 227; and Kenneth Pomeranz, *The Great
Divergence* (Princeton, 2000), ch. 3, discussing consumer incentives elsewhere in
Eurasia.

[295] On 17th- early 19th-century foreign trade, *supra* nn. 285–93, plus Li, *Cochinchina*, ch. 4;
Robert Innes, "The Door Ajar: Japan's Foreign Trade in the Seventeenth Century"
(Univ. of Michigan Ph.D. diss., 1980), 57–66; Yu, "Law and Family," 103–104, 188–89;
Woodside, *Vietnam*, 261–76; idem, "Trading World." Cf. Marks, *Tigers, Rice*, chs. 5, 8
on trends in Guangdong and Guangxi.

As usual, the political apparatus simultaneously inhibited and stimulated production. On the one hand, we find the typical depressants: warfare, official corruption, and arbitrary taxation, about which Europeans never tired of complaining. On the other hand, the Trinh craved the revenues of Chinese mines, and like the Nguyen, sought foreign guns and customs receipts. To this end, both seigneuries and the post-1802 Nguyen regime offered merchants incentives within a system of bureaucratic regulation. The Trinh and Nguyen also provided genuine, if limited legal protection in matters of contracts, torts, and property, and encouraged market integration by standardizing weights and measures, improving roads, and reducing internal tolls.[296] Palaces, forts, armories, and shipyards concentrated urban demand, while taxes, increasingly assessed in cash, drove peasants to the market. Through military settlements, generous tax incentives, and extensive land grants, the post-1802 Nguyen continued to encourage landlord-led colonization of the Mekong delta.[297]

Alongside foreign trade and government action, local initiatives and domestic population growth had a major economic impact. Whether producing for subsistence or local sale, peasants remade the landscape with incremental improvements. One late 18th-century source counted 94 rice strains adapted to local soil, insect, hydrological, salinity, and stalk demands. The ratio between strains of fifth- and tenth-month rice gradually shifted toward the latter because they ripened more rapidly. By 1800 Vietnamese peasants also grew three varieties of maize, four of sweet potatoes, and ten of beans, plus a growing list of commercial fruits and vegetables, all primarily for domestic consumption. Nor did technique stagnate. Impelled by demographic pressures and local market incentives, peasants in the north and center experimented with new methods of plowing, transplantation, multiple-cropping, and fertilization. The latter included nitrogen-fixing legumes, systematic rotation to enhance soil fertility, and wider use of green fertilizer, silkworm waste, and night-soil, chiefly around the cities.[298] Reinforcing the demographic benefits of these changes and of New World crops were: a) an expansion in rural handicraft employment; b) improved rainfall in much of Vietnam c. 1700–1776, followed by a deterioration in Dong Kinh to the

---

[296] Richard, *Histoire naturelle*, I, 94; Nguyen and Ta, *Le Code*, I, 70–80, 191 ff.; Nguyen, *Tableau*, 177–81.
[297] Choi, "Southern Vietnam," 185–96; Nguyen Dinh Dau, "Early Cochinchinese Trade."
[298] Pham Ai Phuong, "Tim hieu," 48–54, 94; Nguyen, *Tableau*, ch. 1; Woodside, "Political Theory," 254–55.

mid-1790s, followed by modest improvement to c. 1830[299]; and c) the restoration of peace in 1802. Together, these factors pushed northern Vietnam's population by 1840 near its previous peak of 6.5 million. Central Vietnam also experienced renewed growth.[300] In the Mekong delta from 1820 to 1847 cultivated acreage – and presumably, population – may have expanded by 50 percent.[301] Although delta rice exports rose in the late 18th century, in the early 1800s and perhaps as late as 1830 rice shipments outside the country appear to have remained a modest portion of shipments to rice-deficit areas in central Vietnam itself.[302] Most of the latter shipments were consumed not by Vietnamese suppliers of foreign markets, but by administrators, soldiers, and domestic producers. In short, at least on present evidence, as in Burma so in Vietnam we cannot look to foreign demand to provide the principal explanation for frontier settlement. This judgment holds through the late 18th century, and probably the early 19th century as well.

Domestic demand joined foreign trade to encourage occupational and regional specialization, for which we have considerable evidence after 1650 and, especially, 1750. Northern and central districts became famous for commercial fruits and vegetables. Villages and urban quarters producing cottons, boats, agricultural implements, ceramics, woodblocks, paper, metal goods – chiefly for local markets – formed production chains with numerous intermediate stages. If we define

---

[299] T. Mikami, ed., *Proceedings of the International Symposium on the Little Ice Age Climate* (Tokyo, 1992), 231, 237, 315, 321, 329, 338; Marks, *Tigers, Rice*, 195–225; Nguyen The Anh, "Quelques aspects economiques et sociaux du problem du riz au Vietnam dans la premiere moitie du XIXe siecle," *Bulletin de la Societie des Etudes Indochinoise*, 1967: 14–15; Forest, *Les missionnaires*, II, 57–59, 97–99; Dutton, "Tay Son Uprising," 190, 196, 232–45.

[300] Li, *Cochinchina*, 159–72; and Sakurai, "Age of Commerce," 3.

[301] Li, "Rice Trade," 10, claims cultivated land "in the country [presumably the entire realm]" grew by over 33 percent." Since Dong Kinh increases were modest, a 50 percent increase in the south is a conservative estimate.

[302] Domestic shipments involved both rice tribute and private trade. As late as 1822 Crawfurd, *Journal of an Embassy*, 510–13 claimed that 2,000 (sic) junks of 30–45 tons from Saigon supplied Hue with rice, salt, oil, and iron, while another 60 junks of 50–75 tons carried provisions from Dong Kinh to Hue for a total of c. 86,000 tons; whereas only 116 junks carrying 20,000 tons traded from all Vietnamese ports to China. Possibly, trade with other ports in SE Asia would have raised the foreign figure considerably – see *supra*, nn. 224, 232, 287 – but Crawfurd's neglect of such trade and the minimal nature of Vietnamese rice shipments to pre-1831 Singapore (Li, "Rice Trade," graph p. 9) leave the issue uncertain. Choi, "Southern Vietnam," 64–67; Nguyen Dinh Dau, "Early Cochinese Trade," 4; and Woodside, *Vietnam*, 139–40 all emphasize the domestic, rather than foreign rice trade.

proto-industrialization as the "widespread development of rural out-work to produce commodities for distant markets,"[303] these develop-ments may qualify. Suppliers of raw materials and food to handicraft villages, mines, and cities benefited accordingly. By 1700 in Thuan Hoa, Quang Nam, and Dong Kinh, even isolated villages relied on markets to dispose of surpluses, with daily transactions in currency rather than in kind. At Thang Long the population spilled beyond the walls, knitting smaller settlements into urban zones, while on the frontier, small towns grew out of military centers and markets.[304]

IMPLICATIONS OF GROWTH: FORCES OF INSTABILITY AND FRACTURE

To return to the issue with which we opened the discussion of economic change, how did such growth influence political and cultural integration between 1650 and 1840? As usual, the effects were ambiguous. Let us consider first localizing and destabilizing implications.

I have emphasized that economic expansion led to political overex-tension, precisely because growth was concentrated at the extremities. There is no need to contrast again the centrifugal implications of south-ern settlement to 1800 with the centripetal effects of colonization in Burma and Siam. But even after 1800, to recall Taylor's argument, the attempt to rule from Hue ran up against the fact that the depressed seaboard economy of central Vietnam could not survive without mas-sive rice shipments from north and south, which left it dangerously vulnerable to market forces no less than to political revolt.[305] In the far south the cultural counterpart to economic and political localism was – in Hue's eyes – a distressingly commercial, indecorous, non-scholarly elite ethos; a dialect barely understood at the capital; and a penchant for Cham and Khmer religious cults.[306]

---

[303] Karen Wigen, *The Making of a Japanese Periphery, 1750–1920* (Berkeley, 1995), 8.

[304] On artisanry, commerce, and urbanization, see contemporary accounts at Baron, "Description," 3–7; Dampier, *Voyages*, 33–50; "Voyage de Pierre Poivre," 107–21; Richard, *Histoire naturelle*, I, 285–351, II, 65–74; and secondary analyses at Pham Ai Phuong, "Tim hieu," 48–54, 94; Li, *Cochinchina*, 94–95, 145, and chs. 4, 5; Woodside, "Trading World"; Li and Reid, *Southern Vietnam*; Yang, *Contribution*, ch. 3; Nguyen, *Tableau*, pt. I, ch. 2, pt. II, chs. 1–2; Yu, "Law and Family," 188–89.

[305] Taylor, "Surface Orientations," 969; Woodside, *Vietnam*, 139–40.

[306] Choi, "Southern Vietnam," 101–12, 160–61; Woodside, *Vietnam*, 28–30, 220–21; Tai, *Millenarianism*, 3–43.

Meanwhile, in 19th-century Dong Kinh renewed population growth and maldistribution of land contributed to yet another round of peasant distress, tax evasion, and unrest, aggravated, we have seen, by anti-Nguyen, pro-Le sentiment. Insofar as demographic renewal fed commercial exchange, it also rendered specie – which by 1810, meant chiefly silver – increasingly scarce. At the same time, Chinese demand for bullion to lubricate internal trade and, by the 1820s, to pay for British opium began pulling large quantities of silver out of Vietnam. The ensuing coin famine weakened exchange, aggravated rural distress, and drained the strength of the new dynasty.[307]

Another tension rooted in economic change was the generic conflict, familiar from Burma and Siam, between fixed social/administrative categories, on the one hand, and market-based mobility of people and goods, on the other. I have already suggested that disorders in late 18th-century Dong Kinh drew strength from commercial as well as demographic pressures, but this was hardly the earliest instance of commerce acting as a solvent. Starting, as noted, in 1658 and with greater urgency thereafter, the Trinh sold offices regardless of education or social qualification.[308] The following passage, remarkable despite its moralistic hyperbole, described a northern examination site of the mid-1700s where anyone who could pay was admitted:

> Up there you had everybody – merchants, butchers, shopkeepers, all wanted to take part. On the opening day the crowd and the stampede were such that some people died in the crush. You could see in the arena some going round with books, some offering to sell their services – all this going on quite openly. Mandarins hawked their good offices around – as though they were petty traders. Since this period the examination system has been completely discredited.[309]

In Thang Long and other cities, the population's mobility, heterogeneity, and anonymity eroded controls on theatres, taverns, nocturnal entertainments, and occupational segregation.[310] In 18th-century Thang Long and more especially Quang Nam, the growing availability of luxury goods once reserved for high officials threatened the maintenance

---

[307] Nguyen, "Quelques aspects," 7–22; Sakurai, "Abandoned Villages"; Whitmore, "Monetary Flow," 388; R. B. Smith, "Politics and Society in Vietnam during the Early Nguyen Period (1802–1862)," *JRAS* 1974: 164–68; Woodside, *Vietnam*, 135, 277–79.

[308] *Supra* n. 175. On commutation and sale of office in Dang Trong, Li, *Cochinchina*, 94–95.

[309] Hodgkin, *Vietnam*, 79; Le Thanh Khoi, *Le Viet-Nam* (Paris, 1955), 252–53, translated from the *Cuong muc*.

[310] Nguyen, *Tableau*, 132–34.

of proper hierarchy. In a refrain reminiscent of anti-parvenue critiques by Late Ayudhya officials and by Rama I (see *supra,* pp. 301, 316), Le Quy Don lamented in 1776 that central Vietnam had become a bespangled silk-wearing plutocracy.[311] But even in Dong Kinh the erosion of traditional social categories appeared in the interpenetration of scholar-officials and merchants. Notwithstanding the latter's low official status, mandarins married into wealthy families – *minh huong* Chinese as well as Vietnamese – and traded either on their own or through their wives or intermediaries. For their part, successful traders sought to acquire the lifestyle, culture, and insignia of scholar-officials and were among the first to buy offices and admission to the examinations.[312]

As Woodside has shown, similar contradictions between Confucian norms and evolving practice beset 18th and early 19th century economic policy.[313] Originally the throne retained a monopoly on casting coins, a policy that maintained uniformity while ritually affirming the ruler's legitimacy. But as monetary demands intensified, in the 1700s Trinh and Nguyen rulers abandoned that prerogative. In the early 19th century the final barrier yielded when for the first time gold and silver ingots circulated legitimately in private trade. Likewise at Saigon, in the 1830s Nguyen efforts to obtain tribute rice for Hue began to founder before the determination of private brokers to export rice to south China and Singapore.

The market's growing claims did not go uncontested. Ironically, the same commercial vitality as challenged bureaucratic management of the economy provided the books, schools, and theoretical perspectives by which an expanding, fundamentalist literati class demanded that property again be subject to Confucian moral principles as embodied in state regulation. In part, this movement built upon the Confucian ferment of the late 18th century when, as we have seen, leading scholars invoked classical norms as the key to restoring social harmony. In keeping with these perspectives, Minh-mang's court in 1839–1840 organized two ambitious programs to expand communal and public lands at the expense of private holdings, most notably in Binh Dinh. The fact that these reforms generally failed suggests, in Woodside's view, that the state was becoming hostage to an intractable tension, rooted in economic

---

[311] Woodside, "Trading World," 166. Also Nguyen, *Tableau,* 149–50.
[312] Yang, *Contribution,* 180; Cooke, "Confucianization," 298; and esp. Nguyen, *Tableau,* 134–41.
[313] Discussion follows Woodside, "Political Theory," 245–68; idem, *Vietnam,* 139–40, 221.

expansion, between a more literate, broadly based radical classicism and the economic power of private landlords.[314] Minh-mang's reforms recall largely unsuccessful attempts in Kon-baung Burma to protect service and glebe lands against money-lending and market inroads, as discussed in Chapter 2. But Vietnam's situation was also unique, because Buddhism was less concerned with social regulation and lacked an antimercantile bias. Although Siamese and Burmese courtiers worried about social disorder, their approach to economic and social questions was basically pragmatic. Thus the revolution in finances, the total surrender to maritime trade embodied in early Chakri reforms met no principled opposition from either Siamese monks or courtiers. More speculatively, I would suggest that whereas in Siam (and to a lesser extent, Burma) the geographic conflation of political-moral center with commercial center encouraged a thoroughgoing accommodation, in Vietnam the physical separation between Hue and Dong Kinh, on the one hand, and the most commercially unfettered region, the far south, on the other hand, provided Confucian moralists with greater insulation, hence purity.

Intellectual debate leads to a final source of tension and instability, the continued proliferation of religious and discursive perspectives that a resurgent Neo-Confucian classicism could not entirely restrain. Despite fierce persecution, from the 1790s Vietnamese Christianity, with growing French missionary support, strengthened its indigenous priesthood, doctrinal orthodoxy, and organizational independence from non-Christian communities. In the far south a Mahayana-derived millennial Buddhist sect, the Buu Son Ky Huong religion, which took root after 1849, reflected the peculiar anomie and ethnic tensions of an essentially illiterate frontier society.[315] But perhaps the chief spur to cultural experimentation, especially in the Red River plain and other developed areas, was the combination of social disorder from the late 1700s with gradual commercial intensification and a corresponding increase in literacy and intellectual synergy. Such developments contributed to new demonstrations of Buddhist piety and an unprecedented output of printed

---

[314] Woodside, "Political Theory," esp. 252–53. Also Nguyen Dinh Dau, "Note on the Analysis of Ancient Land Registry in Binh Dinh," in *The Traditional Village in Vietnam* (Hanoi, 1993) 402–18; and Choi, "Southern Vietnam," 185–96, emphasizing Minh-mang's support for landlordism in the far south.

[315] On these religious currents, Cooke, "Historicizing Vietnamese Christianity"; Choi, "Southern Vietnam," 160–61; Woodside, *Vietnam*, 28–30, 190, 262–64, 284–89; Tai, *Millennarianism*, 3–33.

Buddhist texts and engravings – prayers, commandments, genealogies, stories – at major pagodas in Dong Kinh and Hue.[316]

More especially, intellectual/aesthetic ferment and expanded literacy supported the flowering in the 18th and the early 19th centuries of an extensive lay literature in the demotic script, *nom*. Available in local variants and thus accessible to a far wider audience than Chinese writing, *nom* could promote discourses that were weakly related to the official social order, and in some cases, clearly subversive. Thus in the 1820s and 1830s *nom* became the propaganda medium of peasant rebels and Christian proselytizers alike.[317] More broadly, demotic writing was used for stories, fables, songs, histories, and most especially for poetry in six/eight-syllable verse, including the emergent verse novel. If the bulk of this literature promoted Confucian pieties and stereotypical moralizing, some works voiced satire and protest, questioned received orthodoxies, and focused with a rare intensity on private emotions, particularly love relations, which now became the subject not of stricture, but of sympathetic description. This new emphasis on individual sensibility extended to the use of the female voice to register complaint and to reexamine verities. At the same time the rather simple plots of 17th-century works yielded to more complex stories, with multiple episodes and vivid characters, among whom women often were central. We see these trends, for example, in two famous "female lament" poems; in the poetry of Ho Xuan Huong, a witty female iconoclast; and in the enormously popular early 19th-century epic poem *Kim Van Kieu* by Nguyen Du, which explored issues of cosmic justice through the tale of a virtuous woman reduced to prostitution.[318] Likewise Chinese-language writings in Vietnam, which remained prolific, exhibited greater interest in individual actors. Recall that in the late 18th and 19th centuries Burmese and Siamese literatures also experimented with new folk-influenced genres, more realistic social settings, and more spontaneous, individuated emotions. To what extent did these trends reflect wider readerships, more competitive economic environments, and

---

[316] Nguyen, *History of Buddhism*, 313–67, esp. 324; Cooke, "Myth of the Restoration," 279–88.

[317] Woodside, *Vietnam*, 57–58.

[318] Durand and Nguyen, *Vietnamese Literature,* chs. 7–9; Huynh, *Heritage of Vietnamese Poetry*, esp. intro.; Nguyen Ngoc Bich, *A Thousand Years of Vietnamese Poetry* (New York, 1975); Le, *Histoire*, 294–300; Nguyen et al., *Vietnamese Literature*, 62–84, 281–382; Nguyen Du, *The Tale of Kieu*, Huynh Sanh Thong, tr. (New York, 1973); Woodside, *Vietnam*, 46–50; Nguyen Khac Vien et al., *Anthologie* II, esp. 7–25.

the enhanced possibility that individual action could determine one's fate?

SPURS TO CULTURAL INTEGRATION, C. 1650–1840

In these ways, economic change bred cultural experiment, specialization, tension, and fracture. Yet if a wider circulation of texts encouraged innovation and debate, it also provided marginal social and geographic groups with greater exposure to elite, centrally-defined norms. The resultant homogenizing thrust between 1650 and 1840 probably would have proceeded even if Neo-Confucianism had lost its hegemony. One thinks, for example, of 18th-century France, where the erosion of provincial cultures and the disintegration of Christian-absolutist ideology went hand in hand. But in Vietnam, in part perhaps because commercial solvents were weaker than in France, Neo-Confucianism retained its preeminence within an increasingly integrated cultural system.

Although the mechanisms of vertical and horizontal standardization overlapped, it is convenient to discuss these two processes separately. As regards the former, I acknowledge that in Vietnam as in Burma and Siam, cultural flows were never unidirectional. Popular influences on *nom* literature, including the six/eight style of poetry which drew on village talents; literati interest in peasant legends and tales, royal patronage of local deities, the so-called communal style of architecture, popular traditions in court music – all point to plebeian, non-Sinic influences on elite outlook.[319] Nonetheless, lower social groups responded to, if they did not adopt completely, the norms of their superiors in a way that was never genuinely reciprocal.

I have already suggested that expanded literacy provided the chief vehicle for the vertical diffusion not only of Buddhist texts and new forms of literature, but of Neo-Confucian teachings. Because Confucian education by its nature was more elitist than Theravada Buddhism (and also, as noted, because Chinese ideograms were more difficult to acquire than phonetic syllabaries) functional literacy rates almost certainly were more modest than in Theravada Southeast Asia.[320] Minh-mang denied

---

[319] Previous nn. on southern culture, plus Tran, "Popular Culture"; idem, "The Legend of Ong Dong from the Text to the Field," in Taylor and Whitmore, *Essays*, 13–41; Nguyen, "Vietnamization of Po Nagar"; and Alexander Woodside, "Conceptions of Change and of Human Responsibility for Change in Late Traditional Vietnam," in David Wyatt and Woodside, eds., *Moral Order and the Question of Change* (New Haven, 1982), 144–45.

[320] I have found no figures, but male literacy may have been in the order of 20 percent. See Yu, "Law and Family," 109.

that anyone outside the scholar class had any need to read.[321] Yet clearly the near universal illiteracy of the early 1400s receded, because greater urban and rural prosperity, printing, government patronage, and local reform movements combined to multiply schools, teachers, texts, and readers. These trends, if not their incidence, paralleled long-term changes in Burma and Siam. While the key agents of orthodox acculturation in those lands were monks, in Vietnam it was village school teachers – retired officials, failed scholars, or scholars who declined to hold office. Such teachers relied on local contributions, particularly from landlords and rich peasants.[322] Apart from books imported from China, elementary education employed Sino-Vietnamese textbooks, written in imitation of Chinese prototypes, which may not have been much less standardized than their Theravada counterparts. The policy, pursued by both Trinh and post-1820 Nguyen regimes, of trying to centralize printing at the capital reinforced a conservative intellectual outlook. Over time sanctioned (and illicit) printings joined with relative prosperity to expand the circulation of Chinese-character texts. As Woodside has emphasized, libraries of the size available to early 19th-century northern scholars would have been inconceivable, for sheer economic reasons, 200 years earlier.[323]

More popular, less conventional forms of literature, much of it in *nom*, also extended the social reach of Confucian norms, while providing a more distinctively Vietnamese vehicle. If late 18th to early 19th century *nom* literature was potentially subversive, it also was remarkably well suited to bring legacies of Chinese culture to a wider audience, including semi-literates and illiterates able to memorize *nom* rhymes. Chinese poetry, novels, and drama, for example, could be read only by a very few, but when translated into six/eight poetry, partly in Chinese and partly in *nom*, readers and listeners became more numerous.[324] Likewise, in response to the 18th-century crisis, we have seen that northern intellectuals strove to restore Confucian morality, hence social order, by producing simplified extracts from the classics, abridged versions, versified forms, and most important, translations of Chinese classics into

---

[321] Woodside, *Vietnam*, 190.
[322] Woodside, *Vietnam*, 188–92. On social stratification, Nguyen Tu Chi, "The Traditional Village in Bac Bo," in *Traditional Village in Vietnam*, esp. 53–60.
[323] Woodside, "Political Theory," 249–51. On printing and orthodoxy, also idem, *Vietnam*, 186–94; idem in David J. Steinberg, ed., *In Search of Southeast Asia* (Honolulu, 1985), 72–73; Huynh, *Heritage of Vietnamese Poetry*, "Introduction."
[324] Woodside, *Vietnam*, 56–57.

nom. The Tayson leader Nguyen Hue, acceding to northern literati pressure, extended this program of Confucian popularization and, like Gialong, used *nom* for some official communications. Although Minh-mang tried to reverse course, he too was forced to accept the use of *nom* in school primers, and *nom* literature continued to flourish.[325] Thus, while Chinese retained a larger functional role in Vietnam than did Latin in 18th-century France, Pali in Burma, or Sanskrit in Siam, in each realm a more inclusive, national communications network promoted the vernacular at the expense of an elitist, universal, and sacred language.

To encourage cultural orthodoxy, the Le/Trinh and imperial Nguyen regimes sponsored a range of interventions among which the three-tiered civil service examinations arguably remained most influential. Far more extensive than monastic exams in Burma, Vietnam's civil service exams owed their vertical integrative power to a) their express concern with problems of social and moral propriety and b) their ability, through material and prestige rewards, to ensare upwardly mobile families in state-approved culture. Before they could take the exams, candidates had to be certified as upholding Confucian norms in their private lives. As Samuel Baron noted c. 1683, the Dong Kinhese "have a great inclination for learning, because it is the only step to acquire dignity and preferments, which encourageth them to a studious and diligent application to learning."[326] Besides supervising exams and textual production, Vietnamese rulers supplemented private academies with district, prefectural, and provincial schools, to which approved texts and model examination answers were distributed. At a lower social level, they persecuted Christians and ethnic minorities, sought to bring village conflicts under the purview of Confucian-based law, and obliged officials to lecture ignorant commoners at regular intervals on Confucian principles such as "The 47 Rules for Teaching and Changing the People."[327]

---

[325] Dutton, "Three Case Studies," 6–8, 37–38; idem, "Tay Son Uprising," 378–79; Woodside, *Vietnam*, 54–56; Durand and Nguyen, *Vietnamese Literature*, chs. 8, 9.

[326] Baron, "Description," 15. On civil service examinations, Yu, "Law and Family," 213–15; Woodside, *Vietnam*, 170–81, 194–233.

[327] On standardizing state cultural interventions, Yu, "Law and Family," 43, 190, 213–20; Woodside, *Vietnam*, 27, 134–35, 184–90, 262–89 *passim*; idem, "Political Theory," 251–52; Nguyen and Ta, *Le Code*, I, 60–61, 68; Choi, "Southern Vietnam," 116–24; Cooke, "Historicizing Vietnamese Christianity"; Whitmore, "Administrative Control of the Spirits" (ms). Note too that Minh-mang burned non-conforming private history books.

Trade circuits provided another avenue for popular acculturation insofar as peasants visiting urban markets and fairs gained greater exposure – via entertainments, public competitions, gossip, observation – to elite usages. Urban contacts offered a practical incentive to literacy and numeracy. In the opposite direction storytellers, actors, and singers transmitted aspects of literati culture to peasant audiences.[328]

How deeply did elite norms penetrate society? By Theravada standards, perhaps not very deeply. Whereas Burma knew no dramatic difference between the administrative class (*min*) and commoners (*hsin-yei-tha*) as regards female roles, inheritance, or religious knowledge, even in Dong Kinh most peasants differed from scholar officials in the following respects: among peasants women were more independent physically and financially, parental authority and kinship ties were weaker, marriage prohibitions and mourning less strict, teknonymy more common, inheritance more bilateral, ethnic boundaries more porous, Buddhist and animist beliefs more dearly held, and illiteracy more widespread.[329] In turn, relatively widespread illiteracy and fluid Buddhist-Confucian interactions suggest that popular notions of orthodoxy were less coherent than in Theravada villages. By Burmese standards, dress, housing, conspicuous consumption, and probably speech were also class specific. With their betel chewing, stained teeth, and bare feet, Baron said Vietnamese peasants resembled other Southeast Asians more than Chinese.[330] Almost a century and a half later, Crawfurd drew a similar distinction between the "lower orders [who] are remarkable for their liveliness ... [and t]he higher classes ... [who] affect the grave and solemn demeanour of the Chinese."[331] Among the countries covered in this study, only Russia and Mughal India – whose imperial elites also looked abroad for linguistic and cultural norms – may have had a wider elite-mass cultural gap.

Nonetheless, Sinic models of social organization and deportment did become more influential on the village level from the 16th century, and

---

[328] Neil L. Jamieson, *Understanding Vietnam* (Berkeley, 1993), 40; Yu, "Law and Family," 189. Cf. Woodside, *Vietnam*, 26–27; Evelyn S. Rawski in David Johnson, Andrew J. Nathan, and Rawski, eds., *Popular Culture in Late Imperial China* (Berkeley, 1985), 6–7.

[329] Yu, "Law and Family," chs. 3–7; Taylor, "On Being Muonged."

[330] Baron, "Description," 19, echoed in Richard, *Histoire naturelle*, II, 2; Woodside, *Vietnam*, 199. On class-specific speech, Dampier, *Voyages*, 46; Richard, *Histoire naturelle*, I, 97–99; Henley, "Ethnogeographic Integration," 300.

[331] Crawfurd, *Journal of an Embassy*, 487–88.

more especially in the 18th and 19th centuries. Virtually all strata were affected to some degree. In the northern and central lowlands, in particular, Confucian/Sinic influence could be seen in growing peasant identification with patrilineages (*ho*), a corresponding sense of filial obligation and kinship, expanded popular emphases on ancestor cults and male inheritance, and greater female modesty and subordination than among nearby hill peoples. We also find the spread of Confucian-oriented village codes, a wider ceremonial and social role for the male-dominated village communal house (*dinh*) and for patrilineage-dominated neighborhood groups, and the spread of Confucian family terms, including Chinese words for peripheral kin positions.[332] Whereas in earlier periods the most honored seats in Dong Kinh communal houses automatically were reserved for village elders, from the late 17th century these seats, and control over village politics, usually went to those with Confucian training.[333] As early as 1700–1710, French missionaries commented on growing Confucian influence in the villages of Dong Kinh.[334] This same current nourished the aforementioned Confucian popularization movement that sought to quell the 18th-century social crisis, as well as the "more literate and broadly-based radical classicism" of the early Nguyen era that Woodside has studied.[335] One is reminded of popular, textually-based Theravada reform movements in late 18th/early 19th century Burma and Siam, where demands for renewed social order were instinctively sympathetic to central authority. Note too that whereas anti-Confucian, Buddhist millennial elements had dominated early 16th-century popular revolts in Dong Kinh, during anti-Nguyen Dong Kinh revolts in the 19th century, such themes were conspicuously absent.[336]

Let us turn now from vertical to horizontal standardization. Having already discussed assimilationist pressures against Chams, Khmers and

---

[332] Yu, "Law and Family," chs. 3–7, esp. 87–98, 133–42, 199–201; idem, "Changing Nature," 162; Richard, *Histoire naturelle*, I, 107–108; essays by Nguyen Khac Tung, Nguyen Tu Chi, and To Lan in *Traditional Village in Vietnam*, esp. 67–76; Ha Van Tan and Nguyen Van Ku, *Dinh Viet Nam* (Ho Chi Minh City, 1998), 70–126; John Kleinen, "Village-State Relations in 19th-Century Vietnam," in Nguyen and Forest, *Guerre et paix*, 175–209; Woodside, personal communication, Sept. 14, 1999; Taylor, personal communication, Aug., 2001.

[333] Yu, "Changing Nature," esp. 159–62, 171–72.

[334] Forest, *Les missionaires*, II, 65–66.

[335] Dutton, "Three Case Studies," 8 ff; Woodside, "Political Theory," 253.

[336] Not surprisingly, on the less Confucian southern frontier in the 19th century, millennial Buddhism remained important.

hillpeoples, here I am chiefly interested in cultural change among lowland Vietnamese-speakers. Southern settlement obviously provided the overarching context. In addition, some of the same mechanisms as promoted vertical acculturation – more schools, wider circulation of texts, urban markets, rural fairs, popular entertainments – increased interaction among far-flung communities. As in Burma and Siam, by bringing together soldiers and refugees from widely separated locales, the disorders of the late 18th probably helped to erode local custom. Critical too were government interventions, including Hue's systematic patronage of Confucian schools and examinations in the far south.[337] For all their drawbacks as an instrument of popular pedagogy, as an aid to horizontal elite integration Chinese ideograms were remarkably efficient because, unlike phonetic alphabets, they conveyed precisely the same information to speakers of different dialects.[338] Moreover, civil service examinations obliged candidates to leave their villages to write about issues of expressly empire-wide significance, while laws of avoidance sought to weaken particularistic loyalties among officials.[339] Although *nom* was quasi-phonetic and thus tended to capture local speech differences, by disseminating new intellectual and aesthetic perspectives, *nom* literature too may have had a horizontal standardizing impact.

The invaluable scholarship of Taylor, Whitmore, Li, and Cooke allows us to appreciate: a) the continuous localization of culture that southern settlement entailed; b) the fragility of bureaucratic ideals in the face of patrimonial expectations; c) the vulnerability of Neo-Confucian culture vis-a-vis other Sinic as well as non-Sinic currents; and d) the pivotal role of regional loyalties within each Vietnamese-speaking polity.[340] Even in the mid-1800s Nguyen gazeteers had no difficulty listing highly idiosyncratic provincial customs, especially at the popular level and especially south of Phu Yen.[341] Yet especially at the elite level, we also see a recurrent, long-term tendency for Sinic practices to move south through diffusion within Vietnam and through direct borrowing from China; and for Neo-Confucianism to achieve a hegemonic position within a fluid Confucian-Buddhist-animist synthesis. Military families could challenge the literati in a physical sense, but so intellectually and socially dominant was Neo-Confucian thought after c. 1450 that in the early Le,

---

[337] Choi, "Southern Vietnam," 112–26, 198–200.
[338] See Richard, *Histoire naturelle*, I, 97–99; Dampier, *Voyages*, 46.
[339] Albeit, less successfully than in China. Woodside, *Vietnam*, 82–83.
[340] See *supra*, n. 2.
[341] "Cooke Critique," 54.

the Trinh, the imperial Nguyen (and more superficially, the southern Nguyen) – that is to say, in virtually every early modern dynasty – the heirs to military authority moved to (re)establish Neo-Confucian primacy. The literati never showed a comparable willingness to yield the ideological high ground to other systems.

Consider in this light the cultural evolution of the successive frontier areas, Thanh Nghe and Thuan Quang. Still a bastion of non-Sinic culture well into the 15th century, Thanh Nghe by the mid-1600s had become a site of Confucian scholarship. Indeed, in the 1730s the Thanh Nghe faction at court advanced their fortunes by proposing Confucian reforms more orthodox than those advocated by their Dong Kinh literati rivals.[342] Farther south, Thuan Quang in 1600 was no less a backwater than Thanh Nghe had been in 1400, having bred only three palace examination winners in 137 years. What social dynamics and administrative incentives allowed this area to develop its Confucian resources? How critical were *minh huong* Chinese? Did a viable scholarly tradition antedate the Tayson? Whatever the answer to such queries, northern Thuan Quang, we have seen, was already sporting Chinese-style political trappings by 1744. The subsequent progress of Confucian learning is suggested by Thuan Quang's respectable rates of mid-level exam graduates under Minh-mang (who showed only limited favoritism) and by the mid-century concentration of scholarly talent around Hue, which along with Hanoi, had become the center for the Vietnamese importation of scholarship and books from China.[343] Moreover – and here is the main point – so prestigious was Confucian culture that Thuan Quang leaders at the mid–19th-century Nguyen court, rather than halt the examination system or oppose Mahayana Buddhism to Confucianism, felt obliged to rig examination results and to bias promotion procedures so as to pay themselves with the only cultural coin that had any true value.[344]

In other words, Confucian symbols of achievement that were predominantly northern in the early 1700s had been fully appropriated by Thuan Quang families four or five generations later. Even Saigon and

[342] Yu, "Law and Family," 47–48. See also Cooke, "Regionalism," 136; idem, "Confucianization," 310.

[343] Woodside, *Vietnam*, 180–81, 220–23; Cooke, "Confucianization," 306–12.

[344] Cooke, "Confucianization," 307–12; idem, "Composition," 759–64; Ralph Smith, "The Cycle of Confucianization in Vietnam," in Walter Vella, ed., *Aspects of Vietnamese History* (Honolulu, 1973), 21–23; Woodside, *Vietnam*, 219–23. Likewise Dutton, "Tay Son Uprising," 380–83, 390, 410 emphasizes that after entering Dong Kinh, the southerner Nguyen Hue championed a Neo-Confucian agenda that adumbrated 19th-century Nguyen cultural policy.

the lower Mekong area, where schoolteachers traditionally competed with magicians and soothsayers for influence, showed some scholarly attainment in the early and mid–19th century. Not only did the number of schools and examination candidates grow, but more candidates hailed from the west side of the Mekong. According to Choi, by the 1840s Hue had succeeded in displacing Christians and Chinese settlers in favor of loyal Confucian scholars and allied landlords as opinion-makers and leaders of southern society. Accordingly, the latter groups led the local anti-French, pro-Hue resistance of the 1860s and 1870s.[345]

Fragile though Vietnamese political unity surely remained by Burmese or Siamese standards, a shared cultural and institutional framework thus helps explain Woodside's observation that regionalism in 1847 was far less formidable than in 1802.[346] This tentative Hue-focused reconciliation resembled on a national scale the merger of Thanh Nghe and Dong Kinh elites at the northern court c. 1460–1760.

Finally I would point to two other long-term spurs to imperial integration, spurs that depended more directly on the expanding economy than did cultural currents, namely, changes in the revenue system and in firearms. According to Li, in 1800 revenue from overseas trade in Saigon alone was 489,790 *quan*, whereas from 1746–1752 annual Nguyen state revenues from domestic and foreign sources together had averaged between 338,000 and 423,000 *quan*. Admittedly, if one includes mandarinal kick-backs and non-tax sources of royal income, mid–18th century Nguyen revenues must have been substantially larger than 423,000 *quan*. Still, these figures suggest a marked expansion in the southern tax base between 1750 and the early 1800s.[347] Moreover, in the empire as a whole the number of men registered on the tax rolls between 1819 and 1847 almost doubled, from 613,000 to 1,024,000, as a result of improved controls and natural increase.[348] Thus the base for conscription, corvees, schools, cultural patronage, government salaries, and outlays of all sorts expanded.

---

[345] On southern cultural change, Choi, "Southern Vietnam," 112–26, 197–200; Woodside, *Vietnam*, 220–21.

[346] Woodside, *Vietnam*, 135.

[347] I assume that the 1746–1752 figures represent average annual income, not total income for all six years. Li, "Rice Trade," 6. No one knows total "royal" income c. 1750, but "Cooke Critique," 56 argues it was substantially larger than "state" income. It is unclear how price trends (Li and Reid, *Southern Vietnam*, 136–41) affected Li's figures. On Saigon's expansion, see too Wheeler, "Cross-Cultural Trade," 207–211.

[348] Nguyen, "Quelques aspects," 15–16. Cf. Li, "Rice Trade," 10.

Meanwhile commercial growth and monetization transformed the very structure of the political economy. In the southern seigneury between 1650 (?) and 1769 indirect taxes on the sale and transport of domestic merchandise alone rose from very modest proportions to one-fifth the value of all cash taxes on persons and land.[349] In the north, average annual returns from each interior customs post increased from a maximum of 4,000 ligatures in 1705 to an average of 10,000 by 1729.[350] To compensate for problems with communal lands, in the 1720s the Trinh began taxing private lands, internal shipping, commercial fisheries, and numerous articles of daily use, including salt. Many of these collections were entrusted to tax-farmers, Vietnamese and Chinese. Chinese-run mines provided another source of income that, as noted, by the 1760s became a pillar of Trinh finances.[351] After 1802 the Nguyen not only retained most 18th century commercial taxes, but accelerated a trend, apparent as early as 1720, toward the commutation of in-kind rice taxes.[352] At the same time the Nguyen, much like their Chakri contemporaries, reduced their direct dependence on maritime taxes in favor of internal tolls, taxes on the production of goods, and market taxes.[353] On the other side of the ledger, cash also transformed the system of remuneration. Under the 17th century Trinh, land grants to officials were still the norm. In the 1720s, if not earlier, an intermediate system evolved whereby officials received in lieu of land the specific obligations, in kind or cash, of a number of taxpayers in certain villages. Under the imperial Nguyen, at the latest by 1839, a straight-forward salary system was in place for soldiers as well as officials, with amounts fixed in cash according to grade and with special allocations to nourish incorruptibility.[354]

Ideologically ambiguous and socially destabilizing though commercial growth was, in the long term commercial taxes and cash revenues offer additional explanations for the relative success of Nguyen unification: these changes magnified the range of government income, facilitated extraction from the rural economy, simplified the transmission of resources, and in the case of salaried officials, strengthened

---

[349] Nguyen, *Tableau*, 151. The 1650 base is speculative since the passage talks of growth to 1769 without specifying a base line.

[350] Nguyen, *Tableau*, 150. Cf. Richard, *Histoire naturelle*, II, 74–75.

[351] On Trinh taxes, Dang, *Institutions*, 106–21; Nguyen, *Tableau*, 32–34, 150–51; Woodside, "Political Theory," 259; Le, *Histoire*, 259–60.

[352] Woodside, *Vietnam*, 139; Smith, "Politics and Society," 164–65.

[353] Wheeler, "Cross-Cultural Trade," 33, 171.

[354] Smith, "Politics and Society," 164–65; Woodside, *Vietnam*, 79–81; Crawfurd, *Journal of an Embassy*, 493; Hodgkin, *Vietnam*, 105.

administrative discipline. Many of these changes, of course, are familiar from 18th- and early 19th-century Burma and Siam.

No less significant was the expanded role of firearms. After the Ming invasion of the 15th century and the Nguyen-Trinh conflicts of the 17th century, the civil wars of the late 1700s provided a third major spur to Vietnamese military arts. As noted, the Nguyen victory over the Taysons stemmed in large measure from their success in tapping the military technology and strategies of their European and South China Sea allies. This maritime connection was not lost after 1802, despite the Nguyen move from the Mekong to Hue. In return for permission to export delta rice, Chinese junks provided the new dynasty with strategic metals – pig iron, wrought iron, copper, tin, and sulfur – as well as gunpowder.[355] Unable to temper iron and steel or to manufacture useful gunlocks for flintlock rifles, the Nguyen also depended on European weapons, which it now purchased directly from Bangkok, Singapore, or off-shore traders. Over these weapons the court sought to enforce a strict monopoly. In 1822 not only did half the line troops carry European-style muskets and bayonets, but a substantial portion were dressed in English woolens and trained, presumably via the legacy of French officers and European manuals, in European tactics. Massive Nguyen citadels, at least 31 between 1802 and 1844 alone, also were built to French or, in some cases, Chinese design.

Thus equipped and positioned, Minh-mang's standing army – put by some sources at 115,000, perhaps twice that of the Trinh – was, in Crawfurd's words, "a powerful instrument of oppression towards [the king's] subjects, or even of aggression against his smaller native neighbours."[356] Along with a navy of some 25,000, these forces allowed Minh-mang to compete for Cambodia, and served as ultimate guarantor of control over a restive Dong Kinh and the far south. From 1802–1841 the Nguyen faced, by some accounts, over 300 revolts, most of which opposed fresh centralizing demands and a handful of which were quite formidable.[357] To ignore this coercive component is to misconstrue the bases of Nguyen success.

355 Li, "18th and Early 19th Century Mekong Delta," 8; idem, "Late 18th Century Mekong Delta," 13.
356 Crawfurd, *Journal of an Embassy*, 495. On army size (estimates differ), organization, and technology, ibid., 483, 493–95, 513; Hodgkin, *Vietnam*, 110, 119; Alastair Lamb, *The Mandarin Road to Old Hue* (London, 1970), 231, 262–63; Mantienne, "Military Technology Transfers"; and esp. Dutton, "Flaming Tiger," a fine survey of the pre-1802 period.
357 Woodside, *Vietnam*, 135; Nguyen, "Quelques aspects," 14.

CONCLUSIONS

The Nguyen unification was the last and most contingent of three post-1750 consolidations that transformed the mainland. The antecedent crises to which the Nguyen, Kon-baung, and Chakri dynasties responded were comparable insofar as all three breakdowns reflected the intersection of administrative weaknesses with intensifying warfare, commercial and/or demographic growth. All three dynasties tapped novel military and fiscal sources, including Chinese trade. All rapidly extended their territories, and all benefited from – even as they encouraged – wider literacy and a broadly-based yearning for renewed social order and textual authority. In varying degrees all three dynasties also struggled to reconcile market impulses with the inherited ideal of an administered economy.

Nor, of course, did the late 18th century offer the only substantive parallels. In their demographic vigor, personalized governance, decentralized structure, and indifference to cultic orthodoxy, the Ly and Tran polities resembled charter principalities elsewhere on the mainland, and all may be opposed to more effective post-1450 structures. The Tran collapse of the 14th century coincided substantially in timing and etiology with the decline of Angkor and Upper Burma, while Dai Viet's 16th-century fragmentation recalls the slightly later collapse of Toungoo Burma and Early Ayudhya. In its dependence on new educational systems and its sympathy for royal authority, the Neo-Confucian revolution paralleled Theravada reform. The grand engines of political expansion after 1500 – frontier settlement, commercial intensification, interstate competition, Chinese immigration, new ideological formulae – are broadly familiar, as are feedback loops among these phenomena. Here as elsewhere, political and cultural integration accelerated sharply in the 18th and 19th centuries. And in all three lowland sectors, wider literacy promoted literary movements that were both more variegated and more dependent on vernacular languages.

How, then, did the eastern mainland differ? During the 14th century Vietnam suffered less severe dislocations than any other sector of the mainland. Obviously too Dai Viet's Sinic heritage was unique, as was her tortured geography. The two latter factors produced an ironic set of contrasts. On the one hand, compared to Burma or Siam, Vietnam remained socially and geographically disparate. Not only did class distinctions tend to be more pronounced than in Theravada lands, but cleavages between regions were almost fatal to any sense of pan-Vietnamese identity.

If the 14th-century inaugurated a crisis less prolonged than in the west or center, the 16th century began a split that was far more durable. On the other hand, Sinic intolerance of minority cultures, high population densities, and the absence of large upland valleys had yielded by 1840 the most homogenized ethnic/linguistic makeup of any mainland empire and the most uniform system of lowland administration.

Let me offer a final perspective on east mainland history by playing devil's advocate: given the fact that the Trinh-Nguyen split duplicated a far older north-south division in the eastern corridor, did anything really change after 1600? After all, Dang Trong resisted northern invasions at roughly the same place that the Chams had opposed northern attacks for hundreds of years. People whom we call Vietnamese regarded the northern power with much the same fear as had their Cham predecessors, while adopting deities and customs from those earlier communities.

In truth, such an emphasis on continuity cannot withstand scrutiny. Whereas Champa, highly decentralized, with weak population, had barely held its own against Angkor, by 1770 the Nguyen, along with Siam, was en route to destroying Cambodia as an independent state. In this sense, whether southern Vietnam remained independent or reunited with the north left unaffected the basic trend: in lieu of three viable charter polities in the east in 1300 (Dai Viet, Champa, and Angkor), by 1770 there were only two. Much the same could be said of cultural change: whatever subjective feelings separated southern Vietnamese-speaking cultures from those in Le-Trinh Vietnam, objectively the Sinic-oriented cultures of late 18th-century Dang Trong were far closer to those of the north than Cham or Khmer practices ever had been. In other words, continuous Vietnamese settlement joined with Chinese contacts to promote a simplification of the cultural map that corresponded broadly to the simplification of the political map. Recall too that if accidents contributed to the southern-led (re)unification of Vietnamese-speaking lands in the late 18th and early 19th centuries, that historic movement also built upon intellectual, family, and political ties to the north for which Champa and Cambodia supplied no precedent whatever.

Conclusion and Prologue

This volume makes five large and, I believe, quite novel claims. First, during roughly a thousand years each sector of mainland Southeast Asia experienced a sustained trend towards political consolidation which was punctuated by periodic collapse but which by the early 19th century had yielded an unprecedentedly powerful and extensive formation. Second, during this thousand years, eras of political collapse and consolidation across the mainland, especially in the western and central sectors, substantially coincided. Third, within each sector, most particularly the lowlands, wider political unity reflected and encouraged easier cultural exchange and a growing standardization of ethnicity and cultic practice. Fourth, political and cultural integration derived from fluid synergies between demographic, agricultural, military, and foreign commercial pressures, all of which, including maritime stimuli, remained potent throughout the period under review. Finally, and in more preliminary fashion, I suggest that integration in mainland Southeast Asia correlated in basic chronology and dynamics to changes in other outlying sectors of Eurasia.

Chapter 1 set forth the argument for the mainland as a whole. The introductions and conclusions to Chapters 2–4 applied the thesis in summary fashion to each sector of the mainland, while calling attention to local idiosyncracies. Rather than offer another recapitulation, I conclude on a cautionary note by emphasizing the elements of contingency and causal uncertainty that are intrinsic to my narrative, and by suggesting how these issues can shape future research.

To argue that economic elaboration, interstate competition, and so forth favored some sort of consolidation in each sector is not to claim that the resultant structures were determined with much specificity. Like all people, Southeast Asians periodically faced critical, if poorly understood choices. In the Irrawaddy basin, for example, Bayin-naung's by no means inevitable decision in the 1560s to conquer Siam, and his son's determination in the 1580s to preserve that legacy, altered both the ethnic profile and internal structure of the western empire, because ultimately those choices exhausted the dynasty's Lower Burma base and compelled a return to the north. Until that time there had been a reasonable prospect of a Mon-Burman dyarchy. But by constricting both maritime and Mon influences, the move upriver strengthened the link between Burman exclusiveness and imperial loyalty. Fully realized in the early Kon-baung period, this orientation distinguished Burmese culture from its more incorporative and cosmopolitan Siamese counterpart and contributed to a higher degree of ethnic homogeneity – and psychological solidarity? – in the Irrawaddy than the Chaophraya basin. Whether it also weakened commercial stimuli is unclear, but I am convinced that by recentering the empire in the agricultural heartland, the early 17th-century shift greatly reduced the danger of north-south warfare such as had plagued the valley since the 14th century and had erupted again on Bayin-naung's death. It thus provided an element of stability without which both Toungoo and Kon-baung consolidation would have been far more difficult. Indeed, had the capital stayed in the delta, it is conceivable that north-south warfare would have prevented reunification entirely.

In the central mainland I know of no short-term decisions by Siamese officials that changed the basic complexion of empire. A concentration of maritime and agricultural resources rendered the lower Chaophraya basin the inescapable center of gravity for the area drained by that river and its northern tributaries. Far less predictable was the 13th–15th century shift in the central mainland as a whole from Khmer, Cambodian-plain primacy to Siamese, Chaophraya-basin primacy. Had Cambodia not lost its hegemony, had it been able to capture resources that subsequently went to Ayudhya, not only would many Siamese and Laos have become provincial Khmers, but the Mekong delta would not have fallen under Vietnamese control as readily as it did, if at all. What, then, accounted for this historic shift? I see three possibilities. First, as Richard O'Connor has argued, superior agronomic technique may have given Tai newcomers access to new ecological niches, which in turn ensured demographic and political superiority. Second, whether because of rapids on the middle Mekong, inadequate port sites in the delta, or inferior access to interior zones producing forest exports, the lower Mekong may have been an intrinsically less appealing commercial site than Ayudhya. Third, although Khmer elite factionalism was a symptom of east-west interventions, it also opened the door to those interventions. What subtle elements in Khmer culture were at work? Cultural self-doubt following the decline of Angkor? A less proprietary sense of territorial space? Different notions of patron-client loyalty? How much can we read into the fact that whereas royal succession in Ly-Tran Dai Viet and Pagan was normally peaceful, at Angkor usually it was bitterly contested?

The eastern mainland presents several obvious turning points, including the defeat of successive Chinese invasions and the late 18th-century reunification. It was entirely possible that southern Vietnamese-speakers could have separated permanently from northern Vietnamese much as the latter split from China, and the interplay between cultural bonds and local accidents in forestalling that possibility after 1774 deserves far more attention than it has received. No less contingent and seminal was the failure of Ming reconquest. Had Dai Viet been permanently reannexed in the early 1400s, Cham and Khmer areas probably would have been absorbed anyway, but under the aegis of the Chinese empire, perhaps at a slower pace, and with poorer prospects for a southern breakaway regime.

If specific political outcomes within each sector were indeterminate, the same may be said about our understanding of long-term integrative and dislocative pressures. To explain each transition – the genesis of charter states, their 14th-century debility, resumed centralization in the late 15th and 16th centuries, and so forth – invariably I have cited a mix of domestic and external factors. Yet we still lack adequate data – on population, output, trade, prices, incomes, rainfall – to weigh individual elements or to chart their interactions with much confidence or precision. For example, in seeking to explain the more or less coordinated 10th–14th century florescence of charter states, I have called attention to the Medieval Climate Anomaly and improved monsoon flows. But without better information, we cannot easily separate climate from autonomous changes in agricultural technique, religious organization, or foreign commerce. Even after 1450 or 1500, although maritime trade seems to have become more critical to mainland development, Smithian specialization and the search for comparative advantage still proceeded simultaneously on the local, interregional, and international levels. In any given period, therefore, how much responsibility for reclamation in

Vietnam and the Chaophraya plain should we assign to foreign demand for rice? How much to domestic social, political, and military pressures? How can we decode demographic coordination across the mainland? In explaining the crises of the late 16th and 18th centuries, how important was price inflation and what were its causes? Was Chakri Siam's novel military success primarily the result of growing maritime contacts, and if so, was Burma disadvantaged more by policy or by physical distance from the China coast?

One thing is clear: in conditions of limited local data, a comparative approach can be exceptionally useful. Scholars usually have sought to explain the rise of Pagan, the collapse of Angkor, the First Toungoo conquests, and so forth in purely local terms, institutional or political. But the fact that these changes coincided with more general regional transitions obliges us to treat skeptically explanations that are entirely *sui generis*.

A similar logic commends Eurasian perspectives. By itself, of course, extraregional experience cannot resolve problems in Southeast Asian history, but it can modify our weighting of local factors and alert us to new possibilities. To extend the discussion of charter success, if the prosperity of Pagan, Angkor, and Dai Viet corresponded closely to that of medieval Western Europe, Kiev, Kamakura Japan, and Song China, and if it can be demonstrated that all these areas shared novel climatic or epidemiological features, historians again would be ill-advised to concentrate on purely local developments. Expanding the number of case studies makes it easier to isolate variables. Likewise, by considering instances of limited or aborted integration, as in South Asia and island Southeast Asia, we can better understand why integration proceeded doggedly in Burma and Siam, and why Vietnam was something of an intermediate case

Finally, placing Southeast Asia in extraregional context promises to modify our image not only of Southeast Asia but of Eurasia itself. As the emphasis on European exceptionalism and, its corollary, Southeast Asian encapsulation, recedes, we sense that peninsulas at Eurasia's northwestern and southeastern extremities were part of a coherent, loosely coordinated ecumene. To the challenge of Eurasian comparison we turn in Volume Two.

Index

Note: An f following a page number indicates a figure. An n. indicates a footnote.